# Non-Tariff Barriers, Regionalism and Poverty

**Essays in Applied International Trade Analysis**

## World Scientific Studies in International Economics

(ISSN: 1793-3641)



---

Vol. 36 Trade Policy in Asia: Higher Education and Media Services
*edited by Christopher Findlay (University of Adelaide, Australia), Hildegunn Kyvik Nordas (Organisation for Economic Co-operation and Development, France) & Gloria Pasadilla (APEC Secretariat, Singapore)*

Vol. 37 The Path of World Trade Law in the 21st Century
*by Steve Charnovitz (The George Washington University, USA)*

Vol. 38 International Trade, Distribution and Development: Empirical Studies of Trade Policies
*by Paul Brenton (The World Bank, USA)*

Vol. 39 Evolving Patterns in Global Trade and Finance
*by Sven W. Arndt (Claremont McKenna College, USA)*

Vol. 40 Shadow Banking Within and Across National Borders
*edited by Stijn Claessens (International Monetary Fund, USA), Douglas Evanoff (Federal Reserve Bank of Chicago, USA), George Kaufman (Loyola University Chicago, USA) & Luc Laeven (International Monetary Fund, USA)*

Vol. 41 Modeling Developing Countries' Policies in General Equilibrium
*by Jaime de Melo (FERDI, France & University of Geneva, Switzerland)*

Vol. 42 Developing Countries in the World Economy
*by Jaime de Melo (FERDI, France & University of Geneva, Switzerland)*

Vol. 43 Farm Policies and World Markets: Monitoring and Disciplining the International Trade Impacts of Agricultural Policies
*by Tim Josling (Stanford University, USA)*

Vol. 44 Non-Tariff Barriers, Regionalism and Poverty: Essays in Applied International Trade Analysis
*by L. Alan Winters (University of Sussex, UK)*

The complete list of the published volumes in the series can be found at
http://www.worldscientific.com/series/wssie

World Scientific
Studies in
International
Economics

# Non-Tariff Barriers, Regionalism and Poverty

## Essays in Applied International Trade Analysis

**L Alan Winters**
University of Sussex, UK

**World Scientific**
NEW JERSEY • LONDON • SINGAPORE • BEIJING • SHANGHAI • HONG KONG • TAIPEI • CHENNAI

*Published by*

World Scientific Publishing Co. Pte. Ltd.
5 Toh Tuck Link, Singapore 596224
*USA office:* 27 Warren Street, Suite 401-402, Hackensack, NJ 07601
*UK office:* 57 Shelton Street, Covent Garden, London WC2H 9HE

**Library of Congress Cataloging-in-Publication Data**
Winters, L. Alan.
[Essays. Selection.]
Non-tariff barriers, regionalism and poverty : essays in applied international trade analysis / L. Alan Winters, University of Sussex, UK.
pages cm. -- (World Scientific studies in international economics ; Vol. 44)
Includes bibliographical references.
ISBN 978-9814571265 (hardcover : alk. paper)
1. Non-tariff trade barriers. 2. International trade. 3. Regionalism. 4. Europe, Eastern--Commercial policy. 5. Europe, Eastern--Foreign economic relations. 6. Poverty--Developing countries. 7. Doha Development Agenda (2001–) I. Title.
HF1430.W56 2015
382'.5--dc23

2015004303

**British Library Cataloguing-in-Publication Data**
A catalogue record for this book is available from the British Library.



In-house Editor: Rajni Gamage

Typeset by Stallion Press
Email: enquiries@stallionpress.com

Printed in Singapore

# Table of Contents

# About the Author

**L Alan Winters** is Professor of Economics in the University of Sussex. He is a Research Fellow and former Programme Director for International Trade at the Centre for Economic Policy Research, London and a Fellow of IZA, Bonn. From 2008 to 2011, he was Chief Economist at the British government's Department for International Development (DFID), and from 2004 to 2007 Director of the Development Research Group of the World Bank. He has previously worked as Division Chief and Research Manager (1994–99) and Economist (1983–85) in the World Bank and in the Universities of Cambridge, Bristol, Bangor and Birmingham. He has been editor of the *World Bank Economic Review*, associate editor of the *Economic Journal*, and is now editor of *The World Trade Review*, and he serves on several other editorial boards. He is Chief Executive Officer of the Migrating Out of Poverty Research Programme Consortium (based in Sussex and funded by DFID), Chairman of the Board of the Global Development Network and a member of the Council of the UK's Economic and Social Research Council. He has also advised, *inter alia*, the OECD, the Commonwealth Secretariat, the European Commission, the European Parliament, UNCTAD, the WTO and the Inter-American Development Bank. He was made a Companion of the Most Honourable Order of the Bath in 2012.

# Credits

The author would like to thank the following publishers for granting permission to reprint respective chapters.

**Reprinted with kind permission from Oxford University Press:**

Chapter 2: JJ Nogu'es, A Olechowski and L Alan Winters, "The Extent of Nontariff Barriers to Industrial Countries' Imports," *The World Bank Economic Review*, 1(1) (1986), 181–199.

Chapter 4: WE Takacs and L Alan Winters, "Labour Adjustment Costs and British Footwear Protection," *Oxford Economic Papers*, 43(3) (1991), 479–501.

Chapter 9: L Alan Winters, "British Imports of Manufactures and the Common Market," *Oxford Economic Papers*, 36(1) (1984), 103–118.

Chapter 10: L Alan Winters, "Regionalism and the Rest of the World: The Irrelevance of the Kemp-Wan Theorem," *Oxford Economic Papers*, 49(2) (1997), 228–234.

Chapter 17: J Litchfield, N McCulloch and L Alan Winters, "Agricultural Trade Liberalization and Poverty Dynamics in Three Developing Countries," *American Journal of Agricultural Economics*, 85(5) (2003), 1285–1291.

**Reprinted with kind permission from Elsevier:**

Chapter 3: J de Melo and L Alan Winters, "Do Exporters Gain from VERs?" *European Economic Review*, 37 (1993), 1331–1349.

Chapter 5: PA Brenton and L Alan Winters, "Voluntary Export Restraints and Rationing: U.K. Leather Footwear Imports from Eastern Europe," *Journal of International Economics*, 34(3–4) (1993), 289–308.

Chapter 8: L Alan Winters, "Separability and the Specification of Foreign Trade Functions," *Journal of International Economics*, 17(3–4) (1984), 239–263.

Chapter 19: L Iacovone, F Rauch and L Alan Winters, "Trade as an Engine of Creative Destruction: Mexican Experience with Chinese Competition," *Journal of International Economics*, 89(2) (2013), 379–392.

**Reprinted with kind permission from John Wiley and Sons:**

Chapter 6: L Alan Winters, "VERs and Expectations: Extensions and Evidence," *The Economic Journal*, 104(422) (1994), 113–123.

Chapter 7: L Alan Winters, "Digging for Victory: Agricultural Policy and National Security," *The World Economy*, 13(2) (1991), 170–190.

Chapter 12: HG Overman and L Alan Winters, "Trade and Economic Geography: The Impact of EEC Accession on the UK," *The Manchester School*, 79(5) (2011), 994–1017.

Chapter 13: L Alan Winters, "Trade Liberalisation and Poverty: What are the Links?" *The World Economy*, 25(9) (2002), 1339–1367.

Chapter 15: L Alan Winters, "Trade Liberalisation and Economic Performance: An Overview," *The Economic Journal*, 114(493) (2004), F4–F21.

Chapter 18: TW Hertel, R Keeney, M Ivanic and L Alan Winters, "Why Isn't the Doha Development Agenda More Poverty Friendly?" *Review of Development Economics*, 13 (4) (2009), 543–559.

**Reprinted with kind permission from the American Economic Association**

Chapter 11: W Chang and L Alan Winters, "How Regional Blocs Affect Excluded Countries: The Price Effects of MERCOSUR," *The American Economic Review*, 92(4) (2002), 889–904.

Chapter 14: N McCulloch, A McKay and L Alan Winters, "Trade Liberalisation and Poverty: The Evidence so far," *Journal of Economic Literature*, XLII (2004), 72–115.

**Reprinted with kind permission from the Centre for Economic Integration, Sejong University**

Chapter 16: Y Niimi, P Vasudeva Dutta and L Alan Winters, "Trade Liberalisation and Poverty Dynamics in Vietnam," *Journal of Economic Integration*, 22(4) (2007), 819–851.

## Chapter 1

# Introduction

This book contains a selection of my articles on international trade and trade policy, written over a period of about thirty years. This introduction is intended to place them in several contexts. It attempts to locate the papers' contributions at the time they were written and also to ask how much of that contribution remains today. It also briefly desribes their origins in terms of my own voyage, both intellectually and in terms of policy engagement and prescription.

Even after forty years, I find some pieces of economics elegant and exciting in purely intellectual terms — for example, the Stolper-Samuelson Theorem and the Kemp-Wan Theorem still thrill me in almost the same way as Mozart does. But, possibly for a want of ability, theoretical development *per se* has never motivated my research. If economics were really just a branch of moral philosophy, as a discipline with only theory would basically be, it would be impossible to justify a profession of even one tenth of the size that economics has now attained. Rather, I believe profoundly that economics and economists exist to be useful, and that to be useful we need to relate theory to the real world in as precise a fashion as possible.

Given this slightly grandiose starting point, it is hardly surprising that almost all my research has been driven by either empirical or policy questions — wanting to know whether a particular piece of theory actually reflected the 'real' world and/or trying to apply it to answer specific policy challenges. I have found deciding what research to do among the most difficult parts of academic life, and have rarely, if ever, been successful at dreaming up research topics in the abstract or identifying things that will 'sell well' in journal terms. Rather almost all my research stems from one of three origins. In some cases I have found statements by fellow economists (academic or policy-based) to be surprising and have set off to test them;

in others my own research has posed questions, so that one thing has led to another; and in yet others, I have been asked whether I can solve or offer advice on a particular policy question. While the last motivation is not strongly represented in the papers included here — possibly because many policy questions do not lend themselves to outputs that are attractive to leading journals — I have benefitted enormously from talking to policy-makers and policy-advisors and taking their concerns seriously and/or at face value. For example, my research on small countries — e.g., Winters and Martins (2004) — and my work quantifying the potential benefits of liberalising temporary labour mobility (so-called Mode 4 of the GATS) — e.g., Winters et al. (2003) — were both stimulated by insightful but practical questions (and a small amount of funding) from Roman Grynberg, a top-rate practitioner, who then worked for the Commonwealth Secretariat. In the first case, I thought his views were wrong, but the data proved quite the opposite! One of my main pieces of advice to young economists is to listen carefully to policy-makers and try to work out what is behind their questions and views.

The three topics covered by this book have been the major themes in my research life.

## Part A: Non-Tariff Barriers

I joined the World Bank's International Economics Research Division led by J Michael Finger, an extraordinarily wise economist and manager, in 1984 at a time when Anne Krueger was Vice-President and Chief Economist. Together, they had taken several steps towards changing the prevailing view of trade and development, both in the world and in the World Bank, from import substitution to a more liberal and open conception. The original Asian tigers (Hong Kong, Korea, Singapore and Taiwan, China) had demonstrated the virtues of trade as an aid to development, and trade policy reform was beginning to catch on in the Bank's operational work. A major problem for developing country governments wanting to pursue a more liberal policy — and by so doing to eliminate a number of comfortable rents in their own economies — was that the developed countries seemed to be saying 'do as I say, not as I do'. Opponents of reform would constantly claim that the developed countries restricted access to their markets especially in the commodities of interest to developing countries. To the extent that this was true, it would not only have set a bad example, but would also have curtailed developing country exports and hence incomes. And in this way, it would tend to weaken the contribution that trade liberalisation could make towards development and undermine the forces arguing for it.

The Tokyo Round of GATT talks, which had ended in 1979, had reduced tariffs in many developed countries quite significantly, and the General System of Preferences (GSP), exempted developing countries completely or partially from many tariffs. But on the other hand, developing country exports of many products were subject to quantitative and other trade restrictions: among the worst, agricultural trade was hugely distorted by a plethora of opaque barriers, clothing exports were subject to restraints by the Multi-Fibre Arrangement, and footwear was also subject to quotas and other measures. One such barrier was the so-called Voluntary Export Restraint (VER), whereby developing country exporters (and also Japan in a number of products) were invited to restrict their exports to the USA and Europe and agreed to do so for fear of facing something worse. Because these restrictions were voluntary, it was argued — speciously — that VERs were consistent with the GATT. They were about as voluntary as the response to the old highwayman's offer of 'your money or your life'.

Both to induce some discipline on the part of developed countries, which in the first half of the 1980s restricted trade with almost no provocation, and also to help put the criticisms of developing countries into some perspective (i.e., to explain that Europe might restrict imports of shirts via the MFA, but that this was not the same as having 300% tariffs on many imports as developing countries sometimes had), it became imperative to measure and analyse these non-tariff barriers. For international trade economists, this presented a happy coincidence of interesting analytics and deep policy relevance, and both the World Bank International Economics Division and several leading scholars responded to the challenge.

My first task (I do not think I had heard of non-tariff barriers before joining the World Bank) was to try to measure the extent of developed countries' non-tariff barriers (NTBs). Scholars in UNCTAD had started to record the restrictions that existed as best they could (they were often declared to be secret), but to make these data work in the policy world they had to be quantified (and implicitly compared across countries). Andrzej Olechowski in UNCTAD and Julio J Nogues in the Bank had started to work on this problem, and I joined them in the autumn of 1984. One job was to persuade UNCTAD to share these (sensitive and possibly valuable) data with the Bank, which Jurek Rozanski and I did in December 1984, and he and I then analysed them over the following spring, ready to present to the World Bank's Development Committee. By today's standards the dataset was small, but then it seemed massive and it required huge ingenuity on Jurek's part and many overnight sessions at a facility in Mclean Virginia, which had a larger computer than the Bank to get them into order.

We also had to devise appropriate measures for NTBs. Guided significantly by the work of Robert Stern and Alan Deardorff (see the references in Chapter 2), we used the frequency ratio and the coverage ratio, the first reporting the share of headings in a standard classification of international trade that were affected by one or more NTB, and the second the proportion of total trade that occurred in the affected headings. Neither is powerful as a measure (for example, not all trade headings are equally important and a prohibition on imports receives a zero weight in the coverage ratio) but it is not clear that we have devised any better measures in the intervening three decades — see, for example, page 82 of UNCTAD (2010).

Clearly just counting up how many headings and how much trade gives a very incomplete picture of trade barriers. What we really want to know is by how much the barriers restrict trade and, from that, what their implications are for the things that matter such as economic welfare and its distribution. So this was the next frontier and one on which we started to work immediately. Many fine scholars such as Rob Feenstra and Jim Anderson were working on this problem, and the decade from 1985 to 1995 produced many exciting estimates and uncovered several different routes through which NTBs — especially VERs — affected economic welfare.

My own efforts hinged substantially around a big programme that I put together with Carl Hamilton and Jim de Melo, both of whom I met via the International Economics Division of the World Bank and Mike Finger. I decided we should focus on the footwear sector: it was technologically fairly simple (unlike, say, autos) and while it was heavily distorted by quantitative restrictions, there were a number of flows and years in which trade was relatively free. These would provide the evidence for a counter-factual analysis — the *sine qua non* of any policy analysis. All told, we produced nearly a dozen papers on footwear, which caused Carl to quip — more aspirationally than accurately — that footwear would become the fruit-fly of NTB research (a reference to the way in which the fruit-fly under-pinned so much genetic research at the time). Three of these papers appear here as Chapters 3 to 5.

Rob Feenstra had investigated two important aspects of VERs in the USA market for autos where Japanese exports were subject to VERs. (It is salutary to recall today the 1980s fears that Japanese manufacturing was unstoppably competitive and that Japan would dominate the world economy). First, Feenstra, along with several others, showed that, by reducing the supply of imported goods relative to the demand, VERs increased the prices of imports, worsened the USA's terms of trade, and transferred welfare to the Japanese suppliers. This is part of what made VERs such good politics — the exporter was dissuaded from complaining about selling fewer units by earning higher rents on each of of the units he/she did sell. Second, Feenstra showed that VERs also led to product upgrading. A VER acts like a specific duty on an import (imagine that the licences to export to the USA were auctioned — each would command the same price). The cost of the licence (duty) is proportionately lower, the higher the price of the good, and so producers will tend to use their limited stock of licenses to sell high quality (and, therefore, high price, high margin) variants of their products.

Jim de Melo and I found little evidence of quality upgrading in the case of footwear exports (De Melo and Winters, 1993). We also argued, however, in Chapter 3 of this book that even the rents generated by a VER were not a sufficient compensation for the fact that VERs (a) distorted allocation decisions across markets because the goods that could not be sold in the VER-restrained market were diverted to other markets in which they drove down prices, and (b) reduced the size of the exporting industry. Moreover, even if a VER generated higher profits in the exporting industry, any associated contraction in production reduced wages in it. Thus the generally prevailing view in the 1980s and 1990s that VERs imposed little hardship on developing country exporters was, we argued, misleading. These findings are still relevant today, although quantitative restrictions are rarer and VERs are prohibited by the WTO.

The last result about wages pointed out a further irony about VERs and other quantitative restrictions. They were frequently introduced precisely to protect the interests of workers in the import-competing industry in developed countries — in particular to reverse or reduce the decline in jobs that competition might induce and thus to reduce or avoid the adjustment costs of workers having to find new jobs. Taking these aspirations seriously, Wendy Takacs and I used employment records from a British footwear company to quantify adjustment costs — see Chapter 4. We developed a measure of adjustment costs and estimated it for the British footwear sector and also modelled the labour displacement that was averted by UK quantitative restrictions on footwear imports. Even ignoring the fact that jobs protected in footwear might reduce jobs elsewhere in the British economy, we found that the costs that such protection imposed on consumers far outweighed the adjustment costs avoided by restricting trade.

The main reason that adjustment to reduced labour demand was not very costly in the UK footwear sector was that the sector had high labour turnover: any jobs lost could be fairly well-accommodated by natural wastage as workers moved off to other jobs naturally and, because the firms were in the market to recruit frequently, wages in the sector were close to competitive levels. In addition, the restrictions were not very effective at reducing imports — partly because being country-specific, they could be circumvented by trade diversion. There is not a great deal of work estimating the labour adjustment costs of import competition and the chances of reducing them by import controls, and so this work is still periodically cited.

The third footwear paper in this book — Chapter 5 written with Paul Brenton — was certainly the hardest to produce. Its starting point is that any binding quantitative restriction induces rationing somewhere in some economy. If, for example, producers facing a VER do not raise their prices at all (perhaps because they want to preserve consumer goodwill), consumers are rationed — they want to buy more than they are allowed to at the prevailing price. If, on the other hand and as is more commonly assumed, the prices of the imports are raised to eliminate excess demand (i.e., to clear the market at the exogenously fixed quantity permitted by the VER), producers are rationed in the sense that, at these prices, they wish to sell more in the restricted market. In the former case, consumers' choices among varieties or among goods are distorted and in the latter case, it is producers' decisions about which markets to supply that are distorted.

In Chapter 5 we considered the consumer side of the issue — allowing for the possibility that when the UK imposed restrictions on imports of leather footwear from Eastern Europe, prices were not raised to market-clearing levels. Our aim was as much methodological as substantive, showing how one could identify quantity rationing in the data and then allow for this in estimating the parameters of economic behaviour. We identified significant rationing in a number of periods and found that it had strong effects on the quantities imported: for example, we estimated that Poland would have had a 40% share of UK imports of men's leather footwear in the absence of trade restrictions, compared with an actual share of 10%.

The approaches in Chapter 5 are fairly complex to implement and so we have not seen a great deal of use made of them. However, the results of our exercise do suggest that where rationing is a possibility, it is important to take it into account, and thus I hope that if in future quantitative restrictions were to proliferate, this methodology would be helpful in identifying their costs.

As noted above, VERs were quite common and attracted a good deal of academic attention in the 1980s. Exporters — especially from smaller countries — found VERs very burdensome and pressed hard to 'outlaw' them in the Uruguay Round of trade talks that ran from 1986 to 1994. And they prevailed! VERs were prohibited and while the agreement did not seem completely water-tight at the time, it has proved quite effective with many fewer VERs now in evidence. It is not possible to attribute credit for this major improvement in trade policy in any accurate fashion. However, it is not implausible to believe that the academic community's findings that VERs were costly both to the countries imposing them and to the affected exporters as well — played a significant role in informing wider audiences about the problem and in providing credible ammunition to those who wished to prevent them in the future.

In a final postscript to the work on quantitative restrictions, I observe that export restrictions have become more common in the last few years, especially in response to rising food prices but also with respect to raw materials. Their analysis calls for much the same tools as were developed in the 1980s and 1990s. In 2013 and 2014, I worked on the WTO Dispute between the European Union, Japan, and the USA on the one hand and China on the other, over the latter's export restrictions on rare earths, tungsten, and molybdenum. In describing how to infer the effects of such restrictions, I found myself drawing on this old literature, including my own papers on footwear, such as Brenton and Winters (1991).

Chapter 6 reflects a different part of the debate about VERs, but actually stemmed less from that than from an attempt to clothe a popular idea in empirical garb. It had been argued that while a VER might curtail exports from a particular source to a particular market, the anticipation of a VER would have the opposite effect. The total level of exports under a VER needed to be allocated across firms in the exporting country, and since obtaining the right to export granted the firm the right to sell in a market that had been artificially restricted and hence would generate rents, firms had strong incentives to get an allocation. In many cases export rights were allocated in proportion to firms' exports in the last unrestricted year, so higher exports in that year were essentially the key to obtaining rents the next year when the VER had been introduced. In Chapter 6 I showed that this reasoning depended critically on the structure of the exporting industry.

If it contained many small firms, competition to win export rights would have the effect just indicated. If, however, it was subject to monopoly, the monopolist may have the incentive to cut exports back as soon as the idea of a VER was mooted in order to avert its introduction — that is, the monopolist would impose its own limits in order to avoid tighter limits from the importing countrys authorities. Between these extremes the outcome depended on the degree of competition in the export industry.

The empirical part of Chapter 6 concerned reactions to the European Communities' import surveillance — heightened statistical monitoring of import volumes in sensitive sectors which often preceded a VER. Reactions to surveillance varied by markets in precisely the way predicted. I thought of the exercise as an empirical application of so-called strategic trade policy. The latter theory of trade policy from the mid-1980s argued that in imperfectly competitive industries, governments could bias oligopolistic export markets in favour of their own firms, often merely by threatening to intervene and relying on foreign firms to adjust — see, for example, the papers in Krugman and Smith (1994). It was an exciting theoretical idea (now largely defunct) but one which depended on behaviours that were barely observable let alone measurable. I wanted to bring some evidence to the party and characterised import surveillance as a particularly simple form of strategic trade policy.

The final paper in this section is one of my favourites. During my first period working for the World Bank, I joined the team producing the World Development Report, 1986 on Agricultural Trade Policy. It was an exhilarating experience; as a complete novice to agriculture, I worked very intensively with acknowledged leaders such as Bruce Gardner, Dale Johnson, Ulrich Koester, and Kym Anderson and over about four months soaked up, albeit doubtless imperfectly, huge amounts of information. I became particularly interested in the political economy of agricultural policy. On returning to Britain, I produced two papers on this subject for OECD (Winters, 1987b, 1989–90), which has had a long-standing involvement with agriculture and was, at the time, producing the path-breaking quantification of agricultural trade barriers that allowed the Uruguay Round to start to negotiate their reduction.

Agricultural protection and support was huge and costly throughout the Western world during the 1980s, and on many occasions during the hard-fought policy debates about it, I encountered the argument that it was necessary in order to maintain food, and hence national, security. Moreover this argument was almost always delivered in ways that indicated, explicitly or implicitly, that it was therefore beyond economic analysis and that economists should make way for the 'serious' players (or 'grown ups' as was once put to me). Of course national security is of huge importance, but because we would not pay an infinite amount for it, we must conclude that even it is not immune to the trade-offs that are the domain of economics. And even if it were, there are still questions about choosing efficient means of achieving it and minimising its cost in other dimensions.

I gradually evolved responses to these arguments but, given its heavily political nature, the OECD Secretariat felt they could not risk my setting them out in the second *OECD Economic Studies* article. With the story straight in my own mind and fire in my belly, therefore, I sat down to write it out in an intensive burst over two weeks. The result, with almost no revision, is Chapter 7 of this book. Briefly the argument is that: there *are* trade-offs between food security and other issues; exclusion from world food markets to the extent of starvation is almost inconceivable because there are so many potential suppliers of food and food can be shipped in technologically quite unsophisticated ways, although an emergency diet might not be pleasant[1]; contemporary European agricultural policy stressed current production and intensive farming methods which tend to exhaust the land's fertility; as a result, an oil embargo — which *is* quite conceivable — would devastate European food production by curtailing mechanical cultivation and supplies of fertilizer; and consequently if one were serious about food security, one would keep food stocks for the shorter run, and stocks of simple agricultural implements and of fallow land (i.e., currently unused agricultural land) for the longer-run. Maybe, I concluded, actual agricultural policy was about something other than national security.

## Part B: Regionalism

The articles on footwear trade restrictions in Part A involved the econometric estimation of systems of equations describing the demand for imports or the supply of exports. This approach was not common in trade policy work at the time and I was able to implement it because in another stream of work I had invested heavily in understanding (and programming) the requisite techniques. I studied non-tariff barriers because they were an important policy issue and intellectual challenge of the 1980s, but it was

[1] In the course of this step, I realised that nutritionists disagreed over the necessary minimum diet far more than economists disagreed about virtually anything.

certainly fortunate in terms of getting published that I was able to bring relatively sophisticated tools to it.

My experience in systems econometrics arose from the research I did on British exports as a member of the Cambridge Growth Project in the 1970s. As a comprehensive model of the British economy, the Growth Project model required predictions of UK exports, and this was the topic I volunteered to work on when I arrived in 1971. Much of that work is described in Winters (1981), and in the course of doing it, I started to wonder why my predictions differed from those of the other modellers such as the London Business School and the National Institute of Economic and Social Research. One reason was that I related UK exports directly to measures of the demand for goods and services in export markets, whereas the other researchers adopted a two-stage procedure, which first predicted aggregate imports in the major markets and then, taking that as given, predicted the UK share of those imports.

Winters (1981, 22–24) sets out a rather clumsy analysis of the different modelling strategies arguing that mine was preferable.[2] Having moved to the University of Bristol, I showed this to Angus Deaton who explained that I had stumbled into an area of which the leading demand theorists had a well-developed understanding, in terms of separability and two-stage budgeting. Equipped with Angus's seminal book — Deaton and Muellbauer (1981) — I struggled to re-cast my problem in demand theory terms and to estimate and test the assumption of separability more formally. I did so by studying the geographical composition of UK *imports* of manufactures.

Separability and two-stage budgeting implies that UK consumers of cars, say, first decide how to divide their spending between UK and foreign cars and then allocate the latter over, say, German, Japanese, and Italian cars in a second stage. Among the assumptions necessary to permit this formally are that the first stage depends only on the overall price index of cars, not directly on the prices of the individual sources of cars, and that in the second stage, the demand for cars from each source responds in exactly the same way to changes in the aggregate demand for imports, no matter what caused it. Thus, for example, if demand for imported cars rose because British incomes had increased, that was required to be allocated

[2]The natural question of who was better at predicting UK exports was not easy to answer, since the other modellers were quarterly forecasters looking perhaps two years ahead, whereas the Cambridge model was for medium-term projections (3–7 years ahead) and had considerable commodity disaggregation.

over sources of supply in exactly the same way as if it had risen because the UK industry had become uncompetitive. The example of cars shows just how unrealistic this is: rising incomes might boost the demand for all cars proportionately or perhaps be biased slightly towards better quality ones. The collapse of UK sales, on the other hand, would tend to shift demand towards those foreign varieties that were most like British ones — perhaps French and Italian cars. I was able to show that given total UK imports of manufactures, the allocation of this total over sources did in fact depend on the price of UK manufactures. This was sufficient to reject separability and two-stage budgeting, and thus reject the approach of first predicting imports and then dividing them over suppliers. Extending the insight to UK exports, which was where I started, I had justified my approach of relating exports directly to demand in the markets concerned rather than to the market's aggregate imports.

Chapter 8 is still cited, but as with results on rationing and non-tariff barriers above, adhering to its conclusions has the cost of making empirical work much more complicated, so it is not actually applied very often. Experience of the uptake of these two pieces of research has certainly brought home to me the first lesson of economics: the cheaper things are (in the case of methodological research read 'easier to use') the greater, *ceteris paribus*, the demand they face.

The econometrics for Chapter 8 were frustrating; with data on only ten sources of imports over twenty-eight years, I was trying to estimate ten income effects and fourty-five price effects, with the result that I was frequently confronted with poorly determined parameter estimates. One set of co-efficients stuck out, however, and caught my interest: I consistently found that accession to the European Economic Community (the forerunner of the European Union) appeared to boost UK imports from other member countries, curtail imports from some non-member countries, and strongly curtail the UK's sales of manufactures in its own market. In other words, I had found, using more sophisticated methods than were common at the time, that regional integration affected trade flows in the ways suggested by Jacob Viner. Again at Angus Deaton's suggestion, I wrote these results up, located them in their literature and found a ready market — see Chapter 9.

The serendipity of noticing the economic integration results in Chapter 9 uncovered what turned out to be a rich seam of future research for me. I rapidly applied the same model to UK exports by looking at import allocation in three European and two non-European countries and found that, *ceteris paribus*, exports to Europe increased and exports to non-European destinations decreased following accession — Winters (1985). I also thought about how one should estimate integration effects (Winters, 1987a) and, first at the request of Helen Wallace then at Chatham House, worked on the hot topic of the period, the European Single Market or '1992' — Pelkmans and Winters (1988).

A vital part of my professional life since the mid-1980s has been the Centre for Economic Policy Research (CEPR). The CEPR strongly encouraged my work on trade policy and European integration, and helped me to meet and work with leading policy-makers in those areas. I led a major CEPR programme on '1992', which turned out to provide the organisational template for many later CEPR projects — e.g., Winters (1992a,b) — and with colleagues produced several reports on *Monitoring European Integration.* The CEPR also strongly promoted work on the integration of the newly liberalised Central and Eastern European Countries (the CEECs), for which a sensible trade policy and policy towards integration with the European Communities (as they had now become) were key policy questions.[3] One key issue was to estimate how much trade Western Europe might expect from the CEECs, which I worked on with my wife Zhen Kun Wang (e.g., Wang and Winters, 1992), and another, for which I believe we were the first to make the point, that at least the Central European countries had considerable stocks of educated labour, which would affect their trade patterns heavily — Hamilton and Winters (1992). It is impossible to prove, but my belief is that the CEPR had a significant impact on the trade relations between the CEECs and the European Communities — partly because of the advice we offered the former (although these countries had access to plenty of strong academic economists returning home from the USA as they liberalised), and partly because we influenced the European Commission and gave ammunition to the more liberal parts of it in their internal debates.

In April 1994, I returned to the World Bank as Division Chief for International Trade. I was obliged to cease work on Central and Eastern European trade issues (which was not currently a World Bank priority because it was believed that the European Commission would take care of it), and also on global warming and international trade in which I had become interested (another Department's turf). I was, however, immediately immersed in the

[3]My introduction to Eastern Europe was via Carl Hamilton, who within days of the reforms in Poland had the idea that we should watch and document how the huge Soviet-era firms adjusted to real markets and invited me to help. We found it impossible to get funding directly for this excellent bit of science, but as soon as I added promises of policy conclusions to the prospectus, we had plenty of potential funding.

issues surrounding the completion of the Uruguay Round of trade talks and the creation of the World Trade Organisation and also in regional trading arrangements (RTAs) between developing countries. On the latter, Maurice Schiff and I created a wide-ranging programme on Regionalism and Development, some of which was summarised in Schiff and Winters (2003). Probably the most interesting academically was the effect of regionalism on the members' terms of trade.

The stimulus for the terms of trade work came on the plane to take up my post in the Bank. I was due the next day to appear in front of the Bank's Board to discuss a paper on regional trading arrangements written by two of my new colleagues, Carlos Primo Braga and Patrick Low. It contained a section on the effects of RTAs on excluded (i.e., non-member) countries and in passing referred to the Kemp-Wan Theorem (Kemp and Wan, 1976). Excluded countries had exercised my mind quite a lot in terms of European integration and, given a few clear hours to think about it (and probably some wine), I concluded that while Kemp and Wan had barely dealt with the issue, they did provide the key (well, at least *a* key) to exploring it.

Kemp and Wan (1976) is one of the most elegant pieces of international economics extant. In three pages it shows that, given a few not uncommon assumptions, any customs union (an RTA with a common external tariff that applies to every member country's trade with the rest of the world) can be constructed to be globally Pareto improving. The 'trick' is as follows: before the customs union is signed, the members collectively have a particular trade pattern with the rest of the world (the excluded countries). When the customs union removes the trade barriers between members, this trade is disturbed, but it is always possible to design a common external tariff that returns it to precisely the same level as before the customs union. (In using the terms 'before' and 'after', I am assuming that nothing else at all changes through time.) Since the trade between the customs union and the rest of the world is at precisely the same level as before, the terms of trade will be the same and the rest of the world will achieve exactly its pre-customs union level of welfare. Kemp and Wan then show that given the unchanged trade with the rest of the world, there are still efficiency gains for the member countries from reducing the barriers on their mutual trade to zero. Members gain, non-members do not lose and so we have a Pareto improvement.

There are two observations to make: first, Kemp and Wan show that the common external tariff *can* be set to prevent the rest of the world from losing or gaining, not that it actually *is* so set. Second, Kemp and

Wan quite deliberately make no statement about how any common external tariff structure other than the one that holds the rest of the world's welfare constant would actually affect its welfare. The elegance of their work lies substantially in their ability to avoid having to answer that question. So here was a research agenda stimulated by policy needs: first, like Carlos and Patrick much of the profession had started to talk about Kemp-Wan and the rest of the world's welfare, so there was a target, and, second, how might we more appropriately estimate the effects on the rest of the world's welfare? The answer was 'look at the their terms of trade'. In fact, it turned out that Robert Mundell had laid out a simple model of the terms of trade effects of a customs union in 1964 which showed that excluded countries would lose (Mundell, 1964), but this had lain largely ignored for over thirty years, with roughly one citation a year up until 1994 (and four times as many since).

Chapter 10 sets out the argument that the Kemp-Wan Theorem is not about the rest of the world's welfare. It was followed by several other papers laying out the arguments in more practical terms and seeking evidence of the postulated effects in modelling exercises in the literature. In addition, with Won Chang, I also undertook two empirical exercises — the first on Spain's accession to the European Communities and the second on the creation of Mercosur, the customs union between Argentina, Brazil, Paraguay, and Uruguay, both of which confirmed that non-member countries tended to suffer terms of trade losses when customs unions were formed.

The research on Mercosur is reported in Chapter 11. The basic idea is that when Argentinian firms receive a competitive advantage in Brazil because Mercosur means that they no longer have to pay tariffs, other counties exporting to Brazil will feel the need to reduce their own prices somewhat even though they, being excluded from the customs union, have no such advantage. To estimate these effects we considered five non-Mercosur exporters (Chile, Germany, Japan, Korea, and the USA) and looked at the ratio of the prices of their exports to Brazil relative to the prices of their exports of the same commodities to other markets. (By considering relative export prices we could eliminate any exporter-specific effects.) We related these price relatives to various control variables and to the tariffs faced by Argentina in Brazil, and found, as expected, that the latter played a significant role in the non-member's pricing decisions. Given these estimates, we calculated by how much, on average, the excluded country exporters would have reduced their prices when Argentinian exporters moved from paying the normal (most favoured nation) tariff to paying zero.

The final paper on regional trading arrangements takes us back to the beginning — what has been the effect of European economic integration? The 1990s saw the advent of the new economic geography in which international trade economists tried to answer the pressing policy question of what would happen as the European Communities expanded to include new members. The simple extant models suggested that the gains from trade would benefit every country, but there was a popular undercurrent that worried that integration would allow a favoured core of regions to gain at the expense of the periphery.

The first analytical exposition of the new economic geography, by Paul Krugman and Tony Venables (1990), was in a CEPR policy book, and from it flowed a multitude of refinements and journal publications. The basic idea was that once international trading costs and fixed costs were put into the same model, one could get an agglomeration of economic activity — i.e., a core-periphery pattern: the question hinged around whether it was cheaper for a firm to supply a market by local production or by producing elsewhere and exporting to it. The former is more attractive if transport costs are high relative to fixed costs and the latter if they are low. To this, Krugman and Venables added the observation that firms would want to locate where most of their demand was located, because in that way they avoided the additional costs of exporting relative to selling from a local factory on the majority of their sales. This gave the model a positive feedback loop whereby if one firm chose to locate in country A, it increased demand in country A, and so made it slightly more attractive for other firms also to locate in A. This was sufficient to explain agglomerations. It also implied that while an industry might not relocate in response to small trade liberalisations, because the benefits of staying with the crowd still applied, as trade liberalisation deepened sufficiently for one firm to find it worthwhile to move, many would, and one would get a large discontinuous change — think, say, of industrialisation in Asia.

The geography model is potentially immensely fruitful — it gave us for the first time, a way to model formally processes that simple observation confirmed but which we had up to that point had no means to analyse (and hence tended to deny the existence of). The problem was that it was all theory and that while identifying the switch points in an agglomeration process empirically would be a triumph both intellectually and practically, our empirical tools were not up to the job. Demand followed supply and supply followed demand so that everything seemed to be endogenous and we had almost no way to sort out the various relationships. What we needed was a big exogenous economic-cum-geographical shock. I thought that UK's accession to the EEC, which actually came about fairly suddenly in 1973, might fit the bill, and in 2001, I persuaded Henry Overman, who knew all about UK locational issues and data, that we might try to model the effects.[4]

The key argument in Chapter 12 was that international trade took place through ports — sea and air — and that different ports tended to relate to different countries — partly, although not exclusively, for reasons of geographical proximity — e.g., Dover trading with Western Europe. We argued that as trade with the EEC was encouraged by accession, the hinterlands of different ports would be affected differentially, and that UK employment would tend to migrate towards the hinterlands of those ports that were more heavily implicated in EEC trade. Firms would be attracted to these areas either by better access to European intermediate inputs and/or better access to export markets. Our results were not overwhelming, but in one third of sectors of the UK economy we detected the predicted drift towards the South and East. One of the side products of this exercise was that we compiled a large dataset of UK trade by port and went some way towards explaining it — Overman and Winters (2005).

## Part C: Trade and Poverty

When I rejoined the World Bank in 1994 as Division Chief for International Trade, our largest concern was to analyse and proselytise the outcome of the Uruguay Round. The Round had achieved a large degree of trade liberalisation and created the World Trade Organisation, perhaps its crowning glory. However, even at the outset, various activists expressed concern that developing countries had received a poor deal and that too little had been done to ensure that the benefits of trade liberalisation reached the poor. The same voices were also raised against the World Bank, and James Wolfenson, its new President, refocussed the Bank directly on poverty. I was speaking fairly often about the benefits of the Uruguay Round and why we thought they would help to reduce world poverty and gradually became conscious that we had only theory (albeit good theory — the Stolper-Samuelson Theorem) to support this view. At a seminar in the University of Michigan,

[4] Subsequently, Stephen Redding and Daniel Sturm (2008) came up with a much better case — the division and reunification of Germany and several scholars have exploited the geographical variance in World War II bombing.

Jim Levinsohn challenged me about whether I *knew* the poor would benefit and I guess I mumbled and waved my hands a lot. Afterwards Jim and I sat down and agreed that we had to do better than this and the idea of a research project on the subject was born. We talked to the poverty experts in the Bank and raised some money internally, and Jim started work on a project in 1996, with the eventual output — Friedman and Levinsohn (2002).

Although I actively supported the poverty project, I found it hard to find the time to engage on it personally and so it seemed as if here was another great idea that just would not get off the ground. However, in 1997 three things happened: the activist resistance to trade liberalisation increased, ultimately culminating in the riots at the third WTO Ministerial Meeting in Seattle in 1999; I decided to return to academia in the UK, and the new UK government created the Department for International Development (DFID) as a fully fledged department of government with a seat in the Cabinet. Among the many enlightened decisions that DFID took in its early life was that it could most rapidly start to improve the lot of poor people by engaging internationally and drawing on the expertise of the International Organisations. DFID supported international trade work within the World Bank handsomely — and in doing so was instrumental in overcoming management plans that the Bank should pull out of that area of work. And when they heard I was returning to the UK, DFID staff agreed to support — again handsomely — serious research on trade liberalisation and poverty in the University of Sussex. From the moment I returned in January 1999, this topic became my principal research theme, along with various colleagues of whom Neil McCulloch was the most heavily involved.

The earliest products of this effort were a background paper for the World Development Report, 2000 and a policy paper for the WTO. Then followed a book length exposition — McCulloch, Winters and Cirera (2001) — dealing with both the topic in general and a series of issues that looked ripe for negotiation in a round of WTO talks (and which did actually figure in the initial agenda for Doha Round, which started in December 2001). A more analytical version of the initial papers was published in 2002 and is reproduced here as Chapter 13, and a recast and definitive version in 2004, here reproduced as Chapter 14. These papers, which have, I think, been quite influential, are 'mere' literature surveys — 'all' they do is lay out a taxonomy for thinking through the poverty effects of trade liberalisation and collect together from a large range of literatures what we actually know about its various elements. Thus there is, in one sense, nothing original in the papers, but by organising the topic and collating the evidence we were able to help both academic and policy analysis considerably.[5]

Chapters 13 and 14 build their analysis around four themes. One is macroeconomic — the extent to which trade liberalisation stimulates economic growth, to which I return below. The others detail three microeconomic channels through which shocks and policy interventions at the border (trade shocks and trade policy) can be transmitted to the poor. First, households and markets, which focuses on the prices that households pay and receive in goods and services markets, including whether the markets actually exist and also their degree of variability; many of the extreme poor depend on producing things directly for their livings, not the sale of their labour, so this is their key channel of transmission. The second channel is factor markets, in effect labour markets for less skilled labour when we are talking about poverty. This is where the Stolper-Samuelson Theorem and its generalisations fit in. The third is government revenue: although not very sophisticated analytically this is almost always the first objection that policy makers make to the advice to reduce tariff rates on imports — "the government will lose revenue and the resulting adjustment will harm the poor". In fact, partial tariff reductions frequently increase tariff revenue rather than cut it and even where they do cut it, there is no law of economic behaviour that implies that this must impinge on the poor. It does so because someone decides, either actively or passively, that that is where the burden should fall.

The policy thrust of these chapters is that there can be no simple general conclusion about the relationship between trade liberalisation and poverty. There is a strong presumption that trade liberalisation will be poverty-reducing in the long run and on average through its effects on the level of national income, but there is no guarantee that the static and microeconomic effects will always be beneficial for the poor. Because they alter relative prices significantly, trade liberalisations will almost inevitably reduce the well-being of some people (at least in the short term) and some of these people may be poor: the precise effects of a liberalisation depend, *inter alia*, on factors such as the pre-liberalisation economic situation, the trade

[5] One colleague thanked me for writing the paper because it saved him the trouble of doing so! I was rather affronted at first, but the truth is that the paper and the stream of work that emerged from it rely not so much on a clever and isolated bit of insight as on the painstaking use of what was known to answer a practical question. Somebody else could indeed have written it.

reforms actually undertaken, who the poor are and how they sustain themselves. On the plus side, however, poverty effects are relatively straightforward to predict provided that analysts garner the basic information required, and so liberalisation may be tailored to avoid the worst poverty impacts and accompanied by targeted compensatory measures. Recently Antonio Martuscelli and I have updated this survey work and concluded that while the economics profession has produced a lot of interesting work on trade and poverty, neither the methodologies nor the overall conclusion has changed much — Martuscelli and Winters (2014).

The macroeconomic component of the trade and poverty story actually represents a whole sub-theme of its own: the connection between trade policy and income, in either levels or growth rates, has long fascinated economists, which, as Dani Rodrik has observed, suggests that the profession has no settled view about it. In 2000, the OECD Secretariat asked me to review this literature critically and Tony Thirlwall kindly suggested that he should include a version of the resulting paper in a Symposium that he was constructing for the *Economic Journal*. That paper, which both reviews evidence and tries to clarify some methodological and conceptual points has proved popular and is included as Chapter 15 in this book. It argues that the relationship is between openness to trade and the *level* of income per head, or between trade liberalisation and the *growth* in that income, that it is fairly reliably positive and that with reasonable certainty we can say that it is causal. It does note, however, that the positive causal relationship is not guaranteed and thus that there remains work to be done to understand why and when it breaks down. In particular, this chapter discusses the role of institutions, which is clearly likely to be important in getting the best out of liberalisation and continues to attract a lot of attention today.

Chapters 13 and 14 argue strongly that the question of whether trade liberalisation reduces or increases poverty is an empirical one and thus should be tackled to the greatest extent possible by examining real data and considering the actual outcomes of real policies. This actually turns out to be quite difficult and Chapters 16 and 17 present two of my attempts to do so by putting into practice the conceptual framework provided in the previous chapters. The former, written with former students Yoko Niimi and Puja Vasudeva Dutta, was a product of a large study of Vietnam which at the time was one of the very few countries which had the appropriate data and experience. We sought countries which had undertaken a significant trade liberalisation and for which we could observe the same households both before and after it. We had a panel covering over four thousand households in 1992/3 and 1997/8. Vietnam's trade liberalisation over this period was part of a longer process of dismantling non-tariff barriers rather than a discrete step change in tariffs which we could easily measure, and this made it difficult to identify its effects with complete confidence (and to the satisfaction of journal referees, too!).

Using the official poverty line, we characterised each household's poverty status (poor (P) or not (N)) in the two surveys and sorted them into sets according to this pair — i.e., into the sets ($P_{92}$,$P_{97}$), ($P_{92}$, $N_{97}$), ($N_{92}$, $P_{97}$), and ($N_{92}$,$N_{97}$). We then applied a multinomial logit model to explain which households fell into which set. The effect of trade liberalisation was captured by whether, in 1992, the household produced major export crops (coffee and rice) or had employees in the major export industries (all of which boomed massively over the period) or had employees in import competing industries. Export engagement was strongly associated with getting out of poverty, but there was not a well-defined relationship between poverty changes and import competing employment. The latter presumably reflected the general dynamism of the Vietnamese economy during the period, which meant that even import competing industries did not contract much and that any workers displaced could easily find other employment.

Chapter 17 summarised the work in Vietnam and added accounts of similar attempts to identify trade effects on poverty in Sichuan and Zambia during the 1990s. In the former, the 'trade' shock was the changes in the centrally determined price of grain at which Sichuan was obliged to trade. Exactly as we would predict, net producers of grain benefitted when the price was higher and showed a stronger ability to get out of poverty. Net consumers showed the opposite. In Zambia, we had to construct pseudo-panels and while our estimated effects had the signs predicted by theory, few of them were statistically significant. This wider agenda of work showed, *inter alia*, that the most important element in predicting the poverty effect of a trade reform on a given household is the way in which the household earns its living. Differences in consumption patterns do mean households are affected differently by non-uniform price changes, but generally to nothing like the extent to which differences in crop mixes or employment sectors do. This is because households have relatively similar consumption patterns but great differences in employment.

True empirical work relies on the *ex post* analysis of past events — The Oxford English Dictionary defines empirical as 'based on, concerned with, or verifiable by observation or experience rather than theory or pure logic'. Thus if one is concerned, as policy makers often are, with predicting the effects of a future trade liberalisation, pure empiricism is not possible. Rather one has to turn to simulation modelling in which one builds a computable model of (parts of) the economy and solves it under different assumptions about trade policy. The models may be heavily reliant on past empirical research to identify the form and parameters of economic behaviour, but the effect on poverty is predicted not actual. The most common type of modelling for trade policy is Computable General Equilibrium Modelling and the leading exponents of this art are probably the members of the GTAP (Global Trade Analysis Project) Consortium which is managed from Purdue University. Chapter 18 is a modelling exercise in which I cooperated with Tom Hertel, founder and Director of GTAP, and two young colleagues, Roman Keeney and Maros Ivanic. It looks at a possible outcome of the Doha Development Round of trade talks in the WTO and shows why it is not as poverty-friendly as it might be.

Chapter 18 considers a world trade liberalisation that, in 2007, seemed conceivable as an outcome to the WTO's Doha Development Agenda, particularly its agricultural trade dimension which was among the most contentious. The chapter argues that despite the rhetoric of a 'Development Round', it was fundamentally less poverty-friendly than it could be, in large part due to the absence of tariff cuts on staple food products in developing countries. Such cuts would give the poor access to food at world prices, thereby reducing the cost of living at the poverty line. It also explores the question of whether such tariff cuts would hurt the poor working in agriculture and concludes from an analysis of fifteen developing countries, that there is some danger of this occuring. However, such adverse effects are minimized by ensuring that agricultural tariffs are cut in all developing countries so that intra-developing country trade can increase. Note that the key to poverty reduction is developing countries' *own* tariffs, not the tariffs or the agricultural subsidies of developed countries. Subsidies are a bit of a red herring so far as world poverty is concerned, because, while they hurt those producers in developing countries who compete with the developed countries' temperate agricultural goods, they benefit net consumers in developing counties, among whom most of the very poor are to be found. We documented this in Hertel et al. (2007).

The final chapter in this section is less directly about poverty, but has potentially strong distributional implications. The chapter concerns the effect of competition from Chinese exports on manufacturing firms in Mexico. The research theme started with Leo Iacovone's excellent PhD thesis in the University of Sussex, in which he compiled a unique dataset on Mexican firms and used it to explore Mexican trade liberalisation — see, for example, Iacovone (2012). We realised that the same data could start to answer the China question — which was not only of great policy concern then, but had also become an interest of mine when I was asked to create a project on China in the World Bank in 2006.

Written with Leo and Ferdinand Rauch, Chapter 19 calculates the exposure of different Mexican manufacturing firms to competition from China, much of which was experienced not in Mexico but in the USA because Mexico and China were major suppliers and strong competitors there. It then relates these firms' performances to this degree of exposure and finds that while smaller and weaker firms suffered considerably, larger and more productive ones seemed to weather the storm nearly untouched. Part of their defence mechanism was that they were better able to take advantage of cheaper and better supplies of intermediate inputs once China had penetrated the Mexican market. The same pattern was observable at the product level — firms cut back on their 'minor' products in the face of competition but managed a stronger performance on core products.

Clearly there is more to economic welfare that just firm performance, but the obvious policy message of this work is that coping with foreign competition is one of the ways in which a sector or an economy replaces weaker performers by stronger ones and hence raises mean productivity and incomes. Attempts to respond to Chinese competition by restricting access to the Mexican market, as many had advocated, would reduce this 'clearing out' process, reduce access to intermediates and, of course, completely miss the more important domain of competition, namely in major export markets. On the other hand, if it is the case that small and weaker firms employ weaker, poorer workers, the latter could suffer short-run costs as the firms cut back or disappeared. In the absence of strong mobility, these workers could then experience quite a significant loss of welfare. These trade-offs between the short and long runs and between the stronger and weaker members of society are what makes the political economy of trade liberalisation and poverty so interesting and so sensitive — as Ravi Kanbur (2001) has so fascinatingly laid out.

## Finale

The subject of this book is international trade policy and its approach is entirely empirical. The combination reflects my profound belief that economics is about the real world and trying to make it a better place to live in: we need to understand how the economy works and we also need to be able to measure the parameters of behaviour and the extent of distortions if we are to calibrate policy correctly. I also hope that the chapters of this book illustrate that making these measurements is not necessarily a simple task and, thus, that policy research is not a second rate activity to be fitted in between bouts of 'pure science' but that it can be intellectually challenging and rewarding. Early in my career Alan Brown[6], who taught me as an undergraduate and to whom I think I owe both my first job in Cambridge and my first contact with the World Bank, impressed on me the importance of getting the technical details right when tackling even the most practical of questions. I hope that these chapters would not disappoint him in that respect.

I greatly respect the people who develop new theories and new econometric techniques, but perhaps for lack of talent, those pleasures have never fallen to me. I do not, however, greatly respect people who choose their topics in order to show that they are able to use the latest techniques: research students often tell me that they need to have this or that bit of technique in order to get a PhD and I reply that, on the contrary, they need a good question (for me, a real one, not an artificial one) and then to use the most appropriate tools we have to answer it. Some questions seem to defy satisfactory answers and I sympathise with young academics who feel they must avoid these because they have to get published in journals which seem to believe in some absolute standard of identification or proof. This seems to me to confuse ends and means; the criterion should be how important (or genuinely interesting) is the question and have we answered it convincingly to the best of the profession's current ability. I greatly enjoyed my work in the World Bank's Research Department because the Bank's practical work on development served up a constant flow of interesting questions and yet we had carved out enough distance from the hurly burly of operations to be able to tackle at least some of them rigorously.

What lessons would I draw from all this about the process of doing research on policy matters? First, as I have already said, listen to policymakers, try to answer their questions and to work out why they posed them in the first place. Of course, not all such questions are well-formulated research questions and not all require original research to answer them, but

[6] He was often known as 'Log-Normal Brown' after his great book with Aitcheson (1957).

some of them meet these criteria and I have found them a very useful stimulus. Second, collaborate: looking back over this chapter I am reminded of how much I gained from working with other people and how grateful I am that they put up with my foibles to see the work through to its conclusion. Third, be patient: most of the articles reprinted here took at least six years between the glimmer of the idea and actually getting into print. The practice of judging research on a five or six year cycle encourages cleverness but shallowness, not care and breadth. Policy-makers require answers a lot more quickly than this and one has to be prepared to respond to them on something approaching their timetable, but many of the issues warrant a longer and closer look over a longer time horizon. This is a major problem for researchers in institutes that require a continuing flow of new grants to pay the bills. I would like to think that if university researchers responded a little bit more positively to requests from policy-makers, more questions would flow to them and over the years we would get deeper analyses of policy questions.

## References

Aitchison, J and JAC Brown (1957). *The Lognormal Distribution with Special Reference to Its Uses in Economics.* Cambridge: Cambridge University Press.

Brenton, PA and LA Winters (1991). "Quantifying the Economic Effects of Non-Tariff Barriers: The Case of U.K. Footwear." *Kyklos,* 44, 71–92.

Deaton, A and JA Muellbauer (1980). *Economics and Consumer Behavior.* Cambridge: Cambridge University Press.

De Melo, J and LA Winters (1993). "Price and Quality Effects of VERs Revisited: A Case Study of Korean Footwear Exports." *Journal of Economic Integration,* 8(1): 33–57.

Fujita, M, PR Krugman and AJ Venables (2001). *The Spatial Economy: Cities, Regions, and International Trade.* Cambridge, Massachusetts: MIT Press.

Hamilton, CB and LA Winters (1992). "Opening up International Trade with Eastern Europe." *Economic Policy,* 14, 78–116.

Hertel, TW, R Keeney, M Ivanic and LA Winters (2007). "Distributional Effects of WTO Agricultural Reforms in Rich and Poor Countries." *Economic Policy,* 22(50), 289–337.

Iacovone, L (2012). "The Better You Are the Stronger It Makes You: Evidence on the Asymmetric Impact of Liberalization." *Journal of Development Economics,* 99(2), 474–485.

Kanbur, R (2001). "Economic Policy, Distribution and Poverty: The Nature of Disagreements." *World Development,* 29(6), 1083–1094.

Kemp, MC and HY Wan Jr (1976). "An Elementary Proposition Concerning the Formation of Customs Unions." *Journal of International Economics*, 6(1), 95–97.

Krugman, PR and A Smith (1994). *Empirical Studies of Strategic Trade Policy.* Chicago: University of Chicago Press.

Krugman, PR and AJ Venables (1990). "Integration and the Competitiveness of Peripheral Industry." In C Bliss and J De Macedo. *Unity with Diversity in the European Community.* Oxford: Oxford University Press, 56–77.

Martuscelli, A and LA Winters (2014). "Trade Liberalisation and Poverty: What Have We Learned in a Decade?" *Annual Review of Resource Economics*, 6. DOI: 10.1146/annurev-resource-110713-105054.

Mundell, R (1964). "Tariff Preferences and the Terms of Trade." *The Manchester School*, 32(1), 1–13.

Overman, HG and LA Winters (2005). "The Port Geography of UK International Trade." *Environment and Planning A*, 37(10), 1751–1768.

Pelkmans, J, LA Winters and H Wallace (1988). "Europe's Domestic Market." Chatham House Paper No. 43.

Redding, SJ and DM Sturm (2008). "The Costs of Remoteness: Evidence from German Division and Reunification." *American Economic Review*, 98(5), 1766–1797.

Schiff, M and LA Winters (2003). *Regional Integration and Development.* Oxford: Oxford University Press.

United Nations Conference on Trade and Development (UNCTAD) (2010). *Non-Tariff Measures:* Evidence from Selected Developing Countries and Future Research Agenda. UNCTAD, Geneva.

Winters, LA (1981). *An Econometric Model of the Export Sector: U.K. Visible Exports and Their Prices, 1955–73.* Cambridge: Cambridge University Press.

Winters, LA (1985). "Separability and the Modelling of International Economic Integration: UK Exports to Five Industrial Countries." *European Economic Review*, 27(3), 335–353.

Winters, LA (1987a). "Britain in Europe: A Survey of Quantitative Trade Studies." *Journal of Common Market Studies*, 25, 315–335.

Winters, LA (1987b). "The Economic Consequences of Agricultural Support: A Survey." *OECD, Economic Studies*, 9, 7–54.

Winters, LA (1989). "The 'So-Called Non-Economic Objectives' of Agricultural Policy." *OECD Economic Studies*, 13, 237–266.

Winters, LA (1992a). *Trade Flows and Trade Policy After '1992'.* Cambridge: Cambridge University Press.

Winters, LA (1992b). "The Welfare and Policy Implications of the International Trade Consequences of '1992'." *The American Economic Review Papers and Proceedings*, 82, 104–108.

Winters, LA and PMG Martins (2004). "When Comparative Advantage is Not Enough: Business Costs in Small Remote Economies." *World Trade Review*, 3(3), 347–383.

Winters, LA, T Walmsley, Z Wang and R Grynberg (2003). "Liberalising Temporary Movement of Natural Persons: An Agenda for the Development Round." *The World Economy*, 26(8), 1137–1162.

Winters, LA and ZK Wang (1992). *Eastern Europe's International Trade*. London: Manchester University Press.

# Part A

# Non-Tariff Barriers

THE WORLD BANK ECONOMIC REVIEW, VOL. 1, NO. 1: 181–199

# The Extent of Nontariff Barriers to Industrial Countries' Imports

Julio. J. Nogués, Andrzej Olechowski, and L. Alan Winters

*This article examines the extent of nontariff barriers (NTBs) to the visible imports of sixteen industrial countries. It uses three alternative measures to show that governmental commodity-specific border measures affect more than 27 percent of all imports and more than 34 percent of imports from developing countries. It also shows that during the period from 1981 to 1983, NTBs became significantly more extensive. Detailed statistics reveal considerable variations in NTB coverage by commodity, type of barrier, importer, and exporter. The data on which these conclusions are based were compiled from official information at the highest level of disaggregation and are described in the article.*

Since the 1940s, considerable progress has been made in liberalizing tariff barriers to international trade through a series of multilateral negotiations. For example, the Tokyo Round of the General Agreement on Tariffs and Trade (GATT) concluded in 1979 with an agreement to lower industrial countries' tariffs by about 25 percent on average, and the Geneva (1956), Dillon (1962), and Kennedy rounds (1968) produced similar reductions. In consequence, the average tariff level of industrial countries was reduced from about 40 percent in the mid-1930s to 4–8 percent after the Tokyo Round.

As the GATT rounds have brought about a significant decline in tariff obstacles to trade, nontariff barriers (NTBs) have become more prevalent. The GATT specifically allows countries to impose several kinds of measures, for example, safeguard and antidumping restrictions and countervailing duties. In addition, governments and import-competing interests have been quite inventive in expanding trade barriers. These restrictions have come about through the development and implementation of restrictions which are outside the GATT, such as "voluntary" export restraints, and through the addition of provisions to the

The authors are on the staff of the World Bank. They would like to thank J. Michael Finger for his direction and comments during the article's progress. The programming skills of Jerzy Rozanski have also been of great help. This article, first published in February 1986 in a somewhat different form as World Bank Staff Working Paper 789, is based on a joint study by the United Nations Conference on Trade and Development and the World Bank.

GATT to sanction widespread restrictions, including those on agricultural products when the GATT was initially negotiated, and later, the adoption of the Multifibre Arrangement for textiles and clothing.

Behind this paper lies an interest in moving the international community toward the elimination of such restrictions, but we do not directly address that topic here. This paper takes up an important prerequisite to such work: the presentation of credible information on the nature and extent of nontariff barriers in international trade.[1] The quantitative work reported here concentrates on a basic dimension, the amount of trade subject to or covered by NTBs. Within this quantitative dimension, the paper addresses three questions:

- What is the prevalence of the major nontariff barriers to imports of industrial countries?
- Has that prevalence increased in recent years?
- Are imports from developing countries particularly subject to NTBs?

Section I describes the types of NTBs included in this study and discusses the way each type restricts international trade. Section II discusses the concepts, data, and statistical indicators used, while Sections III to V present the results of the analysis. Section VI provides a summary and conclusions.

## I. The Nontariff Barriers Included

The array of governmental nontariff barriers to trade is very wide. For example, the table of contents of the inventory of nontariff measures which is used by the GATT Secretariat in its *Report of the Group on Quantitative Restrictions and Other Non-Tariff Measures* enumerates more than forty categories of measures.

There are many political and administrative mechanisms through which import restrictions are put in place, and many reasons, legal, political, and otherwise, why a government might argue against the application of the label "protection" or "import regulation" to its policy measures. In certain circumstances, the GATT allows the use of some types of import restrictions, but whether or not an action conforms to the GATT is not an adequate basis for defining a measure as protective. The GATT allows "safeguard actions" to protect domestic producers from injury caused by tariff binders when "unforeseen developments" occur, despite the fact that such measures are universally interpreted as trade restrictions or protection. We deal here only with the economics of such measures—only with the fact that they impose conditions on import sales which are not imposed on sales by domestic firms.

This article investigates a restricted selection of the measures included in the GATT table of contents; specifically, we examine those which are product-specific

1. Other recent attempts to estimate the extent of NTBs include Balassa and Balassa (1984) and Cline (1985), which lack precision due to the incomplete information on NTBs and aggregated trade data, and Jones (1983), which deals only with the United Kingdom.

border measures for which comprehensive and internationally comparable data are available. While there is room for debate about the composition of a complete set of NTBS, our selection, drawn from official definitions and based on official sources, represents a minimum list of nontariff trade policies. It comprises five groups of the most common and explicit border measures used to control the inflow of foreign goods.

*Quantitative Import Restrictions*

- *Prohibitions and embargoes on the importation of a product.* A prohibition may be total, may admit exceptions at the discretion of the competent authority, or may operate only under certain conditions.
- *Quotas.* Ceilings (specified in value or quantitative terms) are imposed on the importation of a product for a given period of time; they may be global, country-specific, or seasonal.
- *Discretionary import authorizations.* Permission to import is granted at the discretion of competent authorities. These are often used for the administration of quantitative limits.
- *Conditional import authorizations.* Permission to import is subject to the importer undertaking commitments in areas other than importation, or to specified overall economic conditions (such as export performance, or the purchase of an equivalent quantity of domestic output) or the unavailability of domestic supply.

*"Voluntary" Export Restraints*

"Voluntary" export restraints (VERS) are agreements between an exporter and an importer as to the maximum amount of exports (specified in value or quantity terms) to be purchased within a given period of time. This category includes, inter alia, bilateral agreements on textile trade reached within the framework of the the Multifibre Arrangement (MFA) that indicate specific limits, consultation levels, and export controls. Although voluntary export restrictions are administered by exporting countries, they are monitored by importing countries, and their imposition is the result of successful protectionist requests in importing countries.

*Measures for the Enforcement of Decreed Prices*

- *Variable levies.* Import charges set periodically to equalize the import price with a decreed domestic price.
- *Minimum price systems.* A minimum import price is set by the importing country, and import prices below the decreed minimum trigger an additional duty or some other penalty.
- *"Voluntary" export price restraints.* This category covers agreements between the exporter and the importer on the minimum price to be observed by the exporter.

*Tariff-type measures*

• *Tariff quotas.* Two tariff rates are applied, the higher rate coming into operation when the quantity of imported goods exceeds a specified level.
• *Seasonal tariffs.* Different tariff rates are applied to the same (agricultural) product according to the time of year.

*Monitoring measures*

• *Price and volume investigations, surveillance.* Formal investigations of charges by domestic producers about unfair trading practices of an exporting country; formal monitoring of the evolution of imports of sensitive products with or without prior import authorization being required. While an investigation is obviously necessary to determine the facts, there is evidence that the inquiry process itself has a protective effect, independent of the eventual findings (Finger 1981).

The investigative process or continued surveillance generates uncertainty about an exporter's continuing access to the market and creates an incentive for the exporting firm to raise its price, whether or not it is guilty of an illegal practice. A surveillance process is often the means by which a government monitors "voluntary" price maintenance agreements or volume restraint agreements contracted between exporting and import-competing industries or governments. Surveillance is often the precursor to more formal import restrictions,[2] or a signal to exporters to practice "self-restraint" to avoid a more formal "voluntary restraint." "Automatic" import licensing procedures are often restrictive; for example, they serve to police bans on imports from certain countries or to funnel all imports of a product through a government-authorized association of import-competing local producers of that product or of producers of a finished good made from that product.
• *Antidumping and countervailing duties.* In theory, antidumping duties are levied on a product that is sold in the importing country at a lower price than in the exporting country. Countervailing duties are levied to offset export rebates or subsidies with the rationale that such measures create a situation which more closely approximates the outcomes that would exist under free and fair trade regimes. William Dickey's study of antidumping practices in the United States (1979) finds that such measures have a greater disincentive effect on imports than do comparable "fair trade" (mainly antitrust) regulations on domestic firms' sales and that they do, in fact, constitute protection of domestic producers. There is evidence that the outcome of the pricing test in dumping and countervailing duty cases is significantly influenced by the economic variables usually used in the parallel injury test to measure injury, that is, that the *economics* of dumping and countervailing duties is much the same as the economics of safeguard cases (Finger, Hall, and Nelson 1982).

2. Indeed, the European Communities (EEC) regulations (for example, Council regulation; see EEC 1982, p. 288) explicitly refer to surveillance for this purpose. (See EEC 1982.)

While our selection of NTBs includes a broad range of policies, it still constitutes only a subset of the trade restrictions included in the GATT and United Nations Conference on Trade and Development (UNCTAD) lists (UNCTAD 1985). For example, it does not include domestic policy measures (such as subsidies to import-competing producers, government procurement, or restrictions on domestic sale of foreign goods), generalized procedures applying to all imports, restrictive business practices, the use of technical or sanitary requirements as barriers to trade, or subtle forms of import restriction such as changing ports of entry; any of these could seriously affect the level of international trade.

## II. Measurements of NTB Coverage

The principal unit of measure used in this study is the amount or share of a country's imports subject to NTBs.[3] Operationally, this concept is quantified by marking on each line of a country's import list the types of NTBs which are applied to that line. Many such restrictions apply only to imports from particular countries and are not global or subject to the "most favored nation" clause; hence the import list must be disaggregated by both product and country of origin. We calculate the NTB prevalence or coverage ratios as the sum of import lines or value subject to NTB divided by the sum of all import lines or value.

The prevalence or coverage ratio is a more elementary concept than a tariff average; a more appropriate parallel is the ratio of dutiable to total (dutiable plus duty free) imports. While a tariff rate provides a measure of the intensity of restriction it entails, nontariff barriers provide no such obvious measure of intensity, nor has the analysis of NTBs yet created an estimated set of intensity figures for NTBs. We have only a "yes or no" indicator—a strictly qualitative indicator of whether or not governmental considerations, as opposed to just normal commercial considerations, influence the amount or the direction of international trade.

### *The Statistical Indicators*

Three indexes of the prevalence of NTBs are used below. Each summarizes the presence or absence of NTBs on several tariff headings simultaneously, but each uses a different scheme to combine observations. While one might wish to combine NTBs on the basis of the amount by which they reduce trade or of the levels that trade would attain in the absence of NTBs, this is not possible. Neither of these is observable. Indeed, one *purpose* of developing an NTB coverage index is to move *toward* estimating the trade effects of these NTBs, *toward* construction of the counterfactual "free trade" pattern of imports.[4]

3. For a recent and extensive discussion of the measurement of NTBs, see Deardorff and Stern (1985).

4. There are many jokes about economists assuming away the problem, and the suggestion that the coverage ratio be based on "free trade" values is an example of why such jokes have an element of valid criticism in them.

We construct and compare three measures of nontariff barriers—the first based on the value of each country's own imports of particular commodities, the second on the world trade value of these commodities, and the third on the number of flows of these commodities. The first, the *own imports coverage ratio*, $I_c$, measures the sum of the value of a country's import groups affected by NTBS over the total value of its imports of that group. The *world trade coverage ratio*, $I_w$, for each of the commodities imported by a country, measures the sum of the value of world trade of an import group affected by that country's NTBS, over the total value of world trade in that commodity group. The *frequency ratio*, $I_f$, simply registers the relative frequency with which countries impose NTBS on their commodity imports; it counts the number of a country's import flows covered by NTBS and divides this sum by the total number of import flows for that country.

For the actual calculation of the three ratios, for any importer ($i$) and type of nontariff barrier ($b$) let $N_{qx} = 1$ if there is a barrier on imports of the commodity, $q$, from exporter $x$, and $= 0$ otherwise. For sets of commodities ($Q$) and exporters ($X$), all three indexes take the form:

$$I = \frac{\sum_{q \epsilon Q} \sum_{x \epsilon X} W_{qx} N_{qx}}{\sum_{q \epsilon Q} \sum_{x \epsilon X} W_{qx}}$$

We define $W_{qx}$ differently for each ratio.

- $I_c$ defines $W_{qx}$ as the value of $i$'s actual imports of $q$ from $x$.
- $I_w$ for each of the commodities, $q$, imported by $i$, defines $W_{qx}$ as the value of world imports of $q$, aggregated across all exporters.
- $I_f$ defines $W_{qx}$ as the presence or absence of a flow of $q$ from $x$ to $i$; thus $W_{qx} = 1$ if imports of $q$ from $x$ are non-zero, $= 0$ otherwise.

Note that while both $N_{qx}$ and $W_{qx}$ must refer to particular years, these need not be the same, provided that, as here, both have been converted to the same classification.[5]

Each of the three indexes has strengths and weaknesses. The own imports coverage ratio is possibly the most appropriate in that the extent of an NTB is represented by the size of the particular trade flows it affects. Its drawback is that more restrictive NTBS tend to receive lower weight than less restrictive ones because they reduce imports by more. In the extreme, a total prohibition shows up as zero imports covered by NTBS. This difficulty is reduced by allowing $W_{qx}$ to refer to a year in which there were relatively few barriers.

5. The UNCTAD converts NTB information from the trade classification current when they are reported to the 1981 classification used for the trade data. To the extent that this is occasionally impossible, such data are not used and thus our figures may slightly understate the prevalence of NTBS.

To the degree that a country's own restrictions are not correlated with those on world trade, the weight that the world trade coverage ratio applies to a particular NTB will be largely independent of the latter's restrictiveness. If all importers restrict a particular commodity (such as textiles), however, its weight in world trade will presumably be understated relative to the free trade case and the NTBs it faces correspondingly underweighted in the overall index. The exceptions would include cases in which discriminatory NTBs result in trade diversion to higher-cost sources of supply. Also, the upgrading effect of NTBs could result in an observed value of trade above the free trade level. There are two major drawbacks of $I_w$ as a measure of the "free trade" coverage of individual countries' NTBs. First, world imports may not be representative of the import pattern of a particular importer because import bundles differ across countries quite independently of the level of NTBs. Second, there are inevitable inaccuracies in estimating world trade for each tariff line of each importer's trade classification.[6]

Most current protection is of recent origin and is intended to prevent further increases in import shares rather than to roll back imports drastically. Moreover, most industrial countries do tend to protect the same sectors, for example, agriculture, textiles, and iron and steel. Thus, when comparing NTB *coverage* between countries, we believe that "own imports" is a better proxy for free trade imports than are our constructed "world trade" data.

The frequency ratio goes still further toward avoiding the downward bias in $I_c$ relative to free trade imports coverage. The extent of NTBs is measured by the number of trade flows that are affected, so that every barrier to every observed trade flow receives equal weight.[7] Its difficulties are twofold, however. First, it ignores differences in the sizes of trade flows of the various commodity categories. Second, it is exaggerated by the tendency of trade classifications to become more fragmented for the more sensitive and restricted categories of trade.

None of our indexes allows for the fact that some barriers are inherently more restrictive than others. For example, discretionary licenses could reflect either just the threat of, or the actual presence of a restriction, but our measures are insensitive to such dimensions. Thus it remains a large and speculative step to draw conclusions about the restrictiveness of trade regimes on the strength of these indexes.

In making comparisons of NTB coverage across time, we use import values from *one* period to calculate NTB coverage for both periods. Thus we get a reliable indicator of changes of the *extent* of NTBs but, as the reader has been reminded before, not of the changes in their restrictiveness.

6. See appendix 1 of Nogués, Olechowski, and Winters (1986) for details.

7. The use of "observed" trade flows means that prohibitions are still excluded in $I_f$. This could be overcome by defining $W_{qx}$ as unity wherever $N_{qx} = 1$, even if actual imports were zero. This involves a certain arbitrariness, however, since it is not guaranteed that every zero trade subject to an NTB would be positive in the absence of the NTB. For example, suppose an importer has a global quota of zero on bananas: thus $N_{qx} = 1$ for all $x$ when $q$ = bananas. While we may like to have $W_{qx} = 1$ for Trinidad, we would not wish it so for Iceland.

### *The Data*

The import data used in construction of the coverage ratios are provided by national authorities to the GATT and thence to UNCTAD. These data classify imports by tariff line and distinguish trade with all partner economies, except for EEC countries, in which intra-Community trade is ignored. All trade data are annual and refer to 1981.

Sixteen industrial country markets are examined in this paper: the ten EEC countries (with Belgium and Luxembourg combined), Australia, Austria, Finland, Japan, Norway, Switzerland, and the United States. In 1981, these markets accounted for about 60 percent of total world imports and about 70 percent of imports from developing countries.

The data on nontariff barriers have been collected by UNCTAD within the framework of its Data Base on Trade Measures. This contains information on governmental product-specific border nontariff measures applied in most developed market-economy countries. The data are recorded at the tariff-line level (that is, the level at which they are legally defined and applied) and are derived from official national and intergovernmental (for example, the GATT) publications. After the preliminary collection of information, or if substantive changes are introduced, governments are invited to verify and comment upon the accuracy of the data on their import regimes.[8] Since the data use the same definition of commodities as do the legal instruments defining them, there is no loss of information through aggregation. Either all imports in a particular tariff line are subject to the particular NTB, or none are. This means that our trade-based indexes, $I_c$ and $I_w$, are quite independent of the level of fragmentation of the trade classification.

The UNCTAD data contain information on the dates of introduction and elimination (if applicable) of individual NTBs and thus make possible the investigation of changes in NTB import coverage over time. Our estimates refer to periods of one year, and we set $N_{qx} = 1$ for a barrier even if it has applied for only part of the period concerned. This possibly imparts an upward bias to our ratios, but it allows us to capture a more representative sample of short-term and seasonal barriers than would a snapshot view.

## III. Results: NTBs on Imports of Industrial Countries

Tables 1, 2, and 3 below summarize the prevalence in sixteen industrial economies of the NTBs we have been able to document. The discussion in this section will be focused on aggregate results. However, an earlier paper (Nogués, Olechowski, and Winters 1986) provides detailed estimates for particular markets, products, and barriers. The figures quoted in the discussion, except for those shown in the tables and documented in the notes, have been drawn from that source.

8. For fuller details of the Data Base on Trade Measures, see UNCTAD (1983a, 1985).

Table 1. *The Extent of Industrial Countries' NTBs by Product Category, 1983*

| Imports | Coverage ratios: Own Imports ($I_c$) | Coverage ratios: World trade ($I_w$) | Frequency ratio ($I_f$) |
|---|---|---|---|
| All products | 27.1 | 21.8 | 12.8 |
| All products, less fuels | 18.6 | 18.5 | 12.7 |
| Fuels | 43.0 | 31.0 | 23.9 |
| Agricultural | 36.1 | 40.4 | 29.5 |
| All manufactures | 16.1 | 14.9 | 10.8 |
| Textiles | 44.8 | 37.8 | 38.1 |
| Footwear | 12.6 | 17.7 | 13.5 |
| Iron and steel | 35.4 | 35.8 | 18.3 |
| Electrical machinery | 10.0 | 10.8 | 5.4 |
| Vehicles | 30.4 | 25.9 | 7.4 |
| Other manufactures | 8.8 | 7.2 | 3.2 |

*Note:* Sixteen industrial markets, all exporters, all NTBS.

### *The Overall Prevalence of NTBs*

Overall, 13 percent of these countries' tariff lines are subject to NTBS, and 27 percent of their imports fall into these categories. In comparison, tariff concessions negotiated at the Tokyo Round covered about 18 percent of the imports of the major developed countries.[9] The value of imports influenced by the nontariff trade policies of these sixteen industrial country governments (some $231 billion, based on 1981 trade flows) is almost half again as large as the *total* imports of the state-trading East European centrally planned countries.

### *Sectoral Coverage*

While NTBS affect almost all internationally traded goods,[10] table 1 shows that in the case of industrial countries they are especially prevalent in certain sectors. In particular, textiles, agricultural products, mineral fuels, and iron and steel generally show a greater prevalence of NTBS than other product groups. It is quite common for imports of agricultural products to be regulated to such an extent that their origin, quantity, quality, price, and time of entry are specified in advance by the importing country authorities. While the management of imports is particularly elaborate in the EC, in which, for example, minimum import prices for certain products are adjusted almost daily, agricultural products face a wide array of NTBS in all industrial countries. Among the measures employed are various kinds of quotas (global, bilateral, seasonal); varying (seasonal) tariff duties; minimum import prices; and import authorizations which include permits dependent, for example, on the purchase of equivalent quantities of locally

9. The total value of trade affected by most favored nation (m.f.n.) tariff reductions and bindings at prevailing rates amounted to 17.8 percent ($125 billion; billion is 1,000 million) of 1976 imports of the major developed import markets (see GATT 1979, p. 118).

10. For example, about 98 percent of four-digit Customs Cooperation Council Nomenclature (CCCN) product groups face some sort of volume restriction somewhere in the world (UNCTAD 1983b, p. 11).

grown products. Their use is so widespread that they cover 73 percent of imports in Switzerland, 42 percent in Austria and Japan, and 36 percent in Australia.

Even so, agriculture is certainly a case where our indexes underestimate the extent of NTBS. First, we do not account for such measures as quality standards or state trading, which are particularly frequent in agriculture and can restrict imports just as effectively as volume or price measures. Second, existing trade restrictions are quite strenuous[11] and hence tend to push both the own imports and world trade coverage ratios downward; international trade in those agricultural products currently subject to restriction would certainly be considerably greater under free trade.

Textile imports generally face NTBS to the same or a higher degree as does agriculture. Most international trade in textiles and clothing is governed by the MFA, an umbrella Multifibre Arrangement under which voluntary export restraints of varying restrictiveness are negotiated between (industrial country) importers and (developing country) exporters. Countries which do not apply the MFA restrictions resort to other devices. Australia, for example, imposes tariff quotas (with higher rates set at prohibitive levels), Switzerland applies automatic licensing and monitors prices of products from certain suppliers, and Norway implemented global quotas until July 1984, when it introduced MFA measures.

As in the case of agriculture, our indexes probably underestimate the extent of NTBS on textiles. First, textile trade regulations are generally highly restrictive. For example, under the current MFA, the annual growth rate of U.S. imports from Hong Kong is limited to 1.5 percent for textiles and 0.7 percent for clothing, while EEC imports of textiles from Colombia are allowed to grow by 0.3 percent and from Mexico by 0.1 percent. The GATT Textiles Surveillance Body recently concluded that "under MFA III, restraints have been more extensive and in many cases more restrictive [than under MFA II]. Most importing countries, in restraining imports under the MFA, had recourse to extensive invocation of 'exceptional circumstances' or of the need to maintain 'minimum viable production' " (GATT 1984a, p. 10).

Second, volume and price restrictions are frequently accompanied and reinforced by other measures, particularly requirements of origin, which our indexes do not include. Recent instances suggest that these measures are becoming progressively more restrictive; for example, the new Customs Regulating Amendments Relating to Textiles and Textile Products in the United States provide more stringent guidelines for the determination of the origin of textile imports.

Contrary to a popular belief that raw materials are free of trade barriers, mineral fuels are among the product groups most subject to government control. The average own-import coverage ratio for fuels is a high 42.9, which reflects the licensing or quota requirements for all or selected imports of hydrocarbons into Australia, Finland, France, Norway, Switzerland, and the United States.

11. See, for example, Bale and Koester (1983).

For example, in France, petroleum imports are subject to a global quota. In the United States, a license is required for imports of natural gas, petroleum, and all petroleum products. In all these categories, the licensing is "intended to restrict the quantity of imports" (GATT 1983, p. 10) and, in the case of natural gas, to exclude those imports which are not "consistent with the public interest" (U.S. Natural Gas Act 1938, section 3). Because of falling consumption, current petroleum imports are not formally restricted, but the authority to license imports enables government to affect the source and level of petroleum trade; for example, imports into the United States from Libya are prohibited.

The fourth product group strongly affected by nontariff barriers is iron and steel. Iron and steel imports, which were relatively free in the 1970s, have become—in a remarkably short period of time—almost as tightly regulated as the textile trade, particularly in the EEC, the United States, and Australia. These economies shield their structurally ailing iron and steel industries from foreign competition. The EEC closely monitors its imports through a system of automatic licenses "to ensure that traditional trade patterns in steel products are not disturbed" (GATT 1984b, p. 4). A number of voluntary export arrangements limit imports from the major suppliers, and minimum ("basic") import prices are established for selected products.

In the United States, additional duties and a global quota were imposed on the imports of specialty steel in 1983, and subsequently a number of voluntary export restraint (VERs) arrangements have been concluded with major suppliers.[12] For certain carbon and alloy steel products, a maximum level of import penetration was set (18.5 percent) and is enforced by VERs and "surge control" arrangements with major suppliers and countries whose exports have increased rapidly.

In Australia, the Steel Industry Plan provides for an "import watch system" and reviews of levels of protection (which rely on tariffs and bounties) if the domestic producers' market share falls below 80 percent or rises above 90 percent in specified product categories.

A common feature of iron and steel protection is a frequent resort by all the countries to antidumping and countervailing actions. For example, in 1982 149 cases were initiated in the United States, 19 in the EEC, and 13 in Australia (UNCTAD 1984a, p. 8). Antidumping and countervailing duty actions are explicitly provided for in the presidential decision on protection for the U.S. steel industry, while a "fast track dumping mechanism" is one element of the Australian Steel Industry Plan (Australian Industries Assistance Commission 1983–84, pp. 21–27). Both are examples of measures that were established to regulate trade practices being applied to problems of a structural character.

Other product groups are less restricted by NTBs. The relatively high ratios for

12. To "encourage" such agreements, the United States has advised its suppliers that the global quota would be divided between countries which concluded orderly marketing arrangements and that only a small part (about 5 percent) would be left for other producers.

vehicles reflect VERs on Japanese exports and surveillance of car imports in the EEC. Ratios for footwear and electrical machinery are moderate. This latter group includes electronics (particularly from Japan, Republic of Korea, and Hong Kong), which meets increasing restrictions. However, because of the still relatively low value of trade in this category and the selective nature of import restrictions (usually VERs or quotas by country), the ratios for the whole group of electrical products are not large.

### *Types of Barriers*

Table 2 gives the breakdown of NTBs by type. Monitoring measures and quantitative import restrictions are the most pervasive of barriers according to all three indexes. Since these measures are predominantly concerned with the quantity of imports, it seems that quantitative measures outweigh price measures in the set of NTBs we examine.

At a more detailed level, it is obvious that different policies are emphasized in different sectors. Agricultural protection comprises mainly price measures and quantitative restrictions. The former are particularly important in the EEC, where much trade is subject to variable levies, but in other countries direct quantity restrictions are relatively more important. In Japan, for example, more than 46 percent of imports from developing countries are affected; in Switzerland, 47 percent of imports from industrial countries are covered. Manufacturing is primarily protected by quantity and monitoring measures. In Europe, surveillance is common—much of it quite explicitly warning exporters to restrain themselves (see note 2)—but so too are more rigid controls in the form of quantitative restrictions and VERs. The United States's protection of manufacturing, which appears to be both more limited and more subtle, relies almost exclusively on monitoring through mechanisms intended to police trade practices and on voluntary agreements. Japan's manufactured imports appear to face very few barriers of the type discussed here.

### *Country Comparisons*

All three indexes in table 3 point to France, Australia, and Switzerland as the countries where NTBs are most prevalent, while the two coverage ratios are also

Table 2. *The Extent of Industrial Countries' NTBs by Type of Measure, 1983*

| *Index* | *Quantitative import restrictions* | *Voluntary export restrictions* | *Decreed prices* | *Tariff-type* | *Monitoring measures* | *All NTBs*[a] |
|---|---|---|---|---|---|---|
| Coverage ratios: | | | | | | |
| Own imports ($I_c$) | 8.6 | 3.0 | 1.7 | 1.3 | 14.8 | 27.1 |
| World trade ($I_w$) | 9.5 | 1.4 | 3.4 | 1.6 | 9.8 | 21.8 |
| Frequency ratio ($I_f$) | 5.0 | 3.4 | 1.7 | 1.4 | 4.6 | 12.8 |

*Note:* Sixteen industrial markets, all exporters, all products.

a. This represents the union of the first five columns of the table. The sums of the ratios across groups of measures frequently exceed the totals quoted. This is because individual trade flows are often subject to NTBs of two or more classes. Such flows are counted once for each class and once (only) for the total.

Table 3. *The Extent of Industrial Countries' NTBs by Importing Country, 1983*

| Industrial country market | Coverage ratios: Own imports ($I_c$) | Coverage ratios: World trade ($I_w$) | Frequency ratio ($I_f$) |
|---|---|---|---|
| EEC | 22.3 | 18.9 | 13.8 |
| Belgium and Luxembourg | 26.0 | 21.0 | 11.6 |
| Denmark | 11.7 | 13.3 | 11.4 |
| France | 57.1 | 44.2 | 24.0 |
| Germany, Fed. Rep. | 12.4 | 14.7 | 12.5 |
| Greece | 13.4 | 19.0 | 13.6 |
| Ireland | 13.4 | 13.0 | 9.1 |
| Italy | 6.9 | 10.0 | 9.7 |
| Netherlands | 25.5 | 21.4 | 13.1 |
| United Kingdom | 14.3 | 13.9 | 13.8 |
| Australia | 34.1 | 44.4 | 18.3 |
| Austria | 4.9 | 7.5 | 5.4 |
| Finland | 34.9 | 34.3 | 13.4 |
| Japan | 11.9 | 9.0 | 9.3 |
| Norway | 5.7 | 6.1 | 9.7 |
| Switzerland | 32.2 | 42.9 | 19.4 |
| United States | 43.0 | 34.3 | 7.0 |
| All sixteen markets | 27.1 | 21.8 | 12.8 |

*Note:* All products, all exporters, all NTBS.

high for the United States and Finland. However, when fuels are excluded from the product coverage, the United States and Finland shift to the group of countries with small or moderate ratios. Thus, NTBS on fuels are the prime source of their high coverage indexes.

Whether or not restrictions on imports of fuels are taken into account, France, Australia, and Switzerland remain among the countries with the highest NTB ratios. For the first two, this is a reflection of an extensive system of quotas and licensing: about 10 percent of import flows accounting for more than 47 percent of import value face these measures in France, and about 13 percent of import flows or 27 percent of imports in Australia. Quantitative restrictions are also significant in Switzerland (8 percent of import flows, or 12 percent of import value, is subject to these restrictions), but the most extensive barrier is the system of automatic licensing, which covers about 11 percent of Swiss import flows and 32 percent of total imports.

Imports into Austria and Norway appear to face relatively few border NTBS, but both countries apply other trade-restricting measures such as state trading, import charges, technical standards, and direct assistance to several import-competing industries. In addition, Austria maintains relatively high tariff duties.[13]

13. The post–Tokyo Round weighted average ratio for Austria is 10.1 percent compared with a 3.6 percent average for the major developed economies (see Olechowski and Yeats 1982, p. 81).

Table 4. *The Extent of Industrial Economies' NTBs to Exports from Industrial and Developing Economies, 1983*

| | | *Developing economies* | | |
|---|---|---|---|---|
| *Index* | *Industrial economies* | *All* | *Major manufacturing exporters* | *Major borrowers* |
| Coverage ratio | | | | |
| Own imports ($I_c$) | 21.0 | 34.3 | 26.5 | 35.4 |
| World trade ($I_w$) | 17.1 | 27.0 | 24.6 | 29.4 |
| Frequency ratio ($I_f$) | 8.8 | 18.6 | 18.1 | 19.4 |

*Note:* Sixteen industrial market importers, all products, all selected NTBS.

The NTB ratios are also relatively low for Italy and Japan. Italy appears to apply fewer but tighter border measures than other EEC countries; its frequency ratios consistently and significantly exceed its own-import coverage ratios. Japan, as is well known, is often suspected of using measures not covered in our exercise—for example, testing procedures, restrictions on retail outlets for foreign products, and administrative guidances—to restrict imports.

In comparing the NTB coverage figures between countries, the reader should remember that the information we have measures the *extent* of NTBS and not their restrictiveness. It would be inappropriate to use these figures to argue, for example, that countries with higher indexes "owe" the international community a unilateral "round" of trade liberalization or that a country with a low coverage index is justified in imposing restrictions against its trading partners.

## IV. The Extent of NTBs on Exports of Developing Countries

Having discussed the prevalence of NTBS in the aggregate, we now turn to the question of whether NTBS impinge more heavily on the exports of developing countries than on intra-industrial country trade. The indexes in table 4 are aggregates for the sixteen industrial markets for which we have NTB information and present NTB coverage ratios for imports from four groups of exporters—industrial countries, all developing economies, developing economies that are major exporters of manufactures, and developing economies that are major borrowers (these groups are defined in the appendix).

Table 4 shows that NTBS are significantly more prevalent on imports from developing economies than from industrial economies and this is replicated for nearly all individual markets.

Not only the relative but also the absolute extent of NTB coverage is larger in the case of developing economies' products. For example, the value (in 1981 U.S. dollars) of imports from developing economies subject to NTBS is $86 billion compared with $81 billion in the case of imports from industrial countries (Nogués, Olechowski, and Winters 1986).

Another important implication of table 4 is that NTBS are relatively extensive on the exports of the developing economies that are major borrowers. For these

Table 5. *A Comparison of Industrial Economies' NTBs on Agricultural and Manufactured Exports of Industrial and Developing Economies, 1983*

| | Industrial economies | | Developing economies | |
|---|---|---|---|---|
| Index | Agriculture | Manufactures | Agriculture | Manufactures |
| Coverage ratio | | | | |
| Own imports ($I_c$) | 40.5 | 14.5 | 31.2 | 21.3 |
| World trade ($I_w$) | 46.1 | 13.2 | 30.5 | 20.5 |
| Frequency ratio ($I_f$) | 31.9 | 6.7 | 25.6 | 17.4 |

*Note:* Sixteen industrial markets, all selected NTBS.

economies, all three indexes assume values which are 1–2 percentage points higher than those for all developing economies and 7–8 percentage points higher than those for all exporters. This difference is partly caused by the presence of three large oil exporters (Indonesia, Mexico, and Venezuela) among the major borrowers. However, even if fuels are excluded, the coverage indexes for major borrowers remain higher than those for all developing economies while the frequency ratio is marginally lower.[14] Given that the major borrowers' ability to cope with their current balance of payments difficulties depends to a large degree on their ability to export to the industrial economies, these figures emphasize how closely linked are debt and trade policy issues.

In the case of major exporters of manufactures, the evidence is less clear-cut. It is often alleged that the newly industralized economies are the prime targets of protective actions, but the figures in table 4 do not support this thesis. However, when fuels are excluded, the values of all three indexes for the exporters of manufactures are higher than those for all developing economies.[15] And our analysis, of course, has not considered the comparative effect of tariff barriers.

The structure of the apparent discrimination against developing economies is explored in table 5. It shows that, almost universally, NTBS are less prevalent on industrial economies' imports of agricultural goods from developing economies than on those from other industrial economies, but that the reverse is true for manufactures. Nonetheless, developing economies still generally face more barriers to agricultural exports than to manufactures, and since agriculture accounts for a higher share of imports from developing economies than from industrial ones, agricultural protection still contributes to the differential incidence at the aggregate level. In the manufacturing sector, developing economies face more barriers than industrial ones to their large-volume exports, such as in textiles and footwear, and fewer to their small-volume ones, such as electrical machinery and vehicles.

A striking feature of the restrictions on imports of manufactures from developing economies is the much greater prevalence of VERS than in the case of

14. The respective values are 25.5 (own imports coverage ratio), 24.0 (world trade coverage ratio), and 18.1 (frequency ratio) for major borrowers and 22.4, 22.7, and 18.5 for all developing exporters.

15. They are: 23.8 (own imports coverage ratio), 24.5 (world trade coverage ratio), and 19.4 (frequency ratio).

Table 6. *The Change in the Extent of Industrial Economies' NTBs on Imports from Industrial and Developing Economies*

| *Index* | *All economies* | *Industrial economies* | *Developing economies* |
|---|---|---|---|
| Coverage ratio | | | |
| Own imports ($I_c$) | 1.5 | 2.2 | 1.1 |
| World trade ($I_w$) | 1.8 | 2.3 | 1.1 |
| Frequency ratio ($I_f$) | 0.3 | 0.1 | 0.9 |

*Note:* Sixteen industrial markets, all products, all selected NTBs, differences between indexes for 1983 and 1981 in percentage points.

imports from industrial ones. For example, the overall world imports coverage ratio of VERs for developing economies' manufactures is 10.9 percent, compared with 0.4 percent for industrial ones, and this pattern is repeated for every market with VERs. While our figures do not reflect the restrictiveness of trade regimes, the evidence of a widespread bias in the application of voluntary export restraints seems overwhelming.

## V. The Growth of NTBs

The final issue we examine is the expansion of NTB coverage through time. Table 6 compares the coverage of NTBs in 1981 and 1983. The UNCTAD data base does not provide precise information on the dates of introduction before 1981 and, at the time our investigation was carried out, did not contain data on measures imposed after June 1984.

All three measures indicate that NTBs have encroached further on international trade. For the sixteen markets whose NTBs have been tabulated, there was, between 1981 and 1983, a net increase of 2,486 in the number of NTBs recorded. The NTBs in place in 1983 covered $12.8 billion more of 1981's imports than did those in place in 1981. This additional $12.8 billion which came under NTBs was approximately 1.5 percent of these countries' total imports in 1981 and approximately 6 percent of the value of imports subject to NTBs. Note that these figures refer only to new NTBs and not to any tightening or reinforcement of existing ones.

According to the coverage ratios, the new measures seem to be aimed mostly at imports from the industrial economies.[16] When the coverage and frequency indicators are compared, it appears that new NTBs were imposed on a larger number of small trade flows from developing economies and a smaller number of large flows from industrial ones. This is a reflection of concentration of new NTBs in areas such as iron and steel and electrical machinery, where developing economies are only now entering international trade. This pattern does not mean, however, that developing economies were exempt from the rise in protec-

16. For a description of new NTBs, see UNCTAD (1984, 1985) and IMF (1984).

tionism, for their main exports (such as textiles and clothing) experienced a considerable tightening of the existing restrictions.

## VI. Summary and Conclusions

Given the lack of sound empirical evidence on the extent of nontariff barriers, this article has attempted to identify some basic features of the situation. By employing the most comprehensive and detailed existing NTB and trade information and calculating three indexes of the prevalence (but not restrictiveness) of NTBs we have generated the most comprehensive analysis extant.

Four major conclusions emerge from the results. First, the extent of NTBs is indeed large. At least 27 percent of the sixteen major industrial economies' imports, some $230 billion of 1981 imports, would have been covered by one or more of the selected NTBs as they applied in 1983. NTBs are particularly widespread in agricultural products, textiles and clothing, mineral fuels, and iron and steel.

Second, quantitative controls appear to be the most prevalent of individual NTBs—much more so than price controls, which are applied mainly to agricultural imports.

Third, all the measures investigated indicate that NTBs are significantly more prevalent on imports from developing economies than from industrial ones. The NTBs applied in 1983 by the sixteen industrial markets examined here would have covered $86 billion of imports from developing economies and $79 billion of imports from industrial ones if 1981 trade flows remained unchanged. Particularly significant is the higher coverage of the exports of the most heavily indebted developing economies.

In relative terms, developing economies face more barriers than industrial ones in manufactured trade and fewer in agricultural trade. However, developing economies still generally encounter more barriers to agricultural exports than to manufactures, and since agriculture accounts for a higher share of their exports than of industrial economies' exports, protection in this sector contributes to the differential incidence observed at the aggregate level.

Finally, the results provide evidence that the use of NTBs has increased and has done so at a significant pace. In the period from 1981 to 1983, a net increase of 2,486 NTBs covering $12.8 billion of 1981 imports was observed. Since this increase does not reflect the tightening or reinforcement of existing measures, the growth of NTBs and their effect on international trade should be taken very seriously.

## Appendix. *Definitions of Product and Country Groups*

| *Product* | *TSUSA*[a] *headings* | CCCN[b] *four-digit headings* |
|---|---|---|
| All | 10001–87045 | 0101–9906 |
| All, less fuels | 10001–47462, 48005–52121 52141–87045 | 0101–2604, 2801–9906 |
| Agricultural goods | 10001–19324 | 0101–2402 |
| Manufactured goods | 20003–47462, 48005–49520, 53101–54805, 60502–87045 | 2801–9906 |
| Textiles | 30010–39060 | 5001–6302 |
| Footwear | 70005–70095 | 6401–6406 |
| Iron and steel | 60600–61081 | 7300–7399 |
| Electrical machinery | 68205–68847 | 8501–8528 |
| Vehicles | 69202–69260 | 8701–8714 |

*Economy Groups*

*Developing economies that are major exporters of manufacturers*
Argentina, Brazil, Hong Kong, Israel, Republic of Korea, Philippines, Portugal, Singapore, South Africa, Taiwan, Thailand, Yugoslavia

*Developing economies that are major borrowers*
Argentina, Brazil, Chile, Egypt, India, Indonesia, Israel, Korea, Mexico, Turkey, Venezuela, Yugoslavia
All had more than $15 billion in long-term debt at the end of 1983.

*Industrial and developing countries*
World Bank definitions (World Bank 1984), except that Greece is transferred from developing to industrial countries because its trade policy is determined with that of other industrial countries in the EEC.

a. Tariff Schedules of the United States, Annotated.
b. Customs Cooperation Council Nomenclature.

## REFERENCES


Australian Industries Assistance Commission, 1983–84. *Annual Report.* Canberra.

Balassa, B., and C. Balassa. 1984. "Industrial Protection in the Developed Countries." *World Economy* 7, no. 2 (June): 179–96.

Bale, Malcolm D., and Ulrich Koester. 1983. "Maginot Line of European Farm Policies." *World Economy* 6, no. 4 (December): 373–92.

Cline, W. 1985. *Imports of Manufactures from Developing Countries: Performance and Prospects for Market Access.* Washington, D.C.: Brookings Institution.

Deardorff, A., and R. Stern. 1985. "Methods of Measurement of Non-Tariff Barriers to Trade." UNCTAD/ST/MD/28.

Dickey, William L. 1979. "The Pricing of Imports into the United States." *Journal of World Trade Law* 13 (May–June): 238–56.

EEC. (European Communities). 1982. *Official Journal of the European Communities.* Legislation. EEC 288/82. Luxembourg.

Finger, J. M. 1981. "The Industry-Country Incidence of 'Less than Fair Value' Cases in U.S. Import Trade." *Quarterly Review of Economics and Business,* Summer: 260–79.

Finger, J. M., H. K. Hall, and D. R. Nelson. 1982. "The Political Economy of Administered Protection." *American Economic Review* 72:452–66.

GATT (the General Agreement on Tariffs and Trade). 1979. *The Tokyo Round of Multilateral Trade Negotiations.* Geneva.

———. 1983. Reply to the questionnaire on Licensing: USA. L/5131. Geneva.

———. 1984a. Developments in the Trading System. C/W/448, April 1984–September 1984. Geneva.

———. 1984b. Report of the Group on Quantitative Restrictions and other Non-Tariff Measures. L/5713. Geneva.

IMF (International Monetary Fund). 1984. *Exchange Arrangements and Exchange Restrictions. Annual Report.* Washington, D.C.

Jones, C. D. 1983. "Visible Imports Subject to Restraint." *Government Economic Service* Working Paper 62. London: Her Majesty's Stationery Office.

Nogués, J., A. Olechowski, and L. A. Winters. 1986. "The Extent of Non-Tariff Barriers to Imports of Industrial Countries." World Bank Staff Working Paper 789. Washington, D.C.

Olechowski, A., and A. Yeats. 1982. "Implications of the Tokyo Round for East-West Trade Relations." *Oxford Bulletin of Economics and Statistics,* February:79–96.

UNCTAD (United Nations Conference on Trade and Development). 1983a. *Non-Tariff Barriers Affecting the Trade of Developing Countries and Transparency in World Trading Conditions: the Inventory of Non-Tariff Barriers.* TD/B/940. Geneva.

———. 1983b. *Protectionism, Trade Relations, and Standard Adjustment.* TD/274. Belgrade.

———. 1984. *Protectionism and Standard Adjustment in the World Economy. Part I: Analysis of Major Issues and Policy Requirements.* TD/B/981. Geneva.

———. 1985. *Problems of Protectionism and Structural Adjustment. Part I: Restrictions to Trade and Structural Adjustment.* TD/B/1039. Geneva.

U.S. Natural Gas Act. 1938. Act of 21 June. C556. 52 Stat. 821–833. 15 USC 717–717w.

World Bank. 1984. *World Development Report 1984.* New York: Oxford University Press.

European Economic Review 37 (1993) 1331–1349. North-Holland

# Do exporters gain from VERs?

Jaime de Melo*

*The World Bank, Washington DC, USA and Centre of Economic Policy Research, London, UK*

L. Alan Winters

*University of Birmingham, Birmingham, UK and Centre of Economic Policy Research, London, UK*

Received October 1989, final version received October 1991

Previous literature has concentrated on the rent transfer accruing to exporting countries when a voluntary export restraint (VER) is binding. This paper studies the efficiency and distributional effects arising when VERs force factors out of industries in which they are most productive. A theoretical model of the industry under the VER is developed to establish qualitative conditions under which a VER will result in: Spillovers of exports to unrestricted markets; industry contraction; and loss in national welfare. Key parameters of demand and supply are estimated for leather footwear exports from Taiwan subject to the U.S. Orderly Marketing Agreement, and their implications explored in a calibrated simulation exercise. The results make a strong indictment of VERs. For most plausible parameter values, VERs distort exports, reduce industry size and cause overall economic losses, especially if the affected industry is large.

## 1. Introduction

The distinguishing feature of voluntary export restraints (VERs) is that they are administered by exporting countries. So long as the VER is binding, exports of the product under the VER earn a scarcity premium. Much work has been done to estimate the cost to importing countries – and hence the

*Correspondence to*: L. Alan Winters, Department of Economics, University of Birmingham, Edgbaston, Birmingham B15 2TT, U.K.

*Our thanks to two referees and to Arvind Panagariya and Jean Waelbroeck for helpful suggestions that led to substantial improvements over an earlier draft (de Melo and Winters 1990b, WPS discussion paper 326, World Bank, Washington, DC). We are very indebted to Ramon Lopez for suggesting and helping with the simplified presentation of the model in section 2. Helpful comments were also received on an early draft by Bela Balassa, Paul Brenton, Shanti Chakravarty, Nicóla Rossi, Wendy Takacs and to participants of the STEP-CEPR Conference 'Adjustment in Developing Countries' (May 1989), the European Research Workshop in International Trade (June 1989) and the George Washington University Economics Seminar. We thank Alexander Pfaff, Julie Stanton and Rebecca Sugui for logistic support. The views contained herein are those of the authors and do not necessarily reflect those of the World Bank. This research has been financed by World Bank Research Project 672-40.

0014-2921/93/$06.00 

gain to exporting countries – from this transfer.[1] There are, however, other effects in exporting countries arising from a binding VER. These effects stem from the contractionary pressure on the industry subjected to the VER and hence against factors employed in it. By forcing factors out of industries in which they are most productive, VERs can impose significant efficiency losses on exporters. Curiously, these losses, which must be balanced against the rent transfer from abroad, have been neglected in the literature. The purpose of this paper is to explore these effects systematically by econometric estimation and simulations in the context of the U.S. Orderly Marketing Agreement (OMA) for Taiwanese leather footwear exports during 1977–1981.

This paper is organized as follows. In section 2, we develop a simple theoretical model of a perfectly competitive industry subject to the VER. The industry sells its output to two markets, one restricted and one unrestricted. We examine the effects of a VER in the restricted market on sales in the unrestricted market (spillover effect), on industry size and national welfare. The analysis suggests that the effects of a VER depend crucially on a few product supply and factor demand elasticities. This leads us, in section 3, to estimate these key elasticities for the case of leather footwear exports from Taiwan during the U.S. OMA. Although not as precise as desirable because of data limitations, these econometric estimates suggest that the demand and supply of footwear are quite elastic. They also lend strong support to the qualitative prediction that the OMA induced some spillover to unrestricted markets and some contraction of the industry with attendant efficiency losses. Finally, in section 4, we combine the results of the previous two sections into a partial equilibrium simulation model which analyzes the likely effects of a VER on national welfare and income distribution, taking into account efficiency losses.

For plausible elasticity values we establish that a typical VER will lead to a worsening income distribution, as profits in the affected industry rise and the returns to other factors – notably labour – fall. We also establish that exporting countries are likely to incur an overall welfare loss in spite of the rent transfer gain even when the industry under the VER is of non-negligible size. The results of this paper are therefore a strong indictment of VERs. To be sure, VERs are less harmful to exporting countries than are equivalent-sized import quotas administered by the importing country, but nonetheless, they can impose notable welfare losses wherever they restrict industries accounting for significant shares of the exporters' economic activity, or when these industries make use of particular and relatively immobile skills or physical capital.

[1]See, e.g., Greenaway and Hindley (1985), Tarr and Morkre (1984), and Feenstra (1984). On the developing country side most work has concentrated on detecting rents and quality upgrading [see Aw and Roberst (1986); de Melo and Winters (1989)].

In previous work [de Melo and Winters (1990a)], we investigated the effects of the U.S. OMA for Korean leather footwear producers. We relied, however, on a restrictive technology allowing for separability between the input decisions (how much footwear to produce) and the allocation of sales to restricted and unrestricted markets. This led us to the econometric estimation of an export allocation model that concentrated on establishing that in the short run a VER reduced the marginal revenue product of factors in the Korean footwear industry and that sales were diverted from the restricted towards the unrestricted markets. This paper develops a substantially more general model of a competitive industry subject to a VER, and provides econometric estimation for the Taiwanese footwear industry that go well beyond our earlier export allocation approach. It analyzes a full supply–demand model of the footwear industry, and is to our knowledge, the first empirical attempt at the econometric estimation of the welfare (and distributional) effects of a VER on the exporting industry.

## 2. A simple model of a competitive industry subject to a VER

Consider the following partial equilibrium model of the effects of a VER. For convenience we call the restricted industry footwear, but the results generalize to virtually any competitive industry. Assume that many identical firms in an exporting country produce two different types of footwear for two markets, U and R (for unrestricted and restricted), using a single composite variable factor of production, $Z$. To simplify the welfare analysis, suppose that the entire output of the representative firm is exported. Assume, however, that the two types of footwear may differ and allow for the possibility that the marginal costs of one may depend on the output of the other. One possible justification for this is the existence of a second implicit factor of production which is fixed in supply, e.g., entrepreneurship or infrastructure. The one-input two-output technology, $G$, corresponding to our empirical formulation is given by

$$G(X_{\mathrm{U}}, X_{\mathrm{R}}, Z) = 0, \tag{1}$$

where $X_{\mathrm{U}}$ and $X_{\mathrm{R}}$ are outputs and $Z$ is a composite input. The technology is well behaved in the sense that a well-behaved profit function exists,[2] and $G$ is also assumed to be twice differentiable.

We assume many identical price-taking representative firms in the footwear industry. Each firm maximizes profits $\tilde{\pi}$, defined as

[2]The assumptions are that $G$ is nonempty, closed and convex, bounded from above, with free disposability of $X$ and $Z$ and satisfies the assumption of weak essentiality. For further discussion see, e.g., Fuss and McFadden (1978) or Chambers (1988, chapter 7).

$$\tilde{\pi} \equiv p_U X_U + p_R X_R - wZ, \tag{2}$$

subject to the technology described in (1). For the technology described in (1) and under the assumption of price-taking behavior for firms in both export markets and in the market for the composite input $Z$, one can write a profit function $\tilde{\pi}(p_U, p_R, w)$ which describes the maximum profits attainable by the representative firm. Profit maximization insures convexity of the profit function.

The purpose of the model is to consider the consequences of imposing a VER on exports to market R while exports to market U remain unrestricted. A VER in market R, restricting exports to level $\bar{X}_R < X_R^*$ – where $X_R^*$ is the free trade level at price $P_R^*$ – will introduce a wedge between the price received by the firm, $p_R^s$, and the price paid by footwear importers, $p_R^d$. Assume that the rents associated with the VER, defined as

$$R \equiv (p_R^d - p_R^s)\bar{X}_R \tag{3}$$

are redistributed such that they do not affect marginal decisions. For example, assume a lump-sum redistribution. Then firms' allocation decisions are unaffected by the presence of rents,[3] and the representative firm's restricted profit function can be written as

$$\pi = \pi(p_R^s, p_U, w), \tag{4}$$

where the firm's subscript has been omitted.

The industry faces an upward sloping inverse supply curve for its composite factor $Z$:

$$w = w(Z), \quad w' > 0, \tag{5}$$

and downward sloping demand curves for sales in U and R:

$$X_U = X_U(p_u), \; X_R = X_R(p_R^d), \qquad X_R', X_U' < 0. \tag{6}$$

The price-taking behavior assumption implies that firms cannot exploit monopsony in the market for $Z$, nor can they exploit monopoly power in their respective export markets. This price-taking behavior assumption on the part of firms may not be representative of industries with few producers of a highly differentiated product, but it certainly approximates the Taiwanese footwear industry where there is a large number of small firms producing relatively undifferentiated footwear.

Since $\pi$ is differentiable in its arguments, the unique industry profit

[3] With few exceptions (e.g. Korea), rents are redistributed lump sum. If, however, rents affected firms' allocation decision as in the case of the two-tier quota allocation mechanism used by Korea [see Bark and de Melo (1989)], one would include a description of the rent allocation mechanism as an argument in the restricted profit function (4).

maximizing supply functions and derived-demand function can be obtained by application of Hotelling's lemma.[4] Therefore, under a binding VER, equilibrium in the industry will be described by the following three equations:

$$\pi_1(p^s_R, p_U, w) = \bar{X}_R, \tag{7}$$

$$\pi_2(p^s_R, p_U, w) = X_U(p_U), \tag{8}$$

$$-\pi_3(p^s_R, p_U, w) = Z, \tag{9}$$

where $\pi_i$ is the partial derivative of $\pi$ w.r.t. its $i$th argument and the demand function in the restricted market has been replaced by the VER in (7).

With a few more restrictions on technology to be given shortly, it is a straightforward comparative statics exercise to show that in this simple two-output, one-input model, a VER will lead to a contraction of the industry. To parallel the empirical work that follows, we consider two cases. The first case (corresponding to model I in section 3) is one where the industry is small in the market for its variable factor of production so that $w' = \infty$ in (5) and the industry faces a perfectly elastic supply for $Z$. In the second more plausible case (corresponding to model II in section 3), we allow for the upward sloping supply curve for $Z$ in (5) to take into account the possibility that the industry is large in the market for $Z$.

To establish that the industry will contract when the VER is tightened ($\mathrm{d}\bar{X}_R < 0$) we need to establish the conditions under which $(\mathrm{d}Z/\mathrm{d}\bar{X}_R) > 0$, i.e., that $\mathrm{d}Z < 0$. Totally differentiate (9) with respect to $\mathrm{d}\bar{X}_R$ to obtain

$$\mathrm{d}Z/\mathrm{d}\bar{X}_R = -\pi_{31}(\mathrm{d}p^s_R/\mathrm{d}\bar{X}_R) - \pi_{32}(\mathrm{d}p_U/\mathrm{d}\bar{X}_R) - \pi_{33}[(\partial w/\partial Z)(\mathrm{d}Z/\mathrm{d}\bar{X}_R)]. \tag{10}$$

For the first case (model I), the last term on the RHS of (10) is zero. Therefore, consider the general case (model II). To sign (10) we make the further assumption of normality of $Z$, i.e., that an increase in $w$ causes profit maximizing outputs to decline. Then $\pi_{3i} < 0$, $i = 1, 2$ and $\pi_{33} > 0$ by convexity of the profit function. Rewrite (10) as

$$\mathrm{d}Z/\mathrm{d}\bar{X}_R = (1 + \pi_{33}\,\partial w/\partial Z)^{-1}[\cdots], \tag{10'}$$

where the expression in brackets corresponds to the first two terms on the RHS of (10). The expression in parentheses is positive by (5) and by the

[4] Profit maximization under price-taking behavior on the part of identical firms implies that the conditions for aggregation (that industry supply be independent of output distribution across firms) are met.

assumption of convexity. To sign the expression in brackets, totally differentiate (7) and (8). This yields

$$\mathrm{d}p_{\mathrm{R}}^{\mathrm{s}}/\mathrm{d}\bar{X}_{\mathrm{R}} = |H|^{-1}(\pi_{22} - X'_{\mathrm{U}}) > 0, \tag{11}$$

$$\mathrm{d}p_{\mathrm{U}}/\mathrm{d}\bar{X}_{\mathrm{R}} = -|H|^{-1}\pi_{12} > 0, \tag{12}$$

where

$$|H| \equiv \begin{vmatrix} \pi_{11} & \pi_{12} \\ \pi_{21} & \pi_{22} - X'_{\mathrm{U}} \end{vmatrix} < 0 \quad \text{by convexity of } \pi.$$

The positive sign of expression (11) follows from the property of the profit function that it is non-decreasing in the price of one of its outputs and from the sign of (6). The positive sign of expression (12) follows from the gross complementarity of $X_{\mathrm{U}}$ and $X_{\mathrm{R}}$ imposed by adding up for the two-output technology, $G$. This implies that the expression in brackets is positive so that (10′) is positive. Thus, in the two-output case, normality of $Z$ in production of both goods insures that the industry subjected to the VER will contract. In the multiple-output case, one would also have to impose gross complementarity as it would no longer follow from adding-up as in the two-output case.[5]

The sign of expression (12) also establishes that there will be a deflection of sales towards the unrestricted market. Thus competitive firms will respond to a VER by increasing sales in unrestricted markets, the cause of what Hamilton (1989) terms the domino effect, or in the terminology here, the ‘domino diversion’ of exports. This is an important effect since it also explains why importing countries not participating in a VER follow suit and negotiate VERs with major exporters so as to avoid having their own markets flooded by deflected sales from restricted markets.

Finally, what are the effects of the VER on the national welfare of the exporting country? As the simulation model demonstrates, this will depend on demand elasticities in the restricted and unrestricted markets, on the elasticity of factor supply to the affected industry, and on the parameters of the production function.[6]

## 3. Estimation

We now describe two attempts to estimate the principal parameters of the

[5]In a multiple-output technology, gross complementarity would be satisfied provided that there are no strong economies of joint production. For exact conditions, see Lopez (1984).

[6]For expressions of the determinants of national welfare in terms of demand and supply elasticities, the interested reader is referred to our earlier (and more detailed) version of the paper [de Melo and Winters (1990b)].

above model for Taiwanese exports of leather footwear (CCCN 6402). The purpose of this estimation is to establish the plausibility of our approach and to obtain 'ball-park' estimates of the critical parameters for later policy simulations. Thus we have not experimented with large numbers of specifications, nor have we concerned ourselves much about insignificant but implausible estimates of non-critical parameters. Most Taiwanese footwear exports are sold in the U.S.A. and were subject to an OMA between July 1977 and June 1981. The OMA has been investigated several times from the U.S.A.'s point of view [e.g., Pearson (1983) and Aw and Roberts (1986)] but with the exception of Aw's (1989) analysis of quality upgrading, not for Taiwan. We estimate the model for leather footwear sales because they were all affected by the OMA, whereas the other major aggregate available to us (CCCN 6401), although accounting for a larger share of Taiwanese footwear exports, comprises rubber and plastic footwear, the former of which was not limited by the OMA. We distinguish two markets for footwear, the U.S.A. and the rest of the world and use quarterly data for 1974–1986.[7,8]

In our application, we represent the profit function by Diewert's (1974) generalized Leontief form. The corresponding profit function is

$$\pi \equiv \sum_i \sum_j \gamma_{ij}(-p_i^{1/2} p_j^{1/2}), \tag{13}$$

where $i = \mathrm{R, U, Z}$ and $p_{\mathrm{Z}}$ is just the wage ($w$). Concavity of the profit function requires $\gamma_{ij} = \gamma_{ji}$ and $\gamma_{ij} \geqq 0$ if $i \neq j$. Outputs $(X_{\mathrm{R}}, X_{\mathrm{U}})$ are measured with positive signs and inputs ($Z$) with negative signs. Differentiating (13) yields the general 'netput' equation ('netputs' are both inputs and outputs):

$$X_i = \gamma_{ii} - \sum_{j \neq i} \gamma_{ij}(p_j/p_i)^{1/2}. \tag{14}$$

Eq. (14) presumes unfettered optimization in response to prices. When $X_{\mathrm{R}}$ is considered, however, it requires modification, even for the unconstrained variables, $X_{\mathrm{U}}$ and $X_{\mathrm{Z}}$. Neary and Roberts (1980) show that a constrained equilibrium can be expressed in terms of the parameters of the unconstrained compensated demand or supply functions by means of virtual prices. Virtual prices are the prices at which the actual quantities traded would have been traded voluntarily according to the compensated functions. For unconstrained netputs, virtual prices equal actual prices, and for constrained netputs they may be derived by inverting the compensated netput functions.

[7]We assume that all output is exported and that the exports to the rest of the world are not constrained.

[8]We estimate the various parameters of the model presented in section 2 in a simultaneous system of non-linear equations using three stage iterative instrumental variable methods from SAS's SYSNLIN procedures.

Solving (14) for $\tilde{p}_\mathrm{R}$, the virtual price of sales to market R given a value of $\bar{X}_\mathrm{R}$ and substituting into the two unconstrained netputs functions yields

$$\bar{X}_k = -\left[\gamma_{kk} - \frac{\gamma_{k\mathrm{R}}^2}{(\bar{X}_\mathrm{R}+\gamma_\mathrm{RR})}\right] - \left[\gamma_{kl} - \frac{\gamma_{k\mathrm{R}}\gamma_{\mathrm{R}l}}{(\bar{X}_\mathrm{R}+\gamma_\mathrm{RR})}\right]\left[\frac{p_l}{p_k}\right], \quad k,l=\mathrm{U},\mathrm{Z}. \quad (14')$$

Our first attempt at estimation (model I) recognized the paucity of data on the production side of the model. We therefore estimated a system comprising only demand curves and an export allocation model to divide a given volume of exports between markets. We fix total inputs ($Z$) exogenously and, as suggested by an allocation model, proxy $Z$ by total exports of footwear ($X$). This allows us to write $X_\mathrm{R}=F(\tilde{p}_\mathrm{R},p_\mathrm{U})X$, which, using a generalized Leontief form, specializes to

$$X_\mathrm{R}/X = -\gamma_\mathrm{RR} - \gamma_\mathrm{RU}(p_\mathrm{U}/\tilde{p}_\mathrm{R})^{1/2}. \quad (15)$$

The corresponding equation for $X_\mathrm{U}$ is implicit in (15) given adding up.

Eq. (15) was estimated along with demand functions for leather footwear for the U.S.A. and for the rest of the world. These were normalized to express the price of Taiwanese footwear relative to a linear combination of the prices of locally produced footwear ($p_i^\mathrm{L}$) and Korean exports to the market concerned ($p_i^\mathrm{K}$) as the dependent variable. Normalizing the demand curve on price is necessary if the data are to have the opportunity to record infinitely elastic demands. The additional explanatory variables were a cyclical variable (the index of industrial production, $Q_i$) and the quantity of exports. Thus the two demand curves were of the form

$$p_i=(\beta_0^i+\beta_1^iQ_i+\beta_2^iX_i)(1-\beta_3^i)p_i^\mathrm{L}+\beta_3^ip_i^\mathrm{K}), \quad i=\mathrm{U},\mathrm{R}. \quad (16)$$

All three equations were given seasonal dummies and, in view of the evident serial correlation when estimated straightforwardly, were also adjusted for first-order serial correlation. The resulting model is labelled model I in table 1.

During the OMA the demand equations still applied, relating actual prices and quantities, but the allocation function was over-ridden by the VER and its implication, given $Z$, for sales $X_\mathrm{B}$. Thus the quarters 1977,3–1981,2 had to be removed from the estimation of eq. (15).[9] The set of instrumental

[9]When the serial correlation adjustment was made, 1981,3 also had to be dropped because no unrestricted lagged value of $X_\mathrm{R}$ was available from 1981,2. For the omitted quarter, actual values of $X_\mathrm{R}$ and $X_\mathrm{U}$ were used in eq. (16) because they were exogenous. Following Neary and Roberts (1980), we set virtual prices equal to actual prices for unconstrained netputs, and for constrained netputs we obtain virtual prices by inverting the corresponding compensated demand function.

Table 1

Estimates of supply and demand functions for Taiwanese footwear.[a]

| | Model I | | Model II | |
|---|---|---|---|---|
| | Coefficient | *t*-statistic | Coefficient | *t*-statistic |
| $\gamma_{RR}$ | −4.67 | (1.81) | – | |
| $\gamma_{RU}$ | 4.31 | (2.14) | 1.32 | (0.90) |
| $\gamma_{RZ}$ | – | | 0.49 | (0.19) |
| $\gamma_{UU}$ | – | | – | |
| $\gamma_{UZ}$ | – | | −0.05 | (0.09) |
| $\rho$ | 0.87 | (0.12) | 1.00 | (–) |
| R | | | | |
| $\beta_1$ | 0.0003 | (0.0094) | 0.0010 | (0.0080) |
| $\beta_2$ | −0.0016 | (0.0018) | 0.0009 | (0.0012) |
| $\beta_3$ | −0.308 | (0.366) | −0.087 | (0.242) |
| U | | | | |
| $\beta_1$ | 0.0389 | (0.0564) | −0.0031 | (0.0519) |
| $\beta_2$ | 0.0108 | (0.0130) | 0.0073 | (0.0103) |
| $\beta_3$ | 0.5941 | (0.171) | 0.625 | (0.147) |
| $R^2$/DW | $R^2$ | DW | $R^2$ | DW |
| $X_R$ | 0.903 | 1.93 | 0.964 | 1.98 |
| $X_U$ | – | – | 0.958 | 2.06 |
| $P_R$ | 0.985 | 1.86 | 0.988 | 2.08 |
| $P_U$ | 0.955 | 2.46 | 0.965 | 2.52 |

[a]For description of models, see text.

variables included the exogenous variables used in (15) and (16). The initial estimates of (16) were highly unstable: The serial correlation coefficients fluctuated around unity and consequently the resolution on the constant terms $\beta_0^i$ was very weak. The only solution appeared to be to estimate the demand equations in first difference form, dropping the constants. Table 1 reports these results as model I.

The most striking feature of model I is its strong positive estimate of $\gamma_{RU}$: Given total exports the share allocated to market A rises strongly as their relative prices rises. This result confirms negative spillovers between markets and consequently that 'domino diversion' certainly occurs, at least in the two-market case. The elasticity of the U.S.A. share of exports with respect to its price implied by the estimate is about 3.5 in 1976/1977; that is, holding total exports constant, a 1% increase in the price available in the U.S.A. would have increased exports to the U.S.A. by 3.5%.

On the demand side, the results indicate that the U.S.A.'s demand for Taiwanese footwear is insensitive to the state of the business cycle and appears to be related only to local footwear prices rather than to those of competing suppliers from Korea. The price is, however, negatively related to the quantity of exports with an elasticity of about −14, evaluated at the mean levels of exports and prices in the year prior to the OMA (1976,3–

1977,2).[10] The demand in the rest of the world seems to be fairly strongly influenced by the state of demand (prices rise with the cycle), and to be related to the prices of both local footwear and competitive footwear from Korea. The positive term on exports is very fragile, depending on the dynamics of the equation system; it is probably best interpreted as indicating a horizontal demand curve rather than a perverse one. Thus comparing the U.S.A. market in which Taiwan is an important supplier with the world market in which it is less so, we find a lower elasticity of demand ($-14$ vs. $-\infty$) and less direct competition from Korea. This seems intuitively plausible. Omitting the two implausible coefficients ($\beta_3^R$ and $\beta_2^U$) has little effect on the other parameter except for increasing absolutely $\gamma_{RR}$ and $\gamma_{RU}$ by about 0.25. Finally, the $R^2$ and Durbin–Watson statistics are acceptable.

The second estimation exercise (model II) attempts to incorporate the size of the industry into the system of estimating equations. As argued above, this is most easily accomplished by means of the profit function. Thus in addition to the two demand curves (16), we attempted to estimate three supply functions: Eqs. (14) for $i=\mathrm{R,U}$ and (14) for $i=\mathrm{U}$. Eqs. (14) rule during periods of free trade and eq. (14) during the OMA. The factor demand equation, (14) with $i=\mathrm{Z}$, is not estimable because no data exist on factor inputs, but with the exception of $\gamma_{ZZ}$, its parameters are recoverable from the other equations by symmetry. If the stochastic behavior of the supply model is unaffected by the OMA, the error structure of (14) is derivable from that of (14).[11] However, it would be exceedingly complex to do this, as Brenton and Winters (1990) have shown using other functional forms, so it seemed most rational to treat (14) as a separate equation with its own stochastic errors.

We approached the incorporation of supply responses with great trepidation. The factor price data necessary for eqs. (14) are available only on ISIC rather than on SITC commodity classifications and refer only to wages. Data were also available to us only annually for the earlier part of our sample, and thus had to be interpolated into quarterly series. Moreover, it is possible that wages are endogenous. Hence, wages have to be instrumented in our estimation procedure. For instruments, we used employment and wages in the whole of Taiwanese manufacturing. Thus, one should not place great reliance on the results of the expanded estimation.

The results of the full estimation are reported as model II of table 1. As previously, severe serial correlation suggested that working in first differences was a necessary simplification, but this time it affected all equations. This

[10]Our estimate of the U.S. price elasticity of demand for Taiwanese footwear may appear on the high side. For example, Aw (1989) reports an average price elasticity of demand of about 3.0, a result higher than previous global estimates [Szenberg et al. (1977)].

[11]The term $(X_R+\gamma_R)$ in (14′) would become $(X_R+\gamma_{RR}-u_R)$ where $u_R$ is an error term distributed identically throughout our sample period.

made it impossible to estimate the constants of the supply functions which, in turn, meant that (15) was inestimable. Thus our final system comprised four rather than five equations. The estimates of the demand functions are even less well defined in model II than in model I; the only notable change is that the coefficient relating prices to the quantities of exports in the U.S.A. is significantly positive. As before, we interpret this as indicating a horizontal, not an upward-sloping, demand curve.

Turning to the supply responses, we find them reduced by the inclusion of factor prices. For sales to the U.S.A. – the major market – both terms are positive: Exports to the U.S.A. depend positively on their price relative to the prices of both sales elsewhere and factor inputs. The implied elasticity of supply is around 3.1 in 1977. The coefficients on relative prices for exports to the rest of the world are positive relative to the price of U.S.A. sales but just negative relative to factor inputs. The latter sign implies implausible behavior at some set of prices, but does not disturb the signs of the elasticities at the prices experienced over our sample period. The own price elasticity of supply for exports to the rest of the world is about 1.0 in 1977, but grows to 1.5 by 1986.

The results for model II are disappointing in their lack of precision. However, they do suggest that important supply responses exist and that a more detailed study with better data would be rewarding. They also suggest that responses are around the levels suggesting that it is fruitful to study the effects of VERs on resource allocation and welfare. Thus, until firmer empirical work is undertaken, we take the estimates here as bases from which to explore the effect of different elasticity assumptions on the costs of VERs to developing country exporters.

## 4. Welfare and distributional effects of VERs: Some illustrative simulations

The econometric estimates in section 3 for Taiwanese leather footwear exports suggests that factor demand and output supply responsiveness are sufficient to produce 'domino diversion' towards unrestricted markets and industry contraction. However, both because we were unable to estimate precisely all the demand and supply parameters, and because our estimates may not be representative of those in other sectors subject to VERs, we complete the analysis with some counterfactual simulations inspired by our earlier results. We loosely base these calibrated simulations on Taiwanese leather footwear exports to the U.S.A. and to the ROW using volume and price data at the eve of the OMA agreement.

The partial equilibrium model consists of two constant-elasticity export demand curves (17), a constant elasticity supply curve (18) and the generalized Leontief allocation model described in section 3. Bars over a variable indicate an exogenous parameter, stars denote the initial unconstrained equilibrium, and a tilde over a variable, ~, refers to the prices at which unconstrained producers would replicate the input and output allocation decisions imposed on them by binding constraints in the relevant market.

$$X_k = \bar{A}_k P_k^{-e_k}, \quad e_k > 0, \; k \in \{\mathrm{R}, \mathrm{U}\}, \tag{17}$$

$$X_z = Z = \bar{A}_z \tilde{P}_z^{e_z}, \quad \tilde{P}_z = \tilde{P}_3, \; e_z > 0, \tag{18}$$

$$X_i = -\gamma_{ii} - \sum_{j \neq i}^{3} \gamma_{ij} (\tilde{P}_j | \tilde{P}_i)^{1/2}, \quad i,j \in \{\mathrm{R}, \mathrm{U}, \mathrm{Z}\}, \tag{19}$$

$$\tilde{P}_{\mathrm{R}} < P_{\mathrm{R}} \quad \text{when} \quad \bar{X}_{\mathrm{R}} < X_{\mathrm{R}}^*. \tag{20}$$

Eqs. (17) and (18) describe the output demand and factor supply curves facing the all-around price-taking firms in the industry subject to the VER. Eq. (19) is obtained from applying Sheppard's lemma to the generalized Leontief restricted profit function

$$\pi(P;\alpha) = K\left( \sum_{i=1}^{3} \sum_{j=1}^{3} \gamma_{ij} [-(\tilde{P}_i \tilde{P}_j)^{1/2}] \right), \tag{21}$$

where $K$ is a fixed factor (not modelled) which ensures a determinate firm size. Eq. (20) states that when export volumes in the restricted market are below their free trade values, the price $\tilde{P}_{\mathrm{R}}$ at which unconstrained suppliers would have voluntarily supplied the restricted quantity $\bar{X}_{\mathrm{R}}$ is less than the premium-ridden price at which sales are actually made, i.e., $P_{\mathrm{R}} > P_{\mathrm{R}}^* > \tilde{P}_{\mathrm{R}}$ where $P_{\mathrm{R}}^*$ is the free trade price in the restricted market.

Industry profits, $\pi$, is the difference between sales revenues and costs, both evaluated at the VER-ridden prices, whereas 'virtual' profits given by (21) are evaluated at virtual prices $\tilde{P}$. The welfare measure is

$$\Delta W = W_1 - W^* = (\Delta\pi + \Delta P_Z L)/P_Z^* Z_3 \tag{22}$$

where $W_1(W^*)$ is the value of the welfare indicator with (without) the VER, and $L$ is a scalar indicating the size of the industry in the market for $Z$. $\Delta W$ is the sum of the changes in profits and factor incomes divided by their free trade values.

The elasticities in tables 2 and 3 are used to calibrate the parameters $\gamma_{ij}$ appearing in the factor demand equations. Calibration is completed by treating parametrically initial price and quantity data and by choosing an initial parametric value for $Z$ so that profits are initially equal to zero.

Table 2

Sensitivity results to elasticity specification (small industry case) (10% reduction in exports to restricted market).[a]

| Elasticities | (1) | (2) | (3) | (4) | (5) | (6) | (7) | (8) | (9) |
|---|---|---|---|---|---|---|---|---|---|
| Factor demand elasticity ($\varepsilon_Z^d$)[b] | −1 | −1 | −1 | $-\frac{1}{4}$ | $-\frac{1}{4}$ | $-\frac{1}{4}$ | −2 | −2 | −2 |
| Output supply elasticities ($\varepsilon_R^s = \varepsilon_U^s$)[c] | 2 | 2 | 2 | $\frac{1}{2}$ | $\frac{1}{2}$ | $\frac{1}{2}$ | 4 | 4 | 4 |
| Export demand elasticities ($\varepsilon_R^d = \varepsilon_U^d$) | $\frac{1}{2}$ | 2 | 4 | $\frac{1}{2}$ | 2 | 4 | $\frac{1}{2}$ | 2 | 4 |
| Exports to unrestricted market (% change) | 0.016 | 0.036 | 0.046 | 0.034 | 0.049 | 0.053 | 0.009 | 0.026 | 0.036 |
| Factor use (% change) | −0.053 | −0.045 | −0.041 | −0.041 | −0.036 | −0.034 | −0.056 | −0.050 | −0.045 |
| Change in profits[d] | 7.954 | 1.452 | 0.592 | 6.702 | 0.989 | 0.259 | 8.375 | 1.649 | 0.708 |
| Change in 'virtual' profits[e] | −3.287 | −2.709 | −2.428 | −9.699 | −7.997 | −7.541 | −1.778 | −1.540 | −1.381 |

[a]Initial values: $P_R = 1.54$; $X_R = 27.5$; $P_U = 1.25$; $X_U = 22.0$. Small industry case, i.e., $P_Z$ fixed.

[b]Holding output prices constant.

[c]Holding $P_Z$ constant.

[d]Initial profits equal to zero. Change in sales revenue minus change in value of factor inputs.

[e]Initial profits equal to zero. Restricted profits evaluated at virtual prices.

Table 3

Distributional and welfare effects of a VER.

| Elasticities | Factor supply elasticity = 1 Low[a] | Medium[b] | High[c] | Factor supply elasticity = 5 Low[a] | Medium[b] | High[c] | Factor supply elasticity = 10 Low[a] | Medium[b] | High[c] | Factor supply elasticity = ∞ Low[a] | Medium[b] | High[c] |
|---|---|---|---|---|---|---|---|---|---|---|---|---|
| Exports to unrestricted markets (% change) | 0.042 | 0.065 | 0.084 | 0.036 | 0.043 | 0.051 | 0.035 | 0.040 | 0.044 | 0.049 | 0.036 | 0.036 |
| Factor use (% change) | −0.038 | −0.033 | −0.027 | −0.041 | −0.042 | −0.040 | −0.041 | −0.043 | −0.043 | −0.036 | −0.045 | −0.045 |
| Factor price (% change) | −0.038 | −0.033 | −0.027 | −0.008 | −0.009 | −0.008 | −0.004 | −0.004 | −0.004 | 0.0 | 0.0 | 0.0 |
| Change in profits | 8.849 | 3.302 | 2.198 | 7.166 | 1.924 | 1.156 | 6.936 | 1.696 | 0.947 | 0.987 | 1.452 | 0.708 |
| Change in virtual profits | −8.451 | −1.775 | −0.647 | −9.429 | −2.472 | −1.162 | −9.563 | −2.586 | −1.265 | −7.997 | −2.709 | −1.381 |
| Change in welfare[d] (1) | 0.088 | 0.014 | 0.005 | 0.094 | 0.019 | 0.008 | 0.095 | 0.020 | 0.009 | 0.0 | 0.0 | 0.0 |
| (5) | −0.065 | −0.120 | −0.103 | 0.061 | −0.015 | −0.024 | 0.078 | 0.002 | −0.008 | 0.0 | 0.0 | 0.0 |
| (10) | −0.257 | −0.287 | −0.237 | 0.020 | −0.058 | −0.065 | 0.057 | −0.020 | −0.030 | 0.0 | 0.0 | 0.0 |
| (20) | −0.641 | −0.621 | −0.506 | −0.063 | −0.143 | −0.146 | 0.015 | −0.064 | −0.073 | 0.0 | 0.0 | 0.0 |

[a]Same elasticities as table 2, column (5).
[b]Same elasticities as table 2, column (2).
[c]Same elasticities as table 2, column (9).
[d]Numbers in parentheses refer to factor market size in relation to initial factor allocation in the industry. Change in welfare calculated from eq. (20) and expressed as a percentage of initial factor income in the industry before the VER.

The results of simulations under different assumptions about demand and supply elasticities are reported in table 2. All simulations refer to a negotiated 10% cut in exports of Taiwanese leather footwear to the U.S.A. The objective of the simulations is to establish how sensitive the results are to systematic variations in demand and supply elasticities. At this stage, we assume that the footwear industry is small in the market for its factor $Z$, so that $P_Z$, the price of the factor, is fixed.

In all the simulations, we rely on pairwise variations in the parameters of the generalized Leontief production function. For all pairwise variations, the conditions for local concavity of the profit function (i.e., $\gamma_{ij}>0$) are met, as suggested by our econometric estimates. All simulations assume identical pairwise supply and demand elasticities, since we have no a priori ground for presuming that supply elasticities to restricted and unrestricted markets should be different or for presuming that export demand elasticities should be different (although market shares in the restricted and unrestricted markets are different, however).

The simulations in columns (1–3) show that the spillover is an increasing function of export demand elasticities. The results of varying export demand elasticities also show that, other things equal, the rent transfer gain decreases as the size of the spillover increases. This is because with more spillover there is less contraction and less reduction in costs.

More interesting are the results of varying factor demand and output supply elasticities. Raising output supply responses alone increases the spillover and hence reduces profit to the industry as there is less contraction. This negative effect on industry profits is offset if the elasticity of demand for the factor of production is raised. Doubling the elasticity of factor demand approximately halves the size of the spillover effect. Holding export demand elasticities constant, doubling all production function elasticities [columns (1)–(3) to columns (7)–(9)] reduces the spillover effect by about 35% and increases marginally the amount of contraction and hence profits.

The VER breaks the equality of marginal revenues of the industry factor between sales to the restricted and unrestricted markets and creates an inefficiency [see de Melo and Winters (1990a)]. A measure of that inefficiency is provided by industry profits evaluated at 'virtual' prices. Virtual prices are the set of prices which would cause actual quantities to be supplied voluntarily i.e., the set of prices which, with maximizing behavior, would support the observed quantity outcome. Given such prices, 'virtual' profits are the maximum that exporters could earn and thus changes in them represent the efficiency losses that the VER imposes. In the absence of the VER, actual profits equal virtual profits, both being equal to zero. As can be seen from the last row of table 2, virtual profits are more negative (i.e., efficiency losses are greater) the lower demand and supply elasticities.

In practice, however, industries that enter into VERs are not small in their domestic economy. Indeed, it is precisely because these industries have been rapidly gaining market shares in developed-country markets, that VER arrangements are negotiated in the first place. In table 3, we recognize that the industry faces an upward sloping supply curve for its factor, $Z$, so that contraction is accompanied by a fall in the wage of the industry, $P_Z$. Because the share of the industry in the market for $Z$ is likely to vary from case to case, we report welfare effects for different assumptions about the size of the industry in the factor market. Welfare calculations are reported in the bottom of table 3 as a percentage of the income of factors in the industry prior to the VER and for factor market sizes ranging from 1–20 times the initial allocation of factors in the industry. Of course, the elasticity of factor supply to the industry is not independent of its size in the market for factors, so that the welfare estimate grid should be interpreted accordingly with high values of the elasticity of factor supply corresponding to cases where the industry is small in the market for its factors. For example, elasticities of factor supply in the range between 1 and 5 and factor market sizes in the range between 1 and 5 times the initial factor allocation, could be taken as representative for analyzing a VER in textiles. On the other hand, for a smaller industry like footwear, a more likely factor supply elasticity range would be between 5 and 10 with a correspondingly higher range for the size of the factor market in relation to the footwear industry.

With wage flexibility, the distributional effects of a VER are more pronounced than earlier. Industry profits rise relatively more as they shed factors and use remaining factors at a lower wage. Taking the medium elasticity scenario as a reference, with an industry factor supply elasticity of 5, profits rise by 30% more than in the case of infinite supply elasticity, and industry wages fall by one percent. In addition to producing redeployment, a VER raises profits and lowers wages. Thus it has a strong adverse effect on the distribution of income.

The harmful effects of a VER, however, are not confirmed to the adverse distributional shifts arising from higher profits, lower wages and lower factor use. In addition, as can be seen from the grid of welfare changes displayed in the bottom of table 3, for most factor market sizes and for factor supply elasticities of below 10, the VER results in a net welfare loss. For example, with medium elasticities as a reference, a VER reducing exports to the restricted market by 10% would lead to a welfare loss of 12% of factor income (prior to the VER) for a factor supply elasticity of 1 and a factor market 5 times the size of the initial factor allocation in the industry. Of course, higher factor supply elasticities mitigate the welfare loss and so would differential export demand elasticities (with relatively lower demand elasticities in the restricted market). However, the results in the bottom of table 3 suggest that for most plausible elasticity configurations, a VER is more likely than not to reduce national welfare in the exporting country.

## 5. Conclusions

Most work on VERs has focused on establishing the welfare loss to the importing country arising from the conjunction of an income transfer loss and a distortionary efficiency loss in the importing country. Implicit in that work is that the exporting country is likely to receive adequate compensation for any induced inefficiency losses through the often large rent transfer. This paper has argued that this view is misconceived. A fairly general theoretical model of a competitive industry subject to a VER shows that a VER is likely to lead to both industry contraction and spillover to unrestricted export markets. We call spillover 'domino diversion' since it lends support to the pre-occupation of countries that have not negotiated VERs with seeing their markets flooded by sales diverted from the restricted markets. Our econometric estimates for Taiwanese leather footwear exports to the U.S.A. lend support to the fairly general conditions under which spillover and industry contraction will occur, namely that with rising marginal costs in the production of sales to both restricted and unrestricted markets, any increase in the output of one product does not reduce much (or increases) the marginal cost of the other product.

We also show that in addition to the expected contraction of the industry, a VER will lead to rising private profits (because of the rent transfer from abroad), and to a lower wage for the factors employed in the industry, especially those with skills with few alternative uses in other industries. Thus VERs have strongly negative distributional implications for exporting countries as profits rise and wages and employment fall. Finally, illustrative simulations show that for a plausible range of elasticities and relative sizes of the restricted industry, national welfare may well fall in spite of the rent transfer from abroad.

## Appendix A: Data sources for econometric estimates

Exports and export unit values. Foreign Trade of China, Taiwan Province CCN 6402; pairs and US$ per pair;
Korean export unit values. Korean Customs data [see de Melo and Winters (1989) for details];
Domestic prices/unit values. U.S.: Bureau of Census Current Industrial Report non-rubber footwear RoW: British Footwear Manufacturers Federation, U.K. domestic production unit value and I.F.S. average exchange rate (rf);
Indices of industrial production.

Wholesale prices. I.F.S.,
RoW = OECD less U.S.A. weighted by GDP weights;

Exchange rate.

Wages and unemployment. Yearbook of Labor Statistics, Republic of China wages and employment in leather footwear and average exchange rate.

All data were quarterly except for Taiwanese wages and employment for which only annual data were available consistent form. These were interpolated into quarterly series as follows.

We assume each series grows by a constant amount throughout each year. Thus in any year

$$q_{tj}=x_t+(j-2.5)y_t, \qquad j=1\ldots4,\ t=1\ldots n,$$

where $q_{tj}$ is the observation for quarter $j$ year $t$, $x_t$ is the annual observation, $y_t$ is the quarterly growth in year $t$.

Observation $x_t$ is centered between quarters 2 and 3 and $q_{tj}$ at the centers of their respective quarters.

In addition, there is a requirement that the continuous function represented by $x$ connect at the end of each year and at the beginning of the next. Thus

$$x_{t+1}+2y_t=x_{t+1}-2y_{t+1},$$

from which

$$2y_t+2y_{t+1}=x_{t+1}-x_t=\Delta x_{t+1}.$$

Writing this in matrix form yields

$$\begin{bmatrix} 2\,0 & \cdots & 0 \\ 2\,2\,0 & \cdots & 0 \\ 0\,2\,2\,0 & \cdots & 0 \\ . & & . \\ . & & . \\ . & & . \\ 0 & \cdots & 0\,2\,2 \end{bmatrix} \begin{bmatrix} \\ \\ \\ y \\ \\ \\ \\ \end{bmatrix} = \begin{bmatrix} \\ d \\ \\ \Delta x \\ \\ \\ \\ \end{bmatrix}, \tag{A.1}$$

where $d$ is an arbitrary starting condition. (A.1) is solvable once $d$ is known and we choose $d$ to minimize the variance in growth rates (i.e., we choose to make the quarterly series $q_{tj}$ as smooth as possible).

Minimizing $y'y$ w.r.t. $d$ yields

$$d = -\left[\sum_{t=2}^{n} \Delta x_t(m_{t1} + m_{it})\right] \Big/ 2m_{11},$$

where $m_{ij}$ is an element of $M$, and $M = N'N$, where $N$ is the matrix in (A.1).

## References

Aw, B.Y., 1989, An empirical model of mark-ups in a quality differentiated export market, Mimeo. (The Pennsylvania State University, University Park, PA).

Aw, B.Y. and M. Roberts, 1986, Measuring quality change in quota-constrained import markets, Journal of International Economics 21, 45–60.

Bark, T. and J. de Melo, 1989, Efficiency and export earnings implications of two-tier quota allocation rules, International Economic Journal 3, no. 3, 31–42.

Brenton, P.A. and L.A. Winters, 1990, Non-tariff barriers and rationing: UK footwear imports, discussion paper no. 365 (CEPR, London).

Chambers, R.G., 1988, Applied production analysis: A dual approach (Cambridge University Press, Cambridge).

Diewert, E., 1974, An application of the Sheppard duality theorem: A generalized Leontief production, Journal of Political Economy 79, 481–507.

Feenstra, R., 1984, Voluntary export restraints in US autos: 1980–1981: Quality, employment and welfare effects, in: R. Baldwin and A. Krueger, eds., The structure and evolution of recent US trade policy, NBER (University of Chicago Press, Chicago, IL).

Fuss, M. and D. McFadden, 1978, Production economics: A dual approach to theory and applications (North-Holland, Amsterdam).

Greenaway, D. and B. Hindley, 1985, What Britain pays for voluntary export restraints, Thames essay no. 43 (Trade Policy Research Centre, London).

Hamilton, C., 1989, The political economy of transient 'new' protectionism, Weltwirtschaftliches Archiv, 522–546.

Lopez, R., 1984, Estimating substitution and expansion effects using a profit function framework, American Journal of Agricultural Economics 66, 358–367.

Melo, J. de and L.A. Winters, 1989, Price and quality effects of VERs revisited: A case study of Korean footwear exports, WPS discussion paper 216 (World Bank, Washington, DC).

Melo, J. de and L.A. Winters, 1990a. Voluntary export restraints and resource allocation in developing countries, World Bank Economic Review 4, no. 2, 209–233.

Melo, J. de and L.A. Winters, 1990b, Do exporters gain from voluntary export restraints?, WPS discussion paper 326 (World Bank, Washington, DC).

Neary, P. and K.W.S. Roberts, 1980, The theory of household behavior under rationing, European Economic Review 13, 25–42.

Pearson, C., 1983, Emergency protection in the footwear industry, Thames essay no. 36 (Trade Policy Research Centre, London).

Szenberg, M., J. Lombardi and E. Lee, 1977, Welfare effects of trade restrictions: A case study of the U.S. footwear industry (Academic Press, New York).

Takacs, W. and L.A. Winters, 1991, Labour adjustment costs and British footwear protection, Oxford Economic Papers.

Tarr, D. and M. Morkre, 1984, Aggregate costs to the Unites States of tariffs and quotas on imports: General tariff cuts and removal of quotas on automobiles, steel, sugar and textiles (Federal Trade Commission, Washington, DC).

*Oxford Economic Papers* 43 (1991), 479–501

# LABOUR ADJUSTMENT COSTS AND BRITISH FOOTWEAR PROTECTION*

*By* WENDY E. TAKACS** *and* L. ALAN WINTERS***

## 1. Introduction

The British footwear industry has faced severe pressure from import competition since the early 1950s. Footwear consumption has grown only slowly, while imports have increased dramatically. Domestic manufacturers have faced not only a shrinking market share, but also two decades of absolute decline in domestic sales and output.

One of the industry's responses to import pressure during the 1970s was to try to persuade the government to control international trade. Imports from EEC producers had increased significantly, but given Britain's membership of the EEC nothing could be done about them. The government was prepared, however, to curtail the increases in imports from other sources as and when they became burdensome.

Imports from Eastern European countries increased strongly during 1974 and 1975, which prompted the UK government, at the urging of the industry, to request 'voluntary' export restraints from Poland, Czechoslovakia, and Rumania. These countries agreed to restrain their exports of men's leather shoes during 1975 to a level 5–10% below the 1974 levels, and by 1977 they had agreed to extend the restraints to other leather footwear as well. These 'voluntary' restraints have continued until very recently.

Imports from Taiwan increased rapidly during 1976 and early 1977. In September of 1977, the British government, with the agreement of the Commission of the EEC, imposed quotas on non-leather footwear imports from Taiwan.[1] The quotas limited imports from Taiwan, but Korean footwear shipments to Britain then mushroomed in 1978, so they, in turn, became candidates for restriction. In this case, however, the government suggested that the British Footwear Manufacturers' Federation (BFMF) should negotiate a voluntary restraint arrangement directly with the Korean industry.[2] BFMF and Korean

* This research was supported by the Department of Trade and Industry and the Ford Foundation, to whom we are most grateful. Work for this paper was started during a visit to the Institute for International Economic Studies, Stockholm. We are grateful to Paul Brenton for help with the data and to Bela Balassa and Paul Brenton for comments on an earlier draft.

[1] Taiwan is not a member of GATT, so it is much more vulnerable to actions of this type, which would otherwise be contrary to the terms of the agreement. This action may have been prompted by concern over diversion of shipments to the UK after the US negotiated an Orderly Marketing Agreement (a VER) with Taiwan in July of 1977.

[2] Korea, as a member of the GATT, was not as vulnerable as Taiwan. It is interesting to note how the course of action decided upon by the government and the BFMF was explained by the industry: 'By October it was seen that imports from South Korea were running at over double the previous year, and the Government accepted our case that action needed to be taken against them. For procedural reasons it was agreed that it was better that there should be inter-industry negotiations with the threat of unilateral action by the European Commission in the background, rather than negotiations between the Commission and the South Korean government.' British Footwear Manufacturers' Federation, *Annual Report of the Council*, 1979, p. 8.

industry representatives reached an agreement which limited non-leather footwear shipments in 1979 to about 25% below the levels then projected for 1978 and leather footwear shipments to a level just above projected 1978 shipments. The agreements have been renewed each year through 1987.[3]

In 1980, the industry pressed the government to extend the quotas on footwear imports from Taiwan to cover leather as well as non-leather footwear. According to industry reports, the government's response was to suggest an industry-to-industry arrangement similar to the agreement with Korea. Negotiations failed to reach agreement for 1980 and so the government renewed the quota, but in 1981 the Taiwanese agreed to restrain leather as well as non-leather footwear exports in return for a 22% increase in the level of non-leather restraints.[4] At this point the government abolished the import quota. After the government was no longer actively involved, however, overshipping became a contentious issue, and the British industry eventually decided that continuing the agreements was futile. The last agreement referred to 1985.

The popular justification for import restrictions such as these is that they protect jobs. They increase the price of imported footwear and/or reduce its availability, and so increase the demand for UK footwear and increase its price. Higher output prices increase domestic production and increase the demand for labour. Higher demand for labour maintains employment in the sector above what it would be without the restrictions, avoiding redundancies that would otherwise take place, and avoiding the costs of displacing workers from their jobs.

This paper takes this argument at face value and explores the issues surrounding labour displacement and adjustment costs in the British footwear industry. It discusses the concept and measurement of adjustment costs caused by labour displacement (section 2), develops a method of estimating adjustment costs based on labour turnover in the industry (section 3), develops a model of the production sector to estimate the magnitude of the labour displacement avoided by the non-tariff barriers described above (section 4), and estimates the adjustment costs and compares them with the social costs of the import restrictions themselves (section 5). The estimates of adjustment costs are derived from labour turnover data for footwear plants collected especially for this project, and the model of the production sector makes allowance both for variations in labour-output ratios and for complex interactions between different inputs and outputs of the footwear sector. Thus our estimates of the impact of trade policy on employment are more firmly grounded in real data than previous studies (e.g. Greenaway (1986)).

The paper does not estimate the extent to which the import restrictions boosted the demand for British footwear, but uses the results from Brenton and Winters (1989). Neither does it quantify the extent to which increased

[3] The 1988 BFMF *Annual Report* reports that negotiations with the Korean industry over limits for 1988 had reached agreement on four of five types of footwear (leather was still under discussion). Although formal limits were negotiated each year, actual imports after 1982 were considerably below the ceilings between 1982 and 1987.

[4] British Footwear Manufacturers' Federation, *Annual Report of the Council*, 1980, p. 8.

employment in footwear is offset by reductions elsewhere in the economy. Even ignoring these spillover effects, however, we find that the adjustment costs avoided by protection were far smaller than the costs of protection.

## 2. The concept and measurement of adjustment costs

This section discusses the concept and measurement of adjustment costs in the context of a simple model of the labour market. Takacs (1989) contains a more extended discussion of the issues.

Any reduction in the demand for an industry's product will also decrease its demand for factors of production. Given that labour is usually the most easily variable factor of production in the short run, it will often feel the brunt of the adjustment. The exact impact of the decrease in demand for labour on wages and employment depends upon the structure of the labour market, but lower demand will cause some combination of lower wages and lower employment (higher unemployment), and hence provide an incentive for workers to move to other jobs in other sectors. This is the mechanism through which a market economy responds to changes in demand conditions and ensures the efficient allocation of resources among the various sectors.

In a perfectly functioning labour market with no rigidities and instantaneous adjustment, the labour no longer employed in the declining industry would be immediately reabsorbed into some other sector. If displaced labour were immediately and costlessly transferred to an alternative job with an identical value of the worker's marginal product (and therefore an identical wage), there would be no adjustment problem and no loss of private or social income from the adjustment.

If workers cannot instantaneously and costlessly move between jobs, changes in conditions will impose losses on individual workers and society as a whole. The private and social losses are not usually equal because the former include elements of income transfer and capital gains and losses. Consequently a number of authors draw a distinction between 'private' adjustment costs and 'social' adjustment costs. 'Private' adjustment costs are identified as the losses borne by displaced workers: they may suffer periods of unemployment; they may have to pay to move or to undergo retraining for a new job; they may be re-employed at lower wages than in their previous occupation; and they may suffer capital losses such as a decline in the market value of their homes. On the other hand, these losses may be counterbalanced by unemployment compensation and the value that the workers place on increased leisure time.

Some of the losses and compensating factors, such as unemployment compensation, welfare payments and changes in the market prices of existing assets, are merely transfers from one group to another. They determine the net *private* costs to the individuals affected, but should not necessarily be included as part of net social costs. The *social* adjustment costs, which are the main focus of this paper, are the net losses incurred by society during the adjustment process. As shown below, they may be identified as the value of the output lost when workers are unemployed during the transition between jobs.

Takacs (1989) shows that the nature of adjustment costs depends upon the structure of the labour market in the industry. In perfectly functioning, perfectly competitive labour and product markets with no distortions, no rigidities, and free movement of homogeneous workers among different occupations, there are no identifiable losses to workers, adjustment problems or adjustment costs. If labour is not homogeneous because workers acquire skills specific to a particular industry, then a decrease in the demand for the industry's output will cause workers to move out of the industry imposing private adjustment costs, but no social adjustment costs because there is no way of avoiding the losses inherent in the lower market evaluation of their skills.

However, if imperfections in the labour market prevent workers from moving between industries or maintain rigid wages because of institutional constraints, then social adjustment costs can arise from sudden decreases in the demand for labour. If wages are flexible downward but workers cannot transfer between industries, social adjustment costs arise from the temporary misallocations of labour between industries. If, on the other hand, wages are inflexible downward, the decrease in demand for labour will create excess supply in the labour market and workers will be displaced. This displacement imposes a social cost because there is a social opportunity cost to the idle labour.

The rigid-wage model is the one relevant to the British footwear industry. The labour market for the British footwear industry exhibits a high degree of wage inflexibility due to union contracts and customary practice. Workers in the industry belong to one of two industrial unions, the National Union of Footwear, Leather, and Allied Trades (NUFLAT) or the much smaller Lancashire-based Rossandale Union of Boot, Shoe, and Slipper Operators (RUBSSO). Almost all firms with more than 25 employees belong to the British Footwear Manufacturers' Federation (BFMF), which has a closed shop agreement with NUFLAT. The payment system is a combination of piecework rates, which are set to the establishment level, and day rates.

BFMF and NUFLAT representatives negotiate a national collective agreement every two years. The agreements cover conditions of employment, minimum day rates, increases in piecework rates (piecework plussages), and partial cost-of-living adjustments. When new styles require an operation for which there is no standard rate, the generally accepted method for determining new compensation rates is to 'maintain customary earnings levels for workers'.[5] The union agreements, the practice of maintaining customary earnings levels, and the escalator clause limit the downward flexibility of wages, at least over the adjustment periods that are relevant for this study.

The model of the labour market in this paper assumes that firms and workers negotiate a nominal wage rate for a given contract period. Suppose that the demand and supply curves for labour are $D_0$ and $S_0$ in Fig. 1, and that the labour contract specifies the equilibrium wage $W^*$ for the period of duration of the contract. The industry employs $L_0$ labour. If the demand for the industry's output declines during the period of the contract because of import competition,

[5] See Craig, Garnsey, and Rubery (1982), especially pp. 98–108.

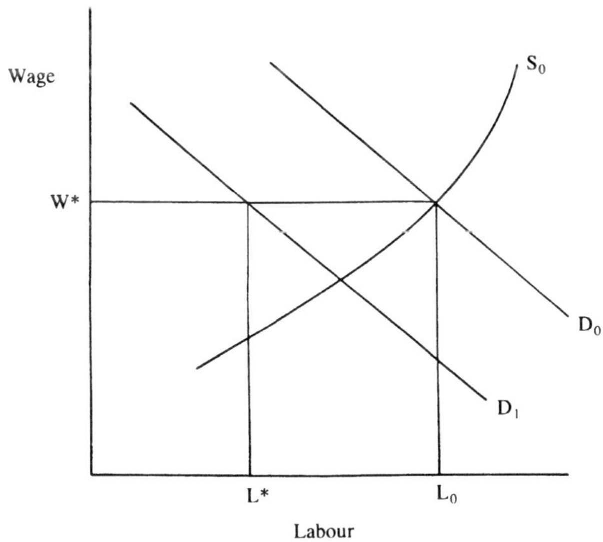


FIG. 1.

the demand for labour would fall, say, to $D_1$, and employment would fall to $L^*$. The fixed wage generates 'involuntary' unemployment of $L_0 - L^*$.

When labour is unemployed, there is a private cost to the individual in terms of lost income, but also a social cost due to foregone output. The social cost of the unemployment in the period of the displacement would be $(L_0 - L^*)$, multiplied by the wage these workers could earn in their next best alternative employment. Given the decline in the demand for the industry's output, the value of the marginal product of the $(L_0 - L^*)$ displaced workers would be less than their previously contracted wage $W^*$. Thus evaluating displaced labour at the wage in its original occupation would overestimate the social opportunity cost of displacement because the value of the human capital specific to the declining sector has decreased since that wage was agreed.[6]

Output would be foregone for as long as displaced workers remained unemployed. Previous studies of adjustment costs have estimated the periods of unemployment of displaced workers,[7] but given the lack of such information for displaced British footwear workers, this study uses a different approach based on labour turnover data obtained from British footwear firms. We assume that as employed labour in the footwear industry turns over, displaced workers

[6] Mutti (1978) evaluates the opportunity cost of displaced workers at the current wage payment including all fringe benefits. Wolf (1979) correctly points out the overestimation that this entails.

[7] See, for example, Bale (1976), Mutti (1978), and Baldwin, Mutti, and Richardson (1980), all of which rely on a US Department of Labor study on the duration of employment for trade-displaced workers.

move out of the pool of unemployed back into work in the footwear sector. Thus following an employment shock the pool of unemployed workers would fall over time due to turnover among the $L^*$ workers still employed, and turn-over (exits) within the pool itself. Workers would have retired, left the industry for jobs elsewhere,[8] or left the industry for other reasons, and we assume that such behaviour continues within the pool of unemployed just as it did during employment.[9] As the pool of unemployed decreases, the social cost incurred will decrease accordingly.

In terms of Figure 1, suppose that import competition decreases the demand for labour and generates a pool of displaced workers equal to $L_0 - L^*$. Assume that the unemployment generates no more movement into other industries than would be captured by normal turnover rates. The supply of workers to the industry ($L_0$ in time period zero) would decline at rate $\theta$ by normal attrition alone, so that in each time period following the decline in demand, the remaining pool of displaced workers ($D_t$) would be:

$$D_t = L_0(1 - \theta)^t - L^*$$

The present discounted value of the adjustment costs of the labour displacement ($C$) can then be expressed as:

$$C = \sum_{t=1}^{\tau} W_A(L_0(1 - \theta)^t - L^*)(1/(1 + r))^t \qquad (1)$$

where:

- $\tau$ is the time period at which all of the displaced labour has been re-employed or left the labour force 'voluntarily'; $\tau$ will be given by: $D_\tau = 0 = L_0(1 - \theta)^\tau - L^*$
- $W_A$ is the wage earned by labour in its next-best alternative;
- $L^*$ is the quantity of labour demanded after the shock that displaces labour;
- $r$ is an appropriate social rate of discount.

There are a number of reasons why this approach may overestimate or underestimate true adjustment costs. The method will tend to overestimate the costs because: (1) we assume that the pool of unemployed decreases only at the rate of estimated normal turnover rates, while unemployment will undoubtedly spur workers to seek jobs more actively outside the industry; (2) we evaluate displaced labour at the wage in the footwear industry, which, for the reason cited above, will overestimate the social opportunity cost of the displaced labour;

[8] Mussa (1986), for example, examines a model of adjustment in which the rate at which resources move out of protected industries depends upon the amount of unemployment experienced by those continuing to seek employment in the industry.

[9] As noted below the assumption that workers leave the pool of unemployed at the same rate that they would leave employment in the industry is very conservative. If displaced workers leave the pool of unemployed faster than the normal labour turnover, our method will overstate adjustment costs.

(3) we ignore the value of increased leisure time or non-market activities to unemployed workers, and (4) we measure lost output relative to the idealized world in which workers move instantaneously into their next best alternative occupation, when in fact this movement would take time and involve an optimal period of job search.

On the other hand, the method may underestimate adjustment costs because we treat labour as homogeneous, while the actual production process for footwear uses different types of workers at different stages. The cutting of leather into pieces (clicking) employs primarily men, the sewing together of the pieces (closing) employs primarily women, the joining of tops and soles (making) employs primarily men, and the finishing and boxing employs primarily women. Demand for these different activities would presumably decrease more or less proportionately as output falls. The skills in these different areas are not readily transferable, so it would be very unusual for a clicker to become a closer as labour demand fell. Thus differences in turnover between men and women will matter because a given decrease in the demand for workers with high turnover rates may not 'displace' any of these workers because they would have left the industry in any event, but the same decrease in the demand for workers with lower turnover rates may displace workers who would not have 'voluntarily' left their jobs. Normal turnover may re-employ displaced female closers very quickly, while displaced male clickers or makers remain unemployed for a longer period because their natural rate of turnover is lower. The use of aggregate turnover rates obscures this distinction and thus may underestimate the mean time it would take for complete adjustment.

There are also other caveats to the interpretation and application of aggregate turnover rates. A 10% turnover rate could be generated from quite different underlying patterns. One possibility is that workers are all alike and each individual worker has an equal 10% probability of leaving during the year. Alternatively, out of every 100 workers there may be 90 who are lifelong employees, and 10 who come and go during the year. In the latter case, employment could contract by 10% the first year and not displace anyone. However, if employment contracted another 10% the next year, workers would be made redundant who would not have left voluntarily.[10]

In the same vein, the discussion above treats a decrease in demand for labour as if each firm contracts proportionally with industry output. However a 10% decline in industry output can entail either the loss of 10% of the firms or a 10% loss of output for each firm. If the industry contracts by closing down individual, geographically scattered plants, displaced workers may not be able

[10] Available evidence indicates that footwear firms in Britain seem to have a hard core of stable, long-service employees, with high turnover rates concentrated among younger workers who are recruited into the industry but subsequently leave. The factors cited for turnover among younger workers include long learning periods before achieving reasonable earnings (due to the piecework system), attractive employment alternatives both within and outside the industry, the demanding nature of the work, the low social status of footwear workers, and the difficulties of integrating young workers with a predominantly middle aged and elderly work force. See Craig, Garnsey, and Rubery (1982), esp. pp. 43 and 138.

to move easily and quickly into a job opening created by normal turnover in a factory that is still operating. We do not dismiss this possibility, but we do not consider it a major problem for the year we are considering because the number of firms in the industry was actually growing at the time and British footwear production is geographically concentrated.

Data on the number of establishments of different sizes in the industry over time appear in Table 1. The comparison for the entire period is complicated by the change in the definitions of the categories, but a clear picture still emerges. The number of establishments in the industry declined drastically across all size categories between 1970 and 1975. This pattern is consistent with a scenario in which firms go out of business and shut down individual factories. The number of establishments actually increased between 1975 and 1980, however, and again between 1980 and 1985. Both increases took place entirely in the smallest category, with concurrent declines in the number of firms in the larger categories. It is impossible to tell from these data alone whether larger establishments shut down and were replaced by completely different new establishments in the smallest category, or whether existing firms shifted into smaller size classifications as they 'downsized'. Given that the restrictions under question became effective between 1975 and 1979, there is no presumption on the basis of the data that additional industry contraction would have taken the form of closure of individual factories rather than lower employment and output on the part of existing firms. This evidence gives some support to the view that labour turnover among workers in existing factories could be relied upon to reduce the pool of displaced workers.

Geographical contraction of the industry may also serve to ease adjustment because if the industry did contract by shutting down entire establishments, displaced workers could find jobs to replace workers who leave other

TABLE 1
*Distribution of footwear establishments by size, 1970–1985*

| *Average Number Employed* | | *1970* | *1975* | *1980* | *1985* |
|---|---|---|---|---|---|
| 1–99 | | 443 | 410 | 448 | 676 |
| 100–199 | | 104 | 62 | 57 | 44 |
| 200–499 | | 76 | 51 | 50 | |
| | (200–399) | | | | 40 |
| 500–999 | | 23 | 20 | 15 | |
| | (400–749) | | | | 14 |
| 1000+ | | 13 | 12 | 5 | |
| | (750+) | | | | 5 |
| Total | | 659 | 555 | 575 | 779 |

Source: BFMF, Footwear Industry Statistical Review, various years.

establishments in the area.[11] Footwear production takes place in many regions of the country, but within them is concentrated locally in areas such as Northampton, Kettering, Leicester, Norwich, Bristol, Street, and Kendal. We do not want to make too much of this point, however, because some footwear production facilities are located in remote villages with no opportunity for workers to find other employment within the footwear industry without moving if the facility that employs them were to shut down.

### 3. Data on labour turnover

We obtained information on labour turnover from the personnel departments of two British footwear firms: K Shoes, which has production facilities in and around Kendal, in Cumbria, and the British Shoe Corporation (BSC), which has production facilities in various parts of the country. Both sets of information cover periods corresponding approximately to April 1984–April 1985 and April 1985–April 1986. The information from K Shoes distinguished between attritions (workers who had left due to retirement, pregnancy, other employment, domestic reasons, and dismissals) and workers who had been made redundant. The information from BSC identified 'leavers' but it is not absolutely clear that all of these were voluntary separations, so the turnover data were adjusted to correct for declines in the numbers employed, where relevant. A more detailed explanation of the data and the adjustments made appears in Appendix A. The BSC data were disaggregated by individual plants, located in different areas of the country, and by departments within these plants. The total number of employees covered by the two sets of information was about 10% of total industry employment. The turnover rates indicated by these two sources of information are shown in Table 2.

The data indicate an 11–13% annual labour turnover for K Shoes and, when averaged across all factories and departments, about a 23% annual turnover for BSC. Given their locations it seems reasonable that BSC would have a higher turnover than K Shoes. K Shoes is located in a relatively small and isolated town. It has outlying factories, but also in small towns or villages. The weighted average turnover rate for the entire sample, using the corrected turnover rates for BSC and 1986 employment as weights, is 16.9% per year.

These turnover rates may appear high, but they are modest compared to turnover data for the footwear industry in the United States. The last available data on quits in the footwear industry are for 1981, at which point the monthly labour quits were 2.9 per 100 employees, which is equivalent to an annual rate of 40.9%.[12] And even this figure was low by historical standards. Between 1972

[11] The argument presented here that geographic concentration of the industry can reduce adjustment costs by allowing turnover to more easily re-employ displaced workers runs counter to Mutti and Rosen (1987, p. 31) who express the view that regional concentration of affected industries compounds adjustment costs. Craig, Garnsey, and Rubery (1982, p. 148) report that one large firm that was closing down outlying factories began 'bussing' skilled workers into the central factory.

[12] Due to budget cuts the Bureau of Labor Statistics curtailed collection of labour turnover data in 1981.

TABLE 2
*Labour turnover data*

| | *K Shoes* | | |
|---|---|---|---|
| | *April–April 1984–1985* | | *April–April 1985–1986* |
| Number employed | 2915 | | 2853 |
| 'Voluntary leavers' | 370 | | 320 |
| Turnover | 12.7% | | 11.2% |
| | *British Shoe Corporation* | | |
| | *Turnover by Department* | | |
| | *Year to April 1985* | *Year to April 1986* | *Corrected* |
| Clicking | 13.1 | 18.2 | 12.7 |
| Closing | 36.8 | 35.0 | 32.3 |
| Making | 23.7 | 19.7 | 12.2 |
| Shoe Room | 26.5 | 38.9 | 28.4 |
| All Departments | 31.4 | 31.9 | 27.8 |
| | *Entire Sample* | | |
| | *Year to April 1985* | *Year to April 1986* | *Corrected* |
| Weighted Average Entire Sample | 19.1 | 18.2 | 16.9 |

and 1981 monthly quits per 100 employees reached as high as 8.6, with an average for the entire period of 4.3. When disaggregated by department, the turnover rates are consistent with the pattern of different turnover rates for male and female employees discussed above. The clicking and making departments, traditionally male, show corrected average turnover rates of 12.7% and 12.2%, respectively. The closing departments, almost exclusively female, show an average corrected turnover rate of 32.3%, and the shoe room, predominantly female, an average corrected turnover rate of 28.4%.

These figures may give an inflated view of turnover rates in the industry because 1984 through 1986 were relatively good years for the British footwear industry, years of relative stability in employment. Work on the time series analysis of labour turnover suggests that the quit rate is lower in depressed than in prosperous times.[13] The data on turnover within firms may also overstate turnover for the industry because some of the 'leavers' have gone to other footwear firms. Finally, the data are from two of the relatively large firms in the industry where turnover may be larger than that in smaller firms.

## 4. The production model

This section estimates the labour displacement that was avoided by maintaining VERs in the footwear sector in 1979. The extent of the shift of demand towards UK produced footwear is estimated in other papers in this series (Winters, 1989b, and Brenton and Winters, 1989). Here we present a model to translate

[13] This evidence is presented in Brechling (1978) and more recently in Jones (1988).

these demand shocks into changes in employment, taking account of the different factor inputs of different footwear types and allowing for variations in labour: output ratios. In these latter respects our work is considerably more sophisticated than most studies of the employment effects of trade policy. The model used is based on a multi-input multi-output profit function, fuller details of which are available in Winters (1989a).

The profit function is now a well-established component of the economist's tool-kit, see, for example, Varian (1978) or Fuss and McFadden (1978). It defines the maximum profit a representative firm can earn as a function of the prices of its inputs and outputs (collectively netputs). Under well-known conditions its derivatives define a set of mutually consistent output supply and input demand functions. For both theoretical and practical reasons, we take the stock of capital to be exogenous in the medium-term, and thus estimate a restricted profit function which explains profit per unit of capital. Trading off

TABLE 3
*Output supply and input demand function for footwear*

| | *Stage 2 (GLS)* | | |
|---|---|---|---|
| | *Coefficient* | *Standard Error* | *Asymptotic t-statistic* |
| $\alpha_{LL}$ | −9.458 | 2.591 | −3.650 |
| $\alpha_{LN}$ | 3.904 | 2.551 | 1.530 |
| $\alpha_{NN}$ | −8.665 | 2.913 | −2.975 |
| $\alpha_{LE}$ | 3.119 | 1.269 | 2.459 |
| $\alpha_{NE}$ | 0.374 | 1.237 | 0.302 |
| $\alpha_{EE}$ | −2.349 | 0.944 | −2.487 |
| $\alpha_{LM}$ | 5.147 | 2.556 | 2.014 |
| $\alpha_{NM}$ | 3.592 | 2.526 | 1.422 |
| $\alpha_{EM}$ | −1.915 | 1.721 | −1.113 |
| $\lambda$ | 0.805 | 0.044 | 18.467 |
| $\delta$ | 0.752 | 0.226 | 3.326 |
| *Covariance matrices* | | | |
| | *Leather* | *Non-leather* | *Employment* |
| | 4.088 | −0.339 | −0.827 |
| | −0.339 | 1.784 | 0.029 |
| | −0.827 | 0.029 | 0.853 |
| *R-squared* | | | |
| | 0.948 | 0.825 | 0.986 |
| *LM-test*[a,b] | | | |
| | −0.825 | −0.818 | −0.288 |
| Observations | | 72 | |
| Degrees of freedom | | 61 | |
| Residual Sum of Squares[b] | | 2.930 | |
| Std error of estimate[b] | | 0.219 | |
| Total Sum of Squares[b] | | 1290.3 | |
| $F(11, 61)$[b] | | 2436.8 | |

[a] *LM*-test for first-order serial correlation (Durbin). Test-statistic is asymptotically normally distributed $N(0, 1)$.

[b] In the second stage estimates, these statistics are calculated from the (transformed) regression data, rather than from residuals obtained by applying the estimated coefficients to the crude data as is done for the covariance matrix and the $R$-squared.

flexibility against tractability we use Diewert's Generalized Leontief form:

$$\Pi(p;\alpha) = K \sum_{i=1}^{N} \sum_{j=1}^{N} \alpha_{ij}(-(p_i p_j)^{1/2}) \tag{2}$$

where:

| | |
|---|---|
| $K$ | is the capital stock, |
| $p_i$ | are input or output prices, |
| $\alpha_{ij} = \alpha_{ji}$ | are parameters, |

and

$i$ and $j$ count over both inputs and outputs.

It is easy to show that (2) is a proper convex profit function if $\alpha_{ij} \geqslant 0$ for all $i$, $j \neq i$; however, it may also be convex for a subset of prices ($p$) even if some $\alpha_{ij} < 0$.

Although (2) has the minimum number of parameters required for flexibility (in Diewert's sense), it is still very demanding of our data. Thus we keep the dimensionality to the absolute minimum, identifying only two outputs, (1) leather footwear and (2) non-leather footwear, and two variable inputs (1) employment and (2) materials. Price series are available for all four variables, but quantities for only the first three. Given symmetry, however, most of the co-efficients in the last equation can be recovered from the first three. Unfortunately, we can not exploit any explicit adding-up constraints because neither total profits nor the return to capital is observable to the same extent as the other variables.

Differentiating (2) yields the following general form:

$$\frac{\partial \Pi}{\partial p_i} = x_i = -K \sum_{j=1}^{4} \alpha_{ij}(p_j/p_i)^{1/2} \qquad i = 1, 2, 3 \tag{3}$$

This was specialized into the following set of estimating equations, which show four minor developments of the general form to allow as parsimoniously as possible for particular features of the UK footwear sector.

$$1/K = -[\alpha_{LL} + \alpha_{LN}(\hat{p}_N/\hat{p}_L)^{1/2} + \alpha_{LE}(p_E/\hat{p}_L)^{1/2} + \alpha_{LM}(p_{ML}/\hat{p}_L)^{1/2}] + \lambda L(1/K) \tag{4a}$$

$$n/K = -[\alpha_{LN}(\hat{p}_L/\hat{p}_N)^{1/2} + \alpha_{NN} + \alpha_{NE}(p_E/\hat{p}_N)^{1/2} + \alpha_{NM}(p_{MN}/\hat{p}_N)^{1/2}] + \delta D + \lambda L(n/K) \tag{4b}$$

$$-e/K = -[\alpha_{LE}(\hat{p}_L/p_E)^{1/2} + \alpha_{NE}(\hat{p}_N/p_E)^{1/2} + \alpha_{EE} + \alpha_{EM}(p_{ME}/p_E)^{1/2}] - \lambda L(e/K) \tag{4c}$$

where:

| | |
|---|---|
| 1 | is output of leather footwear (in tens of millions of pairs), |
| $n$ | is output of non-leather footwear (in tens of millions of pairs), |

$e$ is employment in footwear (tens of thousands),

$\hat{p}_L$ is an *instrumental estimate* of the price of leather footwear (£ per thousand pairs),

$\hat{p}_N$ is an instrumental estimate of the price of non-leather footwear (£ per thousand pairs),

$p_E$ is the average wage (£ per annum),

$p_{ML}$ is a materials price index pertinent to leather footwear (1975 = 1000),

$p_{MN}$ is a materials price index pertinent to non-leather footwear (1975 – 1000),

$p_{ME}$ is a general materials price index for footwear (1975 = 1000),

$K$ is the capital stock in £1970 millions,

$D$ is a dummy variable, 0 over 1963–82, 1 over 1983–86,

$L$ is the lag operator,

and

$\alpha_{ij}$, $\delta$ and $\lambda$ are parameters.

The four modifications to (3) require explanation: first, the different materials prices in different equations. The profit function strictly explains all quantities as functions of the same set of prices, and ideally we should have included the prices of leather and of others inputs separately. Doing so, however, would have added an extra term to each equation, and, given the multi-collinearity of prices and the absence of quantity data, threatened serious numerical problems. We therefore specialized the general system to include leather prices ($p_{ML}$) in the leather equation, other prices ($p_{MN}$) in the non-leather equation, and the general index ($p_{ME}$) in the labour equation. Thus we implicitly assume that the supply of leather footwear is independent of non-leather costs, and that the output of non-leather footwear is independent of leather costs. While this is restrictive it is not entirely implausible, and since our principal interest is not in the effects of materials prices, such a pragmatic approximation was felt justifiable.

The lagged dependent variable in each equation reflects firms' costs of adjustment. We have insufficient data to model adjustment explicitly in this section, and so we have adopted the expedient shown in equation (4). The use of a common speed of adjustment for all questions is the only system-consistent alternative to full vector autoregression, which proved both numerically unreliable and unnecessary statistically.[14] Intuitively it implies a form of partial adjustment in which firms commence the year with a commitment to producing Ll and Ln with Le of labour, and the substitutions reflected in the Generalised Leontief component of (4) are merely modifications to this plan. The larger is $\lambda$, the relatively more costly such modifications are.

The dummy variable in (4b) reflects a change in the productivity of capital in the non-leather footwear sector. Discussions with industry representatives

[14] That is, model (4) was not statistically rejected by the model with full autoregression.

identified a significant technical change in the early 1980s with the advent of automatic computer-controlled stitching, computer-aided design and injection molding of soles. Although this evidence is patchy, it provides sufficient justification for modelling the change in productivity that is so evident in the data from around 1982. The simplest approach is to include a step function dummy, which implies that none of the substitution effects of the system is affected by the technical change.

The final modification of (3) is the substitution of instrumental estimates of output prices for actual prices. The footwear production sector is undoubtedly competitive, but there is still scope for simultaneity at the industry level given the relatively low elasticities of demand for UK footwear estimated elsewhere, e.g. Brenton and Winters (1989). These authors' preferred demand system for footwear is complex, involving hierarchies of suppliers and footwear types, so full information estimation methods are presently quite infeasible. We therefore adopted a simple instrumental variable approach. Each of the leather and non-leather output prices was regressed on aggregate leather footwear import prices, aggregate non-leather footwear import prices (both of which are assumed exogenous in the demand studies), UK retail prices and UK consumers' expenditure, as well as the exogenous variables from (4)—wages, capital stock and materials prices. The instrumental estimates were then substituted into (4). Although this approach has obvious short-comings, its linearity and simplicity have much to recommend it in the present data-scarce circumstances.

The most obvious feature of the UK footwear sector's history has been its decline.[15] British output of leather footwear roughly halved over 1963–86, while non-leather footwear output, the smaller part of the sector, showed mild net growth. Employment has also roughly halved over the period. The strong decline in output would suggest that the capital stock should also have declined. However conventional calculations by Allard (1982) for the period 1963–78 and analogous calculations by the authors subsequently, suggest otherwise. These calculations are based on a perpetual inventory of constant-price investment, depreciated by historical average asset lives. The latter are derived from periods of technological stability and growing output, however, and make no allowance for economic obsolescence. It seemed desirable, therefore, to construct a more sensitive measure of capital stock, designed to reflect the extent to which the fixity of capital may have constrained footwear output during our period of change and decline. With declining output and employment it seemed unlikely that buildings would provide a serious constraint on output, while vehicle stocks were probably sufficiently flexible not to represent a fixed constraint. Given the changing output mixes and rate of technological change, we felt that for plant and machinery a moving average of investment over ten years would roughly reflect the economically useful capital stock. Thus for year $t$ we approximate $K$, the capital stock, by $\sum_{i=1}^{10} I_{t-1}$, where $I_j$ is (constant price)

[15] Much fuller details of the sector and our data are available in Winters (1989a). The output data used here exclude slippers and parts of footwear, and the input quantities have been scaled appropriately.

investment in year $j$. This series grows by 30% over 1963–74 and declines by a similar amount thereafter with a small upturn in 1986.

The model was estimated on annual data covering the period 1963–86 using a non-iterative 'seemingly unrelated regression' approach. All estimation and subsequent manipulation was conducted in GAUSS. The final results are given in Table 3. The regression equations are obviously highly significant and appear to be free from first-order serial correlation. With so few degrees of freedom it was felt inappropriate to save data for forecasting tests, but tests of structural stability suggested that, with the possible exception of 1964, there were no worries about regime changes provided that the dummy variable for 1983–86 was included. The residuals show minor negative contemporaneous correlations between those for leather and the others. This is as one would expect given the sign conventions: higher than expected output of leather footwear is associated with lower non-leather output but higher (more negative) employment.

The lag co-efficient $\lambda$ is rather high, indicating slow adjustment to exogenous shocks: only 20% of any disequilibrium is taken up in the year in which it occurs. While this seems rather slow a priori, it captures graphically the problems besetting the sector: with almost continuous decline in demand and in employment, the industry is always trying to catch up but never really achieving equilibrium.

The co-efficient $\delta$ measures the step change in capital productivity from 1983 onwards. Almost certainly the step change is too sudden, but over a few years we believe that its effect is about right. With actual output of non-leather footwear at 40 to 50 million pairs, the dummy variable suggests a productivity increase of between 15% and 19%.

Economically the most important co-efficients in the estimation are the Generalised Leontief terms, $\alpha$. These are less well determined than the other co-efficients, but are nontheless statistically significant as a group.[16] The results suggest a strong connection between the price of leather footwear and the quantity of employment ($\alpha_{LE}$), but a much weaker one between non-leather output and employment. This is consistent with the view generally held in the industry that non-leather is the more capital-intensive of the two sorts of footwear distinguished. There is also a strong substitution relationship between leather and non-leather footwear output, a rise in the price of one reducing the output of the other.

The positive co-efficients $\alpha_{LM}$ and $\alpha_{NM}$ show that a rise in the price of material inputs reduces the output of footwear *ceteris paribus*. It also, however, appears to reduce inputs of labour, for $\alpha_{EM}$ is negative. Although this response could lead to non-convexities and implausibilities at some sets of prices, it is not problematic at the prices observed over the sample. Materials and intermediate service inputs account for over half of the gross value of output, and thus have a significant effect on total costs. If output prices are fixed, rising input prices

[16] While having individual estimates significantly different from zero would have been nice, the joint test is the relevant one for asking the question 'do prices affect input and output decisions?'. The answer is yes.

will cut the level of output and with it the demand for all inputs. The negative co-efficient $\alpha_{EM}$ merely indicates that this indirect activity effect outweighs the negative substitution effect between materials and labour.[17]

Table 4 reports the simple medium-term partial elasticities implied by our estimates. These are the short-term elasticities multiplied by $(1 - \lambda)^{-1}$; they are not genuinely long-run elasticities because the model still assumes the fixity of the capital stock. Taken as a whole they are surprisingly low. The footwear industry appears to have sharply rising supply curves and sharply falling demand curves for labour. This suggests that quantities are fairly unresponsive to price shocks but that conversely exogenous shocks requiring particular adjustments to quantities have large price effects.

Elsewhere we have calculated the effects of UK quantitative restrictions on footwear imports on the prices and quantities of imports and the demand for UK output–Winters (1989b) and Brenton and Winters (1989). Very briefly, these studies find that the QRs induce both increases in certain import prices and evidence of non-price rationing in certain restricted markets. The elasticities of substitution between the demands for footwear from different sources are

TABLE 4
*The price elasticities of supply and demand 1963–86*

| | *Elasticities with respect to:* | | | |
|---|---|---|---|---|
| *Year* | *Leather Output Prices* | *Non-leather Output Prices* | *Wages* | *Materials Prices* |
| | *(A) Output of Leather Footwear* | | | |
| 1963 | 0.340 | −0.130 | −0.086 | −0.124 |
| 1970 | 0.554 | −0.204 | −0.152 | −0.198 |
| 1980 | 0.599 | −0.217 | −0.178 | −0.204 |
| 1986 | 0.597 | −0.203 | −0.179 | −0.215 |
| | *(B) Output of Non-Leather Footwear* | | | |
| 1963 | −0.853 | 1.344 | −0.052 | −0.439 |
| 1970 | −0.601 | 0.923 | −0.042 | −0.280 |
| 1980 | −0.807 | 1.231 | −0.059 | −0.365 |
| 1986 | −0.533 | 0.814 | −0.041 | −0.239 |
| | *(C) Employment in Footwear* | | | |
| 1963 | 0.268 | 0.025 | −0.201 | −0.092 |
| 1970 | 0.351 | 0.033 | −0.267 | −0.117 |
| 1980 | 0.432 | 0.039 | −0.335 | −0.136 |
| 1986 | 0.489 | 0.043 | −0.370 | −0.161 |

[17] At actual prices the profit function was convex for every year of our sample except for 1963, 1964 and 1978 when the smallest eigenvalue of the Hessian matrix was of the order of -1E-06 compared with a next smallest of 1E-003 in 1963 and 1964, and half that in 1978. Given that our interest is not focused on the materials prices effects, this degree of non-convexity seems supportable.

−2.7, −1.9, −2.2, and −0.8 for men's leather, women's and children's leather, rubber and plastic, and textiles, respectively; in addition we assume an elasticity of substitution between the four footwear types of −1.5 and a price elasticity of demand for total footwear in Britain of −0.75. Combining these demand parameters with the supply functions calculated here, it is possible to estimate the effect of the import restrictions on the prices of UK footwear and hence, via the employment equation, on the demand for labour.

The experiment considered here is the abolition of the various quantitative restrictions on UK imports of footwear applying in 1979. This was the year in which restrictions were most widespread, and Brenton and Winters (1989) calculate that even had they not affected the prices of UK production they would have cost UK consumers some £46 million in all. Once we allow for changes in UK output, prices, and profits, the net cost of the restrictions was about £57 million. Both the demand modules and the production module above allow for gradual adjustment to shocks, but it is best to assess trade policy from a medium-term perspective. Thus, Table 5 reports the effects of abolishing import restrictions after allowing for the various effects to work themselves out. This will cause us to over-estimate the labour costs of adjustment.

Although the effects of the QRs on import prices are quite large and the effects of non-price rationing (not shown in Table 5) even larger, they do not

TABLE 5
*The effects of abolishing quantitative restrictions on footwear, 1979*

| | | |
|---|---|---|
| *Decreases in actual import prices* | | |
| leather mens | Poland | 19% |
| leather womens and childrens | Poland | 19% |
| textile | Korea | 27% |
| | Taiwan | 16% |
| rubber and plastic | Korea | 28% |
| | Taiwan | 12% |
| *Decrease in demand for UK output at fixed prices* | | |
| leather mens | | 13.9% |
| leather womens and childrens | | 7.5% |
| rubber and plastic | | 11.1% |
| *Decrease in prices of UK output* | | |
| leather | | 4.0% |
| non-leather | | 5.4% |
| *Decrease in UK output* | | |
| leather | | 1.2% |
| non-leather | | 0.0% |
| Decrease in employment (workers) | | 1,064 |
| Increase in consumer welfare (equivalent variation) | | £79.2 million |
| Loss of profits and tariff revenue | | £22.4 million |

translate into large effects on UK quantities, prices, and employment. This is because it is generally the smaller suppliers which are restricted and because, with relatively high degrees of substitution between demands for different suppliers' output, small reductions in price allow UK producers to protect their market shares.

**5. Estimates of labour adjustment costs avoided**

We estimate the adjustment costs avoided by the quantitative restrictions on UK footwear imports under three different scenarios, each of which in turn uses low, medium, and high values of turnover rates to generate a range of estimates of adjustment costs. The weighted average turnover rate in our sample was 16.9% per year, but, because some departments show lower and higher turnover rates, we also estimate adjustment costs using 8% and 25% annual turnover rates.

All of the scenarios start with the presumption that abolishing the quantitative restrictions at the beginning of 1979 would have immediately displaced 1064 workers. The three scenarios differ in the underlying assumptions as to how quickly the trade-displaced workers are re-employed relative to workers displaced from the industry for other reasons. In 1979 output and employment in the industry were in decline because of the recession and labour-saving technological change. If the nontariff barriers on footwear had been removed, additional workers would have been displaced. Our three scenarios are: (1) trade-displaced workers are the first claimants on jobs that open up due to turnover; (2) trade displaced workers have a probability of being re-employed equal to that of workers displaced for other reasons; and (3) trade-displaced workers are residual claimants on jobs that open up due to turnover, coming after all workers who have been displaced during the adjustment period for other reasons. The duration of the adjustment period ($\tau$, in weeks) and the present value of the adjustment costs avoided, discounted back to January, 1979, at 10% per annum for each of our three scenarios, assuming low, average, and high turnover rates are presented in Table 6.

TABLE 6

*Adjustment costs avoided by 1979 restrictions*

January 1979 Present Value (Millions of £)
Discounted at 10% annual rate
Period of Adjustment ($\tau$, in weeks) in parentheses

| | *Turnover rates ($\theta$)* 8% | 16.9% | 25% |
|---|---|---|---|
| SCENARIO 1: | 0.70 | 0.37 | 0.28 |
| First Claimants | ($\tau = 14$) | ($\tau = 7$) | ($\tau = 5$) |
| SCENARIO 2: | 0.84 | 0.41 | 0.30 |
| Equal chance | ($\tau = 21$) | ($\tau = 9$) | ($\tau = 6$) |
| SCENARIO 3: | 1.01 | 0.44 | 0.31 |
| Residual Claimants | ($\tau = 21$) | ($\tau = 9$) | ($\tau = 6$) |

Using the 'first claimants' scenario and the weighted average turnover rate of 16.9%, the displaced workers would be reabsorbed, or would have left the pool of unemployment, within seven weeks. The January 1979 present value of the adjustment costs avoided by continuing the restrictions is £0.37 million. Even with the low estimate of turnover of 8% the adjustment period lasts only 14 weeks, and the adjustment costs avoided total £0.70 million.

The 'equal chance' scenario takes into account the decline in total employment that occurred even with the trade restrictions. The total pool of footwear workers made redundant during the adjustment period ($U_t$), the pool of trade-displaced footwear workers ($D_t$), and the expected re-employment of trade-displaced workers ($R_t$) in each week are calculated using (5a–c), starting with $U_1 = 1064 + O_1$; $R_1 = 0$; $D_1 = 1064$:

$$U_t = U_{t-1} + O_t - \theta L_t \tag{5a}$$

$$R_t = (D_t/U_t)\theta L_t \tag{5b}$$

$$D_t = D_{t-1} - R_{t-1} \tag{5c}$$

where:

$O_t$ is the observed weekly decline in the labour force and

$L_t$ is the labour force employed in week $t$.

The adjustment is considered complete when 99% of the original trade-displaced workers have been re-employed or have left. Under this scenario, the adjustment period increases to 21 weeks under the slowest turnover assumption, but the adjustment costs are still relatively low at £0.84 million, because the bulk of the displaced workers are re-employed fairly quickly, even though a few have to wait rather longer.

The 'residual claimants' scenario takes the extreme view that trade-displaced workers are re-employed only after all the workers displaced during the adjustment period for other reasons have taken the jobs that open up due to turnover. Under this scenario:

$$\begin{aligned} R_t &= \theta L_t - O_t &\quad \text{if } \theta L_t - O_t > 0; \\ &= 0 &\quad \text{otherwise.} \end{aligned} \tag{6}$$

Even under this pessimistic assumption and at 8% turnover, it takes only 21 weeks to absorb the trade-displaced workers at a total cost of just over £1 million. The residual claimants scenario does, however, raise the possibility of higher adjustment costs. If turnover had been as low as 5% per annum—and we stress that this is far outside any plausible range based on our data—adjustment would have taken 236 weeks and cost £9.57 million. The significantly longer adjustment period is due to the effect of the 1980 recession, which added significantly to the pool of workers displaced for other reasons. With a 5% turnover rate, some workers displaced in January 1979 would remain unemployed when this group of workers arrived on the job market and pushed them down the queue. As a result, no trade-displaced worker would have been re-employed between July 1980 and July 1982. This estimate of adjustment costs must be considered an upper bound, however, because 5% is very low compared to our observed turnover data, and the method evaluates displaced workers at earnings in their former occupation, makes no adjustment for the value of leisure time, and uses the pessimistic scenario that trade-displaced workers are the last workers re-employed.

In all but this 'worst case' scenario, the results indicate that, because of the high labour turnover in the industry, it is unlikely that labour displacement caused by the removal of British footwear NTBs would have been a major problem. This result might seem surprising in light of the magnitude of the decline in employment in the industry over the last quarter century, but it is consistent with descriptive studies of the footwear industry in which there are frequent references to a *shortage* of labour in the industry during the 1960s and 1970s.[18] Such shortages are not consistent with the existence of large pools of unemployed footwear workers.

The avoidance of adjustment costs can be considered a 'benefit' of the non-tariff trade barriers, to be compared with the 'costs' involved. The demand model and production sector yield estimates of the consumer welfare losses and producer gains from the restrictions. The estimated consumer losses from the set of restrictions in 1979 are £79 million, while, based on the figures in Tables 4 and 5, the increase in profits to the industry is £22 million. The estimated net loss to the society in 1979 is thus £57 million. It is important to note, however, that the adjustment costs are a 'once-and-for-all' cost, incurred only during the adjustment period, while the consumer and net welfare losses continue year after year, as long as the restrictions are in effect and bind. Thus, the present discounted value of the adjustment costs avoided must be compared with the present discounted value of the net social cost of the restrictions. The present value of such costs, discounted at a 10% annual rate, would be £570 million. Moreover, this figure is likely to underestimate the net costs because the annual costs of quantitative restrictions tend to increase over time as fixed quotas confront increasing demand.

The large estimated consumer and net losses relative to the adjustment costs avoided arise because of the combined effects of the relatively low substitutability of British footwear with footwear from the restricted sources especially for non-leather footwear, the inelasticity of British footwear output as prices rise, and the insensitivity of the demand for labour to footwear prices. The combination of these factors implies that the restrictions raise the prices of imported footwear and British footwear without generating much extra output and employment.

**6. Summary**

One argument for protecting domestic industries from import competition is to avoid labour displacement. This paper investigates the adjustment costs

[18] See, for example, Craig, Garnsey, and Rubery (1982), pp. 11 and 194, and Economist's Advisory Group (1976), p. 134.

avoided by maintaining quantitative trade restrictions on British footwear imports from Taiwan, Korea, Czechoslovakia, Poland and Rumania, and compares them with the social costs of the restrictions themselves.

Our estimate of adjustment costs is based on a model of the footwear labour market characterized by contractually determined rigid wages, and emphasizes the role of labour turnover in decreasing the pool of displaced workers. Data on labour turnover in the British footwear industry indicate a relatively high turnover rate of 16.9% per year.

We estimate labour displacement avoided by maintaining quantitative restrictions by deriving a labour demand equation from a multi-input–multi-output profit function for the industry. The results indicate that quantities of inputs and outputs are fairly unresponsive to price changes, and we estimate that the quantitative restrictions in effect in 1979 prevented the displacement of only 1,064 workers. Restrictions on footwear were most widespread during 1979, so this was almost certainly the year in which they had the greatest direct employment effects.

Using the model of adjustment costs, a range of turnover rates that appears reasonable given the data, and the estimated labour displacement, we estimate the adjustment costs avoided by the restrictions under three different scenarios regarding the rate at which trade-displaced labour is re-employed relative to labour displaced for other reasons. The results indicate that, except under unrealistically pessimistic assumptions, the labour displacement caused by the removal of British footwear NTBs would not be a major problem. Even the most pessimistic scenario results in adjustment costs of £9.6 million, compared with social costs of the restrictions of £570 million. The adjustment costs avoided by the protection are far smaller than the costs of protection.

** *University of Maryland*
*** *University of Birmingham and CEPR*

## APPENDIX A

It is not clear whether the data for British Shoe Corporation include only voluntary separations. To generate a conservative estimate of labour turnover, we adjust the data to correct for the overall decrease in the labour force. The percentage turnover rates for April 1985 to April 1986 were applied to the average number employed at each location in 1985 to generate an estimated number of 'leavers' between April 1985 and April 1986. If the average number employed in the year to April 1986 was less than the average number employed in the year to April 1985, the decline in the number employed was subtracted from the estimated number of leavers. This assumes that the observed decline in the number employed was intentional on the part of the firm and these workers did not leave 'voluntarily'. This generates an estimate of separations not accounted for by the decline in the labour force. The turnover rates were then calculated as a percentage of average 1985 employment.

The data for one relatively small factory (Shingler and Thetford) were dropped from the sample because of an obvious error in the data (a tenfold increase in the number employed in one department with no corresponding increase in employment in other departments).

Turnover data by department and factory are shown in Table A1.

TABLE A1

| | Year to April 1985 | | Year to April 1986 | | |
|---|---|---|---|---|---|
| Factory | Number Employed | Turnover (% per yr.) | Number Employed | Turnover (% per yr.) | Corrected |
| | | Clicking Departments | | | |
| Wellingborough Rd. | 58 | 12.0 | 55 | 9.3 | 4.1 |
| North Park | 54 | 17.0 | 52 | 28.0 | 24.3 |
| Leicester St. | 33 | 9.1 | 32 | 12.5 | 9.5 |
| Barry Rd. | 26 | 11.5 | 23 | 30.4 | 18.9 |
| Bardolph St. | 36.5 | 13.7 | 34 | 14.7 | 7.9 |
| Weighted Average | | 13.1 | | 18.2 | 12.7 |
| | | Closing Departments | | | |
| Wellingborough Rd. | 109 | 70.0 | 118 | 50.5 | 50.5 |
| Atherstone | 106 | 15.0 | 100 | 32.5 | 26.8 |
| Brackley | 48 | 32.0 | 51 | 41.5 | 41.5 |
| North Park | 164 | 39.5 | 168 | 33.0 | 33.0 |
| Corby | 62 | 75.5 | 64 | 40.0 | 40.0 |
| Leicester St. | 51 | 37.5 | 39 | 64.1 | 40.6 |
| Sleaford | 51 | 31.4 | 49 | 28.6 | 24.7 |
| Ibstock | 40 | 22.5 | z 39 | 10.3 | 7.8 |
| Shepshed | 58 | 29.3 | 52 | 28.8 | 18.5 |
| Barry Rd. | 51 | 49.0 | 47 | 76.6 | 68.8 |
| Bristol | 59 | 27.1 | 61 | 21.3 | 21.3 |
| Bardolph St. | 82 | 41.0 | 85 | 41.2 | 41.2 |
| Kilmarnock | 141 | 15.0 | 147 | 13.8 | 13.8 |
| Weighted Average | | 36.8 | | 35.0 | 32.3 |
| | | Making Departments | | | |
| Wellingborough Rd. (I) | 33 | 28.0 | 27 | 27.0 | 8.8 |
| Wellingborough Rd. (II) | 35 | 39.0 | 31 | 22.5 | 11.1 |
| Barry Rd. | 33 | 12.1 | 34 | 17.7 | 17.7 |
| Kilmarnock | 19 | 8.3 | 21 | 9.5 | 9.5 |
| Weighted Average | | 23.7 | | 19.7 | 12.2 |
| | | Shoe Room | | | |
| Wellingborough Rd. (I) | 35 | 46.0 | 32 | 53.5 | 44.9 |
| Wellingborough Rd. (II) | 20 | 31.0 | 19 | 53.0 | 48.0 |
| Barry Rd. | 26 | 30.8 | 25 | 36.0 | 32.2 |
| Bardolph St. | 22 | 9.1 | 19 | 52.6 | 39.0 |
| Kilmarnock | 13 | 13.0 | 14 | 6.7 | 6.7 |
| North Park | 54 | 20.5 | 43 | 28.0 | 7.6 |
| Weighted Average | | 26.5 | | 38.9 | 28.4 |

## REFERENCES


ALLARD, R. (1982). 'Estimates of Capital Stock for Manufacturing Industry by MLH', mimeo, Office of Fair Trading, London.

BALDWIN, R. E., MUTTI, J. H. and RICHARDSON, J. (1980). 'Welfare Effects on the United States if a Significant Multilateral Tariff Reduction', *Journal of International Economics*, 10: 405–423.

BALE, M. D. (1976). 'Estimates of Trade Displacement Costs for US Workers', *Journal of International Economics*, 6: 245–250.

BHAGWATI, J. N. (1982). 'Introduction' in Bhagwati, Jagdish, (ed.) *Import Competition and Response* Chicago: University of Chicago Press.

BRECHLING, F. (1978). 'A Time Series Analysis of Labor Turnover', in US Department of Labor, *The Impact of International Trade and Investment on Employment*, Washington, D.C.: US Government Printing Office.

BRENTON, P. A. and WINTERS, L. A. (1989). 'Non-tariff Barriers and Rationing: UK Imports of Footwear', Discussion Paper No. 365. Centre for Economic Policy Research, London.

BRITISH FOOTWEAR MANUFACTURERS' FEDERATION (1969–70 through 1987). *Annual Report of the Council.*

CRAIG, C., GARNSEY, E. and RUBERY, J. (1982). 'Payment Structures and Smaller Firms: Women's Employment in Segmented Labour Markets', Industry Working Papers No. 4, Footwear, University of Cambridge, Department of Applied Economics, Labour Studies Group.

DEPARTMENT OF INDUSTRY (1977). *Report on the Footwear Industry Study Steering Group*, London: Department of Industry.

DHRYMES, P. (1970). *Economics*, Harper and Row, New York.

ECONOMISTS ADVISORY GROUP, LTD. (1976). 'British Footwear—The Future: Vol. II, The Industry', London, Economists Advisory Group.

FUSS, M. and MCFADDEN, D. (1978). *Production Economics: A Dual Approach to Theory and Applications*, North Holland, Amsterdam.

GLENDAY, G., JENKINS, G. P. and EVANS, C. (1980). 'Worker Adjustment to Liberalized Trade: Costs and Assistance Policies', World Bank Staff-Working Paper No. 426.

GREENAWAY, D. (1986). 'Estimating the Welfare Effects of Voluntary Export Restraints and Tariffs: an Application to Non-leather Footwear in the UK', *Applied Economics*, Vol. 18, pp. 1065–83.

HALL, R. E. (1973), 'The Specification of Technology with Several Kinds of Output', *Journal of Political Economy*, Vol. 81, pp. 878–92.

JONES, D. R. (1988). *Redundancy and Re-employment*, unpublished Ph.D. Thesis, University College of North Wales, Bangor.

LEAMER, E. E. (1980). 'Welfare Computations and the Optimal Staging of Tariff Reductions in Models with Adjustment Costs', *Journal of International Economics*, 10: 21–36.

MCFADDEN, D. (1978). 'The General Linear Profit Function', in Fuss and McFadden (eds.) (1978), Vol. I, Chapter II.2, pp. 269–286.

MUSSA, M. (1986). 'The Adjustment Process and the Timing of Trade Liberalization' in Choksi, Armeane M. and Demetris Papageorgiou, eds., *Economic Liberalization in Developing Countries*, New York: Basil Blackwell.

MUSSA, M. (1982). 'Government Policy and the Adjustment Process', in Bhagwati, Jagdish, (ed.) *Import Competition and Response*, Chicago: The University of Chicago Press.

MUTTI, J. (1978). 'Aspects of Unilateral Trade Policy and Factor Adjustment Costs', *Review of Economics and Statistics*, 60: 102–10.

MUTTI, J. H. and ROSEN, H. F. (1987). 'US Labour Market Adjustment', Paper prepared for the project 'Domestic Adjustment and International Trade', Institute for International Economics, Washington, D.C.

PEARSON, C. S. and SALEMBIER, G. (1983). *Trade, Employment, and Adjustment*, Montreal: The Institute for Research on Public Policy.

TAKACS, W. E. (1989). 'Non-tariff Trade Barriers and Labour Adjustment Costs: The Case of the British Footwear Industry', Department of Economics, UMBC, Working Paper 89-004.

VARIAN, H. (1978). *Microeconomic Analysis*, Norton, New York.

WINTERS, L. A. (1989a). 'A Multi-input Multi-output Model of the UK Footwear Sector', Working Paper No. 89/2, School of Accounting, Banking and Economics, University of Wales, Bangor.

WINTERS, L. A. (1989b). 'The Effects of Voluntary Export Restraints on the Prices of UK Imports of Footwear', Discussion Paper No. 374, Centre for Economic Policy Research London.

WINTERS, L. A. and BRENTON, P. A. (1988). 'Non-tariff barriers to International Trade: UK Restrictions on Imports of Leather Footwear from Eastern Europe', mimeo, School of Accounting, Banking and Economics, University of Wales, Bangor.

WOLF, M. (1979). 'Adjustment Policies and Problems in Developed Countries', World Bank Staff Working Paper No. 349.

Journal of International Economics 34 (1993) 289–308. North-Holland

# Voluntary export restraints and rationing
## U.K. leather footwear imports from Eastern Europe*

Paul A. Brenton and L. Alan Winters

*Department of Economics, University of Birmingham, Edgbaston, Birmingham B15 2TT, UK*

Received December 1989, revised version received May 1992

Following the imposition of a quantitative import restriction someone somewhere must be quantity rationed. Concentrating on demand we develop methods to test and allow for the presence of rationing in the estimation of demand equations and in the calculation of the welfare effects of quantitative restrictions. Using a CES model we analyse the voluntary export restraints on U.K. imports of two types of leather footwear from Comecon countries. The results suggest that, even if prices did not rise to clear the market, U.K. consumers could have lost up to £60 million in 1986 from these restrictions.

## 1. Introduction

An important feature of international trading relations since 1970 has been the increasing use of quantitative restrictions (QRs). Fundamental to the analysis of non-tariff barriers (NTBs) is the modelling of quantity constraints, and in this paper we develop a general approach to them by allowing for the possibility that they lead not only to a rise in import prices, but also to non-price rationing. The paper develops statistical methods of identifying rationing, given information of when a QR is in place, and of allowing for it in the estimation of demand systems and in making welfare calculations. We also place much more emphasis than previous studies of NTBs upon the *estimation* of the parameters of behaviour in the presence of binding quantitative restrictions.[1]

Although this paper concentrates on the demand side of the market, the techniques developed are of general relevance to the modelling of QRs.

*Correspondence to*: L.A. Winters, Department of Economics, University of Birmingham, Birmingham B15 2TT, UK.

*We are grateful to two anonymous referees, the participants of seminars at the Universities of Surrey and Cambridge, the University College of North Wales, the Institute for International Economic Studies, Stockholm, and the European Workshop on International Trade, and to our collaborator Wendy Takacs for comments, and to Sue James for typing. This work was conducted in the University of Wales, Bangor, in conjunction with the Centre for Economic Policy Research, London, and was financed by The Ford Foundation, the Department of Trade and Industry, and the World Bank (under project RP 672-40) to whom we are grateful.

[1]This paper is a condensation of some of the work described in Brenton and Winters (1990).

0022-1996/93/$06.00 

When a QR is imposed, someone somewhere is rationed. If suppliers do not raise their prices sufficiently, demanders are rationed as we assume here. If, on the other hand, prices are raised to a level where there is no excess demand, then suppliers must be rationed in the sense that at the new higher price, they would wish to provide more than the quantity permitted. Thus a consistent treatment of rationing is a necessary part of the complete empirical analysis of QRs.

Having developed a model of non-price rationing we use it to assess the effects of the U.K.'s restrictions on two classes of leather footwear (men's, and women's and children's) imported from Poland and Czechoslovakia. The aim of the paper is as much methodological as substantive, but the latter aspect is significant. To our knowledge this is the most detailed study of European footwear protection and the first of imports from Eastern Europe. Given the recent liberalisation of such trade our conclusion that consumer rationing has occurred and is costly assumes considerable policy relevance.[2]

## 2. The basic model of demand[3]

To explore rationing resulting from geographically discriminatory quantitative import restrictions, we require a demand system that admits the simultaneous estimation of quantity-constrained as well as regular quantity-endogenous equations, permits explicit welfare judgements and allows the simple treatment of hierarchies to cope with groups of suppliers. In Winters and Brenton (1988) we developed a model of non-price rationing using the Rotterdam system. This met these criteria and, in principle, allowed a fairly general set of substitutions between different suppliers/product types. However, in empirical application it proved difficult to fit, gave imprecise parameter estimates and proved estimable only for Comecon as a whole. In the present paper, therefore, we try to obviate some of those problems by adopting a more constrained functional form – the constant elasticity of substitution (CES) model. CES functions have a long history in applied international trade; see, for example, Armington (1969) and Hickman and Lau (1973). Being separable and linear homogeneous they permit only restricted substitution possibilities between goods and frequently appear to impose too much structure on the data; see, for example, Winters (1984) or Brenton (1989). However, by concentrating all price responses into the estimation of a single parameter, they allow us to make sense of very noisy

[2]The policy implications of our work are spelt out more fully in Winters and Brenton (1991), which integrates the results of this study with similar research on Taiwan and Korea, an investigation of the price effects of the VERs [Winters (1990)] and a production/employment model [Takacs and Winters (1991)].

[3]Further details of the model may be found in Brenton and Winters (1990) and Winters and Brenton (1991).

data sets such as those presently available to us. Since our concern here is with rationing, we take the CES's separability and homotheticity as maintained hypotheses and exploit its greater focus to allow us to disaggregate our study by footwear type and supplier.

Taking a single type of footwear supplied in differentiated form by $n$ sources, we assume that consumers maximise the sub-utility function

$$U=\left[\sum_{i=1}^{n} a_i q_i^{\delta}\right]^{1/\delta} \tag{1}$$

subject to the budget constraint

$$M=\sum_{i=1}^{n} p_i q_i,$$

where $q_i$ and $p_i$ are, respectively, the quantity and price of footwear from source $i$, $U$ is the sub-utility level, $M$ is expenditure on all footwear of the type under consideration, assumed to be determined by a previous higher-level budgeting decision, and $a_i$ and $\delta$ are parameters.

The elasticity of substitution is $-1/(1+\delta)\equiv\sigma$, which must be negative in order that (1) constitute a proper sub-utility function. Standard manipulations – see Armington (1969) – produce the demand functions

$$q_i=a_i^{-\sigma}\left(\frac{p_i}{p^*}\right)^{\sigma} U, \tag{2}$$

where $p^*$ is the CES dual price function, $p^*=[\sum_j a_j^{-\sigma} p_j^{(1+\sigma)}]^{1/(1+\sigma)}$.

This may be further transformed – see Hickman and Lau (1973) – into

$$s_i=\alpha_i p_i^{\sigma} p^{-1}+\varepsilon_i, \tag{3}$$

where

$\alpha_i \equiv a_i^{-\sigma}$,
$s_i \equiv q_i/\sum_{j=1}^{n} q_j$,
$\varepsilon_i$ is a stochastic error, and
$p$ is a fixed-weight price index $=\sum_{j=1}^{n} \alpha_j p_j^{\sigma}$.

Expressing (3) in share form helps to avoid the heteroskedasticity that frequently results from having quantities on the left-hand side, and emphasises the usual adding up constraints that $\sum_i \alpha_i=1$ and that $\sum_i \varepsilon_i=0$, for all observations.

Eq. (3) is usually estimated with exogenous prices, but it is equally applicable when a quota or a VER is imposed and prices become endogenous. Assume, without loss of generality, that commodity $i$ alone is subject to the QR, we can 'partially invert' (3) to substitute $p_i$ out of the equations for commodity $k$ to get the conditional demand curves (conditional on $s_i$)

$$s_k = (1 - s_i)\alpha_k p_k^\sigma J^{-1} + \alpha_k p_k^\sigma J^{-1}\varepsilon_i + \varepsilon_k, \quad k \neq i, \tag{4}$$

where $J \equiv \sum_{j \neq i} \alpha_j p_j^\sigma$ is the component of the price index referring to the exogenous prices – see Winters and Brenton (1991). Thus allocation among the unconstrained commodities depends on the product of a term in the relative prices of the unconstrained products and a scale factor which reflects the fact that only $(1 - s_i)$ of total expenditure remains to be allocated; there is also a complex error term.

Although we have fixed the quantity (share) of good $i$ in total consumption, nothing so far mentions rationing. The usual assumption in studies of protection is that the import restriction causes the price of imports of commodity $i$ to rise sufficiently to reduce the demand for $q_i$ to the constrained supply, i.e. to clear all markets perfectly. If so, the inverse of eq. (3) reflects demand for $i$, and it, plus eqs. (4), for $k \neq i$, may be used to estimate the parameters of the demand system. Assuming that the distribution of the basic errors is invariant with respect to which variable is exogenous, transformation of the demand equations to make their stochastic components well behaved merely takes us back to (3). We refer to this as the market-clearing model below: although imports of $i$ are constrained, they are not rationed, since their price has increased sufficiently to curtail demand.

We do not face the problems discussed by Richard (1980). He showed (a) that statistics based on the residuals of equations normalised in different ways – i.e. $q = \theta(p) + \varepsilon$ and $p = \Psi(q) + \mu$ – cannot shed light on switches in the exogeneity of $q$ and $p$, and (b) that estimates of the parameters of $\theta(p)$ and $\Psi(q)$ depend upon the parameters of the joint distribution of $(q, p)$ and the distributions of $\varepsilon$ and $\mu$. But we have no need to test for switches in exogeneity, because prior information identifies the change from an endogenous quantity to an endogenous price regime, i.e. we know fairly accurately when the trade restrictions were in place. What we seek below by way of regime change is evidence that in the latter regime demanders are rationed. Second, our transformations of the observations for which $p = \Psi(q) + \mu$ would be the natural regression model back into the form $q = \theta(p) + \varepsilon$ are designed expressly to cope with Richard's point (b).

Richard also argues the implausibility of assuming that the distribution of $\varepsilon$ is invariant with respect to changes in exogeneity; this view commands some respect, but in our problem the prices of other goods and changes in taste – probably the two major contributors to $\varepsilon$ – are likely to be independent of exogeneity.

The remainder of this section explores the statistical implications of rationing and develops some tests for its presence. Suppose that, at the ruling price, $p_i$, consumers are unable to obtain the share indicated by (3) for $q_i$ but are rationed to consume less. Clearly the observed pair $(p_i, q_i)$ will lie below the demand surface, but because we cannot observe directly by how much below, we cannot use the pair to identify that surface other than directionally. This might appear to suggest that almost no information from the rationed period may be used to estimate the parameters of the demand function, but in fact this is too pessimistic. Neary and Roberts (1980) show that even while the ration binds, the demand for unrationed goods may be expressed as a function of the parameters of the demand systems, observed prices, and the ration; this in turn permits us to identify a sub-set of the parameters empirically even while the ration binds. This is done by inverting the Hicksian demand curves (2) for the rationed goods to estimate their 'virtual prices' and substituting these into the demand functions for unrationed goods. Since for homothetic systems such as the CES inverting (2) is equivalent to inverting (3), this amounts to no more than estimating (4) directly – see Winters and Brenton (1991) for details.

The error affecting commodity $i$, $\varepsilon_i$, cannot be separated empirically from the degree of rationing, but if we assume that the stochastic element of demand is unaffected by rationing we can write the $(n-1)\times(n-1)$ matrix of error covariances for eqs. (4) as

$$\tilde{\Sigma}_t = E(\tilde{\varepsilon}_t \tilde{\varepsilon}_t') = G_t' \Sigma G_t, \tag{5}$$

where $\tilde{\varepsilon}_t$ is the vector of errors for the unconstrained commodities for observation $t$, $G_t' = [\tilde{\beta}_t I_{n-1}]$, $\tilde{\beta}_t$ is the $(n-1)$ vector of $\beta_{jt} = \alpha_j p_{jt}^{\sigma} J_t^{-1}$, and where we have assumed that commodity 1 is constrained.

A common way of estimating the effects of a distortionary trade policy is to fit the demand system on pre-distortion data and then to use the estimates to define an anti-monde for the distorted period. Our approach is more efficient for we combine observations from periods with no quantitative restrictions, (3), with observations on the unrationed commodities from the periods of rationing, (4) and (5), in the same estimation. Making efficient use of the information to hand can be a very significant advantage when there are only a few unconstrained observations. In this crucial regard our work differs from Deaton's (1981). His Almost Ideal Demand System is not invertible analytically and hence precludes the combination of rationed and unrationed observations.[4]

As well as defining an estimation procedure, the previous analysis also

[4]It was to allow such combination that our earlier, more general, modelling used the Rotterdam System. Deaton is careful to note the lack of relation between the AIDS and his Rationed AIDS (RAIDS) model.

offers a means of distinguishing between market clearing and Neary–Roberts rationing through the distribution of the residuals. Assuming market clearing we may estimate (3) on all observations. Letting a caret ( ^ ) denote observed residuals, $H_0$ (market clearing) entails that

$$\text{distribution}\,(\hat{\boldsymbol{\varepsilon}}_t, t \in T_2) = \text{distribution}\,(\hat{\boldsymbol{\varepsilon}}_t, t \in T_1),$$

where $T_1$ is the period with no constraints and $T_2$ is the period of suspected rationing. The alternative hypothesis $H_1$ (Neary–Roberts) is that

$$\hat{\boldsymbol{\varepsilon}}_t = \boldsymbol{\varepsilon}_t + \boldsymbol{r}_t, \quad t \in T_2, \tag{6}$$

where $\boldsymbol{r}_t$ is the vector of the effects of rationing. By comparing the distributions of $\hat{\boldsymbol{\varepsilon}}_t$ in $T_1$ and $T_2$ we might identify whether rationing distorts observed behaviour. Several tests for this are described briefly in the appendix.

## 3. Extensions of the basic model

This section makes three extensions to the basic model: the introduction of time trends in the share parameters, the introduction of dynamics and the extension to two or more constrained commodities.

Following Hickman and Lau (1973) we permit the share parameters, $\alpha_j$, to evolve through time according to

$$\alpha_{jt} = \alpha_j^0 \exp(\sigma\gamma_j t) \approx \alpha_j^0 (1 + \sigma\gamma_j t), \tag{7}$$

where $t$ is centred to be zero in mid-sample. The adding-up constraint requires that $_j\sum \alpha_j^0 \gamma_j = 0$, which is imposed during estimation.

Experience in Winters and Brenton (1988) suggested the need for some form of dynamics. It is not practicable to estimate a full vector autoregressive scheme on the vector of shares, and so we are obliged to use the rather restrictive approach of adding the terms $\sum_{l=1}^{4} \lambda_l L^l s_i$ to each eq. (3), $i = 1 \ldots n$, where $L^l$ is the lag operator and the $\lambda_l$ are dynamic coefficients which are common to all suppliers. No position intermediate to full autoregression or this common parameter form preserves adding up – see Anderson and Blundell (1983). In practice our quarterly data needed only lags one and four. Similar manipulation as before yields

$$s_k = (\bar{s}_i - \lambda_1 L\bar{s}_i - \lambda_4 L^4 \bar{s}_i)\beta_k + \lambda_1 L s_k + \lambda_4 L^4 s_k + \beta_k \varepsilon_i + \varepsilon_k, \tag{4'}$$

where $\bar{s}_i \equiv 1 - s_i$ and $\beta_k \equiv \alpha_k p_k^\sigma J^{-1}$, see Brenton and Winters (1990). This is perfectly analogous to eq. (4), and may be estimated in exactly the same way. Simple manipulation shows that (4′) still adds up.

The extension of the model to two rationed commodities is also straightforward, if tedious. The final estimating equations with both $i$ and $j$ rationed are

$$s_k = (\tilde{s} - \lambda_1 L_1 \tilde{s} - \lambda_4 L^4 \tilde{s})\beta_k + \lambda_1 L s_k + \lambda_4 L^4 s_k + \beta_k(\varepsilon_i + \varepsilon_j) + \varepsilon_k, \qquad (4'')$$

where $\tilde{s} \equiv 1 - s_i - s_j$ and previous terms are defined as before.

## 4. Estimation

The equations above are all estimated by maximum likelihood methods using GAUSS. As is well known, allocation models are singular in their variance–covariance structure, which entails either omitting one commodity from the system or substituting $(\Sigma + ii')$ for $\Sigma$ in the likelihhod functions. The present work entails three further complications.

First the demands on the data of estimating a full variance–covariance matrix, $\Sigma$, are fairly heavy, for it entails $n(n+1)/2$ freely estimated parameters. If $n$, the number of commodities included in the system is large, $\Sigma$ can absorb considerable amounts of sample information, and even preclude convergence. In this paper, therefore, we adopt a restriction due to De Boer and Harkema (1984) and De Boer et al. (1987). They suggest the characterisation

$$\Sigma'' = \hat{d} - (d'i)^{-1} d\, d', \qquad (8)$$

where $d$ is a vector of parameters of dimension $n$, the number of commodities, and $i$ is a unit vector also of dimension $n$. Harkema and de Boer show how maximum likelihood systems using $\Sigma''$ may be estimated iteratively from a concentrated likelihood function, but we preferred to treat the $d$ as genuine parameters and use a full likelihood function.

The second complication in estimation involves the change in regime discussed above. In the absence of rationing we have an $n$-equation system with $\varepsilon_t \sim \mathrm{N}(0, \Sigma'')$, whereas with one rationed good we have an $(n-1)$ equation system (still subject to adding up) with $\tilde{\varepsilon}_t \sim \mathrm{N}(0, G_t' \Sigma'' G_t)$. These must be combined into the log-likelihood function

$$\left(\frac{T_1 n_1}{2} + \frac{T_2 n_2}{2}\right) \log 2\pi - \frac{n_1}{2} \log|\Sigma'' + ii'| - \frac{1}{2} \sum_{\tau \in T_1} \varepsilon_\tau' (\Sigma'' + ii')^{-1} \varepsilon_\tau$$

$$- \frac{n_2}{2} \log|G_t \Sigma'' G_t' + ii'| - \frac{1}{2} \sum_{\tau \in T_2} \tilde{\varepsilon}_\tau' (G_t \Sigma'' G_t' + ii')^{-1} \tilde{\varepsilon}_\tau, \qquad (9)$$

where

$T_1$ and $T_2$ are the numbers of observations in the unconstrained and constrained periods,
$n_1$ and $n_2$ are the numbers of commodities which are never constrained and sometimes constrained,
$\varepsilon_\tau$ are vectors of residuals in $T_1$ (of order $n_1$),
$\tilde{\varepsilon}_\tau$ are vectors of residuals in $T_2$ (of order $n_2$).

This again requires us to use a full rather than a concentrated likelihood function, for no satisfactory concentration exists.

Clearly (9) may be generalised to cope with two constrained commodities, although in that case there are potentially four regimes to be combined: no rationing, $i$ rationed, $j$ rationed, and $i$ and $j$ rationed. When $\Sigma$ is unconstrained – save, of course, for its usual adding-up and symmetry – (9) provides no interpretational difficulties. When $\Sigma$ is constrained, however, as in (8), there is no reason other than convenience for believing that it is $\Sigma$, rather than $\tilde{\Sigma}$, that satisfies the particular constraints. In this case, however, convenience wins the day.

Finally, given our assumption that rationing occurs in particular periods the likelihood function should contain additional terms reflecting the likelihood that in the absence of rationing imports would exceed the actual level of imports. Writing $s_{\mathrm{Hi}}$ for the 'Hicksian' share of imports of origin $i$ – the level predicted by the estimated Hicksian demand curve at the observed vector of prices – and recognising that actual imports would differ from this by a stochastic component $\varepsilon_i$ even in the absence of rationing, the probability of rationing is

$$\operatorname{prob}(s_i \leqq s_{\mathrm{H}i} + \varepsilon_i) = \operatorname{prob}(\varepsilon_i \geqq s_i - s_{\mathrm{H}i}). \tag{10}$$

Given our previous assumption that the vector $\boldsymbol{\varepsilon}$ has the multivariate normal distribution with covariance matrix $\Sigma''$, $\varepsilon_i$ is $N(0, \Sigma''_{ii})$, where $\Sigma''_{ii}$ is the $(i,i)$th element of $\Sigma''$. Thus, given $s_{\mathrm{H}i}$, the probability of rationing is

$$\int_{(s_i - s_{\mathrm{H}i})/\sqrt{\Sigma''_{ii}}}^{\infty} \mathrm{N}(0,1)\,\mathrm{d}t, \tag{10'}$$

the log of which for each rationed observation may be added to (9).[5]

## 5. The welfare effects of QRs

The previous section discussed the identification of different regimes and the methods of estimating demand appropriate to them. Once the parameters

[5]The additional factor required when both $i$ and $j$ are rationed is described in Brenton and Winters (1990).

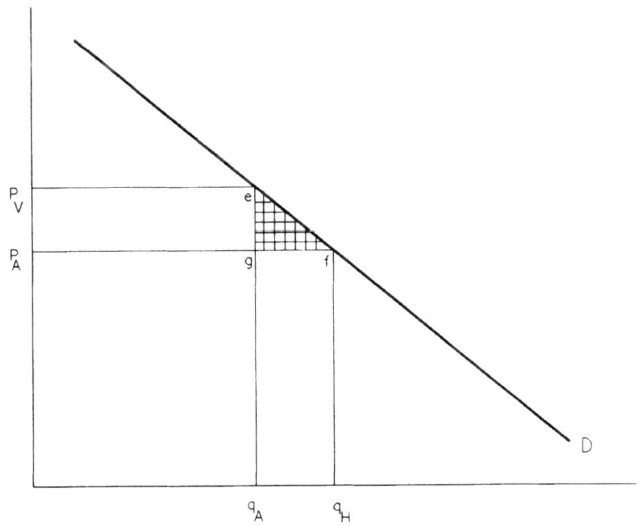


Fig. 1

of demand have been identified, we wish to use them to estimate the welfare effects of the NTBs under consideration. Here we concentrate on rationing, taking the actual price of the constrained imports as given and seeking evidence that, at that price, markets do not clear. The issue of post-QR price rises is discussed by Winters (1990).

The costs of rationing are illustrated in fig. 1. The actual price and quantity $(p_A, q_A)$ lie off the compensated (Hicksian) demand curve. The virtual price, $p_V$, is the price at which quantity $q_A$ would have been bought voluntarily at the given level of utility, while $q_H$, the 'Hicksian' quantity, is the quantity that would have been bought at $p_A$ in the absence of rationing. Neary and Roberts (1980) and Johansson (1987) show that the area shaded under the compensated demand curve (*efg*) for the constrained goods represents the loss of welfare due to rationing. Intuitively, the loss of the units $(q_H - q_A)$ would reduce consumers' surplus by $p_V efp_A$ if it were achieved by an increase in price, but under rationing the expenditure $p_V egp_A$ remains with consumers, leaving a net loss of *efg*. We calculate the welfare effects on consumers directly from the cost functions underlying the CES demand system, holding utility constant at its level under rationing and subtracting the area $q_A(p_V - p_A)$.

All this implicitly supposes that observed prices and quantities pertain directly to final consumers, and that it is the latter who are rationed.

However, the price data available to us refer to imports measured cif plus tariffs and domestic supplies at the factory gate. If somewhere along the domestic distribution chain profit margins are raised as a result of the QR so that final prices reach the market-clearing level, consumers are no longer rationed, and they suffer the usual loss of welfare associated with a price rise – $p_V efp_A$. A model of quantity rationing is still required, however; someone's margins have risen and in an unfettered market, higher returns would surely cause this individual to increase his level of activity – i.e. to buy in more footwear – and the fact that the VER prevents this means that he is rationed. Whether the national welfare loss in this case included the transfer rectangle would, of course, depend on whether the enhanced price–cost margin accrued to residents or not.

## 6. Measurement issues: Imports and import restrictions

To estimate the demand system we require data of the volume and value of U.K. imports distinguished by supplier and domestic sales (domestic production minus exports) for both women's and children's, and men's leather footwear.[6] In common with previous research, the absence of actual import prices has led us to use unit values to approximate the prices of traded goods.[7] To maintain conformity and to permit our desired degree of disaggregation, unit values are also used as the measure of the prices of domestically produced footwear. The basic data are quarterly and cover the period 1971 quarter I to 1986 quarter IV.[8]

Here we concentrate on modelling separately the allocation of pre-determined expenditure on the two types of leather footwear across suppliers. Initially there are 14 separate country/country group suppliers of imports which we treat in a hierarchical manner. The allocation of countries to sub-groups of the hierarchy is determined by our a priori views as to the main substitutions that have occurred [see Brenton and Winters (1990)]. Prices and quantities are passed to higher levels of the hierarchy using the correct CES aggregators,

$$p_t=\left(\sum_j \alpha_{jt}p_{jt}^{(1+\sigma)}\right)^{1/(1+\sigma)} \quad \text{and} \quad q_t=\left(\sum_j \alpha_{jt}q_{jt}^{(1+\sigma)/\sigma}\right)^{\sigma/(1+\sigma)},$$

[6]Initially we had hoped to model the demand for women's and children's footwear separately, but major tariff classification changes in 1978 necessitated that the two groups be combined. These categories correspond to the groupings used to define the U.K. import restrictions.

[7]All import values are tariff inclusive.

[8]The original source of the trade data is HM Customs and Excise, whilst the domestic data are taken from Business Monitor PQ450. Many of the data were provided to us, however, by the British Footwear Manufacturers Federation, to whom we are most grateful.

except for the lowest levels of the hierarchies where, for numerical reasons, we used the simple sum of volumes and a current weighted index of unit values.

The QR which we analyse is the set of voluntary export restraints (VERs) on imports of leather footwear from Czechoslovakia, Poland and Romania, which were imposed in the mid-1970s. We treat imports from Poland and Czechoslovakia as separate goods, but combine the small and barely restrained imports from Romania into a rest of the world category.

There is a surprising degree of confusion in official sources about the timing and nature of the VERs in their early years, and their precise conditions are still confidential. Contemporary and current issues of *Hansard* and *British Business* conflict as to whether the restrictions on women's and children's and men's footwear were agreed from 1975, 1976 or 1977, while the Polish import agents, whom we interviewed, suggested that effective restraint did not occur unti mid-1977 or even 1978. We have, however, received official confirmation (on a private basis) of the existence of the VERs for years since 1978. Taking all this information into account, it seems clear that the VERs were not fully operative until 1977 at the earliest.

In the men's leather group actual imports from Czechoslovakia fell sharply in 1977 and 1978 and then fluctuated between 50 and 60 percent of permitted levels. The trend increase in imports from Poland was halted in 1977, and the volume of imports began to fall in 1978. However, actual quantities did not fall below the VER level until 1979 and then were stabilised at around 80 percent of the agreed volume. In the women's and children's group imports from Poland declined rapidly in 1977 and 1978 and then remained at about 50 percent of the quota level, while those from Czechoslovakia fell rapidly in 1978, rose during 1979 and 1980 (the VER level was increased in 1979) only to decline continuously thereafter. Simultaneously with the restrictions on Eastern Europe, home sales stabilized temporarily while Italian and other suppliers' sales in the United Kingdom increased.

The fact that actual imports fell below permissible levels raises the question of whether the VERs were actually binding after 1977. We believe so. The importers of Polish footwear – Skorimpex Rind plc, whom we interviewed – reported that they could easily have obtained at least 25 percent more orders and that their sales were immune to cyclical fluctuation. Their failure to fill their quota appeared to reflect two phenomena. First, informational and coordination problems. They felt an exaggerated concern not to overshoot their quotas (saying they feared penal reprisals), and since they arranged most of their sales at two major annual fairs could not readily replace cancelled orders. (This absence of aggressive marketing is perhaps further evidence of a perceived binding constraint.) Second, aggregation: Skorimpex reported that when the demand for sandals fell below the agreed

VER level, permission was refused to transfer this quota to other footwear types; unfortunately, data are not available to remove sandals from our exercise.[9] Finally, we note that British industry sources (The British Footwear Manufacturers Federation) reported that they feared a huge expansion of Comecon exports if the VERs were removed. That is, they felt that the VERs bound.

For modelling purposes we assume that each VER binds at the actual level of imports. This seems a natural procedure, but it has two possible dangers. First, because exporters have to allocate their annual quotas across quarters, they have some flexibility in most periods and thus the observed quantities are not wholly exogenous; see Anderson (1987). While this is clearly true in principle, we believe that the traditions of quantity targetting and rigid planning would make the required flexibility hard to achieve in the Eastern bloc.[10] Second, taking actual imports as the binding limit makes it necessary to be careful in identifying periods of rationing. As actual imports fall progressively below the quota level, the likelihood that the VER is actually binding falls, but the tightness of the constraint, if it does indeed bind, increases because the assumed bound level falls with the level of actual imports. Whenever imports persistently fall more than 30 percent below quota we consider it unrealistic even to contemplate the restrictions binding.

A related question is: If the VER binds, why do exporters not raise their prices to market-clearing levels? A plausible, if somewhat unsatisfying answer is that Eastern bloc economies operated entirely on quantity plans and at domestic prices; thus firms experienced no incentive to raise prices, and planning authorities were ill-prepared to exploit their market position. A second explanation could arise from the fact that the U.K. importers of Polish footwear were wholly owned by the single footwear exporting agency in Poland and that this agency was also charged with importing Western machinery back into Poland.[11] By keeping cif import prices down the exporters were able to reduce payments of the U.K.'s ad valorem tariff and yet still reap any scarcity rents by raising prices inside the United Kingdom. As we noted above, such behaviour entails the loss of rents to the U.K. economy just as if prices were at market-clearing levels, but it does not change the fact that someone is rationed and that the VER pushes us off the

[9]The VERs included 'inner limits' on various types of footwear, although it has not proved possible to identify one on Polish sandals in official source documents. Nevertheless, the basic difficulty over aggregation still stands.

[10]Moreover, given the particular form of our model, such endogeneity is not a major problem econometrically. In eq. (6), $p_i$, the price of constrained sales plays no direct role, while any shock in $s_i$ affects all $s_k$ proportionately and hence their shares in $(1-s_i)$ not at all. Indeed, the term $\alpha_k p_k^\sigma J^{-1}\varepsilon_i$ precisely counteracts any such effect. In a more sophisticated demand model endogeneity might be a potential difficulty.

[11]Such arrangements were common for state trading countries. Information made available to us by the licensing authorities suggests that during our sample period Czech footwear was also imported into the United Kingdom by a single agent.

Table 1

Estimates of market-clearing model.

| | Italy | R.O.W. | Czechoslovakia | Poland | U.K. |
|---|---|---|---|---|---|
| (a) Men's leather | | | | | |
| $\alpha_i$ | 0.1562[a] | 0.0989[a] | 0.0090 | 0.0086 | 0.7273 |
| $\gamma_i$ | 0.0060 | 0.0041 | −0.0073[a] | 0.0041[a] | −0.0018 |
| $\sigma$ | 2.7850[a] | | | | |
| $\delta_1$ | 0.4567[a] | | | | |
| $\delta_4$ | 0.2759[a] | | | | |
| $R^2$ | 0.9690 | 0.8266 | 0.5150 | 0.3529 | 0.9600 |
| LM(1–4) | 9.3636 | 18.1086 | 25.8603 | 17.6438 | 18.4961 |
| (b) Women's and children's leather | | | | | |
| $\alpha_i$ | 0.1659[a] | 0.1444[a] | 0.0032[a] | 0.0059[a] | 0.6807 |
| $\gamma_i$ | 0.0116[a] | 0.0093[a] | −0.0168[a] | −0.0055 | −0.0047 |
| $\sigma$ | 1.7503[a] | | | | |
| $\delta_1$ | 0.3124[a] | | | | |
| $\delta_4$ | 0.3155[a] | | | | |
| $R^2$ | 0.8901 | 0.9246 | 0.6024 | 0.4605 | 0.9438 |
| LM(1–4) | 9.5693 | 17.5178 | 7.0762 | 4.1762 | 3.8180 |

[a]Represents $t>2$; the parameter estimates for the United Kingdom were derived from the adding-up conditions and standard errors were not evaluated.

notional import demand schedule.[12] Even if there were no rationing, our model would provide a useful response to the problems posed by unobservable consumer prices.[13]

## 7. The results

One further extension of the basic model proved necessary. Footwear trade is highly seasonal, and ideally we would have treated this by adding seasonal dummies to the estimating equations. However, this was precluded because the additional 12 parameters would have over-stretched our data and estimation ability and so we were forced into using de-seasonalised data. The de-seasonalisation was applied to the regression data, i.e. $s_{it}$ and $p_{it}$, by regressing them on seasonal dummies constrained to sum to zero over a year. The model is non-linear so this is not equivalent to including dummies in the estimating equations; however, we never detect signs of residual seasonality in the following results.

The estimates of the market-clearing model with trends and lagged dependent variables are reported in table 1. They use the De Boer and Harkema covariance matrix, although the unrestricted version produced

[12]Under these circumstances, however, interpreting the model is somewhat more complex than in this paper – see Brenton and Winters (1990).

[13]We are grateful to a referee for noting this.

similar results. To this model we apply the statistics discussed in the appendix to test our prior views about rationing over the period 1977–1986. Starting with the men's leather group and testing individual quarters for the start and finish of rationing by (T1) we found, as expected, no evidence of regime changes over 1975–1976. There was, however, a strong market disturbance in 1977 QIII, the $\chi^2$ statistic of 15.5 being significant at 1 percent. Associated with this statistic was a large negative residual for Czechoslovakian imports (algebraically the lowest residual observed) followed by a string of negative residuals. The residual for the Polish share in this quarter was just positive,[14] although several large negative residuals were apparent immediately afterwards. These latter observations produced relatively high values of the test statistic (T1).

These results corroborate our institutional information, namely that imports from both Poland and Czechoslovakia were quantity rationed towards the end of 1977. As noted above, imports from Czechoslovakia fell away quickly after the imposition of the constraint and, as expected, in 1979 QIII a high positive residual for Czechoslovakia is accompanied by a relatively high, although not quite significant, value of the test statistic. No subsequent quarter appeared to reflect the removal of restrictions on Polish imports, which suggests, along with our institutional information and interview results, that the VER on Polish suppliers still bound in 1986. Thus these tests identify two periods of rationing, for Czechoslovakia and Poland together during 1977 QIII–1979 QII, and Poland alone over 1979 QIII–1986 QIV. The portmanteau tests for the whole period 1977 QIII to 1986 QIV broadly confirm this: the $F$-test on the difference in the constrained and unconstrained covariance matrix, (T3), was not significant, but the likelihood-ratio statistic (T4) was strongly so, taking the value 388.7 compared with a critical value of 15.5 at 5 percent.

With regard to the women's and children's leather group a strong disturbance, significant as 5 percent, was apparent in 1977 QIV. Its associated large negative residuals for Czechoslovakia and Poland followed by a further series of negative residuals (including algebraically the lowest residual observed for both suppliers) and fairly high test statistics seemed to confirm a switch in regime. Rationing of both sources of imports appeared to cease in 1980 QII with large positive residuals for both suppliers and a high, although not significant, value of the test statistic for this observation. Again this confirms our prior view that with falling imports rationing no longer applied. The portmanteau tests of rationing over the period 1977 QIV to 1980 QI provide much stronger evidence of a change in regime, with both the $F$-test (T3) and the likelihood-ratio test being overwhelmingly significant.

[14]However, when rationing was admitted, as the Czechoslovakian result required, this residual also became negative.

Table 2

Estimates of the Neary–Roberts model.

| | Italy | R.O.W. | Czechoslovakia | Poland | U.K. |
|---|---|---|---|---|---|
| (a) Men's leather | | | | | |
| $\alpha_i$ | 0.1602[a] | 0.0998[a] | 0.0114[a] | 0.0193 | 0.7092 |
| $\gamma_i$ | 0.0058 | 0.0040 | −0.0079[a] | 0.0242[a] | −0.0024 |
| $\sigma$ | 2.7511[a] | | | | |
| $\delta_1$ | 0.5038[a] | | | | |
| $\delta_4$ | 0.2642[a] | | | | |
| $R^2$ | 0.9674 | 0.8338 | | | 0.9657 |
| LM(1–4) | 9.9514 | 16.2677 | | | 19.0887 |
| (b) Women's and children's leather | | | | | |
| $\alpha_i^0$ | 0.1926[a] | 0.1517[a] | 0.0091[a] | 0.0118[a] | 0.6348 |
| $\gamma_i$ | 0.0082 | 0.0094 | −0.0089 | −0.0034 | −0.0046 |
| $\sigma$ | 1.8793[a] | | | | |
| $\delta_1$ | 0.2412[a] | | | | |
| $\delta_4$ | 0.5377[a] | | | | |
| $R^2$ | 0.8964 | 0.9284 | | | 0.9445 |
| LM(1–4) | 5.5257 | 17.4359 | | | 8.1930 |

[a]See table 1.

In response to these tests the model was re-estimated with rationing for Polish and Czech footwear over the periods detailed above. In the women's and children's case we experienced severe convergence difficulties, and hence turned to a more restrictive form of the covariance matrix [see Deaton (1975)] whereby $\Sigma = s^2(I_n - (1/n)i_n i_n')$, where $s^2$ is a parameter to be estimated.

Although the results, which are presented in table 2, appear at first glance to be similar to the previous set, in fact they differ in crucial respects. When we allow for rationing the estimated base year shares ($\alpha_i$) for the constrained countries increase strongly as, in the case of men's leather, do the trend rates of growth. There are also large differences in the dynamic adjustment parameters. Hence, although the slopes of the demand curves for constrained footwear do not change greatly (see the elasticities of substitution) their positions shift markedly. Moreover, the coefficient estimates involved in identifying these shifts are generally well determined.

Turning to the economics of the results, we consider first the changes in sales induced by the VERs. These are calculated by comparing actual quantities under the ration with the corresponding Hicksian quantities calculated on the assumption that changes in demand are met at constant-prices and that total demand is given.[15] For men's leather the market share losses to Poland are considerable; our equations suggest that without the VER Poland would have supplied around 40 percent of the market rather

[15]That is, applying the parameters from table 2 to actual prices and total sales in eq. (3) modified for trends and lags.

than its actual 10 percent in 1986. These losses to Poland are balanced by increases in sales for other suppliers which are distributed fairly evenly amongst producers in Italy, the United Kingdom, and the rest of the world. For women's and children's leather the share of the market for both constrained suppliers under the VERs is less than half the share that would have occurred in their absence.[16]

It may seem surprising that trade restrictions could have had such strong effects on market shares, and we recognise the possibility that we have over-estimated the suppliers' ability to expand sales in Britain at constant costs. On the other hand, with relatively long-lived restrictions such as those imposed on Poland, and with the pattern of price movements that actually occurred, it is difficult to find convincing a priori reasons to reject the shifts in the patterns of demand that we have identified. Indeed, we suspect that the traditional insensitivity of demand patterns that colleagues implicitly use as a benchmark when they wonder at our results, stems from the existence or threat of restrictions of the sort that we have been analysing.

The concomitants of the strong effects of the VERs on relative market shares are their implications for virtual prices.[17] A small difference between the actual and virtual prices of men's leather imports from Poland emerges in the latter two quarters of 1977 and in 1978 and grows strongly thereafter. By 1986 the ratio of virtual to actual price exceeds 2.5.[18] The strength and duration of this effect reflects the tightness of the restriction whilst its growth shows the economic distortions that occur when a constant VER is confronted by expanding demand.

For women's and children's leather footwear the actual and virtual prices of both Poland and Czechoslovakia diverge sharply in the first quarter of rationing and the differences increase to a factor of over 3 for Czechoslovakia and 1.6 for Poland in the middle of the constrained period. There is a marked tendency for the virtual and actual prices to converge during 1979, however, as rationing becomes less important.

The final statistics of interest are the welfare costs of rationing. These are shown in table 3. The first column under each type of footwear shows the deadweight loss to the consumer corresponding to the shaded area of fig. 1. The losses to U.K. consumers range from £3.04 million in 1978 (both women's and children's, and men's) to £32 million in 1986 (men's only). The increasing costs of the VER on imports from Poland of men's leather footwear reflect the increasing burden implied by a roughly constant quota

[16]The size of these effects dwarfs any possible under-fulfilment of the quota. Hence even if we could somehow have modelled the VERs as binding at their nominal limits these results would still have suggested a strong degree of restriction.

[17]For reasons explained in Brenton and Winters (1990), we refer here to the 'equilibrium' virtual price not the 'dynamic' one.

[18]During the short period in which Czechoslovakian imports of men's leather footwear are bounded the Czechoslovakian virtual price exceeds the actual price by approximately 40 percent.

Table 3

Estimated welfare costs of VERs on men's and women's and children's, leather footwear (£million).

| | Men's rationing | | Women's and children's rationing | | Men's, and women's and children's, price rise | |
|---|---|---|---|---|---|---|
| | Deadweight loss | Transfer | Deadweight loss | Transfer | Deadweight loss and transfer | Total |
| 1977 | 0.15 | 0.53 | 0.34 | 0.56 | 1.84 | 3.42 |
| 1978 | 0.78 | 2.71 | 2.26 | 2.54 | 4.57 | 12.86 |
| 1979 | 2.04 | 4.14 | 2.26 | 2.88 | 5.78 | 17.10 |
| 1980 | 2.35 | 4.19 | 0.30 | 0.62 | 7.55 | 15.01 |
| 1981 | 3.37 | 4.78 | | | 5.62 | 13.77 |
| 1982 | 7.01 | 6.73 | | | 4.50 | 18.24 |
| 1983 | 12.20 | 9.15 | | | 4.36 | 25.71 |
| 1984 | 18.13 | 12.72 | | | 4.07 | 34.92 |
| 1985 | 22.99 | 15.14 | | | 4.50 | 42.63 |
| 1986 | 32.49 | 20.18 | | | 5.59 | 58.26 |

in the face of growing demand. Annual costs (in current prices) more than double between 1983 and 1986.

The deadweight losses to consumers are compounded if one allows for increases in price somewhere between the exporter and the final consumer. The second column under each type of footwear in table 3 is a measure of the rectangle $(p_V - p_A)\, q_A$. As noted above, this represents the transfer from consumers to domestic distributors if the latter raise their margins, or the transfer abroad if the foreign-owned importers sell at the market-clearing price and gather themselves the VER-scarcity rents. In 1986 this adds an extra £20.2 million to the welfare costs faced by consumers of men's leather footwear.

The estimates of the welfare costs of the VERs given here refer only to the effects of rationing at a given import price. Winters (1990) has estimated the extent to which exporters raised their prices in response to the VERs. On admittedly rather crude data he finds no evidence of increases in Czechoslovakian or Romanian prices, but suggests that the Poles raised their leather export prices by around 19 percent between 1977 and 1986. The additional welfare losses of these price rises are given in the fifth column of table 3.

Yet further losses of welfare from footwear protection are identified in Brenton and Winters (1991) which considers restrictions on imports of non-leather footwear from Korea and Taiwan. They show that while the VER on the relatively concentrated Korean industry never resulted in rationing – that is, prices rose to market-clearing levels – the U.K. administered import quota on the competitive Taiwanese industry did result in rationing. That is, competition between exporters appeared to prevent the Taiwanese from collecting the scarcity rents. Moreover, once the quota on Taiwan was converted into a VER in 1981 the rationing of textile footwear soon ceased.

## 8. Conclusion

The imposition of a quantitative trade restriction necessarily leads to either demanders or suppliers being rationed. This paper has made two contributions stemming from this observation. First, it has developed a means of identifying and modelling rationing: we have applied the approach to a system of demand equations, but it is of equal relevance ot supply relations, and, as noted above, any empirical work on quantitative restrictions must grapple with rationing somewhere in the market. Second, we have shown that for U.K. leather footwear imports from Eastern Europe there is a strong presumption that demand-side rationing occurred. Complete proof is, of course, impossible, but from institutional and interview data we identified periods when rationing was plausible and then with detailed data found that in those periods market clearing was rejected in exactly the fashion predicted by rationing theory. These results – the most detailed on European footwear markets and the first on Eastern Europe – suggest that even in the absence of price rises to the market-clearing level, British consumers have been materially penalised by the VERs which restricted their access to men's, and women's and children's footwear from Czechoslovakia and Poland.

## Appendix: Tests for rationing

Under the null hypothesis that the model is perfectly specified the residuals $\varepsilon$ from systems estimation of (3) are asymptotically normal with mean zero and variance $\sigma^2$, and

$$\frac{1}{T}\sum_{k=1}^{T} \varepsilon_k \varepsilon_k' \rightarrow \Sigma,$$

where $\varepsilon_k$ is $\varepsilon$ for observation $k$. Thus for period $k$

$$\varepsilon_k'(\hat{\Sigma} + ii')^{-1}\varepsilon_k \sim \chi^2_{n-1} \tag{T.1}$$

and for several periods ($T'$ in all)

$$\sum_{k=1}^{T} \varepsilon_k'(\hat{\Sigma} + ii')\varepsilon_k \sim \chi^2_{T'(n-1)}, \tag{T.2}$$

where $\hat{\Sigma}$ is the estimate of $\Sigma$, and $n$ the number of commodities.

Following Harvey (1981, p. 157) these tests might be more powerful if the estimate of $\Sigma$ were based not on the whole sample but on only that part for which the market-clearing model was strongly believed to be correct. However, in our case this period is too short to give reliable estimates of $\Sigma$, and so the whole of the period is used.

Harvey also suggests an exact test for heteroskedasticity based on single equation recursive residuals. However, data limitations and the complexity of calculating recursive residuals for systems estimated by maximum likelihood require that an approximation be used. In vew of (T.1)

$$\frac{\sum_{t\in T_1} \varepsilon_t'(\hat{\Sigma}+ii')^{-1}\varepsilon_t}{\sum_{t\in T_2} \varepsilon_t'(\hat{\Sigma}+ii')^{-1}\varepsilon_t} \tag{T.3}$$

will be distributed approximately $F_{(n-1)T_1,(n-1)T_2}$, where $T_1$ and $T_2$ are sets of unconstrained and constrained observations.

Finally we consider maximum-likelihood tests of the variance–covariance structure. Under $H_0$, $\Sigma$ is common to both regimes, whereas under $H_1$ the variances $\Sigma_1$ and $\Sigma_2$ vary between regimes. A rather crude approximation of a standard likelihood-ratio test is given by

$$2{*}LL \approx T\log|\hat{\Sigma}| - \sum_{i=1}^{2} T_i \log|\hat{\Sigma}_i|, \tag{T.4}$$

with $\hat{\Sigma}_i$ appproximated by the residuals of the estimation under $H_0$. This test essentially considers the first step of a maximum-likelihood search for the parameters under $H_1$ (different $\Sigma_i$) starting from the estimate of $H_0$ (identical $\Sigma_i$). If it suggests rejection of $H_0$ one can be sure that further steps towards convergence, all of which increase the likelihood, would not reverse that conclusion. The derivation of these tests are described in more detail in Brenton and Winters (1990).

## References

Anderson, G. and R. Blundell, 1983, Testing restrictions in a flexible dynamic system: An application to consumers expenditure in Canada, Review of Economic Studies 12, 397–410.

Anderson, J.E., 1987, Quotas as options: Optimality and quota licence pricing under uncertainty, Journal of International Economics 22, 21–39.

Armington, P.S., 1969, A theory of demand for products distinguished by place of production, IMF Staff Papers 16, 159–176.

Brenton, P.A., 1989, The allocation approach to trade modelling: Some tests of separability between imports and domestic production and between different imported commodity groups, Weltwirtschaftliches Archiv 125, 230–251.

Brenton, P.A. and L.A. Winters, 1990, Non-tariff barriers and rationing: UK footwear imports, Discussion Paper No. 365, Centre for Economic Policy Research, London.

Deaton, A.S., 1975, Models and projections of demand in post-war Britain (Chapman and Hall, London).
Deaton, A.S., 1981, Theoretical and empirical approaches to consumer demand under rationing, in: A.S. Deaton, ed., Essays in the theory and measurement of consumer behaviour (Cambridge University Press, Cambridge) 55–72.
De Boer, P.M.C. and R. Harkema, 1984, Undersized samples and maximum likelihood estimation of sum-constrained linear models, Report 8331/E, Economic Institute, Erasmus University, Rotterdam.
De Boer, P.M.C., R. Harkema and B.J. van Heeswijk, 1987 Estimating foreign trade functions: A comment and a correction, Journal of International Economics 22, 369–373.
Greenaway, D., 1986, Estimating the welfare affects of voluntary export restraints and tariffs: An application to non-leather footwear in the UK, Applied Economics 18, 1065–1083.
Harvey, A.C., 1981, The econometric analysis of time series (Philip Allen, Oxford).
Hickman, B.G. and L.J. Lau, 1973, Elasticities of substitution and export demands in a world trade model, European Economic Review 4, 347–380.
Johansson, P.-O., 1987, The economic theory and measurement of environmental benefits (Cambridge University Press, London).
Neary, J.P. and K.W.S. Roberts, 1980, The theory of household behavior under rationing, European Economic Review 13, 25–42.
Quandt, R.E., 1982, Economic disequilibrium models, Econometric Reviews 1, 1–63.
Richard, J.F., 1980, Models with several regimes and changes in exogeneity, Review of Economic Studies 47, 1–20.
Takacs, W.E. and L.A. Winters, 1991, Labour adjustment costs and British footwear protection, Oxford Economic Papers 43, 479–501.
Winters, L.A., 1984, Separability and the specification of foreign trade functions, Journal of International Economics 17, 239–263.
Winters, L.A., 1990, Voluntary export restraints and the prices of UK imports of footwear, Weltwirtschaftliches Archiv 126, 523–542.
Winters, L.A. and P.A. Brenton, 1988, Voluntary export restraints: UK restrictions on imports of leather footwear from Eastern Europe, Discussion Paper 283, Centre for Economic Policy Research, London.
Winters, L.A. and P.A. Brenton, 1991, Quantifying the economic effects of non-tariff barriers: The case of UK footwear, Kyklos 44, 71–91.

*The Economic Journal*, **104** (*January*), 113–123. © Royal Economic Society 1994. Published by Blackwell Publishers, 108 Cowley Road, Oxford OX4 1JF, UK and 238 Main Street, Cambridge, MA 02142, USA.

# VERs AND EXPECTATIONS: EXTENSIONS AND EVIDENCE*

*L. Alan Winters*

This paper analyses the effects of an expected future voluntary export restraint on the level of firms' current exports to a market. The traditional result that current exports increase is shown to depend on the degree of collusion in the exporting industry and the anticipated restrictiveness of the VER. The former relationship is tested by reference to the effect of EC import surveillance on its imports. Surveillance is argued to indicate an increased probability of a VER in the future, and it is found that while competitive industries respond to it by increasing exports to the EC, less competitive ones curtail exports. This constitutes one of the few empirical tests of the strategic part of strategic trade policy.

In a recent paper Yano (1989) explored the effects of anticipated voluntary export restrictions (VERs). He showed that if a future VER will generate rents and the rights to export under it will be allocated proportionately to current exports then the threat of imposing the VER will increase current levels of exports. That is, anticipated future VERs disprotect import-competing firms in the current period. Essentially, a marginal unit of current exports earns the current margin between marginal revenue and marginal costs (if any) *plus* the right to share in the VER-induced rents next period.

Yano's model had one domestic firm and two foreign exporting firms playing a Cournot game, and assumed that the probability of a future VER was exogenous. Subsequently Hariharan and Wall (1992) showed that his result applies even if there is only one exporting firm, so long as future sales under the VER are positively related to current sales. Hoekman and Leidy (1990), in independent work, showed that the latter assumption induced the Yano effect even if there are no rents to exporting and extended the model by endogenising the VER probability. Anderson (1992) also endogenised the VER probability and found Yano effects for price-taking competitive exporters. Ethier (1991) explored these effects in a general model.

This paper combines these extensions to Yano's model. First it considers a full range of conjectural variations in the exporting game rather than assuming just Cournot conjectures; second, it allows for many exporting firms; and third, it endogenises the VER probability. These extensions are of some interest directly, especially in allowing us to gauge the importance of industry structure to the Yano effect, but their real attraction is that they permit a crude empirical test of the expectational effects of VERs.

Winters (1990) explores the effects of import surveillance on the levels of EC imports. Import surveillance formally entails merely the enhanced statistical

* Part of this work was conducted under the Centre for Economic Policy Research's programme 'Empirical Models of Strategic Trade Policy', funded by the Ford Foundation (No. 860-0312A). The paper has benefited from discussions in seminars at City University, the University of Bristol, the University of Bordeaux and the Catholic University, Leuven. I also thank Paul Brenton, Michael Leidy and two referees for comments.

monitoring of imports, but it is governed by the same EC legislation as quantitative import restrictions and its introduction is frequently justified in terms more appropriate to restriction than to monitoring. It is arguable that the principal effect of surveillance is to indicate an increased probability of import restriction – very frequently a VER. The model below shows that where the export industry is relatively collusive, it may pay export firms to curtail their exports when surveillance is imposed in order to head-off a more coercive VER. Less collusive industries, on the other hand, may find it difficult to achieve the coordination necessary to curtail trade, and may not find it desirable to do so even if they can. The data do, in fact, suggest that industries with different structures differ in their responses to surveillance, and thus offer some support for the sort of expectational effects postulated above.

## I. AN ANTICIPATED VER

I distinguish period o, the current period, from period 1, the future, in which there is a probability $\phi$ of a VER being imposed. In that eventuality, denoted by superscript $V$, I assume that exporting firm $i$'s permitted level of exports, $q_i^V$, will be proportional to its share of total exports to the country in period o. Thus

$$q_i^V = \frac{q_i^0}{\sum_{j \in M} q_j^0} \bar{Q} = \frac{q_i^0}{q_m^0} \bar{Q}, \tag{1}$$

where $\bar{Q}$ is the total permitted level of trade under the VER, $j \in M$ indicates the set of import-supplying (i.e. exporting) firms, and $q_m^0$ is total imports in period o.

The alternative situation for period 1 is free trade, denoted $F$, which occurs with probability $(1-\phi)$. I assume that all firms supply an identical good, so there is only one price in each situation, $p^k, k = 0, V, F$. For convenience I also assume constant marginal costs, $c$, identical across all firms, and, because I deal only with a fixed number of firms, ignore fixed costs. Finally, I assume that there is a domestic industry, subscripted $d$, and that there is no time discounting.

The endogeneity of the VER, which is the only intertemporal link between periods o and 1, is represented by writing

$$\phi = \phi(q_m^0), \quad \phi' > 0. \tag{2}$$

That is, the probability of a VER being imposed in period 1 is a function of *total* imports in period o. This simple function does not capture the richness of the political economy of VERs but it suffices for our purposes with one further minor, and fairly realistic, assumption. I assume that the legislation under which VERs are imposed prevents the domestic firm from reducing its own quantity of output in period o with a view to encouraging imports in order to induce a VER in period 1. This essentially rules out a form of Stackelberg leadership by the domestic industry and erases the intertemporal link for domestic industry.

The problem for each exporting firm is to choose $q_i^0$ to maximise expected profits. That is

$$\max E_i(\pi) = (p^0-c)\,q_i^0+\phi(p^V-c)\,q_i^V+(1-\phi)\,(p^F-c)\,q_i^F, \tag{3}$$

where $q_i^V$ is given by (1), $\phi$ by (2), and $p^k = p^k(q^k)$ $k = 0, V, F$, where $q^k = q_d^k+q_m^k$ is total supply in period $k$.

The first order conditions for the exporting firms with respect to period 0 output is:

$$(p^0-c)+p^{0\prime}\delta_i\,q_i^0+\phi(p^V-c)\,\bar{Q}\,\frac{q_m^0-\lambda_i\,q_i^0}{q_m^{02}}+\phi'\lambda_i[(p^V-c)\,q_i^V-(p^F-c)\,q_i^F] = 0, \tag{4}$$

where $\lambda_i$ is $i$'s conjectural variation about total imports, i.e. its perceived value of $dq_m^0/dq_i^0$ and $\delta_i$ is $i$'s conjectural variation about total supplies, i.e. $dq^0/dq_i^0$.

The difference between $\lambda_i$ and $\delta_i$ is exporters' conjectures about *current* domestic output. Having ruled out the intertemporal link for domestic firms, these conjectures are quite separate from those about domestic responses to the VER; the latter are embodied in exporters' expectations about $p^V$ (the price in period 1 under a VER fixed at $\bar{Q}$), which they are assumed to hold with certainty.

The first two terms of (4) are the usual static first order conditions setting perceived marginal revenue equal to marginal cost. The third term comprises the margin under the VER multiplied by the effect of $dq_i^0$ on $i$'s sales under a VER allocated according to (1), all multiplied by the probability of a VER arising. The last term reflects the endogenous probability of a VER. $\phi'\lambda_i$ is the expected effect that $dq_i^0$ has on the VER-probability, while the term in brackets is merely the difference between profits under a VER and under free trade. Note that since we are dealing with period 0 decisions, $p^V$ and $p^F$ are forecasts not actual values, and thus depend on conjectures about future behaviour.

Imposing symmetry on the exporting firms and summing (4) across, $i = 1,\ldots,n$, we obtain

$$p_0+\frac{1}{n}p^{0\prime}\delta q_m^0+\phi\left(1-\frac{\lambda}{n}\right)(p^V-c)\,v+\phi'\lambda(\pi^V-\pi^F) = c, \tag{5}$$

where $\pi^V, \pi^F$ are the representative firm's export profits under $V$ and $F$, and $v = \bar{Q}/q_m^0$ is the 'restrictiveness' of the VER.

If the VER were not possible, i.e. if $\phi = \phi' = 0$, (5) is the traditional oligopolistic equilibrium condition. Perceived marginal revenue, $p^0+p^{0\prime}\delta q_m^0/n$, is set equal to marginal costs.

The third term of (5), is non-negative: if price covers marginal cost under free trade, so it will under a VER which restricts sales; $v \geqslant 0$; $\phi \geqslant 0$; and $\lambda \leqslant n$, given the usual stability assumptions of the oligopolistic model. Ignoring the endogeneity of the VER, i.e. setting $\phi' = 0$, a positive value implies that, given $c$, marginal revenue must be reduced if (5) is to remain satisfied. Thus, relative to the absence of VER-threats, supplies must be expanded. This is the pure Yano effect ($Y$), and surveillance would *boost* imports if it were the only effect.

Now allow for VER-endogeneity. Standard assumptions guarantee $\lambda \geqslant 0$, so the direction of the effect of endogenising the VER depends entirely on the relative sizes of profits under a VER and free trade. If $\pi^V$ is the greater, the 'endogenous probability effect' (call it $E$), is positive, and supplies in period 0 are stimulated further as exporters rush headlong into the VER. If, on the other hand, $\pi^V < \pi^F$, exporters would try to resist the imposition of the VER and would curtail exports. If $\phi$ were sufficiently low, or if the VER were expected to be highly restrictive, $E$ could dominate $Y$ and lead exporters to cut supplies below those in the absence of a VER threat.

The overall effect of a VER threat depends on the relative sizes of $Y$ and $E$. These will vary first with the subjective and unobserved probability $\phi$ and its derivative $\phi'$, and second with various market structure variables. Suppose, for example, that one could raise the number of exporters, $n$, without changing anything else in equation (5). This would increase $Y$ relative to $E$: firms scramble to get quota rights if the VER is introduced but are less convinced that they can influence the probability of the VER. Hence industries with many small firms are less likely to curtail exports following the introduction of surveillance than are those with few players.

Of course, it is not wholly plausible to vary $n$ while holding the conjectural variation, $\lambda$, and the relative profit levels, $\pi^V$ and $\pi^F$, constant, but the likely variations in these values only strengthen the conclusion. As $n$ rises, industries tend to become less collusive, which reduces $\lambda$ and thus raises $|Y|$ relative to $|E|$. Moreover higher $n$ and lower $\lambda$, imply less collusion, which will tend to reduce free trade profits ($\pi^F$) relative to those under the VER ($\pi^V$). This increases $E$ algebraically and thus increases the incentive to expand sales in response to a threatened VER. Section II formalises this relationship.

## II. VERS AND PROFITS

The difference in exporters' period 1 profits between the free trade and VER situations is the crucial determinant of the effects of a threatened VER. Several authors have noted the dependence of this difference on the degree of industry collusion. Harris (1985) notes that a VER imposed on a competitive industry at the free-trade level of imports will raise its profits by increasing, from zero, its effective degree of collusion. It is also obvious that under Cournot conjectures such a VER has no effect: it merely confirms firms' conjectures about each other. Finally, Mai and Hwang (1988) have shown that in duopolies which are more (less) collusive than Cournot, a VER on one firm reduces (raises) its profits.

Two further factors increase the likelihood that $\pi^V$ will fall below $\pi^F$ when a VER is introduced. First, VERs are almost always tighter than the free-trade level. Even if in their first year they are fairly close to initial free-trade levels, they are designed to curtail natural export growth and thus tend to become progressively tighter – see, for example, Hindley (1985) or Brenton and Winters (1989). While a VER at free-trade levels ($v = 1$) may allow $\pi^V$ to exceed $\pi^F$, at $v = 0$ they obviously do not; by continuity, therefore, for a less than perfectly competitive industry, $\pi^V - \pi^F \leqslant 0$ for some $v < 1$.

The second factor is the threat that a VER may be discriminatory. Most VERs single out only the more dynamic exporters, so there is a real possibility that an 'over-enthusiastic' exporter is curtailed while other suppliers move into its forcibly vacated market. In the limit trade diversion to unrestricted suppliers may keep the market price at its free-trade level in the presence of a partial VER; in this case, if the VER restricts a firm's sales, it reduces its profits, i.e. for the restricted firms $\pi^V - \pi^F < 0$.

The rest of this Section formalises these arguments in order to gauge the extent to which different industries have different incentives to encourage or avoid VERs.[1]

Following Mai and Hwang (1988) I consider a symmetric linear model with conjectural variations, but unlike them I allow for any number of firms both in the industry and subject to the VER. For simplicity I suppose that there are $n$ identical firms in all, of which $m$ are subject to the VER.[2] All firms supply the same homogenous product, which has everywhere marginal cost of $c$. Like Mai and Hwang I find that a VER will raise (lower) exporters' profits relative to free trade according to whether conjectures are less (more) collusive than Cournot. In addition, however, I show that the strength of these effects is related to the number of firms and to the restrictiveness and the scope of the VER.

With a linear demand curve

$$p = \alpha + \beta q \quad \text{where, by symmetry} \quad q = \sum_{i=1}^{n} q_i = nq_i,$$

and with constant marginal costs, it is easy to show that, under free trade, each firm produces

$$q_i^F = -\frac{\alpha - c}{\beta(\delta + n)}, \tag{6}$$

where $\delta = [1 + (n-1)\gamma) > 0$ is $i$'s conjectural variation about industry output – as above – and $\gamma$ is its conjecture about each of its competitors.

If a VER is imposed on $m$ of the firms, and if crucially, it does not affect the remaining $(n-m)$ firms' perceptions of $\gamma$, the unconstrained firms have first order conditions

$$\beta[1 + (n-m-1)\gamma]\, q_i^U + p^V - c = 0, \tag{7}$$

where $q_i^U$ is the quantity supplied by an *un*constrained firm when some other firms are constrained and $p^V$ is the price ruling under those circumstances. If the $m$ constrained firms can each supply $vq_i^F$, total supply will be $mvq_i^F + (n-m)\, q_i^U$, and using (6) and (7)

$$q_i^U = \left[\frac{\delta + n - mv}{\delta + n - m(1+\gamma)}\right] q_i^F. \tag{8}$$

[1] Further details of the derivations below are available in Winters (1992).
[2] Hence I now drop the distinction between domestic and foreign firms.

This allows us to express the change in total industry sales resulting from the VER as

$$\Delta q = \frac{m[v(\delta - m\gamma) - (1-\gamma)]}{\delta - m\gamma + n - m} q_i^F. \tag{9}$$

Harris and Mai and Hwang set the VER at free trade levels ($v = 1$), in which case it may be readily verified that: if conjectures are Cournot ($\gamma = 0, \delta = 1$), $\Delta q = 0$; if conjectures are less collusive than Cournot ($\gamma < 0, \delta < 1$), industry sales fall, industry price rises and constrained firms, which still produce $q_i^F$, make higher profits; and if conjectures are more collusive than Cournot, constrained firms' profits fall.

When constrained firms are restricted to sell less than $q_i^F$ the situation is more complex, and I tackle it by comparing $\Delta q$ from (9) with $\Delta w$, the change in industry sales that would just leave constrained firms' profits unchanged. This is

$$\Delta w = -\left(\frac{1-v}{v}\right)\delta q_i^F. \tag{10}$$

Equating (9) and (10) defines a locus along which constrained firms will be indifferent between a VER and free trade.[3]

In Winters (1992) I analyse some special cases of this locus, but the general results are most easily seen by plotting it in $v$ and $\gamma$ space for various $n$ and $m$, see Fig. 1. Combining Cournot conjectures ($\gamma = 0$) and $v = 1$ ensures that

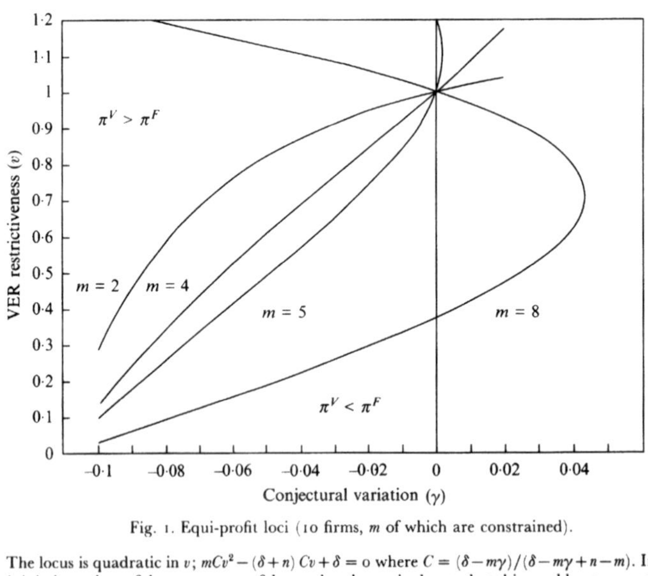


Fig. 1. Equi-profit loci (10 firms, $m$ of which are constrained).

[3] The locus is quadratic in $v$; $mCv^2 - (\delta + n)Cv + \delta = 0$ where $C = (\delta - m\gamma)/(\delta - m\gamma + n - m)$. In the linear case it is independent of the parameters of demand and marginal costs, but this would not generalise to other functional forms.

$\pi_i^V = \pi_i^F$, so the point (0, 1) always lies on the locus. If $\gamma < 0$, however, while $v = 1, \pi_i^V > \pi_i^F$, so points to the left of (0, 1) imply higher profits and an incentive for restricted firms to seek a VER.

Fig. 1 is drawn for an industry of 10 identical firms of which 8, 5, 4 and 2 respectively face a VER. Variation in $m$ represents the different proportions of total supplies that emanate from potentially constrained firms. Two types of relationship are evident. For high $m$ ($\geqslant 6$) restricted firms in a Cournot industry ($\gamma = 0$) gain from a moderately restrictive VER and even those in more collusive industries could do so. For lower levels of $m$, however, firms in Cournot industries never gain if $v < 1$, and as the number of firms affected declines those in relatively competitive industries could suffer. Thus, for example, when $m = 5$ and $\gamma = -0.02$ the threatened firms prefer $v = 0.8$ (a 20% reduction in sales) to free trade – the point $(-0.02, 0.8)$ lies left of the locus – whereas when $m = 2$ and $\gamma = -0.02$ even $v = 0.94$ (a 6% reduction) reduces profits.

Equations (9) and (10) show that the loci also depend on the number of firms in the industry. However, if one varies $n$ while holding constant both the proportion of firms constrained ($m/n$) and firms' conjectural variation about industry output ($\delta$), the differences are, in fact, rather minor:[4] larger industries show only slightly greater incentives towards VERs.

Although they have been based on very special assumptions, Sections I and II have provided a number of testable predictions. If they are not refuted by the data we may conclude at least that the expectational aspects of trade policy are worthy of further consideration. The analysis suggests that if a VER will affect only a relatively small proportion of total sales of a good there are quite strong incentives for the firms which expect to be constrained to avoid it. These incentives are stronger for collusive industries and for industries which have fewer firms. They are never likely to become so strong, however, that a highly competitive industry (low $\gamma$) would seek to behave in that way. Recall that I have modelled *total* supplies in this section so it is perfectly plausible that the principal foreign suppliers, who are the usual targets of VERs, have market shares of below 20%.

## III. MODELLING SURVEILLANCE

A plausible way of representing import surveillance is as a shift in the subjective probability of there being a future VER, $\phi$, and its derivative, $\phi'$, from zero to positive values. The previous sections suggested that this is more likely to curtail exports the fewer firms and countries threatened, the smaller their share of total supplies and the more collusive the industry initially.[5]

In Winters (1990) I examined the evolution of EC imports subject to import surveillance over the 1970s and 1980s. I examined all instances of surveillance

[4] This seems the most satisfactory basis for comparing industries with different $n$.

[5] Of course, these industry effects could be confounded by variations in $\phi$ and $\phi'$ between cases. Because these variations are uobservable I have to assume them away below, but I find that I can explain the observed facts quite well without recourse to them.*

since 1976, excluding those cases where its effects could be confounded by those of other trade policy changes, such as in agriculture, steel and textiles and clothing. After excluding a few other cases because of data inadequacy the sample comprises thirty-five trade-headings subject to surveillance which I subdivided into five groups according to the details of their surveillance and their industry characteristics. In nearly all cases surveillance reduced the growth rate of EC imports. Thus, I sought to identify surveillance effects by comparing the market share of surveyed exporters during surveillance with their share in the last pre-surveillance year. I similarly compared the unit value of EC imports from those countries with that of intra-EC trade in the same commodities.

Table 1 summarises the results. Part (a) reports the number of instances in which the import share or relative unit value exceeded the pre-surveillance value, and Part (b) the unweighted means of the proportionate deviations of actual from pre-surveillance values. Unweighted sums and means are appropriate because I am investigating the *existence* of trade effects rather than trying to quantify their significance. The table reports data for up to seven years of surveillance, although given the usual amounts of change in trading conditions the later years should not be taken too seriously. The number of cases varies from year to year because not all surveillance lasted or could be observed for seven years. Group III refers to goods from Japan first surveyed in 1981 for which the years 1983–5 were covered by 'moderation' agreements. Hence the three missing years. Group I includes goods with different starting dates for surveillance, but the remaining groups are homogeneous in that regard; Group II, starting in 1978; Group III, 1981; Group IV, 1983; and Group V, 1986.

*Prima facie* the totals at the foot of the table suggest no systematic effects of surveillance at all. The loss of import share is consistently negative, but the mean effect is small and at least for the first three years no more than half the individual instances record declines in share.

The results for the individual groups are more informative, however. Three groups display a consistent tendency for surveillance to be accompanied by rising relative unit values and declining market shares – cases of universal surveillance (Group I) and the two Japanese groups (III and IV). The latter pair are consistent with several of our hypotheses: the goods are sophisticated and hence have relatively few supplying firms, only one country was surveyed, and Japan is sometimes held to have well-developed mechanisms for industrial co-operation.[6]

By contrast Groups II and V generally record negative responses in relative unit values and positive import share responses. These also appear explicable in terms of the arguments above. For footwear (Group II), imports from eleven developing countries were surveyed and footwear is a highly fragmented

[6] The main concern about this result is the possibility that there were covert 'export moderation' agreements covering these groups for more years than I have allowed. However, in Winters (1990) I also considered a more restrictive selection of years and trade headings, including only those commodities for which this problem could be ruled out and found the results largely unaffected.

Table 1

*The Effects of Import Surveillance Relative to 'No-change' Anti-monde*

| | (a) No. of positive deviations | | | (b) Mean proportionate deviation | |
|---|---|---|---|---|---|
| Years | Market Share | Relative Price | No. of cases | Market Share | Relative Price |
| | | Group I. Universal surveillance | | | |
| 1 | 3 | 4 | 6 | −0·034 | 0·108 |
| 2 | 1 | 3 | 3 | −0·010 | 0·241 |
| 3 | 1 | 3 | 3 | −0·029 | 0·304 |
| 4 | 1 | 3 | 3 | −0·021 | 0·348 |
| 5 | 1 | 2 | 3 | −0·023 | 0·331 |
| | | Group II. Footwear | | | |
| 1 | 2 | 0 | 6 | −0·019 | −0·076 |
| 2 | 4 | 3 | 6 | 0·000 | −0·023 |
| 3 | 5 | 3 | 6 | 0·048 | −0·059 |
| 4 | 3 | 3 | 6 | 0·056 | 0·064 |
| 5 | 3 | 4 | 6 | 0·047 | 0·074 |
| 6 | 4 | 2 | 6 | 0·069 | −0·016 |
| 7 | 4 | 3 | 6 | 0·069 | 0·095 |
| | | Group III. Japanese goods from 1981 | | | |
| 1 | 3 | 6 | 8 | −0·019 | 0·131 |
| 2 | 3 | 4 | 8 | −0·066 | 0·049 |
| 3 | | | | | |
| 4 | | | | | |
| 5 | | | | | |
| 6 | 1 | 6 | 8 | −0·075 | 0·129 |
| 7 | 1 | 6 | 8 | −0·102 | 0·088 |
| | | Group IV. Japanese goods from 1983 | | | |
| 1 | 7 | 12 | 15 | −0·019 | 0·183 |
| 2 | 9 | 13 | 15 | −0·015 | 0·184 |
| 3 | 7 | 14 | 15 | −0·024 | 0·203 |
| 4 | 2 | 9 | 10 | −0·045 | 0·161 |
| 5 | 3 | 8 | 8 | −0·054 | 0·148 |
| | | Group V. Korea video-recorders | | | |
| 1 | 1 | 0 | 1 | 0·050 | −0·234 |
| 2 | 1 | 0 | 1 | 0·142 | −0·217 |
| | | Total | | | |
| 1 | 16 | 22 | 36 | −0·009 | 0·071 |
| 2 | 18 | 23 | 33 | −0·005 | 0·117 |
| 3 | 13 | 20 | 24 | −0·007 | 0·137 |
| 4 | 3 | 17 | 19 | −0·017 | 0·111 |
| 5 | 4 | 16 | 17 | −0·013 | 0·117 |

industry in most of them. Thus the industry is highly competitive and effective restraint would be hard to organise.

Group V contains only one case, which does not lie very happily in our analysis because of its dynamic nature. Korea had a very small share of the EC video tape recorder market when surveillance was imposed in 1986. Despite earlier restrictions on Japan, the sector was still sensitive in the EC in 1986 and Korea had experienced many previous instances of restrictions. Thus in this case $\phi$ was perhaps rather high and $\phi'$ correspondingly low. Thus an aggressive attempt to establish a market position while the opportunity lasted looks like a rational response to surveillance. In 1987, the EC instituted anti-dumping actions against Korean VCRs;[7] however even if this was in retaliation for Korea's 'aggressive selling' during 1986 and 1987, the 'aggression' may well have been optimal because Japanese exporters were also faced by anti-dumping investigations at the same time. Thus Korea had arguably managed to attain a reasonable share of the market before the undertakings extracted by the EC anti-dumping authorities cartelised it.

Group I – the six cases of universal surveillance – appears to refute the theory above. Because surveillance refers to all countries, one might expect import supply to be competitive and anticipate the same outcome as for footwear (Group II), but in fact it is consistently one of rising relative unit values and falling market shares. This almost certainly reflects the structure of imports. Although ostensibly universal, surveillance was effectively focused on only one or two countries because of their high shares of EC imports. For the two types of slide fasteners, Japan accounted for 73% and 88% of the last pre-surveillance year's extra-EC imports, while for phosphate fertilisers the USA's share was 92% and for titanium the United States and Japan jointly accounted for 99% of each of the three headings. Thus overall a high degree of collusion looks plausible, and the negative effect of surveillance on imports seems explicable.

The consistency of the results in Table 1 is striking, but the observed changes are only rarely significantly different from zero. Under a null hypothesis of no surveillance effect on quantities, the five declines in market share recorded for Group III in years 1 and 2 could have occurred by chance with probability 15%, and the seven declines in years 6 and 7 only with probability 3·5%. Otherwise the sign counts on market shares are wholly insignificant. Those on the relative unit values are stronger, but even then not overwhelmingly so. I also calculated standard deviations for year-on-year changes in the two indicators from data on the four years before surveillance in order to check the statistical significance of the first year's results for each group in Table 1. The relative increases in unit values for Groups I, III and IV are the only significant ones. The market share changes generally have ratios to their standard errors of just over unity.

The lack of statistical significance in the results is disappointing, but it is not surprising given the small sample and the extreme noisiness of finely disaggregated trade data. Moreover, although the data cannot generally reject the hypothesis of no surveillance effects at 95% significance, they nonetheless suggest that the alternative hypothesis of some effect provides a better explanation of observed phenomena than the null hypothesis of no effect.

[7] Anti-dumping action is the most frequent precursor to the imposition of VERs; it gives the latter an apparent legitimacy that is lacking if one jumps straight from surveillance to VER. Thus the interpolation of this step does not reduce the signalling role of surveillance and hence its effect on $\phi$.

## VI. CONCLUSION

This paper has argued that exporters are more likely to curtail their exports in response to a threatened VER the more collusive they are and the more discriminatory and restrictive the threatened restriction. Moreover it has found that actual responses to EC import surveillance were consistent with this view, even if they were not statistically significant. Thus I have shown that it is at least plausible to believe that import surveillance cuts EC imports and that firms respond to potential as well as actual trade policy. The latter observation offers one of the few empirical tests of the strategic element of strategic trade policy.

*University of Birmingham*

*Date of receipt of final typescript: June 1993*

### References


Anderson, J. E. (1992). 'Domino dumping, I: competitive exporters.' *American Economic Review*, vol. 82 (1), pp. 65–83.

Brenton, P. and Winters, L. A. (1993). 'Voluntary expert restraints and rationing: UK leather footwear imports from Eastern Europe.' *Journal of International Economics*, vol. 34, pp. 289–308.

Ethier, W. (1991). 'Voluntary export restraints.' Chapter 1 in (A. Takayama, M. Ohyama and O. Michihiro) *Trade Policy and International Adjustments*. New York: Academic Press, pp. 3–18.

Hariharan, G. and Wall, H. J. (1992). 'Intertemporal optimisation under threat of VER.' *Journal of International Economic Integration*, vol. 7, pp. 45–57.

Harris, R. (1985). 'Why voluntary export restraints are voluntary.' *Canadian Journal of Economics*, vol. 18, pp. 799–809.

Hindley, B. (1985). 'European venture: VCRs from Japan.' Chapter 2 in (D. Greenaway and B. Hindley) *What Britain Pays for Voluntary Expert Restraints*. Thames Essay 43, Trade Policy Research Centre, London, pp. 29–63.

Hoekman, B. M. and Leidy, M. P. (1990). 'Policy responses to shifting comparative advantage; designing a system of emergency protection.' *Kyklos*, vol. 43, pp. 25–52.

Mai, C. C. and Hwang, H. (1988). 'Why voluntary export restraints are voluntary: an extension.' *Canadian Journal of Economics*, vol. 21, pp. 877–82.

Winters, L. A. (1990). 'Import surveillance as a strategic trade policy.' Discussion Paper No. 404, Centre for Economic Policy Research, London, forthcoming in (P. R. Krugman and A. Smith) (1993). *Empirical Studies of Strategic Trade Policy*. Chicago: Chicago University Press.

Winters, L. A. (1992). 'VERs and expectations: extensions and evidence.' Discussion Paper 91.25, Department of Economics, University of Birmingham.

Yano, M. (1989). 'Voluntary export restraints and expectations: an analysis of export quotas in oligopolistic markets.' *International Economic Review*, vol. 30, pp. 707–23.

# Digging for Victory: Agricultural Policy and National Security

*L. Alan Winters*

## 1. INTRODUCTION

AGRICULTURAL policy has been one of the most contentious issues in economic relations between industrial countries over the last decade, and has threatened to scupper the Uruguay Round of GATT talks. In debating agricultural policy protagonists appear to be more ready to put forward arguments which go beyond mere economic efficiency than they are when discussing other sectors. Such issues include environmental amenity, cultural heritage, the vitality of rural communities and national security. These are certainly all important aspects of modern life and are legitimate objectives of government policy, but, in fact, they all have an essential economic dimension because their achievement diverts scarce resources from other objectives. For this reason Winters (1989) characterises them as SNOs — So-Called Non-Economic Objectives — of agricultural policy.

Once the economic dimension is recognised it is possible to ask whether agricultural policy is an efficient means of delivering SNOs. For the various social and distributional concerns analysed in Winters (1989) the answer was almost universally 'no', and the present paper subjects the national security argument for agricultural support to the same sort of analysis. The purpose of this paper is to show that the national security argument for agricultural policy is amenable to examination on exactly the same criteria as are, say, industrial policy, energy policy and education policy. Consequently, it should be subjected to the same sort of rational debate as surrounds those policies. The paper accepts the legitimacy — indeed, the paramountcy — of national security, but asks whether current

---

L. ALAN WINTERS is from the Department of Economics, University of Birmingham, UK. The work for this paper was conducted at the University of Wales, Bangor. The author is grateful to David Greenaway, Richard Howarth, Ian Kelso and John Sheehy for discussions and to Sue James for typing. An earlier draft of this paper (1988), was presented at the Centre for Economic Policy Research at their workshop on Economic Aspects of International Security. The author and the CEPR are grateful to the John D. and Catherine MacArthur Foundation for financial support. Any remaining errors are the author's own.

agricultural policies are an efficient means of achieving it. It concludes in the negative, and even finds some grounds for believing that policy may harm security. The arguments in this paper relate to the United Kingdom for the sake of concreteness, but the same set of issues must be confronted by any government wishing to support agriculture on national security grounds.

We ask whether current agricultural policy contributes to national security commensurate with its cost; in crude terms, is agricultural policy good value for money in terms of security? We do not attempt to measure the value of different degrees of security directly, but explore whether current policy is the best, i.e. the cheapest, means of delivering any given level of security. We conclude that, while some form of agricultural intervention may be justified on national security grounds, current policies may not. The paper consists of seven parts: part 2 briefly analyses the economics of preparing for an embargo of imports; part 3 considers the costs of a food embargo; part 4 deals with the probability of an effective embargo; the production of food under a general embargo including material inputs for agriculture is examined in part 5; part 6 considers the roles of stocks; and finally, part 7 draws some conclusions from the analysis.

## 2. THE ECONOMIC THEORY OF EMBARGOES

Despite its age and popularity the national security argument for protection has received relatively little formal attention (see Winters, 1988, for reference to various informal analyses of the case of agriculture). Only in the late 1970s did economists, stimulated by the oil crisis, start to build formal models of import embargoes and to evaluate their implications for policy: see, Bhagwati and Srinivasan (1976), Mayer (1977), Tolley and Wilman (1977), Arad and Hillman (1979), Thompson (1979) and Bergstrom, Loury and Persson (1985). In all cases the argument proceeded by seeking to maximise expected social welfare given a finite probability that imports of some or all goods would be cut off at some time in the future.

The social welfare functions used by these economists contained only consumption of goods and services as arguments, and thus their analysis amounted to maximising some appropriately discounted function of the consumption stream. Superficially this appears rather limiting, because it places no explicit value on factors such as political freedom. Conceptually, however, the latter can be incorporated by assuming that the ability to resist aggression — i.e. to maintain freedom — is related to the national use (consumption) of certain goods and/or to the overall level of social welfare, (in other words, that countries capitulate when the costs of not doing so become too great). This approach will be used implicitly below, although two caveats should be recorded. First, the 'technology' of translating goods or welfare into military resistance is not explored at all, and second, any direct link from policy to military performance (as opposed to indirect links via consumption) are not modelled.

Although the various models of embargo differ in their details, they are virtually unanimous in identifying the necessary conditions for economic policy in the non-embargoed state to contribute to welfare under the embargo. First, there must be an intertemporal link. If production and consumption under embargo were quite independent of pre-embargo conditions, no pre-embargo policy would be worthwhile. In Bhagwati and Srinivasan (1976) and Mayer (1977) the link comes through production adjustment costs, in Tolley and Wilman (1977) through consumption rigidities, in Arad and Hillman (1979) through learning-by-doing, and in Thompson (1979) through durable capital. Among earlier commentators Black (1959) stressed adjustment costs.

Second, public policy is justified only if private information or incentives differ from social ones. Bhagwati and Srinivasan (1976), Mayer (1977) and Arad and Hillman (1979) assume implicitly that the private sector does not perceive the threat of embargo; Tolley and Wilman (1977) impute external costs to the embargo situation — e.g. unemployment and political costs; Thompson (1979) allows existing capital to deter aggression (which is a public benefit) and also assumes that private agents believe that, under embargo, governments will not permit the prices of the embargoed good to rise sufficiently to clear their markets. For critical food embargoes the last seems to be the most plausible assumption, and we shall adopt it below. The first-best policy response differs acceding to the nature of the market failure to be corrected: production subsidies in the first group, tariffs in Tolley and Wilman, and capital subsidies in Thompson.

Third, the extent of policy intervention depends directly on the probability of embargo, and also on the costs that it would impose. The latter, in turn, depend partly on the adjustment costs mentioned above.

Fourth, stock-piling represents an alternative response to the threat of embargo — see Tolley and Willey (1977), Thompson (1979) and Bergstrom, Loury and Persson (1985). The choice between stock-piling and output-based policy during the non-embargo period depends on their relative costs: each should be used until its expected marginal costs equals the expected value of the marginal unit of consumption under embargo.

The remainder of this paper analyses current agricultural support policies in terms of these parameters. It argues that while embargoes could obviously entail costs — quite serious costs — these are quantifiable and commensurable with the costs of trying to reduce vulnerability to foreign supply interruptions. In other words, the national security arguments for current agricultural policy is amenable to rational discussion and analysis — even by economists.

### 3. THE REQUIREMENT FOR FOOD

Henderson (1986) identified a fallacy of 'essentailism' in popular discussion of economic policy; this holds that some particular good is absolutely essential to economic welfare, and, implicitly, therefore, that any cost is worth bearing to ensure its continued supply. The unit of food which just prevents starvation may fall into this class, as might a unit of life-saving drugs, energy, shelter, transport, or clothing. Until starvation appears on the horizon, however, food is subject to trade-offs just like any other good: as its effective price rises, so people maximise their economic welfare by replacing it in the consumption basket by other goods such as shelter or clothing. That such trade-offs are made every day is obvious from empirical studies of demand, which show that food consumption in the UK is quite flexible. Such studies also allow us to estimate the value of marginal units of food.

*a. Food Demand*

Deaton (1975) analyses the patterns of demand for the main categories of food in Britain, and finds a reasonable degree of substitution between types. For example, in 1963 a 10 per cent increase in the price of cereals and bread would have reduced consumption of these goods by 3.3 per cent and increased consumpion of, say, meat by 0.9 per cent holding constant the amount of utility derived from food consumption overall. This flexibility over the basket of food to be consumed suggests that interruptions to the supply of certain foods could be accommodated, even if some loss of welfare is involved.[1]

Perhaps more important is the substitution between food and other goods as reported in Table 1. The table shows the substitution possibilities between food and other goods from two different models of consumer demand. The columns headed (A) are based on a model admitting wide substitution possibilities (the Rotterdam model) estimated over 1900-70 (Deaton, 1974), while the columns headed (B) come from a more restricted model (the Linear Expenditure System) estimated over 1954-70 (Deaton, 1975). The first pair of columns reports the changes that would be made to consumption bundles if food consumption were forcibly cut by 10 per cent. For all except the last row, we assume that consumers are compensated in order to allow them to achieve the same level of utility as before the cut. The relatively modest increases necessary in the consumption of other goods suggests no over-riding role for food in determining welfare. The last row reports the compensating variation of the enforced reduction in food consumption — that is the percentage change in income necessary to compensate for the forced reduction in food if there is no change in prices. It too, suggests nothing resembling a critical role for food. The second pair of columns confirms this view by recording the effect on consumption of a 25 per cent increase in the price of food, holding overall welfare levels constant. Again, food does not appear to be particularly special, its

[1] Results are quoted for 1963 because per capita incomes were some 35 per cent lower than now, and hence are more representative of what might be experienced during a political crisis. Lower incomes typically cause food to account for a larger share of total expenditure and to exhibit rather lower substitutability for other goods. Thus, if anything, the quoted results may understate substitutability.

consumption falling by around 7 per cent. Moreover, the final elements of the columns report the increase in income that would be necessary to compensate for the rise in food prices: it is significant, but provided that distribution was not a problem, not catastrophic.

TABLE 1

Substitutions Between Food and Other Goods

| | *Changes in consumption necessary to compensate for a 10% reduction in food consumption* (A) % | (B) % | *Changes in consumption as a result of a 25% increase in the price of food* (A) % | (B) % |
|---|---|---|---|---|
| Commodity: | | | | |
| Food | −10.0 | −10.0 | −6.4 | −7.3 |
| Clothing | 2.9 | 3.9 | 5.3 | 1.73 |
| Housing | 1.4 | 1.9 | 1.7 | 0.75 |
| Fuel | 0.3 | 3.2 | 1.1 | 1.39 |
| Drink & tobacco | 1.5 | 2.6 | 2.0 | 1.10 |
| Travel, communication | 5.8 | 4.0 | 10.9 | 1.78 |
| Entertainment | −1.9 | n.a. | −10.6 | n.a. |
| Other goods | −0.2 | 4.0 | −0.7 | 1.77 |
| Other services | 0.2 | 2.7 | 0.3 | 1.14 |
| Overall welfare | 0.6 | 1.5 | 7.1 | 5.8 |

n.a. not applicable
Sources: Author's calculations based on Deaton (1974, 1975). See Appendix A of Winters (1988) for details.

While there is scope to argue about the precise nature of the substitution within the food bundle and between food and other goods, Table 1 shows quite clearly that substitutions are feasible and are not catastrophic in terms of welfare. Moreover, these results refer to periods of lower incomes and higher food shares of expenditure than apply at present, and hence probably understate current substitution possibilities. Thus at post-war levels of consumption, food is just like any other good. There is no reason to treat it specially in either analysis or policy-making. Small shocks, such as the loss of one or two imported foods or moderate price rises for a wide range of foods, are manageable at finite, indeed relatively slight, cost. As economic contingencies they are no more damaging or disruptive than would be similar shocks to, say, clothing, vehicles, or electrical goods supplies. Moreover, since their costs may be assessed, the costs and benefits of self-sufficiency as a means of avoiding them may be analysed in a perfectly straight-forward way.

### *b. Food Needs*

Empirical demand studies apply functional approximations to historical data, and once one considers shocks outside the range of previous experience it is no longer feasible to rely on such behavioural relationships. Besides, in the face of a major food shock social institutions would change — or be changed by government policy — so that past data would no longer be very informative about peoples' behaviour. Thus, on both counts we now turn to the technical analysis of food requirements.

Nutritionists appear to differ between themselves even more than economists, and we therefore have only the crudest of indicators of food requirements and the realisable nutritional value of particular foods. CAS (1979) quotes several current estimates of the recommended daily intakes (RDIs) for various nutrients. The range of values suggested by different national authorities is very wide: for each of the six major nutrients reported, the maximum RDI is at least twice the minimum! Neither are the distributions of requirements over individuals well known. RDIs are typically calculated as mean requirements plus 20 per cent, in the hope, more than the expectation, that this will prove adequate for 97.5 per cent of the population. For protein, UK officials fix the recommendation arbitrarily as 10 per cent of total energy requirements.

To the extent that these nutritional data convey any information, it is about steady states and averages across individuals. For a finite period they could probably be trimmed somewhat and there may be scope for further economy in the averaging process. Moreover, the required nutrients may be delivered from a wide variety of diets, so that, at a technical level, there is very high substitutability between different types of food. Thus, at the expense of dietary choice, it would be possible to keep the population alive on the basis of a vastly reduced variety and quantity of food than is presently consumed. For example, it would be feasible to extract more human nutrition per animal slaughtered than is currently obtained, while switching from the indirect consumption of crops via animals, to the direct consumption of the crops would increase nutritional efficiency several-fold. In 1981-83, the UK's production of seven major crops — wheat, barley, potatoes, sugar, beef, lamb, and milk — yielded 146 per cent of her requirements for human energy, even after allowing for some losses in food preparation and for seed requirements (CAS, 1986). Moreover, although other nutrients are not considered directly, 'the products listed will also contain most of the protein and other nutrient needs of the population, and the fruit and vegetable crops have still to be added'. This is not to be read as implying that self-sufficiency is either (a) actually achievable or (b) desirable but merely as indicating the very substantial wedge that exists between current eating habits and those that would be required at times of a national security crisis.

The economic analysis in this section suggests that the costs of a reduction in food supplies would not be as high as is sometimes suggested, and thus that the costs that should be incurred to avoid such a reduction are similarly bounded. A 25 per cent rise in final food prices is equivalent to a more than 50 per cent rise in the price of 'raw food', once processing, distribution and taxes have been taken into account. This would represent a considerable shock and yet it would reduce welfare by only about seven per cent. Obviously, such a situation would be worth protecting against, but not at any cost. The analysis has shown that even if all imports of food were stopped — a situation never yet encountered — current production would be more than adequate to maintain a minimal diet. Consequently, the infinite costs of starvation occasionally alluded to in the national security debate could not possibly be imposed even by the most effective food embargo.

## 4. THE PROBABILITIES OF AN EFFECTIVE EMBARGO

In terms of national security the attractions of food self-sufficiency are argued to lie in the ability it confers on governments to resist extreme political pressure from an outside power. This section explores the probabilities of an embargo occurring, first, in any form, and second, in a form amenable to alleviation by food self-sufficiency. The discussion deals first with embargoes short of physical force and second with active hostilities.

### *a. Embargoes*

Embargoes are rare events. Hufbauer and Schott (1985) in a comprehensive study of economic sanctions have identified 104 such occurrences since 1914. They restricted themselves to embargoes imposed for political reasons (including war) — the sort usually alluded to in discussions of national security; but even if the count were extended to cover those of economic origin e.g. the USA's prohibition of exports of soya beans in 1974 — the total would not be very large. This is especially so when one recognises that policy discussion concerns not goods whose export is regularly or perpetually embargoed (domestic supply would be the obvious solution in those cases), but goods whose export is embargoed occasionally and unpredictably.

Of the cases identified by Hufbauer and Schott, some 85 have occurred since 1950, and of those ten have entailed the embargo of food. In nine of these the target country (the country whose imports were curtailed) was a developing country and in the tenth it was the USSR. In eight cases, the USA was the 'sender' — the country which imposed the embargo. These data suggest that political relationships would have to change dramatically before OECD and NATO countries such as Japan or the UK were likely to face a food embargo.

Of the ten food embargoes recorded by Hufbauer and Schott, five were almost complete failures — in terms of their political consequences, judged informally by the authors; two resulted in short-term pressure on the target country but no long-term effects; one was successful overall, but the contribution of food policy was judged to be very slight; and two were successful. Of these last, the success of one (USA vs India) occurred largely because the trade restrictions coincided fortuitously with unfavourable Indian weather conditions to generate very considerable pressure on the Indian government.

Not all of these incidents reflected determined efforts to bring the target country to its knees (or 'senses' as the senders would say), and so it may be that greater pressure would have generated greater results. Overall, however, two themes emerge repeatedly from Hufbauer and Schott's discussion. First, unilateral sanctions were easily overcome by resort to alternative suppliers and, for several developing countries, alternative sources of finance. Indeed, target countries were frequently 'rescued' by the sender's political foes — e.g. the USSR for the US's sanctions, China for the USSR's — which supplied food from home or imported sources. Second, even when hardship was imposed, it rarely led to political capitulation. Thus, it appears that given minimal food supplies, target countries are willing and able to resist 'food pressure' for long periods of time. They may suffer increased costs of supply and some shortfall of supplies below normal levels, but they appear not to suffer intolerable pressure.

In a number of cases, food was only one of several goods embargoed. This raises the issue of whether there are not more efficient means of exerting political pressure than by curtailing imports of food. The obvious alternative is energy — specifically oil. Few countries are self-sufficient in oil, and in the short run there are few opportunities for substituting other goods for oil. Moreover, for Japan and most European countries food supplies are probably as vulnerable to oil embargoes as they are to food embargoes: although these countries currently produce a high proportion of their own food, they can do so only on the basis of imported oil and chemicals. It is true that the set of countries that could exert food pressure is different from the set that could exert oil pressure, but it is difficult to imagine circumstances short of actual war in which the former countries were so unified that they could totally embargo food without the co-operation of the latter countries. In other words, it would be a rare event, indeed, in which it was materially better to be able to convert foreign oil into food by means of domestic agriculture than to rely directly on foreign food. In fact given recent experience, one may plausibly argue that for many countries it is the ability to import food in times of need which reduces the danger to domestic food consumption posed by insecure oil supplies.

An important determinant of the likelihood of a successful embargo is the number of countries producing and selling the good concerned. Production is as relevant as exports because exports are more variable and more distorted by current policies, and because production originally destined for a country's home consumption may well be diverted to her allies in times of crisis. On the other hand, export data refer directly to excess supplies and also identify countries which already have the infrastructure necessary for supplying other countries.

Table 2(A) analyses the production of major agricultural commodities and agricultural inputs, while Table 2(B) reports the same data for exports. The Herfindahl Index summarises the overall concentration of production (exports) of each good, ranging from just above zero (wholly unconcentrated) to unity (wholly concentrated). The five-country concentration ratio reports the share of total output accounted for by the five largest producers. (In both statistics EC countries are treated individually, not as a group.) These data show that the production of oil and other inputs is more concentrated than that of agricultural commodities. Surprisingly, however, the story is reversed for exports with greater concentration in the agricultural commodities. On the other hand, there is perhaps a suggestion that the materials exporters are less reliable politically than those of food-stuffs, especially, with the exception of the UK, in the oil sector. It seems that it would be easier to fall out with all the major oil producers than all the major food producers, especially given the wide range of foods produced around the world. Moreover, it is probably easier for allies to start shipping grain at short notice and without experience, than oil. Thus while these data do not suggest dangerous concentrations of economic power in any sector, except perhaps oil, they may suggest a slight security advantage in food over materials.

TABLE 2(A)

The Concentration of World Production

| *Commodity* | *Year* | *Herfindahl Index* | *Five-Country Concentration Ratio* | *Top Five producers (and share of world output)* % |
|---|---|---|---|---|
| Cereals[(a)] | 1982 | 0.096 | 0.59 | USA (20), China (18), USSR (10), India (8), Canada (3) |
| Wheat[(a)] | 1982 | 0.094 | 0.61 | USSR (18), USA (16), China (14), India (7), Canada (6) |
| Beef[(a)] | 1982 | 0.093 | 0.54 | USA (24), USSR (15), Argentina (6), Brazil (5), France (4) |
| Crude petroleum[(b)] | 1982 | 0.114 | 0.64 | USSR (22), Saudi Arabia (17), USA (16), Mexico (5), Iran (4) |
| Motor gas[(b)] | 1982 | 0.206 | 0.66 | USA (43), USSR (12), Japan (4), Canada (4), FRG (3) |
| Pesticides[(b)] | 1978 | 0.127 | 0.70 | USA (24), China (20), USSR (11), FRG (10), Spain (5) |
| Tractors[(b)] | 1981 | 0.110 | 0.64 | USSR (34), Japan (12), France (7), FRG (6), Italy (6) |
| Fertilizers: | | | | |
| nitrogen[(b)] | 1981 | 0.100 | 0.59 | USA (19), USSR (17), China (16), India (4), Romania (3) |
| super-phosphates[(b)] | 1980 | 0.145 | 0.65 | USSR (33), China (12), USA (10), Australia (5), France (5) |
| phosphates[(b)] | 1980 | 0.322 | 0.83 | USA (54), France (12), Brazil (7), Canada (7), S. Korea (3) |
| potassium[(b)] | 1982 | 0.197 | 0.85 | USSR (32), Canada (14), GDR (14), FRG (8), France (7) |

Data Sources: (a) FAO Production Yearbook, vol. 37
(b) Industrial Statistics Yearbook

The most recent example of a food embargo was the US refusal to sell grains to the USSR in 1980 — see Paarlberg (1980) or Lundborg (1987). This is widely recognised as having been a failure and was reversed within two years. The

TABLE 2(B)

The Concentration of World Exports

| *Commodity* | *Year* | *Herfindahl Index* | *Five-Country Concentration Ratio* | *Top Five producers (and share of world output)* % |
|---|---|---|---|---|
| Cereals[(a)] | 1982 | 0.196 | 0.74 | USA (40), Canada (12), France (10), Australia (7), Argentina (5) |
| Wheat[(a)] | 1982 | 0.234 | 0.88 | USA (40), Canada (21), Australia (12), France (10), Argentina (4) |
| Meat[(a)] | 1982 | 0.061 | 0.44 | Netherlands (13), Australia (9), France (8), New Zealand (8), USA (7) |
| Crude petroleum[(b)] | 1982 | 0.126 | 0.56 | Saudi Arabia (30), Nigeria (7), Mexico (6), United Arab Emirates (6), UK (6) |
| Petroleum products[(b)] | 1982 | 0.053 | 0.40 | Netherlands (13), Venezuela (7), Singapore (7), Italy (6), USA (6) |
| Pesticides[(a)] | 1982 | 0.107 | 0.66 | FRG (20), USA (16), UK (12), France (10), Switzerland (8) |
| Tractors[(a)] | 1982 | 0.110 | 0.68 | USA (20), FRG (13), Japan (13), UK (11), Italy (11) |
| Crude fertilizers[(a)] | 1982 | 0.166 | 0.79 | Morocco (28), USSR (19), USA (19), Jordan (8), Togo (4) |
| Manufactured[(a)] fertilizers | 1982 | 0.069 | 0.49 | USA (17), Canada (10), Netherlands (8), Belgium-Luxembourg (7), USSR (6) |

Data Sources: (a) FAO Yearbook of Trade Statistics
(b) Yearbook of International Trade Statistics

principal reason for failure was trade deflection: although the USA's allies agreed not to increase their sales to the USSR above 'normal levels', the latter were not defined and the agreement did not extend to other markets. Thus USSR consumption was supported as other Eastern European countries reduced their grain imports from her and Argentina and the allies increased their exports to her. The USA — with excess supplies on her hands — had displaced some of these other exporters from their traditional markets, undermining their willingness to keep supplies from the USSR, and a spot market for re-exports of grain grew up in Italy. Moreover, not only grains but also soya and meat trade was deflected and increased. Although the costs of food to the USSR rose somewhat, the effect of the embargo on quantities was very small. Consequently, although the embargo was designed to reduce USSR grain imports by 17 million tons, it did so by only 6.5 million tons; the reduction in USSR meat consumption was three per cent rather than the twenty per cent that President Carter had intended. Considering the political forces ranged against the USSR at the time, the ease with which she overcame the embargo must suggest that the probabilities of OECD countries experiencing effective food embargoes are minimal.

*b. Warfare*

Actual warfare would obviously entail the break-down of all trade between the protagonists but would probably also entail a blockade against neutral shipping. Under these circumstances it is difficult to know whether food or oil would be more vulnerable, although it is worth noting that food arriving from more origins may be traded in smaller units and along more diverse routes.

Discussion of war raises again the issue of who the enemy is. The British tradition has been that for so long as the North Atlantic is open, long-term survival is possible and this, of course, would almost certainly allow the provision of food. If this route were not available it is not clear how long a war could be sustained even if food were not an issue, for many war materials would be available only from abroad. I am not party to the strategic plans of the UK government, but to the extent that they presume alliance with the USA and some degree of movement across the North Atlantic, it seems that food self-sufficiency would not be a requirement for continuing hostilities.

A further important consideration for the UK is the vulnerability of her oil supplies if active hostilities broke out. While local production may be more secure than imported supplies under non-war conditions, it is hard to imagine North Sea oil installations lasting very long in a war. Thus in these circumstances Britain would rapidly find herself in the same position as import-dependent countries, except perhaps for having rather greater storage facilities.

*c. The Time Dimension*

Whether one is considering embargoes or active hostilities it is necessary to examine the time frame over which food self-sufficiency would be an asset. Domestic cultivation delivers most of its food to domestic warehouses during the period May to October. A loss of food imports expected to be confined to months outside this period would be unaffected by whether current stocks had been grown at home or not. All that would matter would he how full the warehouses were. For embargoes covering the harvest period, home supplies would be an advantage, but only in the sense of being stocks in the ground. Virtually all the decisions affecting the level of output would have been taken months ago, and so 'live' stocks would offer little gain over 'dead' ones already in the warehouse. Similar arguments also pertain to livestock. Meat on the hoof may be slaughtered at any time, but the total amount available at any instant depends on past decisions.

It is impossible to forecast precisely how long a political crisis would last, but there are several reasons for believing that one so deep that it curtailed all imports of food would be relatively short-lived. First, it seems likely that it would break out into active warfare rather than persist as a complete embargo. Second, such comment as is available — e.g. Hackett (1982) or Clancy (1987) — suggests that active warfare among super-powers would be short and sharp. The massive material requirements of modern warfare mean that strategic shortages are likely to be critical well before food shortages are. The futility of 'digging in' as a defence against modern weapons suggests a war of movement, which will be more likely to be resolved quickly than previous wars of attrition. Finally, a crisis so deep as to prevent all trade must be a candidate for resolution by nuclear weapons. Indeed, that very threat, even if not executed, would speed efforts to find a resolution by other means. Moreover, once nuclear weapons have been used, even if only in a limited way, the advantages of being able to grow one's own food in the war zone look, to say the least, of limited value.

If strategic immunity depends on stocks in the short run, it depends on production in the long run; but the long run is not now. Provided that stocks could tide the country over the transitional period, it would matter not what was produced before the crisis, but whether domestic production could be expanded sufficiently to meet minimum domestic needs over the course of the crisis. The maximum rate of expansion of agriculture is debatable, but it can certainly be enhanced by adequate prior planning, as we show below.

An important dimension here is the amount of notice of the embargo that a country would have. Political crises do not appear from nowhere, thus the degree of readiness to withstand an embargo should be related to its probability, which in turn should be related to the current degree of tension. While tension is difficult to measure, and its rate of change difficult to predict, military planning already makes use of the concept in terms of weapon availability, personnel training and levels of readiness. Agricultural policy should do likewise, with low embargo-preparedness in times of relaxation, and stock-piling and preparations for expansion occurring as tensions rise. All told it is difficult to imagine a complete embargo arising without a period of at least one year's worsening relations.

The issues of stocks and expansion will be taken up in more detail below. Here all we need to note is that the probability of the UK being entirely cut off from foreign food is very slight, and that the probability of food self-sufficiency helping to overcome that situation is also small. Together they imply minute expected returns to current self-sufficiency.

## 5. AGRICULTURAL PRODUCTION UNDER EMBARGO

Section 2 of this paper noted that a crucial link in the case for national security protection is that production under the embargo be related positively to production prior to it. This is the implicit assumption in much policy discussion, but it is not beyond question. There are two dimensions to be considered: first, will it be feasible to maintain, let alone increase, current subsidised agricultural output levels under an embargo; and second, if current output were reduced, how rapidly could it be expanded in time of need.

### *a. Maintaining Current Output*

If food imports alone were embargoed, UK current agricultural output could be maintained and probably expanded somewhat. On the other hand, we have argued above that it is far more likely that the country would face the loss of nearly all imports, in which case current agricultural output would be threatened because it relies so heavily on vulnerable material inputs. Table 3 reports the direct and indirect requirements of certain inputs per £100 worth of agricultural output in 1979. It also reports the share of these inputs coming from abroad, as a partial indicator of vulnerability. The indicator is partial because it ignores the vulnerability of domestic oil and the geographical differences in the origins of imports of the different goods.

TABLE 3

Requirements of Major Inputs for Agriculture, 1979

| | *Inputs per £100 output* | *(in total)* | *Percentage of Imports in Total Supplies* |
|---|---|---|---|
| | *direct* £ | *indirect & direct* £ | |
| Extraction of Oil and Natural Gas | 0.0 | 1.1 | 40 |
| Mineral Oil Processing | 2.5 | 3.8 | 20 |
| Electricity | 1.0 | 2.2 | 5 |
| Fertilizers | 5.4 | 5.9 | 11 |
| Chemicals for Industry and Agriculture | 0.2 | 0.4 | 19 |
| Agricultural Machinery | 0.2 | 0.4 | 21 |

Source: UK Business Statistics Office (1983)

The working assumption behind input-output analysis (from which these data were derived) is that each input is *essential* to the output — that to reduce inputs of any single material would reduce output *pari passu*. This assumption is plainly too extreme, for there are bound to be opportunities for substitution, especially in a sector like agriculture. Nevertheless, it does raise the question of how well output would hold up during a deep crisis of the kind considered here.

Let us consider energy first. The UK is largely self-sufficient in energy and so it might appear that there is nothing for her to fear. Short of war that may be true, but if it came to war not only would UK oil production be extremely vulnerable, it is not clear that agriculture would have a strong claim on what remained. Modern non-nuclear warfare is likely to be extremely energy and material intensive, see, for example, Hackett (1982) or Clancy (1987). It is also, as argued above, likely to be short-lived. In such circumstances, it is difficult to envisage much fuel being allocated to tractors before tanks, shipping, munitions and transportation. Thus, if war lasted long enough for domestic agriculture to matter, the latter would probably no longer be able to operate on its present high-energy, high yields basis.

Chemicals pose similar problems. The data in the input-output tables are too aggregated to identify particular products, but Jollans (1985) reports that around half of the potash used and most of the phosphates in Britain come from abroad. Moreover, although nitrogen fertilizers are mostly produced locally, they are very energy intensive — absorbing, with production and delivery, over one per cent of total UK energy supplies.

Inputs of fertilizer have increased many times over since the second world war. For example, between 1945 and 1980 average applications of nitrogen grew by 7.5 times for winter wheat, and by factors of 4, 2 and 41 for spring barley, potatoes, and temporary grass respectively. The use of phosphates roughly doubled, while that of potassium grew (from a rationed base year) even faster than that of nitrogen (Cooke, 1982, p.47). The productivity of fertilizer application is beyond doubt. Cooke presents detailed data and Jollans (1985) offers a useful summary. The effects of withdrawing fertilizers are much less well documented, and will, of course, vary considerably by soil-type and climate, as well as by fertilizer.[2] In the south-east of England phosphates have actually been accumulating over recent years (Cooke, 1982), so their withdrawal would hardly be noticed. The situation is probably similar with potassium. In the west of Britain, with much greater leeching, accumulations are lower and so some drop in productivity would probably occur if these two inputs were curtailed. The critical fertilizer in Britain is nitrogen. The moist climate means that very little artificially fixed nitrogen persists from one season to the next. Hence repeated applications are required, and in their absence yields would plummet, probably to levels below those recorded on wholly untreated land. Falls in yield of 50 per cent are probably conservative estimates.

There is one factor which might mitigate the shock to agricultural output. As Bolin et al. (1986) observe, an import embargo is also an export embargo. The loss of exports will not necessarily save energy and materials directly, but it may well release a large amount of labour. Many labour-intensive peace-time tasks would disappear during a deep crisis of the sort we are considering — e.g. service export

[2] For example, experiments at Rothampstead show that while plots of land with optimal applications of fertilizers over many years yield 5 tonnes of wheat per hectare, similar plots which have received no applications since 1852 yield only 2.2 tonnes per hectare. Similar returns to fertilizers apply to potatoes and grass, and via the latter, to livestock. The author is grateful to Ian Kelso for advice on crop yields and fertilizer use.

sectors. Moreover, while the armed forces and supporting bureaucracies would have to expand, they are unlikely to do so to the extent experienced in previous wars, because deficiencies in training and equipment would nullify such an expansion. As a result, agriculture may be able to become more labour intensive than in peace time. Labour cannot displace fuel as an input into current technologies, but with suitable tools and techniques it may be able to contribute something to crisis output levels.

These arguments suggest that current levels of output could be very vulnerable to outside pressure, and thus that current policies, which encourage material-dependence, in fact do little to improve food self-sufficiency.

*b. Expanding Agricultural Output*

Although artificial fertilizers are leeched out of British soils very quickly, natural nitrogen-fixation is slightly longer-lived. The use of grass-clover ley as a means of fixing nitrogen and enhancing subsequent output has been known for centuries, but it is still useful in current strategic thinking. Newly ploughed grass-lands give arable crop yields well above their long-run (untreated) averages for two or three years cropping, and are still significantly more fertile than permanently arable land twenty years after they have first borne arable crops (Cooke, 1982). Therefore, if the strategic aim is to maximise food output during an embargo it would be more sensible to 'rest' the land beforehand with grass and clover than to use it intensively through the use of artificial nitrogenous fertilizers.

The arguments of the previous paragraph apply even if one does not expect a total loss of fertilizer supplies. Fresh land requires less fertilizer than exhausted land. Wheat crops grown after just three years of grazed ley appear not to require any additional nitrogen in their first year to achieve maximum yields (Cooke, 1985, p.243), and require considerably lower than average dressings for two subsequent years. Qualitatively similar results are found for other crops, and even just one year's ley improves nitrogen availability to subsequent crops. Thus, there exist well-tried methods for transferring fertility forward in time, if only land is not over-exploited in the non-embargo situation. The strategic implications are obvious.

Richard Body (1982) argues that the ploughing of new land was a principal reason for the rapid expansion of crop outputs during the Second World War. While there is undoubtedly some truth in this, it is unfortunate from a scientific point of view that nitrogen and phosphate fertilizer inputs also increased significantly. However, that period of history is still of interest in showing how rapidly agriculture could expand from a low base in times of need. Table 4 presents some basic data on the situation, taken from the Official History, Murray (1955).

Few preparations had been taken towards securing food supplies by the start of the war, and even then matters did not proceed with the greatest expedition.

Nevertheless, within three years the output of staple crops had nearly doubled and output of other crops had risen by nearly one-half. This expansion was at the expense of livestock numbers, reflecting the latter's relative inefficiency in providing nutrients. It is difficult to generalise these data to current conditions

TABLE 4

Agriculture in the Second World War

| | *Output (gross)* | | | | | | | | | *Index Numbers 1936-7 to 1938-9 = 100* *Inputs of* [a] | | |
|---|---|---|---|---|---|---|---|---|---|---|---|---|
| | *grains* | *potatoes* | *sugar beet* | *vegetables* | *fodder crops* | *meat* | *milk* | *eggs* | *N* | $P_2O_5$ | $K_2O$ |
| 1940 | 132 | 131 | 116 | 110 | 98 | 97 | 90 | 90 | 129 | 115 | 113 |
| 1941 | 155 | 164 | 118 | 122 | 127 | 65 | 88 | 75 | 213 | 136 | 63 |
| 1942 | 182 | 193 | 143 | 156 | 133 | 69 | 93 | 57 | 280 | 168 | 97 |
| 1943 | 195 | 202 | 137 | 133 | 135 | 66 | 96 | 51 | 285 | 177 | 138 |
| 1944 | 186 | 187 | 119 | 144 | 140 | 68 | 97 | 54 | 303 | 202 | 153 |
| 1945 | 179 | 201 | 141 | 137 | 132 | 71 | 100 | 63 | 287 | 203 | 148 |

[a] 1938-9 base;
Source: Murray (1955), Tables 16, 18, 22 and Appendix Table VI

because there are, for example, new varieties of crops and new efficient feeding techniques for livestock (especially poultry), but they do suggest reasonable possibilities for expanding output rapidly if needs be. On the other hand, it must be recognised that Britain was nowhere near self-sufficient in food, even at the height of the Second World War, so that the evidence refers to expansion from a low base, not the levels of output currently experienced.

## 6. STRATEGIC STOCKS

Stocks play two roles in the strategic arguments about national security. First, they could be a substitute for output self-sufficiency if one was confident that they were large enough to outlast any emergency. Second, and more relevant, they may last sufficient time to expand output to meet a very long-lived embargo.

Tolley and Wilman (1977) and Bergstrom, Loury and Persson (1985) discuss optimal stock-holding rules. While their models differ slightly in the details of what is assumed known, both conclude that stocks should be held until their marginal cost (including building extra stock-holding facilities if necessary) equals the expected returns to relaxing the embargo consumption constraint by one unit. The latter depends, in turn, on the probabilities of embargo, its effectiveness, and the demand for food under the embargo.

Food stocks are already very high. For example, MAFF (1987) reports UK stocks of wheat and barley equal to nearly one year's 'disposals'. The latter include certain exceptional export contracts as well as use as feed-stuffs, and so human consumption of these products could already be supported for approaching two years. Stocks of dairy products range from around three months' consumption (milk powder) to eighteen months' (butter), while those of apples and potatoes amount to about three months' consumption at the end of the season (MAFF, 1987). Stocks of other products are not reported, and are probably not as large. Nevertheless, it seems that intervention and private stocks (not to mention any strategic stocks that might exist) already afford the UK a reasonable degree of strategic food security.

Storing food involves costs in terms of handling and deterioration as well as financially, but compared with the economic losses entailed by current output levels they are very small. The costs of the CAP are frequently put at over ECU 10 billion per annum in the early 1980s, see Winters (1987), and are almost certainly substantially higher today. The EAGGF (1986) estimates that the handling and financial costs of intervention stocks in 1985 were around ECU 1.35 billion, or about 15 per cent of total stock value, split roughly evenly between the two components. The financial cost and the valuation are exaggerated, of course, because they are calculated on inflated domestic prices, but so too is the handling cost relative to those of a properly handled strategic stock. Intervention stocks require far greater flexibility than strategic stocks which would be of roughly constant size and regularly rolled-over. Overall, therefore, it would be probably be an over-estimate to say that stock-holding costs for food would amount to 15 per cent of the value of stocks.

Stocks come in many forms other than food, e.g. growing crops, live animals for slaughter, seed, breeding stock, fertilizers, oil, equipment and fertility. It is likely that optimality will require mixtures of several, if not all, of these. While stocks of food are the simplest to manage and understand, they are not necessarily the most efficient. They may deteriorate more quickly than other things and they also tie up their gross value in capital, rather than just some of it as would be the case if certain crucial inputs are stored. Therefore grain worth £100 million requires, say, £10 million p.a. in capital costs, while the fertilizers required to grow that grain (£5.4 million's worth) require only about £0.54 million p.a.

Obviously the decision of whether to store outputs or inputs depends on the relative valuations of *all* inputs under embargo and non-embargo. Thus, if the oil required for agricultural production were not available under embargo, it might not be worth storing fertilizers. On the other hand, if less directly energy-intensive methods of farming were feasible under embargo, it would be desirable to ensure that suitable inputs were available. 'Rested' land and nitrogen fertilizers fall into this category, as might breeding stock and certain non-energy-intensive capital equipment. Thompson (1979) argues that the private sector may be encouraged to carry such stocks through tax-breaks and subsidies on investment. He emphasises, however, that it is the intertemporal transfer that should be subsidised, not current output, in order that farmers always carry greater stocks than they otherwise would. Tax-breaks on investment income may be sufficient to encourage the holding of breeding stock, for which technology is fairly precisely defined. For capital equipment, however, further policy may be necessary to persuade the private sector to select technologies appropriate for the embargo, given that they do not expect to benefit from so doing.

Given a detailed planning model and a specific strategic threat it would be possible to calculate roughly the optimal strategic stock. That task is beyond the scope of the present paper, but a few simple calculations may identify appropriate orders of magnitude. Suppose the intention was for the UK to be able to survive a two year total embargo. Assume that domestic output would fall to supply half of current consumption and that, with economies in use, stocks would have to supply one-third of current human consumption of crops plus one-fifth of current consumption by livestock and of livestock. Strategic stocks of wheat, barley, potatoes, beef and poultry-meat would need to be worth about $2.8 billion at 1983 prices, so that storage costs would be around $430 million. This is almost certainly an over-estimate, not least because cheaper forms of stock-holding probably exist, but it serves as a focus for considering the issues at stake.

First, the cost of stocks places an upper-limit on the price that should be paid for strategic security via other means. The figure quoted is not insignificant as an annual cost, but it is smaller than typical estimates of the UK losses from the CAP — see, for example, Brechling, Thorpe and Stoeckel (1987). Moreover, much of the cost of stocks is already being borne at present, and current policy does not generate much security anyway.

Second, if it costs so much to have totally secure food supplies, is it worthwhile? Equating the expected costs of embargo with the known costs of alleviating it, suggests that given the low probabilities of embargo occurring, very high costs would have to result from it before total alleviation appeared rational.

Third, if embargoes can be predicted, perpetually full store-houses may not be necessary. Provided that storage facilities existed, emergency supplies could be imported as international tension rose. Moreover, since strategic stocks would be held by the government, this would be easy to bring about outside the glare of publicity.

## 7. CONCLUSIONS

This paper has made an economic analysis of the national security argument for agricultural protection. It took as given the economic nature of the problem

— namely, the allocation of scarce means over conflicting ends, one of which is freedom from undue political pressure — and it also assumed the existence of significant market failures in the private provision of national food security. It then considered four groups of issues. First, it showed that there is currently great flexibility in the amount and composition of food consumption, and thus that food and agriculture need not occupy a special position relative to other goods. Starvation is most unlikely to occur, and short of starvation embargoes of food are no more or less serious than those of other goods.

Second, we argued that it was very improbable that the UK, or indeed any OECD country, would suffer a complete embargo of food. Limited embargoes are possible from specific partners or covering particular foods, but taken as a whole oil and chemical supplies are more vulnerable than food. Moreover, only for a subset of embargoes would food self-sufficiency offer any alleviation: in the short run food stocks are the critical variable (regardless of the origin of the food), while in the long run it is future, not current, food output that matters.

The third set of issues concerned long-run agricultural output. The paper argued that given the vulnerability of oil and chemical supplies, a serious import embargo or war could halve UK agricultural output. However, it also showed that reasonably high levels of output are feasible during a relatively long embargo, provided that fertility had been conserved beforehand.

Finally, we argued that stock-holding, not current output, is the real key to strategic security. It is feasible to hold sufficient food stocks to endure a total blockade for two years and the costs of doing so are not massive. The country could, of course, hold even greater stocks, but two years would be enough to bring output up to acceptable levels, and it is, anyway, virtually inconceivable that such a blockade could last so long. We also argued that it would be rational to store agricultural inputs, especially nitrogen fertilizers and natural fertility, in preparation for an embargo.

The final conclusion of this paper must be that the national security argument for agricultural protection cannot withstand serious analysis. This is not say that national security does not matter, but that governments do not pursue agricultural policies even vaguely consistent with it. Indeed, their policies probably hinder it. That the argument continues in currency, if only implicitly, owes more to the need of politicians and the farm lobbies to find unchallengable excuses for supporting farming than to the facts of the case. What better way to scare the public into submission than to invoke threats to national security?

## REFERENCES

Arad, R.W. and A.L. Hillman (1979), 'Embargo Threat, Learning and Departure from Comparative Advantage', *Journal of International Economics*, Vol. 9, pp. 265-275.

Bergstrom, C., G.C. Loury and M. Persson (1985), 'Embargo Threats and the Management of Emergency Reserves', *Journal of Political Economy*, Vol. 93, pp. 26-42.
Bhagwati, J.N. and T.N. Srinivasan (1976), 'Optimal Trade Policy and Compensation under Endogenous Uncertainty: The Phenomenon of Market Disruption', *Journal of International Economics*, Vol. 6, pp. 317-36.
Black, J. (1959), 'Arguments for Tariffs', *Oxford Economic Papers*, Vol. 11, pp. 191-208.
Body, R. (1982), *Agriculture: The Triumph and the Shame*, Temple Smith, London.
Bolin, O., P. Meyerson and I. Stahl (1986), *The Political Economy of the Food Sector: The Case of Sweden*, SNS Förlag, Stockholm.
Brechling, J., S. Thorpe and A. Stoechel (1987), 'Effects of EC Agricultural Policies: A General Equilibrium Approach', Bureau of Agricultural Economics, Canberra, Australia.
CAS (1979), *National Food Policy in the UK*, CAS Report 5, November 1979, Centre for Agricultural Strategy, Reading.
— (1986), *The Case for Agriculture: an Independent Assessment*, (eds) G.M. Craig, J.L. Jollans and A. Korbey, CAS Report 10, May 1986, Centre for Agricultural Strategy, Reading.
Clancy, T. (1987), *Red Storm Rising*, Fontana, London.
Cooke, G.W. (1982), *Fertilizing for Maximum Yield*, 3rd edition, Granada, St. Albans.
Dahlby, T. (1978), 'The Dilemma of Japan's Protected Agriculture', *Far Eastern Economic Review*, September 1978, pp. 40-2.
Deaton, A.S. (1974), 'The Analysis of Consumer Demand in the United Kingdom, 1900-1970', *Econometrica*, Vol. 42, pp. 341-67.
— (1975), *Models and Projections of Demand in Post-War Britain*, Chapman and Hall, London.
EAGGF (1986), *Annual Report*, 1985, EC Commission, Brussels.
Guither, H.D. (1980), *The Food Lobbyists*, Lexington Books, Lexington, Mass.
Haberler, G. (1936), *The Theory of International Trade with its Applications to Commercial Policy*, Translated by A. Stonier and F. Benham, Hodge, London.
Hackett, J. (1982), *The Untold Story*, Sidgwick and Jackson, London.
Henderson, P.D. (1986), *Innocence and Design*, Basil Blackwell, Oxford.
Hufbauer, G.C. and J.J. Schott (1985), *Economic Sanctions Reconsidered: History and Current Policy*, Institute for International Economics, Washington DC.
Johansson, P.-O. (1987), *The Economic Theory and Measurement of Environmental Benefits*, Cambridge University Press, London.
Jollans, J.L. (1985), *Fertilizers in UK Farming*, CAS Report 9, June 1985, Centre for Agricultural Strategy, Reading.
Lundborg, P. (1987), *The Economics of Export Embargoes*, Croom Helm, Beckenham, Kent.
Marcks Von Würtemberg, J. (1987), *The Cost of Present Agricultural Policies in the EFTA Countries*, Occasional Paper No. 18, EFTA, Geneva.
Mayer, W. (1977), 'The National Defence Tariff Argument Reconsidered', *Journal of International Economics*, Vol. 7, pp. 363-77.
MAFF (1987), *Annual Review of Agriculture*, 1987, H.M. Stationery Office, London.
Murray, K.A.H. (1955), *Agriculture*, H.M. Stationery Office, London.
OECD (1987), National Policies and Agricultural Trade, OECD, Paris.
Paarlberg, R.L. (1980), 'Lessons of the Grain Embargo', Foreign Affairs, Vol. 20, pp. 144-163.
Paul, A.A. and D.A.T. Southgate (1978), *McCauce and Widdowson's The Composition of Foods*, HMSO, London.
Pigou, A.C. (1929), *The Economics of Welfare*, Macmillan, London.
Smith, A. (1776), An Inquiry into the Nature and Causes of the Wealth of Nations, ed. E. Cannan, 1937, New York.
Takeishi, K. (1987), 'Rice Self-Sufficiency Spells National Security', *The Yomiuri Shimbun*, April 1987, p. 38.
Thompson, E.A. (1979), 'An Economic Basis for the "National Defence Argument" for Aiding Certain Industries', *Journal of Political Economy*, Vol. 87, pp. 1-36.
Tolley, G.S. and J.D. Wilman (1977), 'The Foreign Dependence Question', *Journal of Political Economy*, Vol. 85, pp. 323-47.

Winters, L.A. (1987), 'The Economic Consequences of Agricultural Support: A Survey', *OECD Economic Studies*, No. 9, pp. 7-54.
— (1988), 'The National Security Argument for Agricultural Protection', Discussion Paper No. 287, Centre for Economic Policy Research, London.
— (1989), 'The So-Called Non-Economic Objectives of Agricultural Policy', *OECD Economic Studies*, No. 13, pp. 237-266.

# Part B

# Regionalism

Journal of International Economics 17 (1984) 239–263. North-Holland

# SEPARABILITY AND THE SPECIFICATION OF FOREIGN TRADE FUNCTIONS

L. Alan WINTERS*

*University of Bristol, Bristol, UK*

Received June 1982, revised version received August 1983

A universal assumption of models allocating a country's imports among suppliers is that demand is separable over foreign and domestic sources. Nearly as common are the assumptions that import demands are homothetic and mutually separable. This paper explores the theoretical implications of these assumptions and then tests them, applying Deaton and Muellbauer's 'Almost Ideal Demand System' to U.K. data on manufactures covering 1952–79. It uses Lagrange Multiplier tests. Both homogeneity and separability are overwhelmingly rejected. A model of import demand without these restrictions is introduced which, while not entirely satisfactory, suggests a direction for future research.

## 1. Introduction

Much effort has been devoted over the last few decades to building models of world trade. The purposes of this activity have been many, but prominent among them is the desire to explain and predict the effects of relative price changes. Following Ranuzzi (1981) we might distinguish three broad approaches: (i) direct bilateral linkage, in which the flow from country $i$ to country $j$ is explained by direct reference to the countries' internal economic variables; (ii) total trade models where each country's total exports and imports are projected but no bilateral predictions are made; and (iii) a trade allocation approach in which first each country's total imports are projected and then the total is allocated over suppliers to get bilateral figures. The last is by far the most popular approach — see, for example, Armington (1969), Barten (1971), Hickman and Lau (1973), Deppler and Ripley (1981) and Ranuzzi (1981) — and it is the purpose of this paper to question whether it is really up to the task in hand.

The trade allocation model assumes a two-stage budgeting procedure in which each importer's total imports of some good or aggregate of goods is explained by an equation of the form:

$$M = M(Y, p_m, p_d, Z_1), \tag{1'}$$

*I am grateful to C.L.F. Attfield, A.S. Deaton and other members of the Department of Economics at Bristol for comments on early drafts of this work. Naturally they bear no responsibility for its remaining shortcomings.

and this is then split up among suppliers by equations like

$$M_i = M_i(M, p_1, p_2, \ldots, p_n, Z_2), \qquad i = 1, \ldots, n. \tag{2'}$$

where $M_i$ is imports of the good concerned from $i$, $i = 1, \ldots, n$,

$M$ is total imports of the good $M = \Sigma M_i$,

$p_i, i = 1, \ldots, n$, are import prices,

$p_m$ is an index of import prices,

$p_d$ is an index of domestic prices, and

$Z_l$, $l = 1, 2$, are vectors of other variables.

The salient features of this system are that total imports depend only on the import price index ($p_m$) and not the individual prices ($p_i$), and that the allocation of imports is independent of the determinants of total imports except via total imports themselves. We shall argue that the assumptions necessary to justify these points are inappropriate to a model whose prime interest is relative price effects. We shall also consider a popular approach adopted to render (2′) tractable (as specified it includes $n$ price and one 'income' effect), and find it similarly wanting. Finally, we will suggest and test a more satisfactory method of modelling import allocation.

The allocation, by a country, of its domestic expenditure between domestic and various foreign goods is formally similar to the allocation problem faced by a single individual or firm. Abstracting from aggregation effects — over both commodities and agents — most researchers have, therefore, used methods based on the utility-maximising individual or profit-maximising firm. As well as the convenience of ready-made theories this also justifies the imposition of several restrictions on (1′) and (2′) which help in both their estimation and application to foreign trade data; these include homogeneity, adding-up, and symmetry, all of which have a strong intuitive appeal in the latter context. This paper is no exception, being based almost entirely on the analysis of consumers' expenditure by Deaton and Muellbauer (1980a).[1]

The paper starts with a brief discussion of the theoretical implications of two-stage budgeting, and the use made of it currently in the study of import behaviour. Following that we discuss our tests of the assumptions underlying the two-stage procedure, introducing both a more general allocation model than is currently found and our approach to the econometric estimation. This is followed by some results. The present paper is a reduction of Winters (1982), which is available from the author.

Throughout the discussion we shall abstract from the problem of aggregation over goods, being concerned only with the allocation of the demand

[1]So many of our results are taken from Deaton and Muellbauer (DM) that we do not explicitly acknowledge each one below.

for a particular sort of good over the varieties supplied by different countries. Formally, we are assuming that some higher budgeting procedure determines the demand for our type of good, and that different (national) suppliers of this good provide differentiated versions of it ('products distinguished by place of production' in Armington's words). In most empirical work, including the present, the 'type of good' considered is the broad aggregate manufactures.

## 2. Two-stage budgeting

This section briefly lists the assumptions necessary for, and consequences of, two-stage budgeting, illustrating them with certain trade allocation models extant. The theory is drawn largely from DM and full details of both theory and its applications in this area are available in Winters (1982).

In general notation the two-stage procedure may be written:

$$x_g = f_g(x, \bar{p}), \qquad g = 1, \ldots, \Gamma, \tag{1}$$

$$q_{gi} = q_{gi}(x_g, p_g), \qquad i = 1, \ldots, n_g, \tag{2}$$

where $x_g$ is expenditure on group $g$,

$x$ is total expenditure,

$\bar{p}$ a $(\Gamma \times 1)$ vector of price indices of the various groups,

$q_{gi}$ consumption of good $i \in g$, and

$p_g$ a $(n_g \times 1)$ vector of prices, $p_{gi}$, in group $g$.

There are $\Gamma$ groups of goods, each comprising $n_g$, $g = 1, \ldots, \Gamma$, individual goods. In our context $x$ is total expenditure on manufactures (assumed given) and $q_i$ is manufactures from one particular source; $x_g$ represents expenditure on manufactures from some group of suppliers — in our case all foreign sources. Hence, the models we consider contain two groups ($\Gamma = 2$); home supplies, comprising just one item, and imports comprising one item for each supplying country.

Eqs. (1) and (2) raise (at least) three questions. First, when is it legitimate to express the demand for good $i$ entirely in terms of expenditure on its group ($x_g$) and intra-group prices? Second, when is it legitimate to compress the influence of individual prices in group $g$ into a single price index with which to determine, along with total expenditure and other prices, overall expenditure on group $g$; i.e. when is broad group allocation independent of individual prices? Third, how can the general demand equations in (1) and (2) be rendered tractable without imposing undue restriction on the estimated price responses? As specified, the first step budgeting could contain upto $\Gamma$ price effects and the $g$th second step upto $n_g$; given the collinearity of prices they will be difficult to estimate without further restriction if $\Gamma$ and/or $n_g$ are other than small.

### 2.1. Intra-group allocation

The necessary and sufficient condition for the allocation model for group $g$ to be expressed as (2) is that the utility function generating behaviour is weakly separable over the groups $g=1,\ldots,\Gamma$; namely

$$u(q)=f(v_1(q_1),v_2(q_2),\ldots,v_\Gamma(q_\Gamma)), \tag{3}$$

where $q$ is a $[(n_1+n_2+\ldots+n_\Gamma)\times 1]$ vector of consumption of all goods.
$q_g$ the vector of consumptions in group $g$, and
$v_g$ the quantity indicator for group $g$, i.e. a sub-utility function.

Separability has three implications for the responses of demands to exogenous shocks. First, the marginal rate of substitution between two goods from the same group,

$$\left[\frac{\partial v_g}{\partial q_i}\bigg/\frac{\partial v_g}{\partial q_j}\right],$$

is independent of the quantities consumed of goods in other groups. Second, the substitution effect between goods in different groups is determined by intra-group 'income' effects but only inter-group price effects, i.e. given the substitution of fuels for beverages, the substitution of coal for tea depends only on income effects. Third, is the following link between price and income effects:

$$\left.\frac{\partial q_i}{\partial p_j}\right|_{u\,\text{const.}}=\frac{\partial q_i}{\partial x_g}\frac{\partial x_g}{\partial p_j}, \qquad i\in g,\quad j\in h,\quad g\neq h,$$

$$\left.\frac{\partial q_i}{\partial x}\right|_{u\,\text{const.}}=\frac{\partial q_i}{\partial x_g}\frac{\partial x_g}{\partial x}, \qquad i\in g. \tag{4}$$

Hence, no matter what factors cause $x_g$ to change, the effect on $q_i$ is the same, i.e. $\mathrm{d}q_i=\eta_i\,\mathrm{d}x_g$, where $\eta_i=\partial q_i/\partial x_g$.

Now if the groups over which utility is separable are genuinely unrelated, these restrictions do not seem unreasonable. But if, on the other hand, the groups contain similar goods but originating from different suppliers, then the constraints are indefensible. For instance, one might well accept that the substitution between, say, tea and coffee is independent of the consumption of coal, i.e. that beverages and fuels are separable, but it is hard to accept that the British substitution between German and Japanese cars (Mercedes and Hondas, say) is independent of the consumption of British cars (Jaguars), as would be implied if imports and home sales were separable. Neither is it plausible to argue that because imports from country $i$ are relatively unresponsive to changes in incomes, they will always be similarly unresponsive to changes in local prices; but this is a consequence of separating imports and local sales, for the low income response ($\partial q_i/\partial x$) would be manifest in a low $\eta_i$ ($=\partial q_i/\partial x_g$), and this must be reflected in a low price response through (4).[2]

*2.2. Inter-group budgeting — the import function*

Consider now the upper stage of the two-stage budgeting — the allocation of expenditure between groups. Following DM only two sets of circumstances permit the aggregate import function to be precisely of the form (1).

The first is when the group cost, or expenditure, functions have the form:

$$c_g(u_g, p_g) = \theta_g(u_g)\,b_g(p_g), \tag{5}$$

for each of the separable groups $g$, where

$\theta_g(\cdot)$ is a monotonic increasing function,

$b_g(\cdot)$ is a linear homogeneous function, and

$u_g$ is the sub-utility level for which the cost function is defined, with $u_g = v_g(q_g)$.

Unfortunately, (5) implies that the within group budget shares are independent of group expenditure,[3] i.e. the income elasticities of all goods within a group are equal. This is very restrictive, especially in the context of international trade, for it implies that exporters' shares of particular markets would not change except through price changes, a proposition that is immediately refuted by the British export experience. It also, incidentally, further restricts the price responses, see (4) above, for it implies that $\partial q_i/\partial x_g = q_i/x_g$.

The second, and most general, form that permits (1) precisely is due to Gorman: (1) follows if the indirect utility function takes the Gorman generalised polar form and overall utility is explicitly additive in the sub-utilities, namely:

$$\psi_g(x_g, p_g) = F_g(x_g/b_g(p_g)) + a_g(p_g) = u_g \tag{6}$$

[2]For example, Germany's imports from Britain may display low income elasticities (a frequently mentioned problem with British exports), but there is no evidence that they are atypically unresponsive to German prices.

[3]By Shepherd's lemma $\partial c/\partial p_i = q_i$; hence, the budget share

$$w_i = \frac{p_i q_i}{x} = \frac{\partial c}{\partial p_i}\frac{p_i}{c} = \frac{\partial \log c}{\partial \log p_i}.$$

Therefore, given (5), $w_i = \partial \log b/\partial \log p_i$, which is independent of utility and hence of expenditure.

and

$$u(q)=\sum_k v_k(q_k)=\sum_k u_k, \tag{7}$$

where $F_g(\cdot)$ is monotonically increasing, and $a_g(\cdot)$ is some undefined function homogeneous of degree zero.

Unfortunately, conditions (6) and (7) are also highly restrictive, for, as shown in DM, additivity enforces an approximate proportionality between the income and price elasticities of different groups. This approach is much less common in international trade literature than the previous one, but it is used by Strombach (1980) in a linear expenditure system for imports.

Two further possible justifications of the import function exist (see DM). The first involves the decomposition of each group cost function into a component measuring costs at constant prices (a quantity or utility indicator) and a cost of living index. If the latter can be represented by a computable price index this can be used legitimately in the import function. Second, we could appeal to Theil's (1980) differential demand system. This defines first-order approximations to the demand functions for individual goods and then simply adds up the resulting linear equations into appropriate groups. If the derivatives used in the approximation are constant, the resulting import-function is a Rotterdam model, and if, additionally, separability is assumed, the trade allocation model is one also.

### 2.3. Three models

The most popular trade allocation model extant is Armington's (1969). He initially assumed demand to be separable over goods but not over suppliers. Hence, for example, he separated food from machinery, but within each group treated home and all foreign suppliers symmetrically. Then, requiring a precise justification of two-stage budgeting and also a tractable allocation model, he made his groups homothetic — as in (5); but, by adopting a CES specification, he also made them separable over all pairs of sources. Hence, the separability of domestic and foreign supplies essentially slipped in by the back door, the consequence of a particular simplifying assumption in the specification of the group 'sub-utility' functions, rather than as a necessary consequence of two-stage budgeting. A similar comment also applies to the homotheticity. Since even precise two-stage budgeting does not require homotheticity, this other restrictive feature of Armington's model is also unnecessary. Hence, the two most notable characteristics of Armington's model — its ability to separate import allocations from domestic sales and the constancy of import shares given constant relative prices — are not inherent in his initial exploitation of separability. Rather, they appear later as consequences of a particular simplifying assumption.

Armington's specification is remarkably economical of parameters. For any one good there is just one parameter to characterise the price responses — the elasticity of substitution, $\rho$. Hence, once the import function splitting home and foreign demands has been estimated (which involves estimating $\rho$) the import allocation model is entirely determined. This is a powerful result, and a useful one in the absence of much price variation, but it does stretch one's credulity. Below, the crucial 'Armingtonian' assumptions are subjected to test.[4]

Two other studies have conjoined separability and imports. Neither considers separability over sources, however, and both are conducted in a production rather than a consumption framework. The first is Theil and Clements (1978). Using the Rotterdam model they examine U.S. imports disaggregated into four commodity groups. The United States is presumed to generate its GDP in a cost-minimising fashion from a function separable over foreign and domestic inputs, and then to split total imports (foreign inputs) over four commodity groups. The latter allocation assumes strong separability, and this is partially tested and found acceptable. The test is partial because the estimated model with strong separability (and hence symmetry) is tested against an unrestricted model which eschews both separability and symmetry; the test statistic is such that it is possible that compared with a non-separable but symmetric alternative the published model would be rejected.

The second study is Burgess (1974). Again within a production framework Burgess explicitly tests the separability of imports (in total) from domestic labour and capital. He uses a translogarithmic production function and tests and imposes homotheticity and symmetry. He then tests the further imposition of separability and finds it rejected. This implies that when dividing imports among sources, labour and capital prices must appear in the import allocation model, for weak separability is both necessary and sufficient for the second stage budgeting.[5]

## 3. A test of separability

We have argued that existing import models are defective in as much as they (i) invariably assume separability between home and foreign goods, and (ii) usually assume separability between different sources of imports. In this section we introduce our tests of these assumptions. The former is our main concern but some light is shed on the latter.

[4]In private correspondence Armington has explained that his objective was to define 'reasonable' or 'likely' price responses relying as much as possible on actual data and as little as possible on unknown parameters and estimation. Thus, the CES approximation as was advanced as a means of summarising data into a usable form rather than as an econometric hypothesis. Indeed, although others have published econometric estimates based on his model, Armington has never done so.

[5]A much fuller survey of the theory and the literature is available in Winters (1982).

The ideal test of the separability of domestic and foreign goods would be to estimate a non-separable model and then to impose a (nested) restriction implying separability. If the restriction were rejected we would adopt the unrestricted non-separable model for imports, while if it were not we should accept the separable model. Unfortunately, however, there are substantial difficulties in this approach: it is very difficult to find a functional form which admits both separability and non-separability as meaningful, nested, hypotheses, and it is also difficult to formulate consistent separable systems that do not involve other severe restrictions.

In this paper, therefore, we adopt a slightly looser, but more tractable approach. First we do not require both the null (separable) and alternative (non-separable) hypotheses to be fully specified import allocation models, and second, rather than simultaneously test all the implications of separability, we concentrate on only one. This is quite sufficient for our purposes, however, for if we can reject just one necessary consequence of separability we have rejected separability. The implication that we test is that, given total imports, import allocation be independent of the domestic price. We do so by estimating a fully consistent import allocation model under the null hypothesis of separability and testing, by means of the Lagrange Multiplier test, whether domestic prices have anything extra to contribute to that explanation.

This section introduces the null model and the Lagrange Multiplier test and shows how to use them to test separability. It then presents some data on which the approach is tried and concludes by mentioning two extensions to the basic tests.

### *3.1. The import allocation model*

As already indicated, we wish to estimate a model of import allocation embodying the assumption that import and domestic demand are separable. Basically this means that the allocation model should contain only 'import-specific' information. Since we are concentrating on the separability of imports and domestic demand, the import model should be as general as possible, in order to minimise the probability of any other mis-specifications. Specifically, when we come to consider adding domestic prices to the function, we want to be sure that if they are significant, they are so in their own right and not as a proxy correcting some other mis-specification.

Among the most general of consistent demand systems, but still among the most tractable, is Deaton and Muellbauer's AIDS — the Almost Ideal Demand System — see DM (Chapter 3) or Deaton and Muellbauer (1980b). We shall not describe the derivation of the AIDS here but move straight on to the estimating equations. Assuming away any biases from mis-specified dynamics, aggregation or simultaneity, the budget share of imports from country $i$ among total imports ($w_i$) may be written (ignoring the time dimension) as:

$$w_i = \alpha_i + \sum_j \gamma_{ij} \log p_j + \beta_i \log(M/P), \qquad i = 1, \dots, n, \tag{8}$$

where

$$\log P = \alpha_0 + \sum_k \alpha_k \log p_k + \tfrac{1}{2} \sum_j \sum_k \gamma_{kj} \log p_k \log p_j, \tag{9}$$

and where $M$ is total (current price) expenditure on imports. Summing (8) over $i$ shows that adding-up requires

$$\sum_i \alpha_i = 1, \qquad \sum_i \gamma_{ij} = 0, \qquad \sum_i \beta_i = 0, \tag{10}$$

and these restrictions will be automatically satisfied by any set of $w_i$ for which $\Sigma w_i = 1$. Homogeneity requires that

$$\sum_j \gamma_{ij} = 0, \qquad i = 1, \dots, n, \tag{11}$$

and symmetry that

$$\gamma_{ij} = \gamma_{ji}, \qquad i, j = 1, \dots, n. \tag{12}$$

Deaton and Muellbauer show that provided (10)–(12) hold, (8) is a proper demand system. Its generality may be seen by inspection: subject to (11) and (12) the price responses are quite unrestricted; budget shares may change in the absence of price changes via the 'real expenditure' term $(M/P)$ — positive $\beta_i$ corresponding to luxuries; and there is no separability between import sources.

From an empirical point of view the AIDS' attraction is its tractability. The restrictions for homogeneity and symmetry are linear restrictions and so are handled by standard estimation techniques. Also, the system is non-linear only through the aggregate deflator $P$. This has led Deaton and Muellbauer to suggest that provided $P$ can be proxied by some price index whose weights are independent of the parameters — $P^*$, say — (8) may be estimated linearly with $P^*$ replacing $P$. They propose — and we adopt — Stone's index:

$$\log P_t^* = \sum_k w_{kt} \log p_{kt}. \tag{13}$$

Now provided that $P \simeq \phi P^*$, the only estimate affected by the substitution is the constant ($\alpha_i$), which has $\beta_i \log \phi$ subtracted from it. Even if one does not wish to use the substitution in the final estimates, it does at least provide plausible starting values for the non-linear estimates. Notice also that if we use $P^*$ and do not impose the symmetry condition (12), eq. (8) may be estimated separately for each $i$ in turn. Once symmetry is imposed, however, the $n$ equations of (8) have to be estimated as a single system, because symmetry involves across-equation constraints.

The price of the generality we seek in the import allocation model is the large number of parameters that the AIDS involves. Below we use it to test U.K. imports from ten countries, using annual data for 28 years. With $n=10$ the AIDS involves, even with all the restrictions, 64 independent parameters. In fact, it is virtually impossible to identify $\alpha_0$ if the other $\alpha_i$ are unconstrained, and so following Deaton and Muellbauer, we impose it exogenously.

The AIDS also presents further estimation problems, relating to the structure of the error covariance matrix. To be an estimating equation (8) clearly requires the addition of a stochastic error — $u_i$ say. But the adding-up condition implies that $\sum_i u_{it}=0$, and from this it is obvious that $\Omega_t = E(u_t u_t')$ will have, at most, rank $(n-1)$. One solution to this is to use the adding-up restrictions to eliminate one equation from the system entirely. However, we prefer an alternative explored by Deaton (1975). Instead of minimising $\operatorname{tr}(S\Omega^{-1})$ in the estimation (where $S=[S_{ij}]=[\sum_t \hat{u}_{it}\hat{u}_{jt}]$) we minimise $\operatorname{tr} S(\Omega \rightarrow ll')^{-1}$, where $l$ is an $(n \times 1)$ vector with all elements equal to $n^{-1/2}$. This facility has been programmed into Deaton's non-linear maximum likelihood programme NLFIML, the programme used in this exercise [Deaton (1974)].

There remains one further difficulty. Normally one would replace $\Omega$ by its maximum-likelihood estimator constructed from the residuals $\hat{u}$. This is possible whenever $P^*$ replaces $P$, but when the full AIDS is estimated, 55 of the 63 parameters appear in any single equation of (8)' Hence, with only 28 observations the equation for country $i$ could be made to fit perfectly, rendering the likelihood infinite. Hence, the full AIDS can be estimated only with some restriction on $\Omega$. Furthermore, even when a full $\Omega$ would be estimable in principle, the addition of its 45 parameters stretches our rather inadequate data to their very limit. For this reason, even when using $P^*$, we consider a restricted version of $\Omega$.

Unfortunately there is little information on how to restrict $\Omega$. The most obvious suggestion is to restrict the off-diagonal elements of $\Omega$ to zero; but it would be arbitrary to select some sub-set of covariances for this treatment and so we would appear to have to restrict all off-diagonal elements. This, however, violates the singularity condition discussed above. In fact, as shown in the appendix, the only permissible restricted form of $\Omega$ that treats all flows symmetrically (i.e. which requires no prior knowledge of the way that errors may be related across particular pairs of flows) is:

$$\Omega \propto (I - ll'), \tag{14}$$

where $l$ is, as above, a vector comprising $n$ occurrences of $n^{-1/2}$. This quite clearly imposes homoscedasticity between the various shares. More interesting, however, is its relationship to the singularity adjustment just described: when adjusted for singularity, (14) clearly reduces to $I$. Hence, the maximum likelihood programme instead of minimising the determinant of the matrix of error cross-products, minimises its trace; thus, estimation using (14) amounts to no more than OLS with across-equation constraints.

Based on this discussion we estimated the AIDS at five levels of sophistication. In order of decreasing complexity they are:

*Model P* — the 'proper' AIDS:

- eqs. (8) and (9), but with $\alpha_0$ constrained
- restrictions (11) and (12) [(10) is automatically imposed]
- non-linear system of equations
- least squares, since $\Omega \propto (I - ll')$.

*Model* $S_\Omega$ — the symmetric model, estimating $\Omega$

- eq. (8), $P^*$ substituted for (9)
- restrictions (11) and (12)
- linear system of equations
- generalised minimisation, since $\Omega$ is freely estimated.

*Model* $S_I$ — the symmetric model, constraining $\Omega$

- as$S_\Omega$ except least squares, since $\Omega \propto (I - ll')$.

*Models* $H_\Omega$ *and* $H_I$ — the homogeneous model

- eq. (8), $P^*$ substituted for (9)
- restriction (11)
- single linear equations
- least squares, since single equations.

$H_\Omega$ and $H_I$ are grouped together because they give rise to the same estimates. $H_\Omega$ is basically a SURE model, and it is well known [e.g. Maddala (1977)] that when all equations contain the same regressors, SURE offers no gain over separate estimation. All that differs is the final value of the likelihood and we shall present it on both bases: i.e. assuming $\Omega$ is unrestricted and assuming that $\Omega \propto (I - ll')$.

*Models $N_\Omega$ and $N_I$* — the non-homogeneous model

- as $H_I$ and $H_\Omega$ except for the removal of the homogeneity restriction (11). All the discussion of $H$ carries over to $N$.

### *3.2. The Lagrange multiplier test*

As already stated, we test the hypothesis of most interest in this paper by means of a Lagrange Multiplier (LM) test. This test has been much explored and exploited in recent years — see, for example, Breusch and Pagan (1980) and Harvey (1981). Here we merely note the two forms we use.

The Lagrange Multiplier statistic involves estimating the equation under the null hypothesis (of separability) and then examining whether relaxing the restrictions of the null in some particular direction would significantly improve the fit. In least squares models this is particularly simple. We merely estimate the null model with the addition of extra terms in domestic prices. If, by standard tests, e.g. likelihood-ratio tests, the latter are significant, the null hypothesis is rejected. In terms of our exercise we merely estimate (8), including for each $i$ a term of the form $\delta_i \log p_d$, and test the composite hypothesis $\delta_i = 0$, all $i$.[6] Among our models, $N$, $H$ and $S_I$ are estimated by least squares.

In more general models Breusch and Pagan show that if the algorithm used calculates its step by the method of scoring, as does NLFIML, the Lagrange Multiplier statistic may be calculated as:

$$\mathrm{LM} = (\tilde{\theta}_1 - \hat{\theta}_0)' \mathscr{I}(\theta_0)(\tilde{\theta}_1 - \hat{\theta}_0), \tag{15}$$

where

$\hat{\theta}$ is the (converged) ML estimate of the parameter vector under $H_0$,

$\tilde{\theta}_1$ is the result of taking one step from $\hat{\theta}_0$ towards $H_1$ (i.e. relaxing the restrictions in $H_0$), and

$\mathscr{I}(\hat{\theta}_0)$ is the information matrix evaluated at $\hat{\theta}_0$.

Under $H_0$, LM is distributed as $\chi^2$ with $r$ degrees of freedom, where $H_0$ imposes $r$ restrictions on $H_1$.

The attractions of the Lagrange Multiplier statistic are first computational — estimating the general ($H_1$) model and restricting it is complex — and second data-based. To estimate an AIDS model without separability between home and import demand would require data on home sales; we avoid this by our approach.

[6]Actually since we are not specifying what relationship may exist between $w_i$ and $p_d$, we can use any transform of $p_d$ as the additional variable.

### 3.3. The data[7]

The data used to illustrate our hypothesis are crude, although no cruder than those used in most import models extant.[8] They are annual, covering the period 1952–79, consider only manufactures — defined as SITC(R)5–8 — and examine only ten sources of manufactured imports. These are the main OECD industrial nations (see table 1) which account for around 75% of U.K. manufactured imports. Total imports are defined as the sum of imports from the ten included countries.

Table 1
British purchases of manufactures.

| Country | Sales of manufactures in the U.K. 1952 | 1965 | 1979 |
|---|---|---|---|
| | shares in imports (%) | | |
| France | 8.1 | 7.8 | 13.0 |
| Belgium/Luxembourg | 13.7 | 6.2 | 8.2 |
| Netherlands | 5.0 | 7.5 | 7.9 |
| Germany | 12.6 | 16.2 | 22.6 |
| Italy | 4.7 | 5.4 | 8.4 |
| Sweden | 5.2 | 6.9 | 5.4 |
| Switzerland | 3.4 | 5.3 | 10.7 |
| Japan | 4.4 | 3.1 | 6.1 |
| Canada | 17.7 | 12.3 | 2.2 |
| U.S.A. | 25.1 | 29.3 | 15.4 |
| Total imports[a] (£m) | 593 | 1676 | 23925 |
| U.K. domestic sales (£m) | 9929 | 19275 | 71581 |

[a]Inclusive of tariff revenues; total of imports from above countries.

Imports in current prices were collected from Annual Statements of Trade. In the absence of proper data, import prices were represented by the overall export unit value of manufactures for each source, as given in U.N. sources. Inappropriate though they are, these are the series used in most trade allocation models. Obviously, export unit values exclude tariffs, and so changing trade preferences must be represented some other way. We assumed that EFTA did not affect British imports of manufactures significantly, but measured accession to the EEC by a dummy of value zero until 1972 and unity thereafter.[9] This gives rise to nine extra parameters in the system.

When comparing home and import variables, account must also be taken of non-discriminatory tariffs. Source-specific tariff data were not available, so

[7]The data were collected by Martin Snell, to whom I am most grateful. Full details are available in Winters (1982).

[8]A notable exception is Ranuzzi (1981).

[9]A more sophisticated dummy is used in Winters (1984).

all imports were multiplied by the same average tariff rate. The latter, referring to all imports of manufactures, was calculated from data supplied by the Cambridge Growth Project. Domestic prices were measured by the published wholesale price index for manufactures less food, drink and tobacco. This does not precisely match SITC5–8, but since any errors in it would tend to reduce the significance of home prices, it was felt a reasonable approximation. The exchange rate was the daily average rate as given by the IMF.

Finally, despite all the misgivings expressed below, we did try to explain imports without assuming separability, and this required a series on domestic sales. Imports cover goods at all stages of production and so the corresponding measure of domestic sales is related to gross rather than net output. A series of gross ouput at current prices was provided by the Cambridge Growth Project and from this we subtracted exports (SITC5–8), taken from the Annual Statements of Trade.

### *3.4. Some subsidiary tests*

#### *3.4.1. Separability between import sources*

There is no difference in principle between testing the separability of ten import shares from domestic prices and testing the separability of nine import shares from the price of a tenth. Hence, the whole of the above methodology may be adapted to the latter, by isolating imports from each source in turn. Indeed, one could generalise the approach to consider the separability of any set of $m$ import shares from the remaining $(10-m)$, but the case already mentioned of $m=1$ is sufficient for our purposes.

In section 2 we made particular mention of Armington's work which assumed both separability between sources and homotheticity. Unfortunately Armington showed that his CES functions were the most general form that simultaneously admitted these two restrictions, and since the CES is not a specialisation of the AIDS, we clearly cannot conduct a straightforward nested test of Armington's model. Nevertheless, some progress is possible. Homotheticity implies that in the absence of price changes budget shares will not change. It is obvious from (8) that AIDS is homothetic if and only if $\beta_i=0$, all $i$. Hence, homotheticity is simply tested.

We can now combine the tests of the last two paragraphs to get something like a nested test of the Armington model. Suppose we estimate a homothetic AIDS for nine import sources and then test its separability from the tenth price. If the two crucial features of the Armington model were correct, we would expect the extra price to be insignificant. A (slight) problem with this test is that the AIDS cannot simultaneously reflect the homotheticity and separability between the nine import sources,[10] so that it would be possible to argue that a significant coefficient on the tenth price was merely a compensation for forcing 'Armingtonian' data into an AIDS mould. This seems, however, a rather implausible view. A further, and probably more important, difficulty is that our test considers only the separability of the $n$th source, not its homotheticity as well. Hence, the failure to reject separability does not necessarily imply the acceptability of Armington's model.

### 3.4.2. *A complete model*

Negative results are not popular with economists and so having rejected the various separability hypotheses that are the main concern of this paper, one is tempted to try to explain import shares non-separably. The obvious way is to consider an eleventh source of manufacturing sales — U.K. domestic industry — and estimate an eleven-fold extended AIDS explaining sales to U.K. residents from ten foreign sources and one domestic. This we have done, despite our very strong misgivings about the data.

The output of the extended AIDS may be compared with that from the import allocation model by examining its implications for the import shares alone. Hence, if a residual from the extended AIDS is $\hat{u}_{it}$, the error in the prediction of $i$'s import share, $\hat{v}_{it}$, is given by

$$\hat{v}_{it} = \hat{u}_{it}(E_t/M_t), \tag{16}$$

where $E$ is total expenditure including domestic supplies, and $M$ total import values. The $\hat{v}_{it}$ are directly comparable with the errors from our original import allocation AIDS.

We should observe that by adjusting the two models to work in identical units we are not undertaking any formal statistical test — that has already been conducted by the Lagrange Multiplier Statistics — rather we are examining just one dimension of the performance of the extended model. Also, in view of the data difficulties of the extended model in the present study, it is not guaranteed that its theoretical superiority will actually be manifest in the results.

## 4. Results

### 4.1. *The import allocation model*

We start the description of our results by introducing the basic (separable) import allocation model. This gives some feel for the data as well as defining

[10] A homothetic AIDS can, with constant parameters, be made separable only at one point of the data space at a time.

the base from which we start our experiments. It will be recalled that our a priori view is that this model is misspecified. Hence we are not surprised by its shortcomings.

The results are summarised in column 1 of table 2. Starting with the non-homogeneous model, $N$, we gradually move through the models defined above. Under both specifications of the error structure both homogeneity and symmetry are rejected. This is not an unusual result — see, for example, Murray and Ginman (1976) or, for consumers' demand, Deaton and Muellbauer (1980a). It probably owes as much to the inadequacies of our data and our neglect of dynamics as to the theoretical shortcomings of our static model. It is noticeable from the strength of the rejections that the more general error structure compensates for the inadequacies of the deterministic parts of the model. Indeed, in models $N$ and $H$ the error covariance restrictions are not rejected but they become so as the model becomes more tightly specified (mis-specified?).

Table 2
Adding domestic prices to the import allocation model.

| Model | 2* log-likelihood[a] | $\chi^2$-statistic (9.d.f.)[b] $p^d$ | $p^d/P^*$ |
|---|---|---|---|
| $N_I$ | 2090.4 | 102.8 | 96.3 |
| $H_I$ | 2043.9 | 52.7 | 78.3 |
| $S_I$ | 1611.1 | 58.8 | 82.4 |
| $P^c$ | 1610.4 | 66.5 | 97.2 |
| $N_\Omega$ | 2093.6 | 58.3 | 52.7 |
| $H_\Omega$ | 2062.4 | 38.0 | 40.0 |
| $S_\Omega$ | 1951.4 | 36.0 | 30.0 |

[a]At 5% the critical values are $\chi^2_{10}=18.31$ (for homogeneity), and $\chi^2_{45}=61.66$ (for symmetry and the error-covariance matrix).

[b]All tests are Lagrange Multiplier tests. The critical value at 5 percent is $\chi^2_q(0.05)=16.92$.

[c]The reported model sets $\alpha_0=0$, but estimates with $\alpha_0=\log(0.5)$ and $\alpha_0=\log(0.1)$ produce virtually identical results.

In all models there are considerable problems over plausibility. For instance, in $H_I$ only three of the own-price effects are negative (at this level of aggregation we discount Giffen goods), while in $S_I$ and $P$, the Slutsky matrix, which, for negativity, should have one zero and $(n-1)$ negative eigenvalues, has in fact five negative, one zero and four positive values in 1979.[11] On a more positive note, in virtually all models the integration dummy takes plausible values (positive for the original members of the EEC, negative for other sources) and is statistically significant, and the 'income' effects ($\beta_i$) are collectively significantly different from zero.

[11]The Slutsky matrix varies over time — see DM, p. 76.

There are no signs of serial correlation in the less restricted models, but in $S_I$ and $P$ the Durbin–Watson statistics, calculated separately for each country, show some propensity to fall below two. The fit ($R^2$) of the equations for different countries shows a great range, reflecting partly the different variability of their observed import shares and partly some tendency towards different residual variances. Hence, at least part of the difference between $S_I$ and $S_\Omega$ is due to allowing for heteroscedasticity rather than for contemporaneous correlations. The difference between model $S_I$, which uses an exogenous overall deflator $P^*$, and model $P$, where the deflator is endogenous, is not marked. In the former the correlation between $\log P^*$ and $\log \tilde{P}$, the deflator implied by the estimates in $S_I$ is 0.996.

### 4.2. Adding domestic prices

The remaining two columns of table 2 give the results of adding the log of domestic prices to the various models. In view of the strong rejection of homogeneity by the import data it seemed possible that the statistical significance of the additional terms in $\log p_d$ could have arisen more from the relaxation of homogeneity that they implied than from the fact that they referred to domestic sales.[12] We therefore decided first to examine $\log p_d$ in the context of the non-homogeneous model, and second to repeat all the experiments using a 'homogenised' variable $\log(p_d/P^*)$ instead of $\log p_d$.

The results of table 2 are quite unambiguous. In every model and variant the addition of domestic prices is significant. The explanation of various countries' shares of British manufactured imports is significantly improved by including British domestic prices among the regressors; thus, British imports and home sales are not separable.

The significance of domestic prices is widespread across countries — for instance, in $N$ seven out of ten coefficients on $p_d/P^*$ are individually significant, while in $S_I$ five are. (Individual significance is not calculated in $S_\Omega$ and $P$.) Furthermore, there is a range of responses, stretching in $S_I$ from 0.24 for Germany to $-0.34$ for the United States. The addition of $p_d/P^*$ also slightly improves the plausibility and statistical properties; for instance, in model $S_I$ raising the number of negative own price effects from five to six and removing any hints of first-order serial correlation. Of course we should not make too much out of these comparisons, for the AIDS with added terms in $p_d/P^*$ is not a proper demand system, but overall the evidence suggests that domestic prices, as well as being statistically significant, shift the model in the right direction.

[12]That is to say, it seemed possible that adding any price would have been significant because of the consequence for homogeneity.

### 4.3. A non-separable system

The previous section used Lagrange Multiplier methods to show that imports and domestic sales are non-separable — at least in the case of the United Kingdom. A drawback of these methods is, however, that while they can reject the null hypothesis quite simply, they are rather vague as to the nature of the alternative hypothesis. That is to say, that several (many?) alternative hypotheses give rise to the same test statistic. Hence, while we are quite categorical that separability does not apply, it is not obvious where to proceed from here. It is plain that some reformulation is necessary, however, for merely tacking home prices onto an import allocation AIDS does not realise a proper demand model — i.e. it meets none of the a priori requirements that theorists and model-builders require.

One obvious reformulation is to incorporate home sales and their prices into the AIDS symmetrically with all the import shares, and this is what we now describe. Before going onto the results, however, we should mention the difficulties inherent in such a process.

(a) Data. The U.K. data on gross output and domestic prices are of a quite different nature from the import data and, especially the former, subject to greater observation error.

(b) Simultaneity. There seems a stronger likelihood of simultaneity between the U.K. share of its own market for manufactures and both the price of its output and the overall level of spending, than between import shares and their prices and expenditure.

(c) Increasing size. With a full matrix of Slutsky substitution effects, adding an eleventh equation involves a further ten independent price responses and three other coefficients, hence increasing the ratio of parameters to observations.

(d) Disparate shares. The U.K. share of its own market ranges from 96 percent (in 1954) to 75 percent (in 1979). The largest share ever recorded by any importer is 5.7 percent by Germany in 1979. This causes substantial numerical difficulties, as well as raising the spectre of heteroscedasticity. In fact, the follwoing results have been limited by numerical difficulties and must be treated cautiously.

(e) Dynamics and aggregation. Adding home sales does nothing to overcome the problems of applying static theory to a dynamic world, and of using aggregate data for disaggregate theory.

The main results, given in table 3, are disappointing. Column (1) gives twice the log-likelihoods, while columns (2)–(4) give residual sums of squares on import shares; column (2) gives the crude figures from the present, non-separable, model; column (3) gives an adjusted sum of squares from the present model in which the errors over the ten imported sources are constrained to sum to zero in each year;[13] and column (4) gives the

[13]In terms of eq. (16) above, column (2) gives $\sum_t \sum_{i=1}^{10} \hat{v}_{it}^2$, while (3) gives $\sum_t \sum_{i=1}^{10} (\hat{v}_{it} - \bar{v}_t)^2$.

Table 3
A non-separable allocation model.

| Model | 2* log-likelihood | Residual sum of squares on import shares: Non-separable (i) Crude | (ii) Adjusted | Separable |
|---|---|---|---|---|
| $N_I$ | 3661.6 | 0.02448 | 0.01957 | 0.01613 |
| $H_I$ | 3348.2 | 0.05925 | 0.02909 | 0.01752 |
| $S_I$ | 2258.2 | 0.48198 | 0.44135 | 0.03187 |
| $N_\Omega$ | 3703.2 | 0.02448 | 0.01957 | 0.01613 |
| $H_\Omega$ | 3565.2 | 0.05925 | 0.02909 | 0.01752 |
| $S_\Omega$ | 3394.6 | 0.19045 | 0.07204 | 0.03812 |
| $S_I^B$ | 2659.2 | 0.16290 | 0.06965 | 0.03187[a] |
| $P_I^B$ | 3083.9 | 0.10155 | n.a. | 0.03196[a] |
| $S_\Omega^B$ | 2880.8 | 0.31046 | 0.26354 | 0.03812[a] |

[a]Not strictly applicable; the statistics come from $S_I$, $P_I$, and $S_\Omega$, respectively.

corresponding sums of squares from the import allocation models above. Roughly speaking, column (3) removes any error in the import shares stemming directly from errors in the predicted domestic share. As noted above, the separable import allocation model is estimated to minimise these reported sums of squares (at least in the $I$ models) and so the comparisons are biased in its favour. Nevertheless, the huge differences between the separable and non-separable models is disappointing; furthermore, although the problems with the domestic share are disproportionately large, it is evident that they do not directly explain all the difficulties with the import shares — compare columns (2) and (3).[14]

Table 3 does suggest, however, at least one source of the difficulties. As for the separable model, we find both homogeneity and symmetry rejected, and also observe that, to some extent, allowing a more general error structure compensates for the constraints on the deterministic part of the equation. However, in this case the rejections and the differences between the $I$ and the $\Omega$ models are all much greater than in the separable case. This suggests that at least some of the present problems stem from the domestic price data, although whether it is their quality per se, or just their lack of comparability with the other price data, we cannot say.

Mention should be made at this point of the additional models reported at the foot of table 3 — those superscripted B. The residuals from the standard models all showed strong negative correlations between foreign countries' shares and the U.K.'s share; for instance, in $H$ four were below $-0.9$ and eight below $-0.65$. This is consistent with the pattern identified in the

[14]We cannot of course remove the influence that having to explain the domestic share has on the estimated parameters and hence predicted values; we can only remove the error in the domestic share *remaining after* estimation.

appendix in which one country's share (here the United Kingdom) makes all the compensating variations arising from changes in other countries' shares. Given the U.K.'s predominant share of her own market for manufactures, and given the frequently expressed view about the relatively poor quality of U.K. products, this does not seem an unreasonable hypothesis. Hence, in the models superscripted B the error-covariances between all pairs of foreign shares are constrained to zero, while those between the United Kingdom and country $i$ are constrained such that, in obvious notation, $\sigma_{iu} = -\sigma_{ii}^2$. (Hence the error covariance matrix is 'bordered'.) In $S_I^B$ all $\sigma_{ii}^2$ are constrained to be equal, whereas in $S_\Omega^B$ the ten $\sigma_{ii}^2$ referring to foreign countries are freely estimated ($\sigma_{uu}^2$ is defined from these by the singularity condition).

It is plain from table 3 that this specification of the error covariances considerably improves matters. $S_I^B$ has the same number of degrees of freedom as $S_I$ and yet raises the test statistic by over 400, while the ten parameters that convert $S_I^B$ into $S_\Omega^B$ have a likelihood ratio statistic of 221.6. Comparing $S_I^B$ and $S_\Omega^B$ in more detail finds the latter dominant in every respect except in the explanation of import shares [see column (2)]: it has virtually no sign of serial correlation, it fits all countries except Japan better, and it exhibits greater plausibility.

On this last criterion, however, there is still room for improvement. The Slutsky matrix should, as before, have one zero and $(n-1)$ negative eigenvalues, but in fact has, in 1979, seven negative, one zero and three positive. The last group corresponds essentially to the positive own substitution elasticities for Sweden, the United States and the United Kingdom. The last is the largest and could reflect simultaneity problems.[15] The income effects illustrate Britain's well-known trade problem. With $\beta_{UK} = -0.11$, the United Kingdom loses its shares of the home market rapidly as sales expand; considering the likely simultaneity between U.K. expenditure and the U.K.'s share of that expenditure, which would bias $\beta_{UK}$ towards zero, the observed value is very worrying indeed. Further evidence of poor domestic performance comes from the integration effects. Again the largest effect refers to the U.K.'s own share with a coefficient of $-0.076$; that is, the U.K.'s own share is nearly 8 percentage points lower since 1973 compared with earlier. We should beware of making too strong a causal statement here, however, for the beneficiaries of making the U.K.'s loss include virtually all import sources, with the gains to Switzerland and Japan, as well as to the EEC members, being statistically significant. This issue is discussed in detail in Winters (1984).

[15]This possibility was partially tested by replacing the U.K. price by an instrumental estimate, using as instruments U.K. and OECD unit labour costs in manufacturing, U.K. and OECD industrial production (all lagged from 0 to 2 years), and time. In the event this changed virtually nothing, which may indicate either an absence of simultaneity, or that U.K. labour costs are part of a simultaneous system with prices and import penetration. I am grateful to a referee for suggesting this approach.

The conclusion of the previous section was that domestic prices must be considered in import allocation models. The conclusion of this section is that treating imports and domestic sales symmetrically in an AIDS is not a totally successful way of doing so. While disappointing, this latter conclusion does not undermine the former, it merely shows the need for further research in the direction indicated. That, however, is the topic for another paper.

### *4.4. Testing the Armington assumptions*

We showed above how Armington's influential model made two critical assumptions about the relationships between import sources — namely the homotheticity of import demand and the mutual separability of demands for different imports. This section tests these assumptions using the approaches developed above.

The assumption of homotheticity implies that the import shares are independent of the overall level imports. Statistically this requires that the $\beta_i$ are zero in eq. (8). In all the models applying the AIDS just to imports — i.e. assuming separability of home and foreign demand — we tested this assumption, and in all it was rejected. For instance, five out of ten $\beta_i$ were individually significant in $H$, and the likelihood ratio test for all ten was 50.5 in $H_I$ and 41.0 in $H_\Omega$; similarly, in $P_I$ three were individually significant while the Wald test on all ten was 84.2.

Turning to the simultaneous testing of homotheticity and mutual separability the main results appear in table 4. For each import source in turn we

Table 4
Testing homotheticity and separability between import sources.

| | Wald tests ($\chi^2$-distributed)[a] | | |
|---|---|---|---|
| | Homotheticity $\beta_i=0,\forall_i$ | Separability $\delta_i=0,\forall_i$ | Homotheticity and separability $\beta_i=\delta_i=0,\forall_i$ |
| Degrees of freedom | 8 | 8 | 16 |
| Separable country | | | |
| France | 53.0 | 6.9[b] | 85.2 |
| Belgium/Luxembourg | 51.7 | 33.6 | 115.9 |
| Netherlands | 61.6 | 15.6 | 94.8 |
| West Germany | 84.6 | 10.4[b] | 100.8 |
| Italy | 38.1 | 29.1 | 134.3 |
| Sweden | 33.3 | 40.0 | 118.3 |
| Switzerland | 44.4 | 5.0[b] | 102.5 |
| Japan | 49.0 | 17.2 | 82.0 |
| Canada | 16.1 | 34.1 | 49.9 |
| U.S.A. | 68.9 | 47.6 | 174.6 |

[a]Critical values at 5 percent: $\chi^2_8=15.51$ and $\chi^2_{16}=26.30$.
[b]*Not* significant at 5 percent.

estimated an AIDS excluding it and then tested whether its price had any influence on the shares (among themselves) of the remaining nine. For convenience we used only model $S_I$ for this experiment — this being the most general case for which the Lagrange Multiplier test involves merely including extra terms in a linear regression. Hence, the equation estimated was the AIDS with an additional parameter ($\delta_i$) on the price of the excluded import for each of the nine included flows. We then applied Wald tests to this equation to test homotheticity ($\beta_i = 0$), separability ($\delta_i = 0$), and then both together. It is the last that tests Armington's model.

Homotheticity is rejected in each of the 'nine source' AIDS, as it was in all the ten and eleven source AIDS, and separability is rejected in seven of the ten cases. Homotheticity and separability together are overwhelmingly rejected in every case. Our data are quite unambiguous that the restrictions implied by Armington's model of international trade are not acceptable.

## 5. Conclusion

This paper has argued that the traditional assumption of trade allocation models, that the demand for domestic and foreign goods is separable, is false. We considered first the theoretical implications of separability, rejecting them a priori. We then discussed a tractable but general approach to testing separability and illustrated it on U.K. manufactured imports over 1952–79. The hypothesis of separability was overwhelmingly rejected.

We also used our methods to conduct two further tests. First, we constructed a non-separable model of import allocation. This encountered several problems, not least, we hypothesise, with the data, but was not without hope of generalisation. Second, we tested a popular trade model — the Armington model — which, as well as imposing domestic/foreign separability, imposes separability between all import sources and homotheticity. The additional assumptions were strongly rejected, both individually and together.

On a methodological level this is the first paper to use Deaton and Muellbauer's AIDS for explaining international trade flows, and the preliminary results look promising. As a tool of analysis the AIDS offers generality with tractability — a happy combination. The paper also illustrates the advantages of the Lagrange Multiplier test, allowing relatively simple tests of complex hypotheses.

Our tests are subject to several shortcomings — e.g. in aggregation, dynamics, simultaneity and data — and firm conclusions must await more and better tests. But if our results are supported, the implications for modelling international trade are very serious. First, the Armington model, with its highly constrained price responses, must be put aside, for its restrictions are rejected and, with inflation and floating, we certainly now have sufficient data to estimate a more interesting set of price effects. Thus, even if we stick with separable import allocation models more sophisticated structures — such as the AIDS — must be adopted.

Second, it is no longer legitimate to assume the separability of imports and home sales. This suggests that the popular two-stage budgeting process of import function followed by import allocation is no longer acceptable. For the latter, home prices and probably home sales must be considered, although the simple symmetric treatment adopted here looks inadequate. There are also implications for the former, however. Since we have rejected the homotheticity and separability of different import sources, it is no longer possible to combine information from the various import sources into aggregate import variables. Hence, the import function should contain information from each source country. This amounts to dropping overall import functions in favour of separate equations for imports from each source, taking us back to the extended allocation model mentioned above.

The third implication concerns modelling exports. The origin of the present work was the author's view — see Winters (1981) — that exports were best modelled with respect to income in each market rather than with respect to each market's total imports. (These amount to world income and world trade for an aggregate export function.) If the present results generalise to other countries, this view will be vindicated for it is clear that export demand is merely a different aspect of the import allocation decision, and we have shown how domestic considerations, as well as overall trade levels, influence this.

## Appendix: The form of the error covariance matrix

From the text we know that

$$\sum_i u_{it}=0, \quad \text{all } t. \tag{A.1}$$

Let us use (A.1) to eliminate $u_{nt}$ $(=-\sum_{i=1}^{n-1} u_{it})$. Then $\Omega=E(uu')$ takes the form:

$$\Omega=\begin{bmatrix} \sigma_{11} & \sigma_{12} & \sigma_{13} & \cdots & -\sum_{j=1}^{n-1}\sigma_{1j} \\ \sigma_{21} & \sigma_{22} & \sigma_{23} & \cdots & -\sum_{j=1}^{n-1}\sigma_{2j} \\ \vdots & \vdots & \vdots & & \\ -\sum_{i=1}^{n-1}\sigma_{i1} & -\sum_{i=1}^{n-1}\sigma_{i2} & -\sum_{i=1}^{n-1}\sigma_{i3} & \cdots & \sum_{i=1}^{n-1}\sum_{j=1}^{n-1}\sigma_{ij} \end{bmatrix}, \tag{A.2}$$

where $\sigma_{kl}=E(u_k u_l)$.

Now suppose $\sigma_{ij}=0$, for all $i \neq j$, $i=1,\dots,n-1$. It is clear that the last row (and column) of $\Omega$ would be non-zero, for it contains terms in $-\sigma_{ii}$. This shows that we cannot set *all* off-diagonal terms to zero. Furthermore, unless there are very strong reasons for believing that country $n$'s share responds entirely passively to the other shares, it is arbitrary to single it out for non-zero off-diagonals. Given the arbitrariness of setting some subset of $\sigma_{ij}, i, j=1,\dots,n-1$, to zero, we conclude that zero restrictions are not generally suitable for $\Omega$.

Consider now the possibility that $\sigma_{ii}$ vary over $i$, but that the $\sigma_{ij}$ are all identical, $\sigma_{ij}=k$, say. (This restriction shows a 'symmetry of information' — i.e. that we have no special information about any particular flow — which is, we believe, a requirement of non-arbitrary a priori restrictions.) Consider row $i$; from (A.2) the $n$th element is

$$\sigma_{in} = -\sum_{j=1}^{n-1} \sigma_{ij},$$

from which

$$\sigma_{ii} = -\sum_{\substack{j=1 \\ j \neq i}}^{n} \sigma_{ij} = -(n-1)k.$$

Hence

$$k = -\frac{1}{n-1}\sigma_{ii}. \tag{A.3}$$

But through the symmetry of $\Omega$ we know that column $i$ as well as row $i$ contains $k$ off the diagonal. But since (A.3) applies to any row, the $k$ in row $l$ column $i$ must imply that $k=-[1/(n-1)]\sigma_{ll}$, and hence that $\sigma_{ii}=\sigma_{kk}$, etc. Hence, the only form of $\Omega$ permitting these restrictions must be:

$$\Omega = \sigma^2(I - ll'), \tag{A.4}$$

where $l$ is a vector of elements $n^{-1/2}$.

It may also be shown that the attempt to allow $\sigma_{ii}$ to vary but to have common correlations between all flows also reduces to (A.4). The upshot of this is that in the absence of information about particular flows there is no a priori restriction of $\Omega$ that permits different flows to have different variances. It appears then that either $\Omega$ is to be estimated in full or it is to take form (A.4).

## References

Armington, P.S., 1969, A theory of demand for products distinguished by place of production, IMF Staff Papers XVI, 159–176.
Barten, A.P., 1971, An import allocation model for the Common Market, Cahiers Economiques de Bruxelles 50, 3–14.
Breusch, T.S. and A.R. Pagan, 1980, The Lagrange multiplier test and its applications to model specification in econometrics, Review of Economic Studies XLVII, 239–253.
Burgess, D.F., 1974, Production theory and the derived demand for imports, Journal of International Economics 4, 103–118.
Deaton, A.S., 1974, NLFIML, programme for the estimation of the parameters of non-linear relationships, mimeo, Growth Project Paper, 400, Department of Applied Economics, Cambridge.
Deaton, A.S., 1975, Models and projections of demand in post-war Britain, No. 1 of Cambridge Studies in Applied Econometrics (Chapman and Hall, London).
Deaton, A.S. and J. Muellbauer, 1980a, Economics and consumer behaviour (Cambridge University Press, London).
Deaton, A.S. and J. Muellbauer, 1980b, An almost ideal demand system, American Economic Review 70, 312–326.
Deppler, M.C. and D.M. Ripley, 1981, The world trade model: merchandise trade, IMF Staff Papers XXV, 147–206.
Harvey, A.C., 1981, The econometric analysis of time series (Philip Allen, London).
Hickman, B.G. and L.J. Lau, 1973, Elasticities of substitution and export demands in a world trade model, European Economic Review 4, 347–380.
Maddala, G.S., 1977, Econometrics (McGraw-Hill, New York).
Murray, T. and P.J. Ginman, 1976, An empirical examination of the traditional aggregate import demand model, Review of Economics and Statistics LVIII, 75–80.
Ranuzzi, P., 1981, The experience of EEC Eurolink project in modelling bilateral trade linkage equations, Journal of Policy Modelling 3, 153–173.
Strombach, C.T., 1980, A model of bilateral trade flows — some preliminary results, mimeo, University of Southampton, June 1980.
Theil, H., 1980, A system-wide approach to microeconomics (Basil Blackwell, Oxford).
Theil, H. and K.W. Clements, 1978, A differential approach to U.S. import demand, Economics Letters 1, 249–252.
Winters, L.A., 1980, Aggregation in logarithmic models: some experiments with U.K. export functions, Oxford Bulletin of Economics and Statistics 42, 36–50.
Winters, L.A., 1981, An econometric model of the export sector, No. 4 of Cambridge Studies in Applied Econometrics (Cambridge University Press, London).
Winters, L.A., 1982, Separability and the specification of foreign trade functions, Discussion Paper 82/126, University of Bristol.
Winters, L.A., 1984, British imports of manufactures and the Common Market, Oxford Economic Papers 36, 103–118.

*Oxford Economic Papers* 36 (1984), 103–118

# BRITISH IMPORTS OF MANUFACTURES AND THE COMMON MARKET*

*By* L. ALAN WINTERS

**Abstract**

THIS paper assesses the impact of Britain's accession to the EEC on her imports of manufactures. It argues that account must be taken of the substitutability of imports for home production, and that price effects must be modelled consistently. It applies Deaton and Muellbauer's "Almost Ideal Demand System" to annual data on UK home sales and imports from ten sources. It identifies considerable trade creation, but little or no trade diversion.

This paper has two objectives: first to assess the effect of accession to the EEC on the UK's pattern of imports of manufactures, and second to explore certain methodological issues in the estimation of such effects. It is now ten years since the UK acceded to the Common Market and the time is ripe for an assessment. So far this matter has attracted remarkably little attention from economists despite the continuing debate about membership among politicians—Daly (1978), Fetherston, Moore and Rhodes (1979) and Morgan (1980) are the main sources. Obviously imports are only half of the issue, but we concentrate on them here because they illustrate the methodological points we make. A corresponding study of exports would require substantially more data than we currently have and is left over to another paper.

The principal methodological issue of the paper is whether or not one can consider import flows alone in assessing the effects of economic integration or whether one should simultaneously consider home sales of domestic output. It is our contention that the latter is correct and that the distinction is important. A further, minor, methodological contribution is the model of trade that we use: we explain the allocation of British purchases of manufacturing over competing suppliers by means of Deaton and Muellbauer's (1980) Almost Ideal Demand System. To our knowledge ours is the first application of this system to international trade data.

## I

The most popular way of measuring integration effects is by residual imputation whereby a hypothetical *anti-monde* is constructed to represent

* An earlier version of this paper was presented to the International Economics Study Group and to the European Studies graduate seminar at the London School of Economics. The author is grateful to both these groups, and also to Dr. D. G. Mayes, Dr. F. V. Meyer and two referees for comments on that draft. Naturally he does not blame any of these people for its remaining shortcomings.

trade in the absence of integration and the difference between this and actual trade is attributed to integration.[1] Obviously the crucial question is how to construct the *anti-monde* and there are several alternatives available.[2] Aitken (1973) defines his *anti-monde* by a cross-sectional gravity model of trade, implying that in the absence of integration, trade between partners would be determined by the same relationship with incomes, population and distance as is actual trade between non-partners. This is a powerful approach but is obviously not well suited to examining the effects of integration on a single country.

Other authors define their *anti-mondes* to contain at least some time-series component. For example Williamson and Bottrill (1971) assume that in the absence of integration, partners' shares of each others' import bundles would evolve "in a similar way" to their shares of third markets. Hence their *anti-monde* is a mixture of time series and cross-section effects. Fetherston, Moore and Rhodes (1979), however, are more explicitly time-oriented. They fit import functions (for partner and non-partner trade) containing total final expenditure, relative costs and time over the pre-integration period and extrapolate these over the integration period. Balassa's (1974) ex post income elasticities are basically similar, although here income is the only variable in the import function.[3] Finally Truman (1969, 1975) extrapolates not only the shares of partners' and non-partners' in local sales but also the share of local producers. His extrapolation leaves something to be desired, but we shall argue that his recognition of the role of home sales is fundamentally correct.

Appendix 1 summarises evidence from Winters (forthcoming) that, for Britain, the demand for manufactures from various foreign sources is not separable from that for British manufactures, and furthermore that the demands for manufactures are not homothetic. The former implies that the choice between, say, French and Swiss manufactures (partner and non-partner imports, respectively) is influenced by the British price, while the latter implies that is is also affected, non-proportionately, by the total level of demand. Correspondingly the British share of her own total consumption of manufactures depends on that total and also on the various import prices. This means that the shares of partner, non-partner and domestic suppliers in total demand must be modelled simultaneously. Hence, only Truman's among the time-series procedures above could be truly satisfactory. Truman, however, extrapolated his shares very crudely; leaving them fixed in (1969) and using a trend and cyclical variable alone in (1975). Hence he too is guilty of imposing homotheticity in the former and separability in both. However, unlike the other studies, Truman's approach lends itself more readily to correction.

[1] See Mayes (1978) for a thorough survey of empirical studies of integration.

[2] The following paragraphs are not intended to be a proper survey of work on integration. They merely take the works chosen as representative of classes of methodology.

[3] Balassa's method is discussed further in Appendix 2.

## II

In this section we introduce our own estimates. Our purpose is to examine the consequences of correctly taking account of domestic sales, hence we present two sets of results, the first excluding home sales (i.e. considering only import shares)—the import-only model—and the second including them—the complete model. We start with a very simple 'Trumanesque' approach and then move onto the full Almost Ideal Demand System.

Our data cover 1952–79 annually and refer to UK imports of manufactures from ten sources (see Table 3) covering about 75% of manufactured imports, and to UK gross output of manufactures. Since imports compete with all stages of production within UK manufacturing the correct variable for local sales is gross output rather than value-added. Imports are valued inclusive of tariffs.[4] Prices, when they are required, are derived from export unit value series for the foreign sources, corrected for non-discriminatory tariffs,[5] and from UK wholesale prices for the UK. The discrepancy between the nature of these price series is unfortunate but unavoidable. The term "total imports" refers to imports from the ten identified countries while "total expenditure" refers to this plus home sales. Full details of the data may be found in Winters (forthcoming).

We start with a very simple exercise, essentially following Truman, but one which illustrates the importance of the home sales variables. We estimate the following equations over 1952–72

$$w_{it} = \alpha_i + \beta_i \log (E_t/P_t^*) + \eta_i t + u_{it} \qquad (1)^6$$

where $w_{it}$ is country $i$'s share of $E_t$ in year $t$; $E_t$ is total expenditure when home sales are included and total imports in the imports-only model; $t$ is a time trend and

$$\log P_t^* = \sum_j w_{jt} \log p_{jt} \qquad (2)$$

where $p_{jt}$ is the price of manufactures from country $j$. $P^*$ is calculated over the group of included countries (i.e. it includes UK prices in the complete model but not in the import-only model).

Integration effects are then calculated as the difference between actual trade shares over 1973–79 and those predicted by applying our estimate of equation (1) to the actual values of the independent variables over that period. This is the method of 'residual imputation', and it attributes to integration *any* structural change over the prediction period as well as any random variation in the actual series. Hence, the *anti-monde* implicitly

[4] Total tariff revenue from manufactures was pro rated across all imports of manufactures. Hence our valuation ignores the effects of discriminatory tariff changes.

[5] Hence our price series *do not* reflect the competitive advantage conferred on our partners in 1973.

[6] This is a specialisation of the AIDS that is used below, see equation (3).

TABLE 1
*The effects of integration on the origin of manufactures sold in the UK*

| | *Imports only* | | | *Complete model* | | | | | |
|---|---|---|---|---|---|---|---|---|---|
| | *change in EEC share* | *change in EEC amount £ million* | | *change in shares* | | | *change in amounts £ million* | | |
| | | (a) | (b) | *EEC* | *non EEC* | *home* | *EEC* | *non EEC* | *home* |
| 1973 | 0.072 | 456 | 786 | 0.030 | 0.014 | −0.044 | 1152 | 537 | −1689 |
| 1974 | 0.093 | 807 | 1299 | 0.040 | 0.018 | −0.057 | 1871 | 842 | −2713 |
| 1975 | 0.093 | 862 | 1338 | 0.033 | 0.012 | −0.044 | 1671 | 608 | −2279 |
| 1976 | 0.109 | 1356 | 2003 | 0.046 | 0.016 | −0.061 | 2787 | 969 | −3756 |
| 1977 | 0.122 | 1905 | 2709 | 0.052 | 0.015 | −0.067 | 3777 | 1090 | −4867 |
| 1978 | 0.129 | 2499 | 3361 | 0.064 | 0.022 | −0.086 | 5206 | 1790 | −6996 |
| 1979 | 0.156 | 3732 | 4932 | 0.075 | 0.020 | −0.095 | 7163 | 1910 | −9073 |

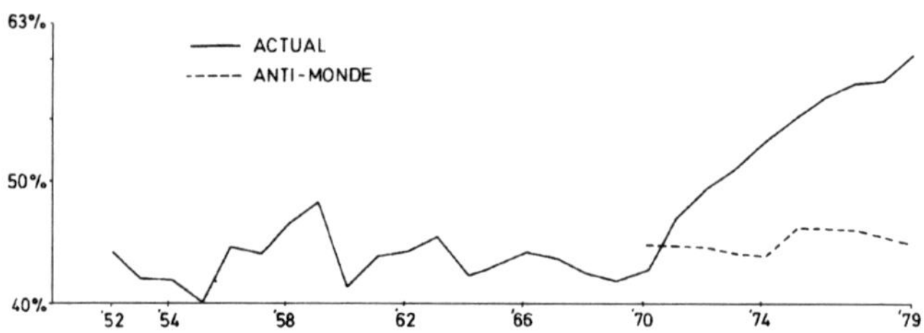


FIG. 1(a). Share of EC(6) in UK imports of manufactures ('imports only').

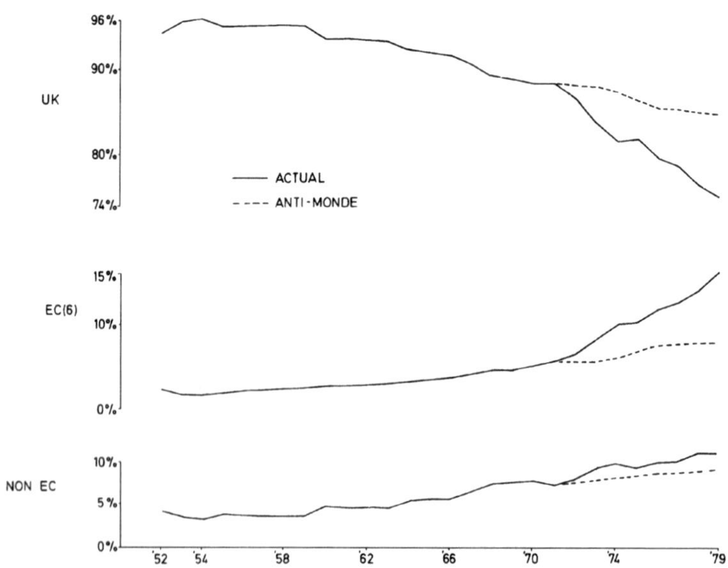


FIG. 1(b). Share of EC(6), non UK and UK in UK sales of manufactures ('complete model').

assumes that there are no other significant changes in behaviour and that the independent variables have not been influenced by integration. This is obviously rather strong, but convincing alternatives are not readily apparent.

The results are summarised in Table 1 and Fig. 1 below, where we sum the import results into partner countries (France, Belgium–Luxembourg, Netherlands, Germany and Italy) and non-partner countries (Sweden, Switzerland, Japan, Canada and USA). Table 1 gives the difference between the actual and *anti-monde* shares of these groups over the extrapolation period, and estimates of the value of trade (at current prices) affected, on various assumptions about the effect of accession on overall expenditure.

The "import-only" model looks essentially at the reallocation of a given level of imports among different sources. Table 1 shows the deviation in the EEC share relative to expected, and in column (a) this is translated into a gain in trade, holding imports constant between the actual outcome and the *anti-monde*. This amounts, of course, to attributing all the change to trade diversion, for any EEC gain must be a non-EEC loss. In column (b) we correct this and, roughly, attribute all the gain to trade creation. The non-EEC share would fall even if non-EEC countries lost no trade absolutely but EEC-trade grew by displacing home production. Hence we construct a new *anti-monde* in which the shares are as in the previous *anti-monde* but in which the total level of imports is lower. They are lower such that the *anti-monde* share of non-EEC sources of the new total yields the actually observed level of non-EEC imports. The difference between the actual and *anti-monde* levels of imports is hypothesised to accrue only to EEC suppliers and roughly measures the amount of trade creation that would be necessary to account for the observed changes.[7]

Consider now the complete model with home sales added. Home sales are dominant throughout the period, but over the seventies they were increasingly displaced by imports. Of the latter, those from the EEC showed the stronger growth. These shifts clearly broke with the trends of previous decades, and assuming again that behaviour changed only because of accession and that total sales were not affected by accession, we have very strong evidence of trade-creation. This is quantified in Table 1.

There is also, however, some evidence of 'external trade creation', to use Balassa's term, whereby non-partners increase their trade. The adoption of the CET did reduce the UK tariff on imports from these countries—see National Institute (1971), table 2—so this result has some a priori justification, but it could just reflect some factor leading to a general increase in imports relative to home sales. If so, the EEC share would have risen above the assumed *anti-monde* level even without integration, and we should have

[7] Under the new *anti-monde* let $\tilde{M}$ be total imports, and $h$ the non-EEC share. Total non-EEC imports are hence $h\tilde{M}$ and those are hypothesised to equal actual non-EEC imports ($aM$), where $M$ is total actual imports and $a$ the non-EEC share. Hence $\tilde{M} = (a/h)M$ and trade created $= (1 - a/h)M$. Clearly if the shares ($a$ and $h$) are non-homothetic the same share will not rule under $M$ and $\tilde{M}$ so this procedure is only approximate.

over-estimated trade-creation. With EEC and non-EEC imports roughly equal, we might expect roughly equal effects from this additional factor, so, on this interpretation, the estimate of trade creation should be that of Table 1 less the estimated rise in non-EEC imports. Either way, there is little evidence of trade diversion for the countries we consider here.

Interesting though these results are they are subject to several limitations, which can be, at least partially, removed. First, in both models the results are strongly influenced by Switzerland. In the complete model she, alone, accounts for three-quarters of the external trade creation! The Swiss share of the British market, having grown steadily over the sixties from 0.28% in 1960 to 0.78% by 1971, then doubles over the next two years and rises further to 2.68% by 1979. Most of this shows up as external trade creation, but examination of the data reveals that most is in fact due to huge rises in the value of diamonds traded.[8]

A second difficulty evident from Fig. 1 is the identification of the start of the integration period. A very strong case can be made for acknowledging anticipations and including 1972 as an integration year. Clearly wrongfully excluding years from the integration period will lead us to understate the integration effects.

## III

The third obvious defect of the analysis above is that it ignores relative prices. We therefore now consider a more general model, based on Deaton and Muellbauer's AIDS model. As is argued in Winters (forthcoming), less general methods of introducing prices—for instance following Armington (1969), using the Linear Expenditure System or adding terms in $(p_i/P^*)$ to equation (1)—are not legitimate, for they impose the unwarranted assumptions of separability and, possibly, homotheticity.

Deaton and Muellbauer's Almost Ideal Demand System (1980) is a very general yet tractable demand system, which satisfies various a priori restrictions arising from demand theory. Ignoring problems of aggregation, simultaneity and lagged responses we postulate that the allocation of demand over sources of supply is governed by:

$$w_{it} = \alpha_i + \sum_j \gamma_{ij} \log p_{jt} + \beta_i \log (E_t/P_t^*) + u_{it} \qquad i = 1 \ldots N \tag{3}$$

where the variables are as defined previously and $\alpha_i$, $\beta_i$, $\gamma_{ij}$ are parameters.

Adding up requires that

$$\sum_i \alpha_i = 1 \quad \text{and} \quad \sum_i \gamma_{ij} = \sum_i \beta_i = 0 \tag{4}$$

and this is satisfied automatically by any set of $w_i$ which add up to unity.

[8] Probably due to price rises, although British trade statistics are sufficiently coy about diamonds to make a complete solution to the mystery impossible.

Homogeneity requires

$$\sum_i \gamma_{ij} = 0 \tag{5}$$

and symmetry that

$$\gamma_{ij} = \gamma_{ji} \tag{6}$$

These are easily imposed, although (6) does mean that all equations have to be estimated simultaneously with cross-equation constraints. The adding-up constraint also means that $\sum_i u_{it} = 0$ where the $u_{it}$ are the errors in equation (3). This makes for some problems in estimating (3) as a system, for the variance-covariance matrix $\Omega \equiv E(uu')$ is singular. In fact estimating $\Omega$ is very difficult, for the deterministic part of (3) alone contains 75 parameters when $N = 11$, and estimating $\Omega$ would add a further 55. We have, therefore, constrained it *a priori*. For the import shares model, where $N = 10$, we assume that

$$\Omega = (I - ll') \tag{7}$$

where the vector $l$ comprises 10 elements of $N^{-\frac{1}{2}}$. When corrected for singularity this amounts to applying OLS to (3) with all cross-correlations set to zero. For the full model there is evidence that random changes in the share of any imports are largely reflected by compensating changes in the UK share, and hence we write, where the UK is the last supplier:

$$\Omega = \begin{pmatrix} \sigma_{11}^2 & & & & -\sigma_{11}^2 \\ & \sigma_{22}^2 & & 0 & -\sigma_{22}^2 \\ & & \cdot & & \cdot \\ & & \cdot & & \cdot \\ & & \cdot & & \cdot \\ & 0 & & \sigma_{10\,10}^2 & -\sigma_{10\,10}^2 \\ -\sigma_{11}^2 & -\sigma_{22}^2 & \cdots & -\sigma_{10\,10}^2 & \eta \end{pmatrix} \tag{8}$$

where $$\eta = \sum_{i=1}^{10} \sigma_{ii}^2.$$

In this case we allow for the non-singularity by suppressing the equation for the UK, calculating its parameters from the adding-up constraints. Full details of the estimation are available in Winters (forthcoming).

We apply the AIDS model to UK imports both with and without home sales. The full model contains fifty-five price parameters ($\gamma_{ij}$). Over the pre-integration period 1952–71 none of our sample of developed countries experienced great inflation and there were very few exchange-rate changes. Hence there is too little variation in the independent data to permit the sensible estimation of the AIDS—we experienced huge standard errors, implausible estimates and a lack of convergence. We therefore estimated the model over the whole data period adding dummies to account for integration effects. In experiments A we added $\delta_i D$ to (3) for each country, where $D$ is zero up to 1972 and unity from 1973. This implies an immediate and complete effect from integration, which seems unlikely. We therefore also conducted experiments B, replacing $D$ by $D'$, which took the following values (constructed informally from the time patterns in Fig. 1):

TABLE 2
*Integration dummy $D'$ in experiments B*

| 1952–71 | 1972 | 1973 | 1974 | 1975 | 1976 | 1977 | 1978 | 1979 |
|---|---|---|---|---|---|---|---|---|
| 0 | 1 | 3 | 4 | 5 | 6 | 7 | 8 | 9 |

The use of dummies rather than extrapolation shifts our model from "the residual imputation" class to the "analytic" class, see Mayes (1978). The former attributes all structural shifts and random variation to integration, whereas the latter attributes to it only the factor specifically being analysed—in our case a single intercept shift in experiments A, or a staggered intercept shift in experiments B. Clearly, therefore, our present procedure is a special case of the more general residual technique used above.

We also introduced two further dummies to allow for the Swiss diamond trade. These took the value zero except for the years 1972–79 and 1978–79 respectively when they were one. These dummies had the effect of raising the Swiss share, but we also had to decide at whose expense.[9] In the complete model we merely assumed it was at Britain's expense, in keeping with her predominant share of her own market, but in the imports-only model others suffered in proportion to their 1971 shares. The first of these dummies differs from the integration dummy D only by one year (1972), so there may be some difficulty in separating their effects. However, there is nothing to suggest that Switzerland should experience such huge external trade creation, and the dominance of the shift in the diamond trade is so obvious in the statistics that we believe strongly that it is correct to include separate effects.

Before proceeding to the results we should perhaps admit to certain problems with the present approach. They should lead us to treat the results cautiously, but it is worth noting that similar problems beset almost every other exercise of this kind. First we analyse manufactures as if they were a single homogeneous good. The Swiss diamond trade illustrates the danger of this but many more similar but less extreme problems must exist; see Winters (1980) on the dangers of aggregation. Second we have no dynamics in the price effects; our excuse is tractability—it is not clear how to incorporate sensible dynamics into allocation models like the AIDS. Third

[9] It was impossible to estimate at whose expense since that would have required an additional eighteen independent parameters.

we ignore any simultaneity problems. Most serious among these is the causation running from the UK share of her own market in manufactures to the UK price index and aggregate level of spending on manufactures. Clearly these problems would be greater if we were considering all output, not just manufactures, but they must exist currently to some extent. The share/expenditure link is present in all share analyses of integration-effects, although obviously it is much worse when home sales are considered. Finally, we should not pretend that our data are perfect.

## IV

Tables 3 and 4 summarise the main results giving both the import-only model and complete model under experiments A and B. In all cases the Swiss dummies are significantly positive. For example in the complete model, in experiments A they have $t$-statistics of 2.80 (1972–9 dummy) and 7.16 (1978–9 dummy), and in experiments B 3.74 and 6.28 respectively. In the former they reduce the 1979 estimate of Swiss external trade creation (and consequent loss of domestic sales) from £2875 m to £363 m, and in the latter from £2195 m to £542 m.

It is also apparent that the time-phased dummy, $D'$, despite its crude construction, is an improvement over the step change dummy, $D$. Nested econometric tests are not possible but the substitution of $D'$ for $D$ raises twice the log-likelihood by 32.3 and 222.4 in the import-only and complete models respectively. There are slightly more signs of serial correlation with $D'$, however, although this appears to relate more to the prediction of pre-integration shares than to post-integration ones. Both dummies show

TABLE 3
*Integration effects in an AIDS model of trade*[a]

| | *actual sales in the UK 1979,*[b] (£m) | *Imports only* | | *Complete model* | |
|---|---|---|---|---|---|
| | | *share* | *value 1979* (£m) | *share* | *value 1979* (£m) |
| France | 3100 | 0.1067 | 400 | 0.0085* | 812 |
| Belgium/Luxembourg | 1967 | −0.0057 | −136 | 0.0028 | 267 |
| Netherlands | 1883 | 0.0371* | 888 | 0.0090* | 860 |
| Germany | 5419 | 0.0199 | 476 | 0.0181* | 1729 |
| Italy | 2012 | 0.0263 | 629 | 0.0062* | 592 |
| Sweden | 1301 | −0.0619 | −1481 | −0.0026* | −248 |
| Switzerland | 2559 | −0.0039 | −93 | 0.0038 | 363 |
| Japan | 1471 | 0.0053 | 127 | 0.0030* | 287 |
| Canada | 529 | −0.0113 | −270 | −0.0002 | −19 |
| USA | 3684 | −0.0225 | −538 | 0.0005 | 48 |
| UK | 71581 | — | — | −0.0492* | −4699 |

[a] Experiments A: AIDS plus dummy D and two Swiss dummies
[b] adjusted for tariffs
* $t$-statistic exceeds 1.96

TABLE 4
*Integration effects in an AIDS model of trade*[a]

| | *actual sales in the UK* 1979,[b] (£m) | *Imports only* | | *Complete model* | | |
|---|---|---|---|---|---|---|
| | | *share*[c] | *value* 1979 (£m) | *share*[c] | *value* 1979 (£m) | *t-statistic*[d] |
| France | 3100 | 0.0060* | 1292 | 0.00225* | 1934 | 2.25 |
| Belgium/ Luxembourg | 1967 | 0.0024 | 517 | 0.00203* | 1745 | 2.03 |
| Netherlands | 1883 | 0.0015 | 323 | 0.00153 | 1315 | 1.53 |
| Germany | 5419 | 0.0080* | 1723 | 0.00436* | 3748 | 4.36 |
| Italy | 2012 | 0.0059* | 1270 | 0.00155 | 1332 | 1.55 |
| Sweden | 1301 | −0.0067 | −1443 | −0.00014 | −120 | −0.14 |
| Switzerland | 2559 | −0.0034 | −732 | 0.00063 | 542 | 0.64 |
| Japan | 1471 | −0.0005 | −108 | 0.00084 | 722 | 0.84 |
| Canada | 529 | −0.0019 | −409 | −0.00027 | −232 | −0.27 |
| USA | 3684 | −0.0112* | −2412 | 0.00138 | 1186 | 1.38 |
| UK | 71581 | — | — | −0.01416* | −12171 | 4.54 |

[a] Experiments B: AIDS plus dummy $D'$ and two Swiss dummies
[b] Adjusted for tariffs
[c] The effect on the share in any year is this coefficient times the value for the year in Table 2
[d] $t$-statistics of coefficients on $D'$. Wald-statistics on the joint significance of the integration effects in this model are:
(i) on all ten independent effects 36.9 (critical value $\chi^2_{10} = 18.3$),
(ii) on five EEC partner effects 33.5 (critical value $\chi^2_5 = 11.1$),
(iii) on five non-partner effects 3.1 (critical value $\chi^2_5 = 11.1$),
* $t$-statistic exceeding 1.96

some signs of being inappropriate during the latter period (i.e. they give rise to sequences of same-signed residuals) but these are rather less under $D'$ than under $D$. Overall, while the serial correlation is uncomfortable, it is not disastrous, for none of the Durbin–Watson statistics for the individual shares lies below the lower limit if we apportion the estimated parameters equally over countries: they range from 1.37 to 2.21 in complete model $A$ and from 1.07 to 1.79 in complete model $B$.[10]

Comparing Tables 3 and 4 clearly illustrates the importance of dynamics in estimating integration effects. The step dummy reflects an average effect over 1973–79, while the phased dummy allows a gradual build up. The mean value of $D'$ over 1973–79 is six, which suggests that the coefficients on $D$ would be, on average, six times those on $D'$. They are, in fact, clearly less than that and this further supports the view that $D'$ is more nearly correct, for if $D$ is merely $D'$ measured with error we would expect its coefficients to be biased towards zero. Overall $D'$ predicts very much greater integration effects than $D$, increasing our estimates by factors of around 2 to 3. More

[10] Since the AIDS is a single system with across equation constraints, the distribution of the D.W. statistic for individual countries is not known. However, we can still consider them informally, as descriptive statistics.

interesting, however, than the average size are the differences in particular countries' effects. Most spectacular is the effect on Belgium–Luxembourg where almost negligible effects under $D$ are transformed to large effects under $D'$, but similar large increases occur for France, Germany, Italy and the U.S.A.

We turn now to the main methodological result of the paper—the difference between the import-only model and the complete model. We have seen above that the distinction affects not only the numerical magnitudes but also the nature of the integration effects measured. This is repeated in Tables 3 and 4. In both, the major difference between models is the trade creation in the complete model, namely the extent to which the UK is shown to have lost her own market. With the step dummy, $D$, this amounts to nearly five percentage points while with the phased dummy, $D'$, it is over twelve and a half percentage points by 1979. It is also clear, however, that modelling the substitution between home and foreign goods, as well as that between different sources of foreign goods, influences the allocation of the gains in market share. Most obviously all non-partner countries appear to suffer in the import-only model, whereas in the complete model only Sweden and Canada appear to lose share. This suggests that trade diversion is much weaker than the import-only model would lead us to expect. Second, it is notable that Italy's gains appear to be largely unaffected by the modelling approach, while Germany's are substantially affected. This suggests that Italy has gained mainly from trade diversion while Germany has gained from trade creation. In other words, Italy's goods compete with those from other exporters to the UK, while Germany's compete relatively more strongly with UK local manufactures. Similarly, Belgium appears to gain relatively more from creation, and France is intermediate; the Netherlands is crucially affected by the dummy used.

It is clear, then, that methodological issues are important. Our results show substantial variation over the different approaches. Our preferred equation is the latter one of Table 4—the complete model, based on the AIDS, with $D'$ and the Swiss dummies—and we conclude the paper by examining its implications more closely.

The ten integration effects are jointly significantly different from zero—see note (d) of Table 4. The main effect is "internal" trade creation—the five EEC partner effects are statistically significant jointly (and nearly so individually) and involve substantial amounts of trade. The non-partner effects, on the other hand, are insignificant and relatively small. At face value these results suggest that accession to the EEC led by 1979 to internal trade-creation of £10 billion, external trade creation of £2 b. and a consequent loss of domestic sales of £12 b. Proportionately these amount to 70%, 22% and 17% of the respective 1979 magnitudes.[11]

[11] Without the (insignificant) non-partner coefficients the overall estimate of internal trade creation is virtually unchanged.

Whilst we would not dispute the large size of trade creation there are perhaps reasons for believing that ours are over-estimates. First, as we noted before, if the external creation figures actually capture some additional general effect we should remove them from the integration estimates, suggesting effects of £8 b., £0 and −£8 b. on partner imports, non-partner imports and home sales respectively.

Second the oil price rise of 1973–4 may have affected the relative competitiveness of EEC and non-EEC goods because they embody differing amounts of oil in either production or transport. Our price indicators (export unit values) will capture the former, but not the latter. Hence our integration measures may be inflated to the extent that EEC and non-EEC imports involve different transport costs. The effect should be slight, however, for fuel oil accounts for at most 25% of transport cost which itself is probably less than 5% of manufactured imports delivered price. Nevertheless, after 1974 this possibility should be considered.

Third the implication of our *anti-monde* is that the consumption of manufactures and all (tariff-exclusive) prices would have been the same with or without integration. In fact there is some reason to believe that accession to the EEC worsened the current account of the balance of payments, see Winters (1983); hence in the *anti-monde* economic policy may have been less restrictive and the exchange rate higher than actually occurred, especially over the crisis years 1976–7. If so, and ignoring any estimation biases these possibilities may entail, *anti-monde* imports would have been higher than we have suggested, and thus integration effects smaller.

It is impossible to quantify all these caveats, but overall we would suggest that by 1979 trade creation amounted to at least £6 billion, and probably rather more.

## V

This paper has explored the impact of Britain's accession to the Common Market on her import behaviour. It has argued strongly that account must be taken of the interactions between home and foreign supplies of manufactures in making this assessment and has shown that bringing in home sales substantially affects the estimates. On a theoretical level it allows one to reflect the fact that imports from some countries compete more closely with indigenous production than others. The paper made use of a sophisticated demand allocation model to incorporate price rigorously, but was careful to avoid the unwanted assumptions of homotheticity of demands and the separability of home and foreign goods. This also represents an improvement on existing methodology.

Empirically the main conclusion was that accession had led to substantial trade creation. Subject to fairly wide margins of error (as must be all estimates) our results suggest that our European partners increased their exports to the UK by at least £6 b. p.a. by 1979, at the expense of UK producers.

## APPENDIX 1 SEPARABILITY AND HOMOTHETICITY IN FOREIGN TRADE FUNCTIONS

This appendix briefly describes some tests of the separability and homotheticity of British manufactured import behaviour. It is based on Winters (forthcoming), and uses the same data as used in the text.

Most models of import behaviour adopt a two-stage procedure of first estimating a single function to explain total imports in terms of home and import prices, incomes, and so on and then estimating an allocation model explaining imports from source $i$, $i = 1...N$, in terms of total imports and the prices of imports from the various sources. Given total imports, import allocation is independent of income and of the domestic price, and to be correct this requires that the process generating the allocation of sales over all sources be separable into a part dealing with imports and a part dealing with home sales.

We have tested this by estimating Deaton and Meullbauer's AIDS on import data alone—to explain import allocation—and then asking whether adding domestic prices to that model significantly improves the explanation of import shares. If it does, import allocation is not independent of domestic prices, separability is rejected and we know we must use a single system to explain import allocation and the import/home sales decision simultaneously.

The tests are conducted using the Lagrange-Multiplier test, which avoids having to construct a fully specified model under the alternative hypothesis (of no separabilty). In our case this greatly reduces the computational burden. The results are very stark. Using four different variants of the AIDS (depending on the imposition of homogeneity and symmetry and the estimation of $P^*$), two different specifications of the variance-covariance matrix, and two different measures of domestic price, the hypothesis of separability is strongly rejected every time. (Of the LM statistics, which are distributed $\chi^2_9$, none falls below 30.0 compared with a critical value of 16.9).

Import allocation models frequently also impose homotheticity, which implies that import shares are invariant with respect to income or expenditure. In terms of the AIDS—equation (3) above—this implies that $\beta_i = 0$, all $i$. This was tested in all the specifications used to test separability and again roundly rejected in every one.

Finally, an influential trade allocation model due to Armington (1969) imposes both homotheticity and also separability between each import source. Ignoring home prices, this implies that the allocation of imports between any nine sources will be independent of the price of the tenth. This was tested, along with homotheticity, by estimating a 'nine-source AIDS' and adding the tenth price. Treating each country in turn as the tenth, mutual separability and homotheticity were jointly rejected in every case.

These results strongly establish the contentions of the text. Foreign trade functions should consider import allocation and the import/home sales decision simultaneously; they should not impose homotheticity; and they should be sufficiently general not to imply the mutual separability of imports from different sources.

## APPENDIX 2 BALASSA'S EX POST INCOME ELASTICITIES

Balassa (e.g. 1974) measures integration effects by means of ex post income elasticities. These are the ratio of the change in imports (over some period) to the change in income, and they are compared before and after integration. Increases in the elasticity for imports from partners are interpreted as reflecting trade creation and decreases for non-partners trade diversion. This appendix argues that this is not an entirely satisfactory method of measuring integration effects.

To the author's knowledge Balassa has never said why integration should increase the *sensitivity* of imports to increases in income, rather than merely increase the *level* of imports associated with any particular level of income in a step fashion. (Of course, transition costs may stretch the step over several years). In Fig. A.1 plotting the log of imports against the log of

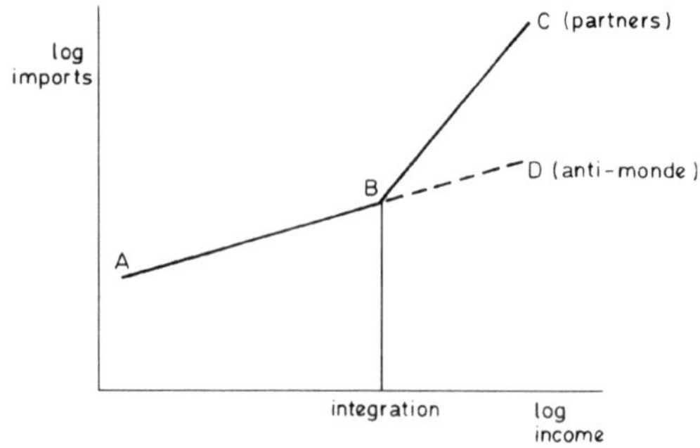


FIG. A1

income,[12] Balassa implies that at the date of integration the relationship of partner imports will shift up to *BC*, and one compares this with the anti-monde *BD* to get the integration effects.

We would argue, however, that rather than shift the slope, integration shifts the intercept of this relationship. Hence the situation really looks as in Fig. A.2.

We can test these conflicting views by examining whether the income coefficients, $\beta_i$, in equation (3) were altered by integration. (The $\beta_i$ are not strictly income elasticities, but they are close enough to provide a satisfactory test of the Balassa hypothesis). The test is conducted by adding to the models in the text terms in

$$\varepsilon_i D(\log E_t/P_t^* - \log E_{72}/P_{72}^*), \qquad i = 1...10.$$

The $\varepsilon_i$ measure the change in $\beta_i$ after 1972, and the $\log E_{72}/P_{72}^*$ is inserted to ensure that in 1973 no step changes occurs in the equation. Step intercept changes are captured by the dummies $D$ and $D'$ as in the text.

Table A1 summarises some results of these tests. From the column of likelihoods we see that both slope and intercept shifts have significant roles to play. However, of the two, the intercepts contribute more—witness the low likelihood when they are omitted. The further details of the results, are disturbing. In two of their three appearances the 'Balassa-partner' effects are implausible (negative) and in two they are insignificant; the corresponding non-partner effects seem better justified statistically but they are very volatile and are (although this is not shown)

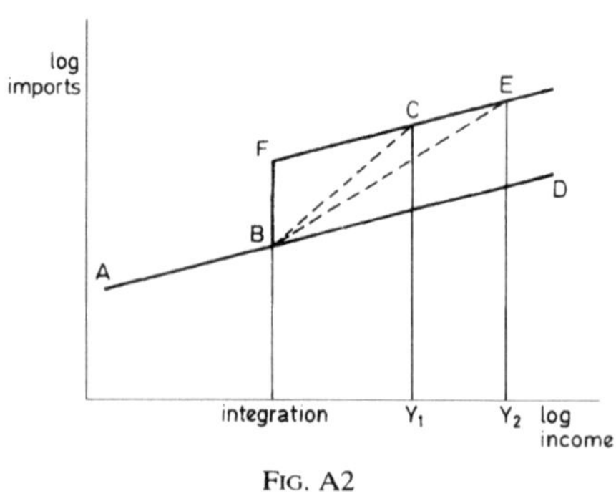


FIG. A2

[12] Hence the slope represents income elasticities.

TABLE A.1
*Intercept vs. slope changes as measures of integration effects*

| Integration variables[a] | 2* log likelihood[b] | *Integration effects sum and (significance)*[c] | | | |
|---|---|---|---|---|---|
| | | *'Balassa terms' (D.B)* | | *intercept terms (D or D')* | |
| | | *partners* | *non-partners* | *partners* | *non-partners* |
| *D, D.B* | 2940.6 | 0.0222 (6.58) | −0.1643 (23.69) | 0.0448 (148.6) | 0.0088 (17.56) |
| *D*[d] | 2914.8 | — | — | 0.0346 (143.1) | 0.0146 (18.32) |
| *D.B.* | 2812.6 | −0.1762 (5.68) | 0.0356 (29.63) | — | — |
| *D', D.B* | 3173.9 | −0.2857 (37.37) | 0.2554 (15.59) | 0.01214 (35.86) | 0.00230 (2.88) |
| *D'*[e] | 3137.2 | — | — | 0.01172 (33.54) | 0.00245 (3.05) |

[a] *D* and *D'* have been defined in the text.
*B* is $(\log E_t/P_t^* - \log E_{72}/P_{72}^*)$, the 'Balassa' effect.

[b] For nested models the difference in 2* log-likelihood between restricted and unrestricted forms is distributed as $\chi^2_{10}$, with critical value 18.31.

[c] The sums of the coefficients on integration terms over partner and non-partner countries, and (in brackets) Wald-tests of the hypothesis that all the relevant coefficients are simultaneously zero. The test-statistic is distributed as $\chi^2_5$, with critical value 11.07.

[d] The complete model from Table 3.

[e] The complete model from Table 4.

disproportionately influenced by the behaviour of Switzerland. The intercept shifts on the other hand seem plausible and robust.

These results cast considerable doubt on Balassa's ex post income elasticities approach. They are not conclusive, but if they are replicated in further research they will provide one explanation of why Balassa's estimates of trade creation have dropped over time (Balassa, 1974). Assume that income grows fairly steadily before and after integration, so that when we come to measure integration effects it has reached $Y_1$ in Fig. A2. (This reasonably represents the case of 'the Six', which Balassa was examining). We argue that the integration effect was *BF* (we ignore dynamics for simplicity), but Balassa measures it by the slope of *BC* less the slope of *BD*. Now consider a few years later when income had grown to $Y_2$. Our estimate is unchanged, but Balassa's, based on *BE*, has fallen.

*University of Bristol*

## REFERENCES

AITKEN, N. D. (1973) "*The Effect of the EEC and EFTA on European Trade: A Temporal Cross-Section Analysis*", American Economic Review, Vol. 63, pp. 881–892.

ARMINGTON, P. S. (1969), "*A Theory of Demand for Products Distinguished by Place of Production*", IMF Staff Papers, Vol. XVI, pp. 159–176.

BALASSA, B. (1974), "*Trade Creation and Trade Diversion in the European Common Market: An Appraisal of the Evidence*", Manchester School, Vol. XLII, pp. 93–135.

DALY, A. E. (1978), "*UK Visible Trade and the Common Market*", National Institute Economic Review, No. 86, pp. 42–54.

DEATON, A. S. and MUELLBAUER, J. (1980), "*An Almost Ideal Demand System*", American Economic Review, Vol. 70, pp. 312–326.

FETHERSTON, M., MOORE, B., RHODES, J. (1979). "*EEC Membership and UK Trade in Manufactures*", Cambridge Journal of Economics, Vol. 3, pp. 399–407.

MAYES, D. G. (1978), "*The Effects of Economic Integration on Trade*", Journal of Common Market Studies, Vol. XVII, pp. 1–25.

MORGAN, A. D. (1980), "*The Balance of Payments and British Membership of the European Community*", in Wallace, W. (ed.) *Britain in Europe*, Heinemann, London.

NATIONAL INSTITUTE (1971), "*Entry into the Common Market: A Comment on Some of the Economic Issues*", National Institute Economic Review, No. 57, pp. 35–61.

TRUMAN, E. M. (1969), "*The European Economic Community: Trade Creation and Trade Diversion*", Yale Economic Essays, Vol. 9, Spring, pp. 201–57.

TRUMAN, E. M. (1975). "*The Effects of European Economic Integration on the Production and Trade of Manufactured Products*", in Balassa B. (ed.) "European Economic Integration", North Holland, Amsterdam.

WILLIAMSON, J. and BOTTRILL, A. (1971), "*The Impact of Customs Union on Trade in Manufactures*", Oxford Economic Papers, Vol. 23, pp. 323–351.

WINTERS, L. A. (1980), "*Aggregation in Logarithmic Models: Some Experiments with UK Export Functions*", Oxford Bulletin of Economics and Statistics, Vol. 42, pp. 36–50.

WINTERS, L. A. (forthcoming), *Separability and the Specification of Foreign Trade Functions*, Journal of International Economics.

WINTERS, L. A. (1983), Evidence presented to the House of Lords Select Committee on the European Communities.

*Oxford Economic Papers* 49 (1997), 228–234

# REGIONALISM AND THE REST OF THE WORLD: THE IRRELEVANCE OF THE KEMP–WAN THEOREM

*By* L. ALAN WINTERS

*International Trade Division, International Economics Department, The World Bank, 1818 H Street NW, Washington, DC 20433, USA*

Many commentators purport to use the Kemp–Wan Theorem to discuss the effects of region integration schemes on non-member countries, and to operationalize the theorem in terms the share of member countries' imports coming from non-members. I show that Kemp ar Wan say nothing about changes in non-member welfare and that the latter is more close related to non-members' imports than to their shares of members' markets. I suggest th a new approach to this issue is required.

## 1. Introduction

TWENTY years ago Murray Kemp and Henry Wan (1976) showed that, und very general circumstances, a customs union between any sub-set of countri could be designed to leave non-member countries indifferent to its creation an member countries better off. This rehabilitation of the idea that a customs unio can represent 'a step in the right direction' came to be known as the Kemp–Wa Theorem and remains today one of the most elegant pieces of reasoning i international economics.

This note shows that most current scholars appealing to what they call tl 'Kemp–Wan Theorem' or 'Criterion' or 'Test' mean something complete different from Kemp and Wan's argument, and frequently something rath misleading. Kemp–Wan is now commonly cited as a basis for determinir whether the creation of a customs union benefits the rest of the world, and operationalized by asking whether the union has increased or decrease non-members' exports to members either absolutely or relative to the latter total imports or consumption. Kemp and Wan never proposed such a test criterion, and in the context of their model, an increase in non-member expor is, at best, only imprecisely and indirectly related to welfare. This paper discuss these two propositions, as well as briefly commenting on possible reforms the GATT's Article XXIV, which governs customs union formation.

## 2. What Kemp and Wan actually said

There are so many examples of the misuse of the epithet 'Kemp–Wan' that is invidious to single out any individual citation. Nonetheless, for the sake concreteness, I quote three in increasing order of confusion. Sapir (1992), in a important and influential assessment of European integration, implies tl existence of an operational test in terms of tariff levels. He observes that tl combination of the formation of the EEC and the liberalizations undertaken in the GATT's Dillon and Kennedy Rounds reduced average tariffs on France, Italy, and Benelux's manufactured imports from non-members and only slightly raised those on Germany's imports. From this he concludes, without further comment, that 'with respect to manufacturing the EC meets the Vanek–Kemp–Wan test. She has sufficiently lowered her common external tariff to ensure that the rest of the world is, in general, at least as well off as it would have been, *ceteris paribus*, in the absence of integration.'

McMillan (1993), in an essay on regional integration arrangements (RIAs) and the rest of the world implies a test and operationalizes it in terms of trade flows. He states:

> I have suggested that the best test for judging whether a RIA is harmful is the simplest possible: does the agreement result in less trade [defined as the volume of imports into the RIA] between member countries and outsider countries? If the answer to this question is no, then the RIA is consistent with open trade, as the Kemp–Vanek theorem shows: the agreement makes its member countries better off without making the outsider countries worse off.

This view is echoed given a simple temporal dimension by the IMF (1994) '[T]he insight of Kemp and Wan might be used to assess welfare effects . . . if the volume of imports into a region is at least as great as the volume imported prior to the regional grouping, it would suggest that the Kemp–Wan criteria have been met and that the grouping is welfare improving.'

But what did Kemp and Wan actually say?

Kemp and Wan (1976), and before them but less clearly, Kemp (1964) and Ohyama (1972), made powerful use of the fundamental theorem of welfare economics to show that, following the creation of a customs union, one can freeze members' trade with the rest of the world by selecting a suitable common external tariff. The fundamental theorem argues that any competitive equilibrium can be supported by some price vector. Kemp and Wan ask what internal price vector within the customs union (i.e. after the removal of tariffs on inter-member trade) would generate just the same level and composition of trade (and hence of prices) with the rest of the world as the partners collectively undertook before union. The required common external tariff is then the difference between this and the (by construction, unchanged) world price vector. This result refers to non-member welfare, but offers no basis for making welfare assessments of the effect of any other integration scheme on the rest of the world, not least because this was not at all the purpose of the exercise.[1]

Kemp and Wan bring the rest of the world into their analysis thus: 'Here we merely note that there exists a common tariff vector which leaves world prices, and therefore the trade and welfare of non-members, at their pre-union

[1] Baldwin and Venables (1996) trace the origins of Kemp and Wan's insight back to Meade (1955). Panagariya (1996), however, rebuts such an attribution. He shows, *inter alia*, that Meade's analysis held trade barriers (*QR*s in his case) fixed, not trade, and that Meade, correctly, made no claim that in his model the rest of the world was hurt, helped, or unaffected by the integration examined.

levels.' There is no further reference to non-members, and no hint that any particular deviation from the 'Kemp–Wan' tariff would help or harm the rest of the world; still less is a Kemp–Wan criterion or test enunciated. The trick of freezing trade and world prices is a means of setting the rest of the world on one side so that changes in union welfare (which in this case must be non-negative) represent changes in world welfare. Indeed, given the extreme generality of the model—which is one of its great beauties—it is difficult to see how it could be more informative about non-member welfare, for with no restriction on pre-union tariffs, taxes or subsidies, and only mild restrictions on utility and production functions, there is no means within the model of identifying whether an increase in a particular trade flow would be welfare-enhancing or not.[2]

## 3. Non-member trade and welfare

Although Kemp and Wan did not deal with changes in non-member welfare, maybe their apparatus can be adapted to this task by others. Certainly, it seems attractive, if we can identify the origin of a welfare measure, to try also to identify its slope around that point. One can, but at the cost of generality—so much, in fact, that the model becomes merely a common or garden competitive neoclassical model. This is illustrated in Fig. 1 which plots the offer curve of the supposed sole non-member country in a two-good world.[3] For convenience the goods are labeled *M*, the non-member's import, and *X*, its export. The terms of trade line and the social indifference curve in the figure refer to the initial, pre-union, equilibrium *E*, and we consider the impact on welfare of movements from that point.

First, assume that the non-member's offer-curve is fixed and that integration, by affecting the union-members' net offer curve affects the point chosen along it. We would normally assume that integration would contract the union's offer curve, for, with more intra-union trade, extra-union trade is less important. This would generate a new equilibrium, *N*, in which non-member welfare is lower and in which non-member exports to the union have fallen.

Alternatively, however, integration may enlarge the union's supply of exportables and/or demand for importables, pushing its offer-curve upwards and generating new equilibria like *P* or *Q*. In the former, both non-member welfare and exports have risen, whereas in the latter, which rests on the inelastic segment of the offer-curve, welfare has risen but exports have fallen. This suggests that while an increase in exports is sufficient to indicate an increase in non-member welfare, it is not necessary, but even this would be incorrect if we had started

[2] See Bliss (1994), Krishna and Bhagwati (1994), and Richardson (1995) for insightful analyses of other aspects of the Kemp–Wan theorem, and Srinivasan and Park (1996) for a useful operationalization of it.

[3] Kemp and Wan require that trade be frozen for every commodity and every non-member country. McMillan (1993) recognizes the potential aggregation errors entailed in his assessment of total non-members exports, but this is not a conceptual problem in a two-good model.

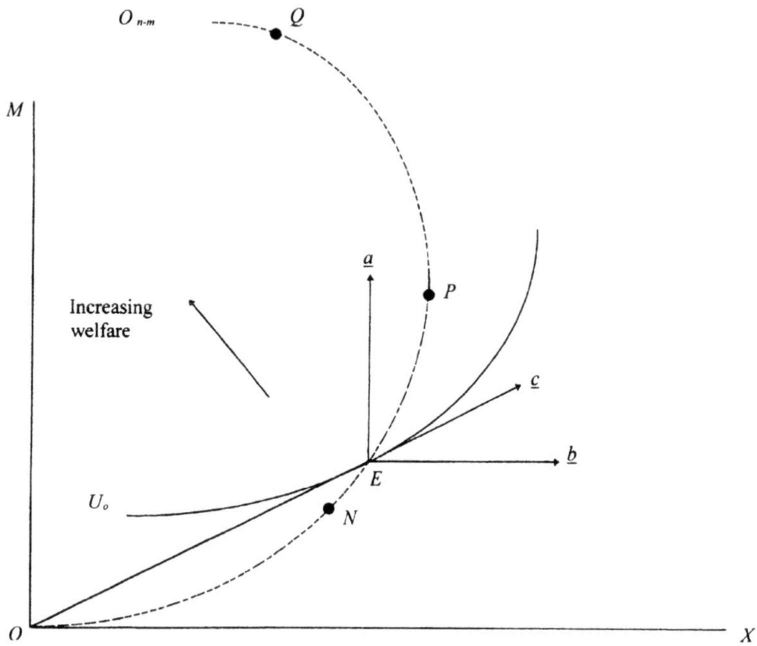


FIG. 1. Non-members' welfare: deviations from the initial equilibrium

from $Q$ and integration had carried us to $P$ or $E$. The two measures which show the direct, necessary and sufficient connection to non-member welfare are non-member imports and non-member terms of trade. It is these that should be the focus of our measurement efforts.

To re-inforce the last point consider the slopes of the welfare surface around the initial equilibrium, $E$. An increase in imports, shown by vector $\underline{a}$, is unambiguously welfare-improving, whereas an (unrequited) increase in exports ($\underline{b}$) is welfare-worsening, as is a balanced increase in exports and imports valued at the initial terms of trade ($\underline{c}$). To identify welfare improvements via increased exports is like judging how good a party was by the size of your hang-over: it may be indicative, but only because more of the measured bad is associated with even more of the unmeasured good.

Figure 1 assumes that the non-member country practices free trade. If instead it levied a tariff on its import ($M$), the indifference curve through $E$ would be tangential to the domestic price ratio rather than to the international price ratio, $OE$. Since the former would have a shallower slope than the latter, this would amount diagrammatically to rotating $U_0U_0$ clockwise about $E$. It is immediately clear that all the propositions advanced above would follow through except for the last: a small expansion of trade at the original terms of trade ($\underline{a}$) would now be welfare enhancing.[4]

To my knowledge, there are no *ex post* studies of integration and the terms of trade (see Winters, 1995) but in Winters (1985) I explored the effect of UK accession on the direction of UK manufactured exports. Interestingly, I found evidence that exports to some non-members—i.e. non-member imports from one of the partners in the enlarged customs union—were lower as a result of integration.

Turning briefly to the practical aspects of measuring the effects of integration, two points should be made. First, one needs to isolate the effect of integration, i.e. to define the *anti-monde*. *Ex post* measurement of the effects of integration occurs over real time, during which the offer-curves will shift for exogenous reasons. It is perfectly possible that while integration shrinks the member offer-curve inwards, and thus *ceteris paribus* reduces non-member welfare, economic growth shifts that of non-members outwards sufficiently to increase non-member exports overall. Again, non-member exports will be a misleading indicator of the welfare effects. Given the rapid growth in the supply of manufactures from Japan and developing countries since the 1960s, it is not difficult to believe, for example, that this problem could beset estimates of the effects of European integration.

Second, the practice of measuring the share of union members' imports or apparent consumption coming from non-members makes some sense for assessing the former's welfare—some rate of decline in this share would indicate trade division and hence threats to members' welfare. It makes less sense for non-members, however, for even setting aside the weaknesses of looking at non-member exports, it is the level of trade, possibly normalized by total non-member trade or GDP, not its share in union imports, that matters. The best justication for considering the share of imports is that one is assuming that in the *anti-monde* shares in total member imports would have been constant.

## 4. GATT's Article XXIV

McMillan (1993), among others, has suggested amending the GATT's Article XXIV to make customs unions 'GATT-consistent' only if they do not cause trade volumes to be lowered. I have a quite different view of that Article. First, as noted above, McMillan actually considers the union's import volume not its trade volume: exports would have been better. Second, it is immensely difficult to define an *anti-monde* in practice and trying to do so would probably tie up the WTO's consideration of customs unions for years. Third, McMillan's proposal is essentially outcome-oriented trade policy not instrument-oriented

[4] I am grateful to a referee for suggesting that I include this case. For an algebraic demonstration of the same point, see Winters (1995).

policy. The latter is better both in theory and in practice, as, for example, the slightest acquaintance with the Multi-Fiber Arrangement demonstrates.

## 5. Conclusion

I have argued that, in assessing the effects of economic integration, a non-member's share of member countries' imports is only tenuously related to its economic welfare. A more direct and useful link would be to the non-member's imports and the terms of trade. That we do not explore these latter variables partly reflects the practical difficulties involved (see Winters and Chang, 1996), but it also reflects, I think, economists accommodating a mercantilist mode of thought among policymakers that cannot conceive of benefits arising from importing nor costs from exporting.

It is true that if we abandon the simple competitive model for a more sophisticated one in which exports generate rents, we would place somewhat more weight on non-members' exports as a welfare indicator. They would still not be the dominant measure, however, but would need to be combined with factors such as the terms of trade, tariff revenue, economies of scale, variety, output, domestic distortions, investment, technology, and various other dynamic factors. In Winters (1995) I have shown how one might explore non-member welfare in these terms using the welfare decomposition developed by Baldwin and Venables (1995).

My second conclusion is that there is no such thing as a Kemp–Wan criterion or test. In particular, economists would be truer to their scientific ideals and fairer to their policymakers if henceforth they completely dissociated the pseudo-scientific term 'Kemp–Wan' from the discussion of non-member exports to a customs union.

## Acknowledgements

I am grateful to Won Chang for research assistance, to Audrey Kitson-Walters and Minerva Pateña for logistical support, and to Richard Baldwin, Jagdish Bhagwati, Uri Dadush, Murray Kemp, Arvind Panagariya, André Sapir, Maurice Schiff, Jim Tybout, and two referees for comments on an earlier version of this paper.

The views expressed here are the author's alone. They do not necessarily represent those of the World Bank or any of its member governments.

## REFERENCES

Baldwin, R. E. and Venables, A. J. (1966). 'Regional Economic Integration', in *Handbook of International Economics*, III, North-Holland, Amsterdam (forthcoming).

Bliss, C. (1994). *Economic Theory and Policy for Trading Blocks*, Manchester University Press, Manchester and New York, NY.

IMF (1994). *International Trade Policies: the Uruguay Round and Beyond—Volume II, Background Papers*, IMF, Washinton, DC.

Kemp, M. C. (1964). *The Pure Theory of International Trade*, Prentice-Hall, Englewood Cliffs, NJ.

KEMP, M. C., and WAN, H. Y. (1976). 'An Elementary Proposition concerning the Formation of Customs Unions', *Journal of International Economics*, **6**, 95–7.

KRISHNA, P. and BHAGWAI, J. (1994). 'Necessarily Welfare-Enhancing Customs Unions with Industrialization Constraints: a Proof of the Cooper-Massell-Johnson-Bhagwati Conjecture', mimeo, Columbia University, New York, NY.

MCMILLAN, J. (1993). 'Does Regional Integration Foster Open Trade: Economic Theory and GATT's Article XXIV', in K. Anderson and R. Blackhurst (eds), *Regional Integration and the Global Trading System*, Harvester Wheatsheaf, Hemel Hempstead, 292–309.

MEADE, J. E. (1955). *The Theory of Customs Unions*, North-Holland, Amsterdam.

OHYAMA, M. (1972). 'Trade and Welfare in General Equilibrium', *Keio Economic Studies*, **9**, 37–73.

PANAGARIYA, A. (1996). 'The Meade Model of Preferential Trading: History, Analytics and Policy Implications', mimeo, University of Maryland, MD.

RICHARDSON, M. (1995). 'On the Interpretation of the Kemp–Wan Theorem', *Oxford Economic Papers*, **47**, 696–703.

SAPIR, A. (1992). 'Regional Integration in Europe', *The Economic Journal*, **102**, 1,491–506.

SRINIVASAN, T. N. and PARK, S. C., JR. (1996). 'The Common External Tariff of a Customs Union: Alternative Approaches', mimeo, Yale University, CT.

WINTERS, L. A. (1985). 'Separability and the Modelling of UK Exports to Five Countries', *European Economic Review*, **27**, 335–53.

WINTERS, L. A. (1995). 'European Integration and Economic Welfare in the Rest of the World,' paper given to a conference on 'European Economic Integration,' Association Française de Science Economiques and Centre d'Etude sur l'Economie Internationale et l'Enterprise, Nantes, June 1995.

WINTERS, L. A. and CHANG, W. (1996). 'Integration and Non-Member Welfare: Measuring the Price Effects,' mimeo, The World Bank, Washington, DC.

# How Regional Blocs Affect Excluded Countries: The Price Effects of MERCOSUR

*By* WON CHANG AND L. ALAN WINTERS*

*The welfare effects of PTAs are most directly linked to changes in trade prices, i.e., the terms of trade. This paper employs a simple strategic pricing game in segmented markets to measure the effects of MERCOSUR on the pricing of "nonmember" exports to Brazil: As Brazil exempts its MERCOSUR partners from tariffs, the resulting competitive pressure leads other exporters to reduce their prices. Working with detailed data on unit values and tariffs we find that the creation of MERCOSUR was associated with significant declines in the prices of nonmembers' exports to the region.* (*JEL* F13, F15).

Preferential Trading Arrangements (PTAs) are an integral and enduring part of the multilateral trading regime. Between 1990 and 1999, 87 PTAs were notified to the World Trade Organization (WTO), and nearly all signatories of the WTO are currently members of at least one PTA. Despite such widespread existence, concerns continue about the welfare effects of PTAs, especially on excluded countries. The effects of PTAs on the volume and quantities of trade are studied quite frequently but, as Winters (1997a, b) argues, these variables are not a reliable guide to welfare effects for nonmember countries. The latter are more directly related to price effects, and of these little is known. Indeed, there is, to our knowledge, only one published *ex post* study of the price effects of a PTA on its trading partners: Winters and Chang (2000).

This paper examines the effect of MERCOSUR (a customs union between Argentina, Brazil, Paraguay, and Uruguay) on the prices of its imports from nonmembers. We focus on the Brazilian import market since it is large (eighth in the world by GDP) and, by far, the largest in MERCOSUR. It also provides good data over the time period of interest.

We postulate that nonmember firms' export prices to Brazil will be influenced not only by the tariffs that they face, but also by the tariffs that their rivals in member countries face, via the effect of the latter on the rivals' prices. We estimate both such responses from commodity-level export data from Brazil's major overseas suppliers. The first effect, known as "pass-through," has previously been estimated for other markets, but the second, which is a result of competitive price interactions between member and nonmember firms, has never been investigated before.

MERCOSUR nations have made significant tariff adjustments over our sample period (1991–1996). In addition to unilateral most-favored nation (m.f.n.) reforms over 1989–1995, they

* Chang: International Economist, U.S. Department of the Treasury, Office of International Trade, 1500 Pennsylvania Avenue, NW, Washington, DC 20220 (e-mail: won.chang@do.treas.gov). Winters: Professor of Economics, School of Social Sciences, University of Sussex, Falmer, BRIGHTON, BN1 9QN, United Kingdom (e-mail: L.A.Winters@Sussex.ac.uk); Centre for Economic Policy Research, 90-98 Goswell Road, London, EC1V 7DB, England; and Centre for Economic Performance, London School of Economics, Houghton Street, London WC2A 2AE, England. This work was partly conducted while the authors were consultant and research manager in the Development Research Group of the World Bank. The views expressed in this paper are those of the authors and should not be attributed to the World Bank, its member governments, or the U.S. Department of the Treasury. The authors are grateful to Kyle Bagwell, Jagdish Bhagwati, Stephen Cameron, Richard Clarida, Antoni Estevadeordal, Junichi Goto, Ann Harrison, Ken Leonard, Will Martin, John McLaren, Andrew Newell, Robert Mundell, Marcelo Olarreaga, Maurice Schiff, Forhad Shilpi, Isidro Soloaga, Anthony Venables, and Stan Wellisz, to two anonymous referees, and to participants in the seminars at the Inter-American Development Bank, the World Bank, the Universities of Kent, Nottingham, and Sussex, and Columbia University for excellent comments. They are also grateful to Rosie Bellinger for logistical help.

largely abolished tariffs on intra-MERCOSUR trade over 1991–1995 and adopted a new common external tariff (CET) over 1995–1996. The sizes and different phasing of these adjustments, plus the exceptions to both the CET and internal free trade—see Marcelo Olarreaga and Isidro Soloaga (1998)—mean that the margins of preference on internal trade show considerable variation both through time and across commodities. This helps us to identify their effects empirically.

In the remainder of the paper, Section I summarizes the literature on the effects of PTAs on nonmembers and on identifying price effects empirically. Section II discusses some stylized facts and descriptive statistics on the major exporters to the Brazilian market. They suggest quite strong movements in relative prices. Section III briefly presents a model of pricing, from which we derive a reduced-form estimation equation. The model has two firms, a "nonmember" and a "member" firm, exporting a differentiated product to the Brazilian market and to the rest of the world (RoW). The two firms respond to each other's prices (as well as to their own tariffs, exchange rates, and costs), playing a Bertrand pricing game within the Brazilian market. We explore the game by examining the prices of nonmember exports to Brazil relative to those of their exports to the RoW. Section IV discusses the empirical implementation of the model and provides details of MERCOSUR's tariff policy during the integration period. Section V presents some results that suggest strongly that both m.f.n. and preferential tariff changes affect supplier prices significantly, and that MERCOSUR's preferential tariffs caused significant declines, ceteris paribus, in the prices of nonmembers' exports to Brazil.

## I. Price Effects of Trade Policy

One of the major influences on the welfare of any trading economy is its terms of trade, and thus questions surrounding trade policy should be concerned with this variable. But given its importance in theory this issue is addressed surprisingly rarely in empirical studies. The seminal contribution was Mordechai E. Kreinin (1961) which considered the effects of U.S. m.f.n. tariff concessions during the postwar years. Kreinin argues that a reduction in U.S. tariffs would most directly affect posttariff import prices and that only through this medium would changes in the volume of imports occur. He also shows that U.S. m.f.n. tariff concessions did indeed lead to considerable changes in foreign export prices.[1]

By the same token the empirical analysis of the effects of PTAs should be at least as concerned with price as with volume effects. An elegant but relatively unremarked theoretical examination of the terms of trade effect of regional integration is given by Robert Mundell (1964). He elucidates the terms of trade effects in a three-country general-equilibrium model in which goods are gross substitutes, and in which price changes occur to restore balance of payments equilibrium after an initial preferential tariff shock occurs. He shows that for a single tariff change by one member, the preferred exporting partner's terms of trade unambiguously improve, while the excluded country's deteriorate. The net effect of the active country's tariff concessions on its own terms of trade is ambiguous, but when two countries swap preferential concessions, as in a PTA, they collectively improve their terms of trade vis-à-vis the rest of the world.

More recent studies focusing on PTAs such as Kyle Bagwell and Robert W. Staiger (1998, 1999) also show that the multilateral negotiations of the GATT based on the principles of *reciprocity* and *nondiscrimination* foster efficient outcomes which allow governments to escape from a terms-of-trade-driven Prisoner's Dilemma. The authors argue that PTA formation could enable member countries to exploit greater market power over their terms of trade and potentially undermine the efficient outcome of multilateral negotiations.

The last result is potentially very significant, for the terms of trade is by far the most direct way in which PTAs affect economic welfare in the RoW. Precisely paralleling Kreinin's complaint, the usual empirical approach to assessing the effects of a PTA is to ask whether, as a result of integration, the RoW's exports to the

[1] Kreinin states that "less than a third ... of the tariff concessions granted by the U.S. were passed on to the U.S. consumer in the form of reduced import prices, while more than two-thirds ... accrued to the foreign suppliers and improved the terms of trade of the exporting nations."

integrating bloc increase (which is held to be good) or decrease (bad). Winters (1997a) shows that this is a very inadequate indicator: first, RoW welfare will be related to its imports not its exports, and second, in a competitive economy, marginal changes in quantities hardly matter, whereas changes in the prices of traded goods matter considerably.[2]

Winters (1997b) observes that the RoW's terms of trade do figure in a number of *ex ante* studies of PTAs (although frequently with little emphasis), but that surprisingly, at that time, no *ex post* empirical study addressed the issue. Winters and Chang (2000) started to do so in the case of Spanish accession to the EC, but were severely hampered by a number of data difficulties that rendered their results indicative rather than definitive. This paper continues our efforts in a much more satisfactory empirical environment and generates stronger and more interesting results.

The empirical literature on which we build relies on the microeconomic foundations of imperfectly competitive and segmented markets. "Pass-through" studies examine the apparent lack of import price response following shocks in the exchange rate, and the consequent implication that foreign suppliers absorb exchange-rate shocks into their markup in order to maintain some degree of local currency price stability.[3] Notable contributions include Knetter (1989, 1993) and Robert C. Feenstra (1989). Knetter estimates the degree of price discrimination of major industrialized exporters employing very detailed commodity-level trade data and finds that price discrimination is prevalent even in industries whose products are seemingly homogeneous. His results suggest that the level of discrimination varies by supplying country as well as with the importance of the destination markets.[4] They imply that trade policy will affect export prices in ways that differ from the competitive law of one price. Feenstra (1989) estimates a markup model incorporating tariff changes in the U.S. market for motorcycles and trucks and obtains the useful result that changes in the exchange rate and in tariffs have equal effects on the final price of imports—his so-called "symmetry" hypothesis.

Feenstra and Knetter considered only the rivalry between domestic and imported varieties, with the former behaving wholly nonstrategically: they examined only the pass-through of the exchange rate and the m.f.n. tariff. For estimating the effects of PTAs, however, we have explicitly to model the pricing game that occurs between rival foreign suppliers within a market under consideration. In this setting, a firm's price depends not only on the tariff it faces on its own export product, but also on that charged on its rivals' product. When a member-country firm benefits from a preferential tariff concession it becomes more competitive in the PTA market, and nonmember firms are likely (although not bound) to reduce their prices in compensation. On the assumption that no such shock occurs in the RoW markets, the prices of nonmembers' exports to the PTA relative to those of their exports to the RoW will fall. Thus our empirical investigation must go well beyond that of the Feenstra-Knetter approach.

## II. Stylized Facts

Figure 1 plots the average price (unit value) of various suppliers' exports to Brazil relative to those of their exports to the RoW since the formation of MERCOSUR in 1991.[5] To render

[2] Winters also shows that, contrary to the common belief, Murray C. Kemp and Henry Y. Wan, Jr. (1976) said nothing about whether RoW's welfare increases or decreases in the face of a PTA. They showed how it could be kept constant, completely obviating the need to discuss its determinants.

[3] Several papers analyze incomplete pass-through in the face of exchange-rate fluctuations: for example, theoretical papers by Rudiger Dornbusch (1987), Paul R. Krugman (1987), and Richard Baldwin (1988), and cross-sectional industry empirics by Catherine L. Mann (1986), Kenneth Froot and Paul Klemperer (1989), Michael M. Knetter (1989, 1993), Lawrence Schembri (1989) and Richard C. Marston (1990).

[4] For example, Knetter (1989) shows that U.S. exporters' prices were generally rather insensitive, or even amplified the effect of exchange-rate fluctuations, while German exporters, on the other hand, were likely to exhibit "local currency price stabilization" in destination markets, especially the United States. He attributes the latter to the high shares of the U.S. market in their total sales.

[5] Because no price data are available we have to use unit value data, but since these are available at the 6-digit level of the Harmonized System (HS-6) that distinguishes 5,113 commodities, we can have reasonable confidence in their accuracy. The 6-digit Harmonized System became the standard

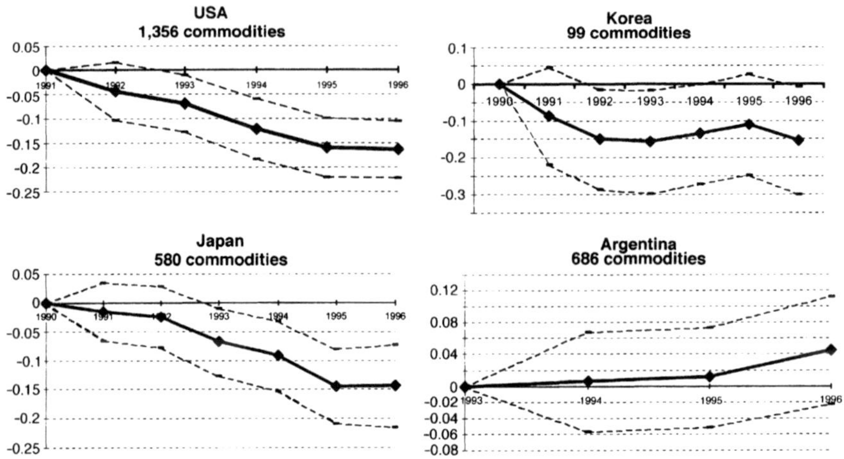


FIGURE 1. EXPORT PRICES TO BRAZIL RELATIVE TO EXPORT PRICES TO THE REST OF THE WORLD

commodities comparable, the starting-year price has been normalized to be 1 for each commodity so that we are essentially measuring price changes. To be precise we plot the following statistic:

$$\frac{1}{N}\sum_{i=1}^{N}\ln\left(\frac{\bar{p}_{1it}/\bar{p}_{2it}}{\bar{p}_{1i90}/\bar{p}_{2i90}}\right)$$

$$i = (1, \ldots, N) \quad t = (1, \ldots, T)$$

where the first subscript (1 or 2) represents prices paid in Brazil and RoW, respectively, the second ($i = 1, \ldots, N$) indicates the commodity, and the third ($t = 1, \ldots, T$) is time, with the beginning year as base. The bars above the prices indicate that these are pretariff prices in U.S. dollars ($).

The figure averages prices only over the set of commodities for which we have observations for all years for both markets, and considers four major exporters to Brazil: the United States (for which 1,356 commodities were exported to both markets in all years), Japan (580), Korea (99), and Argentina (686). The broken lines give the 95-percent confidence interval about the means. To infer from Figure 1 an effect of MERCOSUR on prices, we have implicitly to employ RoW as the *anti-monde*. On this basis nonmembers' relative prices of exports to Brazil declined by approximately 15 percent between 1991 and 1996, a phenomenon that certainly requires some explanation.[6] Conversely, for Brazil's PTA partner, Argentina, relative pretariff prices to Brazil increased, as predicted by theory. This latter result is weak, however, presumably because data on the critical years 1991 and 1992, during which the major tariff reductions occurred, are missing.[7]

classification for trade and tariff data across countries starting in 1989. Unfortunately, many countries started reporting well after that date, and there is no other way to obtain data of this level and precision for earlier years. This means that our sample of exporters is severely constrained, and that even among our chosen set, sample sizes vary.

[6] Similar results for U.S. exports have been obtained using the data provided in Feenstra (1997).

[7] We have also examined absolute export prices—see Chang and Winters (1999). The United States' and Korea's absolute prices to Brazil declined by approximately 10 percent following the shock of MERCOSUR while their absolute prices to the RoW were stable or moderately increasing. Absolute dollar prices of Japan to Brazil rose (reflecting the yen's appreciation with respect to the dollar during this period) but by less than her export prices in general.

These descriptive statistics match our expectations surprisingly well and clearly make a prima facie case for further investigation. Moreover, they refer to significant volumes of international trade. In 1996, for example, Brazilian imports of goods amounted to $56.5 billion: $12.5 billion from the United States (22.2 percent of the total), $7.1 billion from Argentina (12.6 percent), $5 billion from Germany (8.8 percent), $3.1 billion from Italy (5.4 percent), and $2.9 billion from Japan (5.1 percent). The other suppliers for which we can get data are Korea and Chile, which account for $1.3 and $1.0 billion (2.2 percent and 1.8 percent), respectively. At the commodity level the United States has a share of 10 percent or more of Brazilian imports in 60 percent of the 5,113 HS-6 product headings, Argentina in 17 percent, Germany in 30 percent, Italy in 16 percent, Japan in 12 percent, Korea in 5 percent, and Chile in 5 percent. These last statistics indicate that these exporters may well have significant market power in Brazil.

## III. The Model

While Figure 1 is impressive, it is a weak basis for inference because any number of things could have affected prices over that period. Thus, we now have to include a series of controls and model the effects of MERCOSUR more formally. We use a parsimonious model of export pricing to illustrate the effects we expect to find and guide our formal estimation. For each good we distinguish two segmented markets, Brazil and the RoW, and two exporting firms, a nonmember firm from outside MERCOSUR and a member firm from inside (always Argentina in our case).[8] The firms supply differentiated products and maximize profits in their own currency by manipulating duty-paid prices in their markets ($p$). They take their input costs, exchange rates, and tariffs as given. Costs ($\tilde{c}(x, w)$) are homogeneous of degree one in the price of a composite factor, loosely referred to here as the wage ($w$). Thus $\tilde{c}(x, w) = wc(x)$ where $x$ is output and $c(x)$ is unit costs.

The demand for the nonmember's differentiated product in Brazil (market 1) is given by $x_1(p_1, p_1^*, Q_1, Y_1)$, a function of its own price, $p$, its major rival's (Argentina) product price, $p^*$, the aggregate price index, $Q$, and nominal national income, $Y$, in Brazil. The demand for its product in the RoW (market 2) is a function of its own price, the aggregate price level and national income in RoW, $x_2(p_2, Q_2, Y_2)$. We are assuming here that Argentina is a sufficiently large supplier to the Brazilian market that the nonmember firm's demand may be related to Argentina's prices, but that it is so insignificant in RoW markets that no separate Argentina price effect will be identifiable.[9] The nonmember firm's objective function and first-order condition in market $i = \{1, 2\}$ may be written as

$$\text{(1)} \qquad \max_{p_1, p_2} \left[ \frac{e_1}{\tau_1} p_1 x_1(p_1, p_1^*, Q_1, Y_1) + \frac{e_2}{\tau_2} p_2 x_2(p_2, Q_2, Y_2) - c_1(x_1)w - c_2(x_2)w \right]$$

$$\text{(2)} \qquad p_i \left[ 1 + \frac{1}{\eta_{ip}} \right] - \frac{w\tau_i}{e_i} c_{ix}(x_i(p_i, p_i^*, Q_i, Y_i)) = 0$$

$$\eta_{ip} = \frac{\partial x_i}{\partial p_i} \frac{p_i}{x_i}$$

where, in addition to the variables already defined, $\tau_1$, and $\tau_2$, are the ad valorem tariff factors $(1 + t)$ charged by Brazil and RoW, and $e_1$, and $e_2$, the supplier countries' currency prices of a Brazilian REAL and RoW currency. Note that the price elasticities, $\eta_1$, and $\eta_2$, are potentially affected by the same variables as demand, and that as noted above $\partial x_2 / \partial p_2^* \equiv 0$.

[8] We concentrate on the two largest traders of MERCOSUR, Argentina and Brazil, because Paraguay and Uruguay are so small and their data so sparse.

[9] The assumption is reasonable. Argentina's share of Brazil's imports exceeds 5 percent in 22.6 percent of all HS-6 headings, but in only 3.1 percent of headings in the RoW even using our limited set of exporters to define world sales.

The first-order conditions imply that, for any market and supplier, an increase in either the tariff or the supplying country's exogenous wage, or a decrease in the exchange rate will increase the marginal cost of delivering exports. The supplying firm must therefore increase its marginal revenue by altering its landed price ($p$). Exactly how depends on how the price elasticity of demand changes as we move along the demand curve.

The member (Argentine) firm's objective function chooses prices $p_1^*$ and $p_2^*$ to maximize peso profits. It generates precisely analogous first-order conditions to (2) except in that demand in RoW depends explicitly on both Argentine and nonmember prices, with the latter being treated as exogenous.

By assuming that the two markets are segmented and have independent cost functions we are making them strategically separable, so that we can develop two separate pricing equations.[10] In Brazil the U.S. firm prices according to

$$p_1 = f_1\left(\frac{w\tau_1}{e_1},\, p_1^*,\, Q_1,\, Y_1\right) \tag{3}$$

and correspondingly (excluding $p_2^*$) in the RoW. Again, Argentina's pricing equations are perfectly analogous. Each of these pricing equations is homogeneous of degree one in costs, competitor's price, the aggregate price, and nominal income in local currency.

Firms are assumed to play a Bertrand game in the Brazilian market, so solving the nonmember's reaction function for Brazil and the analogous equation for the Argentine firms and taking a log-linear approximation we obtain a reduced-form equation.[11]

$$\ln p_1 = A_1 + \beta_1 \ln \frac{w\tau_1}{e_1} + \delta_1^* \ln \frac{w^*\tau_1^*}{e_1^*} + \alpha_1 \ln Q_1 + \lambda_1 \ln Y_1. \tag{4}$$

The corresponding equation for the RoW market is recursive, with Argentine firms reacting to U.S. prices but not vice versa. That is, the term relating $p_2$ to Argentinian costs $(w^*\tau_2/e_2^*)$ is omitted.[12]

Feenstra (1989) uses a variant of equation (4) to show that for U.S. imports of Japanese trucks and cycles, the long-run pass-through of tariffs and exchange rates are statistically identical. Essentially, he focuses on the m.f.n. changes, $\beta_1$ in the equation. We, however, focus on the policy effects of PTAs on the nonmember exporter, i.e., on $\delta_1^*$ which captures the effects of the rival's preferential tariff changes, $\tau_1^*$. If marginal costs are fixed then the expected sign of $\delta_1^*$ depends only on how the nonmember firm's "perceived" price elasticity of demand is altered by the preference-induced reduction of its rival's price. If the nonmember's demand becomes more elastic, then the optimal response is to reduce price; $\delta_1^* > 0$, and in the framework of Jeremy I. Bulow et al. (1985), the rivals' prices are "strategic complements." This is what one would expect under price competition. The less likely (strategic substitutes) outcome is that a reduction in the Argentine price causes the nonmember's demand curve to become less elastic locally, hence making it optimal to raise its price.[13]

While equations of type (4) are estimable directly it is intuitively easier and econometrically more efficient to combine them into a series of relative price equations. We are interested in the price changes in exports to Brazil relative to those of exports to the RoW which we treat as our *anti-monde*. Using the homogeneity assumption (i.e., $\alpha_1 = 1 - \beta_1 - \delta_1^* - \lambda_1$) we get the following:

[10] There is strong evidence to support that markets are in fact segmented—see, for example, Knetter (1989) and Marston (1990).

[11] In accordance with the symmetry hypothesis, we have given the tariff and wage the same coefficients in equation (4), but in our estimations we separate out the tariffs and test for symmetry.

[12] In addition, we have practically to write the RoW equation without the tariff terms, i.e., without $\tau_2$, because this variable is considered fixed over our sample period. In fact these rates did change slightly over time, but very much less than the MERCOSUR tariff rates. In any case, since we have no data on "world" tariffs, these variables must either be taken as constant, or absorbed into the error term as white noise.

[13] Further analysis and interpretations of the coefficients and comparative statics is given in Chang and Winters (1999).

$$(5)\quad \ln\frac{p_1/Q_1}{p_2/Q_2} = C + \beta_1 \ln\left[\frac{w\tau_1}{e_1 Q_1}\right] - \beta_2 \ln\left[\frac{w}{e_2 Q_2}\right] + \delta_1^* \ln\left[\frac{w^*\tau_1^*}{e_1^* Q_1}\right] + \lambda_1 \ln\left[\frac{Y_1}{Q_1}\right] - \lambda_2 \ln\left[\frac{Y_2}{Q_2}\right].$$

Knetter (1989) develops a slightly different approach to the relative price equation. For each exporter, he makes export prices to each market proportional to marginal costs (which are common across markets) applying a market-specific markup in the base period. Then allowing exchange-rate-induced movements along the demand curve to change the elasticity of demand, and hence the markup, he adds a term in the exchange rate whose coefficient determines the extent of pass-through. The ratio of two export prices determined in this way is independent of costs, which is very neat empirically. Unfortunately, however, it is not clear to us why a movement along the demand curve induced by an exchange-rate shock changes the elasticity of demand, while an equivalent movement due to a cost change does not.[14] We prefer the two shocks to have the same (market-specific) effect on the elasticity. This allows us to use a single parameter on $[w\tau_1/e_1Q_1]$ in equation (5) but at the expense of costs remaining in the relative price equation because markets might differ in the extent to which the elasticity of demand varies along the demand curve.

In summary, equation (5) is a price-discrimination model showing how much the nonmember's export price to Brazil changes relative to its export price to RoW.[15] Assuming that the latter is wholly independent of the formation of MERCOSUR, the coefficient on $\tau_1^*$ from equation (5) tells us how the tariff preferences inherent in MERCOSUR changed nonmember export prices. Figure 1 suggests that there were significant price effects through time and (5) helps to identify whether those are due to tariff changes (MERCOSUR) or to other factors.

## IV. Empirical Implementation

### A. *MERCOSUR's Tariff Policy*

MERCOSUR (Mercado Común del Sur) was established under the Treaty of Asunción, signed by the presidents of Argentina, Brazil, Paraguay, and Uruguay on March 26, 1991 and ratified on November 29, 1991. Article 5 of the Treaty defined a path of tariff liberalization to achieve zero internal tariffs and the elimination of nontariff barriers by the end of 1994. The immediate reduction of the internal applied tariff rates was by 47 percent of the m.f.n. rate after the ratification of the Treaty. Subsequent preferential reductions relative to prevailing m.f.n. rates were to occur semi-annually and automatically according to the following time table: 54 percent by December 1991, 61 percent by June 1992, 68 percent by December 1992, 75 percent by June 1993, 82 percent by December 1993, 89 percent by June 1994, and finally 100 percent by December 1994.[16] Members were allowed to declare up to 300 exceptions to internal free trade, but by 1995 approximately 95 percent of intraregional trade was duty-free (Sam Laird, 1997). In fact, Brazil had only 27 exceptions and so effectively had open borders for its MERCOSUR partners.

MERCOSUR member countries had originally planned to align their external tariffs on the MERCOSUR common external tariff by January 1, 1995. However, this proved politically impossible and little progress was made in defining the CET until the Protocol of Ouro Preto was signed in December 1994. Under the Ouro Preto Protocol the CET was to be introduced from the beginning of 1995. Each member was again allowed an exceptions list, the tariffs on which were to be aligned by 2001 for

[14] Nor why any changes in elasticities induced by cost changes would be the same (and hence cancel out) across markets.

[15] In Chang and Winters (1999) we also derive the equivalent equation to (5) for Argentine exporters and an equation for the relative prices of nonmember and Argentine exports of each good to Brazil.

[16] Article 3, Annex 1, Trade Liberalization Program, Treaty of Asunción, 1991.

Argentina and Brazil, and 2006 for Paraguay and Uruguay; see Olarreaga and Soloaga (1998). Brazil named approximately 200 tariff lines in the exceptions list, mainly sensitive industries such as computers, electronics, chemical, agroindustry, textiles, capital goods (machinery), and the automotive industry.

Unilateral liberalization, followed by these negotiated changes, reduced tariffs substantially in MERCOSUR countries, from an average of 50 percent in 1988 to a CET average of 12 percent in 1995. However, it remained the case that trade policy in Brazil was subject to vigorous debate and to frequent changes to meet short-run political objectives. For example, tariffs on textiles, toys, and motor vehicles in particular were increased to 70 percent for nonmembers in 1995.[17] The different phasing of internal and external tariff reductions, the large number of tariff rates, and the use of exceptions mean that over 1989–1996 (our sample period) tariffs and preference margins varied widely over time and commodities. This allows us a good chance of identifying their effects empirically.

### B. *Data*

The trade data from which we obtain unit values (as value/quantity) were taken from the UN's Comtrade database, at the Harmonized System (HS) 6-digit level. Although it was introduced in 1989 most countries did not start to use HS until somewhat later. Hence this exercise is constrained by data availability and our sample varies by country. We estimate the model for every significant exporter to Brazil for which we can muster six or more years' data.

HS 6-digit data offer two major advantages over other sources. First, they are very disaggregated: over 5,000 commodities are distinguished. This helps to minimize heterogeneity within each heading, which in turn improves the quality of our unit value data, and reduces the need for tariff averaging within headings. Second, trade and tariff data match very well at the 6-digit level, because at this level the HS classification is universal across countries. At finer levels of disaggregation codes are country specific.[18]

The tariff data were provided by United Nations Conference on Trade and Development (UNCTAD) (1996) and the MERCOSUR Secretariat (1996).[19] Over the years 1991–1994, Brazil and Argentina defined their tariff data at HS 10-digits, while the Common External Tariff (CET) of 1995 and 1996, and the exceptions listed in the agreement of Ouro Preto Protocol, are defined at the HS-8 digit level. In order to concord the tariff and the price data we truncated the tariff codes up to 6-digits and took simple averages. This averaging within the HS-6 level is not a serious problem, however, because there is very little variation in tariffs within the HS-6 digit groups.

As an empirical exercise on the price effects of integration, a study of MERCOSUR is relatively problem free. There are few problems of changes in quotas confounding price movements, since on signing of the Treaty of Asunción, all nontariff barriers (NTBs) were to be removed for all trade including imports from nonmembers.[20] Products having NTB measures before integration which could potentially affect prices over the series were deleted from our sample altogether.[21] Applied tariff rates are entirely ad valorem charged on the c.i.f. (cost, insurance, and freight) value of imports. There

[17] Motor vehicles have always been a special issue within Brazil. Coupled with the 70 percent tariffs, the Brazilian government applied special local content rules, under which firms that produced vehicles locally were given reduced rates of 35 percent. These rules (and similar ones in Argentina) prompted several multinationals to set up automobile plants within the MERCOSUR region.

[18] There is a slight discrepancy between the HS-6 digit codes in HS92 and HS96. Commodities have been deleted when such concordance problems arise between years.

[19] Most of the applied m.f.n. tariff rates charged to nonmembers including exceptions were compiled by UNCTAD. We are grateful to Aki Kuwahara of UNCTAD and Jerzy Rosanski of the World Bank for their help in obtaining them. Detailed information can be obtained in UNCTAD, "A User's Manual for TRAINS" (1996). The internal tariff rates are estimated using these m.f.n. rates and the Treaty of Asunción's time path for reductions. Brazil's detailed import and export data disaggregated by source country were also provided by Aki Kuwahara. Argentina's trade data, which we used later, was provided by Tony Estevadeordal and Raphael Cornejo of the Inter-American Development Bank to whom we are also grateful.

[20] See Laird (1997) and Claudio Frischtak et al. (1996). The abolition may not have been entirely clean in practice, but we understand that, in fact, few barriers persisted.

[21] This list, obtained from UNCTAD, includes products under quantity control measures such as quotas, and voluntary export restraints.

TABLE 1—HS-6 TARIFF AVERAGE (UNWEIGHTED) FOR NONMEMBER, MEMBER, AND PREFERENCE MARGIN YEAR FOR 1,356 PRODUCTS

| Year | M.f.n. | Partner | Preference margin[a] |
|---|---|---|---|
| 1991 | 25.9 | 25.9 | 0.0 |
| 1992 | 21.3 | 8.3 | 11.7 |
| 1993 | 14.9 | 3.7 | 10.7 |
| 1994 | 13.2 | 1.5 | 11.5 |
| 1995 | 13.0 | 0.0 | 13.0 |
| 1996 | 13.5 | 0.0 | 13.5 |

[a] The preference margin is calculated at the commodity level using $\{[(1 + t_{mfn})/(1 + t_{partner})] - 1\} \times 100$.

were no major prior associations between these countries and therefore changes in tariff preferences are defined by the Treaty of Asunción and the Ouro Preto Protocol. Finally, as noted previously, tariffs show a good deal of variation over time and commodities.

Since the tariff reductions took place semiannually (see above) we have averaged them for each year to match the annual trade data. Internal tariff rates were calculated as the m.f.n. rate multiplied by (1 − average reduction rate for that year). We have incorporated the exclusions to this rule included in the agreement of Ouro Preto Protocol in December 1994, which took effect in 1995, as well as the changes that occurred subsequent to this Protocol.[22]

Table 1 illustrates the evolution of Brazil's (unweighted) average tariffs on imports from the United States and Argentina.[23] The trend decline of m.f.n. rates is reversed in 1996, but the rapid approach to duty-free trade within MERCOSUR is evident. In the more detailed data there are many instances of rising m.f.n. rates over 1995–1996 (e.g., in foodstuffs, textiles and clothing, and vehicles) and of fluctuations in the margins of preference granted to MERCOSUR partners.

Member and nonmember wage rates or labor costs could not be obtained at the industry level and certainly not at the commodity level over our time period. Thus in order to obtain data and also to recognize a wider range of inputs than just labor, we used GDP deflators to proxy export country costs. These, and the requisite exchange rate data, were taken from the IMF, *International Financial Statistics*. We also used GDP deflators to represent aggregate price levels in Brazil and RoW.[24]

Finally, note that our sample is restricted to commodity headings that are supplied to Brazil by both the nonmember country we are considering and Argentina for at least three of our sample years. Although this raises the question of whether those product varieties exported by nonmembers but not by Argentina have also been affected by potential entrants within that product category, that is a different issue that will not be examined here.

## V. Results

### A. *Relative Export Prices*

Given the extreme noisiness of unit value data, we estimate equation (5) for each exporter by pooling all commodity data available. All variables are expressed in natural logs and as deviations from commodity-specific means. This is equivalent to allowing commodity-specific fixed effects. We also corrected for heteroscedasticity by collecting the residuals from the estimated unweighted equations and reweighting each of the variables by the inverse of the estimated commodity-specific residual standard deviations.[25] This procedure improves the efficiency of our estimates and permits more accurate inference.

[22] This list was provided by the MERCOSUR Secretariat (1996).

[23] This table refers only to our sample of 1,356 commodities that Brazil imports from the United States. However, Laird's (1997) calculations for all commodities have the same characteristics. More disaggregated data are given in Chang and Winters (1999).

[24] The GDP deflator for the world in dollar terms was taken to be an export-weighted average of the GDP deflators of supplying countries, with weights coming from the International Monetary Fund, *Direction of Trade Statistics: Yearbook* (1996, 1997). The representative countries included in the weighted average are: Belgium, Bolivia, Canada, Chile, China, Colombia, Denmark, France, United Kingdom, Germany, Indonesia, Italy, Korea, Mexico, Malaysia, Netherlands, Peru, Philippines, Singapore, the United States, and Venezuela.

[25] The homoscedasticity assumption was tested by using the loglikelihood-ratio test and the null was always strongly rejected. The prodedure adopted is a two-step Feasible Generalized Least-Squares (FGLS) estimation, which is unbiased. The coefficient estimates in the first-stage regressions were quite similar to the heteroscedasticity-corrected set and can be obtained from the authors on request. They yield very low $R$-squares, however.

TABLE 2—ESTIMATED COEFFICIENTS OF EQUATION (5) OVER ALL COMMODITIES: (A) WITHOUT AND (B) WITH TIME DUMMIES

A.

| Country (years) | $\tau$ | $\tau^*$ | $w/e_1Q_1$ | $w/e_2Q_2$ | $w^*/e_1^*Q_1$ | $R^2$ | EDF |
|---|---|---|---|---|---|---|---|
| Chile (1991–1996) | 1.353 (0.10) | 0.127 (0.08) | 0.828 (0.13) | −0.895 (0.17) | 0.091 (0.13) | 0.89 | 1,042 |
| Germany (1991–1996) | 0.737 (0.09) | 0.447 (0.08) | 1.081 (0.08) | −1.280 (0.17) | −0.033 (0.08) | 0.61 | 4,959 |
| Japan (1989–1996) | 1.071 (0.09) | 0.168 (0.07) | 1.083 (0.03) | −1.055 (0.05) | 0.015 (0.02) | 0.72 | 2,754 |
| Korea (1989–1996) | 0.184 (0.07) | 0.360 (0.06) | 1.385 (0.05) | −0.073 (0.12) | −0.145 (0.03) | 0.75 | 1,372 |
| USA (1991–1996) | 0.883 (0.08) | 0.445 (0.08) | 0.779 (0.16) | −0.843 (0.25) | 0.379 (0.16) | 0.60 | 5,463 |

B.

| Country | $\tau$ | $\tau^*$ | $R^2$ | EDF |
|---|---|---|---|---|
| Chile | 1.126 (0.13) | 0.711 (0.12) | 0.84 | 1,039 |
| Germany | 0.650 (0.10) | 0.827 (0.10) | 0.59 | 4,956 |
| Japan | 1.029 (0.11) | 0.370 (0.09) | 0.70 | 2,749 |
| Korea | 0.373 (0.13) | 0.838 (0.11) | 0.64 | 1,367 |
| USA | 0.881 (0.10) | 0.495 (0.09) | 0.58 | 5,460 |

*Notes:* Standard errors are beside the estimates in parentheses. All variables are in natural logs. EDF is error degrees of freedom.

Since we are primarily interested in the tariff effects, we separate tariffs from the other cost variables in our base equation (i.e., we do not impose symmetry). Also, multicollinearity made it very difficult to identify the real income effects, $\lambda_i \ln[Y_i/Q_i]$, empirically. This is presumably because such effects are small over short time periods and vary across commodities, and because, particularly in Brazil with its rampant inflation over the early 1990's, published data reflect actual income effects very poorly. Real income effects are not central to our thesis, however, so we feel comfortable with the following two responses to this problem.

First, we just dropped the real income terms; the results of doing this are reported in Table 2 (Panel A). Second, we swept out *all* the macroeconomic effects by including time dummies for each year, leaving tariffs as the only explanatory variables in the equation, as in Panel B. Since our focus is on tariff effects, this is quite attractive. All the time-variant but commodity-invariant macro-influences on relative prices are absorbed into the dummies, so we can be confident that what remains really does relate to trade policy. On the other hand, we have to recognize that such equations are likely to offer only very approximate predictions of prices. Accordingly, we prefer to consider both forms of the equation in reaching economic conclusions.

The results reported in Table 2 are quite intuitive. An increase in the exporter's costs ($w$) has hardly any effect on the relative prices of exports to Brazil and the RoW—both sets of prices rise roughly equally (i.e., $\beta_1 - \beta_2 \approx 0$). Changes in the prevailing prices in one or other of the markets ($Q_1$ or $Q_2$) get reflected, ceteris paribus, nearly one-for-one in the price of exports relative to prevailing prices. That is, $(1 - \beta_1 - \delta_1^*)$ and $(\beta_2 - 1)$ are fairly close to zero, so that export prices do not change very much. Changes in the exchange rate between the exporter's and one importer's currency ($e_1$ or $e_2$), on the other hand, do get reflected, again almost proportionately, in the price relatives. Changes in Argentina's costs, which impinge on the dependent variable via their effect on Argentina's export prices to Brazil and hence on other exporters' prices in that market, can be identified only for the United States as exporter. These results seem a little extreme, but given that they are not our focus of interest, not alarmingly so.

Turning to the tariff effects, the results are strong and consistent. In two cases, Chile and Japan, exporters seem to pass the full effect of tariffs on their goods through to purchasers, while for the other three, pass-through ranges from small to substantial. At the extreme, a change in the tariff on Korean suppliers seems to affect its export prices less than proportionately: tariff-inclusive prices rise by approximately one-fifth to one-third of the increase in the tariff, resulting in a substantial loss in revenue for these suppliers. For Germany and the United States the pass-through is much stronger, but still leaves the exporters bearing some of the import tax.

Even more interesting are the estimates of the effects of the tariffs levied on Argentinian exports to Brazil. These also appear to matter in nonmember pricing in the Brazilian market. In Table 2 (Panel A), ceteris paribus around one third of any tariff changes facing Argentinian exports is reflected in their rivals' posttariff (and hence pretariff) export prices. It is interesting to note that, again, Japan shows the least sensitivity of posttariff prices to tariff changes.[26] Table 2 (Panel B) confirms the important effect of Argentinian tariffs on other exporters' prices to Brazil. Its estimated effects are similar for the United States but larger—possibly implausibly so—for the other exporters.

There is no reason to believe that exporters' prices to RoW are responding materially to Brazil's tariffs against Argentina. Thus, overall, we take Table 2 as a strong indication that preferential tariff reductions in MERCOSUR forced down the pretariff export prices of nonmembers, turning, ceteris paribus, the terms of trade against them.

### B. *Additional Evidence*

In Chang and Winters (1999) we report three additional exercises which lend further support to our conclusion that tariff preferences impose terms-of-trade losses on excluded countries. These are briefly described here.

First, we have repeated the above exercise on data for each exporter disaggregated into nine subsets of commodities (Appendix). This allows for sector-specific differences, which seems useful, but at the expense of much smaller sample sizes, which, given the noisiness of our data and simplicity of model, is plainly a problem. The range of results, as reported in the Appendix, is unsurprisingly large, but among the 32 estimates with more than 100 error degrees of freedom, all the own-tariff elasticities except one are positive, with three-quarters below 1 and one-quarter of them significantly so. The coefficients on the rival (members') tariffs are positive and significant in 16 of these 32 cases and positive in seven others; they are positive in seven out of nine cases for the United States, our exporter with the largest sample (the exceptions being simple manufacturers [HS64–83] and miscellaneous manufacturers, art and arms [HS93–96]). There are five cases of significantly negative member-tariff coefficients. These do not seem very plausible intuitively, but cannot be ruled out a priori; as explained in Section III, the reduction in the Argentine posttariff price can cause the nonmember's demand curve to become less elastic. Finally, with fewer degrees of freedom, and greater sample homogeneity, symmetry fares better in the disaggregated results than in Subsection A above. It is accepted about half the time for most exporters, and in seven and eight out of nine cases for the United States' own and rival's tariff effects respectively.

Overall, despite the problems of small sample sizes, the disaggregated results strongly confirm that MERCOSUR's preferential tariff reductions induced widespread cuts in the prices of nonmembers' exports to the Brazilian market.

A second confirmatory exercise is to estimate the equivalent of equation (5) for Argentina's relative export prices. Unfortunately, the crucial years for identifying tariff cuts, 1991 and 1992, could not be included because Argentina started reporting HS data only in 1993. Hence, because tariffs on Argentinian exports were almost zero from 1993 on, we had to combine this variable with other costs and rely on symmetry to identify its effects. The rival tariff (i.e., the effect of the tariffs faced by nonmembers) on Argentina's export prices is positive and significant (0.245); but the estimated pass-through of tariffs and other Argentinian costs to Brazilian consumers is rather small and insignificant (at 0.202). These results are consistent with our basic pricing model and with tariff preferences reducing Argentine posttariff prices and so

[26] These results are broadly confirmed if we impose symmetry on the estimates, with significant coefficients of 0.229 (Chile), 0.113 (Germany), and 0.396 (United States) on $\tau^*$, and insignificant estimates for Japan and Korea. However, symmetry is rejected at 95 percent by all exporters except the United States. This rejection is, strictly, a challenge to our model, but given the obvious data inadequacies and the strong empirical support for there being some effect from partner tariffs, we do not view it as a serious challenge to our basic hypothesis.

squeezing nonmembers' prices. However, the inadequate sample means that we should do no more with these results than conclude that the Argentinian data are not inconsistent with our basic hypothesis.

The final confirmatory exercise moves from comparing one exporter's prices to two markets, to comparing two exporters' (say, the United States' and Argentina's) prices to a single market (Brazil). We subtract equation (4) from a corresponding equation describing the prices of Argentina's exports to Brazil, again suppressing the real income terms. This exercise relies on Brazilian import data to provide unit value series, which is attractive both in terms of extending the sample to 1989–1996, and to 11 main exporters, and in terms of analyzing data that are completely independent of those used above.

This exercise is parallel to Winters and Chang's (2000) estimates of the effects of Spanish accession to the EC. As explained there, it is a weaker test of the terms-of-trade costs to nonmembers than is the main estimation above. This is because even if we can show that MERCOSUR preferences reduced nonmember pretariff export prices relative to member ones, we cannot tell immediately in what proportions this was due to the former falling or the latter rising, both of which are possible in theory. To decompose the relative price changes into these two parts requires one (a) to take the model more literally than is perhaps desirable, and (b) to introduce an extraneous estimate of at least one parameter. Nonetheless, being based on different and more extensive data than our main exercise, this estimation is useful as a confirmation of the latter.

Theory predicts that a change in the Brazilian tariff factor on Argentinian exports, $\tau^*$, will normally lead to a similarly signed but less than proportional change in the relative posttariff prices of Argentinian and nonmember exports to Brazil. This is consistent with full or partial pass-through by Argentinian exporters plus positive or zero emulation of Argentinian price changes by other exporters. For ten out of 12 nonmember exporters (11 major exporters plus one exercise based on Brazilian imports from all nonmembers) this is exactly what we found, with estimated coefficients virtually always significantly different from both one and zero. In the other two cases (Mexico and Japan) the coefficient exceeds unity suggesting greater than full pass-through of Argentinian tariff cuts and little, or no, emulation. This chimes with Japan's relative insensitivity to the member's tariff in the main exercise above.

As noted in Chang and Winters (1999), these results do not prove that nonmembers reduced their export prices to Brazil in response to MERCOSUR. However, the results are strongly consistent with the basic model and interpretation developed above, and as Chang and Winters argue, the failure to reduce prices in the face of member preferences would need extreme parameters in the model. Overall, therefore, these results lend further weight to our concerns about nonmembers' terms-of-trade losses.

### C. *Welfare Implications*

This paper is intended primarily as an exercise in positive economics, but it is interesting to ask whether the effects uncovered are significant in welfare terms. Although welfare calculations based just on our empirical estimates will be crude and incomplete, they represent a significant advancement in estimating the terms-of-trade effects of PTA's on nonmembers.

The first-order estimate of the welfare effect of a price change is $q^*\Delta p$. Assuming that all variables except tariff rates were unaffected by MERCOSUR and taking unweighted averages of the latter, we can use the coefficients of Table 2 to make such estimates (see Table 3, column A). The United States exported \$5.4 billion worth of goods to Brazil in 1991. With partner tariffs falling by an average of 26 percentage points by 1996 and a coefficient of 0.445, this implies a loss of \$624 million in that year. Losses similarly occurred for the other countries that reported export data—Japan (with losses of \$59 million), Germany (\$236 million), Korea (\$14 million), and Chile (\$17 million).[27]

Some have argued (although we would not) that the m.f.n. reductions that accompanied MERCOSUR were also a part of the MERCOSUR program—see Olivier Cadot et al. (2001)

[27] These results are not much changed if they are based on the disaggregated results in Chang and Winters (1999).

TABLE 3—TOTAL EXPORTS TO BRAZIL AND POSSIBLE LOSSES DUE TO MERCOSUR ($ MILLION)

| Country | Exports, 1991 | Welfare change due to MERCOSUR | |
|---|---|---|---|
| | | A | B |
| Chile | 524.4 | −17.3 | −40.4 |
| Germany | 2,030.0 | −236.0 | −169.4 |
| Japan | 1,349.6 | −58.8 | −70.6 |
| Korea | 146.7 | −13.7 | 1.2 |
| USA | 5,395.5 | −624.1 | −545.3 |

*Notes:* Revenue losses were calculated using the elasticities of the rival's tariffs from Table 2A. Column B also incorporates the own tariff effects due to m.f.n. tariff reductions by MERCOSUR members.

for a discussion. If so, these should be included in the pricing calculation (see Table 3, column B). If we incorporate the terms-of-trade gains that nonmembers may have earned as Brazil reduced its m.f.n. tariffs, U.S. welfare losses fall to $545 million, and Germany's to $169 million. Korea now gains and Chile and Japan would lose more because of their coefficients exceeding unity in Table 2. The preference effect dominates the welfare calculation because, first, the "pass-through" of m.f.n. tariff changes to consumers is quite large (close to one in the aggregate, except for Korea) and the changes in m.f.n. tariffs are smaller than those for MERCOSUR members.

The welfare estimates are very crude and are clearly only part of the story. For example, the United States may have had terms-of-trade gains if MERCOSUR stimulated efficiency gains and so reduced Brazilian export prices, and there may have been partly offsetting changes in export quantities as both member and nonmember export prices fell. Quantity increases would be particularly significant if the m.f.n. reductions and other reforms were included as part of MERCOSUR: Brazilian imports increased strongly over the period 1991–1996 and so could have implied major transfers to imperfectly competitive exporters. In models such as ours in which imperfect competition implies positive margins, additional exports induce significant welfare gains. Of course, Brazil is the major winner from the price reductions by nonmember exporters, and, because the reductions imply falling price-cost margins they tend to cure a preexisting distortion (imperfect competition) and hence are likely to imply global net gains overall.[28]

We do not advance the welfare sums above as final calculations of the costs of MERCOSUR to nonmembers. They are, however, indicative of the significant magnitudes of losses in export revenue that countries left out of regional arrangements may suffer. Given the centrality of prices and the terms of trade in economic theory, it is surprising that such large amounts of real income have been ignored by empiricists and policy makers until now.

## VI. Conclusion

We have shown empirically that regional integration does affect the prices of traded goods. This is no surprise from a theoretical point of view, for price effects lie at the very heart of the analysis of international trade policy. It is novel empirically, however, for with the exception of our own earlier work, which used less appropriate data and a much weaker empirical test, there is not a single *ex post* empirical study of the price effects of integration.

We have also shown that the price effects of integration can be quantitatively significant for nonmember exporters supplying an integrating market such as Brazil. An important policy implication is that even if a PTA aims *only* to "facilitate trade between the constituent territories and *not* to raise barriers to the trade of other contracting parties with such territories" (GATT, Article XXIV), the other contracting parties may still be adversely affected. "Nonmember" effects have always been a concern, as is evident in the fact that both Article XXIV and the "Enabling Clause"[29] contain wording that suggests nonmembers should not be harmed. Our results give empirical backing to the well-known theoretical argument that even if external tariffs are unchanged by integration, nonmember countries are likely to be hurt by regional integration.

[28] This statement cannot be categorical because Argentinian margins rise and because of other possible second-best complications.

[29] Differential and More Favourable Treatment, Reciprocity and Fuller Participation of Developing Countries, Decision of 28 November 1979 (L/4903).

APPENDIX: ESTIMATED COEFFICIENTS OF EQUATION (5), BY NINE COMMODITY GROUPS AND SUPPLIER

| HS-2 | Country | $\tau$ | $\tau^*$ | $w/e_1Q_1$ | $w/e_2Q_2$ | $w^*/e_1^*Q_1$ | $R^2$ | EDF | A | B | C |
|---|---|---|---|---|---|---|---|---|---|---|---|
| 01–15 | CHL | 1.384 (0.22) | −0.190 (0.18) | 1.28 (0.27) | −1.26 (0.37) | −0.33 (0.28) | 0.87 | 378 | 0.773 | 0.572 | 0.115 |
| | GER | 0.231 (0.33)* | −0.633 (0.21) | 1.71 (0.10) | −2.22 (0.13) | −0.93 (0.11) | 0.94 | 184 | 0.000 | 0.213 | 0.000 |
| | USA | 0.090 (0.50)* | 0.127 (0.42) | 1.74 (0.46) | −0.53 (0.61) | −0.70 (0.49) | 0.75 | 279 | 0.005 | 0.031 | 0.015 |
| 16–27 | CHL | 0.833 (0.21) | 0.281 (0.17)* | 0.95 (0.32) | −1.91 (0.45) | −0.24 (0.33) | 0.87 | 181 | 0.780 | 0.086 | 0.020 |
| | GER | 0.749 (0.53) | 1.248 (0.44)* | −1.52 (0.75) | 2.82 (1.38) | 2.03 (0.67) | 0.46 | 160 | 0.044 | 0.299 | 0.007 |
| | JPN | 0.033 (0.40)* | 0.996 (0.30)* | 1.46 (0.16) | −1.19 (0.25) | −0.06 (0.12) | 0.85 | 66 | 0.002 | 0.001 | 0.003 |
| | KOR | 0.124 (0.52)* | 0.386 (0.37) | 1.60 (0.30) | 0.39 (0.35) | 0.09 (0.15) | 0.90 | 57 | 0.024 | 0.349 | 0.068 |
| | USA | 0.545 (0.30) | 0.830 (0.31)* | 0.12 (0.85) | −2.65 (1.14) | 1.12 (0.87) | 0.66 | 301 | 0.627 | 0.687 | 0.865 |
| 28–38 | CHL | 3.826 (0.53) | −1.655 (0.44) | 1.07 (0.54) | −2.90 (0.78) | −1.03 (0.60) | 0.78 | 139 | 0.000 | 0.168 | 0.000 |
| | GER | 0.316 (0.19)* | 0.283 (0.17)* | 0.80 (0.14) | −1.52 (0.26) | 0.17 (0.13) | 0.67 | 933 | 0.061 | 0.575 | 0.021 |
| | JPN | 0.343 (0.32)* | 0.642 (0.23)* | 1.09 (0.09) | −1.16 (0.14) | −0.07 (0.06) | 0.76 | 452 | 0.042 | 0.002 | 0.003 |
| | KOR | −0.224 (0.78) | −0.640 (0.55) | 1.62 (0.36) | 0.91 (0.68) | −0.17 (0.21) | 0.57 | 86 | 0.065 | 0.392 | 0.001 |
| | USA | 0.762 (0.23) | 0.639 (0.22)* | 0.64 (0.30) | −0.43 (0.43) | 0.42 (0.32) | 0.62 | 1,300 | 0.675 | 0.317 | 0.030 |
| 39–40 | CHL | −0.655 (2.03) | 2.636 (1.17)* | −1.70 (2.01) | 1.40 (1.81) | 1.85 (1.71) | 0.56 | 49 | 0.767 | 0.723 | 0.103 |
| | GER | 0.916 (0.40) | 0.246 (0.33) | 0.81 (0.33) | −0.22 (0.81) | 0.53 (0.32) | 0.69 | 422 | 0.863 | 0.372 | 0.459 |
| | JPN | 0.889 (0.45) | 0.544 (0.32)* | 1.36 (0.15) | −1.34 (0.25) | 0.11 (0.10) | 0.69 | 270 | 0.360 | 0.182 | 0.386 |
| | KOR | 0.432 (0.60) | 0.120 (0.44) | 2.14 (0.38) | −1.02 (0.55) | −0.78 (0.28) | 0.65 | 142 | 0.024 | 0.057 | 0.072 |
| | USA | 0.354 (0.39)* | 0.118 (0.35) | 2.05 (0.63) | −1.91 (0.66) | −0.61 (0.62) | 0.76 | 475 | 0.013 | 0.076 | 0.023 |
| 41–63 | CHL | 2.566 (0.60) | 0.200 (0.41) | 0.68 (0.43) | −0.40 (0.60) | 0.48 (0.45) | 0.72 | 152 | 0.002 | 0.523 | 0.002 |
| | GER | 0.423 (0.47) | 1.159 (0.37)* | 0.84 (0.25) | 0.46 (0.52) | 0.14 (0.23) | 0.55 | 348 | 0.444 | 0.011 | 0.001 |
| | JPN | 3.546 (0.56) | −1.084 (0.40) | 0.46 (0.15) | −0.54 (0.25) | 0.40 (0.12) | 0.63 | 150 | 0.000 | 0.000 | 0.000 |
| | KOR | −0.710 (0.37)* | 1.245 (0.23)* | 0.90 (0.23) | 0.10 (0.35) | 0.25 (0.12) | 0.65 | 385 | 0.002 | 0.000 | 0.000 |
| | USA | 0.757 (0.42) | 0.607 (0.32)* | 0.85 (0.43) | 0.22 (0.76) | 0.46 (0.45) | 0.58 | 633 | 0.854 | 0.708 | 0.886 |
| 64–83 | CHL | 1.311 (0.42) | 0.775 (0.28)* | 0.02 (0.61) | −0.54 (0.86) | 0.70 (0.63) | 0.89 | 78 | 0.109 | 0.899 | 0.002 |
| | GER | 0.604 (0.38) | 0.717 (0.33)* | 1.28 (0.22) | −2.20 (0.56) | −0.35 (0.21) | 0.57 | 937 | 0.141 | 0.000 | 0.000 |
| | JPN | 0.612 (0.39) | 0.495 (0.28)* | 1.03 (0.13) | −0.90 (0.19) | 0.04 (0.09) | 0.54 | 471 | 0.336 | 0.095 | 0.234 |
| | KOR | 2.810 (0.91) | −0.334 (0.65) | 1.75 (0.40) | −2.63 (0.73) | −0.43 (0.24) | 0.55 | 147 | 0.277 | 0.872 | 0.344 |
| | USA | 1.372 (0.52) | −0.460 (0.48) | 0.88 (0.76) | −0.18 (1.03) | 0.35 (0.77) | 0.34 | 637 | 0.544 | 0.128 | 0.112 |
| 84–85 | CHL | 0.900 (1.88) | −0.238 (1.16) | 1.45 (2.64) | 1.42 (3.37) | 0.49 (2.65) | 0.51 | 22 | 0.878 | 0.761 | 0.601 |
| | GER | 0.909 (0.23) | 0.669 (0.20)* | 1.12 (0.19) | −0.80 (0.51) | 0.08 (0.19) | 0.62 | 1,579 | 0.506 | 0.000 | 0.000 |
| | JPN | 1.148 (0.22) | −0.319 (0.15) | 1.27 (0.07) | −1.44 (0.13) | −0.12 (0.05) | 0.58 | 1,044 | 0.625 | 0.176 | 0.027 |
| | KOR | 0.570 (0.19)* | 0.347 (0.19)* | 1.42 (0.15) | −0.35 (0.31) | −0.17 (0.08) | 0.70 | 312 | 0.000 | 0.002 | 0.000 |
| | USA | 1.177 (0.38) | 0.629 (0.37)* | 0.30 (0.82) | −1.94 (0.91) | 0.73 (0.81) | 0.29 | 1,464 | 0.283 | 0.865 | 0.059 |
| 86–92 | GER | 1.789 (0.43) | −0.450 (0.46) | 2.68 (0.60) | −4.46 (1.54) | −1.58 (0.60) | 0.54 | 269 | 0.251 | 0.017 | 0.048 |
| | JPN | 1.362 (0.32) | 0.559 (0.20)* | 0.99 (0.13) | −0.37 (0.24) | 0.10 (0.09) | 0.71 | 206 | 0.316 | 0.018 | 0.000 |
| | KOR | 0.955 (0.14) | 0.606 (0.40) | 0.35 (0.52) | −1.53 (0.69) | −0.15 (0.32) | 0.64 | 90 | 0.248 | 0.022 | 0.054 |
| | USA | 0.739 (0.40) | 0.077 (0.47) | 1.97 (1.87) | 1.28 (2.45) | −0.39 (1.85) | 0.48 | 183 | 0.531 | 0.756 | 0.520 |
| 93–96 | GER | 0.669 (0.77) | −1.572 (0.73) | 6.50 (1.52) | −13.3 (3.00) | −5.73 (1.35) | 0.45 | 87 | 0.003 | 0.000 | 0.003 |
| | JPN | 2.515 (0.51) | −0.437 (0.52) | 0.37 (0.42) | 0.65 (0.82) | 0.29 (0.28) | 0.52 | 45 | 0.036 | 0.160 | 0.104 |
| | KOR | −0.078 (0.44)* | 0.094 (0.36) | 1.24 (0.43) | 0.84 (1.43) | −0.02 (0.22) | 0.25 | 111 | 0.050 | 0.750 | 0.145 |
| | USA | 0.792 (0.80) | −1.126 (1.06) | 6.90 (3.97) | 1.75 (3.75) | −5.18 (3.93) | 0.30 | 151 | 0.126 | 0.194 | 0.210 |

*Notes:* Estimated coefficients are presented, with standard errors in parentheses. All variables are expressed in natural logs. Estimates are not reported where the error degrees of freedom would be below 20. Columns A, B, C represent the probability of type I error in the $F$ tests of (A) symmetry of the pass-through of the m.f.n. tariff and the real wage, (B) symmetry between the rival's tariff and rival's real wage, and (C) the joint test of (A) and (B). Countries are CHL, Chile; GER, Germany; JPN, Japan; KOR, Korea; and the United States.

* Own tariff estimate ($\tau$) is below unity or the rival's tariff estimate ($\tau^*$) above zero with 95-percent confidence.

## REFERENCES

**Bagwell, Kyle and Staiger, Robert W.** "Will Preferential Agreements Undermine the Multilateral Trading System?" *Economic Journal*, July 1998, *108*(449), pp. 1162–82.

______. "An Economic Theory of GATT." *American Economic Review*, March 1999, *89*(1), pp. 215–48.

**Baldwin, Richard.** "Hysteresis in Import Prices: The Beachhead Effect." *American Economic Review*, September 1988, *78*(4), pp. 773–85.

**Bulow, Jeremy I.; Geanakoplos, John D. and Klemperer, Paul D.** "Multimarket Oligopoly: Strategic Substitutes and Complements." *Journal of Political Economy*, June 1985, *93*(3), pp. 488–511.

**Cadot, Olivier; de Melo, Jaime and Olarreaga, Marcelo.** "Can Bilateralism Ease the Pains of Multilateral Trade Liberalization?" *European Economic Review*, January 2001, *45*(1), pp. 27–44.

**Chang, Won and Winters, L. Alan.** "How Regional Blocs Affect Excluded Countries: The Price Effects of MERCOSUR." Centre for Economic Policy Research (London, U.K.) Discussion Paper No. 2179, June 1999.

**Dornbusch, Rudiger.** "Exchange Rates and Prices." *American Economic Review*, March 1987, *77*(1), pp. 93–106.

**Feenstra, Robert C.** "Symmetric Pass-Through of Tariffs and Exchange Rates under Imperfect Competition: An Empirical Test." *Journal of International Economics*, August 1989, *27*(1–2), pp. 25–45.

______. "U.S. Exports, 1972–1994: With State Exports and Other U.S. Data." National Bureau of Economic Research (Cambridge, MA) Working Paper No. 5990, April 1997.

**Frischtak, Claudio; Leipziger, Danny M. and Normand, John F.** "Industrial Policy in MERCOSUR: Issues and Lessons." Country Department I, Latin America and the Caribbean Region, Working paper, The World Bank, August 1996.

**Froot, Kenneth and Klemperer, Paul.** "Exchange Rate Pass-Through When Market Share Matters." *American Economic Review*, September 1989, *79*(4), pp. 637–54.

**International Monetary Fund.** *Direction of trade statistics: Yearbook.* Washington, DC: International Monetary Fund, 1996, 1997.

______. *International financial statistics: Yearbook.* Washington, DC: International Monetary Fund, various issues.

**Kemp, Murray C. and Wan, Henry Y., Jr.** "An Elementary Proposition Concerning the Formation of Customs Unions." *Journal of International Economics*, February 1976, *6*(1), pp. 95–97.

**Knetter, Michael M.** "Price Discrimination by U.S. and German Exporters." *American Economic Review*, March 1989, *79*(1), pp. 198–210.

______. "International Comparisons of Price-to-Market Behavior." *American Economic Review*, June 1993, *83*(3), pp. 473–86.

**Kreinin, Mordechai E.** "Effect of Tariff Changes on the Prices and Volume of Imports." *American Economic Review*, June 1961, *51*(3), pp. 310–24.

**Krugman, Paul R.** "Pricing to Market When the Exchange Rate Changes," in Sven W. Arndt and J. David Richardson, eds., *Real-financial linkages among open economies.* Cambridge, MA: MIT Press, 1987, pp. 49–70.

**Laird, Sam.** "MERCOSUR: Objectives and Achievements." Mimeo, World Trade Organization, June 1997.

**Mann, Catherine L.** "Prices, Profit Margins, and Exchange Rates." *Federal Reserve Bulletin*, June 1986, *72*(6), pp. 366–79.

**Marston, Richard C.** "Pricing to Market in Japanese Manufacturing." *Journal of International Economics*, November 1990, *29*(3–4), pp. 217–36.

**Mundell, Robert.** "Tariff Preferences and the Terms of Trade." *Manchester School Economic Social Studies*, 1964, *32*(1), pp. 1–13.

**Olarreaga, Marcelo and Soloaga, Isidro.** "Endogenous Tariff Formation: The Case of Mercosur." *World Bank Economic Review*, May 1998, *12*(2), pp. 297–320.

**Schembri, Lawrence.** "Export Prices and Exchange Rates: An Industry Approach," in Robert C. Feenstra, ed., *Trade policies for international competitiveness.* Chicago: University of Chicago Press, 1989, pp. 185–206.

**United Nations Conference on Trade and Development (UNCTAD).** "A User's Manual for TRAINS." United Nations, New York and Geneva, 1996.

**Winters, L. Alan.** "Regionalism and the Rest of the World: The Irrelevance of the Kemp-Wan Theorem." *Oxford Economics Papers*, April 1997a, *49*(2), pp. 228–34.

______. "Regionalism and the Rest of the World: Theory and Estimates of the Effects of European Integration." *Review of International Economics*, Supp. 5(4), 1997b, pp. 134–47.

**Winters, L. Alan and Chang, Won.** "Regional Integration and Import Prices: An Empirical Investigation." *Journal of International Economics*, August 2000, *51*(2), pp. 363–77.

*The Manchester School* Vol 79 No. 5 994–1017 September 2011
doi: 10.1111/j.1467-9957.2010.02171.x

# TRADE AND ECONOMIC GEOGRAPHY: THE IMPACT OF EEC ACCESSION ON THE UK*

by
*HENRY G. OVERMAN*
*LSE, CEP and CEPR*
and
*L. ALAN WINTERS*[†]
*DFID and CEPR*

We combine establishment-level employment data with trade data by port to examine the impact of accession to the European Economic Community on the spatial distribution of UK manufacturing. We test the predictions from economic geography models of how external trade affects the spatial distribution of employment. We treat accession as a natural experiment which helps mitigate problems of endogeneity. Our results suggest that accession changed the country composition of trade and via the port composition induced an exogenous shock to different locations. In line with theory, we find that better access to export markets and intermediate goods increase employment while increased import competition decreases employment.

## 1 Introduction

Work in international trade has long been concerned with what is produced where. That is, in the distribution of economic activity across countries. In contrast, this paper forms part of a small, but growing literature focusing on the relationship between economic integration and the spatial distribution of economic activities *within* a country. We view UK accession to the European Economic Community (EEC) as a 'natural experiment' and use the resulting trade 'shock' as a source of exogenous variation that identifies how trade affects the spatial distribution of activity.

* Manuscript received 5.1.09; final version received 6.8.09.
† We are grateful to two anonymous referees and the editor for suggestions that considerably improved the paper; to Sandra Bulli and Andrea Molinari for research assistance and to the Office for National Statistics (ONS) Business Data Linking Project for facilitating access to the Annual Respondent Database (ARD). The work was largely undertaken while Alan Winters was at the University of Sussex and a senior visitor at the Centre for Economic Performance (CEP; it does not necessarily reflect the views or policies of the Department for International Development). The paper has benefited from comments by seminar participants at the CEP and at two Centre for Economic Policy Research (CEPR) conferences in Cagliari and Paris. This work contains statistical data from ONS which is Crown copyright and reproduced with the permission of the controller of Her Majesty's Stationery Office (HMSO) and Queen's Printer for Scotland. The use of the ONS statistical data in this work does not imply the endorsement of the ONS in relation to the interpretation or analysis of the statistical data. This work uses research data sets which may not exactly reproduce National Statistics aggregates. Financial support from the Economic and Social Research Council (ESRC) (grant number L138251028) is gratefully acknowledged.


Published by Blackwell Publishing Ltd, 9600 Garsington Road, Oxford OX4 2DQ, UK, and 350 Main Street, Malden, MA 02148, USA.

This endogeneity problem arises because trade both affects, and is affected by, the spatial distribution of activity. It is increasingly recognized that natural experiments provide an exogenous source of variation that can help solve the resulting identification problem. We argue that the UK's accession to the EEC can be viewed as such a natural experiment that causes exogenous changes in trade. The fact that UK accession led to a significant re-orientation of trade towards EEC members is well documented—see, among others, Winters (1984) or Begg *et al.* (2003). Less well known is the significant re-orientation in terms of the port through which trade occurred, described in Overman and Winters (2005). Because this changing port composition was a result of accession we argue it induces different *exogenous* shocks in different UK regions. We examine whether the resulting changes to employment are in line with predictions from models of economic geography. To do this, we construct a panel of firms for which we know employment and the Travel To Work Area (TTWA) where these firms are located. We use data on the volume of trade by port and distances from these ports to different TTWAs to construct measures of the import competition and access to export markets and intermediate goods faced by firms. We test whether these three access variables affect firm employment. To address concerns about endogeneity, we assume that the changing country composition of UK trade during this period is driven by accession, not the performance of individual firms and so we use this changing country composition to construct instruments for the three access variables.

The effect of UK accession is interesting for a number of reasons. First, accession occurred when tariffs, generally, were at much higher levels than today, so that impacts should be easier to identify. Second, these tariff changes affected most manufacturing sectors at a time when manufacturing was a significant component of the UK economy. As most studies, ours included, focus on manufacturing, the relative importance of this sector will matter for the magnitude of any effects. Third, we have detailed data on individual firms and the ports (including airports) through which trade flows. This allows us to test the predictions from economic geography models in an original fashion. Finally, the existing literature focuses on the response of developing countries to major trade liberalizations. See, for example, Hanson (1996, 1997, 1998), Pavcnik (2002) and Tybout (2000, 2001). Studying developed countries, however, has one key advantage over looking at developing countries. Frequently, developing country liberalizations form part of a larger package in response to macroeconomic shocks. In contrast, although the early 1970s was a time of significant macroeconomic shocks, accession was *not* a response to these shocks. Thus, we can treat accession as providing a natural experiment in terms of changing trade policy.

The paper is structured as follows. Section 2 summarizes the historical background and details the extent of liberalization that occurred when the UK joined the EEC. Section 3 considers theoretical predictions about the impact of integration on the spatial distribution of activity. Section 4 details the trade and production data. Section 5 constructs measures of import competition, export market access and intermediate good market access and analyses whether these have the predicted impact on firm employment. Section 6 looks at the extent to which changes in the port composition of trade are determined by the country composition of trade. Section 7 then uses these findings to construct instruments and assess whether the effects that we document in Section 5 are actually due to the trade liberalization associated with accession. Section 8 concludes.

## 2 The Background

The UK first applied to join the EEC in 1961. This application, and a second in 1967, failed as a result of a French veto. A third application was successful and the UK joined on 1 January 1973. Even without the French veto, UK membership was far from certain. Edward Heath's narrow majority ensured that parliament accepted the government's accession terms, but the signing of the Treaty was a much closer run thing. This uncertainty ensures that adjustment to accession tended to occur after entry rather than before, even if firms were forward-looking. Moreover, once the need for adjustment had been identified, it is likely it took a while to effect, so we should observe the impact in our data (which start from 1970).

While this uncertainty works in our favour, other contemporaneous macroeconomic uncertainties do not. A number of these were global, some UK specific. Table 1 provides a timeline of major events. These events are likely to affect the composition of overall economic activity. However, our focus is on the impact that integration has on the spatial distribution of economic activity in different sectors *within* the UK taking total sectoral activity as given. It is still possible that these shocks could affect our results, but only if they affect locations asymmetrically in a way that is correlated with the trade shocks we identify. Given their macroeconomic nature, this is unlikely, but the possibility cannot be completely ruled out.

We finish this section with a note on the changes in tariffs associated with accession. In the early 1970s tariffs were considerably higher than now, so that the margins of preference generated by accession were, in some cases, quite large. Table 2 reports average UK and EEC tariffs after the Kennedy Round applicable from 1972 to 1980 (when the Tokyo Round started). In 1972 UK imports from outside the Commonwealth and manufactured imports from the European Free Trade Association (EFTA) faced tariffs reported in the 'UK' column, with a mean of 7.2 per cent but as high as a 19 per cent. By 1979 imports from the EEC, EFTA (manufactures) and the African, Caribbean and Pacific group of states faced zero tariffs broadly speaking. Tariffs on imports from other countries also faced lower tariffs, but as the EEC column shows mean tariffs of 4.9 per cent with peaks of 13.9 per cent were far from zero.

TABLE 1
MAJOR ECONOMIC EVENTS 1970s

| *Year* | *Month* | *Event* |
|---|---|---|
| 1971 | February | Decimal currency introduced |
| | August | End of Bretton Woods era; Pound allowed to float |
| 1972 | January | Miners begin pay strike |
| | February | Most industry begins 3-day week to conserve power supplies; miners return to work |
| | May | Sterling joins the EEC currency snake |
| | June | Sterling out of the snake |
| | November | Counter inflation bill—90-day standstill pay, prices, rents, dividends |
| 1973 | January | UK joins EEC; further controls on prices, pay, rents, dividends |
| | March | Pay Board and Price Commission established |
| | May | 1.6 m workers strike against counter-inflation measures |
| | October | 66% price increase light crude oil |
| | November | 25% cut in oil supplies to West; petrol ration coupons issued |
| 1974 | January | Light crude oil price from $5 to $11.5 per barrel; 3-day working week |
| | February | Miners strike |
| | March | End of miners strike and return to 5-day working week |
| | May | Lifting of restrictions on fuel |
| | July | TUC accept voluntary wage restraint in place of statutory wage controls |
| 1975 | August | £6 per week pay rise limit becomes effective |
| | October | Organization of the Petroleum Exporting Countries (OPEC) 10% price increase |
| | July | Heavy selling of sterling |
| 1976 | September | Treasury announces it will seek $3.9bn loan from the International Monetary Fund |
| | January | Further $3bn loan from Bank of International Settlements |
| 1977 | July | Abolition of tariffs with EFTA |
| | December | OPEC announces new 14.5% (staggered) price increases |
| 1978 | January | 'Winter of Discontent'—series of strikes in public services |
| 1979 | May | Price Commission abolished |
| | June | OPEC announce 15% price increase |

*Note:* http://www.bized.ac.uk, accessed November 2002.

## 3 THEORY

What impact should accession have on the spatial distribution of activity in the UK? Comparative advantage helps understand the changing composition across sectors, and must play a part in the overall decline in UK manufacturing during this period. It could also help us to understand changes in the distribution of aggregate activity if regions are specialized in sectors that perform differently as the UK adjusts. However, our focus is on how integration affects the spatial distribution of activity *within* particular sectors, on which theories of comparative advantage are essentially silent. Thus our theoretical foundation comes from literature that directly considers the impact of integration on economic geography. These effects have been the focus of the recent 'New Economic Geography' (NEG) (see Baldwin *et al.* (2003) for an overview). The analysis of NEG formalizes ideas about the impact of trade from an older literature associated with economic geographers.

TABLE 2
UK/EEC TARIFF RATES 1972–79

| *Product* | *UK* | *EEC* | *Product* | *UK* | *EEC* |
|---|---|---|---|---|---|
| Mineral products | 0.2 | 0.1 | Footwear and headwear | 14.7 | 12.4 |
| Chemical products | 8.1 | 6.9 | Stone, ceramic and glass products | 10.2 | 8.0 |
| Rubber products | 7.4 | 2.0 | Base metals and metal products | 5.2 | 4.2 |
| Hides, furs, leather products | 4.6 | 1.3 | Unwrought, pig iron, scrap | 1.1 | 2.0 |
| Raw hides, skins, fur | N/A | N/A | Basic shapes and forms | 8.9 | 7.0 |
| Articles of leather, fur | 13.1 | 1.3 | Steel | 9.2 | 6.7 |
| Wood and cork products | 2.3 | 1.1 | Other | 7.5 | 8.7 |
| Wood, natural cork | 0.5 | 0.1 | Articles of base metal, misc. | 10.0 | 7.1 |
| Articles of wood, cork | 6.8 | 9.4 | Non-electrical machinery | 8.6 | 6.4 |
| Pulp and paper | 7.8 | 6.9 | Electrical machinery | 12.4 | 9.1 |
| Pulp | 0.1 | 2.5 | Transportation equipment | 9.8 | 9.3 |
| Paper | 13.1 | 11.1 | Precision instruments | 13.5 | 8.4 |
| Textiles | 9.1 | 4.7 | Miscellaneous | 4.2 | 2.4 |
| Natural fibre and waste | N/A | 0.2 | | | |
| Yarn and basic fabrics | 15.0 | 11.1 | | | |
| Special fabrics, apparel, other | 19.0 | 13.9 | | | |
| | | | Total | 7.2 | 4.9 |

*Source:* Preeg (1970).
*Notes:* Table reports simple (i.e. unweighted) average of tariffs for each product group. N/A denotes figures not available in the original source.

This literature argues that the spatial distribution of economic activity depends on the balance between agglomeration and dispersion forces. Firms in big markets benefit from being close to customers and suppliers. That is, from demand and supply linkages. Offsetting this, big markets are more crowded which increases product and factor market competition putting downward pressure on prices and upward pressure on wages. The balance of these forces depends on the trade costs between locations. At higher trade costs, the costs of serving distant customers are large enough to dominate the agglomeration forces and activity is dispersed. At intermediate trade costs, the opposite is true and agglomeration can occur, while at low trade costs, congestion costs are dominant and industry may once again disperse.

What do such models imply for the economic geography of the UK as it opens up to trade with Europe? One possibility is that regions that are close to new trading partners (i.e. 'border' regions) benefit disproportionately from the improved market access that comes with accession. Hanson (1996, 1997, 1998) has tested whether changing export market access helps explain the changing economic geography of Mexican regions. He argues that NAFTA acts as a natural experiment that disproportionately increases the export market access of regions in the north of the country close to the US border. His empirical work tests the prediction that this change should lead activity to relocate from Mexico City to the northern regions driving up employment and wages there. Both of these predictions hold true.

The effect found by Hanson is not the only possibility when a country opens up to trade. While export market access and access to imported intermediate goods rises in border regions, so too does the degree of product market competition from imports. Hanson focuses only on export market access and argues that the employment share of border regions *must* rise. Once we allow for increased import competition, border regions may suffer, while firms in non-border regions are partly protected from increased competition by the fact that imports incur higher transport costs to reach those regions. This line of reasoning has been formalized by Alonso-Villar (2001), Monfort and Nicolini (2000), Paluzie (2001) and Crozet and Koenig Soubeyran (2004). Brülhart and Koenig (2006) provide related empirical evidence for quite aggregate sectoral data (the eight sectors of one-digit NACE) for the Central and Eastern European countries.

In our empirical analysis we view ports as identifying the borders of the UK (i.e. the points through which imports enter and exports leave). We then construct variables that capture all three access effects. We expect activity to rise with better export market access and access to intermediate goods and to fall with increased import competition. As data limitations prevent us from estimating a more structural equation, we see little to be gained from working through a more formal model. Instead, we motivate our reduced-form approach on the basis of the informal reasoning and the intuitive predictions that we have drawn out above and refer the interested reader to the references given.

## 4 Data

### *4.1 Production Data*

Our basic unit of observation will be the employment of UK manufacturing establishments for the period 1970–92 constructed using production data from the Annual Respondent Database (ARD).[1] The ARD is an extremely rich data set which contains information about all UK manufacturing establishments.[2] Griffith (1999) provides a detailed description of these data.

The data available on any particular establishment in any given year depend on whether they were selected to make a detailed return that year. Selected establishments answer a detailed questionnaire. In contrast, data for non-selected establishments are much more limited. As a general rule all

[1]The availability of trade data restricts us to only study 1970–92. We discuss this below.

[2]We exclude Northern Ireland. The smallest unit of observation in the ARD is the local unit ('plants'). Local unit data are not available before 1983 so we use data for reporting units ('establishments'). Reporting units may consist of local units in different locations. In these cases the calculation of access variables is problematic. Local unit data from 1984 onwards show this only affects a small percentage of reporting units (less than 3 per cent have local units in different TTWAs). Given this, we assign all employment to the reporting unit. We also ignore correlation across reporting units part of a larger enterprise group.

larger establishments with more than 100 employees are selected, as are a percentage of those with more than 20 but less than 100 employees. Establishments with less than 20 employees are usually exempt. The precise rules vary by year. See Barnes and Martin (2002) for details.

We use employment data, rather than wages, because employment is constructed consistently across time.[3] There are two possible variables to work with. One is an estimate of employment used when deciding which establishments are selected to return a full questionnaire.[4] This should be recorded for all establishments. This is true from 1980 to 1992, but not in the 1970s where employment has been (accidentally) deleted for non-sampled establishments. As a result, we use *returned employment*. For an establishment to be in our sample, we must have returned employment for at least two years.[5] Given the sampling frame, this means that our sample will be composed of a disproportionate number of larger establishments. Robustness checks show that this does not affect our results.

Given that our unit of observation is employment by establishment, we need to classify establishments by activity and location. All establishments are classified according to their main economic activity using the Standard Industrial Classification (SIC). During our sample period, the SIC changes from SIC 1968 revision (SIC68) to SIC 1980 revision (SIC80). A preliminary mapping from SIC80 to SIC68 was provided by the Office for National Statistics and then supplemented using ARD data on individual establishments' sectoral classifications. For compatibility with the trade data, we then map from SIC68 to the Industry/Commodity group classification used in the 1974 Input–Output (IO) table (IO sectors). IO sectors are basically defined at, or are aggregations of, three-digit SIC68 sectors (minimum list headings). Details of the mappings from SIC80 to SIC68 to IO sectors are available from the authors on request. The list of the 80 IO sectors that we work with in the econometric section is given in Table A1 of the Appendix.

All establishments can be located in one of 10 UK regions. However, we wanted to use a smaller geographical scale to provide more variation with which to identify the effects. After much experimentation, we constructed a consistent set of geographical units based on 307 UK TTWAs (TTWA 1998 revision). Allocating establishments to TTWAs is complicated because the location information provided in the ARD varies significantly over time. The three most important sources of location information are the establishment's local employment office, local authority and postcode. Local employment office codes are provided at the start of our time period but not the end and

[3]That is, we consider the quantity version of the effects rather than the price or wage version. See Head and Mayer (2004).

[4]These employment data are obtained from the various predecessors to the Inter Departmental Business Register.

[5]We need at least two years to estimate firm-specific fixed effects. We also only consider firms that do not change sector.

vice versa for postcode. Again, detailed information on how establishments are located is available on request.

### 4.2 The International Trade Data

Preparing the international trade data required two steps—see the Appendix for a brief account and Overman and Winters (2005, 2006) for detail. First a consistent data set on trade by port, commodity and year had to be constructed for 1970–92 and, second, this had to be converted to an industrial classification to be matched to the firm data.[6] The former entailed working with several commodity classifications, several definitions of ports and a variety of data sources. The output comprised series on the shares of exports and imports for each of 54 commodity groups defined at the two-digit level of the Standard International Trade Classification (Revised) that entered or left through each of 92 ports or groups of ports. No data were available for 1987 and export data were also missing for 1983. For some purposes the ports were further aggregated into 11 regional groups as described in Table A2 of the Appendix. These are more finely disaggregated around the South East because that is where the consequences of integration with Europe seem most likely to be felt. The second stage involved using a series of concordance matrices to map trade flows to the sectors identified in the UK IO table for 1974, to create a data series of trade by port, IO sector and year, which we can merge with the establishment data.

## 5 Import Competition, Access to Export Markets and the Changing Economic Geography of UK Manufacturing

In Overman and Winters (2005) we describe how accession re-orientated UK trade towards ports that were close to EEC member countries. Re-orientation did not occur uniformly across sectors. In this paper, we use this variation to examine whether accession affected the economic geography of manufacturing. The hypotheses that we investigate are (i) that accession re-oriented UK trade by country of origin/destination and that this caused a re-orientation in terms of the ports used, (ii) that this changed the import competition, and the access to intermediate goods and export markets differently across TTWAs, and (iii) that these changes in turn affected the economic geography of manufacturing. We proceed in stages. First, we describe how we calculate import competition, access to intermediate goods and export market access for TTWAs. We show that changes in these measures are correlated with changes in establishment employment in a way consistent with theory. In the following two sections, we consider causality.

[6]Data are not available by port for trade with the EU after 1992 because under the Single Market Programme these flows were treated as internal European trade and were recorded via value added tax returns rather than by Customs and Excise at the port.

Our dependent variable is establishment employment. We know the location (TTWA) and industrial sector of the establishment. We want to explain the evolution in establishment employment in terms of import competition, access to intermediate goods and export markets. We start by using the port trade data to construct proxies for these three access variables.

Although we have trade data by ports, we do not have information on the UK origin of exports and the UK destination of imports. We could assume that imports and exports occur only through the closest port. That is, assume that ports have 'hinterlands' and 'forelands'. Evidence in Hoare (1977, 1985, 1986, 1988) and Chisholm (1992) argues against this. Chisholm reports Hoare's results as showing that:

> If we take the standard region as the geographical unit of analysis, then in 1964, the tonnage of [firm] exports routed through a port in the same standard region accounted for 63% of the total; by 1978 the proportion had fallen to 48%. (Chisholm, 1992, p. 563)

Chisholm's finds that 'the rapid reduction in the strength of local linkages seems to have abated in the period 1978–86' (Chisholm, 1992, p. 563) but clearly establishments are not just linked to their closest port. Instead we assume that distance from *all* ports and the volume of trade through those ports are the key determinants of the access variables. That is, we assume that establishments in TTWAs close to ports with large amounts of imports face more import competition than those a long way from these ports. Similarly for intermediate goods and export market access.

Such a formulation is consistent with NEG theory where love of variety means that consumers purchase all varieties of differentiated manufactured goods, while establishments supply their differentiated goods to all markets. Given that different ports tend to trade with different foreign markets (something we consider empirically below), the idea that distance to all ports matters is consistent with theory. Using this assumption, we construct a measure of import competition faced by an establishment in a given sector located in a given TTWA as

$$\text{IMP}_{jlt} = \sum_p \frac{m_{jpt}}{d_{lp}}$$

where $m_{jpt}$ is the share of imports for sector $j$ coming in through port $p$ at time $t$ and $d_{lp}$ is the distance in kilometres between port $p$ and TTWA $l$. Distances are calculated as straight line distances using data on the location of the port and the centre of the TTWA. We weight port trade flows by the simple inverse of distance, but we discuss other alternatives in Section 7.1. We calculate export market access equivalently:

$$\text{EXP}_{jlt} = \sum_p \frac{x_{jpt}}{d_{lp}}$$

using the share of exports ($x_{jpt}$) through each port. To calculate intermediate market access we weight the imports in different sectors coming in at each port by industries' use of that sector's good in production:

$$\mathrm{INT}_{jlt} = \sum_k \sum_p \frac{a_{jk} m_{kpt}}{d_{lp}}$$

where $a_{jk}$ is industry $j$'s use of intermediate $k$.[7]

Using these measures we run the following regression for each sector:

$$\ln(e_{it}) = \beta_{0j} + \beta_{1j}\ln(\mathrm{IMP}_{jlt}) + \beta_{2j}\ln(\mathrm{EXP}_{jlt}) + \beta_{3j}\ln(\mathrm{INT}_{jlt}) + c_i d_t + \varepsilon_{it}$$

where $e_{it}$ is employment in establishment $i$, $c_i$ is an establishment-specific fixed effect, $d_t$ a series of year dummies, $\varepsilon_{it}$ is an idiosyncratic shock; $\mathrm{IMP}_{jlt}$, $\mathrm{EXP}_{jlt}$ and $\mathrm{INT}_{jlt}$ are as defined above. The betas are coefficients to be estimated. We estimate by sector using data from 1970 to 1992. We exclude 1983 (no export data) and 1987 (no export or import data). We include, but do not report results for, a set of year dummies. Theory predicts a negative coefficient on import competition ($\beta_{1i} < 0$), and positive coefficients on intermediate good and export market access ($\beta_{2i} > 0$ and $\beta_{3i} > 0$).

A few comments are in order. First, we observe no additional establishment characteristics so all we can do is to use the panel dimension of our data to control for an unobserved establishment-specific fixed effects. Second, as the only explanatory variable is at the TTWA level, an alternative would be to aggregate and model employment at the TTWA level. We run the regression at the establishment level, however, because the sampling of establishments means that the unobserved factors are not fixed at the TTWA level (because different establishments are sampled in different years). We report results for TTWA regressions in the robustness section. Third, port trade may be partly driven by changes in the spatial distribution of UK manufacturing rather than vice versa. To control for these problems we report instrumental variable results in Section 7, once we have considered the extent to which the direction of trade determines the port composition. Instrumenting controls for the problem that the included TTWA variables may be endogenous. Providing that other TTWA-level or establishment-level variables are uncorrelated with the country re-orientation of trade (which seems reasonable) this should also control for other omitted variables that might be correlated with the access variables.

Table 3 reports results from the fixed effects specification ignoring these three problems.[8] We get the cleanest results on export market access. Twenty-one coefficients are positive and significant at the 5 per cent level or higher,

[7]Industry $j$'s use of intermediate $k$ is taken from Department of Industry (1980).

[8]There are insufficient observations for sector 61 (other vehicles). No industry is classified in sector 74 (textile finishing). It is not clear why this is the case, but this is true in the raw data and is not a result of our processing of the data.

TABLE 3

ESTIMATES OF EFFECT OF ECONOMIC GEOGRAPHY VARIABLES ON ESTABLISHMENT EMPLOYMENT

| *IO* | *IMP* | *EXP* | *INT* | *N* | *IO* | *IMP* | *EXP* | *INT* | *N* |
|---|---|---|---|---|---|---|---|---|---|
| 10 | –0.18 | 0.36 | –0.14 | 40 | 50 | 0.31 | –0.19 | 0.06 | 215 |
| 11 | 0.49* | 0.15** | –0.55** | 130 | 51 | –0.20** | 0.14* | 0.10 | 926 |
| 12 | –0.20* | 0.02 | 0.17* | 149 | 52 | 16.04** | 1.73** | –18.06** | 223 |
| 13 | 0.03 | 0.03 | –0.06 | 1258 | 53 | 0.61** | 0.06 | –0.70** | 308 |
| 14 | –0.71** | 0.09 | 0.72** | 1031 | 54 | –0.72** | 0.21* | 0.67** | 529 |
| 15 | –0.09 | 0.04 | 0.16 | 512 | 55 | –0.11 | 0.04 | 0.12 | 252 |
| 16 | –4.33 | 0.30** | 4.23 | 39 | 56 | 0.00 | 0.12 | –0.07 | 746 |
| 17 | –0.01 | –0.13** | 0.02 | 215 | 57 | –0.18** | 0.31** | –0.04 | 825 |
| 18 | –0.01 | –0.12** | 0.23** | 375 | 58 | 0.13 | –0.03 | 0.32 | 59 |
| 19 | –0.01 | –0.04 | 0.10 | 121 | 59 | 0.00 | –0.13** | 0.06 | 1529 |
| 20 | 0.34** | 0.06 | –0.31** | 798 | 60 | –0.01 | 0.08 | –0.03 | 579 |
| 21 | 0.00 | 0.09 | 0.07 | 326 | 62 | –0.04 | 0.04 | 0.00 | 1083 |
| 22 | 0.04 | –0.10** | 0.22** | 337 | 63 | –0.40 | 0.18* | 0.26 | 492 |
| 23 | 0.50** | –0.18* | –0.35** | 32 | 64 | –0.53** | 0.25* | 0.42** | 321 |
| 24 | 0.03 | 0.12** | 0.04 | 609 | 65 | 0.03 | 0.02 | 0.06 | 348 |
| 25 | –0.08 | 0.10 | 0.04 | 290 | 66 | 0.26* | –0.23* | 0.13 | 138 |
| 26 | 0.09 | –0.08 | –0.08 | 161 | 67 | 0.06* | 0.03 | –0.05* | 4840 |
| 27 | 0.02 | 0.01 | 0.01 | 213 | 68 | 0.00 | 0.09 | –0.16 | 56 |
| 28 | –0.38** | 0.45** | 0.27* | 111 | 69 | –0.76** | 0.01 | 1.02** | 713 |
| 29 | 0.12 | –0.27** | 0.21** | 422 | 70 | 0.08 | 0.05 | –0.21* | 808 |
| 30 | –0.25 | –0.01 | 0.11 | 75 | 71 | 0.40 | 0.20* | –0.36 | 1030 |
| 31 | –0.07 | 0.19 | –0.04 | 67 | 72 | 0.50* | –0.08 | –0.62** | 166 |
| 32 | –0.09 | 0.09 | 0.03 | 434 | 73 | 0.13 | –0.19 | –0.10 | 275 |
| 33 | 0.10* | 0.12* | –0.07 | 673 | 75 | –0.33* | –0.31* | 0.58** | 165 |
| 34 | 0.07 | 0.03 | 0.00 | 751 | 76 | 0.03 | 0.04 | –0.02 | 733 |
| 35 | –0.35 | 0.00 | 0.64* | 418 | 77 | 0.11** | 0.00 | –0.13** | 3918 |
| 36 | 0.04 | 0.16** | –0.07 | 492 | 78 | 0.13* | –0.02 | –0.01 | 535 |
| 37 | 0.45* | 0.01 | 0.03 | 229 | 79 | –0.12 | 0.20** | –0.10 | 437 |
| 38 | 0.02 | –0.11 | 0.17 | 628 | 80 | –0.13* | 0.13* | 0.13 | 679 |
| 39 | –0.10* | 0.04 | 0.09* | 591 | 81 | –0.01 | –0.17 | –0.27 | 31 |
| 40 | –0.75** | 0.14 | 0.85** | 97 | 82 | –0.04 | –0.01 | 0.11** | 1353 |
| 41 | –0.22 | 0.53** | –0.23 | 244 | 83 | –0.06 | 0.09* | 0.07** | 1650 |
| 42 | 0.02 | –0.11* | 0.08 | 877 | 84 | 0.50 | –0.02 | –0.46 | 3220 |
| 43 | 0.97 | 0.10 | –1.27 | 102 | 85 | 0.65 | 0.22** | –0.82 | 324 |
| 44 | –0.09** | 0.01 | 0.05 | 2269 | 86 | –0.13 | 0.04 | 0.12 | 843 |
| 45 | –0.10** | 0.24** | –0.08* | 1770 | 87 | –0.08 | 0.02 | 0.02 | 830 |
| 46 | 0.01 | –0.05 | 0.09** | 2347 | 88 | 0.04 | –0.09** | 0.00 | 4979 |
| 47 | –0.19** | 0.20** | 0.04 | 1655 | 89 | 0.00 | 0.07 | 0.00 | 535 |
| 48 | 0.04 | 0.00 | –0.11** | 941 | 90 | –0.07 | –0.02 | 0.03 | 2155 |
| 49 | –0.30* | 0.80** | –0.16** | 171 | 91 | 0.10* | –0.12 | –0.01 | 1323 |

*Source:* Authors' own calculations using ARD data and trade data described in Section 4.
*Notes:* The dependent variable is returned employment at the establishment level. IO gives the IO sector number; see Table A2 in the Appendix for sector names. IMP reports the coefficient on import competition, EXP the coefficient on export market access and INT the coefficient on access to intermediate inputs. N gives the number of unique establishments used to calculate the within estimator. * denotes significant at 5 per cent; ** significant at 1 per cent. All specifications include establishment fixed effects and time dummies. Data are for 1970–92 (excluding 1983 and 1987).

with 10 negative and significant and the rest insignificant. Results on import competition and intermediate good access are more mixed. For import competition, 16 coefficients are negative and significant in line with theory, while 13 are significantly positive. For intermediate access, 16 coefficients are positive, in line with theory with 12 negative. Part of the problem here is that the diagonal coefficients on the IO table are often large at the two-digit level so these two variables are quite highly correlated. On balance, our results are more with theory than against it, but we postpone further discussion until we have dealt with the three problems highlighted above. Details of how we construct the instrument are given in Section 6, while Section 7 considers results when we use these instruments.

## 6 Explaining the Port Composition of UK Trade

The basic hypothesis behind our identification strategy is that UK accession acts as a natural experiment exogenously changing the direction of trade. The direction of trade in turn partly determines the port composition of trade which then determines import competition and market access. For this strategy to work there must be a link between the direction of trade and the port composition, and it is that link that we consider in this section. Of course, direction is not the only factor behind the port composition of trade. Clearly other factors (e.g. port facilities) matter. However, even the most casual reflection suggests the likelihood of some link—e.g. roll-on, roll-off ferries for France leave mainly from South-East England, while those for Ireland leave from Wales, North-West England and West Scotland.

We use data for 11 port regions and 54 two-digit SITC(R) commodities.[9] The hypothesis concerns the 'behaviour' of ports and hence we treat ports as the basic units and estimate, for each, a panel of 54 commodities with 21 years of data for exports and 22 for imports. We are interested in the shares of each commodity entering/leaving via specific ports which avoids the need to allow for inflation.[10] The basic equation is

$$S_{pgt} = \sum_{d}^{D} b_{pd} T_{gdt}$$

where subscripts are $p$ for port group, $g$ for commodity, $t$ for time and $d$ ($d = 1, \ldots, D$) for destination of exports (or source for imports). $S$ is the share of the port group $p$ in total trade in good $g$ in year $t$, and $T$ the share of destination $d$ in that trade. Because the shares sum to unity over $d$ (i.e. $\Sigma_d T_{gdt} = 1$, all $g$ and $t$), the equation is rewritten in the form:

$$S_{pgt} = \sum_{d}^{D-1} b_{pd} (T_{gdt} - T_{gDt}) + b_{gD}$$

[9]Given that we do not have a full model of the port composition of trade we do not try to explain the small number of zero flows for port regions. Rather we take them as data, omitting them from the sample, and omitting all observations for a region–commodity pair if it can muster fewer than five observations exceeding 0.000001 over the sample period.

[10]Different ports may import or export different varieties within a commodity heading and the prices of these varieties may move differently. This would drive ports' volume and value shares apart, which could make our value shares misleading. Offsetting this, at least in some categories value shares might reflect economic contribution better than volume shares.

where $D$ refers to the $D$th destination. Further, because the shares all sum to unity over ports ($\Sigma_p S_{pgt} = 1$, all $g$ and $t$), the $b_{gd}$ sum to zero over $p$ and the $b_{gD}$ to unity. Provided that all equations contain the same regressors and no observations are omitted, these conditions are automatically satisfied by linear regressions run on each port separately. In addition we include a time trend in the equations to capture slowly evolving factors affecting ports (allowed to vary over port regions and over commodities), and a dummy variable taking the value of unity from 1980 onwards to represent the abolition of the National Dock Labour Scheme, a highly restrictive labour agreement which applied in around half of UK ports. The coefficients of these variables also sum to zero over port groups.

Given the difficulties of identifying many country effects we assume that while Europe is sufficiently close to the UK that it could be of material importance which UK ports were used for trade, the rest of the world is sufficiently distant that port choice is hardly influenced by the geographical composition of trade within the bloc. Thus, we distinguish the following (groups of) countries as sources for imports and markets for exports: France; Germany; Benelux; Scandinavia; Italy; Austria and Switzerland; Other Western Europe, and Rest of the World (the omitted category, $D$, in the equation above).[11] Given that our sample ends in 1992, trade with the Soviet bloc was small so we do not break it out separately.

Table 4 presents results for exports and imports of manufactures (SITC 5–8). Results for primary exports and imports (SITC 0–4) are available on request. The time trend terms are frequently statistically significant individually and always strongly so collectively. The fit is mostly quite high and the direction of trade variables often highly significant. Collectively they give a good deal of credibility to the hypothesis that West European trade is biased towards the Southern and Eastern ports.

The results are reported with the ports ordered according to the extent to which we expect the port to be tied to European trade. Thus the second column refers to 'other airports', which are scattered about the country, the third to the London airports (Heathrow, Gatwick and Southend) and the remainder to sea ports roughly in order of increasing proximity to Western Europe. The constant, labelled RW, is difficult to interpret because the RW data also appear in all the other independent data. The remaining coefficients describe the effects on a port region's share of exports of a commodity of an increase in the share of that country accompanied by an equal fall in the share of the RW in exports of the commodity.

The results clearly show that the country composition of trade partly explains port composition. The degrees of explanation are quite high, given the simplicity of the model, and the statistical tests quite clear in their

[11]Some trade travels via European entrepôts (e.g. Rotterdam or Antwerp) and hence all trade may have a bias towards South-East ports. This could slightly distort our estimates.

TABLE 4
THE PORT COMPOSITION OF TRADE GIVEN THE COUNTRY COMPOSITION

| | AIROT | AIRLO | RESTP | ESCOT | NEHUM | SSWCO | SUHAM | FELIX | HAVEA | LONDN | THAKE |
|---|---|---|---|---|---|---|---|---|---|---|---|
| Manufactured exports | | | | | | | | | | | |
| Dock Labour | −0.01** | 0.01 | −0.01* | 0.00 | 0.01** | 0.00 | −0.03** | 0.01** | 0.01** | 0.02** | −0.01** |
| France | −0.11** | 0.10 | −0.42** | −0.04** | 0.38** | 0.04 | 0.02 | −0.04 | 0.00 | −0.29** | 0.36** |
| Germany | 0.04 | 0.09 | −0.14 | −0.03 | −0.03 | 0.03 | −0.05 | −0.12** | 0.04 | −0.17 | 0.34** |
| Benelux | −0.03 | −0.29** | 0.25** | 0.04** | 0.01 | 0.04* | −0.05 | −0.01 | −0.05 | 0.09 | 0.01 |
| Italy | −0.14* | 0.46** | 0.12 | 0.03 | −0.23* | −0.13** | 0.01 | −0.17* | −0.01 | 0.05 | 0.01 |
| Scandinavia | 0.09** | 0.04 | −0.29** | 0.02 | 0.07 | 0.06* | 0.03 | 0.21** | 0.09 | −0.04 | −0.27** |
| Other Western Europe | 0.10 | −1.08** | 0.59** | −0.01 | 0.00 | −0.05 | 0.06 | −0.07 | 0.06 | 0.83** | −0.43** |
| Austria/Switz | 0.02 | 0.69** | −0.12** | −0.01 | −0.10** | 0.01 | −0.03 | 0.02 | −0.08** | −0.45** | 0.04 |
| Constant RW | 0.01 | 0.17** | 0.19** | 0.01** | 0.15** | 0.01 | 0.08** | 0.01 | 0.09** | 0.12** | 0.18** |
| $R^2$ (within) | 0.28 | 0.59 | 0.81 | 0.50 | 0.51 | 0.49 | 0.41 | 0.82 | 0.59 | 0.81 | 0.91 |
| $p$ (direcn = 0) | 0.00 | 0.00 | 0.00 | 0.01 | 0.00 | 0.01 | 0.12 | 0.00 | 0.00 | 0.00 | 0.00 |
| N | 564 | 567 | 567 | 567 | 567 | 554 | 567 | 567 | 567 | 567 | 567 |
| Manufactured imports | | | | | | | | | | | |
| Dock Labour | −0.01** | −0.01 | −0.01 | 0.00 | 0.01** | 0.01** | −0.04** | 0.02** | 0.01** | 0.01* | 0.01 |
| France | −0.09** | −0.05 | −0.19** | −0.05 | 0.04 | −0.02 | 0.28** | −0.16** | 0.17** | −0.22** | 0.30** |
| Germany | 0.00 | −0.16** | −0.06 | 0.62 | 0.04 | −0.01 | 0.03 | 0.00 | −0.05 | 0.12* | 0.06 |
| Benelux | 0.01 | −0.11 | 0.15** | −0.09** | −0.09** | −0.03 | 0.12** | 0.00 | 0.04 | −0.08 | 0.08 |
| Italy | −0.03 | 0.02 | −0.13* | 0.02 | −0.09* | 0.18** | −0.13 | −0.09 | −0.21 | −0.12 | 0.58** |
| Scandinavia | 0.00 | −0.42** | 0.03 | −0.06* | 0.09** | −0.05** | −0.09 | 0.26** | 0.28** | 0.28** | −0.31** |
| Other Western Europe | 0.10* | −0.03 | 0.14 | 0.02 | −0.07 | −0.01 | 0.01 | 0.04 | −0.01 | 0.07 | −0.27** |
| Austria/Switz | 0.01 | 0.82** | −0.03 | 0.08** | 0.05 | −0.02 | −0.19** | −0.09* | −0.12** | −0.18** | −0.34** |
| Constant RW | 0.05** | 0.18** | 0.09** | 0.00 | 0.10** | 0.03** | 0.10** | 0.09** | 0.12** | 0.04** | 0.20** |
| $R^2$ (within) | 0.32 | 0.59 | 0.80 | 0.54 | 0.49 | 0.52 | 0.27 | 0.68 | 0.65 | 0.68 | 0.86 |
| $p$ (direcn = 0) | 0.03 | 0.00 | 0.00 | 0.00 | 0.00 | 0.00 | 0.00 | 0.00 | 0.00 | 0.00 | 0.00 |
| N | 591 | 593 | 594 | 594 | 594 | 593 | 594 | 594 | 594 | 594 | 594 |

*Source:* Authors' own calculations using trade data described in Section 4.
*Notes:* Coefficients from regression of port regions shares on dummy for Dock Labour Scheme, country shares and time dummies (not reported). * denotes significant at 5 per cent, ** significant at 1 per cent. $R^2$ (within) reports the within $R$-squared. $p$ (direcn = 0) reports the probability levels for Wald tests of the null hypothesis that the country breakdown explains none of the port composition of trade. N reports the sample size. See Table A2 for definitions of the port groups AIROT, AIRLO etc.

inference. Overall, they are quite sufficient to suggest the plausibility of our hypothesis and the use of country composition as instruments for port composition. Given this, we estimate the same model on individual port data to generate instrumental estimates of exports and imports.[12]

## 7 The UK's Accession to the EEC and the Changing Economic Geography of UK Manufacturing

### *7.1 Instrumental Variable Results*

To construct our instruments, we replace actual port trade shares with predicted shares when calculating our measures of import competition, intermediate good and export market access. Table 5 presents results when we instrument all three access variables using these measures based on predicted shares as instruments. The instrumental variable results are somewhat more supportive of theory. There is a tendency for the significant theory-consistent estimates to come from sectors with larger samples. Overall, 17 sectors show precisely the sign pattern predicted by theory. Before discussing our results further, we briefly discuss a range of robustness checks. Detailed results for the robustness checks are available on request or in the discussion paper version of this paper (Overman and Winters, 2006).

The results in Table 5 are based on reported (or 'returned') employment. This is only available if an establishment has been selected and so the sample favours larger establishments. When an establishment is not sampled, we only have estimated employment. Using both measures of employment significantly increases the number of firms (particularly small firms) but this does not change the core results.[13]

We can also use different distance decay effects when constructing our measures of import competition, export market and intermediate good access. We redefine import competition for sector $j$ in TTWA $l$ as

$$\text{IMP}_{jlt} = \sum_{p} \frac{m_{jpt}}{(d_{lp})^{\rho}}$$

[12]The port data are noisier and subject to more zeros and small values. For some ports we have too few observations to estimate a panel and for many we have to omit some commodities. We take the zeros as exogenous and estimate only on share observations exceeding 0.000001 where there are at least five of them for a particular port/commodity combination over the sample. Some predicted values are negative, but they are small. Before being used as instruments, they are put through the SITC-IO converter, and many are absorbed into other positive values. Then the results by port are distance weighted to generate the TTWA variables so small negative values are dominated by larger positive ones for the larger ports. The estimates for the larger ports are well defined so we do not believe the negative predictions play any material role in the final results.

[13]To be precise, we set establishment employment equal to returned employment when that is available and selected employment otherwise.

TABLE 5
INSTRUMENTAL VARIABLE ESTIMATES OF EFFECT OF ECONOMIC GEOGRAPHY VARIABLES ON ESTABLISHMENT EMPLOYMENT

| *IO* | *IMP* | *EXP* | *INT* | *N* | *IO* | *IMP* | *EXP* | *INT* | *N* |
|---|---|---|---|---|---|---|---|---|---|
| 10 | −0.18 | −0.25 | 0.41 | 40 | 50 | 0.26 | −0.33 | 0.27 | 215 |
| 11 | −1.76* | −0.45* | 2.43** | 130 | 51 | −0.54** | 0.25* | 0.29** | 926 |
| 12 | −0.27 | −0.05 | 0.31** | 149 | 52 | 17.42** | 1.72** | −19.45** | 223 |
| 13 | 0.05 | 0.00 | −0.05 | 1258 | 53 | 0.60 | 0.37 | −0.99 | 308 |
| 14 | −0.66* | 0.12 | 0.65* | 1030 | 54 | −0.74** | 0.27* | 0.64 | 529 |
| 15 | −0.15 | 0.23* | 0.08 | 512 | 55 | −0.25* | 0.33* | −0.07 | 252 |
| 16 | 3.29 | 0.56** | −3.84 | 39 | 56 | 0.00 | 0.09 | −0.03 | 746 |
| 17 | 0.08 | −0.25** | 0.04 | 215 | 57 | −0.50** | 0.67** | −0.17 | 825 |
| 18 | −0.04 | −0.19* | 0.32** | 375 | 58 | −0.09 | −0.12 | 1.61** | 59 |
| 19 | 0.04 | 0.12 | −0.09 | 121 | 59 | 0.06 | −0.42** | 0.35** | 1529 |
| 20 | −0.17 | 0.48** | −0.24* | 798 | 60 | −0.36 | 0.04 | 0.33 | 579 |
| 21 | 0.13 | 0.03 | 0.01 | 326 | 62 | −0.08 | 0.16 | −0.09 | 1083 |
| 22 | −0.11 | −0.07 | 0.27** | 337 | 63 | −0.23 | 0.62** | −0.37 | 492 |
| 23 | 0.66** | −0.19* | −0.69** | 32 | 64 | −0.97** | 0.35 | 0.84** | 321 |
| 24 | −0.12 | 0.18** | 0.15 | 609 | 65 | 0.08 | −0.15 | 0.23* | 348 |
| 25 | −0.06 | 0.04 | 0.10 | 290 | 66 | 0.44* | −0.42* | 0.37** | 138 |
| 26 | 0.06 | −0.07 | −0.07 | 161 | 67 | 0.07 | 0.11* | −0.16** | 4840 |
| 27 | −0.25 | −0.03 | 0.21 | 213 | 68 | −0.05 | 0.16 | −0.22 | 56 |
| 28 | −0.50** | 0.48** | 0.38* | 111 | 69 | −1.50** | −0.23 | 2.03** | 713 |
| 29 | −0.04 | −0.24** | 0.37** | 422 | 70 | 0.44 | −0.46 | −0.16 | 808 |
| 30 | −0.59 | 0.18 | 0.14 | 75 | 71 | 0.28 | −0.30 | 0.25 | 1030 |
| 31 | −0.06 | 0.08 | 0.09 | 67 | 72 | 0.41 | −0.53 | −0.15 | 166 |
| 32 | 0.03 | −0.06 | 0.09 | 434 | 73 | 0.86* | −0.50* | −0.53 | 275 |
| 33 | 0.36** | −0.06 | −0.09 | 673 | 75 | −0.61* | −0.45* | 1.00** | 165 |
| 34 | −0.07 | 0.25** | −0.09 | 751 | 76 | 0.02 | 0.02 | 0.01 | 733 |
| 35 | 0.06 | −0.14 | 0.34 | 418 | 77 | 0.13** | 0.02 | −0.19** | 3918 |
| 36 | 0.10 | 0.26* | −0.18 | 492 | 78 | 0.22** | −0.12* | 0.02 | 535 |
| 37 | 0.14 | 0.30 | −0.08 | 229 | 79 | −0.04 | 0.32* | −0.25 | 437 |
| 38 | −0.05 | −0.09 | 0.23 | 628 | 80 | −0.26** | 0.25* | 0.16 | 679 |
| 39 | −0.22** | 0.06 | 0.18* | 591 | 81 | −0.17 | −0.19 | −0.15 | 31 |
| 40 | −0.69** | 0.46 | 0.52 | 97 | 82 | −0.04 | −0.01 | 0.13** | 1353 |
| 41 | −1.67* | 1.27** | 0.15 | 244 | 83 | −0.22** | 0.26** | 0.06 | 1650 |
| 42 | 0.01 | −0.04 | 0.01 | 877 | 84 | 1.81** | 0.06 | −1.85** | 3220 |
| 43 | −0.51 | −0.77 | 1.06 | 102 | 85 | 1.43 | 0.46** | −1.82* | 324 |
| 44 | −0.14** | −0.11 | 0.21** | 2269 | 86 | −0.55* | 0.13* | 0.47* | 843 |
| 45 | −0.31** | 0.61** | −0.30** | 1770 | 87 | 0.01 | 0.01 | −0.06 | 830 |
| 46 | −0.03 | −0.20** | 0.28** | 2347 | 88 | 0.01 | −0.06 | 0.00 | 4979 |
| 47 | −0.23** | 0.36** | −0.08 | 1655 | 89 | −0.04 | 0.21* | −0.09 | 535 |
| 48 | −0.20* | 0.08 | −0.03 | 941 | 90 | −0.12* | 0.06 | −0.03 | 2155 |
| 49 | −0.42* | 1.04** | −0.30** | 171 | 91 | 0.22* | −0.22 | −0.02 | 1323 |

*Source:* Authors' own calculations using ARD data and trade data described in Section 4.
*Notes:* The dependent variable is returned employment at the establishment level. IO gives the IO sector number; see Table A2 in the Appendix for sector names. IMP reports the coefficient on import competition, EXP the coefficient on export market access and INT the coefficient on access to intermediate inputs. N gives the number of unique establishments used to calculate the within estimator. * denotes significant at 5 per cent, ** significant at 1 per cent. All specifications include establishment fixed effects and time dummies. Data are for 1970–92 (excluding 1983 and 1987).

where, as before, $m_{jpt}$ is the share of imports for sector $j$ coming in through port $p$ at time $t$ and $d_{lp}$ is the distance in kilometres between port $p$ and TTWA $l$. The coefficient $\rho$ varies the distance decay effect: the higher $\rho$ the more import competition declines with distance. The other two market access variables can be defined similarly. Ideally, we would like to estimate the coefficient on distance, but this is computationally infeasible.[14] Instead, we experimented with two values ($\rho = 0.5$ and $\rho = 1.5$) chosen after consulting Disdier and Head (2008) who provide a meta-analysis of results on the distance decay coefficient in the standard gravity model. Results with a distance decay parameter of 0.5 were, if anything, a little stronger, those with $\rho$ equal to 1.5 a little weaker, particularly for import competition and intermediate goods access. This is not particularly surprising, as $\rho = 1.5$ is a fairly strong distance decay and gives much less time-series variation from which to estimate the effects.

Large diagonal elements in the IO matrix mean we might be able to get stronger results if we ignore own intermediate inputs when defining our measure of intermediate good access. In other words, define

$$\mathrm{INT}_{jlt} = \sum_{k \neq j} \sum_{p} \frac{a_{jk} m_{kp}}{d_{lp}}$$

where, as before, $a_{jk}$ is industry $j$'s use of intermediate $k$. Of course, this means that the sign on the import competition variable could be positive if access to own intermediate goods is sufficiently important so as to outweigh the competition effect. This seems unlikely *a priori*, and in fact, this redefinition of intermediate input access does little to change the results and so we pursue it no further.

We considered two final issues. First, we examined what happens if we allow for a more general error structure on the idiosyncratic errors. Results change little if we allow for arbitrary heteroscedasticity at the establishment level. Finally, we aggregated so that the basic unit of observation is TTWA employment by sector. Aggregating up to the TTWA level reduces noise. The cost of doing this is that, as explained earlier, the annual sampling of establishments means that we cannot regard the unobserved variable as fixed at the TTWA level (because different establishments may be sampled in different years). Results for this final robustness check are somewhat mixed. For the TTWA regressions, we struggle to find consistent evidence of the import competition effect. Indeed, we now have roughly equal numbers of coefficients with positive and negative signs. The results on access to intermediates are also slightly weakened, but offsetting this is the fact that our results on export access are strengthened—we now found 31 positive coefficients and only five negative.

Overall, the series of checks that we have presented makes us confident that the core results that we presented in Table 5 are fairly robust. The strongest results are for the role of export market access with those for import market competition and intermediate access somewhat weaker. Partly, this reflects the difficulty in separating out these two effects given the presence of large diagonal elements in the IO table.

[14]For 81 sectors, with 93 ports and 287 TTWAs each iteration requires a minimum of 3 × 2,161,971 calculations.

## 8 Conclusion

This paper has offered a detailed investigation of the effects of the UK's accession to the EEC on the spatial distribution of industry. It has two objectives. First, the drift of industry towards the South East has implications for aspects of economic life and has been the subject of policy interventions, so it is interesting to understand its determinants *per se*. We have undertaken two major data construction exercises, one on the employment and location of establishments and one on the allocation of UK international trade between British ports, to explore the question with a finer geographical and commodity disaggregation than ever before. Our second objective was to propose a way of testing predictions of models of NEG using UK access to the EEC as a natural experiment.

To recap the substantive analysis, UK accession changed the country composition of trade. These changes to the country composition of trade changed the ports through which trade entered and exited the UK with the result that import competition, export and intermediate market access changed differently for firms located in different areas. Firm employment responded to these changes in the way that theory predicts in roughly one-quarter to one-third of UK sectors. In a few sectors, the changes went against theory while for the remainder we can detect no significant effect. Given the multitude of forces operating on local employment and on specific firms, our relatively small samples and the noise in our data, it is not surprising that many of the estimates are insignificant. The significant but implausible estimates are a little more disturbing and suggest that some of the factors omitted from our model are correlated with the changes in geographical trade patterns. For example, it is possible that *within* some of our sectors changes in comparative advantage—i.e. over varieties—favour firms in the North and West or disfavours those in the South East. These could be related to factor inputs (e.g. labour-intensive varieties prosper) or technology or even public policy changes. Overall the tendencies in our results suggest that the simple locational factors underpinning the NEG view of trade are useful for explaining industrial geography, but that other systematic forces are also at work. Overall the results suggest that the re-orientation of trade entailed in joining the EEC did contribute to the relocation of UK industry; equally, however, they indicate that it was not the only factor.

On methodology, our approach provides an original and relatively clean test of theories of economic geography. UK accession to the EEC was a natural experiment that generated an exogenous geographical shock which helps us to identify the causal effect of changing import competition, export market access and intermediate good market access on economic geography. Overall, we find that changes in the spatial distribution of UK manufacturing are broadly consistent with the predictions of the theory, and that by using UK accession as a natural experiment we have been able to identify the causation running from trade to location more securely than in the absence of that exogenous source of variation.

## Appendix

Table A1
IO Sectors

| *Code* | *Industry name* | *Code* | *Industry name* |
|---|---|---|---|
| 10 | Coke ovens and manufactured fuel | 51 | Radio and electronics components |
| 11 | Mineral oil refining, lubricating oils etc. | 52 | Television, radio and sound-reproducing equipment |
| 12 | Grain milling | 53 | Electronic computers |
| 13 | Bread and flour confectionery and biscuits | 54 | Radio, radar and electronic capital goods |
| 14 | Meat and fish products | 55 | Domestic electrical appliances |
| 15 | Milk and milk products | 56 | Other electrical goods |
| 16 | Sugar | 57 | Shipbuilding and marine engineering |
| 17 | Cocoa, chocolate and sugar confectionery | 58 | Wheeled tractors |
| 18 | Animal and poultry foods | 59 | Motor vehicles |
| 19 | Oils and fats | 60 | Aerospace equipment |
| 20 | Other food | 61 | Other vehicles |
| 21 | Soft drinks | 62 | Engineers' small tools |
| 22 | Alcoholic drink | 63 | Cutlery etc., jewelry and precious metals |
| 23 | Tobacco | 64 | Bolts, nuts, screws etc. |
| 24 | General chemicals | 65 | Wire and wire manufactures |
| 25 | Pharmaceutical chemicals and preparations | 66 | Cans and metal boxes |
| 26 | Toilet preparations | 67 | Other metal goods |
| 27 | Paints | 68 | Production of man-made fibres |
| 28 | Soap and detergents | 69 | Cotton etc. spinning and weaving |
| 29 | Synthetic resins etc. and synthetic rubber | 70 | Woollen and worsted |
| 30 | Dyestuffs and pigments | 71 | Hosiery and knitted goods |
| 31 | Fertilizers | 72 | Carpets |
| 32 | Other chemical industries | 73 | Household textiles and handkerchiefs |
| 33 | Iron castings etc. | 74 | Textile finishing |
| 34 | Other iron and steel | 75 | Other textiles |
| 35 | Aluminium and aluminium alloys | 76 | Leather, leather goods and fur |
| 36 | Other non-ferrous metals | 77 | Clothing |
| 37 | Agricultural machinery | 78 | Footwear |
| 38 | Machine tools | 79 | Bricks, fireclay and refractory goods |
| 39 | Pumps, valves and compressors | 80 | Pottery and glass |
| 40 | Industrial engines | 81 | Cement |
| 41 | Textile machinery | 82 | Other building materials etc. |
| 42 | Construction and mechanical handling equipment | 83 | Furniture and bedding etc. |
| 43 | Office machinery | 84 | Timber and miscellaneous wood manufactures |
| 44 | Other non-electrical machinery | 85 | Paper and board |
| 45 | Industrial plan and steelwork | 86 | Packaging products of paper, board etc. |
| 46 | Other mechanical engineering | 87 | Other paper and board products |
| 47 | Instrument engineering | 88 | Printing and publishing |
| 48 | Electrical machinery | 89 | Rubber |
| 49 | Insulated wires and cables | 90 | Plastics products not elsewhere stated |
| 50 | Telegraph and telephone equipment | 91 | Other manufacturing |

TABLE A2
DEFINITION OF PORT GROUPS

| | | | |
|---|---|---|---|
| AIROT | ALL OTHER AIRPORTS | ESCOT | ABERDEEN |
| Other Airports | BELFAST AIRPORT | East Scotland | DUNDEE |
| | GLASGOW AIRPORT | | FRASERBURGH |
| | MANCHESTER AIRPORT | | GRANGEMOUTH |
| | PRESTWICK AIRPORT | | KIRKCALDY |
| AIRLO | GATWICK AIRPORT | | KIRKWALL |
| London | HEATHROW AIRPORT | | LEITH |
| Airports | SOUTHEND AIRPORT | | MONTROSE |
| RESTP | ARDROSSAN | | PETERHEAD |
| Rest of ports | AVONMOUTH | NEHUM | BLYTH |
| | AYR | North East | BOSTON |
| | BARROW-IN-FURNESS | and Humber | GOOLE |
| | BELFAST | | GRIMSBY |
| | CARDIFF | | HARTLEPOOL |
| | COLERAINE | | HULL |
| | DOUGLAS | | IMMINGHAM |
| | ELLESMERE PORT | | MIDDLESBROUGH |
| | FISHGUARD | | SCARBOROUGH |
| | FLEETWOOD | | SUNDERLAND |
| | GLASGOW | | TYNE |
| | GREENOCK | | WHITBY |
| | HEYSHAM | SSWCO | EXETER |
| | HOLYHEAD | South West | FALMOUTH |
| | INVERNESS | and Cornwall | FOWEY |
| | IRISH LAND BOUNDARY | | GUERNSEY |
| | IRVINE | | JERSEY |
| | LERWICK | | PAR |
| | LIVERPOOL | | PENZANCE |
| | LONDONDERRY | | PLYMOUTH |
| | MANCHESTER | | POOLE |
| | MILFORD | | TEIGNMOUTH |
| | MOSTYN | | WEYMOUTH |
| | NEWPORT | SUHAM | COWES |
| | PORT TALBOT | Sussex and | NEWHAVEN |
| | RUNCORN | Hampshire | PORTSMOUTH |
| | SHARPNESS | | SHOREHAM |
| | SILLOTH | | SOUTHAMPTON |
| | STORNOWAY | HAVEA | COLCHESTER |
| | SWANSEA | Haven and | GREAT YARMOUTH |
| | WATCHET | East Anglia | HARWICH |
| | WHITEHAVEN | | IPSWICH |
| | WORKINGTON | | KINGS LYNN |
| LONDON | LONDON | | LOWESTOFT |
| FELIX | FELIXSTOWE | | WISBECH |
| | | THAKE | DOVER |
| | | Thames and | LONDON |
| | | Kent | MEDWAY |
| | | | RAMSGATE |
| | | | WHITSTABLE |

*The International Trade Data*

*UK Trade by Port, 1970–92.* The main international trade data that underpin our analysis describe UK trade by port and commodity from 1970 to 1992.[15] The data set was specially constructed from official sources for the present exercise and, to our knowledge, these sources have never been exploited before at this level of detail. They were supplemented by data for the same commodities and time period on the sources of imports and destination of exports, which reflect the re-orientation of UK trade following accession to the EEC.

Data on UK trade by port have been published in a variety of sources since 1970.[16] The source data contain three major omissions: export data for 1983, both export and import data for 1987, and export data for Harmonized System chapters 84–99 for 1989–90. The structure of the data varies by publication and the classifications evolve from SITC(R) through SITC(2R) and (3R) to the Harmonized System (1988).[17] We have attempted to correct for these evolutions and to convert the data to a common classification. The latter process requires some approximation, e.g. splitting a heading in one classification into two in another. This was done by working with the finest level of aggregation available, but was done for total UK exports and imports and the shares used for each port of partner country.

The most disaggregated continuous series that could be constructed was at the Division (two-digit) level of the SITC(R), which distinguishes 56 headings, of which we have to drop one (35, gas and electricity) and combine one pair into a single heading (33 and 52 which become indissolubly entwined in the later classifications). At this level no volume or deflator data are available, so all data are in value terms. Given the high rates of inflation over much of the period intertemporal absolute comparisons are meaningless, but for our purposes using ports' shares in total UK trade of a commodity is sufficient.

Over the period 1970–92 data are reported for about 120 ports at some point of time. However, the coverage changes through time and there is a fairly continuous process of re-combination of ports into local groups, as the geographical responsibilities of individual customs offices evolved. In most cases we solve these problems by aggregating ports into groups that are invariant over time, but there remain a number of possible minor inconsistencies.[18] Overall we are able to compile consistent data on 92 ports or local groups of ports over 1970–92.[19]

[15]Data are not available by port for trade with the EU after 1992 because under the Single Market Programme these flows were treated as internal European trade and were recorded via value added tax returns rather than by Customs and Excise at the port.

[16]The Annual Statement of Trade, Vol. V (HM Customs and Excise), 1970–75; Statistics of Trade through United Kingdom Ports (HM Customs and Excise), 1976–80; on micro fiche, 1981–87, and then electronically for 1988–92 via the commercial data suppliers, Business Trade Statistics Ltd.

[17]In addition to classifying goods differently, the classifications also have slightly different coverage of goods. For example, variations in the treatment of non-monetary gold, tax-free cars and parcel post.

[18]For example, Avonmouth was included in Bristol 1970–73, the two ports were separated for 1974–80 and after 1980 Bristol disappears as an explicit entry and we take it implicitly to be included in Avonmouth.

[19]The data have been subject to a number of consistency checks as they have been prepared, including checking against independent sources. Unfortunately a small number of

When we turn to the econometric specifications, it is sometimes useful to group ports into 11 groups, loosely based on those used by Chisholm (1992, 1995) in the only previous analysis we know of that considers the effects of accession on the geography of trade (but not production). The 11 groups, along with the acronyms that we use to refer to them, are defined in Table A2 of the Appendix. The grouping is more finely disaggregated around the South East, because we expect integration to affect those ports in particular.[20]

The second stage involved using a series of concordance matrices to map trade flows to the sectors identified in the UK IO table for 1974, to create a data series of trade by port, IO sector and year, which we can marry with the establishment data.

*Mapping Trade Flows to Industries.* The data on trade flows prior to 1977 are available only at Division (two-digit) level of the SITC(R). Thus all subsequent data were converted to this basis. To relate the trade data at two-digit level of the SITC(R) to manufacturing establishments we need to develop a concordance between SITC(R) and UK IO sectors. No such converters were published, so we had to proceed indirectly. Aki Kuwahara of the United Nations Conference on Trade and Development (UNCTAD) kindly supplied us with a 'universal' concordance between eight classifications including the SITC(R) and the International Standard Industrial Classification (ISIC) 1968 from which we generated a mapping from the approximately 1200 basic SITC(R) four- and five-digit headings to four-digit ISIC headings, of which 100 are of relevance for trade in goods.

This mapping was then matched to UK visible export data by SITC(R) collected from the UN Comtrade Database,[21] averaged over 1970–80. In about a dozen cases an SITC heading was mapped to more than one ISIC heading, in which case trade was divided evenly between those headings. In about three dozen cases an SITC heading had not been mapped to ISIC. Most of these were UN 'special' four-digit codes ending in zero which are used when official statisticians cannot allocate trade across four-digit headings but know its three-digit category. Most of these actually recorded no trade for the UK, and so allocating them to ISIC did not matter, but this was not always the case. In addition, there were about half a dozen 'genuine' SITC heading that were unmapped. In these cases we created a mapping from the textual descriptions of the two classifications.[22]

The data set resulting from these manipulations comprised about 1200 rows each containing an ISIC heading, an SITC(R) heading and an export flow. This was then aggregated into SITC(R) two-digit divisions and then into the ISIC headings to create

implausibilities remain in the allocation of trade across ports. The most serious remaining mystery is the sharp changes in the share of exports of engineering goods (SITC(R)7) passing through Heathrow in 1991. We have been unable to explain this or to find a plausible way of adjusting the data.

[20]We separate London from THAKE and Felixstowe from HAVEA because the two named ports are major specialist deep-sea ports which may have different trading roles from their regional neighbours. We do not treat Southampton specially, however, because it entirely dominates its region, nor Liverpool, because we are less interested in the North-West region *a priori*.

[21]For which, thanks are due to Azita Amjadi of the World Bank.

[22]Finally, two SITC headings were mapped to a 'false' ISIC heading, 9999; that is, for these headings there is no corresponding ISIC heading at all. This 'false' heading was treated symmetrically with genuine ISIC headings and mapped via their descriptions.

a matrix of trade cross-classified by ISIC and SITC(R) sections. From this the converter matrix $B^x$ was created by dividing entries by their column sums. Thus $B^x$ reports how exports of an SITC section flow are derived from ISIC four-digit headings. A corresponding matrix was created for imports, $B^M$, using UK imports data from the same source averaged over 1970–80.

Department of Industry (1980) defines UK IO sectors in terms of the minimum list headings (MLHs) of the UK's SIC68. There are 91 sectors which potentially could produce tradable goods. Central Statistical Office (1971) concords the MLHs with ISIC four-digit categories, noting the many places in which the concordance is less than perfect. Most of these are small enough to ignore or are neutralized when MLHs are aggregated into IO sectors. Thus the mapping normally maps the whole of an ISIC heading into a single IO sector. However, 13 major conflicts between ISIC and SIC are explicitly listed in the introduction to Central Statistical Office (1971);[23] these were treated individually wherever possible, as were the 26 cases in which an ISIC heading is mapped to more than one IO sector. In these cases, we reverted to the SITC(R) four- and five-digit trade data to divide the ISIC trade aggregate appropriately between IO sectors, completing separate exercises for exports and imports. The resulting matrices, $C^X$ and $C^M$, report how trade flows by ISIC heading may be allocated across IO sectors. Once the classification matrices have been derived we apply them to the data on SITC(R) Division trade by port to create series of trade by port, IO sector and year, which we can marry with the establishment data.

## References


Alonso-Villar, O. (2001). 'Large Metropolises in the Third World: An Explanation', *Urban Studies*, Vol. 38, pp. 1359–1371.

Baldwin, R., Forslid, R., Martin, P., Ottaviano, G. M. and Robert-Nicoud, F. (2003). *Economic Geography and Public Policy*, Princeton, NJ, Princeton University Press.

Barnes, M. and Martin, R. (2002). 'Business Data Linking: An Introduction', *Economic Trends*, No. 581, April, pp. 34–41.

Begg, D., Blanchard, O., Coyle, D., Frankel, J., Giavazzi, F., Portes, R., Seabright, P., Venables, A., Winters, L. A. and Wyplosz, C. (2003). *The Consequences of Saying No: an Independent Report into the Economic Consequences of the UK Saying No to the Euro*, London, Britain in Europe.

Brülhart, M. and Koenig, P. (2006). New Economic Geography Meet Comecon, The Economics of Transition, *The European Bank for Reconstruction and Development*, Vol. 14, No. 2, pp. 245–267, 04.

Central Statistical Office (1971). *Standard Industrial Classification, National and International*, London, Central Statistical Office.

Chisholm, M. (1992). 'Britain, the European Community, and the Centralisation of Production: Theory and Evidence, Freight Movements', *Environment and Planning A*, Vol. 24, No. 4, pp. 551–570.

Chisholm, M. (1995). *Britain on the Edge of Europe*, London, Routledge.

Crozet, M. and Koenig Soubeyran, P. (2004). 'EU Enlargement and the Internal Geography of Countries', *Journal of Comparative Economics*, Vol. 32, No. 2, pp. 265–279.


[23]This is in addition to a general note about the different treatment of repair work in the two classifications, which we cannot make allowance for.

Department of Industry (1980). *Input–Output Tables for the United Kingdom*, Business Monitor, PA 1004, HMSO, London.
Disdier, A.-C. and Head, K. (2008). 'The Puzzling Persistence of the Distance Effect on Bilateral Trade', *The Review of Economics and Statistics*, Vol. 90, No. 1, pp. 37–48, 09.
Griffith, R. (1999). 'Using the ARD Establishment Level Data: an Application to Estimating Production Functions', *Economic Journal*, Vol. 109, Nos 4–6, pp. F416–F442.
Hanson, G. (1996). 'Localisation Economies, Vertical Organisation, and Trade', *American Economic Review*, Vol. 86, No. 5, pp. 1266–1278.
Hanson, G. (1997). 'Increasing Returns, Trade, and the Regional Structure of Wages', *Economic Journal*, Vol. 107, pp. 103–133.
Hanson, G. (1998). 'Regional Adjustment to Trade Liberalization', *Regional Science and Urban Economics*, Vol. 28, pp. 419–444.
Head, K. and Mayer, T. (2004). 'The Empirics of Agglomeration and Trade' in J.F. Thisse and V. Henderson (eds). North-Holland Handbook of Regional and Urban Economics 2004.
Hoare, G. (1977). 'The Geography of British Exports', *Environment and Planning A*, Vol. 9, pp. 121–136.
Hoare, G. (1985). 'Great Britain and Her Exports: an Exploratory Regional Analysis', *Tijdschrift voor Economische en Sociale Geografie*, Vol. LXXVI, pp. 9–21.
Hoare, G. (1986). 'British Ports and Their Export Hinterlands: a Rapidly Changing Geography', *Geografiska Analler B*, Vol. 68, pp. 29–40.
Hoare, G. (1988). 'Geographical Aspects of British Overseas Trade: a Framework and a Review', *Environment and Planning A*, Vol. 20, pp. 1345–1364.
Monfort, Ph. and Nicolini, R. (2000). 'Regional Convergence and International Integration', *Journal of Urban Economics*, Vol. 48, pp. 286–306.
Overman, H. G. and Winters, L. A. (2005). 'The Port Geography of UK International Trade', *Environment and Planning A*, Vol. 37, pp. 1751–1768.
Overman, H. G. and Winters, L. A. (2006). 'Trade and Economic Geography', *CEP Discussion Paper 588*.
Paluzie, E. (2001). 'Trade Policy and Regional Inequalities Papers in Regional Science', *Springer*, Vol. 80, No. 1, pp. 67–85.
Pavcnik, N. (2002). 'Trade Liberalisation, Exit and Productivity Improvement: Evidence from Chilean Plants', *Review of Economic Studies*, Vol. 69, No. 1, pp. 245–276.
Preeg, E. H. (1970). *Traders and Diplomats: an Analysis of the Kennedy Round of Negotiations under the General Agreement on Tariffs and Trade*, Washington, DC, Brookings Institution.
Tybout, J. (2000). 'Manufacturing Firms in Developing Countries: How Well Do They Do, and Why?', *Journal of Economic Literature*, Vol. 38, No. 1, pp. 11–44.
Tybout, J. (2001). 'Plant and Firm Level Evidence on "New" Trade Theories'. J. Harrigan and K. Choi (eds). *The Handbook of International Trade*, Basil Blackwell, London.
Winters, L. A. (1984). 'British Imports of Manufactures and the Common Market', *Oxford Economic Papers*, Vol. 36, No. 1, pp. 103–118.

# Part C

# Trade and Poverty

# Trade Liberalisation and Poverty: What are the Links?

*L. Alan Winters*

## 1. BACKGROUND

OPENNESS and trade liberalisation have been a major component of conventional economic policy advice for the last fifteen years. There is widespread acceptance that in the long run open economies fare better in aggregate than do closed ones, and that relatively open policies contribute to long-run development. Many commentators fear, however, that in the shorter run trade liberalisation puts great stress on certain actors in the economy and that even in the longer run successful open regimes may leave some behind in poverty. Others additionally argue that being open – rather than just the process of opening up – exposes an economy to shocks that generate uncertainty, cause it to operate with higher levels of poverty than would a less open economy and undermine policy measures designed to alleviate poverty and redistribute income.

This paper attempts to take these concerns seriously; it asks how a developing country's own trade liberalisation could translate into increased poverty, and what information would be required to identify whether it will do so.[1] While companion papers, Winters (2000b and 2001a), describe two partial empirical exercises and address the appropriate policy response to fears of liberalisation-induced poverty, and McKay, Winters and Kedir (2000) survey empirical evidence, this paper concentrates on positive economics, presenting a conceptual framework into which to marshall and assess relevant evidence.[2]

If trade liberalisation and poverty were both easily measured, and if there were many historical instances in which liberalisation could be identified as the main

L. ALAN WINTERS is from the School of Social Sciences, University of Sussex; the Centre for Economic Policy Research, London; and the Centre for Economic Performance, London School of Economics.

[1] While I focus on trade liberalisation, the analysis largely generalises to cover other trade shocks such as commodity price booms and slumps and exchange rate changes.

[2] In addition, McCulloch, Winters and Cirera discuss practical aspects of the trade-party link, and detailed analyses of three cases (Zambia, Vietnam and Sichuan, China) are under way at the University of Sussex.

economic shock, it would be simple to derive simple empirical regularities linking the two. Unfortunately, none of these conditions is met, and so we are thrown back on fragmentary evidence on parts of the argument. The key to assembling this evidence into a coherent picture, as well as to designing policies to alleviate any ill effects, is to understand the channels through which such effects might operate. This is the main job of this paper.

I explore the static effects of trade policy on poverty via four broad groups of institutions: households, distribution channels, factor markets and government, and then consider the dynamic questions of volatility, long-term economic growth, and short-term adjustment stresses. None of the economic analysis for the individual institutions is very complex, but in each case there are both pro- and anti-poor influences. Thus when we come to put them all together, it is hardly surprising that there is no universal conclusion as to whether a particular trade liberalisation will increase or reduce poverty. While there is a strong presumption that the long-run effects on growth will benefit the poor, the detailed and immediate effects differ both between households and across countries. Simple statements about 'the poor' will, at best, lose a lot of information, while simple generalisations about all countries will just be wrong. What I do provide, however, is a checklist that policy-makers might use to guide their thoughts about whether a particular liberalisation is likely to be pro-poor.

An important aspect of any analysis of poverty is the definition and measurement of the phenomenon itself. While recognising that there are many legitimate approaches to this, I adopt here an absolute consumption metric.[3] This entails that poverty is held to have fallen if fewer people fall below a fixed threshold in terms of their claims (entitlements) over goods and services. The threshold is not necessarily the same for all countries, although once one has to aggregate across countries – for example, to consider global effects or effects on subsets of developing countries – it becomes difficult to make the case for differences. In choosing this definition of poverty I am not denying the importance of other aspects based, for example, on social exclusion; however, a sensible first step towards understanding the effects of trade on poverty is to focus on the simplest and most directly observable aspects of the question.

There are many reasons why people are poor, and even within broad groups there are huge differences in circumstances between individual households. Thus the effects of many shocks will differ across 'the poor', and a crucial part of any practical analysis must be to identify different interests within that group. A first step towards this is a poverty profile, including information on the consumption, production and employment activities of the poor. I do not labour the point about heterogeneity below, but in truth it is hard to over-estimate its importance.

[3] Baulch (1996) offers a useful account of different poverty measures.

While poverty profiles are a necessary input to thinking about the links between trade and poverty, they should not lead one to believe that poverty is a static and unchanging state. There is, in fact, a fairly rapid turnover of families into and out of poverty, and the determinants of those transitions appear to be rather different from those turned up by studies of the static correlates of poverty (Baulch and McCulloch, 1998). This is potentially an important insight for present purposes, for if trade affects the transition probabilities it could have significant effects on the stock of 'poor', while apparently having little to do with that stock directly.

## 2. THE HOUSEHOLD

Poverty is a condition of individuals or households, so for convenience I start with a simple model of the farm household (see, for example, Singh, Squire and Strauss, 1986). This is not to be taken literally as referring only to the rural poor, although they are the majority group, but to any household which potentially makes production as well as consumption decisions. In the simplest case, household welfare is expressed as a function of the prices of all goods that the household faces and income. The latter is 'full income' comprising the value of the full complement of time at prevailing wage rates, transfers and other non-earned income (including a wide range of elements such as remittances, official transfers, transfers in kind, etc.) and profits from production decisions.

To a first-order approximation, the effect of a single price change on household welfare is proportional to its net supply position in that good expressed at current prices as a proportion of total expenditure. In practical terms, then, to predict poverty effects we need to know the price changes implied by a shock and poor households' net supply positions.

For finite price changes the household's responses influence the size of the welfare effect, but if there is full optimisation with full information, they will not reverse its sign. Responsiveness is particularly important when one considers the vulnerability aspects of poverty. Policies which reduce households' ability to cope with negative shocks could have major implications for the translation of trade shocks into actual poverty. Moreover, fear of the consequences of not being able to cope with negative shocks might induce households to rule out activities that would raise mean income significantly. Responsiveness is also important in terms of spreading shocks from one market to the next. These factors are all considered below.

Given the prevalence of small-scale agriculture among the poor, the analysis of prices is indispensable. But the poor also derive some of their income (most, in some cases) from labour and other factors of production that they own. The proportionate shock to earned income induced by a trade liberalisation depends on the shares of factors in household income and the proportionate changes in their returns or wages.[4]

An important complication in developing countries is that a given type of labour may have different value to the household according to where it is employed. If different wages are given exogenously, the choice between jobs is easy – take the activity for which the net wage is highest. More interesting, however, is the (very common) case where the trade-off is between explicit wages for 'traded' labour and an implicit or 'virtual' wage for work within the household.

For example, the higher costs of monitoring non-family workers make family labour cheaper than bought-in labour, while the transportation costs entailed in reaching other employers will make outside work less attractive to the family than work at home. When the virtual wage falls between these limits, labour is not traded outside the household. If the range is very large labour is effectively non-tradable as in de Janvry, Sadoulet and Fafchamps (1991) – but by changing the prices of goods produced in the households, trade reforms could switch it between tradable and non-tradable status. Indeed, the ability to switch between activities will be an important aspect of adjusting to potentially impoverishing shocks.

A further necessary generalisation recognises that some transactions may be quantity-constrained. Most obviously, some external jobs may be available only for either $t$ or 0 hours a day – e.g. factory work or service activities such as transportation services. If trade shocks flip workers from $t$ to 0 hours, poverty impacts could be very great. The loss of a job is probably the most common proximate cause of households descending rapidly into poverty.[5]

Finally, of course, the set of factors of production and associated returns that we consider must include land and other assets. The unequal distribution of land is an important contributory factor to poverty, and while addressing it is not strictly a matter of trade policy, it does clearly affect the outcome of trade liberalisation if the latter affects the rate of return to land. If, for institutional reasons, an asset cannot be sold or hired out (as is very frequently true of land) its rate of return is endogenous.

A key extension of the approach just outlined is to recognise the importance of intra-household distribution. It is frequently argued that the costs of poverty fall disproportionately on women, children and the elderly. Two approaches seem possible: either to describe a household and add some analytics for intra-

[4] Lloyd (2000) shows how price and factor effects can be combined formally to predict real income effects.

[5] A general observation is that major shocks to welfare are usually associated with 'corner solutions' such as this. Smooth quantitative adjustments between interior solutions need to be large to matter seriously, whereas at the corners small shocks can induce qualitative changes in life-style. Below I consider collapsing markets and changes in the sets of goods that are available, as well as job loss and creation.

household distribution, or to define welfare for individuals and add some analytics to describe inter-personal transfers. The former is probably the more effective route.[6]

The easiest approach is to assume separability between household activities generating and those distributing welfare. Thus the basic model could describe the former, while the latter would be characterised by a model of distribution. If the determinants of the distributive shares were not affected by trade policy, the welfare of each person in the household would vary in proportion to the whole in response to a trade shock. This would more or less remove gender and age from the picture and would be very convenient.

Unfortunately, however, separability is just not plausible. First, the homotheticity required by separability is unlikely to hold. As household incomes change, relative weights change (Kanbur and Haddad, 1994). Second, for this approach to be useful, intra-household transfers will be necessary to compensate individuals who, because of their non-transferable endowments (labour), bear the brunt of adverse shocks. If subsistence requirements or culture preclude this, the decision is no longer separable and the effects of specific prices or factor shocks impinge directly on individuals. For example, if female external employment increases – because, say, the wage rises or male wages fall – but women receive little compensatory help with their traditional in-home activities, female poverty could result.[7] Unfortunately, gender aspects are likely to be very case-specific and, worse, to be analysable only with data that are not generally available. Thus other than noting that gender and intergenerational issues must be taken seriously, and that they call for attention and flexibility in the application of the basic results, it is difficult to specify how to proceed.

## 3. PRICE CHANGES AND TRANSMISSION

### *a. The Direct Effects of a Price Change: The Distribution Sector*

I start by considering a change in the world price, tariff or exchange rate of a single good. Figure 1 summarises the way in which such shocks might work through to household welfare in a target country. Schematically, it comprises five columns of information. The elements concerning the distribution sector lie in the middle of the figure where I plot the transmission of price shocks from world

[6] The fact that the majority of data and the bulk of interventions refer to households rather than individuals suggests that policy-makers and legislators see households as the fundamental unit.
[7] Elson (1991) and Haddad, Hodinott and Alderman (1994) provide useful overviews of these non-separabilities and their consequences. Fontana and Wood (2000) operationalise some of them in a CGE model.

FIGURE 1
The Transmission of Trade Shocks

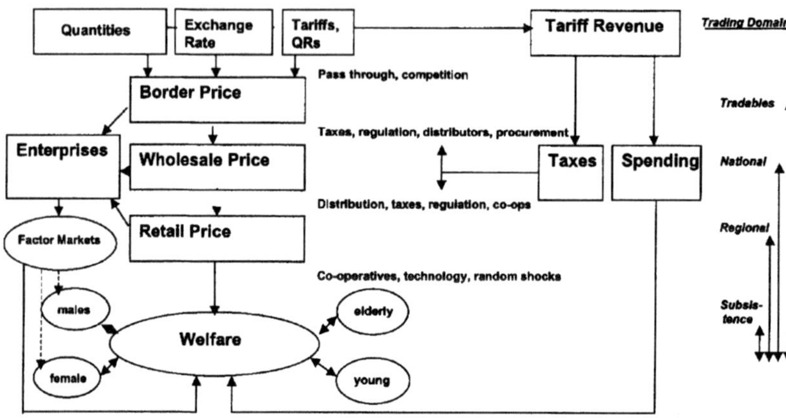


prices through to final consumers, and briefly describe the factors influencing the extent to which shocks at one stage are passed through to the next.

Consider the transmission of price shocks in pure accounting terms. For an import, the world price of a good, the tariff it faces and the exchange rate combine to define the post-tariff border price. Once inside the country, the good faces things like domestic taxes, distribution costs from the port to major distribution centres, various regulations which may add costs or control its price and the possibility of compulsory procurement by the authorities. The resulting price is termed the wholesale price. From the distribution centre the good is sent out to more local distribution points, and potentially faces more taxes and regulations. This stage may involve co-ops or other labour-managed enterprises, which may respond to shocks differently from commercial firms. I term the resulting price the retail price, although of course market institutions may well not resemble retailing in the industrial economy sense. Finally, from the retail point, goods are distributed to households and individuals. Again cooperatives may be involved, plus, of course, inputs from the household itself. More significantly, the translation of price signals into economic welfare depends on the household's endowments of time, skills, land, technology and random shocks such as weather. Anything that increases farm yields, for example, would permit a household greater welfare at any given price vector.

A corresponding taxonomy can be constructed for export goods, starting at the bottom of the column. An export good is produced, put into local marketing channels, aggregated into national supply and finally sold abroad. At each stage the institutions involved incur costs and add mark-ups, all of which enter the final price. If the world price of the good is given, all such additions come off the farm-gate price that determines household welfare.

In determining the effects of world price or trade policy shocks on poor households it is important to have a clear picture of these transmission channels and the behaviour of the agents and institutions comprising them. For example, monopsonistic buyers of export crops will respond differently to price shocks than will producers' marketing cooperatives. Regulations that fix market prices by fiat or by compensatory stock-piling can completely block the transmission of shocks to the household level.[8]

Even more important, all these various links must actually exist. If a trade liberalisation itself – or, more likely, the changes in domestic marketing arrangements that accompany it – lead to the disappearance of markets, households can become isolated from the market and suffer substantial income losses. This is most obvious in the case of markets on which to sell cash crops, but can also afflict purchased inputs and credit. If official marketing boards provided credit for inputs and against future outputs, whereas post-liberalisation private agents do not, no increase in output prices will benefit farmers unless alternative borrowing arrangements can be made. The converse case is that if trade reform opens up new markets, it can have dramatically positive effects on poverty alleviation, as for example in Bangladesh with new sources of work for females (see CUTS, 1998, Ch. 5) and new supplies of farm equipment (see Gisselquist and Harun-ar-Rashid, 1998).

The importance of transmission mechanisms is well illustrated by the contrasting experience of Zambia and Zimbabwe during the 1990s (Oxfam-IDS, 1999). In Zambia, the government abolished the official purchasing monopsony of maize; the activity became dominated by two private firms which probably colluded to keep prices low and which abandoned purchasing altogether in remote areas.[9] In Zimbabwe, by contrast, three private buyers emerged after privatisation of cotton purchasing, including one owned by the farmers. Here the abolition of the government monopoly resulted in increased competition and prices and farm incomes rose appreciably. In a less extreme example, Glewwe and de Tray (1989) show how transport and storage costs attenuated price changes of potatoes following liberalisation in Peru.

[8] Lest this seem automatically a good thing, remember that many shocks are positive and that official bodies have a tendency to take a large cut out of the price in return for providing the 'service' of insulation.

[9] Even if the latter was justified in the aggregate, it still left remote farmers with a huge problem. This was said to have been exacerbated by the difficulties of their re-entering subsistence agriculture, because the necessary seed stocks and practical knowledge had declined strongly during the (subsidised) cash-crop period. I have also heard, however, that in the early 1980s the state marketing system failed to serve the Northern Province effectively and that the economic saviour was illegal cross-border trade with Malawi. It is not clear when, or if, this ceased, nor whether it actually mitigated the shocks of the 1990s.

This discussion prompts three comments. First, and most obviously, the effects of a liberalisation depend on where you set off from. For example, if an import ban plus government monopoly subsidises remote farmers, the first-round effects of liberalisation will be to hurt those groups.[10] The analysis of the poverty impact of trade liberalisation can be no more general than is the pattern of trade restrictions across countries.

Second, usually many goods are liberalised at once, so that the effects on individual households will be the sums of many individual shocks. When some of the goods affected are inputs into the production of others, the net effect is quite complex and it is important to consider the balance of forces. For example, Zambian liberalisation raised the selling price of maize in the 1990s, but even where purchasing arrangements continued, input prices rose by more as subsidised deliveries were abolished; as a result, maize output fell (Oxfam-IDS, 1999).

### *b. Indirect Effects and the Domain of Trade*

Third, one needs to know how the household will accommodate the price changes. An adverse shock may entail large losses of utility if no alternative activities exist, or relatively small losses if they do. Similarly, positive shocks may deliver great benefits if households can switch their activities to take advantage of them.

Accommodating a shock also transmits the shock to other markets and sets off a whole series of second-round price and quantity effects. A critical consideration in assessing these is the domain over which the 'second-round' goods are traded, because this defines the range of agents whose behaviour can be called upon to equilibrate the various markets. The trading domains are summarised on the far right of Figure 1.

The price of a good that is traded internationally will be largely determined by the world price. Hence putting aside endogenous adjustment in the various margins identified above, the prices of such goods will not change further as the market equilibrates and all adjustment will be in internationally traded quantities. At the other extreme, if goods are traded only locally – say because of transportation difficulties, or local taste idiosyncrasies – the trading domain is very small and price is likely to bear part of the adjustment. The impact will be more narrowly focused geographically, but economically more significant within that domain. In between, goods that are traded nationally but not internationally will generate national second-round quantity shocks but probably rather small price changes. While small, however, the price changes will be widespread and through this mechanism shocks could be spread from one region of the target country to another.

[10] Second round effects could, of course, be positive – see below.

The literature on growth linkages – e.g. Timmer (1997), Delgado et al. (1998) and Mellor and Gavian (1999) – argues that agricultural liberalisation and productivity growth are so effective at poverty alleviation because their demand spillovers are heavily concentrated on relatively employment intensive and localised activities in which the poor have a large stake – for example, construction, personal servants and simple manufactures. This literature assumes that developing country rural economies have excess labour and can deliver extra output by taking on more workers without price increases.[11] This, in turn, means that shocks have income multiplier effects. The basic idea, however, generalises to the present approach, in which prices as well as quantities adjust: local spillovers increase local prices and hence local incomes.

Positive shocks to the urban economy, on the other hand, result in more diffuse spillovers, including to imports. In a fix-price world, imports are just a lost opportunity for generating further employment, but in the long run, when prices adjust imports also generate spillovers: output of exports has to grow, because the imports have to be paid for. If the factors used intensively in the export sector or in domestic sectors on which urban residents spend their income are not among the poorest, the spillover from urban shocks will be less pro-poor than agricultural shocks.

Finally, there are two sets of goods for which explicit prices are not observed: first, subsistence goods. By definition these are not directly subject to trade shocks, but they will still be affected by spillovers. Second, there are goods that are just not available. While conceptually simple to deal with – the price is infinity when they are not available – changes in the available set create complex measurement problems in practice.[12] Romer (1994) has noted the large welfare benefits associated with changes in availability, while Booth et al. (1993) show how important they were even for the poor in Tanzania, and Gisselquist and Harun-ar-Rashid (1998) show how liberalisation greatly increased the availability of, for example, small tractors and water pumps to small farmers in Bangladesh.

In many cases, of course, trade shocks will be sufficiently specific and/or small for us to ignore second-round effects, and focus just on the direct impacts described previously, but in others the latter could be important.

## 4. FACTOR MARKETS: WAGES, EMPLOYMENT AND PROFITS

The left-hand side of Figure 1 describes the link from trade to poverty operating via factor markets – most importantly for poverty than for less-skilled labour employed outside the household. Enterprises (loosely defined) determine

[11] See Section 4*b* below for a discussion of whether such changes actually alleviate poverty.
[12] Feenstra (1994) has pioneered solutions to the measurement question.

output by comparing prices and costs. Costs depend on factor prices and factor input-output coefficients which, in turn, depend on technology, on factor prices and possibly on scale. Total output and the factor-mix determine total factcr demand which is equated with total factor supply in the factor markets. In the process, employment and wages (and their equivalent for other factors) are determined. Implicit in this view is that the distribution of assets is given and that any non-pecuniary determinants of employment/factor use remain unchanged. Increasing asset stocks is an issue of economic growth, and perhaps public expenditure (for education and health) which I treat below. Redistributing them is a separate issue independent of trade policy.

### *a. 'Trade Theory' – Fixed Factor Supplies*

Assuming that, for poverty purposes, the critical factor market is for unskilled labour, it is useful to consider two polar forms of that market. The first is that assumed by traditional international trade theory, in which factor supplies are exogenously fixed, wages are perfectly flexible and goods are homogeneous.

Price changes affect the incentives to produce particular goods and the technologies they use. The simplest and most elegant analysis of these incentives – the Stolper-Samuelson Theorem (among the most powerful and elegant pieces of economic analysis on any subject) – generates the powerful result that, under particular conditions, an increase in the price of the good that is unskilled labour-intensive in production will increase the unskilled real wage and decrease that of skilled workers.[13]

Following Wood (1994), imagine a world of two national factors (skilled and unskilled labour) and a third (capital), whose rate of return is fixed by virtue of being perfectly mobile internationally. As the price of the unskilled labour-intensive good rises, production of it increases, drawing factors of production away from the other, skill-intensive, sector. Since the former wishes to employ more unskilled per unit of skilled labour than the former releases (by virtue of their factor intensities), this reallocation increases the demand for and the relative wage of unskilled labour. This change causes both industries to switch to more skill-intensive production methods – i.e. to employ less unskilled labour per unit of skill – which, in turn, raises the marginal product of unskilled labour in both industries. If factors are paid their marginal products, unskilled labour receives a higher wage in terms of each good and so, *a fortiori*, has a higher real wage regardless of its consumption patterns. Similar reasoning shows why skilled labour's real wage falls.

[13] The Stolper-Samuelson Theorem is described in all International Economics textbooks – see, for example, Winters (1991) or, in more detail, Bowen, Hollander and Vianne (1998). A full account appears in Deardorff and Stern (1994).

Unfortunately, for all its elegance, Stolper-Samuelson alone is not sufficient to answer questions of trade and poverty in the real world. Among the complications are:[14]

- *The functional distribution of income is not the same as the personal distribution of income*: household income depends also on the ownership of factors and on intra-household activity, which are both often very difficult to ascertain empirically.[15]
- *Dimensionality*: once one moves beyond a model with two immobile factors and two goods, the results become less definitive.
- *Mobility*: labour is required to be perfectly mobile between all sectors and regions of the economy. If labour markets are segmented, similar labourers in different markets are different factors, and will fare differently from each other.
- *Diversified equilibrium*: to guarantee the Stolper-Samuelson result the country must produce all goods before and after the price change in question. If one distinguishes goods by levels of sophistication, this is unlikely, and perverse results are possible – e.g. Davis (1996).
- *Non-traded goods'* prices are determined by the need to clear the domestic market. These price changes will tend to attenuate the rate at which tradable goods price shocks are translated into changes in the relative demands for different factors. On the other hand, if trade shocks induce changes in the real exchange rate, the relative prices of traded and non-traded goods, and if these goods have different factor intensities, a further source of factor market effects is introduced, as identified by Lal (1986) in the Philippines and, perhaps, Winters (2000b) in India.

Despite these complications, the basic insight of Stolper-Samuelson seems likely to hold very broadly. An increase in the price of a good will increase the incentive to produce it. This will raise the returns to factors of production specific to that good – e.g. labour with specific skill, specialist capital equipment – and, assuming that some increase in output is feasible, will also generally affect the returns to non-specific, or mobile, factors. Generally, the returns to at least one such factor will increase and, provided that economies of scale are not too strong, those to at least one other fall. Thus the presumption on wages remains that if the prices of unskilled-labour-intensive goods increase one would expect unskilled wages to increase.

In world terms developing countries are clearly unskilled labour-abundant, so that freer trade gravitates towards higher wages in general. However, within those

[14] An extended discussion is given in Winters (2000a).

[15] Recently, Lloyd (2000) has shown how to generalise Stolper-Samuelson to the personal distribution of income conditional on both households' endowments and their consumption patterns.

countries it is not clear that the least-skilled workers, and thus the most likely to be poor, are the most intensively used factor in the production of tradable goods. Thus while, for example, the wages of workers with completed primary education may increase with trade liberalisation, those of illiterate workers may be left behind or even fall. One of the reasons that reforming agriculture is such an important element in any future round of world trade talks is that for this sector one can be reasonably confident that very-low-skilled workers in rural areas – the majority group among the poor – will benefit through the production responses.

It is sometimes suggested – at least implicitly – that the factor intensity approach to the distributional effects of trade policy is refuted by the failure of Latin American liberalisation in the 1980s to alleviate poverty. Without denying the need for refinement in the argument, I would rather argue that the alleged surprise arose more from faulty premises than from theoretical failure. Thus, as Wood (1997) argues, by the 1980s Latin America was not obviously the unskilled-labour-abundant region of the world economy: both China's 'arrival' in world markets and Latin America's abundant natural resources suggest otherwise. Similarly the growth of outsourcing, for which Northern firms do not find it most efficient to seek the lowest-grade labour, suggests that Mexican exports are intensive in labour that is relatively skilled by local standards (Feenstra and Hanson, 1995). Finally, of course, it may take time for markets to clear. Thus Chile's liberalisations (trade and otherwise) were associated with worsening inequality over the 1980s, but inequality measures have now returned to pre-reform levels – and at vastly higher average income levels and lower poverty levels (Ferreira and Litchfield, 1999).

### *b. 'Development Theory' – Infinitely Elastic Factor Supplies*

One exception to the rule that an increase in the demand for a factor increases its wage (real return) is if the factor is available in perfectly elastic supply. Then the wage (return) will be fixed exogenously – by what the factor can earn elsewhere, which is assumed to be unaffected by the trade shock – and the adjustment will take place in terms of employment.

First suppose that unskilled labour is the elastically supplied factor. Most generally this will be because the formal sector can draw effectively infinite amounts of labour out of the informal sector or subsistence agriculture at the subsistence wage (Lewis, 1954). Of course, if the formal wage is no more than the subsistence wage, this transfer will have very little effect on poverty. Poverty will only be alleviated if the loss of labour in subsistence agriculture allows the workers remaining in that sector to increase their 'wage', because the sector begins to run short of labour (the case of successful development).

Probably more common will be where the formal sector has an effective minimum wage, at which there is excess supply. Then as labourers transfer to the formal sector they earn higher wages and poverty may be alleviated.[16] If trade liberalisation raises the value of the marginal product of labour in the formal sector, it increases demand and alleviates poverty. (It effectively reduces the cost of the minimum wage enforcement.) If, on the other hand, it reduces the value of the marginal product, it reduces employment, and thus has adverse consequences.

One possibility is that trade could increase *measured* poverty precisely when it raises unskilled wages in the formal sector. If, following Harris and Todaro (1970), workers migrate until the (unchanged) subsistence wage equals the expected wage in the city, a rise in the actual city wage must be balanced by a higher probability of unemployment in the city. Thus although in expected value terms the trade shock would be beneficial (actually benefiting infra-marginal urban workers) and would impose no expected cost on migrants from the subsistence areas, it would lead to an increase in urban poverty and, if measurement methods were urban biased, to an apparent increase in overall poverty.

In fact, neither of the polar extremes is likely to be precisely true, and so in practical assessments of the effects of trade shocks on poverty, determining the elasticity of labour supply and locating the various pre- and post-reform wages relative to the poverty line are important. Also, if labour markets are segmented, wage impacts will be larger in affected sectors, but less widespread. Segmented markets restrict the set of people who can gain from liberalisation, and so probably hinder poverty alleviation in the long run.

International capital mobility tends to increase the effects, positive or negative, of trade liberalisation. An inflow into a sector that has gained from liberalisation is likely to boost wages and/or employment, which will increase the welfare benefits and, if they exist, the poverty alleviation benefits, of a trade liberalisation. However, outflows from losing sectors will also be larger.[17] Conversely, however, if a trade liberalisation would reduce the returns to capital if it were immobile, it will generate a capital outflow if it is mobile and this is likely to reduce income and so tend to be poverty-worsening.[18] However, if capital has been attracted into a country by distortionary policies – e.g. tariff protection and tax holidays – the inflow could have been immiserising. Then, while the outflow resultant on reforming these policies will still hurt workers in the affected sectors, the overall welfare effects taking account of impacts on other sectors will be positive – and larger than if there had been no immiserising investment to undo.

[16] Depending on the measure of poverty used, the relative levels of the 'before' and 'after' wages and the poverty line, and how wages contribute to household income.

[17] Rama (2001), among others, suggests that foreign direct investment is good for wages.

[18] For policy purposes we should note, however, that this is not a cost of globalisation or internationalisation overall. Rather it represents the loss of mitigation that capital mobility brought the unliberalised economy, not a loss relative to never having had an inflow at all.

*c. Differentiated Products*

Of course, if the target country is not a price-taker in every good, developments in the production sector will affect the prices faced by consumers and feed back into the prices column of Figure 1. This is particularly relevant for non-tradable goods and services, of which, given weak infrastructure and trading institutions, there will be many in developing countries. Their prices will be determined by the need to equate local supply and demand and by the influence on supply of endogenous changes in factor prices.

An important distinction in the analysis of the production sector is whether or not goods are homogeneous across foreign and domestic suppliers. Homogeneous goods must have the same prices, and so trade defines the prices of both internationally traded and domestic output. Trade prices essentially determine internal producer and consumer prices and analysis is straight-forward. The alternative case is that goods are differentiated, so that each variety faces its own downward-sloping demand curve, with links between goods depending on the substitutability between varieties. In this case the transmission of trade shocks to domestic prices is diffused, affecting more goods but being quantitatively smaller than with homogeneous goods. Diffusion typically attenuates the shock to factor prices, because, as more goods are affected, it is more likely that changes in factor demand will be off-setting. The degree of substitutability between domestic varieties and those traded varieties that are affected by the trade shock becomes a critical parameter in this view of the world (see Falvey, 1999): the lower it is, the less extreme the effects of a trade shock generally will be.

## 5. TAXES AND SPENDING

The right-hand set of boxes in Figure 1 illustrates the final major static link between trade and poverty: via taxes and government spending. The early stages of trade liberalisation entail converting quantitative restrictions and regulations into tariffs and reducing high tariff rates. Particularly if the latter is accompanied by a reduction in the scope of tariff exceptions and exemptions this stage is likely to increase tariff revenue, rather than reduce it (Pritchett and Sethi, 1994; and Hood, 1998). Removing exemptions could have an impact on the poor, but given that most are the result of political processes, over which the poor have arguably even less influence than they do in markets, this seems pretty unlikely.[19]

Eventually, however, a trade liberalisation will reduce tariff rates so far that government revenue falls. This triggers the more commonly expressed worry about liberalisation and poverty – namely that the government, finding its

[19] Exemptions typically create rents for the exemption holder, not lower prices for consumers.

revenue constrained, will curtail expenditure on social and other poverty-alleviating policies and/or levy new taxes on goods consumed heavily by the poor. Given the association between stabilisation, liberalisation and poverty over the 1980s, these worries have some historical basis, but it would be mistaken to assume that the association is immutable. Ultimately it is a political decision how to raise and spend money.

A further question under this heading is whether trade liberalisation restricts a government's ability to manage spending and taxation in a way that impacts poverty. To start again at the politically incorrect end of the question, a trade liberalisation bound at the WTO, or perhaps as part of a Bretton Woods package, makes the price-reducing effects of tariff cuts less reversible and constrains a government's (or its successor's) ability to manipulate policy in arbitrary ways. Given that such manipulation very often redistributes real income from the poor to the rich, and that uncertainty reduces the incentives to invest, these constraints are likely to be beneficial. Put more positively, WTO or the Bretton Woods organisation may allow governments to tie their own, or their successors', hands in ways that would otherwise be politically impossible.

Much more common is the fear that bindings and/or commitments at the WTO prevent governments from pursuing pro-poor interventions. For example, if price variability is a problem it is argued that the ban on variable levies, which stabilise the domestic prices of internationally traded goods, could hurt the poor by subjecting them to greater uncertainty. It is sometimes argued that the Uruguay Round Agreement on Subsidies precludes production subsidies that could stimulate output and development – see, for example, the positions of India and Korea during the Uruguay Round negotiations (Croome, 1995, p. 201). The Agreement does restrict production subsidies in principle, but for developing countries the disciplines are very weak. A trading partner would have to demonstrate actual harm before acting against them, which seems very unlikely for the sort of subsidies that might help to alleviate poverty. Factor, regional or consumption subsidies are not subject to WTO constraints.

All these arguments are essentially specific examples of the analysis above: they are trade interventions whose direct effects can be traced via the distribution and enterprise sectors. In addition, however, they may have systemic effects because they affect whole classes of policies. Hence, even if some subsidies would be beneficial individually, given the difficulty of identifying these cases and preventing their capture by interest groups, a blanket ban may be advantageous (Winters, 2000d).

Finally, some have argued (e.g. Rodrik, 1997) that increased openness reduces governments' abilities to raise revenue because mobile factors can no longer be taxed. In its direct form this argument applies only to factors that can move in response to tax (or other) incentives, so international trade policy is only indirectly relevant. For example, the general reduction in trade barriers since the mid-1980s has made it easier to 'cut up the value chain', which presumably fosters capital mobility. On the trade side, increasing world competition makes it more costly for an individual country to tax exports in terms of both eroding the tax base and distorting production patterns. However, it is not clear that individual countries have ever had much scope for such taxes in manufactures, which is where trade barriers have come down most strongly in recent decades. Note, also, that in both these examples, it is more other countries' policies than the target country's that matter.

## 6. SHOCKS, RISKS AND VULNERABILITY

The static analysis compares two perfectly stable scenarios, but, in reality, the world is full of shocks. Thus an ideal analysis should try to deal directly with the effects of trade liberalisation on the *chances* of moving into or out of poverty in an uncertain world. This requires information on the way that liberalisation affects the distribution of shocks and households' ability to cope with them. It would also recognise that these factors feed back onto the static level effects just considered, making an already complex story even worse. This is an area that is very important and yet poorly researched and should clearly be a priority for future attention.

The simplest analysis of risk supposes that both foreign and domestic economies are subject to independent random shocks and that despite any trade liberalisation, the economies are not completely integrated. By increasing foreign exposure, trade liberalisation increases the weight of foreign relative to domestic shocks in the determination of domestic welfare.[20] Simple risk spreading suggests that at low levels of trade, further trade liberalisation would tend to reduce overall risk, but if foreign shocks are much greater than domestic ones, one could get the opposite effects.

The most obvious application of the independent risks model is if farmers produce a crop which is transformed from non-tradable to tradable status. Postponing consideration of changes in price stabilisation policies, this seems likely to reduce variability since for most goods world markets are likely to be more stable than local ones. In particular, they may prevent the largest variations in price by permitting trade in extreme conditions. If world markets are more variable than local ones, however, variance could be increased by opening up. One possibility is that, say, for favourable production conditions, the domestic

[20] Foreign shocks are, of course, transmitted through the links discussed above. As above, they will pass through different amounts of the risk onto the poor according to the specifics of the case – e.g. much if a sector makes heavy use of casual labour. Thus sectors with apparently similar distributions of international shocks can have very different implications for the probability distribution of shocks facing the poor.

market is atypically stable and that opening up 'imports' price variation. A more interesting but not very realistic case is that of Newbery and Stiglitz's (1984) 'Pareto worsening trade'. Imagine a good with an elasticity of demand of one and random supply shocks: producer revenue is completely stable with price fluctuation perfectly off-setting quantity shocks. Now put two economies together and let their shocks be perfectly negatively correlated. Trade stabilises the price and destabilises revenue, so if it is the producers who are poor, the poor become more vulnerable.

A third possibility is that, because trade liberalisation alters the set of feasible policies, it affects the ability of governments to operate price stabilisation policies. For example, if prior to liberalisation domestic food prices were stabilised by varying trade policy, moving to a fixed tariff could increase instability.[21] Thus the Uruguay Round constraints on variable levies or on export subsidies could, in principle, increase domestic instability in certain economies even if they raise average incomes. If economies are inherently inflexible, increasing instability could increase the incidence of poverty.

Another possibility, however – observed quite frequently – is that liberalisation leads farmers to switch from crop $x$ (subsistence food, say) to crop $y$ (cash crop). Their risk then switches from var $(x)$ to var $(y)$, and thus could obviously increase. However, if this switch is made knowingly and has no external effects, it is not clear that it is welfare worsening, even if the variance increases. Thus, just as with the Harris-Todaro example above, higher expected welfare might be correlated with increasing observed poverty if farmers accept higher variance in order to reap higher mean rewards and periodically get unfortunate drawings from the distribution.

Of course, the switch from subsistence to cash crops may not be made knowingly (governments do not always convey information on risk accurately) and there may be serious implications for intra-household income distributions. If, for example, adult males receive the returns from cash crops but females and children bear the risks of failure in terms of nutrition or schooling, the decision to switch may not be optimal for the household overall. The important point, however, is that not every *ex post* descent into poverty is the result of an *ex ante* flawed response to trade liberalisation.

An alternative lens on the previous paragraph is the observation that the poor can often not afford the risks of being entrepreneurial (Morduch, 1994). Their inability to bear the downside risks entailed in producing cash crops (because, say, a price fall would push them below subsistence) might explain the unwillingness to pursue higher mean returns created by trade. If so, the poor may

[21] Note, however, that such insulating policies increase the variability of world prices. If all countries eschewed them at once net variability could decline even though insulation had been removed.

suffer the costs of a reform (e.g. higher food prices) without reaping the expected rewards. The policy implication of this is to examine the effectiveness of capital markets (which is where the market failure exists) and safety nets as a means to spreading the benefits of liberalisation.

Turning briefly to country-level data, there is a presumption that more open economies suffer more heavily from terms of trade shocks; e.g. Rodrik (1998). This question has at least two elements. First, if openness encourages specialisation one would expect the net barter terms of trade (NBTT – the ratio of import to export prices) to become more volatile with openness. In fact, this appears not to happen – see Lutz and Singer (1994), and also Easterly and Kraay (2000), who find very small countries have no worse volatility than larger ones. Second, a given volatility in the NBTT implies a greater volatility in national income the more open the economy, which one expects to increase, *ceteris paribus*, with trade liberalisation (and also as size falls). This second element does receive empirical support (Rodrik, 1998; and Easterly and Kraay, 2000). A possible third element is whether open economies generate larger or smaller domestic shocks, which could go either way. Krueger (1990), for example, argues that openness encourages better policy positions all round and receives some empirical support from Romer (1993) on inflation and Ades and di Tella (1997 and 1999) on corruption. Rodrik suggests that open economies have greater income volatility overall, which suggests that the second element predominates, but, of course, this does not necessarily mean greater consumption volatility. Thus, overall, trade liberalisation has ambiguous implications for macro stability.

## 7. ECONOMIC GROWTH AND TECHNOLOGY

Economic growth is the key to permanent poverty alleviation. Unless growth seriously worsens income distribution, the numbers in poverty measured in any absolute way will fall as average incomes increase. This observation makes it tempting to think about the effects of trade liberalisation on poverty as the product of a growth effect and an inequality effect. I discuss the former in this section, but argue that the latter is not a useful component of poverty analysis. Poverty and inequality are different phenomena, with poverty referring only to the lower end of the income distribution. Any simple parameterisation of inequality runs the risk of implying worsening poverty merely because the income distribution has worsened in its upper regions. If one is to focus on the lower end alone, one needs to analyse prices and incomes in the sort of way described in this paper. In short, one should derive one's view of the lower end of income inequality from poverty analysis, not vice versa.

Ultimately the question of whether growth does actually assist poverty alleviation is an empirical one. Recent evidence suggests that *on average* the incomes of the poor grow proportionately to the overall average (e.g. Romer and Gugerty, 1997; Gallup, Radelet and Warner, 1998; Dollar and Kraay, 2001; and White and Anderson, 2001. There are clearly particular cases where this is not so, and it is worth trying to find out why, but there has been no challenge to the general result that the poor gain significantly from growth. In fact, attempts to see if openness was one of the factors leading to unsatisfactory outcomes have suggested otherwise – White and Anderson and the later versions of Lundberg and Squire (2000).

By the same token, the effects of trade liberalisation on growth is an empirical rather than a conceptual matter.[22] There is plenty of theory to suggest a positive link, based on factors such as technology flows, the prices of capital goods, and access to specialist tools and inputs, and, indeed, most economists believe that the link is positive. The evidence, however, is not unchallenged.

The most commonly cited cross-country studies (e.g. Dollar, 1992; Sachs and Warner, 1995; and Edwards, 1998), received rough treatment recently from Rodriguez and Rodrik (2001) on the grounds that their measures of openness were flawed and/or endogenous.[23] They include open trade (the *result* of trade liberalisation) as only one of several indicators of openness and one which generally seems to weigh rather lightly in the overall result (e.g. Harrison, 1996). In part, I suspect, the weakness of the empirical link between liberal trade and growth reflects the difficulties of measuring trade stances once one comes inside the boundary of near autarchy: for example, tariffs need to be aggregated, QRs assessed and aggregated, the degree of credibility and negotiability of trade barriers represented, and the level of enforcement measured (see Winters, 2000d). A second difficulty is that, to be fully effective, trade liberalisation needs to be part of a package of measures promoting greater use of the market, more stable and less arbitrary policy intervention, stronger competition and macroeconomic stability. With the exception of the last, openness is probably essential to the long-run achievement of these stances, and it probably helps with the last as well (Krueger, 1990). Isolating such joint effects is very complex, although Taylor (1998) and Wacziarg (2001) have made some progress.

Overall, the fairest assessment is that trade liberalisation alone has not been incontrovertibly linked to subsequent economic growth, but that the general tendency of the evidence – cross-section and case study – is strongly in that direction.[24] Even Rodriguez and Rodrik concede that liberalisation has certainly not been identified as a hindrance to growth. Thus one would need strong

[22] It is dealt with more fully in McKay, Winters and Kedir (2000) and in Winters (2001b).

[23] Srinivasan and Bhagwati (2000) chide the profession for being too concerned about Rodriguez and Rodrik's critique of the cross-section studies. The latter were not, they argue, the basis on which wise economists believed that liberalisation stimulated growth.

[24] Jones (2001) shows that even Rodriguez and Rodrik's data tend towards positive effects.

evidence to conclude that any particular liberalisation would not eventually boost income and alleviate poverty.

The link from openness to growth operates at least partly via technical progress, for example by making new inputs, new technologies, or new management techniques available to local producers. Such flows could arise from trade – either imports or exports – or from direct flows of technology from abroad.

The evidence that access to imports enhances performance is quite strong (Esfahani, 1991; and Feenstra et al., 1997), while that which postulates a link from exporting to technology is, surprisingly to some, weaker. While macro studies and case-studies have suggested an export link, detailed and formal work based on enterprise data is doubtful: Bigsten et al. (2000) find links for Africa, while Kraay (1998) is ambiguous for China and Tybout and Westbrook (1995) find nothing for Latin America.[25] Similarly it is quite difficult to prove that FDI boosts efficiency (e.g. Haddad and Harrison, 1993). In both cases the problem is one of causation: efficiency and exporting are linked because efficient firms export, FDI and efficiency because investors choose efficient firms and sectors.

Of course technological flows need not depend just on trade or technology policies in a WTO-sense; they may arise autonomously or through direct interventions in research and development in favour of developing countries. An example of the latter is the green revolution, which developed and disseminated high-yield varieties of grain to many parts of the developing world. While most commentators hold the green revolution to have been a significant step forward in poverty alleviation, the mechanisms identified are quite varied. For example, farmers have benefited where markets have been open (because prices are largely fixed), while net buyers of food have gained where policy has meant that agricultural output has to be domestically absorbed rather than exported (Binswanger and Quizon, 1986). Non-farmers have also sometimes been major beneficiaries via increased demand for locally produced inputs or consumption goods (Moseley, 1999) or where demand for local services has increased (Mellor and Gavian, 1999). Whatever the route, effective access to improved seeds and other food technologies is likely to have major effects on poverty.[26]

The fear is often expressed that technological advance hurts the poor by reducing the demand for unskilled labour. This may be true of general technical progress that is biased against unskilled labour, although why any trade-related technical progress should be so is unclear. Such effects might appear to apply,

[25] Tybout (2000) suggests that this may be because the last was able to identify the temporal links between productivity and exporting more accurately than the others. Bigsten et al., on the other hand, suggest the result is substantive and that small poor countries can gain advantages from trade that larger economies can generate for themselves.

[26] IFAD (2001) makes a passionate case that technology is key to solving rural poverty.

however, if liberalisation reduces capital goods prices and leads to substitution against labour (e.g. Robbins and Gindling, 1999).

When technical advance differs across sectors its sectoral composition is as important as its bias. Increases in the efficiency in a sector will increase demand for the good concerned (strongly in open economies) and thus, generally, for the factors that produce it. Factors specific to that sector will benefit, as will mobile factors that are used intensively in the sector (as in Section 4 above).[27] Thus progress in unskilled labour-intensive sectors will probably aid the poor, at least immediately, even if it is biased against unskilled labour use.

Growth does not appear explicitly in the analytical framework of Figure 1, but it is present throughout and vital. Growth will affect relative prices as well as the incomes generated for households by the production sector both in terms of their average level and the number of people working in that sector. By generating greater demand, growth will raise household sales and assist government in raising revenue and spending. To the extent that it is based on technological improvements, growth will increase the output that farm households generate at any given price level and to the extent that it is due to accumulation incomes will rise accordingly. While it may be difficult to identify the effects of trade liberalisation on economic growth directly, they lie at the heart of both the policy and the positive debates on trade and poverty.

## 8. SHORT-TERM ADJUSTMENT

Trade liberalisation is generally held to have long-run benefits, but it requires adjustment in a country's output bundle to achieve them. If adjustment is costly this could lead to periods of decline and/or poverty before things get better.

For assessments of the overall economic benefits of liberalisation, it is important to distinguish between the social costs of adjustment – net losses to society, through, for example, higher unemployment – and private costs that are counterparts to private gains elsewhere – for example, a cut in wages due solely to the loss of a subsidy. For present purposes, however, the distinction is less significant. Our question is just whether individuals or households slip temporarily into poverty as an economy adjusts to more open trade.

The most significant adjustment problem lies in the market for less-skilled labour, especially employment, and so I concentrate on that. There are two separate questions: how long do spells of unemployment/under-employment last and who suffers them?

[27] This argument is spelt out in Haskel and Slaughter (1998) but dates back to Findlay and Grubert (1959).

*a. How Long Does Unemployment Last?*

The key to answering this question lies in the speed of labour turnover and the flexibility of factor markets. Unfortunately, there is apparently very little research directly on labour turnover in developing countries (Matusz and Tarr, 1999). These authors suggest that, in industrial countries where liberalisation more frequently means the contraction of a sector, not its demise, it is surprisingly rapid in most circumstances. If so, unemployment of displaced workers will be relatively short-lived. In some cases workers displaced from low-paid jobs not only found new jobs quickly, but at higher wages (Jacobson, 1978). In developing countries such benign effects are also a realistic possibility, although the evidence is based on aggregate employment data rather than surveys of workers. For example, Mauritius has successfully combined trade liberalisation with poverty reduction (see, for example, Milner and Wright, 1998, who identify increasing unskilled and female wages as exports boomed). Panama is another case: a strong liberalisation of trade in 1996/97 and of domestic regulations in previous years preceded a decrease in unemployment (16.2 to 13.2 per cent in one year) and a reduction in poverty as informal sector wages rose and poor workers entered formal employment (World Bank, 1999). Harrison and Revenga (1998) find manufacturing employment increasing almost immediately after half the liberalisations they study; the other half are mostly transitional economies in which much more than trade liberalisation was happening and in which the general retrenchment created a very unfavourable environment for trade-displaced workers.

Not all is so rosy, however, even in 'regular' (i.e. non-transition) liberalisations. Workers may suffer long-lived and deep losses of income if they have previously enjoyed very high levels of protection or if they had built up strong firm-specific human capital. For example, Jacobson et al. (1993a and 1993b) find that the US workers laid off after long job tenure earned 25 per cent below their pre-dismissal wages after five years. Rama and MacIsaac (1999) find that employees displaced from the Ecuadorian Central Bank in 1994 had regained on average only 55 per cent of their pre-dismissal salaries after 15 months despite generally low unemployment levels. Mills and Sahn (1995) found that of Guinean public sector workers laid off over 1985–88, half of those who found new jobs increased their earnings. However, their average unemployment duration exceeded two years and fully 30 per cent of them were still unemployed by 1992.

It seems likely that transitional losses will be greater the more protected the sector was originally and the greater the shock. In particular, labour markets suffering very large shocks can become dysfunctional because even normal turnover ceases as incumbents dare not resign for fear of not finding a new job. Thus major reforms – e.g. transition – or concentrated reforms – e.g. closing the only plant in a town – do seem more likely to generate transitional losses through unemployment than more diffuse reforms. On the other hand, it is precisely the sectors with highest protection or the economies with most widespread distortion that offer the greatest long-run returns to reform.

### *b. Transitional Unemployment and Poverty*

Transitional unemployment (or a declining reward for skills) is unfortunate for anyone who suffers it, but it does not necessarily lead to poverty. Individuals who have lived beyond the reach of poverty for some time will generally have assets, or access to credit, with which to smooth consumption.[28] Thus for such individuals it is only longer-lived shocks that fall within the remit of this paper. The poor, on the other hand, will have very few assets, and so will be unable to smooth over even short spells of unemployment. Hence, even switching from one unskilled informal sector job to another could cause severe hardship, especially if temporary stress led to permanent or semi-permanent consequences, such as losing one's place in the queue for rented housing or education services.[29] This suggests that attention to transitional unemployment should mainly be focused on those who were poor or near-poor initially. This is not always the case in practice, however, for the middle class will typically be more articulate and more influential politically than the poor.

## 9. TRADE LIBERALISATION AND POVERTY: A CHECKLIST

The link between trade policy and poverty is evidently very complex and case-specific. The framework developed here defies further summary, but it does suggest a series of key questions that might help to explore a trade liberalisation's effects on poverty.[30]

*Will the effects of changed border prices be passed through to the rest of the economy?*

Trade policy and shocks operate primarily via prices. If price changes are not transmitted the most direct effects on poverty (positive or negative) will be nullified.

[28] In case it seems callous to suggest consuming assets, recall that most precipitous declines in income result from losing public support – i.e. from being unable to continue to live comfortably on the proceeds of distortions or transfers that others finance.
[29] Lokshin and Ravallion (2000) find that the effects on the poor of shocks in Hungary are long but not infinitely lived.
[30] Winters, McCulloch and McKay (2002) organises empirical evidence under the questions defined here.

*Is reform likely to destroy effective markets or create them?*
A shock that undermines an important market could well cause poverty, while one that introduces new employment opportunities, goods or services to the poor can greatly enhance their welfare.

*Is reform likely to affect different household members differently?*
Within a household, claims and endowments are typically unevenly distributed. Hence particular members – usually females and children – may lose personally even when the household in aggregate gains. Conversely some reforms directly boost female earnings.

*Will its spillovers be concentrated on areas/activities of relevance to the poor?*
Adjustment to a shock results in it being transmitted from one market to another. Frequently the diffusion will be so broad that it has little effect on any particular locality or sector, but sometimes – e.g. where services are traded only very locally – the transmission is narrow but deep. Then it is necessary to ask whether the second-round effects have serious poverty implications.

*What factors are used intensively in the most affected sectors and what is their elasticity of supply?*
Changes in the prices of goods affect factor rewards according to factor intensities, but if factor supplies show some elasticity, employment will be affected as well as wages. Poverty effects depend heavily on where the various wages lie relative to poverty lines. Moreover, falling unskilled wages generate poverty only to the extent that poor households depend disproportionately on such wages.

*Will the reform* ***actually*** *affect government revenue strongly?*
In the limit cutting tariffs will reduce government revenue – zero tariffs entail zero revenue – but many trade reforms actually have positive revenue effects. Even where revenue falls, it is not inevitable that compensating tax increases or expenditure cuts will impinge on the poor disproportionately. That, ultimately, is a political decision.

*Will reform expose the poor to greater risk?*
Foreign markets may or may not be more variable than domestic ones; even if they are, risk spreading can reduce overall risk as the economy opens.

*Does the reform depend upon or affect the ability of poor people to take risks?*
For the very poor the consequences of even small negative shocks are very serious. Hence they might be unwilling to seize risky income-raising opportunities and so reap only the negative elements of a reform package.

Similarly, if a reform makes it more difficult for the poor to continue their traditional insulation strategies, it may increase their vulnerability to poverty even if it increases mean incomes.

*Will the reform stimulate growth? Will the growth be particularly unequalising?*

Economic growth is the key to sustained poverty reduction and trade liberalisation generally appears to foster growth Thus it will normally have strong long-run poverty alleviation effects.

*Will transitional unemployment be concentrated on the poor? Will it be deep or long-lived?*

Almost by definition the poor, have few assets, so even relatively short periods of transition could induce descent into deep poverty. Adjustment will typically be harsher if the trade reform is associated with macro-stabilisation or is concentrated on a particular locality. However, many reforms show quite rapid positive employment responses.

## ACKNOWLEDGEMENTS

An earlier version of this paper (Winters, 2000a) was part of a background study on 'Trade, Technology and Poverty' prepared for the World Bank's World Development Report 2000/1 and parts of it were published in Winters (2000c). I am grateful to the UK Department for International Development for financial support and encouragement, to Xavier Cirera for research assistance, to Shoshana Ormonde, Rosie Bellinger and Janet Ellis for logistical help and to Max Corden, Tricia Feeny, Ravi Kanbur, Caroline Lequesne, Michael Lipton, Neil McCulloch, Andrew McRay, Pradeep Mehta, Chris Stevens, David Wall and Howard White for comments and advice. Naturally none of these people are responsible for the paper's remaining imperfections.

## REFERENCES

Ades, A. and R. di Tella (1997), 'National Champions and Corruption: Some Unpleasant Interventionist Arithmetic', *The Economic Journal*, **107**, 1023–42.

Ades, A. and R. di Tella (1999), 'Rents, Competition and Corruption', *American Economic Review*, **89**, 982–93.

Baulch, R. (1996), 'Neglected Trade-offs in Poverty Measurement', *IDS Bulletin*, **27**.

Baulch, R. and N. McCulloch (1998), 'Being Poor and Becoming Poor: Poverty Status and Poverty Transitions in Rural Pakistan', Working Paper No. 79, IDS.

Bigsten, A. et al. (2000), 'Exports and Firm Level Efficiency in African Manufacturing', Centre for the Study of African Economies, Working Paper Series 2000-16 (July).

Binswanger, H. and J. Quizon (1986), 'Modelling the Impact of Agricultural Growth and Government Policy on Income Distribution in India', *The World Bank Economic Review*, **1**, 103–48.

Booth, D., F. Lugngira, P. Masanja, A. Mvungi, R. Mwaipopo, J. Mwami and A. Redmayne (1993), *Social, Economic and Cultural Change in Contemporary Tanzania. People-Oriented Focus* (Stockholm: Swedish International Development Authority).

Bowen, H. P., A. Hollander and J. M. Vianne (1998), *Applied International Trade Analysis* (Michigan University Press, Ann Arbor).

Croome, J. (1995), *Reshaping the World Trading System* (Kluwer, The Hague).

CUTS (1999), 'Conditions Necessary for the Liberalisation of Trade and Investment to Reduce Poverty', Final Report to DfID, August 1999.

Davis, D. (1996), 'Trade Liberalisation and Income Distribution', Working Paper No. 5693 (National Bureau of Economic Research).

Deardorff, A. V. and R. M. Stern (1994), *The Stolper-Samuelson Theorem: A Golden Jubilee* (Ann Arbor: University of Michigan Press).

de Janvry, A., M. Fafchamps and E. Sadoulet (1991), 'Peasant Household Behaviour with Missing Markets: Some Paradoxes Explained', *Economic Journal*, **101**, 1400–17.

Delgado, C., J. Hopkins and V. Kelly (1998), 'Agricultural Growth Linkages in Sub-Saharan Africa', Research Report No. 107 (International Food Policy Research Institute, Washington, DC).

Dollar, D. (1992), 'Outward-Oriented Developing Economies Really Do Grow More Rapidly: Evidence from 95 LDCs, 1976–1985', *Economic Development and Cultural Change*, **40**, 523–44.

Dollar, D. and A. Kraay (2001), 'Growth Is Good for the Poor', World Bank Policy Research Working Paper No. 2587.

Easterly, W. and A. Kraay (2000), 'Small States, Small Problems' (Mimeo, Development Research Group, The World Bank).

Edwards, S. (1998), 'Openness, Productivity and Growth: What Do We Really Know?' *Economic Journal*, **108**, 383–98.

Elson, D. (1991), *Male Bias in the Development Process* (Manchester: Manchester University Press).

Esfahani, H. S. (1991), 'Exports, Imports, and Economic Growth in Semi-Industrialised Countries', *Journal of Development Economics*, **35**, 93–116.

Falvey, R. (1999), 'Factor Price Convergence', *Journal of International Economics*, **49**, 195–210.

Feenstra, R. and G. Hanson (1995), 'Foreign Investment Outsourcing and Relative Wages', in R. Feenstra, G. Grossman and D. Irwin (eds.), *Economy of Trade Policy: Essays in Honour of Jagdish Bhagwati* (MIT Press, Cambridge, Mass.).

Feenstra, R. C. (1994), 'New Product Varieties and the Measurement of International Prices', *American Economic Review*, **84**, 157–77.

Feenstra, R. C., D. Madani, Y. Tzu-Han and L. Chi-Yuan (1997), 'Testing Endogenous Growth in South Korea and Taiwan', NBER Working Paper No. 6028.

Ferreira, F. H. G. and J. A. Litchfield (1999), 'Calm After The Storms: Income Distribution and Welfare in Chile, 1987–1994', *World Bank Economic Review*, **13**, 509–38.

Findlay, R. and H. Grubert (1959), 'Factor Intensities. Technological Progress, and Terms of Trade', *Oxford Economic Papers*, **11**, 111–121.

Fontana and A. Wood (2000), 'Modelling the Effects of Trade on Women, at Work and at Home', *World Development*, **28**, 1173–90.

Gallup, A., S. Radelet and A. Warner (1998), 'Economic Growth and the Income of the Poor' (Mimeo, Harvard Institute for Economic Development).

Gisselquist, D. and Harun-ar-Rashid (1998), 'Agricultural Inputs Trade in Bangladesh: Regulations, Reforms and Impacts' (Mimeo, The World Bank).

Glewwe, P. and D. de Tray (1989), 'The Poor in Latin America During Adjustment: A Case Study of Peru', Living Standards Measurement Study, Working Paper No. 56 (The World Bank,

Washington, DC).

Haddad, L., J. Hodinott and H. Alderman (1994), 'Intrahousehold Resource Allocation: An Overview', Policy Research Working Paper, No. 1255 (The World Bank, Washington, DC).

Haddad, M. and A. Harrison (1993), 'Are there Positive Spillovers from Direct Foreign Investment? Evidence from Panel Data for Morocco', *Journal of Development Economics*, **42**, 51–74.

Harris, J. and M. Todaro (1970), 'Migration, unemployment and development: a two sector analysis', *American Economic Review*, **60**, 126–42.

Harrison, A. (1996), 'Openness and Growth: A Time-Series Cross Country Analysis for Developing Countries', *Journal of Development Economics*, **48**, 419–47.

Harrison, A. and A. Revenga (1998), 'Labour Markets, Foreign Investment, and Trade Policy Reform', in J. Nash and W. Takacs (eds.), *Trade Policy Reform: Lessons and Implications* (The World Bank, Washington, DC), 247–76.

Haskel, J. E. and M. J. Slaughter (1998), 'Does the Sector of Skill-Biased Technical Change Explain Changing Wage Equality?', National Bureau of Economic Research Working Paper No. 6565 (May).

Hood, R. (1998), 'Fiscal Implications of Trade Reforms', in J. Nash and W. Takacs (eds.), *Trade Policy Reform: Lessons and Implications* (The World Bank, Washington, DC), 147–88.

IFAD (2001), *IFAD Rural Poverty Report* (Oxford: Oxford University Press).

Jacobson, L. S. (1978), 'Earning Losses of Workers from Manufacturing Industries', in W. Wald et al. (eds.), *The Impact of International Trade on Investment and Employment* (US Government Printing Office, Washington, DC).

Jones, C. I. (2000), Comment on Rodriguez and Rodrik (2000) 'Trade Policy and Economic Growth: A Skeptic's Guide to the Cross-National Evidence', *NBER Macroeconomics Annual 2000* (Cambridge, Mass., MIT Press), 330–36.

Kanbur, R. and L. Haddad (1994), 'Are Better Off Households More Unequal or Less Unequal?', *Oxford Economic Papers*, **46**, 445–58.

Kraay, A. (1998), 'Exports and Economic Performance: Evidence from a Panel of Chinese Enterprises' (Mimeo, Development Research Group, The World Bank).

Krueger, A. O. (1990), 'Asian Trade and Growth Lessons', *American Economic Review: Papers and Proceedings*, **80**, 108–12.

Lal, D. (1986), 'Stopler-Samuelson-Rybczynski in the Pacific: Real Wages and Real Exchange in the Philippines, 1956–1978', *Journal of Development Studies*, **21**, 181–204.

Lewis, W. A. (1954), 'Economic Development with Unlimited Supplies of Labour', Manchester School; reprinted in A. Agarwala and S. Singh (eds.), *The Economics of Underdevelopment* (Oxford University Press, Delhi, 1975).

Lloyd, P. (2000), 'Generalizing the Stolper-Samuelson Theorem: A Tale of Two Matrices', *Review of International Economics*, **8**, 4, 597–613.

Lokshin, M. and M. Ravallion (2000), 'Short-Lived Shocks with Long-Lived Impacts? Household Income Dynamics in a Transition Economy' (Mimeo, The World Bank, August).

Lundberg, M. and L. Squire (2000), 'The Simultaneous Evolution of Growth and Inequality' (Mimeo, The World Bank, October).

Lutz, M. and H. W. Singer (1994), 'The Link between Increased Trade Openness and the Terms of Trade: An Empirical Investigation', *World Development*, **22**, 1697–709.

Matusz, S. J. and D. Tarr (1999), 'Adjusting to Trade Policy Reform', World Bank Policy Research Working Paper 2142.

McCulloch, N., L. A. Winters and X. Cirera (2001), *Trade Liberalisation and Poverty: A Handbook* (London, CEPR).

McKay, A., L. A. Winters and A. M. Kedir (2000), 'A Review of Empirical Evidence on Trade, Trade Policy and Poverty', A Report to DfID prepared as a Background Document for the Second Development White Paper on http://www.dfid.gov.uk

Mellor, J. W. and S. Gavian (1999), 'The Determinants of Employment Growth in Egypt – The Dominant Role of Agriculture and the Rural Small Scale Sector' (Mimeo, Abt Associates Inc.).

Mills, B. F. and D. E. Sahn (1995), 'Reducing the Size of the Public Sector Workforce: Institutional Constraints and Human Consequences in Guinea', *Journal of Development Studies*, **31**, 505–28.

Milner, C. R. and P. W. Wright (1998), 'Modelling Labour Market Adjustment to Trade Liberalisation in an Industrialising Economy', *Economic Journal*, **108**, 509–28.
Morduch, J. (1994), 'Poverty and Vulnerability', *American Economic Review*, **84**, 221–25.
Moseley, P. (1999), *A Painful Ascent: Obstacles to the Green Revolution in Africa*, draft typescript (London, Routledge, forthcoming 2000).
Newbery, D. M. G. and J. E. Stiglitz (1984), 'Pareto Inferior Trade', *Review of Economic Studies*, **51**, 1–12.
Oxfam-IDS (1999), 'Liberalisation and Poverty', Final Report to DfID (August).
Pritchett, L. and G. Sethi (1994), 'Tariff Rates, Tariff Revenue, and Tariff Reform: Some New Facts', *World Bank Economic Review*, **8**, 1–16.
Rama, M. and D. MacIsaac (1999), 'Activity, Earnings and Welfare after Retrenchment: Central Bank Employees in Ecuador', manuscript prepared for The World Bank conference on 'Public Sector Retrenchment and Efficient Compensation Schemes'.
Robbins, D. and T. H. Gindling (1999), 'Trade Liberalization and the Relative Wages for More-Skilled Workers in Costa Rica', *Review of Development Economics*, **3**, 2, 140–54.
Rodriguez, F. and D. Rodrik (2001), 'Trade Policy and Economic Growth: A Sceptic's Guide to the Cross-National Evidence', *NBER Macroeconomics Annual 2000* (Cambridge, Mass., MIT Press) 261–324.
Rodrik, D. (1997), *Has Globalisation Gone Too Far?* (Institute for International Economics, Washington, DC).
Rodrik, D. (1998), 'Why do More Open Economies have Bigger Governments?' *Journal of Political Economy*, **106**, 997–1032.
Romer, D. (1993), 'Openness and Inflation: Theory and Evidence', *The Quarterly Journal of Economics*, **108**, 870–903.
Romer, P. M. (1994), 'New Goods, Old Theory, and the Welfare Costs of Trade Restrictions', *Journal of Development Economics*, **43**, 5–38.
Romer, P. M. and M. K. Gugerty (1997), 'Does Economic Growth Reduce Poverty? Technical Paper', CAER Discussion Paper No. 5 (Harvard Institute for International Development, Cambridge, Mass.).
Sachs, J. and A. Warner (1995), 'Economic Reform and the Process of Global Integration', *Brookings Papers on Economic Activity*, No. 1, 1–95.
Singh, I., L. Squire and J. Strauss (1986), 'A Survey of Agricultural Household Models: Recent Findings and Policy Implications', *The World Bank Economic Review*, **1**, 149–79.
Srinivasan, T. N. and J. Bhagwati (2001), 'Outward-Orientation and Development: Are Revisionists Right? in D. Lal and R. H. Snape (eds.) *Trade, Development and Political Economy: Essays in Honour of Anne O. Krueger* (New York: Palgrave).
Taylor, A. M. (1998), 'On the Costs of Inward-Looking Development: Price Distortions, Growth, and Divergence in Latin America', *Journal of Economic History*, **58**, 1, 1–28.
Timmer, P. (1997), 'How Well do the Poor Connect to the Growth Process?', CAER Discussion Paper No. 17 (Harvard Institute of International Development, Cambridge, Mass.).
Tybout, J. R. (2000), 'Manufacturing Firms in Developing Countries: How Well Do They Do, and Why?', *Journal of Economic Literature*, **38**, 11–44.
Tybout, J. R. and M. D. Westbrook (1995), 'Trade Liberalisation and the Dimensions of Efficiency Change in Mexican Manufacturing Industries', *Journal of International Economics*, **39**, 53–78.
Wacziarg, R. (2001), 'Measuring Dynamic Gains from Trade', *The World Bank Economic Review*, **15**, 3, 393–430.
White, H. and E. Anderson (2001), 'Growth versus Distribution: Does the Pattern of Growth Matter?', *Development Policy Review*, **19**, 3, 267–89.
Winters, L. A. (1991), *International Economics* (London: HarperCollins Academic).
Winters, L. A. (2000a), 'Trade, Trade Policy and Poverty: What are the Links?', Discussion Paper No. 2382 (Centre for Economic Policy Research, London).
Winters, L. A. (2000b), 'Trade Liberalisation and Poverty', Discussion Paper No. 7 (Poverty Research Unit, University of Sussex, UK).
Winters, L. A. (2000c), 'Trade and Poverty, Is There a Connection?', in D. Ben-David, H.

Nordstrom and L. A. Winters (eds.), *Trade, Income Disparity and Poverty*, Ch. 3 (WTO, Geneva, June), 43–69.

Winters, L. A. (2000d), 'Trade Policy as Development Policy: Building on Fifty Years' Experience', *Proceedings for High Level Round Table*, Tenth United Nations Conference on Trade and Development (Bangkok, February, http://www.unctad-10.org/index_en.htm).

Winters, L. A. (2001a), 'Trade Policies for Poverty Alleviation: What Developing Countries Might Do', paper for the Royal Economic Society Annual Conference (Durham, April).

Winters, L. A. (2001b), 'Trade Liberalisation and Growth: Implementation and Complementary Policies', paper given to the ESRC International Economic Study Group Conference (Gregynog, September).

Winters, L. A., N. McCulloch and A. McKay (2002), 'Trade Liberalisation and Poverty: The Empirical Evidence', Economics Working Paper No. 000 (University of Sussex).

Wood, A. (1994), *North-South Trade, Employment and Inequality: Changing Fortunes in a Skill-Driven World* (Oxford: Clarendon Press).

Wood, A. (1997), 'Openness and Wage Inequality in Developing Countries: The Latin American Challenge to East Asian Conventional Wisdom', *The World Bank Economic Review*, **11**, 33–57.

World Bank (1999), 'Panama Poverty Assessment' (Mimeo, World Bank).

*Journal of Economic Literature*
*Vol. XLII (March 2004) pp. 72–115*

# Trade Liberalization and Poverty: The Evidence So Far

L. ALAN WINTERS, NEIL MCCULLOCH, *and* ANDREW MCKAY[1]

## 1. *Introduction*

Most economists accept that, in the long run, open economies fare better in aggregate than do closed ones, and that relatively open policies contribute significantly to development. Many commentators fear, however, that in the shorter run, one of the steps towards openness—trade liberalization—harms poorer actors in the economy, and that, even in the longer run, successful open regimes may leave some people behind in poverty. Liberalization by its nature implies adjustment and so is likely to have distributional impacts, but to what extent are the poor likely to suffer adverse effects? This paper takes these concerns seriously by examining the evidence about whether developing countries' own trade liberalizations have reduced or increased poverty.[2]

If trade liberalization and poverty were both easily measured, and if there were many historical instances in which liberalization could be identified as the main economic shock, it might be easy to derive simple empirical regularities linking the two. Unfortunately, these conditions do not hold, so there is relatively little direct evidence on this question. Analysts therefore are obliged to try to decompose the link into steps and compile the evidence on each of them individually. A conceptual framework decomposing the links between trade policy and poverty has been developed by L. Alan Winters (2000a, 2002a), and the review in this paper is based on an examination of the evidence linking these components.[3] Even

[1] Winters: School of Social Sciences, University of Sussex. McCulloch: Institute of Development Studies, University of Sussex. McKay: University of Bath and University of Nottingham.We are grateful to Enrique Blanco de Armas, Xavier Cirera, Abbi Mamo Kedir, and Carolina Villegas Sanchez for research assistance, to Rosie Bellinger, Janet Ellis, Amy Sheehan and Reto Speck for logistical help, to innumerable colleagues for help and advice and to the editor and three anonymous referees for comments on an earlier version of this paper. Naturally none of these people is responsible for the paper's remaining imperfections.

[2] The paper does not address the issue of global trade reform (through the WTO) on poverty or poorer countries. For evidence of this see, for example, Oxfam (2002), World Bank (2002), and L. Alan Winters (2003). However, the approach and much of the analysis mostly generalizes to other real-side shocks such as other countries' trade-policy shocks, commodity-price booms and slumps, and exchange-rate changes.

[3] In related papers we have examined a subset of relevant empirical results (Andrew McKay, L. Alan Winters, and Abbi Mamo Kedir 2000), explored policy responses to the possibility that liberalization causes poverty (Winters 2002b) and provided an extended treatment for policy makers, including discussion of specific trade negotiation issues (Neil McCulloch, L. Alan Winters, and Xavier Cirera 2001).

this, it turns out, can only be partial, for often there are no direct studies of the poverty effects of trade and trade liberalization. In these cases we have sought evidence from experiences that might have parallels with trade liberalization, such as domestic market liberalization and public sector retrenchments. This latter process, however, has sometimes threatened to open up too large a literature, so a good deal of selection and judgement has been exercised to keep the output manageable.

The paper is explicitly empirical in focus. We report theoretical work if it informs empirical studies, but our emphasis is primarily on the study of ex post data pertaining to actual instances of trade liberalization and related shocks. We include a little of the computable general equilibrium (CGE) modelling literature, which, while fundamentally theoretical, does at least rely on some data.

The paper starts with a brief account of our analytical framework, which provides the organizational framework for the paper. We then survey the evidence on trade liberalization and poverty under four headings: macro-economic aspects (growth and fluctuations), households and markets, wages and employment, and government revenue and spending. While for each component trade liberalization can facilitate poverty alleviation, in none of them can an unambiguous generalization be made either in theory or empirically.

The ambiguity arises partly because of the heterogeneity of poverty: there are many reasons why people are poor; and even within broadly defined groups there are huge differences in the circumstances of individual households. The conclusions of much of the work surveyed below are conditional on these circumstances, so a crucial part of any specific analysis must be to identify the different characteristics of the poor including information about their consumption, production and employment activities. Outcomes will also depend on the specific trade reform measures being undertaken, and the economic environment in which they take place. Given the variety of factors to take into account, it will hardly be surprising that there are no general comparative static results about whether trade liberalization will increase or reduce poverty. Simple statements about "the poor" will lose information, at best, and simple generalizations about all countries will just be wrong.

An important aspect of any analysis of poverty is the definition and measurement of poverty itself. Poverty is a complex and multidimensional phenomenon, and there is considerable controversy in the literature about how it should be defined and measured.[4] However, the majority of the empirical economic literature on poverty, especially in relation to this issue, adopts an absolute income or consumption metric. Therefore, while recognizing that there are many legitimate approaches to the measurement of poverty, the evidence that we review focuses on this approach. Much of the methodological discussion is likely to generalize to other dimensions of poverty.

Finally, it is worth emphasizing that our concern is with poverty, not inequality. Since trade liberalization tends to increase the opportunities for economic activity, it can very easily increase income inequality while at the same time reducing poverty. Consequently, statements about its effects on inequality cannot be translated directly into statements about its impact on absolute poverty. There may be sound positive and normative reasons for interest in inequality, but they are not the concerns of this paper.

## 2. *An Analytical Framework*

As argued already, we approach the question of trade liberalization and poverty by constructing an analytical framework into which to slot the various pieces of theory and evidence. This section briefly outlines such a

[4] Amartya Sen (1993) discusses many of the central issues and World Bamk (2001) provides a discussion of different concepts.

framework—developed by Winters (2000a, 2002a)—and from it extracts twelve key questions around which we organize our survey of empirical results. It considers, in turn, economic growth and stability, the behavior of households and markets, wages and employment, and the government.

*Economic Growth and Stability.* The key to sustained poverty alleviation is economic growth, as is widely accepted by economists and development practitioners. Although growth can be unequalizing, it has to be very strongly so if it is to increase absolute poverty. This appears not to be the case either in general or for growth associated with freer trade. The link that has seen the most sustained debate among economists, however, is that between greater openness and growth. While there is a good deal of empirical support for the argument that trade liberalization and openness stimulate long-run growth and income, the case has certainly not yet been completely proven; there is no evidence, however, that they are harmful to growth. Sustained growth requires increases in productivity, and most of the evidence suggests that trade liberalization operates through this route. This link, however, warns us that in the short run some factor owners could suffer if productivity increases faster than output. Finally, openness is likely to influence the sort of shocks that affect an economy, so we need to consider macroeconomic volatility and its effects on growth.

Section 3 of this paper addresses these issues under three broad headings.

- Does liberalization stimulate growth and relieve poverty?
- Does trade liberalization boost productivity?
- Are open economies less stable?

*Households and Markets.* Given that the majority of the poor in most countries are self-employed, the best way of thinking about poor households is in terms of the "farm household," which produces goods or services, sells its labor and consumes (Inderjit Singh, Lyn Squire, and John Strauss 1986). An increase in the price of something of which the household is a net seller (labor, goods, services) increases its real income, while a decrease reduces it. Poor households typically have several sources of income, including transfers, remittances from absent family members, and income in kind, as well as wages and profits from production. The framework needs to ask how trade liberalization affects all of these, as well as considering consumption. We also note that shocks to a household can impinge differently on different family members. Thus, women might bear the burden of adjustment if they have to start to work outside the home while continuing to bear family responsibilities. Similarly, one needs to consider whether trade liberalization affects household investments in child welfare, such as basic education and health.

If price changes are an important pathway through which liberalization affects the poor, then we must ask how a trade liberalization affects prices. Even simple economies have several stages between the border, where trade policy operates, and the poor household, so one consideration is how much of any price change gets passed through to the poor. Unchanged internal distribution costs attenuate proportionate border price shocks as they pass through to households for importables, but exacerbate them for exportables. Shocks can even get lost completely if distribution is monopolized, as, for example, with official marketing boards or the private monopolies that sometimes replace them.

More important than price changes is whether markets exist at all: trade reform can both create and destroy markets. Extreme adverse poverty shocks are often associated with the disappearance of a market, while strong poverty alleviation can arise when markets are created for previously untraded or unavailable goods. Another critical issue is how households are able to respond to the price (and other) changes that reach them: Can households respond to favorable price movements (e.g. in the price of an agricultural output); are poorer households less able to respond than richer households; and are they less able to protect themselves against adverse movements?

Obviously a household's ability to adjust to a trade shock affects the size of any impact it suffers, but not generally its sign. Adjustment, however, is also the mechanism by which shocks in one market spill over into another. If these spillovers are particularly deep and narrow, they can be very significant locally. For example, a major attraction of liberalizations that increase agricultural prices is argued to be that the direct beneficiaries—farmers—spend much of their extra income on goods and services provided locally by the poor, such as construction, personal services, and simple manufactures.

A common worry is that opening up an economy will expose it and its component households to increased risk. Certainly, it will expose them to *new* risks, but the net effect can be to reduce overall risk because world markets (which have many players) are often more stable than domestic ones, or because they offer portfolio benefits. On the other hand, trade liberalization can increase risk either by undermining existing stabilization mechanisms (either autonomous or policy-based) or because residents consciously switch to a portfolio that offers higher average rewards but greater variability.

Section 4 takes up these issues under five headings.

- Do border price shocks get transmitted to poor households?
- Are markets created or destroyed?
- How well do households respond?
- Do the spillovers benefit the poor?
- Does trade liberalization increase vulnerability?

*Wages and Employment.* In all countries some of the poor, and in some countries most of the poor, rely on labor markets for the bulk of their income. Labor markets are also often an important route out of poverty (when an individual obtains a job) or into it (when a job is lost). Thus the effects of trade reform on wages and employment are important, especially those of unskilled workers. If reform boosts the demand for labor-intensive products, it boosts the demand for labor, and either wages or employment (or both) will increase. However, if the poor are mostly in completely unskilled families, while it is semi-skilled labor that receives the boost, poverty will be unaffected—or, possibly, worsened. If poverty is measured by counting individuals below the poverty line—the headcount index—it is also important where the various wage rates lie relative to the poverty line. If wages are pushed up from poverty line to higher levels, or the expanding sectors offer above poverty-line wages, then headcount poverty will fall. If, on the other hand, wages do not cross critical thresholds, recorded poverty could be unaffected, despite changes in welfare.

While simple Hechscher-Ohlin trade theory suggests that in relatively unskilled-labor-abundant countries trade liberalization will relieve poverty, in practice other factors may need to be considered. For instance, trade liberalization may be accompanied by skill-biased technical change, which can mean that skilled labor may benefit relative to unskilled labor. Also, not all developing countries are abundant in unskilled labor. For example, many Latin American and some African countries have very strong endowments of mineral and agricultural resources, and so liberalization will stimulate these sectors rather than labor-intensive ones. Similarly, if the unskilled are primarily employed in nontraded sectors, while exports draw mainly on the semi-skilled, a liberalization accompanied by a real-exchange-rate depreciation could have adverse effects.

Even if favorable in the long run, static gains from trade rely largely on adjusting a country's output bundle. Hence some people are likely to suffer temporary adverse shocks, most specifically in the form of unemployment. The initially nonpoor can generally tide themselves over these periods, so poverty statistics will—and public policy should—respond mainly to those who are initially relatively poor but who suffer such temporary setbacks.

Section 5 of this paper considers these issues under two key headings:

- Does liberalization raise wages or employment?
- Is transitional unemployment concentrated on the poor?

*Government Revenue and Spending.* Trade reform can affect government revenue, but actually does so less frequently and less adversely than is popularly imagined, because, for example, trade volume and collection rates increase as tariffs fall or because tariff exemptions are removed. Even where revenue falls (as eventually must be true as tariffs fall to zero), it is not inevitable that the poor suffer. Even recognizing the administrative constraints faced by poor-country governments, it is ultimately a political decision whether the new taxes necessary to make up the shortfall, or the cuts in government expenditure that result from falling revenue, impinge heavily on the poor.

Thus the final substantive section of the paper asks:

- Does liberalization actually cut government revenue?
- Do falling revenues from trade taxation hurt the poor?

## 3. *Economic Growth and Stability*

This section examines the macroeconomic links between trade liberalization, openness, and growth. It identifies the growth pathway as the most critical—and the most contentious—asking whether liberalization aids growth and whether growth aids poverty alleviation. In both cases the answer is "yes," but not unconditionally. The section then discusses the effects of liberalization on productivity growth, which are generally strong, and its consequences for macroeconomic stability, which appear to be mixed.

### 3.1 *Does Trade Liberalization Enhance Growth and Hence Alleviate Poverty?*

In the long run, economic growth is the key to the alleviation of absolute poverty. It creates the resources to raise incomes, and even if "trickle-down" is insufficient to bring the benefits to the poor, governments will have scope for stronger redistributive measures when income is higher and growing faster. This section considers the question in the title in two parts.

*From Openness to Growth.* Economic theory offers many reasons to expect trade liberalization to stimulate economic growth. In the medium term, reaping the static (efficiency) benefits of trade could look rather like growth. In the long run, the potential positive forces include access to technology and to appropriate intermediate and capital goods; the benefits of scale and competition; the flexibility induced by relying on market signals, and the constraints on government incompetence or corruption (see Gene M. Grossman and Elhanan Helpman 1991, or Robert Lucas 1988, for discussion). Unfortunately, none of the benefits is guaranteed, and it is not difficult to construct models in which openness pushes countries into less dynamic sectors (e.g. primary extraction) and harms growth—see, for example, Francisco Rodriguez and Dani Rodrik (2001). Therefore, ultimately the openness–growth link is an empirical matter, and it is that literature which this section briefly surveys.

Over the 1990s the conviction that openness is good for economic growth was fostered by several highly visible and well-promoted cross-country studies, for instance by David Dollar (1992), Jeffrey Sachs and Andrew Warner (1995), and Sebastian Edwards (1998). Recently, however, these were subjected to searching criticism and reworking by Rodriguez and Rodrik (2001), who argue that their conclusions rest on very weak empirical foundations such as flawed measures of openness and serious econometric shortcomings. Moreover, liberal trade is usually only one of several indicators of openness used, and one that often seems to weigh rather lightly in the overall result. (See also Ann Harrison 1996.)

The difficulty of establishing an empirical link between a liberal trade regime and income or growth arises from at least three sources. First, once one comes inside the boundary of near autarchy, measuring trade stances is difficult: for example, tariffs need to be aggregated, quantitative restrictions assessed and then aggregated, and the levels of credibility and enforcement measured.[5] These different dimensions of trade restriction are far from perfectly correlated (see, for example, Lant Pritchett 1996) and need to be aggregated into a single index for econometric purposes. James Anderson and Peter Neary's (1996) Trade Restrictiveness Index provides a coherent way of aggregating tariffs (given highly restrictive assumptions about behavior and a pile of data), but can handle nontariff barriers only once their tariff equivalents are known. The latter are difficult to establish (even conceptually) on a case-by-case basis, and quite impossible for all goods in a broad range of countries.

Second, causation is difficult to establish. Rodriguez and Rodrik (2001) rightly observe that actual openness, usually measured by imports plus exports relative to GDP, is likely to be endogenous, but there is also concern that even policy-based measures, e.g. average tariffs, could be so. Recently, Jeffrey Frankel and David Romer (1999) and Douglas Irwin and Marko Tervio (2002) have tried to address this problem by instrumenting openness in the income equation, with populations, land areas, borders and distances between trading partners. This appears to be successful, although Rodriguez and Rodrik (2001) point out that the instruments might be correlated with factors that boost growth independently of trade—for example, health and institutions—and that adding geographical variables directly to the growth equation undermines the result. Deeper investigation of these concerns, however, by Jeffrey Frankel and Andrew Rose (2002) suggests that these worries are misplaced, and so imply that there is evidence for a positive causal relationship between openness and income, and hence between liberalization and medium-term growth.

The third complication is that if it is to have a long-lived or even permanent effect on growth, trade liberalization almost certainly requires combination with other appropriate policies as well. The sort of policies envisaged here are those that encourage investment, allow effective conflict resolution, and promote human-capital accumulation. Unfortunately, the linear regression model, which is standard to this literature, is not equipped to identify the necessity of variables rather than their additivity in the growth process. Hints of the importance of these policies, however, can be found in exercises identifying the structural relationships through which openness affects growth. For example, Alan Taylor (1998) and Romain Wacziarg (2001) both find that investment is a key link and thus that poor investment policies could undermine trade benefits. Rodrik (1999) shows how the negative effects of external shocks on growth are mitigated by better institutions for managing distributional conflict. Robert Baldwin (2002), however, argues that since trade liberalization is never recommended or applied in isolation, trying to isolate its effects from those of associated policies makes little sense.

A further avenue for growth effects is the possibility that openness is correlated with changes in other policies; see Anne Krueger (1978, 1990). Perhaps the most important dimension is corruption: recent evidence from Alberto Ades and Rafael Di Tella (1997, 1999) shows a clear cross-country

[5] Effective openness requires predictability, transparency, and convenience of the trade regime, as well as low barriers per se.

connection between higher rents, stemming from things such as active industrial policy and trade restrictions, and higher corruption. The latter, in turn, reduces investment and hence growth.[6] On standard macroeconomic policy, inflation appears to be lower in open economies. Romer (1993) suggests that this is because real depreciation is more costly in terms of inflation in open economies, so that such economies are less likely to run the risks of excessive money creation.

The majority of this evidence in the recent growth literature relies on cross-country studies. The weight borne by such studies is remarkable, particularly since so many economists profess to distrust them. The cross-sectional (or panel) assumption that the same model and parameter set applies to Austria and Angola is heroic; so too is the neglect of dynamics and path dependency implicit in the view that the data reflect stable steady-state relationships. There are huge cross-country differences in the measurement of many of the variables used. Obviously important idiosyncratic factors are ignored, and there is no indication of how long it takes for the cross-sectional relationship to be achieved.[7] Nonetheless the attraction of simple generalizations has seduced most of the profession into taking their results seriously. One exception is T. N. Srinivasan and Jagdish Bhagwati (2001), who chide economists for forgetting the problems and neglecting other approaches to the openness–growth link. The latter include detailed case studies of particular countries, which consider a wide variety of causes and channels for growth, but frequently find openness at the heart of the matter, as, for example, with Michael Michaely, Demetris Papageorgiou, and Armeane Choksi (1991); Ritva Reinikka and Paul Collier (2001), and Sebastian Edwards and Daniel Lederman (2002).

A second alternative approach is to specify the links between openness and growth and examine them separately. Some studies associate openness strongly with higher accumulation—Ross Levine and David Renelt (1992), Taylor (1998), Wacziarg (2001)—and hence stronger growth, especially over relatively short periods (five years or so). Others examine the link to productivity using sectoral- or firm-level data for particular countries, as well as cross-country methods. The latter are discussed in section 3.2 below.

Despite the econometric and conceptual difficulties of establishing beyond doubt that openness enhances income levels, the weight of experience and evidence seems strongly in that direction. Charles Jones (2001, p. 337) argues that despite the uncertainty about the size of the effect, "our best estimate is that trade restrictions are harmful to long-run incomes." And Rodriguez and Rodrik concede that there is no "credible [post-war] evidence … that trade restrictions are systematically associated with higher growth" (p. 317).

*From Growth to Poverty.* Economists have long maintained that economic growth generally reduces poverty. Many have argued that, on average, growth does not have identifiable systematic effects on income distribution—see, for example, Gary Fields (1989), Ravallion (1995), or Michael Bruno, Martin Ravallion, and Lyn Squire (1998). These early studies were based on rather small samples, but recent work has extended the sample and reached exactly the same conclusions, although at the expense of great controversy. Most controversial has been the study by David Dollar and Aart Kraay (2002), which examines the relationship between growth and

[6] Shang-Jin Wei (2000), on the other hand, suggests that the losses from corruption increase with openness, because corruption impinges disproportionately on foreign transactions, and as a result that open countries have greater incentives to develop better institutions.

[7] Brock and Durlauf (2001) also question the ability of economic theory to specify growth equations tightly enough to permit traditional classical statistical inference in cross-country regressions, especially given that the determinants of growth might genuinely be highly correlated.

poverty both in levels across countries and in changes through time (national growth rates). Dollar and Kraay relate the mean income of the poor (bottom 20 percent of the income distribution) to overall mean income plus some additional variables.[8] They never reject the hypotheses that the mean income of the poor moves proportionally with mean income and, with the exception of inflation, that a variety of other variables (including measures of openness) affect it only via mean income. The residual errors of Dollar and Kraay's equations are large and so are perfectly consistent with there being instances in which growth hurts the poor. On average, however, these are offset by those in which the poor benefit disproportionately.

Howard White and Edward Anderson (2001) categorize growth histories into such "pro" and "anti" poor experiences, and find that in over one-quarter of cases, distributional changes offset growth effects—i.e., that the mean and "poor" incomes moved in different directions. They are not very successful, however, at identifying the factors that make growth pro- or anti-poor. They run "standard" growth equations for the income growth of each quintile and examine differences in the resulting coefficients. It is hard to detect clear patterns, but one stark result is that openness is associated with significantly higher income growth everywhere except in the *top* quintile, and that the greatest effects proportionally are for lower quintiles; that is, openness appears to be progressive.

Several concerns have been raised about the robustness of these studies of growth, openness, and poverty (in addition to those raised above in relation to cross-country regressions). The data on the incomes of the poor are clearly subject to error.[9] Reporting errors and sample biases are likely to be serious at the bottom of the distribution, and in many cases Dollar and Kraay had to infer the share of the lowest quintile from a broader measure of income distribution. The World Bank's sample of income and expenditure Gini coefficients (e.g. Klaus Deininger and Lyn Squire 1996 and later extensions) has been criticized for severe implausibility—e.g. by Tony Atkinson and Andrea Brandolini (2001). Stephen Knowles (2001) shows that the relationship between inequality and growth can change once one distinguishes between data based on income measures of inequality and those based on consumption data.

There is also an increasing body of evidence that income distribution (and by association, poverty) determines growth rates (and hence mean incomes)—see Philippe Aghion, Eve Caroli, and Cecilia García-Peñalosa (1999)—implying a potential endogeneity problem. Alternatively, the share of the poor and mean incomes could be jointly determined by some third factor. Finally, the average income of the poorest quintile is a very crude indicator of poverty—especially absolute poverty.

Ravallion (2001) offers a more widely accepted discussion of the poverty–growth link. By regressing the change in the \$-a-day poverty ratio on the change in mean income, he finds that a 1-percent increase in mean income results, on average, in a fall of 2.5 percent in the proportion of people in absolute poverty, or 2 percent if the mean income measure is instrumented to allow for errors of observation. Of course, individual experience will vary around this average growth elasticity of poverty, with one of the most important determinants being initial levels of inequality. The more compact the income distribution, the greater the share of population likely to be clustered about the poverty line, and hence the greater the effect of moving the distribution in one direction or the other.[10]

[8] This specification was first used by Montek .S. Ahluwalia (1976).

[9] So too, of course, are those on mean income, but probably less so.

As with the openness–growth relationships, more convincing insights may be derived from country case studies. Martin Ravallion and Gaurav Datt (2002) explore the factors behind pro-poor growth more thoroughly in the context of differences between Indian states. Higher farm yields, higher development spending, and lower inflation all appear to reduce poverty. Most interesting, however, is higher nonfarm output: this also helps to reduce poverty but much more strongly where farm productivity is higher, the rural-urban divide smaller and rural education better (all of which indicate higher initial levels of rural income). Translated into terms of national growth, pro-poor growth seems more likely to occur where initial conditions (including openness) give the poor the ability to take advantage of the opportunities it generates.

Despite the methodological challenges to the recent literature, there is no evidence to overturn the traditional conclusion that growth, *on average*, benefits the poor, nor to suggest that growth generated by greater openness is any worse than other growth in this respect (and may even be better). It is quite clear, however, that on occasions growth has been accompanied by worsening poverty and the challenge is to identify why. Indeed, much of this paper can be seen as trying to answer precisely this question in the case of trade liberalization.

### 3.2 *Trade Liberalization and Productivity*

An alternative approach to the links between trade liberalization, growth, and poverty is to consider the first's effects on productivity. By universal agreement, improved productivity is necessary for sustained economic growth and development. However, it may not be sufficient and, because of its distributional implications, its beneficial effects on poverty could be less than those of growth emanating from other sources. Thus, for example, if higher productivity reflected declining inputs rather than increasing outputs, its short-term effect could be to reduce employment and hence exacerbate poverty. Moreover, despite the strong presumption in modern growth theory, with its references to increased competition, access to new technology, better intermediate goods and so on, the response of productivity to trade liberalization is ultimately ambiguous.[11] Thus, as ever, there is an empirical issue to be settled.

An influential cross-country analysis of trade and aggregate productivity is David Coe, Elhanan Helpman, and Alexander Hoffmaister (1997). They construct an index of total knowledge capital (measured by accumulated investment in R&D) in each industrial country. Trading partners get access to a country's stock of knowledge in proportion to their imports of capital goods from that country. Using import-weighted sums of industrial countries' knowledge stocks to reflect developing countries' access to foreign knowledge, they find that, interacted with the importing country's openness, the latter has a statistically significant positive effect on total factor productivity (TFP). Their sample comprises quinquennial observations on 77 developing countries over 1971–90.

Intuitive as these results are, they leave some questions unanswered. First, they do not seriously consider competing explanations of access to knowledge capital. Second, they imply an excessive bilateralism in access to knowledge. Coe, Helpman, and Hoffmaister's measure implies that the only way for, say, Ghana to obtain French knowledge is to import equipment from France. But if Germany imports from France (and so, by hypothesis, accesses French knowledge), and then Ghana imports from

[10] Ravallion (2001) suggests the robust empirical rule of thumb that the elasticity of the poverty headcount with respect to mean incomes is roughly proportional to (1-index of inequality). He also notes that if the income of the poor is proportional to mean income, economic growth benefits the poor far less than average in absolute terms.

[11] Howard Pack (1988) takes a sceptical view of the early literature on the links.

Germany, this should give Ghana at least some access to French knowledge. Olivier Lumenga-Neso, Marcelo Olarreaga, and Maurice Schiff (2001), who advance this explanation, show that recognizing such indirect knowledge flows offers a better explanation of TFP than the earlier studies.

A second approach to the link between trade liberalization and productivity is cross-sectoral studies for individual countries. Many of these have shown that reductions in trade barriers were followed by significant increases in productivity, generally because of increased import competition; see, for example, Donald Hay (2001) and Pedro Ferreira and José Luis Rossi (2001) on Brazil; Gunnar Jonsson and Arvind Subramanian (2001) on South Africa[12] ; and Jong-Wha Lee (1996) on Korea. On the other hand, Euysung Kim (2000), also on Korea, suggests that most of the apparent TFP advance is actually due to the compression of margins and to economies of scale. Import competition makes some contribution via these effects, and also directly on "technology," but overall Kim argues that it was not the major force. Trade liberalization plays a similarly minor role in Kishor Sharma, Sisira Jayasuriya, and Edward Oczkowski's (2000) results on Nepal, although its effects are small mainly, the authors argue, because necessary complementary policies such as infrastructure investment were absent.

The sectoral studies relate TFP to a sector's own trade barriers and thus imply that competition is the causal link. But for general liberalizations it is likely that barriers on imported inputs also fall and this could be equally important. At an aggregate and sectoral level, Hadi Esfahani (1991) and Robert Feenstra et al. (1997) suggest such a link, as do James Tybout and Daniel Westbrook (1995) at the firm level. The last study provides a comprehensive view of Mexican manufacturing firms over the liberalization of 1984–90. Among its more important findings are that rationalization gains (the shrinking or elimination of inefficient firms) are an important contributor to sectoral productivity gains, that cheaper intermediates provide significant productivity and profitability stimuli, and that competition from imports seems to stimulate increases in technical efficiency (with the strongest effects in industries that are already most open).

Firm-level data also allow one to test the perennial claim that exporting is the key to technological advance. While macro studies or case studies have suggested links to productivity, enterprise level data have shown a much more nuanced picture. Arne Bigsten et al. (2000) find a positive stimulus from exports to productivity in Africa, and Kraay (1997) is ambiguous for China, but Tybout and Westbrook (1995) and Bee Yan Aw, Sukkyun Chung, and Mark Roberts (1999) find little evidence for it in Latin America and Asia respectively. The fundamental problem is that of causation: efficiency and exporting are highly correlated because efficient firms export.[13] Hence researchers must first identify this link (by careful modelling of the timing of changes in exports and productivity) if they are then to isolate the reverse one. Tybout's (2000) excellent survey suggests that the positive results for Africa and China may have arisen because data shortages obliged their authors to use much simpler dynamic structures than the Asian and American exercises.

The strong positive relationship between openness and productivity generally found at the sectoral level and the somewhat weaker one at the firm level may be reconciled by noting that exporting will allow more efficient firms to grow faster than less efficient ones and that import competition may pick

[12] Jonsson and Subramanian also conduct a time series exercise which links TFP positively to the openness ratio—(exports plus imports)/GDP.

[13] The same causation difficulty arises in interpreting the observation that where a region exports heavily, all firms are more productive: is it positive spillovers or comparative advantage?

off the weaker domestic firms. Firm turnover is significant in developing countries (Mark Roberts and James Tybout 1996) and evidence for the beneficial rationalization effects of trade liberalization may be found in Tybout and Westbrook (1995) and inferred from the lower productivity dispersion across plants in open economies (James Tybout, Jaime de Melo, and Vittorio Corbo 1991).

Rationalization effects highlight the poverty concerns about openness. Particularly in Africa, significant numbers of industrial enterprises have been unable to cope with increased import competition, and, in places, this has resulted in a substantial contraction in industrial employment. Sanjaya Lall's (1999) study of technological adaptation in the Kenyan, Tanzanian, and Zimbabwean engineering and garment sectors finds the majority of firms responding to pressure by contracting rather than upgrading aggressively. Among the reasons Lall advances for this are the lack of preparation of firms for competition, the absence of policies to promote technological improvement (especially among SMEs), and the poor technological and human infrastructure in these very poor countries. That adjustment is a key consideration is confirmed by direct evidence on micro and small enterprises from five African countries (Ronald Parker, Randall Riopelle, and William Steel 1995); this shows that firms that adapted quickly were net beneficiaries of import liberalization, while those ill-prepared to face competition lost out. Both these studies show that open trade by itself may not be associated with increased productivity if other essential elements, often including an appropriate policy environment, are not present.

Sectoral analyses are applied almost exclusively to industrial sectors. In many cases these will lie at the heart of development strategies and the generally positive link between productivity and openness is a cause for long-run optimism. For most of the poor, however, even if productivity in rural nonfarm activities is important, agricultural productivity will be of the most direct interest. Historically there has been considerable debate about whether agricultural productivity improvements are good for the poor, but recently the tendency has been on the optimistic side; see, for example, Gaurav Datt and Martin Ravallion (1998).

What is less clear is how agricultural productivity is related to openness and trade liberalization. In section 4.2 below we note that the liberalization of farm-input markets stimulated output per head in Bangladesh, but, of course, not all this is productivity gain in the TFP sense. Will Martin and Devashish Mitra (2001) show that TFP increases are generally higher in agriculture than in industry, but do not seek to explain them. They do note, however, a strong tendency for international convergence of productivity levels, which suggests effective transmission forces, although whether these are via trade or via technology transfer is unclear.[14]

Of course, openness in a broad sense—openness to foreign technology—lay behind the greatest leap in agricultural productivity in recent times—the Green Revolution. The huge increase in grain productivity benefited farmers directly and also, in different proportions in different places, consumers, wage laborers and rural nonfarm workers. Mitch Renkow (2000) makes the obvious point that the distribution of the gains depends very much on whether the country is open: if trade determines the price of a food product, productivity increases mainly benefit producers, whereas in closed economies the benefits come mostly as price declines for consumers. Moreover, despite fears expressed at the time, poor farmers were able to take advantage of the advances by learning appropriate technologies and because some high yield varieties were developed for low-input cultivation (IFAD

[14] Their work also raises the general issue that it is actually rather difficult to get accurate measures of productivity or even of factor inputs.

2001).

One complication in virtually all this literature is actually measuring TFP. The prevailing methodology—e.g. Andrew Bernard and Charles Jones (1996)—assumes perfect competition and equates marginal products with factor shares as is implied by Cobb-Douglas technology. Attempts to relax these assumptions by, say, estimating production or cost functions econometrically have proved disappointing especially for developing countries, with apparently implausible estimates very common (e.g. see Zvi Griliches and Jacques Mairesse 1998). Besides, measuring factor inputs (especially capital) is difficult, not only conceptually, but even merely in terms of obtaining data—see, for example, Donald Larson et al. (2000) on agricultural inputs.

Overall the recent empirical evidence seems to suggest that openness and trade liberalization have a strong influence on productivity and its rate of change. In many cases the latter will be immediately and directly poverty alleviating and in the long run they are a necessary part of any viable poverty-reduction strategy. As we noted at the outset, however, the immediate effect of an increase in productivity could be to reduce inputs as well as to raise output. The net effect on employment will then depend on the relative sizes of the output and productivity shocks and will be influenced by factors such as the flexibility of labor and credit markets. It is not difficult to imagine adverse short-term implications for jobs and poverty, and so we review the evidence on these in section 5 below.

### 3.3 *Are Open Economies Less Stable?*

Macroeconomic volatility is one of the most important sources of risk for all households, both poor and non-poor. Hence we examine briefly the links from trade liberalization to output volatility and terms of trade volatility. The presumption is usually that open economies are less stable—see, for example, Rodrik (1998), who explains the positive correlation between openness and government size in such terms—but this is not particularly well-grounded empirically.

As Assaf Razin and Andrew Rose (1992) elaborated, more open capital markets should be associated with smoother consumption but more volatile investment, whereas more open goods markets should be associated with greater output volatility. This is because goods market integration allows economies to specialize and thus reduces risk spreading in production.[15] Moreover, if export markets display random undiversifiable shocks, greater openness increases exposure. In their empirical tests over 1980–88, however, they find no significant correlations between openness and volatility—mainly because many shocks appear to be common across countries.

William Easterly and Aart Kraay (2000), on the other hand, find that small states, which are generally more open than larger states, tend to have more volatile growth rates, albeit around higher averages. The reason is not that their terms of trade are more volatile, but that a given terms of trade volatility has greater effects on output the more open the economy.

Turning to the literature linking openness to terms of trade (ToT) volatility and the impact of such volatility on growth, the Prebisch-Singer hypothesis suggests that, if the supply of primary products is relatively price inelastic (compared to that of manufactures) fluctuations in world demand will make primary commodity prices more volatile than those of manufactures. If trade liberalization encourages specialization towards primary commodities, this suggests that it will increase the volatility of developing countries' terms of trade (ToT). In fact, however, Matthias Lutz and Hans Singer (1994) find the very opposite—a mild tendency for openness to reduce volatility—while Easterly and Kraay (2000) find no relationship between ToT volatility and

[15] These results do depend on the nature of the shocks.

country size (which, in turn, is correlated with openness).

David Bevan, Paul Collier, and Jan Gunning (1990) suggest that the causality between the ToT and openness may operate in the opposite direction, with ToT shocks giving rise to trade reform. They cite the case of Kenya, in which an increase in the world price of coffee raised government revenues and consequently public expenditure on infrastructure. When prices fell, the government liberalized in order to access foreign finance for their expenditure programmes. This is a plausible story, and one which could dominate any empirical relationship between trade liberalization and the terms of trade. However, it concerns a single specific change in the terms of trade, not volatility per se. It is possible that a series of such episodes would suggest a connection between repeated ToT changes and increasing liberalization, but the case remains to be made.

Turning to the effects of ToT volatility on growth, the simple presumption would be that volatility causes uncertainty which, in turn, reduces investment and therefore growth. Empirical tests of this hypothesis however give mixed results, starting with Alasdair MacBean's (1966) classic refutation. Lutz and Singer (1994) provide a fairly detailed empirical analysis. They find no evidence that volatility in the net barter terms of trade harms growth—indeed, signs of the reverse—but they do find that volatility in the income terms of trade does. However, this is not, apparently, true in low-income or primary product exporting countries, the two groups where poverty levels tend to be highest. Parantap Basu and Darryl McLeod (1992) construct a simple open economy stochastic growth model and test it using VARs for twelve developing countries. Their results confirm the existence of persistent effects of ToT shocks on output levels and suggest that greater ToT variability reduces economic growth.

A study by Patrick Guillaumont, Sylviane Guillaumont Jeanneney, and Jean Francois Brun (1999) uses cross-country data to argue that Africa exhibits higher "primary" instabilities (i.e. structural instabilities, including ToT shocks) than countries from other regions, and that this has negatively affected its growth by increasing the instability of investment and the real exchange rate. These latter "intermediate" instabilities affect growth more by reducing the rate of total factor productivity growth than through reductions in the rate of investment. Although such costs of ToT volatility are relevant to open economies, the role of openness in generating these instabilities is not spelled out; hence it is not clear whether, even in the volatility dimension alone, reducing openness would help.

A third possible link is via financial markets. Helena Svaleryd and Jonas Vlachos (2002) argue that protection might deter the growth of financial markets because governments use it to shelter firms from shocks. If so, trade liberalization could promote financial development, as, indeed, their data tend to suggest. In turn, financial development is often claimed to be an important input to growth—see e.g. William Easterly, Roumeen Islam, and Joseph Stiglitz (2000).

### 4. *Households and Markets*

This section turns to households and markets. Treating the household as the basic unit over which poverty is defined, it asks how the price changes generated by trade reforms impinge on poor households given their consumption and production bundles. The starting point is the observation that, given labor and transfer incomes, the first order approximation of the welfare effect of a small change in prices is

$$\Delta W = \Sigma_i \, (q_i - c_i) \, \Delta p_i \qquad (1)$$

where $q_i$ is production of good $i$, $c_i$ consumption of $i$ and $Dp_i$ the price change. Angus Deaton (1997, ch. 3) provides the analytical background as well as interesting examples of this approach applied to domestic reforms.

Even in its simplest form, (1) provides a powerful starting point for identifying the poverty effects of trade liberalization. Christopher Barrett and Paul Dorosh (1996) predict the short-run effects of rice price changes in Madagascar (partly induced by import policy) by applying kernel estimates to household data on net sales as a share of income (i.e. $(q_r - c_r)/y$, where the subscript $_r$ denotes rice). They estimate that one-third of poor rice farmers could lose from higher prices or price variability.

David Sahn and Alexander Sarris (1991) apply basically this methodology to several African countries to determine the consequences of structural adjustment programmes on rural small-holders. (They consider wages as well as sales of output as sources of income). Their work is attractive in its reliance on observed *ex post* price data but unfortunately they do not relate these to trade policy changes. James Levinsohn, Steven Berry, and Jed Friedman's (1999) study of changes in Indonesian price indices by class of household is essentially (1) with quantities set at zero. They find that the poor suffered more from price increases in 1997 than the non-poor, although with significant geographical variations. Theirs are not estimates of the poverty effects of the crisis per se, however, because they ignore changes in income, and any induced changes in consumption.

Duncan Thomas, et al. (1999) and Asep Suryahadi, Widyanti Wenefrida, and Sudarno Sumarto (2003) also examine the consequences of the Indonesian crisis, and conclude that the greatest challenge in making poverty assessments is constructing the correct price deflator, i.e. estimating the price changes appropriate to each household. The former, very thorough, study shows that households in agricultural regions fared relatively well in real income terms, because the relative prices of their output increased, while regions with many civil servants fared particularly badly because wages were held back far behind prices.

This part of the paper comprises sections on: how prices are transmitted from the border to poor households; whether markets for their output, purchases, or services are destroyed or created by trade liberalization; how households respond to trade-related price shocks; whether spillovers between households exacerbate or alleviate poverty; and whether trade reform increases household vulnerability.

### 4.1 *The Transmission of Border-Price Shocks*

In any economy there are several steps of transmission between changes in (tariff-inclusive) border prices following external liberalization and price changes experienced by producers or consumers at local levels. The extent of transmission may be limited by a number of factors including transport costs and other costs of distribution; the extent of competition between traders and the functioning of markets more generally; and infrastructure, domestic taxes and regulations. Some of these costs, such as transport costs, are inevitable (though they may be increased by other factors such as fuel taxes or inadequate infrastructure); others represent direct economic inefficiency such as monopoly or monopsony power exercised by traders.

At its simplest, we can represent the local price of an importable good ($P^m{}_l$) as

$$P^m{}_l = P_w r\,(l+t_m) + \gamma_m \qquad (2a)$$

Where $P_w$ is the world price, $r$ the exchange rate, $t_m$ the proportional tariff or tax and $\gamma_m$ the transaction costs on importables. For an exportable the corresponding equation is

$$P^x{}_l = P_w r\,(l-t_x) - \gamma_x \qquad (2b)$$

These equations illustrate four simple points. First, the proportional changes in $P^m{}_l$ are smaller than those in tax-inclusive border prices $[P_w r\,(l+t_m)]$, while those in $P^x{}_l$ are larger than those in $P_w r\,(l-t_x)$. Second, changes in trade taxes ($t_i$) could be (partially) offset by changes in world prices if the country or countries under consideration are large. For certain export products this is probably true for some developing country producers—see, for example, Lutz and Singer (1994)—but we do not pursue it further here. Third, correcting exchange rate distortions can have major effects on the prices faced by the poor; see, for example, Krueger (1992). Fourth, changes in border taxes ($t_i$) can be offset or exacerbated by changes in $\gamma_i$. These may be exogenous—i.e. due to (domestic) policy changes such as when trade liberalization is accompanied by marketing reforms—or endogenous, as, for example, when an imperfectly competitive distribution sector absorbs some of the border price change into its own margins.

The available evidence on the effectiveness of transmission mainly concerns prices in agriculture (where the issue is perhaps most important) at the national level. Many export crops, especially those of small farmers, are sold through public or private marketing agencies, whose prices are less than the f.o.b. export price (see, for instance, Yair Mundlak and Donald Larson 1992; Tim Lloyd et al. 1999). The differential reflects transport, marketing and the other costs of the agencies (Andrew McKay, Oliver Morrissey, and Charlotte Vaillant 1997), plus, in many instances, monopsonistic profits. In the case of public sector marketing agencies, the purpose of their operations was often to insulate farmers from world price fluctuations and thus trade liberalization per se would not be transmitted at all. The evidence suggests that this aim was not always achieved (Mundlak and Larson 1992) but in any case the net effect was usually to tax farmers on average. In the case of Pakistan, Paul Dorosh and Alberto Valdes (1990) find that farm gate prices received by farmers increased significantly as a result of trade reform, in large measure because of the reduction in the exchange rate overvaluation that had eroded any benefits from trade policy.

The mere presence of transactions costs provides natural protection to local producers of import competing products, a factor found to be important by Chris Milner, Oliver Morrissey, and Nicodemus Rudaheranwa (2001) in Uganda. But such costs also tax prospective purchasers of imports (producers and consumers) and prospective suppliers of exports. Moreover, as just noted, they attenuate and magnify price changes respectively. Paul Glewwe and Dennis de Tray (1989) illustrate the attenuation effect in the potato market in Peru.

Price transmission is likely to be particularly ineffective for poor people living in remote rural areas (where $\gamma_i$ will be higher), in the absence of specific policy interventions to improve it. In extreme instances producers or consumers can be completely insulated from changes taking place at the border—i.e. goods cease to be tradable. Stephan Goetz (1992) reports that high fixed transport costs prevent some households from trading in many parts of sub-Saharan Africa, and IFAD (2001) lays the blame substantially on poor infrastructure. Nicholas Minot (1998) found in Rwanda in the early 1980s that changes in relative prices at the border had little effect on predominantly rural low-income households because of their isolation from the cash economy. This presumably reflects their physical isolation, which curtails their ability to gain from trade (even within Rwanda) and trade liberalization, and thus reduces the level of their income significantly. Thomas et al. (1999) find that isolated regions of Indonesia were insulated from much of the 1997 crisis.

Once internal trade, and hence transmission, is possible, both the level and the (endogenous) change in transactions costs are relevant. For example, Vietnam experienced significant increases in rice producer prices as export restrictions were lifted over the 1990s, and transformed itself from a net importer into a significant exporter (Nicholas Minot and Francesco Goletti 1998).[16] Nonetheless, rice exports are constrained by a relatively underdeveloped marketing system controlled by a small number of state enterprises. Measures to enable competition between central and local state enterprises have helped, but these authors argue that significantly greater liberalization, including the entry of the private sector, is required to enable Vietnam to realise its full potential as a rice exporter. This, they argue, will reduce the level of transactions costs and the extent to which border price changes can be absorbed into distribution rather than being passed on to farmers.

The transmission of price shocks to local levels is related, but not identical, to the issue of spatial market integration. The degree of market integration is typically assessed in terms of comovements in spatial price spreads—the extent to which prices in different regions (including the border) move in parallel (see, for example, Stefan Dercon 1995). If this is high, border changes will be transmitted strongly, but it does not necessarily indicate the competitiveness of local markets (Ousmane Badiane 1997) because it does not take account of the level of costs and so does not demonstrate that price *levels* converge (Bob Baulch 1997). In the Philippines, Baulch finds arbitrage between markets to be quite efficient despite large constant difference in price levels due to transaction costs.

But introducing private distribution will not help if it amounts merely to the creation of private monopolies[17] (Badiane 1997, 1998; Minot and Goletti 1998), as recent evidence on the privatisation of marketing arrangements in Zambia and Zimbabwe illustrates (Oxfam-IDS 1999; L. Alan Winters 2000b). In Zimbabwe, three private buyers emerged after the privatisation of cotton purchasing, including one owned by the farmers. There was increased competition, resulting in higher output prices and better supplies of inputs (including provision of credit), and farm income increased appreciably. In Zambia, on the other hand, when the government abolished the official monopsony in maize, the activity became dominated by two private firms, which possibly colluded to keep prices low and which abandoned purchasing altogether in remote areas. The last point essentially reflected the deterioration of critical infrastructure—rural roads—which raised transaction costs above viable levels. It illustrates the importance of physical as well as policy-based frictions to trade (see also section 4.2) and the need to consider both in assessing the poverty impacts of trade reform.

Ousmane Badiane and Mylene Kherallah (1999) show that the domestic liberalization of food crop farming in Africa has had a strong effect on reducing poverty. They argue that it brought about increased levels of investment by private traders, and an expansion in their activities. This created employment for low skilled labor in itself, but, in addition, it reduced retail prices for food, and various transactions costs. Thus domestic agricultural reforms can amplify the benefits of agricultural trade reform for poverty, even if it reduces natural protection for some.

### 4.2 *Are Markets Created or Destroyed?*

The biggest impacts of trade reform are often associated with the creation or destruction of markets. Greater openness can result in a wider variety of commodities being available, or create new opportunities for production (e.g. by allowing imported inputs). At the same time other markets may cease to exist, for instance due to the effects of increased import competition on a local market. Often, however, it is the measures that accompany trade liberalization, such as the privatisation of marketing arrangements, that eliminate markets, rather than trade liberalization itself.

From a theoretical perspective, Paul Romer (1994) argues that the most substantial welfare costs of trade restrictions come

[16] Equations (2) do not easily cope with quantitative restrictions of this kind, but this case may be thought of as the transmission of border policies despite high domestic transactions costs.

[17] Unless the private sector is immensely more efficient technically.

from the goods and services that they exclude from the market and the loss of productive activities that results from that exclusion. A good or service will not be produced—or imported—if fixed costs make it unprofitable, as Romer elegantly shows by applying Dupuit's bridge building example (Jules Dupuit 1854) to trade policy. Even if a bridge is operated as a monopoly by the firm that constructed it, it can still provide substantial social benefits in terms of the surplus it provides—the "Dupuit triangle." An ad valorem tax on bridge crossings does not affect the monopolists' optimal price or output as long as the bridge is still built. It does reduce the monopolist's profits, however, so that, at some level, profits no longer cover fixed costs and the bridge will not be built; at this point the welfare cost of the tax to society becomes substantial.

This basic point applies widely, including to trade taxes. Substantial welfare benefits can come from technological change and diffusion of knowledge, for which (as discussed above) trade is often a very important vehicle. Romer argues that the main costs of trade restriction may come from its adverse impact on the adoption of new technologies, and on the variety of productive activities, outputs and inputs. The growth literature surveyed above is suggestive, and David Gisselquist and Jean-Marie Grether (2000) report significant direct benefits to agricultural producers in Bangladesh as liberalization increased the availability of inputs. Consumers too benefit from the increased availability of goods. David Booth et al. (1993), in a participatory study in Tanzania, find that, following liberalization, the greater availability of goods at international prices was regarded as a substantial improvement compared with the past, even by quite poor rural people, and particularly by women. On balance, the communities considered the improved availability of goods to have more than compensated for the steep rises in real prices that had accompanied improved supply.

But where trade liberalization, or accompanying changes in domestic marketing arrangements, destroys markets, households can become completely isolated from the market and suffer substantial income losses (L. Alan Winters 2000b). For instance, if official marketing boards provided small farmers with inputs secured against future output, whereas, post-liberalization, private agents or banks do not, such farmers could lose even if output prices have risen substantially. As noted above, the abolition of the official maize purchasing monopsony in Zambia in the early 1990s led to the abandonment of purchasing altogether in remote areas, reportedly causing great hardship.[18] In part this was due to the deterioration of the roads, which made the transactions costs of collecting small consignments in rural Zambia too high to make any trade worthwhile. But it also illustrates a simple, and sometimes neglected, methodological point: the effects of reform depend on the effects of the policies that it is undoing. In Zambia the marketing board's policy of pan-seasonal and pan-regional pricing was essentially a subsidy to small and remote farmers (a large one in view of the poor infrastructure in remote areas). The liberalization removed the subsidy, so it is not surprising that these farmers suffered. The extent of their suffering was emphasized, however, by the discontinuous nature of the change.

Finally, in an environment of trade liberalization, policy interventions can help to create markets that would be viable for the poor but which would otherwise not form. One example is the creation of jobs for young women in the clothing export factories in Bangladesh. Despite their shortcomings by Western standards, it is widely accepted that these jobs have transformed the lives of these women—see, for example, Naila Kabeer (2000). Two other examples

[18] We say "reportedly," for one commentator has argued privately to us that farmers in the remote Northern Province never sold much to the official buyers, preferring instead to trade informally over the border with Malawi.

illustrate the gains from trade by highlighting the problems that its removal causes. Judith Head (1998) reports the widespread distress of female workers in Paarl, a town in South Africa, when the EU scaled back its imports of their canned fruit.[19] Similarly, Spencer Henson et al. (2000) report that the near cessation of EU imports of fish from Tanzania over 1997–98 cut fishermen's incomes by 80 percent. In these examples the loss of trade implies the cessation of the activity concerned. A more modest version of the same story occurs if transactions costs cause a product to become nontradable, as postulated in the simulation model of Alain de Janvry, Marcel Fafchamps, and Elisabeth Sadoulet (1991). They show theoretically how such non-tradabilities could affect the responses of other tradables to market shocks and hence the welfare consequences of the latter. Unfortunately, there is to our knowledge no empirical (as opposed to numerical) implementation of these ideas.

### 4.3 *How Do Households Respond?*

To the extent that the effects of trade reform are transmitted to local levels, the next question is how agents respond to them. To what extent are agents in general—and the poor in particular—able to protect themselves against any potential adverse impacts and to take advantage of potentially favourable effects? Such ability increases the magnitude of a real income shock—although it does not normally change its sign. Again the nature of local markets and the quality of local infrastructure are likely to play an important role. Both the production and consumption responses of household are important.

[19] Head writes that "working in the canning lines for 5 or 6 months of the year … the women workers…developed…a sense of independence" (p.10) which was the first casualty of the retrenchment of the canning plant, and that the workers moved from "a hard but honourable life, to a life of despair and destitution" (p. 2).

*Production.* The most plentiful evidence on production effects concerns responses to changes in prices, usually in agriculture, based on aggregate time series data. Many such supply response studies, whether for individual crops (Marian Bond 1983) or agriculture as a whole (Maurice Schiff and Claudio Montenegro 1997), suggest that in aggregate agricultural producers are quite responsive to price incentives, when they have access to the necessary inputs, information and credit (McKay, Morrissey, and Vaillant 1997), a condition that may well call for complementary government policies such as information and extension services.

But to assess the poverty impact of price changes, it is necessary to focus on the responses of individual producers, especially small farmers. This is most easily explored using micro (farm) level data, though few such studies have been conducted. Using micro level panel data for farm households in Zambia over the period 1993/94 to 1994/95, Klaus Deininger and Pedro Olinto (2000) show that for many households a major constraint on improvements in agricultural productivity following external liberalization was the absence of key productive assets (draft animals, implements). Similarly, based on a small panel of farm households in Mexico, Ramón López, John Nash, and Julie Stanton (1995) find that those with low levels of capital inputs were, on average, less responsive to price incentives than those with higher levels. But farmers with little capital were also those who had more problems obtaining credit, were less likely to use purchased inputs, were less educated and farmed poorer quality land, any or all of which could account for their lower supply response. Rasmus Heltberg and Finn Tarp (2002) obtained similar results for Mozambique. These studies highlight the importance of complementary policies targeted at small farmers to enable them to benefit fully from new opportunities, for example in fostering asset accumulation, improving access to credit, and providing good quality extension services.

A case where constrained responses are frequently alleged to have rendered trade liberalization harmful is the effect of NAFTA on poor corn producers in Mexico. Several *ex ante* studies forecast problems for small farmers—for instance, Santiago Levy and Sweder Van Wijnbergen (1992)—but Alejandro Nadal (2000) is, to our knowledge, the only thorough *ex post* study. He finds that though the corn price fell, small and poor farmers maintained their production levels of corn, even increasing their planted areas.[20] In part this presumably reflected the costs of switching activities, but it was also partly because much of their output was for subsistence purposes, and because the prices of substitute crops also fell sharply. With so little adjustment, the fall in the price of maize reduced these producers' incomes both directly and through reduced nonfarm employment opportunities; increasing the cultivated area could only cushion this marginally. The depth of these farmers' plight, however, seems to lie less with trade liberalization per se, than with how it was done. Following the peso crisis of 1994 the government abandoned its plans to phase in the liberalization gradually, and to provide adjustment support over the transition period. In such a sensitive crop it is not surprising that so sudden a shock caused hardship.

Two other aspects of this story warrant note. First, one aspect of the response of households to the reduced employment opportunities in rural areas was male labor migration, which increased the workloads for women and children remaining behind (Kevin Watkins 1997). Second, the prospective consumer gains from corn liberalization—lower consumer prices—also failed to materialize. Nadal notes that the cartelised tortilla sector was able to maintain prices despite the reduction in its costs following liberalization.

As well as its impact on production, trade liberalization in agriculture frequently provides incentives for such producers to start to supply the market—i.e. for commercialization. Heltberg and Tarp (2002) find this effect to be substantial in the case of Mozambique in 1996-97. They find that the same factors influence both poor and non-poor farmers' decisions about whether to market their output, notably land and capital endowments, and the characteristics of the farms such as yield and risk. However, the non-poor are generally better endowed than the poor with respect to these factors, and so are better placed to respond.

In addition, some agricultural households are better placed than others to deal with the commercialised environment that results from trade liberalization. For instance, in Malawi, trade liberalization encouraged the emergence of traders who buy food commodities from farmers and sell in urban areas or export (Brett Parris 1999). However, because most smallholders are unable to store their output, they tend to sell in the immediate post-harvest period when prices are low rather than wait until prices would be higher. This inability to cope with fluctuating prices can penalize poor farmers and compromise their food security, for as well as selling low they may need to buy in the lean period when prices are high. One cannot know a priori, however, whether these difficulties will fully outweigh the gains from opening up the new market. Thus rather than being an argument against commercialization and trade liberalization per se, this example rather emphasizes the importance of appropriate institutions to allow farmers to cope with fluctuating prices (such as access to storage or credit).

One aspect of a move towards more commercialised agriculture is the switch from food to cash crops. A concern frequently expressed about this is that it could compromise household food security or health

[20] Confusingly, Nadal uses the term "subsistence farmers" for such people.

status. Diane Elson and Barbara Evers (1997) write of Uganda: "... adjustment measures have elicited a positive export supply response but the greater demands on female labor time have damaging repercussions for the health and well being of children. Survey data reveal that the expansion of NTAE [non-traditional agricultural exports] has meant that men work for wages on others' farms to the neglect of land preparation on their wives' food farms. Increasing workloads of women have led to a decline in breast feeding and worsening child care practices and food insecurity has been intensified ...." But the effect on nutrition is not necessarily adverse given that commercialisation often leads to significant gains in smallholder income (Joachim von Braun 1989; von Braun, David Hotchkiss, and Maarten Immink 1989). In addition, increased agricultural commercialisation often has other favourable impacts on poverty, for example on the demand for landless workers (Eileen Kennedy and Bruce Cogill 1987).

*Consumption and Labor Supply.* Equation (1) provides a first order approximation of the welfare effects of a price change. If we take outputs as given (determined by a separable income-generation model), we can use consumer theory to explore how consumption changes in order to take advantage of the new price vector. Such changes are typically calculated by estimating the demand system for a (representative) consumer (or class of consumer) and applying predicted or observed price changes to it. This is very much in the tradition of tax reform analysis, some parts of which include trade taxes; see David Newbery and Nicholas Stern (1987).

A pertinent example of this approach, although only of a hypothetical policy change, is Martin Ravallion and Dominique van de Walle's (1991) study of Indonesian rice reform. They use detailed data to estimate household demand equations and apply to them assumed income and price changes. They show, inter alia, that the results depend partly on how the government passes the budget shock implied by rice price changes onto consumers and on what poverty line is used. The very poor are net consumers of rice and so suffer from the price rises, whereas farmers just below the standard poverty line are net producers and hence benefit and show positive chances of escaping from poverty. Given that much of the worst poverty is among self-employed farmers, changes in input and output prices can be an important determinant of poverty.

A major technical problem with empirical demand systems is that, having data for only one period, researchers have had to rely on the geographical variation of prices to identify the price effects. Deaton (1988) shows that the unit values of purchases reported by individual households will reflect quality, which is endogenous and correlated with income as well as with true prices, which are exogenous. This will bias the estimates unless relatively sophisticated methods are used (see Deaton 1997, for an accessible account). Deaton uses these methods to discuss the implications of tax reform in India and Pakistan. In Pakistan a reduction in the effective domestic subsidies to rice and wheat (due, in the case of rice, to export taxes) would be efficiency enhancing, but in both cases the burden falls relatively heavily on the poor, who have high and relatively inflexible expenditure shares on these items. Ideally, the adverse distributional effects of such tax reform could be addressed by appropriate complementary policies.

Jed Friedman and James Levinsohn (2002) use Deaton's approach to estimate the parameters for their extension of equation (1) to a second-order approximation of the effects of the 1997 crisis in Indonesia. They find that allowing for household responses roughly halves the welfare losses predicted by the first order formulation, as well as affecting their distribution over households a little. They caution, however, that using parameters derived solely from regional price variations to predict the effects of huge price changes over time represents a massive out-of-sample extrapolation and must be treated accordingly.

As hinted above, an important dimension of poor households' response to shocks is labor supply. Although we consider labor markets in section 5 below, we briefly consider supply responses here. The important point is that for poor households with some subsistence activities, wage employment, self employment and consumption are potentially jointly determined, so that shocks to one affect the other. De Janvry, Fafchamps, and Sadoulet (1991) model these interactions numerically and show that missing markets for, say, wage employment, seriously disturb households' responses to commodity price shocks. Serious attempts to reflect such factors in empirical work include Dwayne Benjamin (1992) on Java, and Sylvie Lambert and Thierry Magnac (1997) on Côte d'Ivoire, although neither deals specifically with poor households. These studies conclude that, in general, the separability of consumption and production decisions cannot be rejected, but probably more because of poor data quality than because underlying behavior is separable.

A related literature shows that 'imperfect labor markets' within the household can constrain supply responses. Christopher Udry (1996) and Lisa Smith and Jean-Paul Chavas (1999), for example, show that distortions to the allocation of responsibilities among household members both impose absolute losses (i.e. are inefficient) and prevent optimal responses to price signals.

An interesting recent analysis of Vietnam—Eric Edmonds and Nina Pavcnik (2002)—suggests that trade reform has reduced the incidence of child labor via its income effects. Observing an average increase in the rice price of 29 percent between two household surveys in 1992/93 and 1997/98, Edmonds and Pavcnik find that reductions in child labor are well correlated with rice price increases across households and communes. Many of the households concerned are poor, so this is a powerful result for our purposes provided that trade reform explains the price increase. Edmonds and Pavcnik basically just assert that link, but Yoko Niimi, Puja Vasudeva-Dutta, and L. Alan Winters (2003) produce at least circumstantial evidence that it exists.

A detailed study of short-term adjustment to an external shock is Elizabeth Frankenberg, James Smith, and Duncan Thomas (2003). As noted above, this team found some households gaining despite the 15-percent decline in the Indonesian economy over 1997–98. They also found extensive mitigation of the shock, with falls in real family incomes of only about half of those in individual real earning (James Smith et al. 2002). Coping strategies included re-organizing households to locate dependants in low-cost locations and workers in household that could employ them, increased hours of work, the postponement of "deferrable" expenditure, and dissaving. In the latter case the role of gold stands out. As an internationally traded asset the gold price increased fourfold in rupiah terms, permitting strong consumption smoothing opportunities. Interestingly, most of the gold was owned by women (as jewellery), which arguably affected the uses to which the dissaving was put.

In summary there is plenty of evidence that households will respond to the impacts of trade liberalization that affect them as producers or as consumers, both to take advantage of opportunities and to protect themselves from adverse effects. But the ability to respond varies across households, so there will often be an important role for complementary policies in helping to ensure that poorer as well as richer households are able to respond appropriately, by, for example, enhancing access to key inputs, markets or infrastructure.

### 4.4 *Do the Spillovers Benefit the Poor?*

Even if the poor do not benefit directly from increased demand generated by a trade liberalization, they may do so indirectly, as those who do benefit directly increase their demands for inputs and consumption goods and services. For example, John Mellor and Sarah Gavian (1999) argue that one of the main advantages of stimulating agriculture is that it strongly increases the demand for goods and services produced by the poor.

The literature on growth linkages distinguishes production (or inter-sectoral) linkages (Albert Hirschman 1958) from expenditure linkages (John Mellor 1976). Production linkages can be either "upstream" (or "backward"), which refer to a sector's demand for factors or intermediate inputs, or "downstream" (or "forward") linkages which occur when the expansion of a sector induces investments in processing and distribution in sectors using its output. Expenditure linkages refer to the extent to which increased incomes in one sector (typically farming) increase the demand for the outputs, and hence factor inputs, of another sector (typically the nonfarm sector). This is the standard Keynesian multiplier effect, although for poverty analysis there can be benefits even if the increased demand is reflected in higher factor returns for the poor rather than increased activity.

Given that linkages are often strong in rural areas, a trade liberalization that benefits one group is likely to have strong benefits for the rest of the rural economy. It is now widely accepted that in Asia the increases in agricultural productivity brought about by the green revolution in the 1970s reduced poverty, at least partly because an extra dollar of agricultural income was typically associated with an additional 80 cents of nonagricultural income for local enterprises (Christopher Delgado et al. 1998). Studies point to the importance of both production (John Mellor and Bruce Johnston 1984) and consumption expenditure (Peter Hazell and Ailsa Roell 1983) linkages. In general, surveys show that large shares of rural households' incomes and consumption are related to locally produced nontradeables, such as services, bulky traditional starch items, perishable foods, and locally processed foods. This means that expenditure linkages are particularly important for the rural poor (Christopher Delgado 1996), although as Barbara Harriss (1987) points out, these results depend heavily on untested assumptions.

Until recently, it was thought that growth linkages were weaker in Africa because of smaller inter-industry flows (due in part to thin markets and high transaction costs) and the absence of important construction and maintenance expenditures associated with the Asian irrigated agriculture (Steven Haggblade, Peter Hazell, and James Brown 1989). However, a survey of the evidence by Delgado et al. (1998) drawing on panel data sets from Burkina Faso, Niger, Senegal, Zambia, and Zimbabwe finds the contrary. It finds that adding $1.00 of new farm income could increase total household income by $2.88 in Burkina Faso, $1.96 in Niger, $2.48 in the Central Groundnut Basin of Senegal and $2.57 in Zambia. Peter Hazell and Behjat Hojjati (1995) show that growth multipliers in the Eastern Province of Zambia are driven primarily by household consumption demands and are largely intra-agricultural because of high marginal propensities to consume local non-tradable foods. Bigsten and Collier (1995) also identify strong pecuniary multipliers but relatively weak real multipliers from agriculture in Kenya.

For policy purposes it is useful to know which sectors yield the largest growth linkages. Peter Hazell and Steven Haggblade (1991) show that growth multipliers in India are higher for irrigated than for rainfed agriculture, suggesting that, for example, a boom in rice exports could provide a large stimulus. Early evidence from Malaysia and Nigeria suggested that it is the households operating the largest farms which have the expenditure patterns most desirable for the generation of indirect labor-intensive growth (Mellor 1983). Hazell and Roell (1983) and Haggblade, Hazell, and Brown (1989), on the other hand, contend that the multipliers are bigger for small to medium-sized farms than for very large farms, as does econometric evidence from India (Hazell and Haggblade 1991).

The effectiveness of linkages in raising the incomes of the poor also depends upon local businesses being able to respond to increased demand. If institutional or other rigidities prevent this then the benefits may be dissipated in higher inflation. For example, Delgado et al. (1998) warn that rising food staple prices have the potential to choke off growth from demand-side linkages if the conditions for a high supply response to prices are not in place. Of course, price increases will still raise the incomes of net suppliers of those goods or services and it is still relevant to ask whether these are the poor. But the overall impact on growth will be less in such cases and it seems likely that its impact upon poverty will also be smaller.

### 4.5 *Does Trade Liberalization Increase Vulnerability?*

In addition to its impact on mean income, it is often claimed that trade liberalization increases the risks faced by poor households and their vulnerability to external shocks. Vulnerability is a key element of poverty and a major concern of the poor; see for example World Bank (2001). However, though clearly related, poverty and vulnerability are not coterminous. Almost by definition, poverty reflects well-being *status*, while vulnerability is dynamic and stochastic. Lant Pritchett, Asep Suryhadi, and Sudarno Sumarto (2000) define vulnerability as having a high probability of being below the poverty line over a three-year period, and thus introduce uncertainty of consumption as well as its level.[21]

Trade liberalization will typically affect both the means and variances of a household's sources of income, and could affect household vulnerability in four ways: changes in mean incomes; changes in the portfolio of activities undertaken by households; changes in the variability of existing income sources (and/or the correlation between them); and poverty traps. The impact of trade liberalization on the mean incomes of the poor is the focus of much of the rest of this article; this section considers the other three effects.

*Portfolio Choice.* Household surveys in developing countries have shown that households often have a large number of different sources of income (Thomas Reardon 1997). An optimizing household will choose a portfolio which maximizes its utility, taking into account its degree of risk aversion (Frank Ellis 1993; Michael Lipton 1968), and clearly trade liberalization could alter the optimal portfolio. The obvious example is a liberalization which encourages farmers to switch from subsistence to cash crops. The latter may have higher returns but also a higher variance. Whether this increases the vulnerability of the household will then depend on the relative sizes of these shifts.[22] In fact, whether the change is made at all will depend on these things.

There is an important distinction to be made here between *ex ante* and *ex post* positions. If households are fully informed of the consequences of changing their portfolios, the status quo is still feasible, and such changes are made freely, then we may assume that switches in portfolio will raise welfare *ex ante*. But, of course, *ex post*, a household may lose from an unlucky realisation. Thus increases in observed poverty can be consistent with *ex ante* improvements in welfare if households trade higher mean incomes for higher variances.

The flip-side of this argument is that poorer households may be unable or unwilling to undertake potentially profitable new

[21] The concept of vulnerability is thus closely related to the concept of "expected poverty" introduced by Ravallion (1988). Robert Chambers (1989) gives a broader discussion of vulnerability in developing countries.

[22] A similar argument can be made about employment in an export processing zone (EPZ) which may be better paid, but less secure than, say, employment in government.

activities because of risk aversion. Marcel Fafchamps and John Pender (1997) show that credit constraints faced by poor farmers in India make them unwilling to make non-divisible and irreversible investments in risky tubewells despite the substantially higher returns associated with irrigated production when tubewells are successful. Other studies indicate the impact of risk aversion on poor farmers' portfolios of agricultural investments (Mark Rosenzweig and Kenneth Wolpin 1993) and cultivation patterns (Takashi Kurosaki 1995). In each case, the existence of undiversifiable risk could undermine the potential gains from trade liberalization among the poor and result in poverty traps.

In addition, the poor may lack information about the risks associated with new activities leading to suboptimal choices. However, such information problems are likely to be short-lived as individuals and communities learn the true extent of the risks faced. Besides, trade liberalization usually involves shifts in the relative returns of activities that are already being undertaken, in which case information will already exist on the risks associated with the activity.

*The Variability of Existing Income Sources or Prices.* Trade liberalization could also increase income vulnerability by increasing the variance of important income sources or prices.[23] One possibility is that, say, due to favorable production conditions, the domestic market is typically stable and that opening it up 'imports' price variation. Similarly, trade liberalization (either domestic or international) may eliminate institutions or policies that actually smooth domestic prices.[24] For example, abolishing official purchasing has increased cocoa price variances in West Africa (Christopher Gilbert and Panos Varangis 2002).

On the other hand, trade liberalization can reduce risk if it increases competition, since this will make households less vulnerable to decisions made by individual traders or employers. Liberalization may also reduce price volatility if it allows households to import goods that would otherwise have been subject to large price swings due to the limited size of the local market.[25] Consequently whether liberalization increases or reduces price risk is an empirical rather than a theoretical matter. Unfortunately, evidence on this issue is extremely limited, since it requires time series data on prices before and after liberalization. Carlo Del Ninno and Paul Dorosh (2001) show how trade liberalization helped to mitigate Bangladesh's post-flood food crisis in 1998, with private imports stabilising prices and increasing supplies. P. V. Srinivasan and Shikha Jha (2001) use simulation models to show that trade is stabilizing in Indian food-grain markets (and incidentally for world food prices too). On the other hand, Lloyd et al. (1999) provide evidence that domestic marketing arrangements in Côte d'Ivoire substantially smoothed price fluctuations (although at very high cost) suggesting that liberalization would increase the variance of prices. However, whether this would increase the vulnerability of poor farmers is not clear given the likely concurrent increase in prices associated with liberalization.

Even if liberalization does increase price volatility at the border, whether household vulnerability increases will depend on how prices are transmitted through the economy (see section 4.1), and on the ability of households to insure against income risk and to cope with shocks. The large body of literature on the ways in which households respond to idiosyncratic and covariant risk in developing countries shows that poor households take several steps to insure

[23] Barrett and Dorosh (1996) show formally that the costs of variability increase with the share of the commodity or income source in total income.

[24] Although not all policies designed to do this succeed.

[25] Similarly, exporting may also stabilize local prices.

themselves against bad outcomes,[26] or to protect themselves ex post from the effects of negative shocks.[27]

Unsurprisingly, however, the poor are much less well insured and less able to cope with negative shocks than are the non-poor (Jyotsna Jalan and Martin Ravallion 1999). This makes it particularly important to consider the effectiveness of the mechanisms available to the poor to smooth consumption when introducing trade reforms likely to increase the variability of their incomes. It is also possible that trade reforms disrupt (or enhance) the ability of the poor to cope with shocks. For example, if trade reforms abolish an institution responsible for fixing producer prices at low levels, this may reduce vulnerability even if it increases price volatility; but if the same institution was responsible for providing a social safety net (e.g. by allowing deferred payment or providing subsidized inputs), then it is possible that the trade reform could increase vulnerability overall. The association of state-owned enterprises with the provision of pensions and health coverage in transition economies is one possible example.

*Poverty Traps*. Finally, shocks, including those induced by trade liberalization, may give rise to poverty traps: that is, actual realizations of bad outcomes may of themselves change the inter-temporal distribution of income. Jonathan Morduch (1994) shows how credit constraints on the poor can result in them preferring low-return low-risk activities to potentially highly profitable but risky activities. Moreover poorer households may have less to lose from reneging on credit agreements, and consequently find it harder to borrow and insure (Abhijit Banerjee and Andrew Newman 1994); this too can create a poverty trap (Oded Galor and Joseph Zeira 1993). Alternatively, if households are forced to curtail investment or deplete productive assets in order to maintain consumption, this can reduce their permanent income and create a cycle of poverty.

Overall, however, the little empirical evidence available does not suggest the widespread existence of poverty traps (i.e. situations in which, once a household falls below the poverty line, it is impossible for them to escape). For example, Michael Lokshin and Martin Ravallion (2000) find no evidence of such non-convexities using a panel of Hungarian households in the 1990s, although it generally takes households several years to recover from transient shocks. There is, however, evidence for the existence of spatial poverty traps. Jyotsna Jalan and Martin Ravallion (1997) show that there are geographical externalities in rural China whereby neighbourhood endowments of physical and human capital affect the productivity of a household's own capital. Similarly there can be inter-generational transmission of poverty effects if the response to a trade shock is to reduce expenditure on education—as Thomas et al. (1999) identified for rural families following the Indonesian crisis of 1997—or on child nutrition or health see, for example, John Strauss and Duncan Thomas (1998).

Most of the myriad causes of vulnerability in developing countries have little direct connection with trade liberalization. Furthermore, given the multiple causes of vulnerability it is extremely difficult to unpick the impact of trade liberalization from that of other events influencing households. Thus, although Paul Glewwe and Gillette Hall (1998) use panel data from Peru in the late 1980s to show how some groups are more vulnerable to macroeconomic shocks than others, their results do

[26] These include diversifying income sources (Frank Ellis 1998), precautionary saving, entering into sharecropping tenancy arrangements (Robert Townsend and Rolf Mueller 1998), maintaining buffer stocks of key assets (Rosenzweig and Wolpin 1993), and building social capital (Franque Grimard 1997). See Tim Besley (1995) for a general discussion.

[27] For example, asset depletion (Rosenzweig and Wolpin 1993), borrowing (Christopher Udry 1995), changes in labor supply (Anjini Kochar 1995), temporary migration (Sylvie Lambert 1994) and reductions in human capital investment (Hanan Jacoby and Emmanuel Skoufias 1997).

not explicitly consider trade reforms.[28] They do find, however, that subsistence farmers and other relatively autarchic households are less affected by, and thus less vulnerable to, economic shocks, while those in the construction, manufacturing and agricultural export sectors are more vulnerable, including, presumably, to external shocks.

Although there is little existing evidence directly linking trade liberalization to vulnerability at the household level, it seems likely that some trade liberalizations have increased the risks faced by the poor and that, in some cases, this will have increased their vulnerability. When this does happen the poor will usually be less well placed to insure themselves against its adverse impact. One can certainly identify circumstances where this can happen (e.g. where effective mechanisms of social protection are absent), but there is no evidence about how widespread such outcomes are in practice, or, indeed about cases in which trade liberalization reduces vulnerability.

## 5. *Wages and Employment*

For the self-employed the main determinant of income is the price commanded by their output and inputs, but for employees commodity prices need to be translated into factor prices (wages) or employment opportunities before they have an effect. This Part considers this vital link between trade liberalization and poverty, first, via permanent shifts in wages and employment and second via adjustment stresses.

### 5.1 *Does Liberalization Raise Wages or Employment?*

An important mechanism by which foreign shocks are translated into poverty impacts is through factor markets, especially the labor market. Indeed, obtaining employment is one of the surest ways out of poverty, while the loss of a job is probably the most common reason for the precipitate declines into poverty that catch most public attention. The structure of the labor market is critical to how trade liberalization gets translated into wage and employment changes.

*Wages and Employment.* Traditional international trade theory assumes that factor supplies are fixed and wages are flexible. In a two factor world, the Stolper-Samuelson Theorem predicts that an increase in the price of the good that is labor-intensive in production will increase its production and thus increase the real wage. Unfortunately, however, while its basic insight is almost certainly robust, the Stolper-Samuelson Theorem is not sufficient to answer questions of trade and poverty in the real world. For example, the theorem is less powerful in multi-commodity, multi-factor, models, and the functional and personal distributions of income are only loosely related. Thus even if increases in the prices of unskilled-labor-intensive goods raise unskilled wages, poverty will be alleviated only if poor households rely largely on unskilled wage earners. Peter Lloyd (2000) formalises this issue theoretically. He characterises the effect of a trade shock on a given household in terms of the latter's endowments of factors, its consumption pattern and the matrix mapping changes in commodity prices into changes in factor rewards. Lloyd shows that each household gains from at least one price increase and loses from at least one other, and that, provided households differ sufficiently, a change in the price of a good that is actually produced will benefit at least one household and hurt at least one other.

The alternative polar view of labor markets in developing countries is that labor is available in perfectly elastic supply. In this case the wage will be fixed exogenously by what labor can earn elsewhere and the adjustment will take place in terms of

[28] Glewwe and Hall (1998) define a household as being vulnerable if it has a larger than average percentage fall in consumption.

employment. Then the reason for the fixity of the wage matters. If it is fixed by the existence of a subsistence sector, moving workers into the formal sector will alleviate poverty only if the loss of labor in subsistence agriculture is so large that the workers remaining in that sector increase their "wage." This is the case of successful development, which is generally likely to require far more than just trade liberalization to achieve.

Alternatively, the labor markets may be segmented for, say, legal or institutional reasons. The formal sector may pay a minimum or conventional wage at above what we might loosely think of as "poverty levels," and at which there is excess supply, while the subsistence or informal sector pays wages below "poverty levels." Then poverty will potentially be affected by a trade shock. If the latter raises the value of the marginal product of labor in the formal sector (e.g. by raising the price of its output), trade liberalization reduces the producer real wage, increases employment and alleviates poverty. If, on the other hand, it reduces the value of the marginal product and thus reduces employment, it has adverse consequences. Clearly the poverty impact depends not only on employment but also on where the different wage levels lie relative to the poverty line.[29]

The critical issues, then, are the effects of trade liberalization on the demand for labor—the shock to the labor market—and the elasticity of labor supply—where the economy actually lies between the two polar extremes of vertical and horizontal supply curves of labor. If we recognize several classes of labor, these factors are likely to vary across classes. In addition, empirical analysis should recognize that adjustment takes time, so that short-run effects may differ from long-run ones (see, for example, Sebastian Edwards 1988, and Chris Milner and Peter Wright 1998); allow for non-traded goods and their prices in the analysis; and distinguish between formal and informal labor markets. It is also important to remember that factor market effects depend wholly on trade reform first changing output, which in turn depends on the structure of goods markets and on the substitutability between imports, exports and locally produced varieties (Rod Falvey 1999).

Smith et al. (2002) found that virtually all of the effects of the Asian crisis on Indonesia over 1997–98 were felt in real wages, with employment remaining constant. The real wages of skilled workers appeared to fall equally in both rural urban areas (34 percent for males over just one year!)—suggesting a fairly integrated market—while, among the unskilled, urban workers suffered more than rural ones (–42 percent compared with –32 percent). The real incomes of the self-employed fell in line with wages, except for rural males, where, amazingly, they remained roughly constant. The latter essentially reflects the stability of the prices of tradable staples (especially rice) noted above when we discussed prices.

There are many studies of the labor market effects of trade reform, but most of them presume segmented markets and deal only with the manufacturing sector and so make it difficult to draw conclusions about overall poverty. Moreover, they rely on intersectoral or interfirm variations to identify effects and so have little to say on general equilibrium effects (which one would expect to be smaller than partial equilibrium ones). Nonetheless, the most striking common feature of these studies is the smallness of the wage and employment effects they find whilst the most striking difference is the variety of explanations offered for it.

An early discussion of trade and employment was by Krueger (1983), who argued that developing-country trade liberalization should boost labor-intensive output and increase employment. Her case studies

[29] Winters (2000a, 2002a) offers more discussion of the significance of these alternative views of the labor markets.

showed that developing countries' manufactured exports were, indeed, labor-intensive, but that the employment effects of liberal trade policies were generally rather muted. Calling for more research, she tentatively concluded that this was because of other distortions in factor markets.

More recent exercises have had more liberalizations to consider and better data, and although they show mixed results the general tendency is still towards small effects. For example, Martin Rama (1994), applying a model of monopolistic competition to a panel of 39 sectors in Uruguay over 1979–86, found a significant positive relationship between protection and employment in manufacturing, but no significant effects on real wages. Janet Currie and Ann Harrison (1997) find that employment responses in Morocco depended heavily on firm characteristics (especially public versus private ownership). Where profit margins were slim initially, the liberalization of manufacturing led to job loss, but in most firms it led to lower margins and almost no change in output or employment. Thus trade liberalization here probably raised efficiency and aggregate welfare by addressing goods market imperfections.

Ana Revenga (1997), on the other hand, attributed the low employment effects of Mexican trade reforms to factor–market imperfections. (She found no effect on employment from tariff cuts and a statistically significant but small negative response to quota abolition). She did, however, find real wages falling in manufacturing (3–4 percent on average; 10–14 percent in some sectors), which she attributed to the erosion of rents: with high rates of unionisation, formal labor had been able to appropriate some of the rents created by trade barriers. Again, there are likely to have been overall poverty benefits from this element of trade liberalization, for few formal sector workers are likely to have been pushed into poverty by such wage cuts, while the erosion of rents will presumably have benefited consumers. Similarly small employment effects elsewhere in Latin America are reported by, for example, Gustavo Marquez and Carmen Pagés-Serra (1998) for Latin America and the Caribbean in general, James Levinsohn (1999) for Chile, and Maurício Moreira and Sheila Najberg (2000) for Brazil.

Milner and Wright (1998) explore industry level data on Mauritius and find a slightly more positive response to liberalization. After an initially adverse wage effect they find fairly strong long-run growth in wages and employment in the exportables sector (mainly of female labor producing clothes).[30] But they also find, surprisingly, growth in the import-competing sector, which they attribute to Mauritius' overall strong economic performance.

Deepak Lal (1986) applies a modified Stolper-Samuelson Theorem directly to the Philippines. Distinguishing only tradable and nontradable goods, but allowing for flows of factors between sectors, he explains the periodic declines in real wages in terms of real exchange rate changes. As the relative price of nontradables (the labor-intensive sector) falls, real wages decline.

Winters (2000b) suggests similarly that the real exchange rate depreciation could explain the simultaneous increase in formal and decrease in informal manufacturing employment in India in the 1990s, the non-traded sector being "informal intensive." From a poverty perspective, an important question is what happened to those who lost their informal manufacturing jobs. If they could move back into agriculture or other informal services at approximately the same wage, the answer would be not much, and the increase in observed formal employment at higher wages would be poverty alleviating. If, on the other hand, the loss of an informal manufacturing job signals a descent (deeper) into poverty, the net effects of these changes would be negative for poverty alleviation.

[30] Similarly trade liberalization and trade growth have vastly increased female employment in clothing in Bangladesh.

Unfortunately, we just do not know, although given that urban informal wages average only just over the Indian poverty line for a family of five, we should not be too sanguine.

*Wage Inequality.* Recently at least as much attention has been paid to relative wages between skilled and unskilled labor—the so-called skills gap—as to employment and wages generally. This is frequently linked to income inequality and thence, casually and less justifiably, to poverty. The debate is pertinent to this paper, however, because a widening skills gap could reflect falling unskilled wages (relative to the no-reform counterfactual) and because many commentators have interpreted the widening skill gap in developing countries as a refutation of the factor-abundance model of trade and income distribution in which skilled and unskilled labor are separate factors.

Most of the recent evidence concerns Latin America, and as argued by Adrian Wood (1997), Latin America's increasing skills gap contrasts with the earlier experience of East Asia, where liberalization was accompanied by a narrowing of the gap.[31] Wood considers various explanations for this difference. Some concern the different timing of the liberalizations: the entry of large labor abundant countries into world markets (especially China) in the 1980s and 1990s which meant that Latin America was not actually unskilled labor abundant when it opened up, the burst of skill-biased technical progress in the 1980s and 1990s, the greater international mobility of highly skilled labor and capital in the later period, and the effect of the debt crisis.

A further issue of timing was the growth of outsourcing over the 1990s. Industrial country firms operating abroad may not wish to use the lowest-grade labor in host developing countries; thus while the labor they use is unskilled by, say, U.S. standards, it is relatively skilled by local standards—see Robert Feenstra and Gordon Hanson (1995) on Mexico. Donald Robbins and T. H. Grindling (1999) adduce a similar bias towards skilled workers in Costa Rica's liberalization. They identify the bias using fairly robust nonparametric methods and then offer some regression evidence that it is due to the increasing stock of imported machinery in the economy. If liberalization encourages higher capital goods imports and if these embody recent biases towards skilled labor use, then liberalization could widen the skills gap.

These latter explanations warn us that, within developing countries, it is not guaranteed that it is the least-skilled workers, and thus the most likely to be poor, who are the most intensively used factor in the production of exportable goods. For example, the wages of workers with completed primary education may increase with trade liberalization, while those of illiterate workers may not. One of the reasons that agricultural liberalization is so important for poverty alleviation is that for this sector one can be reasonably confident that very-low-skilled workers in rural areas will benefit through the production responses.

Other explanations for the skills-gap are more structural. For example, from Wood: the Latin American countries are relatively abundant in natural resources, whereas East Asian countries were relatively abundant in (initially) unskilled labor; Latin American liberalization involved mainly import liberalization while East Asian liberalization also involved providing incentives to exporters; and the vast expansion of basic education in East Asia increased productivity and also the relative supply of skilled labor.

In addition, the initial structure of tariffs in many Latin American countries protected unskilled workers, so it is hardly surprising that liberalization reduced their wages; see

[31] Among researchers finding an increased skills gap in Latin America are Feenstra and Hanson (1995), Gordon Hanson and Ann Harrison (1999), Zadia Feliciano (1996) and Michael Cragg and Mario Epelbaum (1996) for Mexico; Harald Beyer, Patricio Rojas and Rodrigo Vergara (1999) for Chile, and Robbins and Grindling (1999) for Costa Rica.

Gordon Hanson and Ann Harrison (1999) on Mexico. And it may take time for markets to clear. Chile's liberalizations were associated with worsening inequality over the 1980s, but inequality measures have now returned to pre-reform levels—and at vastly higher average income levels and lower poverty levels; Francisco Ferreira and Julie Litchfield (1999). Finally, very recent evidence suggests that the skills gap stabilized or even reversed over the 1990s but with no discernible reduction in the speed of trade liberalization.

Among the relatively small amount of recent evidence on countries outside Latin America, Milner and Wright (1998) find that trade liberalization in Mauritius increased the relative wages for female and unskilled labor in the exportables sector.

One potentially important dimension of the skills gap is whether openness stimulates developing countries' demand for education and acquisition of human capital. Simple Stolper-Samuelson theory suggests that the returns to skill will decline and with them the incentives for education; see Adrian Wood and Cristobal Ridao-Cano (1999), who find some suggestion of such a problem empirically. The alternative analyses just discussed, however, have quite the opposite implication.

This section has shown that the effects of trade liberalization on wages and employment are complex to predict in detail. Although liberalization will often raise the demand for relatively unskilled workers in many developing countries and so, on average, be poverty alleviating, there will also be important exceptions, e.g. possibly where natural resources dominate exports and where out-sourcing is important—as well as cases where segmented import-competing sectors suffer adverse shocks.

*Computable General Equilibrium Modelling.* One response to the complexities of using econometric methods to track commodity price shocks resulting from trade policy through factor prices to poor households has been to use computable general equilibrium (CGE) models. These are essentially numerical manifestations of theoretical systems and thus lay out precisely and quantify many of the steps discussed in our framework. They are not strictly empirical (which classically means "without theory"), but if they are carefully constructed and grounded in real data, they can provide useful insight. The danger is that they depend critically on parameters and functions which can barely be tested one-by-one, let alone in combination. CGE models are indeed almost the only tool available for predicting the effects of future trade policy changes, but care must be taken not to fall for their spurious precision.[32]

One approach is to use a CGE model with a single 'representative' consumer to generate changes in commodity and factor prices from a trade liberalization experiment and then apply these to household data to calculate the poverty impacts. This is akin to the first-order approximation exercises described in the introduction to section 4 above. Elena Ianchovichina, Alessandro Nicita, and Isidro Soloaga (2001) take this approach; they simulate setting all Mexico's tariffs to zero and devote considerable effort to matching the income and expenditure classes of the household survey data to those of the CGE model in order to apply the estimated price changes to each household in the survey. The data show that changes in the cost of living vary by income level (because consumption baskets vary), and the authors estimate that, combining price and income changes, all households would gain from trade liberalization with larger proportionate changes for poorer households.

Thomas W Hertel et al. (2001) distinguish five classes of household according to their predominant source of income and disaggregate within each class by twenty income

[32] Neil McCulloch, L. Alan Winters and Xavier Cirera (2001, ch. 5) and Jeffrey Reimer (2002) discuss CGE modelling and poverty in more detail.

levels. They estimate a very general consumption model, and combining the income and expenditure profiles with a CGE model, they explore the effects of possible liberalization on households clustered around the assumed poverty line. They examine the effects of a multilateral liberalization on seven countries; four suggest reductions in poverty (Indonesia, Philippines, Uganda, and Zambia) and three increases (Brazil, Chile, and Thailand).

A second approach is to embed the household disaggregation within the CGE model. This has the advantage of being internally consistent. Also the behavioral changes at the household level which are ignored above, are both modelled and fed back into the macroeconomic solution. An early approach of this sort is by François Bourguignon, William Branson, and Jaime de Melo (1991) and more recent examples include Denis Cogneau and Anne-Sophie Robillard (2000), and Glenn Harrison, Thomas Rutherford, and David Tarr (2003). Cogneau and Robillard estimate a household model from survey data on Madagascar to explain labor income decisions and embed it in a three-sector CGE model. Among their simulations is one of an increase in the world price of export crops, which reduces rural poverty significantly but increases urban poverty slightly. John Cockburn (2001) uses a similar approach for Nepal and concludes that because liberalization mainly reduces agricultural prices, it benefits the urban poor and harms the rural poor.

All of these simulation exercises are instructive and should be important inputs into the policy-making process. In particular they help to identify household types that are vulnerable even when trade liberalizations are beneficial on average. They are all predictions, however, and are complementary to, not substitutes for, genuine empirical studies on ex post data. Only the latter permit us to test our models and really understand the world as it actually is.

### 5.2 *Is Transitional Unemployment Concentrated on the Poor?*

There is always a possibility of temporary unemployment as a liberalising economy adjusts to new prices. Even in cases where the overall aggregate effect is small, change may still be taking place at a more disaggregated level. This adjustment process will be associated with some transitional unemployment as workers lose one job and require time to find another. In Chile, for instance, Sebastian Edwards and Alejandro Cox Edwards (1996) find a positive association between the degree of liberalization a sector experienced and the extent of layoffs; the sectors experiencing the greatest liberalization were also the ones where the duration of unemployment was longest.

There is surprisingly little evidence on the nature and extent of transitional unemployment and even less on its incidence among the poor. A multi-country study of trade liberalization before 1985 (Michaely, Papageorgiou, and Choksi 1991) argued that experiences varied from case to case, but that, on the whole, transitional unemployment was quite small. In a survey of more than fifty studies of the adjustment costs of trade liberalization in the manufacturing sector, Steven Matusz and David Tarr (1999) argue that the adjustment costs associated with transitional unemployment are not high and that unemployment durations are generally quite short. Indeed, in some cases employment appears to increase more or less instantly—as, for example, Ann Harrison and Ana Revenga (1998) report for Costa Rica, Peru, and Uruguay. Overall, however, there is too little evidence to form a general view on manufacturing employment, and still less on whether similar points apply to agriculture or services, or indeed outside the formal sector.

Moreover, the available studies do not answer the question of whether those laid off following trade liberalization are disproportionately poor. To answer this would require information on the characteristics of those losing their jobs, including their re-employability. Enterprise surveys report the responses of firms to trade liberalization, but typically give little information on the characteristics of their employees, while household surveys, which do provide this information, cannot easily be matched to enterprises. The latter do, however, generally suggest that, in many low-income countries, very few of the poorest are employees in the formal manufacturing sector.

Evidence is available on the relationship between public sector job loss and poverty. Although this job loss is not a direct consequence of trade liberalization, it does deal with transitional unemployment resulting from a shock to the formal sector, and so may inform us also about the effects of trade liberalization. Thus, for example, in Ecuador, employees dismissed from the Central Bank earned on average only 55 percent of their previous salary fifteen months later (Martin Rama and Donna MacIsaac 1999). Evidence from Zambia (Neil McCulloch, Robert Baulch, and Milasoa Cherel-Robson 2001) suggests that job shedding occurred in the public sector at the lower end of the earnings distribution, although it does not show definitively whether these people were poor, nor what happened to them following their retrenchment. In Ghana, Stephen Younger (1996) finds that most retrenched civil servants were able to find new work, but at substantially lower income levels suggesting an increase in poverty, although the income levels and incidence of poverty among their households after retrenchment were not substantially different from the average for the whole country.

Thus retrenchment from the public sector typically does lead to transitional unemployment (which may be quite long lasting, as seen in the case of Guinea where the average duration of unemployment was two years; Bradford Mills and David Sahn 1995) and/or lower income levels. However, there is very little evidence on whether transitional unemployment is disproportionately concentrated among the poor, or on whether this loss of employment (even if temporary) is an important cause of poverty. And we do know that in low-income countries the majority of the poor are not likely to be directly affected by retrenchment because they are not working in the formal sector in the first place (although some may be indirectly affected by loss of transfers or remittances).

It is likely that adjustment costs will be greater the more protected the sector was originally and the greater the shock. In local labor markets, large losses of employment can have (negative) multiplier effects on income, and markets can become dysfunctional because even normal turn-over ceases as incumbents dare not resign for fear of not finding a new job. Thus major reforms—e.g. transition or concentrated reforms such as closing the only plant in a town—seem likely to generate larger and longer-lived transitional losses through unemployment than more diffuse reforms. On the other hand, it is precisely the sectors with highest protection or the economies with most widespread distortion that offer the greatest long-run returns to reform. Martin Rama and Kinnon Scott (1999) analyse the effects of retrenching the only plant in a series of one-plant towns in Kazakhstan. They estimate that for a reduction in the employment in the plant equal to 1 percent of the local labor force, labor income in the town falls by 1.5 percent. This is essentially a Keynesian multiplier effect. The hysteresis of the labor market would serve to deepen and prolong it further.

### 6. *Government Revenue and Spending*

The final link from trade liberalization to poverty is via the government account. Trade reforms potentially reduce revenues and, especially for low income countries, this could unbalance the government budget. This section considers first how large the revenue losses typically are and, second, whether adjustment to declines in tariff revenues when they occur typically hit the poor either via replacement taxation or expenditure reductions. We make the point that the extent to which such policy changes impact on the poor is essentially a political decision. While recognizing the administrative difficulties of raising alternative revenues or cutting expenditures more generally, it is not inevitable that the burden falls on the poor.

### 6.1 *Does Liberalization Actually Cut Government Revenue?*

A key concern about trade liberalization is that it will reduce government revenue. The share of trade taxes in total revenue is negatively associated with the level of economic development, with many low-income countries earning half or more of their revenue from trade taxes.[33] Neil McCulloch, L. Alan Winters, and Xavier Cirera (2001) show that, of the 96 countries for which these data are available over 1994–96, 58 report a share exceeding 5 percent, with an unweighted average of 20.3 percent, and sixteen countries report a share of over 25 percent.

Neither theory nor evidence suggests a simple link between trade reform and revenues, however. Theoretically, a number of factors are important (David Greenaway and Chris Milner 1991). In the case of tariffs, revenue will increase with liberalization if the initial tariff level exceeds its revenue maximising level.[34] It can also increase in the many instances where reforms involve the replacement of quantitative restrictions by tariffs, provided, as is usual, that the government did not previously capture the quota rent associated with the restriction. Rod Falvey (1994) shows that a welfare-improving revenue-enhancing (WIRE) tariff reform will always exist unless the compensated radial elasticities of all goods are the same (which is highly unlikely in practice given that tariffs reflect protective as well as revenue-raising motives).[35] However, designing such a package is well beyond most governments (Sebastian Edwards 1997), especially since short and long-run responses may differ (David Bevan 2000). And, of course, once the condition is approximately met, reductions in tariff rates will cut revenues.

Improvements in collection efficiency can also increase revenue. Official ad valorem tariff rates are often substantially higher than the ratio of tariff revenue to import values (collected rates). Lant Pritchett and Geeta Sethi (1994) find for a sample of developing countries that official rates and collected rates are only weakly correlated, and that the divergence between them increases with the level of the official tariff. Evasion and exemptions are the key factors here, and tightening them up can yield substantial revenue gains. For instance, according to official estimates, the revenue foregone via tariff exemptions in Tanzania in 1986 was almost equivalent to total revenue collected (Greenaway and Milner 1991). Trade reforms that simplify tariff structures also often have favourable revenue effects by simplifying administration and reducing opportunities and incentives for evasion (which of course are also reduced by lower levels of tariffs). This is one of the main practical motivations behind proposals for uniform tariff rates.

Turning to the empirical evidence, Greenaway and Milner (1991) focus on five countries which received World Bank Structural Adjustment Loans (SALs) requiring important trade policy reforms. Three of these countries experienced revenue enhancement (Mauritius, Kenya, and

[33] This reliance may reflect various factors, including difficulties in administering a tax system effectively and the relatively small share of the formal sector (Ebrill, Stotsky, and Gropp 1999)

[34] The revenue maximizing tariff will be $t=(\varepsilon_s-\varepsilon_d)/-\varepsilon_s(1+\varepsilon_d)$ where $t$ is the ad valorem tariff rate, $\varepsilon_s$ is the elasticity of import supply, and $\varepsilon_d$ is the elasticity of import demand (Ebrill, Stotsky, and Gropp 1999).

[35] The compensated radial elasticity of good $j$ is defined as the proportionate reduction in purchases of product $j$ with respect to a common proportionate increase in all taxes, holding utility constant—see George Fane (1991).

Jamaica) and two revenue depletion (Morocco and Côte d'Ivoire). The authors identify a number of clues as to why. First, revenue tends to fall if the existing tariffs are below the revenue maximising rate as in Morocco and Côte d'Ivoire, but not in the other three countries. Second, in all the revenue enhancing cases, some kind of temporary tariff surcharge was introduced when quantitative restrictions were removed; in the revenue depleting cases no such taxes were introduced. Third, the induced changes in the import/export base appear to have been important, particularly in the case of Mauritius. And finally, of the two cases where export incentives were planned, the Mauritian reforms were successful because they were administratively simple, funded by the introduction of other nontrade taxes, and the exchange rate was allowed to depreciate. In the other case—Côte d'Ivoire—none of these conditions applied and the reforms failed.[36]

Liam Ebrill, Janet Stotsky, and Reint Gropp (1999) draw a similar set of lessons from detailed studies of trade liberalization in Argentina, Malawi, Morocco, the Philippines, Poland, and Senegal. Furthermore, in a cross-country panel regression they found that countries that reduced tariffs over the period 1980–92 did not have significantly lower revenue from import tariffs as a proportion of GDP than those that did not. On the other hand, those which dismantled quantitative restrictions did have significantly higher revenue from import tariffs as a proportion of GDP than those that did not.

Detailed individual country studies bear all this out. Graham Glenday (2000), for example, examines the impact of Kenyan liberalization between 1989–99 on import duty revenues. The simple average import duty rate was approximately halved over this period and import licensing requirements and foreign exchange controls were abolished. However, duty as a share of imports rose, as did import duty revenues as a proportion of GDP. The expansion of the revenue base appears to have been an important factor here, along with tighter exemption management, increased duty rates on oil products and certain agricultural commodities, and a shift in imports towards high duty classes. However, improvements in customs administration and the introduction of a preshipment inspection program could also have accounted for some of the improvement.

### 6.2 *Do Falling Tariff Revenues Hurt the Poor?*

The previous section suggests that trade reforms need not have revenue costs. However, designing revenue-neutral packages is complex and liable to error, and eventually, as tariffs approach zero, so too must revenue. Hence this section briefly considers responses to falling tariff revenues. From a trade policy perspective such considerations are central, for fiscal crises are one of the strongest correlates of the reversal of trade liberalization.

The first response is to seek alternative non-trade sources of revenue. Clearly the impact of replacement taxes upon the poor depends on the choice of fiscal instrument, and in general there is no economic reason why the burden should fall on the poorest. Nonetheless, both the evidence and common sense suggest caution, particularly where simple low cost trade tax instruments are replaced by more complex and higher cost domestic ones. (See World Bank 1988, on the cost/yield ratios of different taxes.) Some CGE models suggest that the welfare significance of tariff revenue losses depends on the nature of the replacement taxes introduced (Denise Konan and Keith Maskus 2000, and Harrison, Rutherford, and Tarr 2002).[37] But there is little ex post evidence on these issues.

[36] The revenue enhancing cases also involved significant changes in tariff exemption arrangements but this was also at least formally true of the revenue depleting cases.

[37] CGE models have also been used to explore the implication of trade reform for revenue stability (e.g. Christina Dawkins and John Whalley 1997).

The alternative response to a fall in revenue is to cut public expenditure. There is a large literature describing the effects of structural adjustment in developing countries on poverty and the impact felt via public expenditure and social sector expenditure in particular.[38] But the evidence for adjustment resulting in cuts in social expenditure is mixed at best (Jacques van der Gaag 1991; David Sahn 1992). While there have been major declines in social expenditure in some countries, the consensus is that social expenditures have been relatively protected, especially compared with capital expenditures. Van der Gaag (1991) examines spending in the three years before and after donor financed adjustment programmes began, and finds no pattern of increase or decrease in real levels of total and social sector expenditures. Similarly, David Sahn, Paul Dorosh, and Stephen Younger (1997) argue that, except in a very few cases, those declines in social expenditure that have occurred have not been "part of an extended attempt to balance the government's fiscal position."

The East Asian crisis—a shock far greater than any trade shock—also provides evidence that, with political will and careful planning, social sector spending can be protected. World Bank (2001) reports Korea's large expansion of social spending in the face of the crisis, while Lisa Cameron (2002) reports the success of Indonesia's targeted scholarships at keeping up school enrolments in the face of declining incomes.

There is strong evidence that social expenditures in many developing countries are not well targeted to the poor (Florencia Castro-Leal et al. 1999), and Peter Lanjouw and Martin Ravallion (1999) show how some schooling and anti-poverty programmes in India are captured by the nonpoor. However, this does not necessarily mean that cuts on social expenditures have less impact upon the poor; in fact conventional methods for assessing benefit incidence can underestimate the gains to the poor from higher public outlays and underestimate the losses from cuts (Lanjouw and Ravallion 1999). Thus there are latent dangers even in the absence of direct evidence.

In summary, there is no direct evidence relating trade liberalization to reductions in social spending. However, the evidence from other circumstances suggests that, despite the dangers, reductions in public expenditures of importance to the poor are not inevitable even if trade liberalization does result in losses of revenue. Alternative sources of revenue are not necessarily easy to mobilize, but they are generally available and the evidence suggests that, with political will, social spending and especially that oriented towards the poor, may be substantially shielded. Moreover, if liberalization assists economic growth, this should become easier than it was in the face of decline and crisis. Nonetheless, care needs to be taken if trade liberalization is going to be pursued in a political context in which replacement taxation is likely to be regressive or where social expenditures are likely to be cut.

## 7. *Conclusions*

The evidence surveyed in this paper demonstrates that there can be no simple general conclusion about the relationship between trade liberalization and poverty. Theory provides a strong presumption that trade liberalization will be poverty-alleviating in the long run and on average. The empirical evidence broadly supports this view, and, in particular, lends no support to the position that trade liberalization generally has an adverse impact. Equally, however, it does not assert that trade policy is always among the most important determinants of poverty reduction or that the static and micro-economic effects of liberalization will

[38] Tony Killick (1995) provides an excellent short review of the findings of such work; Howard White (1997) provides a comprehensive review of the literature, while Lyn Squire (1991) and Rolph van der Hoeven (1996) provide reviews of the linkages between adjustment and poverty in the 1980s.

always be beneficial for the poor. Trade liberalization necessarily implies distributional changes; it may well reduce the well-being of some people (at least in the short term) and some of these may be poor.

Thus while there are many causes for optimism that trade liberalization will contribute positively to poverty reduction, the ultimate outcome depends on many factors, including its starting point, the precise trade reform measures undertaken, who the poor are, and how they sustain themselves. Even within most of the individual causal channels that we have identified, the outcome will vary from case to case. Lest this seem too depressing, however, let us be clear that we are not saying that these things are unknowable. They are substantially predictable using the framework and evidence laid out here and the largest impacts may be relatively easy to predict provided that analysts garner the basic information required.[39]

A number of key points emerge from this review. Although there remains a residual ambiguity about the links between trade and growth, there is strong evidence for the beneficial impact of trade liberalization on productivity. Concerns that trade liberalization has generally adverse effects on the employment or wages of poor people, or on government spending on the poor due to falling fiscal revenues, are not well founded, even though specific instances of each of these problems can be identified. The analysis also highlights the importance of local institutions in determining the price effects of liberalization, notably the transmission of border price changes to local levels.

But there is also a surprising number of gaps in our knowledge about trade liberalization and poverty, and important questions for further research. Despite the fact that many of the concerns about trade liberalization are focused on those who become unemployed as a result of it, we know very little about the transitional unemployment that results from this. There is also relatively little empirical evidence about the effects of trade liberalization, as distinct from other factors, on poverty dynamics at the household level, and on how households respond to adverse shocks or potential opportunities. In addition, while the importance of institutions in determining price transmission has been stressed, there is little information about the manner in which border price changes are transmitted to local levels and how this may differ between the poor and non-poor. Finally, much analysis is based on a welfare model which assumes small price changes, but, as stressed in the article, many of the big welfare effects come from discrete changes (market creation and destruction). Again we lack empirical evidence on how this happens and the role that trade liberalization plays.

Although policy has not been our principal focus in this paper, we make three points. First, we have repeatedly stressed that the impact of trade liberalization on poverty will depend on the environment in which it is carried out, including the policies that accompany it. Trade liberalization should not be seen in isolation and additional policies will sometimes be needed to enhance its impact, including on poverty. But this is emphatically not to say that complementary policies are always necessary to enable trade liberalization to have poverty-reducing effects—again it depends on country context.

Second, there is quite a lot of evidence that poorer households may be less able than richer ones to protect themselves against adverse effects or to take advantage of positive opportunities created by policy reform. In such circumstances there will be an important role for complementary policies to accompany trade reform, both to strengthen social protection for losers and to enhance the ability of poorer households to exploit potentially beneficial changes. Such policies are likely to be desirable even in the

[39] McCulloch, Winters, and Cirera (2001) give a thorough discussion of the practical dimensions of such predictions.

absence of trade reforms, but they might become more important if trade reforms do have important adjustment effects on the poor or near poor. Of course trade liberalization may be beneficial for the poor even in the absence of such complementary policies and so the lack of such measures is not always a good argument for postponing trade reforms. But clearly it is preferable for there to be a careful analysis of each country's circumstances so that appropriate 'flanking' mechanisms can be devised to accompany the liberalization.

Finally, although trade liberalization may not be the most powerful or direct mechanism for addressing poverty in a country, it is one of the easiest to change. While many pro-poor policies are administratively complex and expensive to implement, the most important bits of trade reform—tariff reductions and uniformity, and the abolition of nontariff barriers—are easy to do and will frequently save resources. Thus trade reform may be one of the most cost effective anti-poverty policies available to governments. Certainly the evidence suggests that, with care, trade liberalization can be an important component of a "pro-poor" development strategy.

## REFERENCES


Ades, Alberto and Rafael Di Tella. 1997. "National Champions and Corruption: Some Unpleasant Interventionist Arithmetic," *Econ. J.* 107, pp. 1023–42.

———. 1999. "Rents, Competition and Corruption," *Amer. Econ. Rev.* 89:4, pp. 982–93.

Aghion, Philippe; Eve Caroli and Cecilia Garcia-Peñalosa. 1999. "Inequality and Economic Growth: The Perspective of the New Growth Theories," *J. Econ. Lit.* 37:4, pp. 1615–60.

Ahluwalia, Montek. S. 1976. "Inequality, Poverty and Development," *J. Devel. Econ.* 3, pp. 307–42.

Anderson, James E. and Peter J. Neary. 1996. "A New Approach to Evaluating Trade Policy," *Rev. Econ. Stud.* 63, pp. 107–25.

Atkinson Anthony B. and Andrea Brandolini. 2001. "Promise and Pitfalls in the Use of 'Secondary' Data-Sets: Income Inequality in OECD Countries as a Case Study," *J. Econ. Lit.* 39:3, pp.771–800.

Aw, BeeYan; Sukkyun Chung and Mark J. Roberts. 1999. "Productivity and Turnover in the Export Market: Micro Evidence from Taiwan and South Korea," NBER.

Badiane, Ousmane. 1997. "Market Integration and the Long Run Adjustment of Local Markets to Changes in Trade and Exchange Rate Regimes: Options for Market Reform and Promotion Policies," IFPRI discus. paper 11.

Badiane, Ousmane. 1998. "Marketing Policy Reform and Competitiveness: Why Integration and Arbitrage Costs Matter," IFPRI discus. paper 22.

Badiane, Ousmane. and Mylène Kherallah. 1999. "Market Liberalisation and the Poor," *Quart. J. Int. Agr.* 38, pp. 341–58.

Baldwin, Robert E. 2002. "Openness and Growth: What's the Empirical Relationship" in Conference held May 24-25, 2002, International Seminar on International Trade in *Challenges to Globalization: Analyzing the Economics*, Robert E. Baldwin and L. Alan Winters, eds. NBER.

Banerjee, Abhijit V. and Andrew F. Newman. 1994. "Poverty, Incentives and Development," *Amer. Econ. Rev.* 84:2, pp. 211–15.

Barrett, Christopher B. and Paul A. Dorosh. 1996. "Farmers' welfare and changing food prices: Non-Parametric Evidence from Rice in Madagascar," *Amer. J. Agr. Econ.* 78, pp. 656–69.

Basu, Parantap and Darryl McLeod. 1992. "Terms of Trade Fluctuations and Economic Growth in Developing Economies," *J. Devel. Econ.* 37, pp. 89–110.

Baulch, Bob. 1997. "Transfer Costs, Spatial Arbitrage, and Testing for Food Market Integration," *Amer. J. Agr. Econ.* 79: 2, pp. 477–87.

Benjamin, Dwayne. 1992. "Household Composition, Labor Markets, and Labor Demand: Testing for Separation in Agricultural Household Models," *Econometrica* 60:2, pp. 287–322.

Besley, Tim. 1995. "Nonmarket Institutions for Credit and Risk Sharing in Low-Income Countries," *J. Econ. Perspect.* 9:3, pp. 115–27.

Bernard, Andrew and Charles Jones. 1996. "Productivity Across Industries and Countries: Time Series Theory and Evidence," *Rev. Econ. Statist.* 78:1, pp. 135–46.

Bevan, David. 2000. "Fiscal Implications of Trade Liberalization," in *Trade and Fiscal Adjustment in Africa*. D. Bevan et. al., eds. NY: St. Martin's Press.

Bevan, David; Paul Collier and Jan W. Gunning. 1990. "Economic Policy in Countries Prone to Temporary Trade Shocks," in *Public Policy and Economic Development*. M. F. G. Scott and D. Lal, eds. Oxford: Clarendon Press, pp. 36–53.

Beyer, Harald; Patricio Rojas and Rodrigo Vergara. 1999. "Trade Liberalization and Wage Inequality," *J. Devel. Econ.* 59:1, pp. 103–23.

Bigsten, Arne and Paul Collier. 1995. "Linkages from Agricultural Growth in Kenya," in *Agriculture on the Road to Industrialization*. J. W. Mellor, ed. Baltimore: John Hopkins U. Press.

Bigsten, Arne; Paul Collier; Stefan Dercon; Marcel Fafchamps; B. Gauthier; J. W. Gunning; J. Habarurema; R. Oostendorp; C. Pattillo; M. Soderbom; F. Teal and A. Zeufack. 2000. "Exports and Firm Level Efficiency in African Manufacturing," Centre for Study of African Economies, work. paper 2000:16, pp. 1–23, U. Oxford.

Bond, Marian. 1983. "Agricultural Responses to Prices in Sub-Saharan African Countries", *IMF Staff Papers* 30:4, pp. 703–26.

Booth, David; F. Lugngira; P. Masanja; A. Mvungi; R. Mwaipopo; J. Mwami and A. Redmayne. 1993. *Social, Economic and Cultural Change in Contemporary Tanzania: A People Oriented Focus.* Stockholm: Swedish Int. Devel. Authority.

Bourguignon, François; William H. Branson and Jaime De Melo. 1992. "Adjustment and Income Distribution: A Micro-Macro Model for Counterfactual Analysis," *J. Devel. Econ.* 38, pp. 17–39.

Brock, William A. and Steven N. Durlauf. 2001. "Growth Empirics and Reality," *World Bank Econ. Rev.* 15:2, pp. 229–72.

Bruno, Michael; Martin Ravallion and Lyn Squire. 1998. "Equity and Growth in Developing Countries: Old and New Perspectives on the Policy Issue," in *Income Distribution and High-Quality Growth.* V. Tanzi and K. Chu, eds. Cambridge, MA: MIT Press.

Cameron, Lisa A. 2002. "Did Social Safety Net Scholarships Reduce Drop-Out Rates during the Indonesian Economic Crisis?" work. paper 2800. World Bank: Washington, DC.

Castro-Leal, Florencia; Julia Dayton; Lionel Demery and Kalpana Mehra. 1999. "Public Social Spending in Africa: Do the Poor Benefit?" *World Bank Res. Observer* 14:1, pp. 49–72.

Chambers, Robert. 1989. "Editorial Introduction: Vulnerability, Coping and Policy", *IDS Bulletin* 20:2, pp. 1–7.

Cockburn, John. 2001. "Trade Liberalization and Poverty in Nepal: A Computable General Equilibrium Micro Simulation Analysis," CREFA work. paper (01-18).

Coe, David T.; Elhanan Helpman and Alexander W. Hoffmaister. 1997. "North-South R&D Spillovers," *Econ. J.* 107:440, pp. 134–49.

Cogneau, Denis and Anne-Sophie Robilliard. 2000. "Growth, Distribution and Poverty in Madagascar: Learning from a Microsimulation Model in a General Equilibrium Framework," Washington DC: IFPRI, Trade and Macroecon. Division.

Cragg, Michael and Mario Epelbaum. 1996. "Why Has Wage Dispersion Grown in Mexico? Is It the Incidence of Reforms or the Growing Demand for Skills?" *J. Devel. Econ.* 51:1, pp. 99–116.

Currie, Janet and Ann E. Harrison. 1997. "Sharing the Costs: The Impact of Trade Reform on Capital and Labor in Morocco," *J. Lab. Econ.* 15:3, pp. S44–71.

Datt, Gaurav and Martin Ravallion. 1998. "Farm Productivity and Rural Poverty in India," *J. Devel. Stud.* 34:4, pp. 62–85.

Dawkins, Christina and John Whalley. 1997. "Tax Structure and Revenue Instability Under External Shocks: Some General Equilibrium Calculations for Côte d'Ivoire," *Rev. Devel. Econ.* 1:1, pp. 23–33.

Deaton, Angus. 1988. "Quantity, Quality, and the Spatial Variation of Price," *Amer. Econ. Rev.* 78:3, pp. 418–30.

———. 1997. *The Analysis of Household Surveys: A Microeconometric Approach to Development Policy*, Baltimore and London: John Hopkins U. Press for World Bank.

Deininger, Klaus and Pedro Olinto. 2000. "Asset Distribution, Inequality, and Growth," World Bank Policy Research work. paper 2375.

Deininger, Klaus and Lyn Squire. 1996. "A New Data Set Measuring Income Inequality," *World Bank Econ. Rev.* 10:3, pp. 565–91.

de Janvry, Alain; Marcel Fafchamps and Elisabeth Sadoulet. 1991. "Peasant Household Behaviour with Missing Markets: Some Paradoxes Explained," *Econ. J.* 101, pp. 1400–17.

Delgado, Christopher L. 1996. "Agricultural Transformation: The Key to Broad-Based Growth and Poverty Alleviation in Africa" in *Agenda for Africa's Economic Renewal*. B. Ndulu and N. van de Walle et al., eds. New Brunswick, NJ: Transaction.

Delgado, Christopher L.; Jane Hopkins and Valerie A. Kelly with Peter Hazell, Anna A. McKenna, Peter Gruhn, Behjat Hojjati, Jayashree Sil and Claude 1998. "Agricultural Growth Linkages in Sub-Saharan Africa," Research Report 107, Washington DC, IFPRI.

Del Ninno, Carlo and Paul A. Dorosh. 2001. "Averting a Food Crisis: Private Imports and Public Targeted Distribution in Bangladesh After the 1998 Flood," *Agr. Econ.* 25:3, pp. 337–46.

Dercon, Stefan. 1995. "On Market Integration and Liberalisation : Method and Application to Ethiopia," *J. Devel. Stud.* 32:1, pp. 112–43.

Dollar, David. 1992. "Outward-Oriented Developing Economies Really Do Grow More Rapidly: Evidence from 95 LDCs, 1976-1985," *Econ. Devel. Cult. Change* 40:3, pp. 523–44.

Dollar, David and Aart Kraay. 2002. "Growth Is Good for the Poor," *J. Econ. Growth* (US) 7:3, pp. 195–225.

Dorosh Paul and Alberto Valdes. 1990. "Effects of Exchange Rate and Trade Policies in Agriculture in Pakistan," IFPRI Research Report 82, Washington DC.

Easterly, William and Aart Kraay. 2000. "Small States, Small Problems? Income, Growth, and Volatility in Small States," *World Devel.* 28:11, pp. 2013–27.

Easterly, William; Roumeen Islam and Joseph E. Stiglitz. 2000. "Shaken and Stirred: Explaining Growth Volatility", in *Annual World Bank Conference on Development Economics 2000.* B. Pleskovic and N. Stern, eds. Washington DC: World Bank.

Ebrill, Liam; Janet Stotsky and Reint Gropp. 1999. "Revenue Implications of Trade Liberalization," Occasional Paper 42, IMF, Washington DC.

Edmonds, Eric and Nina Pavcnik. 2002. "Does Globalization Increase Child Labor? Evidence from Vietnam," NBER work. paper 8760.

Edwards, Sebastian. 1988. "Terms of Trade, Tariffs, and Labor Market Adjustment in Developing Countries," *World Bank Econ. Rev.* 2:2, pp. 165–85.

———. 1997. "Trade Reform, Uniform Tariffs and the Budget", in *Macroeconomic Dimensions of Public Finance.* M.I. Blejer and T. Ter-Minassian, eds. London and NY: Routledge.

———. 1998. "Openness, Productivity, and Growth: What Do We Really Know?" *Econ. J.* 108:447, pp. 383–98.

Edwards, Sebastian and Alejandro Cox Edwards. 1996. "Trade Liberalization and Unemployment: Policy

Issues and Evidence from Chile," *Cuadernos Econ.* 33, pp. 227–50.

Edwards, Sebastian and Daniel Lederman. 2002. "The Political Economy of Unilateral Trade Liberalization: The Case of Chile," in *Going Alone–The Case for Relaxed Reciprocity in Freeing Trade.* J. Bhagwati, ed. Cambridge MA: MIT Press.

Ellis, Frank. 1993. *Peasant Economics: Farm Households and Agrarian Development.* Cambridge: Cambridge U. Press.

———. 1998. "Household Strategies and Rural Livelihood Diversification," *J. Devel. Stud.* 35:1, pp. 1–38.

Elson, Diane and Barbara Evers. 1997. "Gender Aware Country Economic Reports," work. paper 2: Uganda, U. Manchester, Grad. School Social Sciences, Genecon Unit.

Esfahani, Hadi Salehi. 1991. "Exports, Imports, and Economic Growth in Semi-Industrialized Countries," *J. Devel. Econ.* 35:1, pp. 93–116.

Fafchamps, Marcel and John Pender. 1997. "Precautionary Saving, Credit Constraints and Irreversible Investment: Theory and Evidence from Semi-Arid India," *J. Bus. Econ. Statist.* 15:2, pp. 180–94.

Falvey, Rod. 1994. "Revenue Enhancing Tariff Reform," *Weltwirtsch. Arch.* 130:1, pp. 175–90.

———. 1999. "Factor Price Convergence," *J. Int. Econ.* 49, pp. 195–210.

Fane, George. 1991. "Piecemeal Tax Reforms and the Compensated Radial Elasticities of Tax Bases," *J. Public Econ.* 45, pp. 263–70.

Feenstra, Robert C, and Gordon Hanson. 1995. "Foreign Investment Outsourcing and Relative Wages," in *Economy of Trade Policy: Essays in Honour of Jagdish Bhagwati.* R. C. Feenstra; G. M. Grossman and D. Irwin, eds. Cambridge, MA and London: MIT Press.

Feenstra, Robert C.; Dorsati Madani; Tzu-Han Yang and Chi-Yuan Liang. 1997. "Testing Endogenous Growth in South Korea and Taiwan," NBER work. paper 6028.

Feliciano, Zadia. 1996. "Workers and Trade Liberalisation: The Impact of Trade Reforms in Mexico on Wages and Employment," *Industrial and Labor Relations Review* 38:3, pp. 95-115.

Ferreira, H. C. Francisco and Julie Litchfield. 1999. "Calm After The Storms: Income Distribution and Welfare in Chile 1987–1994," *World Bank Econ. Rev.* 13, pp. 509–38.

Ferriera, Pedro C. and José Luis Rossi. 2001. "New Evidence on Trade Liberalization and Productivity Growth," *Ensaios Econo. da EPGE* 433.

Fields, Gary. 1989. "Changes in Poverty and Inequality in Developing Countries," *World Bank Res. Observer* 4, pp. 167–86.

Frankenberg, Elizabeth; James P. Smith and Duncan Thomas. 2003. "Economic Shocks, Wealth and Welfare," *J. Human Res.* 32:2, pp.280–321.

Frankel, Jeffrey A. and David Romer. 1999. "Does Trade Cause Growth?" *Amer. Econ. Rev.* 89:3, pp. 379–99.

Frankel, Jeffrey and Andrew K. Rose. 2002. "An Estimate of the Effect of Common Currencies on Trade and Growth," *Quart. J. Econ.* 117:469, pp. 437–66.

Friedman, Jed and James Levinsohn. 2002. "The Distributional Impacts of Indonesia's Financial Crisis on Household Welfare: A "Rapid Response" Methodology," *World Bank Econ. Rev.* 16, pp. 397–423.

Galor, Oded and Joseph Zeira. 1993. "Income Distribution and Macroeconomics," *Rev. Econ. Stud.* 60:1, pp. 35–52.

Gilbert, Christopher L. and Panos Varangis. 2002. "Globalization and International Commodity Trade with Specific Reference to the West African Cocoa Producers," Conference May 24–25, Int. Seminar on Int. Trade in *Challenges to Globalization: Analyzing the Economics.* Robert E. Baldwin and L. Alan Winters, eds. NBER.

Gisselquist, David and Jean-Marie Grether. 2000. "An Argument for Deregulating the Transfer of Agricultural Technologies to Developing Countries," *World Bank Econ. Rev.* 14:1, pp. 111–27.

Glenday, Graham. 2000. "Trade Liberalization and Customs Revenues: Does Trade Liberalization Lead to Lower Customs Revenues? The Case of Kenya," African Econ. Policy Discus. Paper 44, JFK School Govt., Harvard U.

Glewwe, Paul and Dennis de Tray. 1989. "The Poor in Latin America During Adjustment: A Case Study of Peru," Living Standards Measurement Study, work. paper 56, World Bank: Washington DC.

Glewwe, Paul and Gillette Hall. 1998. "Are Some Groups More Vulnerable to Macroeconomic Shocks than Others? Hypothesis Tests on Panel Data from Peru," *J. Devel. Econ.* 56, pp. 181–206.

Goetz, Stephen J. 1992. "A Selectivity Model of Household Food Marketing Behavior in Sub-Saharan Africa," *Amer. J. Agr. Econ.* 74, pp. 444–52.

Greenaway, David and Chris Milner. 1991. "Fiscal Dependence on Trade Taxes and Trade Policy Reform," *J. Devel. Stud.* 27, pp. 95–132.

Griliches, Zvi and Jacques Mairesse. 1998. "Production Functions: The Search for Identification," in *Economics and Economic Theory in the Twentieth Century: The Ragnar Frisch Centennial Symposium.* Cambridge MA: Cambridge U. Press.

Grimard, Franque. 1997. "Household Consumption Smoothing Through Ethnic Ties: Evidence from Cote d'Ivoire," *J. Devel. Econ.* 53:2, pp. 391–422.

Grossman, Gene M. and Elhanan Helpman. 1991. *Innovation and Growth in the Global Economy.* Cambridge, MA and London: MIT Press.

Guillaumont, Patrick; Sylviane Guillaumont Jeanneney and Jean-Francois Brun. 1999. "How Instability Lowers African Growth," *J. African Economies* 8:1, pp. 87–107.

Haggblade, Steven; Peter Hazell and James Brown. 1989. "Farm-Nonfarm Linkages in Rural Sub-Saharan Africa," *World Devel.* 17:8, pp. 1173–201.

Hanson, Gordon and Ann Harrison. 1999. "Who Gains From Trade Reform? Some Remaining Puzzles," *J. Devel. Econ.* 59:1, pp.125–54.

Harriss, Barbara. 1987. "Discussion: Regional Growth Linkages from Agriculture," *J. Devel. Stud.* 23:2, pp. 275–89.

Harrison, Anne. 1996. "Openness and Growth: A Time-Series, Cross-Country Analysis for Developing Countries," *J. Devel. Econ.* 48:2, pp. 419–47.

Harrison, Anne and Ana L. Revenga. 1998. "Labor Markets, Foreign Investment and Trade Policy Reform", in *Trade Policy Reform: Lessons and Implications*. J. Nash and W. Takacs, eds. Washington DC: World Bank.

Harrison Glenn W.; Thomas F. Rutherford and David G. Tarr. 2002. "Trade Policy Options for Chile: The Importance of Market Access," *World Bank Econ. Rev.* 16:1, pp. 49–79.

Harrison, Glenn W.; Thomas S. Rutherford; David G. Tarr and Angelo Gurgel. 2003. "Regional, Multilateral and Unilateral Trade Policies of MERCOSUR for Growth and Poverty Reduction in Brazil," work. paper 3051, World Bank: Washington DC.

Hay, Donald. 2001. "The Post-1990 Brazilian Trade Liberalisation and the Performance of Large Manufacturing Firms: Productivity, Market Share and Profits," *Econ. J.* 111:473, pp. 620–41.

Hazell, Peter B. R. and Steven Haggblade. 1991. "Rural-Urban Growth Linkages in India," *Indian J. Agri. Econ.* 46:4, pp. 515–29.

Hazell, Peter B. R. and Behjat Hojjati. 1995. "Farm/Non-Farm Growth Linkages in Zambia," *J. African Economies* 4:3, pp. 406–35.

Hazell, Peter B. S. and Ailsa Roell. 1983. "Rural Growth Linkages: Household Expenditure Patterns in Malaysia and Nigeria," Research Report 41, Washington DC: IFPRI.

Head, Judith. 1998. "Ek Het Niks–I Have Nothing: The Impact of European Union Policies on Women Canning Workers in South Africa," U. Capetown.

Heltberg, Rasmus and Finn Tarp. 2002. "Agriculture Supply Response and Poverty in Mozambique," *Food Policy* 27:2, pp. 103–24.

Henson, Spencer J.; Rupert J. Loader; Alan Swinbank; Maury Bredahl and Nicole Lux. 2000. *Impact of Sanitary and Phytosanitary Measures on Developing Countries*. Centre Food Econ. Research, U. Reading.

Hertel, Thomas W.; Paul V Preckel, John A L Cranfield, and Maros Ivanic. 2001. "Poverty Impacts of Multilateral Trade Liberalization," Purdue U.

Hirschman, Albert O. 1958. *The Strategy of Economic Development*. New Haven: Yale U. Press.

Ianchovichina, Elena; Alessandro Nicita and Isidro Soloaga. 2001. "Trade Reform and Household Welfare: The Case of Mexico," work. paper 2667, World Bank, Washington DC.

IFAD. 2001. *Rural Poverty Report 2001: The Challenge of Ending Rural Poverty*, Oxford: Oxford U. Press.

Irwin, Douglas A. and Tervio, Marko. 2002. "Does Trade Raise Income? Evidence from the Twentieth Century," *J. Int. Econ.* 58, pp. 1–18.

Jacoby, Hanan and Emmanuel Skoufias. 1997. "Risk, Financial Markets and Human Capital in a Developing Country," *Rev. Econ. Stud.* 64:3, pp. 311–36.

Jalan, Jyotsna and Martin Ravallion. 1997. "Geographic Poverty Traps? A Micro Model of Consumption Growth in Rural China," *J. Appl. Econometrics* 17:4, pp. 329–46.

Jalan, Jyotsna and Martin Ravallion. 1999. "Are the Poor Less Well Insured? Evidence on Vulnerability to Income Risk in Rural China," *J. Devel. Econ.* 58:1, pp. 61–81.

Jonsson, Gunnar and Arvind Subramanian. 2001. "Dynamic Gains from Trade: Evidence from South Africa," *IMF Staff Papers* 48:1, pp. 187–224.

Jones, Charles I. 2001. "Comment on 'Trade Policy and Economic Growth: A Sceptic's Guide to the Cross-National Evidence' by Francisco Rodriguez and Dani Rodrik," in *Macroeconomics Annual 2000*. Ben Bernanke and Kenneth S. Rogoff, eds. MIT Press for NBER: Cambridge, MA.

Kabeer, Naila. 2000. *The Power to Choose: Bangladeshi Women and Labour Market Decisions in London and Dhaka*. pp. 464. NY: Verso.

Kennedy, Eileen and Bruce Cogill. 1987. "Income and Nutrition Effects of the Commercialization of Agriculture in South Western Kenya," Research Report 63. Int. Food Policy Research Institute, Washington DC.

Killick, Tony. 1995. "Structural Adjustment and Poverty Alleviation: An Interpretative Survey," *Devel. Change* 26, pp. 305–31.

Kim, Euysung. 2000. "Trade Liberalization and Productivity Growth in Korea Manufacturing Industries: Price Protection, Market Power, and Scale Efficiency," *J. Devel. Econ.* 62:1, pp. 55–83.

Knowles, Stephen. 2001. "Inequality and Economic Growth: The Empirical Relationship Reconsidered in the Light of Comparable Data", CREDIT Res. Paper 01/03, U. Nottingham.

Kochar, Anjini. 1995. "Explaining Household Vulnerability to Idiosyncratic Income Shocks," *Amer. Econ. Rev.* 85:2, pp. 159–64.

Konan, Denise E. and Keith E. Maskus. 2000. "A Computable General Equilibrium Analysis of Egyptian Trade Liberalization Scenarios," in *Regional Partners in Global Markets: Limits and Possibilities of the Euro-Med Agreements*. A. Galal and B. Hoekman, eds. CEPR: London.

Kraay, Aart. 1997. "Exports and Economic Performance: Evidence from a Panel of Chinese Enterprises," mimeo, Devel. Research Group, World Bank.

Krueger, Anne O. 1978. "Liberalization Attempts and Consequences, Liberalization, Direction of Bias and Economic Growth", in *Foreign Trade Regimes and Economic Development*, Vol. X, pp. 277–300, NBER, NY.

———. 1983. *Trade and Employment in Developing Countries: Volume 3: Synthesis and Conclusions*. NBER, NY.

———. 1990. "Asian Trade and Growth Lessons," *Amer. Econ. Rev.*, Papers and Proceedings, 80:2, pp. 108–11.

———. 1992. *The Political Economy of Agricultural Pricing Policy*, in: *A Synthesis of the Political Economy in Developing Countries*, World Bank Compar. Study, vol. 5, Baltimore: Johns Hopkins U. Press.

Kurosaki, Takashi. 1995. *Risk attitudes, Consumption Preferences, and Crop Choices in the Pakistan Punjab*, Ph.D., Stanford U.

Lal, Deepak. 1986. "Stopler-Samuelson-Rybczynski in the Pacific: Real Wages and Real Exchange in the Philippines, 1956–1978," *J. Devel. Stud.* 21, pp. 181–204.

Lall, Sanjaya. 1999. *The Technological Response to Import Liberalization in Sub-Saharan Africa.* London: Macmillan.

Lambert, Sylvie. 1994. "La Migration Comme Instrument de Diversification Intrafamiliale des Risques. Application au Cas de la Cote d'Ivoire," *Revue Econ. Devel.* 2, pp. 3–38.

Lambert Sylvie and Thierry Magnac. 1997. "Implicit prices and Recursivity of Agricultural Households' Decisions," CREST work. paper 9731.

Lanjouw, Peter and Martin Ravallion. 1999. "Benefit Incidence, Public Spending Reforms, and the Timing of Program Capture," *World Bank Econ. Rev.* 13:2, pp. 257–73.

Larson, Donald; Rita Butzer; Yair Mundlak and Al Crego. 2000. "A Cross-Country Database for Sector Investment and Capital," *World Bank Econ. Rev.* 14:1, pp. 371–91.

Lee, Jong-Wha. 1996. "Government Interventions and Productivity Growth," *J. Econ. Growth* 1:3, pp. 391–414.

Levine, Ross and David Renelt. 1992. "A Sensitivity Analysis of Cross-Country Growth Regressions," *Amer. Econ. Rev.* 82:4, pp. 942–63.

Levinsohn, James. 1999. "Employment Responses to International Liberalization in Chile," *J. Int. Econ.* 47:2, pp. 321–44.

Levinsohn, James; Steven Berry and Jed Friedman. 1999. "Impacts of the Indonesian Economic Crisis: Price Changes and the Poor," NBER work. paper 7194.

Levy, Santiago and Sweder van Wijnbergen. 1992. "Agricultural Adjustment and the Mexico-USA Free Trade Agreement," in *Open Economies: Structural Adjustment and Agriculture.* I. Goldin and L. A. Winters, eds. Cambridge U. Press: Cambridge.

Lipton, Michael. 1968. "The Theory of the Optimising Peasant," *J. Devel. Stud.* 4:3, pp. 327–51.

Lloyd, Peter. 2000. "Generalizing the Stopler-Samuelson Theorem: A Tale of Two Matrices," *Rev. Int. Econ.* 8:4, pp. 597–613.

Lloyd, Tim; Wyn Morgan, Tony Rayner and Charlotte Vaillant. 1999. "The Transmission of World Agricultural Prices in Cote d'Ivoire," *J. Int. Trade Econ. Devel.* 8:1, pp. 125–41.

Lokshin, Michael and Martin Ravallion. 2000. "Short-Lived Shocks with Long-Lived Impacts? Household Income Dynamics in a Transition Economy," mimeo, World Bank.

López, Ramón; John Nash and Julie Stanton. 1995. "Adjustment and Poverty in Mexican Agriculture: How Farmers' Wealth Affects Supply Response," World Bank Policy Research work. paper 1494.

Lucas, Robert E. 1988. "The Mechanics of Economic Development," *J. Monet. Econ.* 22, pp. 3–42.

Lumenga-Neso, Olivier; Marcelo Olarreaga and Maurice Schiff. 2001. "On 'Indirect' Trade-Related R&D Spillovers and Growth," CEPR Discus. paper 2871, London.

Lutz, Matthias and Hans W. Singer. 1994. "The Link between Increased Trade Openness and the Terms of Trade: An Empirical Investigation," *World Devel.* 22, pp. 1697–709.

Martin, Will and Devashish Mitra. 2001. "Productivity Growth and Convergence in Agriculture and Manufacturing," *Econ. Devel. Cult. Change* 49:2, pp. 403–22.

MacBean, Alasdair I. 1966. *Export Instability and Economic Development.* Cambridge, MA: Harvard U. Press.

Marquez, Gustavo and Carmen Pagés-Serra. 1998. "Trade and Employment: Evidence from Latin America and the Caribbean," WP-366, Inter-American Devel. Bank, Washington DC.

Matusz, Steven J. and David Tarr. 1999. "Adjusting to Trade Policy Reform," World Bank Policy Research work. paper 2142.

McCulloch, Neil; Bob Baulch and Milasoa Cherel-Robson. 2001. "Poverty, Inequality and Growth in Zambia during the 1990s," Discus. paper 2001/123, World Institute for Devel. Econ. Research, Helsinki.

McCulloch, Neil; L. Alan Winters and Xavier Cirera. 2001. *Trade Liberalization and Poverty: A Handbook.* London: Centre Econ. Policy Research.

McKay, Andrew; Oliver Morrissey and Charlotte Vaillant. 1997. "Trade Liberalization and Agricultural Supply Response: Issues and Some Lessons," *Europ. J. Devel. Res.* 9:2, pp. 129–47.

McKay Andrew; L. Alan Winters and Abbi Mamo Kedir. 2000. "A Review of Empirical Evidence on Trade, Trade Policy and Poverty," Report for Dept. Int. Development, London.

Mellor, John W. 1976. *The New Economics of Growth: A Strategy for India and the Developing World.* Ithaca: Cornell U. Press.

———. 1983. "Foreword" in *Rural Growth Linkages: Household Expenditure Patterns in Malaysia and Nigeria.* P. B. S. Hazell and A. Roell eds. Washington DC: IFPRI, Research Report 41.

Mellor, John and Sarah Gavian. 1999. "The Determinants of Employment Growth In Egypt—The Dominant Role of Agriculture and the Rural Small Scale Sector," mimeo, Abt Assoc., Cambridge, MA.

Mellor, John W. and Bruce F. Johnston. 1984. "The World Food Equation: Interrelations among Development, Employment and Food Consumption," *J. Econ. Lit.* 22:2, pp. 524–31.

Michaely, Michael; Demetris Papageorgiou and Armeane M. Choksi. 1991. *Liberalizing Foreign Trade.* Backwell: Oxford.

Mills, Bradford F. and David E. Sahn. 1995. "Reducing the Size of the Public Sector Workforce: Institutional Constraints and Human Consequences in Guinea," *J. Devel. Stud.* 31, pp. 505–28.

Milner, Chris; Oliver Morrissey and Nicodemus Rudaheranwa. 2001. "Policy and Non-Policy Barriers to Trade and Implicit Taxation of Exports in Uganda," *J. Devel. Stud.* 37:2, pp. 67–90.

Milner, Chris and Peter Wright. 1998. "Modelling Labour Market Adjustment to Trade Liberalization in an Industrializing Economy," *Econ. J.* 108, pp. 509–28.

Minot, Nicholas. 1998. "Distributional and Nutritional Impact of Devaluation in Rwanda," *Econ. Devel. Cult. Change* 46:2, pp. 379–402.

Minot, Nicholas F. and Francesco Goletti. 1998. *Rice Market Liberalization and Poverty in Vietnam.* Washington DC: Int. Food Policy Res. Institute.

Morduch, Jonathan. 1994. "Poverty and Vulnerability," *Amer. Econ. Rev.* 84: pp. 221–25.

Moreira, Maurício M. and Sheila Najberg. 2000. "Trade Liberalization in Brazil: Creating or Exporting Jobs?" *J. Devel. Stud.* 36:3, pp. 78–100.

Mundlak, Yair and Donald F. Larson. 1992. "On the Transmission of World Agricultural Prices," *World Bank Econ. Rev.* 6:3, pp. 399–422.

Nadal, Alejandro. 2000. *The Environmental and Social Impacts of Economic Liberalization on Corn Production in Mexico.* Oxfam GB (UK) and WWF Int. (Switzerland).

Newbery, David M. and Nicholas H. Stern. 1987. *The Theory of Taxation for Developing Countries.* NY and Oxford: Oxford U. Press for World Bank.

Niimi, Yoko; Puja Vasudeva-Dutta and L. Alan Winters. 2003. "Trade Liberalization and Poverty Dynamics in Vietnam," work. paper 17, Poverty Research Unit: U. Sussex, Brighton, England.

Oxfam. 2002. *Rigged Rules and Double Standards–Trade, Globalization, and the Fight Against Poverty.* Oxfam Int.

Oxfam-IDS. 1999. "Liberalization and Poverty," Final Report to DFID, London.

Pack, Howard. 1988. "Industrialization and Trade" in *Handbook of Development Economics.* H. Chenery and T.N. Srinivasan, eds. Vol. I, Elsevier Science B.V.

Papageorgiou, Demetris; Michael Michaely and Armeane M. Choksi, eds. 1991. *Liberalizing Foreign Trade.* Vol. 1–7. Oxford: Blackwell.

Parker, Ronald L.; Randall Riopelle and William R. Steel. 1995. *Small Enterprises Adjusting to Liberalization in Five African Countries.* Washington DC: World Bank.

Parris, Brett. 1999. *Trade for Development: Making the WTO Work for the Poor.* World Vision Int.

Pritchett, Lant. 1996. "Measuring Outward Orientation in Developing Countries: Can It Be Done?" *J. Devel. Econ.* 49:2, pp. 307–35.

Pritchett, Lant and Geeta Sethi. 1994. "Tariff Rates, Tariff Revenue, and Tariff Reform: Some New Facts," *World Bank Econ. Rev.* 8, pp. 1–16.

Pritchett, Lant; Asep Suryhadi and Suryhadi Sumarto. 2000. "Quantifying Vulnerability to Poverty: A Proposed Measure with Application to Indonesia," World Bank Policy Research work. paper 2437, Washington DC.

Rama, Martin. 1994. "The Labour Market and Trade Reform in Manufacturing," in *The Effects of Protectionism on a Small Country.* M. Connolly and J. de Melo, eds. World Bank Regional and Sectoral Studies, Washington DC.

Rama, Martin and Donna MacIsaac. 1999. "Earnings and Welfare after Downsizing: Central Bank Employees in Ecuador," *World Bank Econ. Rev.* 13, pp. 89–116.

Rama, Martin and Kinnori Scott. 1999. "Labor Earnings in One-Company Towns: Theory and Evidence from Kazakhstan," *World Bank Econ. Rev.* 13, pp.185–209.

Ravallion, Martin. 1988. "Expected Poverty under Risk-Induced Welfare Variability," *Econ. J.* 98:Dec., pp. 1171–82.

———. 1995. "Growth and Poverty: Evidence for Developing Countries in the 1980s," *Econ. Letters* 48, pp. 411–17.

———. 1998. "On Reform, Food Prices and Poverty in India," *Econ. Polit. Weekly* 33:Jan. 10–16, pp. 29–36.

———. 1999. "On Protecting the Poor from Fiscal Contractions," mimeo, Washington DC, World Bank Devel. Research Group, and U. Sciences Sociales, ARQADE, Toulouse.

———. 2001. "Growth, Inequality and Poverty: Looking Beyond Averages," *World Devel.* 29, pp. 1803–15.

Ravallion, Martin and Guarav Datt. 2002. "Why Has Economic Growth Been More Pro-Poor in Some States of India Than Others?" *J. Devel. Econ.* 68:2, pp. 381–400.

Ravallion, Martin and Dominique Van de Walle. 1991. "The Impact on Poverty of Food Pricing Reforms: A Welfare Analysis for Indonesia," *J. Pol. Modeling* 13, pp. 281–99.

Razin, Assaf and Andrew K. Rose. 1992. "Business-Cycle Volatility and Openness: An Exploratory Cross-Sectional Analysis" in *Capital Mobility: The Impact on Consumption, Investment and Growth.* L. Leiderman and A. Razin, eds. Cambridge: Cambridge U. Press. pp. 48–82.

Reardon, Thomas. 1997. "Using Evidence of Household Income Diversification to Inform Study of the Rural Nonfarm Labor Market in Africa," *World Devel.* 25:5, pp. 735–47.

Reimer, Jeffrey J. 2002. "Estimating the Poverty Impacts of Trade Liberalization," Policy Research work. paper 2790, World Bank, Washington DC.

Reinikka, Ritva and Paul Collier, eds. 2001. *Uganda's Recovery—The Role of Farms, Firms, and Government.* Washington, DC: World Bank.

Renkow, Mitch. 2000. "Poverty, Productivity and Production Environment: A Review of the Evidence," *Food Policy* 25, pp. 463–78.

Revenga, Ana. 1997. "Employment and Wage Effects of Trade Liberalization: The Case of Mexican Manufacturing," *J. Lab. Econ.* 15:3, pt. 2, S20–S43.

Roberts, Mark J. and James R. Tybout. 1996. *Industrial Evolution in Developing Countries.* Oxford: Oxford U. Press.

Robbins, Donald and T. H. Grindling. 1999. "Trade Liberalisation and the Relative Wages for More-Skilled workers in Costa Rica," *Rev. Devel. Econ.* 3:2, pp. 140–54.

Rodriguez, Francisco and Dani Rodrik. 2001. "Trade Policy and Economic Growth: A Sceptic's Guide to the Cross-National Evidence," *NBER Macroeconomics Annual 2000.* Cambridge, MA: MIT Press, pp. 261–324.

Rodrik, Dani. 1997. *Has Globalization Gone Too Far?* Washington D.C.: Institute Int. Econ.

———. 1998. "Why Do More Open Economies have Bigger Governments?," *J. Polit. Econ.* 106, pp. 997–1032.

———. 1999. "Where Did All the Growth Go? External Shocks, Social Conflict, and Growth Collapses," *J. Econ. Growth* 4:4, pp. 385–412.

Romer, David. 1993. "Openness and Inflation: Theory and Evidence," *Quart. J. Econ.* 108:4, pp. 870–903.
Romer, Paul. 1994. "New Goods, Old Theory and the Welfare Cost of Trade Restrictions," *J. Devel. Econ.* 43, pp. 5–38.
Rosenzweig, Mark R. and Kenneth I. Wolpin. 1993. "Credit Market Constraints, Consumption Smoothing, and the Accumulation of Durable Production Assets in Low-Income Countries: Investments in Bullocks in India," *J. Polit. Econ.* 101:2, pp. 223–44.
Sachs, Jeffrey D. and Andrew M. Warner. 1995. "Economic Convergence and Economic Policies," *Brookings Pap. Econ. Act.* 1, pp. 1–95.
Sahn, David 1992. "Public Expenditures in Sub-Saharan Africa during a Period of Economic Reforms," *World Devel.* 20:5, pp. 673–93.
Sahn, David; Paul A. Dorosh and Stephen Younger. 1997. *Structural Adjustment Reconsidered: Economic Policy and Poverty in Africa.* Cambridge: Cambridge U. Press.
Sahn, David and Alexander Sarris. 1991. "Structural Adjustment and the Welfare of Rural Smallholders: A Comparative Analysis from Sub-Saharan Africa," *World Bank Econ. Rev.* 5, pp. 259–89.
Schiff, Maurice and Claudio E. Montenegro. 1997. "Aggregate Agricultural Supply Response in Developing Countries: A Survey of Selected Issues," *Econ. Devel. Cult. Change* 45:2, pp. 393–410.
Sen, Amartya. 1993. "Capability and Well-Being" in *The Quality of Life.* Martha Nussbaum and A. Sen, eds. Clarendon Press: Oxford.
Sharma, Kishor; Sisira Jayasuriya and Edward Oczkowski. 2000. "Liberalization and Productivity Growth: The Case of Manufacturing Industry in Nepal," *Oxford Devel. Stud.* 28:2, pp. 205–22.
Singh, Inderjit; Lyn Squire and John Strauss. 1986. "A Survey of Agricultural Household Models: Recent Findings and Policy Implications," *World Bank Econ. Rev.* 1:1, pp. 149-79.
Smith, James P.; Duncan Thomas; Elizabeth Frankenberg; Kathleen Beegle and Graciela Teruel. 2002. "Wages, Employment and Economic Shocks: Evidence from Indonesia," *J. Population Econ.* 15, pp. 161–93.
Smith, Lisa C. and Jean-Paul Chavas. 1999. "Supply Response of West African Agricultural Households: Implications of Intrahousehold Preference Heterogeneity," IFPRI Food Consumption and Nutrition Division, discus. paper 69.
Squire, Lyn. 1991. "Introduction: Poverty and Adjustment in the 1980s," *World Bank Econ. Rev.* 5:2, pp. 177–85.
Strauss, John and Duncan Thomas. 1998. "Health, Nutrition, and Economic Development," *J. Econ. Lit.* 36:2, pp. 766–817.
Srinivasan, P.V. and Shikha Jha. 2001. "Liberalized Trade and Domestic Price Stability. The Case of Rice and Wheat in India," *J. Devel. Econ.* 65, pp. 417–41.
Srinivasan, T.N. and Jagdish Bhagwati. 2001. "Outward-Orientation and Development: Are Revisionists Right?" in *Trade, Development and Political Economy: Essays in Honour of Anne O. Krueger.* Deepak Lal and R. H. Snape, eds. London: Palgrave, pp. 3–26.
Suryahadi, Asef; Widyanti Wenefrida and Sudarno Sumarto. 2003. "Short-Term Poverty Dynamics in Rural Indonesia during the Economic Crisis," *J. Int. Devel.* 15:2, pp. 133–44.
Svaleryd, Helena and Jonas Vlachos. 2002. "Markets for Risk and Openness to Trade: How Are They Related?" *J. Int. Econ.* 57:2, pp. 369–95.
Taylor. Alan M. 1998. "On the Costs of Inward-Looking Development: Price Distortions, Growth and Divergence in Latin America," *J. Econ. Hist.* 58:1, pp. 1–28.
Thomas, Duncan; Elizabeth Frankenberg; Kathleen Beegle and Graciela Teruel. 1999. "Household Budgets, Household Composition and the Crisis in Indonesia: Evidence from Longitudinal Household Survey Data," mimeo, paper for 1999 Population Assoc. America Meetings, NY, March 25–27.
Townsend, Robert M. and Rolf A. E. Mueller. 1998. "Mechanism Design and Village Economies: From Credit to Tenancy to Cropping Groups," *Rev. Econ. Dynam.* 1:1, pp. 119–72.
Tybout, James R. 2000. "Manufacturing Firms in Developing Countries: How Well Do They Do, and Why?" *J. Econ. Lit.* 38:1, pp. 11–44.
Tybout, James; Jaime de Melo and Vittorio Corbo. 1991. "The Effects of Trade Reforms on Scale and Technical Efficiency: New Evidence from Chile," *J. Int. Econ.* 31:3–4, pp. 231–50.
Tybout, James R. and Daniel Westbrook. 1995. "Trade Liberalization and the Dimensions of Efficiency Change in Mexican Manufacturing Industries," *J. Int. Econ.* 39, pp.53–78.
Udry, Christopher. 1995. "Risk and Saving in Northern Nigeria," *Amer. Econ. Rev.* 85:5, pp. 1287–300.
———. 1996. "Gender, Agricultural Productivity and the Theory of the Household," *J. Polit. Econ.* 104, pp. 1010–46.
van der Gaag, Jacques. 1991. "Poverty in the Developing World: Assessment of the Past, Prospects for the Future," *Europ. Econ. Rev.* 35, pp. 343–49.
van der Hoeven, Rolph. 1996. "Structural Adjustment and Poverty: Review of Experiences in the 1980s" in *Economic Reforms and Poverty Alleviation in India.* C.H. Hanumantha Rao and H. Linnemann, eds. Sage Publications, pp. 90–118.
von Braun, Joachim. 1989. "Commercialisation of Smallholder Agriculture:- Policy Requirements for Capturing Gains for the Malnourished Poor," IFPRI: Washington DC.
von Braun, Joachim; David Hotchikiss and Maarten Immink. 1989. "Non-Traditional Export Crops in Guatemala: Effects on Production, Income and Nutrition," IFPRI Research Report 73: Washington DC.
Wacziarg, Romain. 2001. "Measuring the Dynamic Gains from Trade," *World Bank Econ. Rev.* 15:3, pp. 393–427.
Watkins, Kevin. 1997. "Globalisation and Liberalisation:- Implications for Poverty, Distribution and Inequality," UNDP occasional paper 32.
Wei, Shang-Jin. 2000. "Natural Openness and Good Government," NBER work paper 7765.

White, Howard. 1997. *Poverty and Adjustment in Sub-Saharan Africa: A Review of the Literature*. The Hague: Institute of Social Studies.

White, Howard and Edward Anderson. 2001. "Growth versus Distribution: Does the Pattern of Growth Matter?" *Devel. Policy Rev.* 19:3, pp. 267–89.

Winters, L. Alan. 2000a. "Trade and Poverty: Is There a Connection?" in *Trade, Income Disparity and Poverty*. Ben David, D.; H. Nordstrom and L. A. Winters, eds. Special Study 5, Geneva: WTO.

———. 2000b. "Trade Liberalization and Poverty", Discus. paper 7, Poverty Research Unit, U. Sussex.

———. 2002a. "Trade Liberalization and Poverty: What Are the Links?" *World Econ.* 25:9, pp. 1339–67.

———. 2002b. "Trade Policies for Poverty Alleviation," in *Development, Trade and the WTO: A Handbook*. B. Hoekman, A. Mattoo and P. English, eds. World Bank, pp. 28–38.

———. 2003. "Doha and World Poverty Targets," in *The New Reform Agenda: Proceedings of the Annual Bank Conference on Development Economics*. B. Pleskovic and N. Stern, eds., 2003. Oxford U. Press: Oxford, pp. 91–121.

Wood, Adrian. 1997. "Openness and Wage Inequality in Developing Countries:- The Latin American Challenge to East Asian Conventional Wisdom," *World Bank Econ. Rev.* 11:1, pp. 33–57.

Wood, Adrian and Cristobal Ridao-Cano. 1999. "Skill, Trade and International Inequality," *Oxford Econ. Pap.* 51, pp. 89–119.

World Bank. 1988. *World Development Report 1988*, NY: Oxford U. Press.

———. 2001. *World Development Report 2000/2001*, Oxford U. Press: NY.

———. 2002. *Global Economic Prospects and the Developing Countries*. Washington DC: World Bank.

Younger, Stephen. 1996. "Labor Market Consequences of Retrenchment for Civil Servants in Ghana," in *Economic Reform and the Poor in Africa*. David Sahn, ed. Clarendon Press: Oxford.

*The Economic Journal*, **114** (*February*), F4–F21. © Royal Economic Society 2004. Published by Blackwell Publishing, 9600 Garsington Road, Oxford OX4 2DQ, UK and 350 Main Street, Malden, MA 02148, USA.

# TRADE LIBERALISATION AND ECONOMIC PERFORMANCE: AN OVERVIEW*

*L Alan Winters*

This paper surveys the recent literature on trade liberalisation and economic growth. While there are serious methodological challenges and disagreements about the strength of the evidence, the most plausible conclusion is that liberalisation generally induces a temporary (but possibly long-lived) increase in growth. A major component of this is an increase in productivity. Part 2 stresses the importance of other factors in achieving growth, such as other policies, investment and institutions, but argues that many of these respond positively to trade liberalisation. It also considers the implementation of liberalisation and notes the benefits of simple and transparent trade regimes.

Trade liberalisation has been a prominent component of policy advice to developing countries for the last two decades. Among the benefits claimed to spring from it, economic growth is probably the most important. And yet economists continue to argue about, and conduct research on, the connection between them. This paper samples the resulting literature with a view to assessing the current state of the evidence that trade liberalisation enhances growth and identifying the key steps in actually reaping such benefits.

The paper comprises two parts. The first considers some of the empirical evidence linking trade liberalisation and openness to trade on the one hand with higher incomes and economic growth on the other. The evidence suggests that openness enhances growth, at least over the medium term, but the methodological problems preclude our being wholly certain. Cross-country studies face problems in defining and measuring openness, in identifying causation and in isolating the effects of trade liberalisation. Case-studies avoid some of these problems but cannot confidently be generalised. Attempts to model the links explicitly – specifically to relate productivity to openness – face similar problems of identification but on the whole provide a somewhat more convincing account of the benefits.

Part 2 considers explicitly the role of other policies and institutions in connecting openness and income. While trade liberalisation alone is unlikely to be sufficient to boost growth significantly, in two important dimensions – corruption and inflation – it appears to improve other policies. The paper then stresses the importance of investment – and hence of other policies affecting investment - in translating trade liberalisation into growth and the importance of institutions in permitting growth. I argue that openness can enhance institutional development, although not through the external imposition of institutions on unwilling

* I am grateful to participants at the ESRC International Economics Study Group Annual Conference 2001 and to Raed Safadi, Tony Thirlwall and two anonymous referees for comments on an earlier draft of this paper, to Enrique Blanco de Armas and Carolina Villegas Sanchez for research assistance and to Amy Sheehan, Reto Speck and Nicola Winterton for logistical help. None is to blame for the paper's remaining short-comings.

developing country governments. The final sub-section of the paper briefly considers the implementation of trade liberalisation. It stresses the virtues of simple trade policy (e.g. uniform tariffs) as a means both of achieving transparency and predictability and of releasing skilled administrative and political resources for other tasks. I argue that while a binding commitment to liberalisation should not wait for other policies to be in place, the timing of liberalisation should recognise possible interaction with other policies.

Before starting, I should do a little terminological ground clearing. The received theory of economic growth is concerned with steady-state rates of growth. These are important conceptually but, in fact, are essentially unobservable. In practical terms, therefore, one should also consider long-term transitional growth-rates. If trade liberalisation shifts the economy onto a higher but parallel growth path actual growth rates exceed the steady-state rate while the change occurs. Given that policy reforms are typically phased-in over several years and that their effects can take decades to occur, it is difficult to tell such transitional rates from changes in steady-state rates empirically (Brock and Durlauf, 2001).

The treatment of trade liberalisation raises similar, but more tractable, issues. Conceptually it is important to distinguish openness to trade, a levels or state variable, from trade liberalisation, which refers to its change: in practice, however, they can be difficult to separate. Both should strictly be measured by policy stances but, since that is so complex, outcome measures are often used instead. I briefly allude to these issues below but illustrations of the empirical difficulties they raise can be found in Pritchett (1996) and Harrison (1996).

## 1. Trade Liberalisation and Growth: the Evidence

### 1.1. *Levels vs. Growth Rates*

The literature on trade and growth is rather casual about which of levels or changes it is referring to. The most obvious relationship is that from openness to the level of income. Simple theory predicts a positive relationship, at least if we can measure real income appropriately, although the situation becomes more complex once one allows for effects such as those on the capital, dynamic comparative advantage and agglomeration.[1] If there is such a relationship, taking first differences of it gives us one between trade liberalisation and the growth of income and, as noted above, this could actually be very long-lived.

More recent theory, has also explored whether openness could affect steady-state growth rates. Thus, for example, if greater competition or exposure to a larger set of ideas or technologies increased the rate of technical progress, it would permanently raise growth rates. This is an immensely attractive view of the world but one which is difficult to maintain empirically. Jones (1995), for example, argues that since the US growth rate has displayed no permanent changes over the period 1880–1987, one must conclude either that it cannot have been determined by

[1] Real GDP is a poor measure of the gains from trade. It misses the consumption gains and, by valuing output and pre-reform prices, under-estimates production gains.

factors that change substantially, such as trade policy or openness, or that changes in such factors have been just off-setting, which is not very credible.[2] More positively Hall and Jones (1997) argue that 'there is a great deal of empirical and theoretical work to suggest that the primary reason that countries grow at such different rates for decades at a time is *transition dynamics*' (italics in original, p. 173). Solow (2001) also makes the same point and it is the starting point for what follows.

### 1.2. *A Priori Reasoning*

If the growth effects of trade liberalisation are 'just' transitional dynamics, it is still worth asking how large they are likely to be. Suppose that the transition is spread over, say, twenty years, the issue is essentially what is the income gain due to liberalisation.

Simple Harberger triangles from a competitive model rarely identify losses from trade restrictions larger than 2% of GDP. These are far too small to produce significant changes in growth but there are several reasons for expecting more. Recognising some rectangles, as in Krueger's (1974) model of rent-seeking, considerably increases the static gains. Similarly, if we add imperfect competition to the model the consumption and production gains from trade reform will tend to increase. For example, in CGE modelling exercises, adding in increasing returns and large group monopolistic competition often more than doubles the estimated effects of trade reform (Francois *et al.*, 1996). If one assumes small group models of oligopoly – surely more appropriate to developing countries – the gains are usually larger still as rationalisation effects occur (Rodrik, 1988; Gasiorek *et al.*, 1992). Allowing investment and the capital stock to increase following the efficiency gains from trade liberalisation, as in Baldwin (1992), further doubles or trebles the estimated GDP effects (although not the welfare effects), see, for example, Francois *et al.* (1996) or Harrison *et al.* (1997).

According to Romer (1994) the principal effect of trade restrictions is to reduce the supply of intermediate goods to an economy. Recognising that this can have infra-marginal effects on productivity he argues that overlooking this effect leads to a several-fold under-estimate of the production penalty of protection. Romer's effect will show up in the data as a positive relationship between trade liberalisation and productivity and one can think of further reasons why opening trade may give a one-off boost to productivity – e.g. competition stimulating technology adoption and adaptation, or the elimination of x-inefficiency.

The upshot of all this is that, while eliminating Harberger triangles alone seems unlikely ever to boost transitional growth rates detectably, more sophisticated models of international trade do appear to promise gains that would be significant over two or three decades. One direct verification of this is Rutherford and Tarr (2002) who implement a 'Romeresque' model over a more-or-less infinite horizon.[3] They find that reducing a uniform 20% tariff to 10% increases the under-

[2] Jones finds the same constancy of growth in other OECD countries once he allows for a gradually subsiding post-world-war II catch-up.

[3] They model a 54 year horizon explicitly and set end conditions to reflect optimisation to infinity roughly.

lying steady-state growth rate of 2% p.a. to 2.6% p.a. over first decade and 2.2% p.a. over the first five decades. Even after these fifty years the annual growth rate is 2.1% p.a.

None of this modelling guarantees significant returns to trade liberalisation, but it does suggest that is worth looking for them empirically. Moreover, although Rutherford and Tarr's model contains only level effects and transitional dynamics, their very long duration suggests that it will be difficult to distinguish them from changes in steady-state growth rates empirically, especially in post-war data. Given that levels of openness reflect previous trade liberalisation (since all economies were pretty closed in 1945), it is easy to imagine empirical studies that link openness to observed growth rates even though over an infinite horizon it should have no such effect. For this reason in discussing the various results from this literature below I do not make much out of whether they relate openness or liberalisation to growth, although of course in principle it is a very important distinction.

### 1.3. *The Direct Evidence*

Over the 1990s the conviction that trade liberalisation or openness was good for growth was fostered by some visible and well-promoted cross-country studies, e.g. Dollar (1992), Sachs and Warner (1995), Edwards (1998) and Frankel and Romer (1999). These, however, received, and by and large deserved, pretty severe criticism from Rodriguez and Rodrik (2001), who argue, *inter alia*, that their measures of openness are flawed and their econometrics weak.

Establishing an empirical link between liberal trade and growth faces at least four difficulties – see Winters (2003). First, there is the definition of 'openness'. In the context of policy advice, it is most directly associated with a liberal trade regime (low tariffs, very few non-tariff barriers etc.) but in fact that is rarely the concept used in empirical work. Thus, for example, Dollar's (1992) results rely heavily on the volatility of the real exchange rate, while Sachs and Warner (1995) combine high tariff and non-tariff measures with high black market exchange rate premia, socialism and the monopolisation of exports to identify non-open economies. Pritchett (1996) shows the trade indicators are only poorly correlated with other indicators of openness, while Harrison (1996), Hanson and Harrison (1999) and Rodriguez and Rodrik (2001) show that most of Sachs and Warner's explanatory power comes from the non-trade components of their measure.[4]

Second, once one comes inside the boundary of near autarchy, measuring trade stances across countries is difficult. For example, even aggregating tariffs correctly is complex – see Anderson and Neary (1996), whose measure depends on imports being separable from domestic goods and services and on an assumed elasticity. Then one needs to measure and aggregate quantitative restrictions and make allowances for the effectiveness and predictability of enforcement and collection.

[4] The use of policy-measures equates trade liberalisation with laissez-faire, but for outcome measures, e.g. trade shares, openness might be induced or at least accompanied by considerable intervention, as, for example, is asserted to have applied in East Asia, e.g. Rodrik (1995, 1997).

Such measurement problems are less significant for panel data measuring changes in trade policy for a single country, although even here Anderson (1998) shows that different measures point in different directions. Nonetheless, Vamvakidis' (1999) results, based on a forty-year panel for over one hundred countries, are more convincing than those of purely cross-section studies. Vamvakidis concludes that multilateral liberalisations over the period 1950–89 were associated with increases in rates of growth, while discriminatory regional trading agreements were not.[5]

Third, causation is extremely difficult to establish. Does trade liberalisation result *in*, or *from*, economic growth? Frankel and Romer (1999) and Irwin and Tervio (2002) address this problem by examining the effects of the component of openness that is independent of economic growth. This is the part of bilateral trade flows that is explained by the genuinely exogenous variables: population, land area, borders and distances. This component appears to explain a significant proportion of the differences in income levels and growth performance between countries, and from this the authors cautiously suggest a general relationship running from increased trade to increased growth. The problem, however, as Rodriguez and Rodrik (2001) and Brock and Durlauf (2001) observe, is that such geographical variables could have effects on growth in their own right and that this alone could explain the significance of the instrumental estimate of trade constructed out of them. For example, geography may influence health, endowments or institutions, any one of which could affect growth. These concerns have, however, recently been answered by Frankel and Rose (2002) who repeat the instrumental variables approach of Frankel and Romer and show that the basic conclusion is robust to the inclusion of geographical and institutional variables in the growth equation. This suggests that openness does indeed play a role even after allowing for geography.[6]

Causation is a particular problem in studies that relate growth to openness measured directly – usually, these days, as (*exports* + *imports*)/*GDP*. Such openness could clearly be endogenous for both the export and the import share seem likely to vary with income levels. It could also be a threat even when one works with directly measured trade policy, such as average tariffs, for, at least in the short run, the pressure for protection increases as growth falters – see, for example, Bohara and Kaempfer (1991).

The fourth complication is that for liberal trade policies to have a long-lived effect on growth almost certainly requires their combination with other good policies such as those that encourage investment, allow effective conflict resolution and promote human capital accumulation. Unfortunately the linear regression model, which is standard to this literature, is not well equipped to identify the necessity of variables rather than their additivity in the growth process. Hints of the importance of these policies, however, can be found in exercises identifying the structural relationships through which openness effects growth. Thus, for

[5] Vamvakidis considers liberalisations only up to 1989 in order to leave enough post-reform data to identify growth effects.

[6] I return to this issue in Section 2.4 below.

example, Taylor (1998) and Wacziarg (2001) both find that investment is a key link and thus imply that poor investment policies could undermine the benefits of trade liberalisation.

I return to other policies below, but two methodological points might usefully be made at this stage. Brock and Durlauf (2001), in a fairly complex discussion of the the statistician's concept of exchangeability, argue that growth theory is too open to be adequately tested with the economists' traditional regression tools. There are too many potential variables and too little theory about model structure to allow classical inference to work. Moreover, they argue, the usual search for robustness – the significance and consistency in sign of a particular variable across a range of specifications – is futile if the true determinants of growth are, in fact, highly correlated. Rather, Brock and Durlauf suggest using policy-makers' objectives to identify the trade-offs between different types of error, and from this conducting specification searches and estimation in an explicitly decision-theoretical way, recognising the wide bounds of uncertainty. This is challenging advice, which has yet to be applied to the role of trade liberalisation in growth, but it is a salutary warning about just how cautious we should be about growth econometrics.

The second general observation comes from Baldwin (2002), who argues that the quest to isolate the effects of trade liberalisation on growth is misguided. He argues that trade liberalisation has never been advanced or implemented as an isolated policy so that the only useful question is how it fares as part of a package including, say, sound macro and fiscal policies. Baldwin concludes that, in this context, openness is a positive force for growth. There are clearly questions as to what such packages comprise and it is not difficult to invent examples in which the benefits of other policies are mis-attributed to trade policy. Nevertheless, that liberal trade policy generally has a role within effective stabilisation and structural packages seems hard to deny completely.

Despite the econometric difficulties of establishing beyond doubt from cross-sections that openness enhances growth, the weight of the evidence is quite clearly in that direction. Jones (2001) offers a measured assessment and one might also note the frequency with which some sort of openness measure proves important in broader studies of growth – e.g. Easterly and Levine (2001). Certainly, there is no coherent body of evidence that trade restrictions generally stimulate growth, as even Rodriguez and Rodrik concede. The question, then, is where else can we turn for evidence?

First, there is further evidence from detailed case studies of particular countries and/or growth events. Pritchett (2000) argues that these offer a more promising approach to empirical growth research than do cross-country regressions, and Srinivasan and Bhagwati (2001) chide the economics profession for forgetting these in their enthusiasm for the latter.[7] Case studies find a wide variety of causes and channels for growth, and frequently find openness at the very heart of the matter – see, for example, the NBER study summarised in Krueger (1978). As

[7] They argue that Rodriguez and Rodrik's strictures on the cross-country studies should not undermine one's confidence that openness enhances growth, because that view should never have been based on those studies in the first place.

before, however, the case for openness in general is stronger than that for trade liberalisation alone.

### 1.4. *The Indirect Evidence - Trade and Productivity*

Second, there is also indirect evidence that examines the steps in the causal relationship between trade liberalisation and growth. The main issue here is the effect on productivity. An influential cross-country analysis is Coe *et al.* (1997). Developing countries are assumed to get access to their OECD trading partners' stocks of knowledge (measured by accumulated investment in R & D) in proportion to their imports of capital goods from those partners. Thus import-weighted sums of industrial countries' knowledge stocks are constructed to reflect developing countries' access to foreign knowledge. Coe *et al.* find that, interacted with the importing country's openness, this measure has a statistically significant positive effect on the growth in total factor productivity (TFP).

While these results are instructive, Coe *et al.* do not formally test trade against other possible conduits for knowledge and Keller (1998, 2000) has suggested that their approach is no better than would be obtained from a random weighting of countries' knowledge stocks.[8] One way of reconciling these conflicting results is to relax the strong bilateralism in Coe *et al.*'s access to knowledge measure. The latter implies that the only way for, say, Bolivia to obtain French knowledge is to import equipment from France. But if the US imports from France (and so, by hypothesis, accesses French knowledge) then Bolivia's imports from the US should give it at least some access to French knowledge. Lumenga-Neso *et al.* (2001), who advance this explanation, show that recognising such indirect knowledge flows offers a better explanation of productivity growth than any of the earlier studies.

A second approach to the link between trade liberalisation and productivity is cross-sectoral studies for individual countries. Many of these have shown that reductions in trade barriers were followed by significant increases in productivity, generally because of increased import competition, see, for example, Hay (2001) and Ferriera and Rossi (2001) on Brazil, Jonsson and Subramanian (1999) on South Africa and Lee (1996) on Korea. Kim (2000), on the other hand, also on Korea, suggests that most of the apparent TFP advance is actually due to the compression of margins and to economies of scale. Import competition makes some contribution via these effects, and also directly on 'technology', but overall Kim argues that it was not the major force.

The sectoral studies relate a sector's TFP to its own trade barriers and thus imply that competition is the causal link. But for general liberalisations it is likely that barriers on imported inputs also fall and this could be equally important. At an aggregate and sectoral level Esfahani (1991) and Feenstra *et al.* (1997) suggest such a link, as do Tybout and Westbrook (1995) at the firm level. The last suggest, for Mexico over 1984–90, that there were strong gains from rationalisation (the shrinking or elimination of inefficient firms), that cheaper intermediates stimu-

[8] Coe and Hoffmaister (1999) have, however, challenged the randomness of Keller's 'random' weights.

lated productivity and that competition from imports stimulated technical efficiency (with the strongest effects in the industries that were already the most open).

Firm level data also allow us to test the perennial claim that exporting is the key to technological advance. While macro studies or case-studies have suggested links to productivity, enterprise level data have shown a much more nuanced picture. Bigsten *et al.* (1998) find positive stimuli from exports to productivity in Africa and Kraay (1997) is ambiguous for China; Tybout and Westbrook (1995) and Aw *et al.* (1999), however, find little evidence for them in Latin America and Asia, respectively. The fundamental problem is, again, one of causation: efficiency and exporting are highly correlated because efficient firms export.[9] Hence researchers must first identify this link (by carefully modelling the timing of changes in exports and productivity) if they are then to isolate the reverse one. Tybout (2000) suggests that the differences between his results and those on Africa and China may arise because data shortages obliged the latter pair to use much simpler dynamic structures than he used.

## 2. Trade Liberalisation and Other Policies

I return now to the substantive aspects of the interaction between trade liberalisation and other policies in generating economic growth. Liberal trade policies are likely to boost income in most circumstances, because they enlarge the set of opportunities for economic agents,[10] but a longer term effect on growth requires combination with other good policies as well. The latter point is regurarly made by the Bretton Woods institutions in their policy advice, although Mosley (2000) argues that their attempts to prove it have not been very successful.[11] This Section discusses several ways in which trade liberalisation and growth are linked via other policies and institutions, including the possibility that the latter are influenced by the trade stance, as Krueger (1978, 1990) argued long ago.

### 2.1. *Corruption*

Perhaps the most important dimension is corruption, although in truth there is much we have yet to understand about it. Ades and Di Tella (1997, 1999) show a clear cross-country connection between higher rents, stemming from things such as active industrial policy or low degrees of openness, and more corruption. The latter, in turn, reduces investment and medium-term growth. Wei (2000), however, suggests another reason for the corruption-openness link: open countries face greater losses from corruption than less open ones, because corruption impinges

[9] The same causation difficulty arises in interpreting the observation that where a region exports heavily, all firms are more productive: is it positive spill-overs or comparative advantage?.

[10] The main exception is in the presence of severe second-best complications.

[11] Mosley goes on to argue that growth responds positively to higher levels of effective protection (at least in poorer countries). Unfortunately, however, his empirics seem flawed. Effective protection is significant only when weighted by total factor productivity (TFP) growth, which is clearly likely to be correlated with growth itself.

disproportionately on foreign transactions. As a result they have greater incentives to develop better institutions. He finds evidence for this theory in two cross-country relationships. First, corruption is correlated with 'natural openness' (essentially the Frankel-Romer variable, which is exogenous) but not with 'residual openness' (the difference between actual and natural openness, which is probably related to policies). Second, more open countries pay their civil servants better, suggesting that they value better administration more highly (although there may be difficulties over the direction of causation here).

At a concrete level, trade policy can contribute significantly to the fight against corruption.[12] The most important aspects are the simplest: the less restrictive is trade policy, the lower are the incentives for corruption while simpler more transparent and non-discretionary policies reduce the scope for corruption. Thus if tariffs or other barriers exist there are important benefits to their being uniform, stable, and widely published. Uniformity over sources of imports is at least as important as uniformity over types of import, for the origin of a good is typically easier to falsify than its nature. The rules of origin that accompany preferential trading arrangements, are burdensome to the honest trader and a great opportunity for less honest ones.

A classic example of success in this dimension is Chile, which transformed its economic performance and its public administrative standards over two decades. Chile abolished QRs and reduced tariffs from very high and dispersed rates to a virtually uniform 10% over the period 1974–9. Moreover, although the economic crisis of the early 1980s led to dramatic increases in tariffs (up to 35% in 1984), uniformity was maintained and the various steps in their de-escalation pre-announced and faithfully implemented. Chile's subsequent growth performance was wholly unlike the rest of Latin America's. At a more general level, Gatti and Fisman (2000) makes the argument for tariff uniformity and shows that corruption in trade administration is positively associated with the variance of tariff rates across commodities.

### 2.2. *Inflation*

The other dimension of openness and policy on which we have evidence concerns inflation. Romer (1993) suggests that because real depreciation is more costly in open economies, such economies will be more careful to avoid it. That in turn makes them less likely to run the risks of excessive money creation and inflation. He finds that inflation is, indeed, lower for open economies.

### 2.3. *Investment Policy*

Investment is a likely route through which corruption and inflation reduce growth, but it also has other determinants. These lie at the centre of Rodrik's (1995, 1997) view that the Asian miracle was due to strong incentives to invest (policy or otherwise) which increased both imports of capital goods and the supply of exports

[12] See UNDP (1997) for a general treatment of corruption.

with which to pay for them. He argues that direct export incentives, via subsidies or devaluation, could not explain Korea's or Taiwan's export booms because they did not vary much over time.

It is not correct, however, to infer from this that openness did not matter. Srinivasan and Bhagwati (2001) note that openness (i.e. the ability to export for reasonable returns) was the *sine qua non* of investment because one needs to sell the output on large markets where it will not drive prices down. Similarly, if markets for imported capital equipment had not been open, the whole process would never have got underway. Thus Rodrik's is a more nuanced view of openness and growth than many, but not a fundamentally antipathetic one.

Investment rates appear to be a robust correlate of growth – see, for example, Levine and Renelt (1992) and Sala-i-Martin (1997) – and, as noted, Taylor (1998) and Wacziarg (2001) argue that it is the principal route through which trade liberalisation has been effective. Of course in the basic neo-classical (Solow) model growth is ultimately independent of investment but even it admits medium-term effects (and Wacziarg considers growth only over five year periods). Moreover, endogenous growth models and other classical models (Srinivasan, 1999) imply a direct growth bonus from investment.

The strength of the investment-growth link suggests the need to ensure that investment is both attractive and feasible if trade-induced growth is to occur. Thus issues such as property rights, peace and financial depth are likely to be necessary conditions for success. That warring economies do poorly is incontrovertible – see, for example, Easterly (2001) – while Crafts (2000) identifies the development of domestic institutions to ensure honest and effective financial intermediation as a high priority.

### 2.4. *Institutions for Growth*

It is now widely recognised that institutions play a pivotal role in economic growth and development. This sub-section briefly examines the interactions between institutions and openness. Early contributions identifying the centrality of institutions came from luminaries such as Douglass North and Mancur Olsen – see North (1990) and Olsen (1996) for summaries. However, in the context of openness and growth the main protagonist has been Rodrik.

Rodrik (1999*a, b*) represents the role of institutions as follows

$$\Delta growth = f[-external\ shock(latent\ social\ conflict/institutions\ of\ conflict\ management)]$$

External shocks are represented in a number of ways but most obviously by the change in the terms of trade; latent social conflict is measured by either income inequality or ethnic fractionalisation, and institutions of conflict management measured by democracy, the rule of law or public spending on social insurance.

This equation postulates that the change in growth is a function of the size of the shocks faced by an economy arbitrated by its ability to deal with them. Latent social conflict increases the burden of a negative shock, so that a shock reducing income directly by $x\%$ can cost several times that if it induces political conflict or stalemate in political management. Appropriate institutions, however, can greatly reduce the multiplier, by allowing societies to make the necessary adjustments quickly and without costly side-squabbles. They have two roles in Rodrik's view. They ease the pain of adjustment, possibly spreading it out so that no section of society feels that it is bearing a disproportionate share and they legitimise decisions (implicit or explicit) that certain parts of society must bear costs, so that unavoidable costs can be borne without leading to social or political collapse. Rodrik's cross-section estimates suggest a slightly mixed story but overall he finds the expected relationships between the postulated variables and changes in economic growth between 1960–5 and 1975–89.

Rodrik (2000*b*) addresses the question of what institutions matter and how to achieve them. On the former he identifies five critical areas:

- Property rights – strictly control over property rather than legal rights *per se*;
- Regulatory institutions to correct externalities, information failures and market power – such as anti-trust bodies, banking supervision and, more controversially, co-ordination of major investment decisions, as Rodrik argues was provided by Korean and Taiwanese economic intervention;
- Institutions for macroeconomic stabilisation – e.g. a lender of last resort;
- Social Insurance – these are often transfer programmes but Rodrik argues that other institutions such as jobs-for-life can also play the same role; and
- Institutions to manage social conflict as discussed above.

On the issue of how to acquire institutions, Rodrik argues that there is no single optimal set of institutions. There are many ways of achieving the same objectives and the interactions between institutions mean that the package needs to be considered as a whole rather than piece by piece. He also argues that institutions will typically have to evolve locally by trial and error, even though this takes time and can involve mistakes.

Tests of the long-run effects of institutions include Hall and Jones (1997) and Acemoglu *et al.* (2001). The latter relate development over many decades to institutions but instrument the latter with countries' death rates among European settlers in colonial times. Where benign geography rendered these low enough to make long-term settlement viable, the Europeans imported their domestic institutions and prospered, e.g. in North America, Australasia and South Africa. Where, on the other hand, health hazards discouraged permanent settlement, institutions were exploitative and fragile and development has not occurred.

More recently, Rodrik *et al.* (2002) (RST) have argued that institutions far outperform geography and openness as explanations of real income per head and, indeed, that given institutions, openness has an (insignificantly) negative effect. They find, however, that openness partly explains the quality of institutions and so has a positive indirect effect on incomes. Its total effect, measured in terms of the effects of a one standard deviation change on income level, is about one-quarter of that of institutions. In all of this RST are careful to instrument openness and institutional quality to avoid the danger of their being determined by, rather than determining, growth.

RST measure institutional quality mainly by Kaufmann *et al.*'s (2002) composite index for the 'rule of law', which includes 'perceptions of the incidence of both violent and non-violent crime, the effectiveness and predictability of the judiciary, and the enforceability of contracts' (p. 6). They follow Acemoglu *et al.* (2001), however, by instrumenting this with colonial mortality, or, the shares of the population speaking a European language.

The interpretation of RST's results is quite subtle, as they, themselves, recognise. Perceptions are the key to investment behaviour, so the question of how to influence them is important. Openness apparently explains at least some of their variance and so could have an important signalling role. RST argue clearly that their theory is that institutional quality determines income and that it is, actually, quite variable through time. They stress that settler mortality is only an instrument, not, as Acemoglu *et al.* hint and Easterly and Levine (2001) assert, the driver of the results *per se*. Nonetheless, their empirical methodology leaves them explaining income levels by openness, which is variable through time and manipulable via policy, and colonial mortality and distance from the equator which are obviously not.

If one heeds Brock and Durlauf's advice and thinks about policy-makers' objectives, the implication of RST is to pursue openness vigorously, for it is the only thing in this model that can be manipulated and it is far from ineffective in its indirect effects. Certainly one would also want to pursue other means of improving institutions, but, as RST note, we have little idea how to do this and plenty of indications that doing so is difficult.

In developing institutions a critical issue is their legitimacy. Adopting foreign institutions can often be an efficient way of short-cutting the learning process that Rodrik writes of, and indeed good policy-making will always seek to learn from others' experience. The requirement, however, is that the institutions be sought as solutions to *locally identified* problems and be *adapted to local needs and conditions*. There is a world of difference between a society facing a problem and looking abroad for something to adapt to its own needs and an external force declaring that such-and-such an institution will be good for it.

At least part of the job of institutions is to codify solutions to distributional conflicts. Institutions help to ensure that the same rules apply through time, and thus make it easier for losers in 'issue A' to accept their losses because they believe that on future 'issue B' they will reap corresponding gains. But institutions can only assist in finding such solutions if, broadly speaking, they push in the direction in which society wishes to go anyway.

Although Rodrik (2000*a*) argues passionately that international financial institutions should not impose specific institutional structures on developing countries, he goes on to say that it is reasonable to insist on basic human rights and democracy. He adduces some evidence that while democracy has no significant effect on growth, it is associated with greater stability in growth, investment and consumption, better responses to negative shocks and more equal distributions of personal income and of rents between labour and capital. He concludes of democracy that '[i]f there is one area where institutional conditionality is both appropriate and of great economic value ... this is it'.

I would make two caveats. First, while democracy may be laudable, it is not clear that the international community, let alone international financial institutions, have the right to insist on it. If, in Rodrik's phrase, democracy is a 'meta-institution', this would be meta-conditionality: it would be interference of the deepest kind, and it could undermine the legitimacy of governments and their willingness to interact with the international community at all.

Second, causality is important here as elsewhere. Clague *et al.* (1997) observe that the factors associated with lasting democracy – e.g. equality, racial harmony, clean bureaucracy – are also associated with better economic policy directly. They identify regime stability as an important dimension of the pro-growth environment and note that switches from democracy to autocracy tend to be associated with improving property rights (their touchstone of the institutional contribution to economic growth). In other words, while the call to democracy is doubtless uplifting and something one might encourage within countries, it is far from proven as a tool for the international community to wield in the search for economic development.

### 2.5. *Education*

Possibly top of any *a priori* list of the causes of economic growth is education, although simple exercises that include education variables in cross-country growth equations have frequently not provided convincing proof (e.g. Hanushek, 1995; Behrman, 1999). The role of education is multi-dimensional. It is likely to induce flexibility (education imparts transferable skills). It brings its own rewards in terms of productivity, so that increasing human capital will lead to increased output. Education also appears to have strong payoffs in terms of health and in social and political capital. Finally, it is almost certainly necessary to facilitate the absorption of new technologies – Abramovitz and David (1996). Since in the long run technology is the key to sustained growth – merely accumulating human or physical capital will eventually encounter diminishing returns – this argument is a key one. It is also crucial in the context of openness, for this too is often argued to operate primarily by opening up the economy to new technologies. Education is therefore likely to be another necessary concomitant policy if openness is to bring continuing and extensive, dynamic benefits.

A potentially important dimension of this question for developing countries is whether openness stimulates the demand for education or not. Simple Stolper-Samuelson theory would suggest that as a skill-scarce economy opens up, the returns to skill will decline and with them the incentives for education – see Wood and Ridao-Cano (1999), who find some suggestion of such a problem empirically. Extending the model, however, e.g. by allowing for multi-dimensional Stolper-Samuelson, endogenous growth with constant returns to R & D, or a skills-bias in tradables as opposed to non-tradables, could all restore a positive link between openness and the returns to education (see Arbache *et al.*, in this issue of the Journal). In addition openness might permit more efficient educational technologies - either importing better techniques and equipment, or, for higher education, permitting education abroad, although the latter may raise worries about the brain drain.[13]

[13] See Commander *et al.* (2002) for a general account of recent work on the brain drain.

2.6. *The Practicalities of Liberalisation: Making Trade-offs*

The bulk of this paper has concerned the effects of trade liberalisation but in this final sub-section I turn very briefly to implementing a trade liberalisation. The list of concomitant policies discussed above is formidable but that does not necessarily imply that there are difficult trade-offs to be made. At a technical level, the effects of many of the policies are essentially additive to those of trade liberalisation and so require no trading off at all.

But this is not always true. One trade-off between trade liberalisation and other objectives can arise in the short run if too large a shock would lead to the complete collapse of a market. For example, local labour markets can seize up in the face of large-scale redundancies because natural mobility evaporates: incumbents cease to leave their jobs speculatively for fear of not finding another. This is essentially a matter of timing – perhaps of staggering the trade liberalisation, or ensuring that it does not co-incide with a negative macro shock.

Similarly, balance of payments effects may need addressing. Most trade liberalisations imply larger reductions in barriers to imports than to exports and hence at fixed exchange rates are likely to entail trade-deficits, as Santos-Paulino and Thirlwall (2003) find. The answer is a real depreciation but this, of course, has consequences for inflation and stabilisation. Hence trade-offs are required at least so far as timing is concerned if governments tackle stabilisation and trade reform simultaneously. Poland used depreciation to preserve the balance of trade and stimulate the tradables sector in the 1990s, as did Chile in the 1970s.

Failure to choose and maintain a realistic real exchange rate has been one of the main causes of the failure of trade liberalisations in developing countries according to Nash and Takacs (1998). The other was failure to address the fiscal consequences of tariff revenue losses. These are far from inevitable, especially if non-tariff barriers are converted into tariffs, exemptions are reduced and collections improved, but they can pose a problem for poorer countries in which trade taxes account for large proportions of total revenue. Time may be required to develop alternative sources of revenue, so, again trade-offs over timing may be necessary.

There are also potential political trade-offs. Societies can exhibit reform fatigue whereby they become resentful of too much, or too long a period of, change. In this case, it is necessary to fix priorities and a major problem becomes maintaining credibility. It is probably better to announce the whole package at the beginning but ensure that not everyone has to change at once. Then governments need to recruit the early movers into the coalition to keep the later ones moving.

Very similar is politician/bureaucratic fatigue. If reform requires constant monitoring or political promotion, it might overwhelm a finite bureaucracy or body-politic. The diffusion of effort across too many objectives is a well-known cause of failure both in business and in politics and this may be a constraint in many countries. One implication is to seek reforms that are simple to implement and maintain. In this regard, a uniform tariff has huge attractions: it is simple to administer and simple to defend from interest groups, and thus takes up very little official effort to maintain. The Chilean reform of the 1970s explicitly used tariff uniformity as a buttress against lobbying and special interests – Edwards and Lederman (2001).

The major area in which administrative constraints bind, however, is in the various institutional reforms suggested above. Institutions take time to design technically and, given the importance of building up their legitimacy and ownership among the population, they also require a good deal of political time. Moreover, no one gets institutions right first time: they require continuing monitoring and adjustment. If, as I argue in the next paragraph, there are often advantages to proceeding on a broad front in order to maintain some semblance of fairness, institutional reforms are likely to require a long time and considerable official skill to achieve.

Political trade-offs also occur at a more micro level as governments have to build up support for their policies, even in the most repressive of dictatorships. Edwards and Lederman (2001) document how Chilean firms were compensated for trade reform by depreciation and by labour market reforms to reduce their costs, and how powerful agricultural interests had to be assuaged. Moreover, this is not just a matter of sordid log-rolling; it also resides in what Corden (1984) calls the 'Hicksian optimism', that although any single efficiency-enhancing reform will hurt someone, if you package enough of them together, their negative effects will be netted out and nearly everyone will gain. This is one of the major reasons for proceeding on a broad front.

## 3. Conclusion

This paper has documented the strong presumption that trade liberalisation contributes positively to economic performance. For a variety of reasons, the level of proof remains a little less than one might wish but the preponderance of evidence certainly favours that conclusion. Part of the benefits of trade liberalisation depends on other policies and institutions being supportive but there is also evidence that openness actually induces improvements in these dimensions. Given that trade liberalisation is administratively simple to implement – indeed a transparent and liberal policy releases administrative resources for other tasks – the case for making it part of a pro-growth policy cocktail is very strong.

*University of Sussex, CEPR*

## References

Abramovitz, M. and David, P. A. (1996). 'Convergence and deferred catch-up: productivity leadership and the waning of American exceptionalism', *The Mosaic of Economic Growth*, pp. 21–62, California: Stanford University Press.

Acemoglu, D., Johnson, S. and Robinson, J. A. (2001). 'The colonial origins of comparative development: an empirical investigation', *American Economic Review*, vol. 91 (5), (December), pp. 1369–401.

Ades, A. and Di Tella, R. (1997). 'National champions and corruption: some unpleasant interventionist arithmetic', ECONOMIC JOURNAL, vol. 107, (July), pp. 1023–42.

Ades, A. and Di Tella, R. (1999). 'Rents, competition and corruption', *American Economic Review*, vol. 89 (4), (September), pp. 982–93.

Anderson, J. E. and Neary, P. J. (1996). 'A new approach to evaluating trade policy', *Review of Economic Studies*, vol. 63, pp. 107–25.

Anderson, J. E. (1998). 'Trade restrictiveness benchmarks', ECONOMIC JOURNAL, vol. 108, pp. 1111–25.

Arbache, J., Dickerson, A. and Green, F. (2003). 'Trade liberalisation and wages in developing countries', ECONOMIC JOURNAL, this issue, pp. F73–96.

Aw, B. Y., Chung, S. and Roberts, M. J. (1999). 'Productivity and turnover in the export market: micro-level evidence from the Republic of Korea and Taiwan (China)', *The World Bank Economic Review*, vol. 14 (1), (January), pp. 65–90.

Baldwin, Richard E. (1992). 'Measurable dynamic gains from trade', *Journal of Political Economy*, vol. 100 (1), pp. 162–74.

Baldwin, Robert E. (2002). 'Openness and growth: what's the empirical relationship', in Baldwin and Winters (forthcoming).

Baldwin, R. E. and Winters, L. A. (forthcoming). *Challenges to Globalisation: Analysing the Economics*, Chicago: University of Chicago Press for National Bureau of Economic Research.

Behrman, J. (1999). 'Labour markets in developing countries'. in (O. Ashenfelter, and D. Card, eds.), *Handbook of Labour Economics*, vol. 3, Elsevier Science B. V.

Bigsten, A. *et al.* (1998). 'Exports and firm-level efficiency in African manufacturing', mimeo, Centre for Study of African Economies, Oxford University.

Bohara, A. K. and Kaempfer, W. H. (1991). 'A test of tariff endogeneity in the United States', *American Economic Review*. vol. 81 (4), pp. 952–60.

Brock, W. A. and Durlauf, S. N. (2001). 'Growth empirics and reality', *The World Bank Economic Review*, vol. 15 (2), pp. 229–72.

Clague, C. *et al.* (1997). *Institutions and Economic Development: Growth and Governance in Less-Developed and Post-Socialist Countries*, Baltimore, MD: The John Hopkins University Press.

Coe, D. T., Helpman, E. and Hoffmaister, A. W. (1997). 'North-South R & D spillovers', ECONOMIC JOURNAL, vol. 107 (440) (January), pp. 134–49.

Coe, D. T. and Hoffmaister, A. W. (1999). 'Are there international R & D spillovers among randomly matched trade partners? A response to Keller', Working Paper of the International Monetary Fund, WP/99/18.

Commander, S., Kangasniemi, M. and Winters L. A. (2002). 'The brain drain: curse or boom? A survey of the literature', in Baldwin and Winters (forthcoming).

Corden, W. M. (1984). 'The normative theory of international trade', in (P. B. Kenen and R. W. Jones eds.), *Handbook of International Economics*, vol. 1, ch. 2, Amsterdam: North Holland.

Crafts, N. (2000). 'Globalisation and growth in the twentieth century', IMF Working Paper no. 00/44, March.

Dollar, D. (1992). 'Outward-oriented developing economies really do grow more rapidly: evidence from 95 LDCs, 1976–1985', *Economic Development and Cultural Change*, vol. 40 (3), pp. 523–44.

Easterly, W. (2001). *The Elusive Quest for Growth: Economists' Adventures and Misadventures in the Tropics*, Cambridge, MA: MIT Press.

Easterly, W. and Levine, R. (2001). 'It's not factor accumulation: stylised facts and growth models', *The World Bank Economic Review*, vol. 15 (2), pp. 177–220.

Edwards, S. (1998). 'Openness, productivity, and growth: what do we really know?', ECONOMIC JOURNAL, vol. 108 (2), pp. 383–98.

Edwards, S. and Lederman, D. (2001). 'The political economy of unilateral trade liberalisation: the case of Chile', in (J. Bhagwati ed.) *Going Alone*, Cambridge, MA: MIT Press.

Esfahani, H. S. (1991). 'Exports, imports, and economic growth in semi-industrialised countries', *Journal of Development Economics*, vol. 35 (1) (January), pp. 93–116.

Feenstra, R. C. et al. (1997). 'Testing endogenous growth in South Korea and Taiwan', National Bureau of Economic Research, Working Paper 6028.

Ferreira, P. C. and Rossi, J. L. (2001). 'New evidence on trade liberalisation and productivity growth', Ensaios Economicos da EPGE no. 433.

Francois, J. F., McDonald, B. and Nordström, H. (1996). 'The Uruguay round: a numerically based qualitative assessment', in (W. Martin and L. A. Winters eds.) *The Uruguay Round and the Developing Countries*, Cambridge: Cambridge University Press.

Frankel, J. A. and Romer, D. (1999). 'Does trade cause growth?', *American Economic Review*, vol. 89 (3) (June), pp. 379–99.

Frankel, J. and Rose, A. K. (2002). 'An estimate of the effect of common currencies on trade and growth', *Quarterly Journal of Economics*, vol. 117 (469), pp. 437–66.

Gasiorek, M., Smith, A. and Venables, A. J. (1992). '1992 trade and welfare – a general equilibrium model', in (L. A. Winters ed.), *Trade Flows and Trade Policy After 1992*, Cambridge: Cambridge University Press.

Gatti, R. and Fisman, R. (2000). 'Decentralisation and corruption: evidence across countries', World Bank working paper 2290 (February).

Hall, R. E. and Jones, C. I. (1997). 'Levels of economic activity across countries', *American Economic Review*, vol. 87 (2), pp. 173–7.

Hanson, G. and Harrison, A. (1999). 'Who gains from trade reform? Some remaining puzzles', *Journal of Development Economics*, vol. 59 (1), pp. 125–54.

Hanushek, E. A. (1995). 'Interpreting recent research on schooling in developing countries', *World Bank Research Observer*, vol. 10 (2), pp. 227–46.

Harrison, A. (1996). 'Openness and growth: a time-series, cross-country analysis for developing countries', *Journal of Development Economics*, vol. 48 (2), (March), pp. 419–47.

Harrison, G., Rutherford, W., Thomas, F and Tarr, D. G. (1997). 'Quantifying the Uruguay round', *Economic Journal*, vol. 107 (444), pp. 1405–30.

Hay, D. A. (2001). 'The post 1990 Brazilian trade liberalisation and the performance of large manufacturing firms:- productivity, market share and profits', *Economic Journal*, vol. 111 (473), pp. 620–41.

Irwin, D. A. and Tervio, M. (2002). 'Does trade raise income? Evidence from the twentieth century', *Journal of International Economics*, vol. 58 (1), pp. 1–18.

Jones, C. I. (1995). 'Time series tests of endogenous growth models', *Quarterly Journal of Economics*, vol. 110 (2), pp. 495–525.

Jones, C. I. (2001). 'Comment on trade policy and economic growth: a skeptic's guide to the cross-national evidence', by Francisco Rodriguez and Dani Rodrik, in (B. Bernanke, and K. S. Rogoff eds.) *Macroeconomics Annual 2000*, pp. 330–6, Cambridge, MA: MIT Press for NBER.

Jonsson, G. and Subramanian, A. (1999). 'Dynamic gains from trade: evidence from South Africa', *International Monetary Fund*, Working Paper no. WP/00/45.

Kaufmann, D., Kraay, A. and Zoido-Lobaton, P. (2002). 'Governance matters II – updated indicators for 2000/01', World Bank Policy Research Department Working Paper 2772.

Keller, W. (1998). 'Are international R & D spillovers trade-related? Analysing spillovers among randomly matched trade partners', *European Economic Review*, vol. 42 (8), (September), pp. 1469–81.

Keller, W. (2000). 'Do trade patterns and technology flows affect productivity growth?', *World Bank Economic Review*, vol. 14 (1), pp. 17–47.

Kim, E. (2000). 'Trade liberalisation and productivity growth in Korea manufacturing industries: price protection, market power, and scale efficiency', *Journal of Development Economics*, vol. 62 (1), pp. 55–83.

Kraay, A. (1997). 'Exports and economic performance: evidence from a panel of Chinese enterprises', mimeo, Development Research Group, The World Bank.

Krueger, A. O. (1974). 'The political economy of the rent-seeking society', *American Economic Review*, vol. 64 (3), pp. 291–303.

Krueger, A. O. (1978). 'Liberalisation attempts and consequences, liberalisation, direction of bias and economic growth', *Foreign Trade Regimes and Economic Development*, vol. 10, pp. 277–300, New York: National Bureau of Economic Research.

Krueger, A. O. (1990). 'Asian trade and growth lessons', *American Economic Review*, vol. 80 (2), (May), pp. 108–11.

Lee, J.-W. (1996). 'Government interventions and productivity growth', *Journal of Economic Growth*, vol. 1 (3), pp. 391–414.

Levine, R. and Renelt, D. (1992). 'A sensitivity analysis of cross-country growth regressions', *American Economic Review*, vol. 82 (4), pp. 942–63.

Lumenga-Neso, A., Olarreaga, M. and Schiff, M. (2001). 'On "indirect" trade-related R & D spillovers and growth', CEPR Discussion Paper, no. 2871.

Mosley, P. (2000). 'Globalisation, economic policy and convergence', *World Economy*, vol. 23 (5), (May), pp. 613–34.

Nash, J. and Tarkacs, W. (1998) (eds.). *Trade Policy Reforms: Lessons and Implications*, Washington, D.C: The World Bank.

North, D. C. (1990). *Institutions, Institutional Change and Economic Performance*, Cambridge: Cambridge University Press.

Olsen, M., J. (1996). 'Big bills left on the sidewalk: why some nations are rich and others poor', *Journal of Economic Perspectives*, vol. 10 (2), pp. 3–24.

Pritchett, L. (1996). 'Measuring outward orientation in developing countries: can it be done?', *Journal of Development Economics*, vol. 49 (2), pp. 307–35.

Pritchett, L. (2000). 'Understanding patterns of economic growth: searching for hills among plateaus, mountains and plains', *World Bank Economic Review*, vol. pp. 14 (2), 221–50.

Rodriguez, F. and Rodrik, D. (2001). 'Trade policy and economic growth: a skeptic's guide to the cross-national evidence', in (B. Bernanke, and K. S. Rogoff, eds.), *Macroeconomics Annual 2000*. pp. 261–324, Cambridge, MA: MIT Press for NBER.

Rodrik, D. (1988). 'Imperfect competition, scale economies and trade policy in developing countries', in (R. E. Baldwin, ed.), *Trade Policy Issues and Empirical Analysis*. University of Chicago Press for NBER.

Rodrik, D. (1995). 'Getting interventions right: how South Korea and Taiwan grew rich', *Economic Policy: A European Forum*, no. 20 (April), pp. 53–97.

Rodrik, D. (1997). 'Trade strategy, investment and exports: another look at East Asia', *Pacific Economic Review*, vol. 2 (1), (February), pp. 1–24.

Rodrik, D. (1999*a*). 'Where did all the growth go? External shocks, social conflict, and growth collapses', *Journal of Economic Growth*, vol. 4 (4), (December), pp. 385–412.

Rodrik, D. (1999*b*). 'The new global economy and developing countries: making openness work', Policy Essay no. 24, Washington, D.C., United States of America: Overseas Development Council; distributed by Johns Hopkins University Press, Baltimore.

Rodrik, D. (2000*a*). 'Comments on trade, growth and poverty', by D. Dollar, and A. Kraay, http://ksghome.harvard.edu/~.drodrik.academic.ksg/papers.html.

Rodrik, D. (2000*b*). 'Institutions for high-quality growth: what they are and how to acquire them'. National Bureau of Economic Research, Working Paper no. 7540.

Rodrik, D., Subramanian, A. and Trebbi, F. (2002). 'Institutions rule: the primacy of institutions over geography and integration in economic development', CEPR Discussion Paper, no. 3643. London: CEPR.

Romer, D. (1993). 'Openness and inflation: theory and evidence', *Quarterly Journal of Economics*, vol. 108 (4), (November), pp. 870–903.

Romer, P. (1994). 'New goods, old theory and the welfare cost of trade restrictions', *Journal of Development Economics*, vol. 43 (1), pp. 5–38.

Rutherford, T. F. and Tarr, D. G. (2002). 'Trade liberalisation, product variety and growth in a small open economy: a quantitative assessment', *Journal of International Economics*, vol. 56 (2), pp. 247–72.

Sachs, J. D. and Warner, A. M. (1995). 'Economic convergence and economic policies', *Brookings Papers in Economic Activity*, (1), pp. 1–95.

Sala-i-Martin, X. (1997), 'I just ran two million regressions', *American Economic Review*, vol. 87 (2), pp. 178–83.

Santos-Paulino, A. and Thirlwall, A. P. (2003). 'The impact of trade liberalisation on exports, imports, and the balance of payments in selected developing countries', ECONOMIC JOURNAL, this issue, F50–72.

Solow, R. M. (2001). 'Applying growth theory across countries', *The World Bank Economic Review*, vol. 15 (2), pp. 283–8.

Srinivasan, T. (1999). 'Trade orientation, trade liberalization and economic growth', in (G. Saxonhouse and T. N. Srinivasan, eds.), *Development, Duality, and the International Economic Regime*, Ann Arbor: University of Michigan Press.

Srinivasan, T. N. and Bhagwati, J. (2001). 'Outward-orientation and development: are revisionists right?', in (D. Lal and R. H. Snape, eds.), *Trade, Development and Political Economy: Essays in Honour of Anne O. Krueger*, New York: Palgrave.

Taylor, A. M. (1998). 'On the costs of inward-looking development: price distortions, growth and divergence in Latin America', *The Journal of Economic History*, vol. 58 (1), pp. 1–28.

Tybout, J. R. (2000). 'Manufacturing firms in developing countries: how well do they do, and why?', *Journal of Economic Literature*, vol. 38 (1), (March), pp. 11–44.

Tybout, J. R. and Westbrook, M. D. (1995). 'Trade liberalisation and the dimensions of efficiency change in Mexican manufacturing industries', *Journal of International Economics*, vol. 39, pp. 53–78.

UNDP (1997). *Corruption & Integrity Improvement Initiatives in Developing Countries*, Paris: UNDP.

Vamvakidis, A. (1999). 'Regional trade agreements versus broad liberalization: which path leads to faster growth? Time-series evidence', *IMF Staff Papers*, vol. 46 (1), (March), pp. 42–68.

Wacziarg, R. (2001). 'Measuring the dynamic gains from trade', *World Bank Economic Review*, vol. 15 (3), pp. 393–429.

Wei, S-J. (2000). 'Natural openness and good government', National Bureau of Economic Research, Working Paper no. 7765 (June).

Winters, L. A. (2002). 'Trade policies for poverty alleviation in developing countries', in (B. Hoekman, A. Mattoo, and A. English, eds.), *Development, Trade and the WTO*, pp. 28–37, Washington D.C.: The World Bank.

Winters, L. A. (2003). 'Trade policy as development policy: building on fifty years' experience', in (J. Toye ed.) *Trade and Development: Directions for the 21st Century*, pp. 62–81, Cheltenham: Edward Elgar.

Wood, A. and Ridao-Cano, C. (1999). 'Skill, trade and international inequality', *Oxford Economic Papers*, vol. 51 (1), pp. 89–119.

Journal of Economic Integration
22(4), December 2007; 819-851

# Trade Liberalisation and Poverty Dynamics in Vietnam

**Yoko Niimi**
*The World Bank*

**Puja Vasudeva Dutta**
*The World Bank*

**L. Alan Winters**
*University of Sussex*

## Abstract

*This paper explores the poverty impact of Vietnam's trade liberalisation over the 1990s and asks how well they could have been predicted from prior data. We identify policy changes and their major effects on trade and prices. We then seek the effects of these changes in a panel comprising 4,302 households observed in 1993 and 1998. Using a multinomial logit model, we find evidence that trade liberalisation influenced household poverty status and that considering trade effects would help to identify winners and losers a priori. We also find evidence that trade liberalisation reduced poverty substantially over the period 1993-1998.*

• **JEL classification:** F13, F14, I32, O15, O24

• **Keywords:** Trade policy, Poverty, Vietnam

*Corresponding address: Yoko Niimi, Development Research Group, The World Bank, 1818 H Street NW, Mail-stop MC3-303, Washington, DC 20433, USA. Tel: +1-202-4585912, Fax: +1-202-5221159, E-mail: yniimi@worldbank.org.

**Puja Vasudeva Dutta, Human Development Unit, The World Bank, 70 Lodi Estate, New Delhi 110003, India. Tel: +91(11) 41479156, Fax: +91(11)24619393, E-mail: pdutta@worldbank.org.

***L. Alan Winters, Department of Economics, University of Sussex, Brighton, BN1 9SN, UK. Tel: +44(0)1273-678332, Fax: +44(0)1273-673563, E-mail: L.A.Winters@sussex.ac.uk

# I. Introduction

The link between trade liberalisation and poverty is one of the most contentious areas of debate within the development community. Both sides of the debate, however, rely more on theory, rhetoric and anecdote than on solid empirical research. This paper starts to redress the balance through a study of the recent trade liberalisation in Vietnam using the conceptual framework developed by Winters (2000, 2002). In addition to the long-run effects operating through economic growth, Winters considers the static effects of trade shocks on households, directly via product and factor markets, and indirectly through changes in government revenues and social spending. This paper explores some aspects of the poverty effects of Vietnam's trade liberalisation over the 1990s and asks, in particular, how well the framework would have performed if it had been applied to this case at the outset.

Vietnam is an ideal candidate for such a test in the sense that it has two surveys of substantially the same households in 1992-1993 and 1997-1998 - the Vietnam Living Standards Surveys.[1] Hence throughout the paper we focus on this five year period, and because five years is too short a period to assess the impact of openness on economic growth,[2] on the static effects felt via prices, wages and employment. In another sense, however, Vietnam is less than ideal. Since the start of the *doi moi* reforms in 1986 the Vietnamese economy has been undergoing a more or less continuous transition from a centrally planned socialist to a market-oriented economy. Although this process has, at times, been halting and confused and is certainly not yet complete (see van Donge, White and Nghia (1999)), it seems to have had quite marked effects on the economy. Thus a major challenge for research of this kind is to identify the international trade reforms that have actually occurred, separate them from other shocks and trace their transmission through to poor households.

[1]These surveys were carried out by the General Statistical Office (GSO) and the Ministry of Planning and Investment, with financial assistance from the United Nations Development Programme (UNDP) and the Swedish International Development Agency (SIDA) and technical assistance from the World Bank.

[2]Given that it takes time for trade liberalisation to have an effect on the economy, a longer span of data, for instance between the early 1990s and early 2000s, must also be examined in future research. It should be noted, however, that the Vietnam Household Living Standard Survey (VHLSS) 2002 did not revisit the households that were surveyed both in 1992-93 and 1997-98, so the panel approach we adopt here would no be feasible for that period.

The next section briefly reviews the reforms undertaken in Vietnam during the 1990s and their impact on the Vietnamese economy. In section 3 the mechanisms through which these macro-level reforms impact households are analysed using the framework provided by Winters focusing on the price and the labour market channels. Section 4 explores the effect of trade liberalisation on poverty using the household survey data to estimate a multinomial logit model (and certain other models) of the transition between poverty and non-poverty incorporating the key trade links identified in the empirical analysis in the previous section. Section 5 concludes by asking how liberalisation appears to have affected poverty and, more directly, whether the maintained framework provides insight on the links between trade liberalisation and poverty.

## II. Economic Reform and Trade Liberalisation in Vietnam[3]

The process of 'economic renovation' or *doi moi* was set in motion in 1986 and gathered momentum in the early 1990s with the objective of transforming Vietnam from a centrally planned to a market economy. The institutional reforms during this period included the encouragement of the private sector and establishment of legal basis for contract, banking and financial sector reforms, taxation reforms, establishment of economic courts, consolidation of property rights, land reforms, and the rationalisation of state-owned enterprises (SOEs).

### A. External Sector Reform

An important facet of *doi moi* was the dramatic change in external sector policy from inward-oriented import substitution to outward-orientation. Vietnam's major external sector reforms included (see Niimi *et al.* (2003) for a more detailed review):

- The removal of constraints on trade outside the CMEA bloc;[4]
- The rationalisation and unification of the exchange rate in 1989 and further liberalisation of foreign exchange controls: by 1993 all foreign transactions were in convertible currency,

[3]This review draws on Andersen (1994), CIE (1998), Martin (2000) and CIEM (2001).

[4]The Council of Mutual Economic Assistance (CMEA) consisting of the former Soviet Union, Eastern European socialist countries and Cuba.

- The relaxation of import and export controls and a move towards a tariff based system of trade management,
- Export promotion and the establishment of export processing zones,
- The relaxation of controls on entry into foreign trading activity and the simplification and eventual elimination in 1998 of the licensing procedure,
- The initiation of an 'open door policy' to promote foreign investment and the creation of a legal framework to approve and regulate foreign direct investment (FDI), and
- Integration with the world economy via regional and multilateral trading agreements.

Customs tariffs were introduced in 1988 for the first time and the Harmonised System (HS) was introduced in 1992. By 1998 the management of imports of most consumer goods had shifted from quotas or licensing to tariffs although eight categories of goods remained under quantitative restrictions. The maximum and average tariff rates (especially on consumer goods) have remained high, and although the average tariff rates do not seem out of line with those in other developing countries, most imports fell in the higher tariff brackets (see Table 1). In addition, there have been several retrogressive measures in the form of rising export taxes, temporary prohibitions on imports of consumer goods, and other barriers introduced as anti-smuggling measures. Overall, both the import tariff and export tax systems are complex and suffer from frequent changes (CIEM, 2001), so that despite all the reforms, Vietnam's trade regime must be considered to

**Table 1.** Indicators of Nominal Tariff in Vietnam, 1992-2000

| | 1992 | 1993 | 1994 | 1995 | 1996 | 1997 | 1998 | 1999 | 2000 |
|---|---|---|---|---|---|---|---|---|---|
| Share of tariff lines | | | | | | | | | |
| *0-10 percent* | 68 | 66 | 66 | 66 | 64 | 63 | 63 | 59 | 60 |
| *Above 10-20 percent* | 15 | 14 | 13 | 13 | 12 | 13 | 12 | 10 | 9 |
| *Above 20-40%* | 15 | 15 | 16 | 16 | 18 | 18 | 19 | 21 | 21 |
| *Above 40%* | 2 | 5 | 5 | 5 | 6 | 6 | 6 | 10 | 10 |
| (No. of tariff lines) | (2813) | (2967) | (2934) | (3023) | (3180) | (3126) | (3163) | (6056) | (6341) |
| Average rate[a)] | 10.7 | 11.8 | 12.3 | 12.3 | 12.9 | 13.4 | 13.6 | 16.3 | 16.2 |
| Maximum rate | 120 | 150 | 200 | 200 | 100 | 200 | 60 | 100 | 100 |
| Standard deviation | 14.8 | 16.7 | 17.5 | 17.3 | 16.1 | 17.0 | 15.9 | 18.7 | 19.1 |
| Number of rates | 26 | 31 | 35 | 34 | 30 | 35 | 28 | 12 | 19 |

Source: CIEM (2001:17).
Note: a) Simple average

remain quite restrictive and interventionist (IMF, 1999).

With its multiple interventions and extensive use of administrative fiat, the complexity of Vietnam's trade policy regime makes it impossible to trace the effects of specific policy changes back to households. Hence we are obliged to use outcomes - prices and quantities - in order to identify the impact of the trade liberalisation. Relative prices and the openness of the Vietnamese economy have changed dramatically over the 1990s, so there is a strong presumption that the external sector will have had significant effects on poverty. Moreover, although Vietnam undertook dramatic reforms of both domestic and external policies so that there remains considerable uncertainty about precise attribution, it is entirely reasonable to assume that at least a significant proportion of the trade shock originated in trade policy changes.

**B. Macroeconomic Outcomes**

Despite their incompleteness, the impact of the reforms on the Vietnamese economy has been tremendous. The economy grew at approximately 7-8 percent per annum between 1990 and 2000 and over 5 percent even following the Asian crisis in 1997. Firm domestic credit policies, tight monetary policies and interest rate reforms stabilised the hyperinflation of the 1980s, and the exchange rate remained relatively stable after the rationalisation of the multiple exchange rate system and successive devaluations (CIE, 1998). The reforms induced large FDI inflows averaging 9 percent per annum of GDP between 1993 and 1997 although this declined after the Asian crisis in 1997. The data on FDI are weak, but the broad picture is that the majority was in the form of joint ventures with SOEs and was concentrated in high-cost, capital- and import-intensive industries with low employment impact (IMF, 1999).

Trade

The share of trade in GDP increased from about 52 percent to 71 percent between 1993 and 1998 (GSO statistics).[5] The external sector reforms stimulated strong export growth for commodities in which Vietnam apparently has a comparative advantage. By 2000 the combined exports of the textile and garments industry (one of the fastest growing export sectors) and the footwear industry were

[5]There are discrepancies in trade data between various sources, possibly due to the treatment of transit centres like Singapore, North Korea and Hong Kong (Apoteker, 1998). However, all sources tell the same sort of story about the increase in openness.

higher than those of the four chief agricultural exports - rice, coffee, rubber and marine products (CIEM, 2001; IMF, 1998, 2000). And this was despite the fact that Vietnam switched from being a net importer of rice in the 1980s to being the world's second largest exporter of rice by volume by 1996 (Nielsen, 2002). Imports continued to be dominated by machinery and intermediate goods (amounting to approximately 70 percent of total imports), reflecting both the industrialisation of the Vietnamese economy and the structure of protection with its bias against imports of consumer goods (IMF, 1998, 2000).

The rice sector

Since it figures so prominently in Vietnamese life, we should consider briefly the rice market. Niimi *et al.* (2004) discuss the sector in more detail. The de-collectivisation of agriculture and land reform in 1988 greatly increased the incentives to produce rice. Domestic prices were liberalised in 1989. Simultaneously, international trade in rice was liberalised with the result that exports boomed and prices rose. Between 1993 and 1998, our period of analysis, real rice prices (relative to the CPI) rose by nearly 30 percent. In a related development real fertiliser prices fell by 23 percent between 1992-1993 and 1997-1998. Since nearly all fertiliser requirements were met by imports and these were regulated by quota with the objective of stabilising domestic prices and keeping average prices significantly above world prices (Nielsen, 2002), we interpret this as a significant and conscious trade liberalisation.

To summarise, "the foundation for Vietnam's success - and the core of the *doi moi* program - has been a combination of liberalization, stabilization, institutional changes, and some structural reform" (Kokko, 1997:1). The economic reforms generated high growth during the 1990s characterised by increasing exports and foreign investment, expanding private sector as well as state enterprise activity, and declining inflation. The relatively egalitarian distribution of land, the stress on agriculture during *doi moi* and the subsequent high growth of the economy suggest that the restructuring of the economy might have had a favourable impact on the poor in Vietnam. Glewwe *et al.* (2002) find that, based on the official poverty line, absolute poverty incidence declined from 58.1 percent to 37.4 percent between 1992-1993 and 1997-1998.[6] The next section traces the product and labour market channels through which the trade reforms might be expected to have impacted poor

[6] Justino and Litchfield (2004) find that alternative poverty lines also imply strong declines in poverty.

households.

## III. Trade Liberalisation and Poverty: Prices and Employment

Winters (2002) develops a framework for exploring the links between trade shocks and poverty by considering its effect on the prices of tradable goods and hence to changes in household and individual welfare. A key concept is the so-called 'farm household' - a household which potentially makes production as well as employment and consumption decisions (see, for example, Singh, Squire and Strauss, 1986). In this section the effects of trade policy on poor households are explored via their direct effects on product and factor markets, that is, in terms of product price and labour market changes. The analysis focuses on identifying critical trade links between 1992-1993 and 1997-1998 because these are the two years that representative Vietnam Living Standards Surveys (VLSS) are available. These trade links are then incorporated into the econometric analysis of household poverty dynamics in the next section.

### A. The Price Channel

Trade-induced price changes in product markets affect both the nominal and real incomes of households in their capacity as producers as well as consumers. The lowering of tariff barriers is likely to reduce the price of imported goods in the domestic market, and at the same time export liberalisation may lead to higher prices for exported goods. The direction and strength of these effects on real incomes depend on whether households are net buyers or net sellers of the products concerned (Winters, 2002).

The dramatic policy-induced development of Vietnam's export sector and import liberalisation would lead one to expect significant changes in the prices of some tradable commodities. Table 2 reports the proportionate changes in the real retail prices of the selected consumer goods and services (from GSO statistics).[7]

It is clear that Vietnam's leading export products such as rice and marine products saw relatively higher price increases during this period than did other products. Rice is the most important single source of income for the majority of Vietnamese households, accounting for about 30 percent of household income in

[7]These figures need to be treated with some caution as most of the individual prices increase. The nominal prices were deflated by the CPI obtained from GSO, but the information on how the CPI was constructed is not available.

**Table 2.** Price Movements 1993-1998 (percent)

| Consumer Goods/Services | Change |
|---|---|
| Mackerel | 76.87 |
| Vitamin C | 40.40 |
| Permanent wave | 35.49 |
| Sea shrimps | 33.31 |
| Fish sauce | 32.53 |
| Paddy | 26.15 |
| Spring rice | 26.05 |
| Salt | 21.55 |
| Beef topside | 21.30 |
| Glutinous rice | 20.68 |
| Haircut | 16.50 |
| Cotton fabrics | 13.75 |
| Supply water | 13.65 |
| Chicken carcass | 11.80 |
| Duck's eggs | 10.76 |
| Petrol | 10.39 |
| Papers | 3.46 |
| Fresh carp | 0.90 |
| Shelled nuts | 0.37 |
| Black beans | -0.69 |
| Green beans | -1.95 |
| Soya curd | -1.99 |
| Glutamate | -3.24 |
| Soya beans | -3.66 |
| Pork | -4.03 |
| Kerosene | -4.44 |
| White sugar | -6.29 |
| Electricity | -17.78 |
| Vitamin B1 | -18.17 |
| Beer | -22.45 |
| Photograph | -25.23 |
| Woollens | -37.97 |
| CPI (percent Change) | 48.5 |

Source: Calculations based on GSO statistics (provided by CIEM).
Nominal prices deflated by official CPI index.

1998 (World Bank, 1999). As a result, changes in rice prices following liberalisation would have a significant impact on Vietnamese households. It is not possible to insist that these price increases were due solely to trade liberalisation, but there seems very likely to be a strong trade component. Although the price data are not available for coffee, which was another booming export commodity in Vietnam over our sample period, secondary sources - for example, Minot (1998) - support the favourable effect of liberalisation-induced price changes on producers. However, more recently these households have been shown to be vulnerable to the considerable volatility of international coffee prices so some care must be taken not to interpret relatively short runs of data as implying permanent effects.

In contrast to their benefits for producers, price increases in consumer goods, especially rice, harm net consumers. According to our calculations based on the VLSS 92-93, rice on its own accounted for 44 percent of total food expenditure on average, and 53 percent for poor households: rice alone comprises about 75 percent of the total calorific intake of the typical Vietnamese household (Minot and Goletti, 1998). Clearly rice prices will be a major determinant of poverty, and in Niimi *et al.*, (2004) we offer a full analysis of the rice market and the importance of different household consumption patterns in determining the poverty impacts of the rice price increases.

## B. The Employment and Wage Channel

The other major channel through which foreign shocks are transmitted to poverty is through factor markets. The changes in product prices that accompany trade reform could lead to changes in the composition of output, and hence in the bundle of factors used in production. There are two ways that trade-induced changes in the factor market can affect households - through wage changes or through employment changes depending on whether the labour supply is taken to be fixed or flexible (Winters, 2002). Although the impact of trade reforms via the labour channel is expected to be limited because the bulk of the labour force in Vietnam is self-employed (Gallup, 2004), it is still of sufficient potential interest to warrant attention.

### Employment and wage trends

The *doi moi* reforms had a substantial impact on the sectoral composition of output growth. The industrial and services sectors grew rapidly, outpacing the growth in the agricultural sector during the 1990s. Despite the high output growth, however, total employment apparently grew by only about 2-3 percent in this entire period (IMF, 1998, 2000) and was characterised by the absence of job creation in the industrial sector despite its being the fastest growing sector (Belser, 1999).

Probably related is the fact that the state sector is still predominant in the Vietnamese economy, especially in the industrial and services sectors. Despite the large output share at around 40 percent of the GDP (GSO statistics), the share of the state sector in total employment is only about 10 percent. Both unemployment and underem- ployment[8] in urban and rural areas declined until the Asian crisis hit Vietnam in 1997, reaching about 6.9 percent and 1.4 percent respectively in 1998, although with considerable regional variations (CIEM, 2000, World Bank, 1999). Estimates from the VLSS data reveal that wage employment expanded marginally from 24 to 25 percent of the labour force between 1993 and 1998 (Gallup, 2004).

There is some disagreement about wage movements given the paucity of wage data. Chandrasiri and de Silva (1996) use ILO data to argue that real wages fell following liberalisation, while the IMF (1998, 2000) seems to suggest that real earnings (covering all cash income including payments in kind, bonus payments, and social security contributions) increased strongly. The VLSS data indicate that real hourly earnings grew rapidly at about 10.5 percent per annum between 1993 and 1998. There are wide regional differences, however, with Ho Chi Minh City and Hanoi having higher earnings and experiencing faster growth in earnings (Gallup, 2004).

There are considerable earnings differentials depending on sector of employment (state or non-state, foreign-invested), education and region (Chandrasiri and de Silva, 1996, O'Connor, 1996). Although minimum wage levels have been prescribed for both domestic and foreign-invested enterprises, average unskilled wages are about three times higher than the minimum in all forms of employment, and exceed the minimum even in small household enterprises (Belser, 1999).

The trade-labour link

The macroeconomic trends in employment and wages described above suggest the absence of any significant employment effect. Whether this is because trade effects are minor or because they have been offset by other factors can be explored by formally exploring how trade shocks have been transmitted through the labour

[8]'Underemployed' is defined as working less than 40 hours per week.

[9]We thank Azita Amjadi of the World Bank for assistance with these data.

[10]Partner data are used as Vietnamese data are not available in sufficient detail. Partner data account for approximately 90 percent of Vietnam's total exports and imports (GSO statistics) for each year. See Niimi *et al.* (2005) for further details about the trade data used.

market. A first step towards this is to identify major changes in trade patterns and then to explore whether output or employment in these sectors has identifiable consequences for poverty dynamics.

We use mirror statistics from the UN Comtrade system[9,10] in order to identify the sectors that showed the biggest absolute increases in export and import flows between 1993 and 1998. In the case of exports, light industrial products such as footwear, garments and electrical parts, and primary commodities including rice, coffee, seafood and petroleum are found to be the main export growth commodities. In contrast, imports are dominated by capital and intermediate products. This seems to accord with a factor endowment view of comparative advantage. These key sectors are now carried forward to our econometric modelling of household poverty dynamics in the next section. In Niimi *et al.* (2005), however, we explore the consequences of the trade changes for net labour demand in some detail, including a factor content of trade analysis. This suggests that the employment and wage effects of trade reforms in Vietnam were real but not particularly deep.

## IV. An Econometric Analysis of Household Poverty

The previous section suggested some of the possible poverty impacts of trade reform on the basis of descriptive statistics. This section assesses whether the observable dimensions of liberalisation have influenced household outcomes and contributed to poverty alleviation using formal analysis of household data - mainly by means of a multinomial logit model. Specifically we ask whether production characteristics that would a priori dispose a household towards an escape from poverty actually do so. In essence, adopting Glewwe *et al.*'s model of the structure of Vietnamese poverty, we estimate a model describing the probabilities of a household staying in or escaping from poverty and ask whether the trade links identified above contribute to the explanation. If they do, the framework advanced above and in Winters (2002) is useful analytically and we can start to explore whether the policy changes have helped or hindered poverty reduction.

### A. Modelling the Economics of Liberalisation

A household is considered to be poor in the VLSS if $c'p \leq \bar{c}'p$, where c is its consumption basket, $p$ the vector of prices and $\bar{c}$ the 'poverty' basket. Aggregate consumption can be expressed as aggregate income less savings:

$$c'p \quad q'p + f'w + m\text{-}s \tag{1}$$

where $q$ is the production vector (negative for inputs), $f$ is a vector of holdings of income generating assets or household characteristics, $w$ the related vector of returns, $m$ 'non-produced' income and s savings. Ignoring savings for lack of data, we essentially use a regression framework to explain changes in the sign of $(c'p-\bar{c}'p)$ in terms of changes in income,[11] $(q'p + f'w + m)$, that is, in terms of

$$d(q'p + f'w + m) = [q'dp + (dq)'p + f'dw + (df)'w] + dm \tag{2}$$

For reasons we discuss below, we focus only on predetermined assets or characteristics, so this expression reduces to:

$$d(q'p + f'w + m) = [q'dp + f'dw] + dm \tag{3}$$

where $q$ and $f$ are data, and, where, because they are basically unknown, $dp$ and $dw$ are to be estimated from the coefficients of the regression model. In fact, this 'change in price' interpretation of the coefficients of our estimated functions is too strict given all the missing variables and specification difficulties we face, but the basic idea is useful: we are asking how well can we predict changes in poverty status given households' initial (pre-reform) sets of outputs/inputs characteristics and activities. While it is possible that ignoring the change in assets could generate an omitted variable bias we felt it desirable to focus on initial conditions alone to avoid simultaneity problems. This is particularly likely to be a problem as the available data pertains to output not assets.

The modelling in this section is related to that in Glewwe *et al.* (2002) and Justino and Litchfield (2002), but differs in a number of important respects. First, our work is more closely focussed on the trade effects than the general dynamics of poverty in Vietnam. Second, we explore both urban and rural populations: although the rice story is rural, the growth of light manufactured exports is essentially urban. Third, with one exception, we limit ourselves to pre-determined variables as regressors, so as to avoid any hint of simultaneity; this is a strict discipline, for it expressly excludes the effects of changes in activity in response to trade reform.

[11]This is clearly a heroic assumption, although quite common in household studies with inadequate income data. It would be legitimate if $s$ were a constant plus a random term, although this is not likely. It would also not be serious if savings were proportionate in income for it would merely scale the coefficients on the components of income. In fact, the probability that savings are correlated with our included regressors - e.g. urban households having better access to financial institutions and hence more likely to save - is a possible source of bias. However, as long as these correlations were not changing between our two observations, we would not distrust our evidence of the correlates of escaping from poverty.

However, since our purpose is to explore whether trade has identifiable poverty impacts and to see how the framework of Winters (2002) helps us identify them a priori, the fact that our approach tends to lead us to underestimate the role of trade seems constructive. We discuss this more fully below. Finally, there are small differences in the sets of included demographic variables and their measurement.

## B. Description of the Data

The VLSS contains two waves of data: 4,800 households in 150 communes surveyed over October 1992 to October 1993 and 6,000 households in 194 communes surveyed over December 1997 to December 1998.[12] The samples are believed to be representative for the respective years and, critically, over 4,300 households are identifiably surveyed in both waves. 89.6 percent of households from VLSS 92-93 were questioned in VLSS 97-98, and the remainder in the latter were randomly selected. Although attrition means that our panel is not a nationally representative sample of Vietnamese households in a strict sense, this panel dimension allows us a much better view of the dynamics of poverty than would two similar-sized unrelated cross-sections. Furthermore, Falaris (2003) demonstrates that survey attrition in the VLSS (1992-93 and 1997-98) does not have a major impact on the estimation of statistical models.

Table 3 reports sample sizes for the four groups defined by poverty status in 1992-1993 and 1997-1998. The rural and urban samples are pooled together. The rural sample is sizeable, although, even here, the numbers slipping into poverty are small. The urban sample is smaller - certainly too small to permit independent estimation. The urban sample is included in the analysis in order to identify the role of employment in the export oriented sectors identified above and these sectors are largely concentrated in urban areas.

**Table 3.** Poverty Transition Matrix (1992-1993 and 1997-1998)

| | Rural | | Urban | |
|---|---|---|---|---|
| 1997/98 | Poor | Non-Poor | Poor | Non-Poor |
| 1992/93 | | | | |
| Poor | 1184 | 1037 | 52 | 139 |
| Non-Poor | 187 | 1086 | 17 | 600 |

Source: Calculations based on the VLSS 92-93 and 97-98.

Note: The figures in the table are the actual number (unweighted) of households in the panel data set.

[12]Justino and Litchfield (2004) give more detail.

The poverty line used in this work is the official poverty line, which is based on calorie intake. Based on the consumption basket of the third quintile of households in 1992-1993, the poverty line is the cost of purchasing 2,100 calories per head per day plus an allowance for non-food costs, valued at national prices. Its value is 1.160 million dong in 1992-1993 and 1.790 million dong in 1997-1998. Reported consumption or expenditures in the VLSS are deflated by regional price indices - constructed from CPI data disaggregated by region and rural/urban sector - before applying the poverty line (World Bank, 2001). Glewwe *et al.* (2002) argue that the VLSS data on incomes are too unreliable for analysis, so we follow them and measure poverty in terms of aggregate consumption. For simplicity, we opt for consumption per capita based on Burgess *et al.*'s (2000) argument that using adult equivalent scales makes little difference to this kind of analysis.[13]

One consequence of the definition of poverty adopted (that is, in terms of a standardised consumption basket) is that households' actual consumption baskets do not affect our estimates of their poverty status, thus short-circuiting one of the links from trade reform to poverty discussed in section 3.1. In Niimi *et al.* (2004) we describe the calculation of consumption and poverty lines in more detail and explore the importance of differences in consumption baskets for our results. They turn out to be very robust in this regard and so we do not pursue the issue here. The approach used in this paper differs in this respect from that followed by Minot and Goletti (1998) or Benjamin and Brandt (2004) who consider households' net positions in rice as a way of predicting ex ante the poverty effects of rice reform.[14] Both studies predict that households, especially rural households, experienced rising real incomes (and declining poverty incidence) that could be linked, at least in part, with the rice market liberalisation but do not test their predictions.

## C. The Multinomial Logit Model

The MultiNomial Logit (MNL) model analyses the probability of being in a particular state out of several unordered alternatives. We examine the poverty transition between 1992-1993 and 1997-1998 in terms of multiple (unordered)

[13]Per adult equivalent scales may deal better with differences in the intra-household allocation of goods and household economies of scale (White and Masset, 2003), but we do not believe that latter are likely to be very important, as food, the main expenditure of poor households, is not generally prone to large economies of scale.

[14]The methodology adopted by both studies is closely related to the work carried out by Deaton (1989), which examines the welfare effect of rice price changes on Thai farmers.

choices - specifically (1) being poor in both periods (P→P), (2) being non-poor in the first period and becoming poor in the second period (NP→P), (3) being poor in the first period and becoming non-poor in the second period (P→NP), and (4) being non-poor in both periods (NP→NP). The probability that household $i$ experiences outcome $j$ is expressed as:

$$\text{Prob}(Y_i = j) = \frac{e^{\beta_j' x_i}}{\sum_{k=1}^{4} e^{\beta_k' x_i}}, \quad j = 1, 2, 3, 4. \tag{4}$$

where $Y_i$ is the outcome experienced by household $i$, $x_i$ is the $(n \times 1)$ vector of characteristics for household $i$, and $\beta_j$ is the $(n \times 1)$ vector of coefficients on $x_i$ applicable to households in state $j$. The model is identified only up to an additive vector since adding, say, vector $m$ to each $\beta_k$ leads to the same probabilities of $Y=1$, $Y=2$, $Y=3$ and $Y=4$. Thus, one $\beta_k$ must be chosen as the base category and set to zero. All other sets are then estimated in relation to this benchmark. In most of our analysis, outcome 1 (the household is poor in both periods) is set to zero, since we are primarily interested in whether trade helps households to escape from poverty.

The empirical results in this paper are expressed as odds ratios - the probability of each outcome relative to the probability of the base category - rather than the MNL coefficients per se. If we set $Y=1$ as our base category, the odds ratio for $Y=2$ for a change in each variable $x$ is given by:

$$\frac{\text{Prob}(Y = 2)}{\text{Prob}(Y = 1)} = e^{\beta_2' x} \tag{5}$$

where $e^{\beta^{(?)}}$ is the odds ratio for a unit change in the variable $x$. Since all continuous variables have been standardised, the coefficients represent the impact of a one standard deviation change in each explanatory variable on the odds ratio of the household being in each outcome. A coefficient less than one implies that the variable reduces the probability of the household being in the nominated category.

The MNL is most easily interpreted as giving conditional probabilities. Given that poor→poor is the base category, the coefficients for poor→non-poor (outcome 3) tell us the probabilities of moving out of poverty relative to being poor in both years. Similarly, the differences in the coefficients for non-poor→non-poor and those for non-poor→poor (i.e., remove "the ratio") give us the probabilities of

[15]The results of this regression are not reported as they mirror the first model.

falling into poverty relative to being non-poor in both years. These latter are most easily calculated by re-estimating the equation with non-poor→non-poor as base and examining the coefficients for non-poor→poor.[15]

The MNL is a common formulation for poverty work and was, as we noted, used by Glewwe *et al.* (2002) in their pioneering work on Vietnam. However, it is not without its drawbacks. One possible problem is the dichotomous nature of the poor/non-poor classification, which places arbitrary poverty lines at the heart of the analysis. This can be a particular problem given the inevitable errors of measurement in household expenditures (Deaton, 1997).[16] In one set of experiments we truncate our sample around the poverty line to reduce the importance of random errors and also briefly discuss alternatives to the MNL (see section 4.6). Moreover, in compensation we note that by seeking to explain a categorical variable the MNL avoids measurement problems at the extremes of the distribution, where, arguably, they are likely to be at their worst.

We start from equations that are similar to those of Glewwe *et al.* (2002), and add a number of variables to reflect the trade links: rice production, coffee production, land and fertiliser use,[17] and the ratio of household members working in the leading export industries (seafood, food processing, garments, and shoes) to the number of adults in the household. The inclusion of the output data in 1992-1993 is designed to capture the benefits for self-employed households of prior specialisation in a booming export sector. The inclusion of variables on land is an attempt to see whether liberalisation affected the poor via (implicit) land rents, while the inclusion of fertiliser is to capture the benefits of the latter's significant price decline. The larger the household's use of fertiliser, the larger its net income gain as the price falls. In addition, there may be benefits to having an initial crop-mix that could take advantage of the decline in price and increased availability of fertilisers. For rice, since production is highly correlated with the land and inputs usage, part of the effects of the latter should be captured by the production variable. However, as noted, fertiliser usage also has direct effects via the input vector, and land or irrigation may have asset-type advantages or reflect the availability of technologies that allow stronger or weaker than average responses to price shocks.

[16]Ravallion (1996) provides a useful discussion on the use of dichotomous variables for poverty measures.

[17]Our variable for the fertiliser use is constructed as the total amount of all kinds of fertilisers including urea, phosphoric fertilisers and NPK fertilisers.

Given the centrality of rice to our story of Vietnamese poverty, it is at least worth checking these things. The benefits of being employed in the export sectors initially are represented by the employment variables.

In a few cases we measure certain demographic variables differently from Glewwe *et al.* (2002). In addition, since the VLSS interviews were spread over twelve month periods in both waves we also consider two timing variables. As there are signs of both seasonality and period-length effects, we add the dummy variables for the interview quarter in VLSS 92-93 and the period between surveys.[18] We attempted to identify the effects of the Asian crisis of 1997 using the variables for the date of interviews for the VLSS 97-98. Although there appeared to be signs of the negative effects of the crisis in the later months of VLSS 97-98, none was significantly different from zero and we do not include these results in this paper. Presumably this means that Vietnam was not directly affected to the extent that some other countries were,[19] although it is also possible that the adverse effects took longer to be felt at the household level than in aggregate or that the shock had been fully felt by December 1997, especially given that there was also a typhoon in the in 1997.

## D. Empirical Results

The "basic" equation with no trade variables explains poverty dynamics as a

[18]The period between samplings could range from fifty to seventy-four months - equivalent to about 16 percent growth in income at average growth rates.

[19]This was perhaps partly due to the strict controls on the short- and long-term capital flows imposed by the State Bank of Vietnam.

[20]These regional dummies should capture, among other things, differences across regions on foreign aid and fiscal transfers from the government. We also tried to include a variable to control for fiscal transfers based on the VLSS 1992-93, more specifically social fund from the government. The results are not reported here as the inclusion of this variable might cause some endogeneity problems. However, we found that having received government funds in 1992-93 increased the probability of escaping from poverty and the inclusion of this variable hardly changed the estimated coefficients reported in this paper.

[21]The infrastructure variables are constructed on the basis of the commune questionnaires that were conducted along with the 1992-1993 and 1997-1998 VLSS. These data are available, however, only for rural communes in 1992-1993 and rural and small urban communes in 1997-1998. We used data for 1997-1998 to identify small urban communes which did not have these facilities in 1997-1998 and assumed they did not have them in 1992-1993 either. For the rest of urban communes, we assumed that they had access to these infrastructures. We experimented with an alternative assumption of universal urban provision since even if the facilities are not available in a commune, they are likely to be much more readily available than in rural communes without them. This hardly changed the results except for the coefficient on the urban dummy.

function of region,[20] ethnicity, demography, human capital (education), occupation, health, infrastructure and seasonality is reported in the Appendix.[21] We report results for all three categories (P→P that is, being poor in both years is treated as base): being non-poor in 1992-1993 and poor in 1997-1998 (NP→P), being poor in 1992-1993 and non-poor in 1997-1998 (P→NP) and being non-poor in both years (NP→NP).

In terms of the "basic" variables, although precise comparisons with Glewwe *et al.* (2002) and Justino and Litchfield (2002) are not feasible, they seem to tell a pretty consistent story. Location and regional effects, education and occupation of the household head, and infrastructure variables were among the major factors that increased the probability of escaping poverty relative to being poor in both years, while belonging to a minority ethnic group and illness of the household head increased the probability of falling into poverty relative to being non-poor in both years.[22]

The Appendix also reports the full model with the trade effects identified above added to the "basic" variables. The trade effects are largely orthogonal to the "basic" effects, so we report in the text only the coefficients on the various trade variables as they affect the chance of escaping from poverty.

Table 4 starts with our basic 'trade-inclusive' model (column A). The empirical analysis in section 3 identified rice, coffee, seafood and light manufactures as the principal areas of export growth. Hence we include among the regressors the household's initial production of rice and coffee and the proportion of workers initially holding jobs in export sectors (seafood, food processing - to allow for any processing of the primary exports - clothing and footwear). All have positive effects, the first two are strongly significant, both in the system as a whole and in explaining just the escape from poverty, whereas the last is strongly significant for the system as a whole but is significant in explaining the escape from and the descent into poverty only at the 10 percent level, indicating possible risk associated with these jobs. For example, ceteris paribus, a one standard deviation increase in a household's production of coffee more than doubles its chances of escaping from poverty in 1998, while a one standard deviation increase in rice output increases it by over 50 percent. Adding these three variables increases the pseudo-$R^2$ of the system from 0.23 to 0.26.

[22]See Niimi *et al.* (2003) for details.

[23]The rice production effect in the Mekong in column (B), Table 3 is an increase of 35 percent in the chance of escaping = 100*(2.29*0.59-1)].

**Table 4.** Odds Ratios for Escaping from Poverty (Results for Trade variables)
Model I (columns A-E): Base category - poor in both years
Model II (column F): Odds ratios for falling into poverty: Base category - non poor in both years

| | Model I | | | | | Model II |
|---|---|---|---|---|---|---|
| | A | B | C | D | E | F |
| **Agricultural variables** | | | | | | |
| Quantity of rice production | ***1.55 | ***2.29 | **1.67 | ***1.75 | ***1.77 | *0.51 |
| In Mekong River Delta | | ***0.59 | **0.63 | **0.60 | **0.60 | 1.51 |
| In Red River Delta | | *0.87 | *0.86 | **0.85 | **0.85 | 1.15 |
| Quantity of coffee production | ***3.00 | ***3.02 | ***2.32 | ***2.31 | ***2.31 | 1.00 |
| Quantity of fertiliser - rice | | | ***1.41 | ***1.46 | ***1.46 | 1.13 |
| Qty. of fertiliser - non-rice | | | *1.59 | *1.70 | *1.71 | *0.79 |
| **Employment variables** | | | | | | |
| Ratio of household members working in export | *1.11 | | | ***1.25 | ***1.23 | *1.19 |
| Change in the ratio (export) | | | | **1.17 | *1.14 | 1.06 |
| Ratio of household members working in import | | | | | 1.12 | 1.09 |
| Change in the ratio (import) | | | | | 1.07 | 0.95 |
| Ratio of household members working in manufacturing | | | | | 1.06 | *0.80 |
| Change in the ratio (manufacturing) | | | | | 1.04 | 0.87 |
| Pseudo R2 | 0.26 | 0.26 | 0.26 | 0.27 | 0.27 | 0.27 |

Note: ***significant at 1 percent level; **significant at 5 percent level; *significant at 10 percent
(1) All the variables included in the "basic equation" (see Model 1 in the Appendix) are included as controls in this regression but not reported for brevity.
(2) The export sector includes seafood, food processing, garment and shoes (+rubber and plastic products).
(3) The categories for occupation slightly differ between the VLSS 92-93 and the VLSS 97-98.
(4) The import sector includes textile, machinery, leather, chemical and metal.

One important refinement to the rice result is its regional dimension (column B). The production effect is weaker in the Mekong River Delta than elsewhere.[23] As well as being the major producing region for rice exports, the Mekong is also characterised by larger farms and a much greater use of hired labour (Minot, 1998). Thus, as production increases less of the benefit accrues to the householder as a producer and more to the labour he hires; correspondingly, household income owes more to wages deriving from others' rice production than it does elsewhere in

Vietnam. We tried to test this last effect by including in the equation the proportion of household members reported to be working on someone else's farm (we cannot isolate rice farms). Its effect was positive but not statistically significant. A similar, but weaker, extenuation is also evident in the other major rice area, the Red River Delta. Here, although coefficient is significant only at 10 percent in the escape from poverty equation, it is strongly significant in the system as a whole ($\chi^2$ at 3 degrees of freedom=33.1). Once these two regional variants are permitted the rice production effect elsewhere in the country increases to above two.

Column (C) of Table 4 adds variables for the initial use of fertiliser. Fertiliser prices fell by 23 percent in real terms between 1992-1993 and 1997-1998 and so heavy users could sustain material increases in real consumption. This is verified by estimation. In the table, however, we further refine the variable by distinguishing between rice and non-rice fertiliser effects. The logic is that non-rice use may reflect greater opportunities for exploiting the fall in price because farmers can switch between crops rather than just increase use for a single crop. Large initial users for non-rice crops may grow crops or farm under circumstances which respond to fertiliser usage and thus have greater opportunities for substitution than those who use little fertiliser to start with.[24] The table shows strong positive effects from fertiliser use although non-rice use is significant only at 10 percent.

In Niimi *et al.* (2004) we also explore whether fixed inputs into agriculture (land and irrigation) and/or rice productivity have effects additional to those of the main outputs and inputs. The answer is 'no', which is as it should be: fertiliser has a direct income effect, while a kilo of rice yields the same net income whether you grow it on land to which you have firm rights or not. Hence, we do not pursue these variables further here.

The second major dimension of the trade liberalisation operates via the employment market. In column (A) of Table 4 we explore the benefits of working (initially) in the major export sectors by including the proportion of adults (15 years and older) holding a job in an export sector - seafood, food processing (because some seafood and rice exports are processed), clothing and footwear. The effects is benign - an 11 percent increase in the chance of escaping from poverty from a one standard deviation increase in the proportion of export workers (mean 0.046, standard deviation 0.156) - but it is not highly significant. When we sought separate effects for each export industry, they were mostly positive and that for

[24]We do not include the change in fertiliser use because of the obvious danger of endogeneity.

seafood was significant, but there was no significant improvement relative to the combined variable shown in Table 4.

There are at least three ways of making a link between initial employment in an export sector and the escape from poverty. Existing workers could get real wage increases, which is a straightforward Heckscher-Ohlin or Ricardo-Viner-Jones result (coupled with an auxiliary assumption minimising churning in employment). Existing workers may be able to work longer hours (that is, a reduction in hidden unemployment or underemployment), as one might expect in transitional economies rationalising the state-owned sector. And finally, it may be that initial employment indicates a location close to exporting firms and hence better chances of the household obtaining more jobs as the firms expand.

In order to explore these possibilities more closely, we break our rule of using only initial values as explanatory variables, and add the change in the proportion of adults with employment in export sectors. This captures the third hypothesis above whereby an export boom generates more jobs but at constant real wages. Given the stock of workers in agriculture and SOEs and the relatively low skills required for most manufacturing export jobs, there is little reason to expect that new workers will be less productive than incumbents over the five years between our surveys.

Including the change in employment has negligible effects on all the other coefficients and their significance but quite strong effects on the initial employment. It increases from 1.11* to 1.19**, while the change in employment gets a coefficient of 1.14** (regression not reported). When the change in export employment is added to the model with agriculture modelled more fully (column C), the effects are even stronger - see column (D). Thus incumbency in manufacturing does have advantages in escaping poverty (via wages or hours presumably, neither of which we can test directly because the data are so noisy), but so does a household's ability to supply new workers.

Methodologically the lesson here is that for predicting the poverty effects of trade liberalisation, agricultural shocks may be well captured by initial activity in the affected sector because mobility is relatively low in these sectors.[25,26] For manufacturing, however, although initial employment captures some of the likely

[25]By the same token negative shocks will hit hard in agriculture, as, for example, the decline in coffee prices since 1997 is reported to have done in Vietnam's Central Highlands.

[26]Note that this cannot certainly be generalised if the low mobility is caused by the country-specific institutional factor, namely Vietnam's household registration system.

effects, some will be less predictable because mobility into manufacturing jobs is high.

If the labour market is reasonably well integrated, wage changes will not be restricted to the booming export sectors (as in Ricardo-Viner), but will spillover to other sectors (as under Heckscher-Ohlin). We test this by including in the equation the proportions of workers in import-competing sectors (textiles, leather, chemical, metals and machinery) and in all manufacturing, and changes in these ratios between the two years (column E). From the former we might also detect job losses as additional imports destroy jobs. The effects of employment in manufacturing are all positive, whatever the sector, but largest in exports, followed by imports and then by manufacturing in general. None of the import or manufacturing effects is significant, however.[27] In interpreting column (E), it should be noted that both export and import industries are included in the general manufacturing set, so the gross effects are given by the products of two coefficients (for example, 1.23*1.06=1.30 for export employment). Also, difficulties of classifying sector of occupation in 1997-1998 mean that the change in employment variables for exports and imports both include workers classified to the textiles and garments sectors.

We now briefly consider the descent into poverty. The sample for this is small and so the results in column (F) of Table 4 are poorly defined. In an economy growing at 8 percent per annum with low levels of initial inequality descent into poverty is likely to be mainly an idiosyncratic event. Nonetheless, the results are broadly consistent with the analysis of escape from poverty even if they are not very significant statistically. The chances of falling back into poverty are reduced by higher rice output (in the Mekong and Red River Deltas as well), higher non-rice fertiliser use and prior employment in manufacturing. The last effect appears to be weaker in exporting (1.19*0.80=0.95) than in other sectors, but is nonetheless still negative. One should not make much of this set of results, but they clearly lend some further support to our model of the poverty consequences of trade liberalisation.

While the trade effects appear to be estimated sufficiently precisely to reject the hypothesis that they have arisen by chance, we have not yet discussed their overall contribution to explaining poverty dynamics. We now ask how much better the fit

[27]Their insignificance persists even if the new variables are added one by one, except for import sector employment which is significant at 10 percent.

**Table 5.** Goodness of Fit with and without Trade Variables

*(A) Multinomial logit model without trade variables*
The poverty status of about 59.90 percent of households was correctly predicted.

| Actual | Prediction | | | | |
|---|---|---|---|---|---|
| | P→P | NP→P | P→NP | NP→NP | |
| **P→P** | 844<br>(68.28) | 0<br>(0.00) | 208<br>(16.83) | 184<br>(14.89) | 1236<br>(100.00) |
| **NP→P** | 61<br>(29.90) | 0<br>(0.00) | 30<br>(14.71) | 113<br>(55.39) | 204<br>(100.00) |
| **P→NP** | 324<br>(27.55) | 1<br>(0.09) | 434<br>(36.90) | 417<br>(35.46) | 1176<br>(100.00) |
| **NP→NP** | 145<br>(8.60) | 2<br>(0.12) | 240<br>(14.23) | 1299<br>(77.05) | 1686<br>(100.00) |
| | 1374 | 3 | 912 | 2013 | 4302 |

*(B) Multinomial logit model with trade variables (equation D-Table 4)*
The poverty status of about 61.46 percent of households was correctly predicted.

| Actual | Prediction | | | | |
|---|---|---|---|---|---|
| | P→P | NP→P | P→NP | NP→NP | |
| **P→P** | 861<br>(69.66) | 1<br>(0.08) | 215<br>(17.39) | 159<br>(12.86) | 1236<br>(100.00) |
| **NP→P** | 61<br>(29.90) | 2<br>(0.98) | 31<br>(15.20) | 110<br>(53.92) | 204<br>(100.00) |
| **P→NP** | 317<br>(26.96) | 1<br>(0.09) | 468<br>(39.80) | 390<br>(33.16) | 1176<br>(100.00) |
| **NP→NP** | 127<br>(7.53) | 4<br>(0.24) | 242<br>(14.35) | 1313<br>(77.88) | 1686<br>(100.00) |
| | 1366 | 8 | 956 | 1972 | 4302 |

Note: The predicted probabilities of falling into the 4 different categories were first calculated and each household was allocated to the category for which the probability was the highest.

is for equation (D) of Table 4 (our preferred equation) than for the base equation with no trade component (see Appendix). The increase in the pseudo-$R^2$ from 0.234 to 0.266 suggests that trade adds a further 3.2 percent to the explained variation in poverty experience but that much of the latter remains unexplained. The proportions of correct predictions from the MNL model tell a similar story (see Table 5). The basic model classifies 59.9 percent of households correctly, over-predicting no-change outcomes (P→P and NP→NP) and under-predicting the changes - see block A. Its inability to pick up descent into poverty is palpable but hardly surprising, but it also misses a significant number of 'escapees': indeed only 36.9 percent of actual escapees are correctly identified.[28] Adding the trade variables improves the overall success rate, though slightly, by about 1.5 percentage points or 2.5 percent - see block (B). In particular, we correctly identify more of the escapees from poverty increasing the success rate to 39.6 percent. These are modest improvements, to be sure, but let us re-iterate that they are statistically significant in the estimating equation and that in terms of targeting compensatory policies even a 2 percentage point improvement is worth achieving.

## E. The Effect on Poverty

The results so far offer some plausible evidence that international trade reform has affected individual household poverty dynamics in Vietnam, and that by taking it into account we are better able to predict which households prosper and which do not. This lends considerable weight to the analytical approach proposed and to the view that 'trade matters'. It does not, however, tell us directly whether trade reform reduced poverty. For that, we need to create a counterfactual - '1998 without trade reform' - and it is here that the uncertain division of responsibility between trade policy, other policies and exogenous shocks really takes its toll.

As noted above we use initial household characteristics as variables and infer the change in their value between 1992-1993 and 1997-1998 from the coefficients. Hence, we can estimate the effects of trade reform on overall poverty by setting the 'trade-related' coefficients to zero (the corresponding odds ratio to unity) and recalculating the predicted changes in poverty.[29] For some effects, however, the change in the value of a characteristic is due to things other than trade, so the appropriate reduction for this exercise may be less than 100 percent. For the sake of illustration we also consider reductions of one-half in these coefficients.

Table 6 summarises the effects of setting various 'trade' coefficients in the MNL model to zero [odds ratio, OR=1] and to one half of their estimated value [OR'≈1+1/

[28]The predictions underestimate the degree of change at least partly because, unlike the actuals, they ignore the random variance in the system (around 75 percent of the total). If our interests were in predicting the proportion of changes per se we would replicate these simulations many times adding in a suitably distributed random variable and calculate an average transition matrix over these replications. However, we are interested in comparing two simulations (with and without trade) so we do not need to do this.

[29]Because we standardised the variables in the regression equation, we also need to subtract $\beta\bar{x}/s$ from the constant to ensure that the equations go through the same mean point as before, where $\bar{x}$ is the mean value of the trade variable, $s$ its standard deviation and $\beta$ the trade coefficient set to zero.

**Table 6.** Poverty Reductions due to Trade Reforms

| | A: Solely due to trade reforms | | B: Partially (half) due to trade reforms | |
|---|---|---|---|---|
| | Escape from Poverty | 1998 Poverty | Escape from Poverty | 1998 Poverty |
| Rice | -1 (0.02%) | -226 (5.25%) | -1 (0.02%) | -113 (2.63%) |
| Coffee | +8 (0.19%) | -12 (0.28%) | +5 (0.12%) | -7 (1.63%) |
| Fertilisers | +186 (4.32%) | -292 (6.79%) | +87 (2.02%) | -141 (3.28%) |
| Export employment | -12 (0.28%) | -61 (1.42%) | -11 (0.26%) | -31 (0.72%) |
| All | +250 (5.81%) | -668 (15.53%) | +96 (2.23%) | -296 (6.88%) |

Note: The coefficients on the variable for rice production and on those interacted with the regional dummies (the Mekong River Delta and the Red River Delta) are controlled for rice. For fertilisers, the coefficients on the quantity of fertilisers used for rice as well as for non-rice are controlled. As for export employment, the coefficients on the ratio of household members working in the export sector and on the change in the ratio are controlled. The figures are the unweighted number of households and those in parentheses are the percentage of the households in the panel data set.

2(OR-1)], in equation from column (D) of Table 4. The predicted numbers of households in each category from equation (D) are given at the foot of Table 5 block B. These figures were then recalculated with various combinations of trade coefficients set to zero to isolate the contribution of trade.[30] Thus, for example, if none of the trade effects had applied, about 250 fewer households would have escaped from poverty and 668 more would have been in poverty in 1998. Out of 4,302 households in total, these are considerable contributions. The table also reports the figures for individual trade effects and reveals that the critical variable appears to be fertiliser use. The small negative figures for rice and export employment arise because, although these variables have a positive partial effect on the chances of escaping from poverty, they also affect the predictions of the household's chances of being in another category and the prediction is made by choosing the category with the highest predicted probability. In both cases the suppression of the trade effects switches households from P→NP to P→P, as we would predict, but this is dominated numerically by those who are switched from NP→NP to P→NP. If trade effects are set to half the estimated coefficients (block B), the contribution of trade reform is still large - nearly 100 additional households escaping from poverty (about 10 percent of those that did) and nearly 300 fewer households in poverty (about 10 percent again).

[30]This exercise is essentially a simulation. We are comparing predictions under two sets of conditions, not actual and predicted values.

## F. Sensitivity Tests

The results just described allow some confidence that we have located some of the effects of trade reform in the dynamics of individual households. Two caveats are in order, however. First, the trade effects included in this exercise are not exhaustive: there will be other channels through which trade has impacted poverty dynamics. This is not a problem with the regression results, unless these other factors are correlated with our included effects. We have identified systematic effects and these will continue to exist even if there are others. It is a problem for calculating the net effect of trade reform on poverty because the omitted effects could be either reinforcing or offsetting to our included effects. All we claim is that the channels we have identified had a beneficial effect. The second caveat is that while it would be desirable to control for unobserved household characteristics that may influence poverty transitions it is not possible to do so as there are only two waves of data.

Despite these caveats, the econometric analysis suggests that the trade reforms of the 1990s influenced the poverty transitions of Vietnamese households. The significant effects accord well with the shocks identified in the discussion of trade policy (although not all those identified could be included), and given that we use only initial variables we are free from worries about endogeneity. Indeed the predictive power of the initial variables gives strong support to their use in ex ante predictions of the effects of liberalisation as made by, for example, Ravallion and van de Walle (1991) for Indonesia and Minot and Goletti (1998) for Vietnam. Nonetheless, it is desirable to push the model a little harder to test its sensitivity. We conducted two such tests.[31]

First, we re-estimated the multinomial logit model with a wider band at which households change their status. This enables us to check whether the errors of observation or random shocks to income flows are correlated with our independent data. We find that re-estimating equation (D) in Table 4 excluding any household that was within ±10 percent of the poverty line in either year leaves the results largely unscathed.[32] Among the trade variables, the results on falling back into poverty are even less significant, while for escaping from poverty the most notable

[31]The results of these alternative models are not reported here (see Niimi *et al.* (2003) for details).

[32]This is a demanding test because it excludes the households most likely to change their poverty status. This may introduce some selection bias, but our prime purpose of this exercise is to examine the robustness our earlier results.

differences are the insignificance of rice production in the Mekong River Delta, the smaller and less significant effects of coffee production, and the larger effects of fertiliser use. Among non-trade variables, the major change is the decline into insignificance of the household head having university education.

The second sensitivity test asks, quite independent of poverty lines, what determines changes in income? It is a simple regression of changes in total household expenditure on the various determinants discussed so far. Given the absence of any information about poverty at all, this approach is even more vulnerable to concerns that it is dominated by the experiences of a few households and so we estimate the regression model on both the full sample and a truncated sample comprising the second to sixth deciles of the initial income distribution. The results differ very significantly between the samples. Overall, the trade variables are jointly significant at 5 percent even if they are not so individually, but their signs are not plausible. It is worth re-iterating, however, that all our independent data refer to initial conditions, so this is a far tougher test than, say, the decompositions used by Dercon (2002) for Ethiopia, in which expenditure changes are related to initial characteristics and changes in them. These results are disappointing for our maintained view that trade policy has affected poverty directly, but they are not entirely nugatory. Since poverty is our focus we draw comfort from the MNL model over the less robust linear regression approaches.

## V. Conclusion

This paper makes two contributions. Methodologically, for the first time it implements and examines empirically the usefulness of a conceptual framework linking trade liberalisation and extreme poverty. While clearly not explaining anything like the full extent of Vietnam's poverty dynamics, it shows that the framework is plausible and adds significantly to our understanding of and ability to predict the poverty impact of trade reform. Substantively, the paper has suggested that despite its incompleteness and hesitancy, trade reform in Vietnam over the 1990s reduced poverty. Exports and imports boomed and the prices of some tradable goods increased strongly. We find signs of these effects in the household data, with the real incomes of the poor tending to increase via their engagement in the rice, coffee and light manufactures sectors. These last results are significant both statistically and economically, and although they are not wholly robust, they are suggestive and represent, we believe, the first time that international trade variables have been formally traced through into ex post household poverty data.

## Acknowledgements

This paper is part of the project "The Impact of Trade Reforms and Trade Shocks on Household Poverty Dynamics" (ESCOR-R7621) funded by the UK Department for International Development, for the benefit of developing countries, as part of their Globalisation and Poverty Research Programme. Views and opinions expressed in the paper are, however, those of the authors alone. We are grateful to the World Bank for making the trade data available for the DFID-funded Globalisation and Poverty Research Programme's projects on Vietnam. The paper draws freely on work by and discussion with our colleagues in the Poverty Research Unit, Sussex, Patricia Justino and Julie Litchfield. We are also grateful for comments on earlier drafts from colleagues in The Economics Subject Group at Sussex, participants in the University of Warwick's Conference on "Globalisation, Growth and (In)Equality", March 2002, the DfID Seminar on "Globalisation and Poverty" in Hanoi, September 2002, and the OECD Development Centre Conference on "How are Globalisation and Poverty Interacting?" in Paris, December 2002, and from Bob Baulch, Rhys Jenkins, Niel McCulloch, Andy McKay, Chantal Nielsen, David O'Connor, Lina Song, Finn Tarp, Shujie Yao and Linxiu Zhang.

*Received 18 June 2005, Accepted 26 June 2007*

**APPENDIX: REGRESSION RESULTS OF MULTINOMIAL LOGIT MODELS (Odds Ratios)**

Model 1: Without trade variables
Model 2: With trade variables

| | NP → P | | P → NP (Escaping Poverty) | | NP → NP | |
|---|---|---|---|---|---|---|
| | Model 1 | Model 2 | Model 1 | Model 2 | Model 1 | Model 2 |
| **Geographic characteristics** | | | | | | |
| Urban | 0.911 | 0.998 | **1.716 | ***1.979 | ***2.442 | ***3.231 |
| Northern Uplands | 1.412 | 1.726 | 1.188 | 1.257 | 1.155 | 1.325 |
| Red River Delta | 1.082 | 1.814 | **1.445 | **1.667 | 1.261 | ***2.489 |
| (North Central) | | | | | | |
| Central Cost | 1.523 | 1.650 | 0.986 | 0.970 | ***2.658 | ***2.706 |
| Central Highlands | 1.282 | 0.830 | **2.256 | 1.019 | ***6.600 | **3.177 |
| South East | ***3.965 | ***3.879 | ***5.423 | ***4.736 | ***19.678 | ***18.482 |
| Mekong River Delta | ***5.027 | ***4.580 | ***2.126 | ***2.175 | ***9.605 | ***8.213 |

| | NP → P | | P → NP (Escaping Poverty) | | NP → NP | |
|---|---|---|---|---|---|---|
| | Model 1 | Model 2 | Model 1 | Model 2 | Model 1 | Model 2 |
| **Ethnicity** | | | | | | |
| (Kinh) | | | | | | |
| Chinese | 1.806 | 1.905 | 0.765 | 0.715 | *3.952 | **4.883 |
| Other ethnicity | 0.864 | 1.006 | ***0.386 | ***0.430 | ***0.359 | ***0.453 |
| **Demographic characteristics** | | | | | | |
| Female head of household | 0.994 | 1.058 | 0.984 | 1.016 | 1.085 | 1.197 |
| Age of household head | 0.951 | 0.959 | ***1.305 | ***1.316 | ***1.456 | ***1.464 |
| No. of males 60+ | 0.968 | 0.925 | 0.918 | *0.895 | *0.879 | ***0.829 |
| No. of females 55+ | 1.122 | 1.085 | 1.092 | 1.074 | *1.118 | 1.076 |
| No. of males 19-59 | 0.997 | 0.933 | 0.993 | 0.942 | 0.977 | *0.892 |
| No. of females 19-54 | 1.138 | 1.070 | *1.115 | 1.073 | **1.152 | 1.073 |
| No. of children 15-18 | 0.969 | 0.889 | 1.029 | 0.969 | **0.893 | ***0.782 |
| No. of children 6-14 | ***0.460 | ***0.411 | **0.887 | ***0.807 | ***0.631 | ***0.538 |
| No. of children 3-5 | ***0.604 | ***0.560 | ***0.760 | ***0.725 | ***0.520 | ***0.475 |
| No. of infants 0-2 | ***0.581 | ***0.558 | ***0.784 | ***0.765 | ***0.548 | ***0.515 |
| **Education variables** | | | | | | |
| **Head** | | | | | | |
| (No education) | | | | | | |
| Primary school | **1.688 | **1.706 | ***1.835 | ***1.833 | ***2.126 | ***2.066 |
| Lower secondary school | **1.779 | **1.836 | ***2.844 | ***2.834 | ***3.455 | ***3.548 |
| Upper secondary school | 1.584 | 1.764 | ***3.227 | ***3.343 | ***6.734 | ***7.564 |
| Tech/voc school | 1.275 | 1.383 | ***1.989 | ***2.023 | ***4.696 | ***5.132 |
| University | ***1.35e-14 | ***2.00e-14 | **10.061 | ***12.707 | ***46.400 | ***69.795 |
| **Spouse** | | | | | | |
| (No spouse) | | | | | | |
| No education | 1.097 | 1.038 | 0.938 | 0.887 | 1.128 | 1.083 |
| Primary school | 1.061 | 1.043 | 1.073 | 1.087 | **1.637 | **1.699 |
| Lower secondary school | 1.222 | 1.209 | 1.061 | 1.052 | 1.273 | 1.294 |
| Upper secondary school | **2.966 | **3.096 | 1.454 | 1.426 | ***2.399 | ***2.447 |
| Tech/voc school | *2.913 | **3.230 | ***2.735 | ***3.021 | ***6.234 | ***7.334 |
| University | ***4.62e-15 | ***4.43e-15 | 2.409 | 2.251 | ***6.413 | ***6.214 |
| **Occupations (Head)** | | | | | | |
| White collar | ***5.733 | ***6.111 | ***3.291 | ***3.528 | ***7.465 | ***8.349 |
| Sales/Services | 1.657 | *2.168 | 1.498 | **1.846 | ***3.252 | ***5.065 |
| (Agriculture) | | | | | | |
| Production | 1.185 | 1.234 | 0.966 | 1.167 | 1.249 | **1.608 |

| | NP → P | | P → NP (Escaping Poverty) | | NP → NP | |
|---|---|---|---|---|---|---|
| | Model 1 | Model 2 | Model 1 | Model 2 | Model 1 | Model 2 |
| Not working | 0.678 | 0.745 | ***0.604 | **0.634 | 0.783 | 0.939 |
| **Illness shock** | | | | | | |
| Household head ill for more than a week in past 4 months | **1.828 | **1.995 | 1.221 | 1.249 | 1.030 | 1.090 |
| **Infrastructure** | | | | | | |
| Access to electricity | 1.422 | 1.381 | ***1.541 | ***1.446 | ***3.481 | ***3.364 |
| Road | 0.620 | 0.733 | ***1.666 | **1.605 | **0.680 | 0.768 |
| Food shop | 1.409 | 1.459 | ***1.611 | ***1.766 | ***2.190 | ***2.317 |
| Daily market | ***2.015 | ***2.205 | 1.093 | 1.208 | ***1.512 | ***1.613 |
| Primary school | 0.456 | 0.441 | 0.782 | 0.767 | *0.496 | **0.483 |
| Lower secondary school | 1.110 | 1.030 | 0.872 | 0.792 | **1.382 | 1.164 |
| Upper secondary school | 1.091 | 1.175 | 1.042 | 1.098 | **1.565 | ***1.736 |
| Post office | ***0.566 | **0.561 | ***0.622 | ***0.619 | ***0.378 | ***0.363 |
| Clinic | 1.634 | 1.531 | ***1.923 | ***1.756 | **1.701 | ***1.841 |
| **Agricultural variables** | | | | | | |
| Quantity of rice production | | 1.769 | | ***1.753 | | ***3.445 |
| In Mekong River Delta | | 0.752 | | **0.601 | | ***0.505 |
| In Red River Delta | | **0.710 | | **0.845 | | ***0.612 |
| Quantity of coffee production | | ***2.358 | | ***2.315 | | ***2.359 |
| Quantity of fertiliser for rice | | ***1.679 | | ***1.460 | | ***1.491 |
| Quantity of fertiliser for non-rice | | 1.557 | | *1.696 | | **1.969 |
| **Trade variables** | | | | | | |
| Ratio of household members working in export (1) to number of adults | | ***1.649 | | ***1.254 | | ***1.517 |
| Change in the ratio (2) | | *1.186 | | **1.173 | | **1.169 |
| **Duration between two surveys** | 0.932 | 0.920 | ***1.500 | ***1.432 | ***1.375 | ***1.394 |
| **Seasonality** | | | | | | |
| (Interviewed 1st quarter) | | | | | | |
| Interviewed 2nd quarter | 0.626 | 0.629 | 1.054 | 1.065 | 0.928 | 0.960 |
| Interviewed 3rd quarter | 0.941 | 1.156 | **1.341 | ***1.594 | ***1.821 | ***2.190 |
| Interviewed 4th quarter | 0.820 | 0.788 | ***1.845 | ***1.668 | ***1.965 | ***1.994 |

| | NP → P | | P → NP (Escaping Poverty) | | NP → NP | |
|---|---|---|---|---|---|---|
| | Model 1 | Model 2 | Model 1 | Model 2 | Model 1 | Model 2 |
| **No. of observations** | 4,302 | 4,302 | 4,302 | 4,302 | 4,302 | 4,302 |
| **Pseudo $R^2$** | 0.234 | 0.266 | 0.234 | 0.266 | 0.234 | 0.266 |

Source: Calculations based on the VLSS 92-93 and 97-98.
Note: *** significant at 1 percent level; ** significant at 5 percent level; * significant at 10 percent level.
(1) The export sector includes seafood, food processing, garment and shoes (+rubber and plastic products).
(2) It should be noted that the categories for occupation slightly differ between the VLSS 92-93 and the VLSS 97-98.

## References

Andersen, H. (1994) Vietnam at the Crossroads, *Macroeconomic Studies*, 55/94, Stockholm: Planning Secretariat, SIDA.

Apoteker, T. (1998) Vietnam: Trade and Investment Analysis: 1998 Update, *A Report for the European Commission*, Vietnam.

Belser, P. (1999) Vietnam: On the Road to Labour-Intensive Growth?, *Policy Research Working Paper*, No.2389, Washington, D. C.: World Bank.

Benjamin, D. and Brandt, L. (2004) Agriculture and Income Distribution in Rural Vietnam under Economic Reforms: A Tale of Two Regions, in *Economic Growth, Poverty, and Household Welfare in Vietnam* (Ed.), Glewwe, P., Agrawal, N. and Dollar, D., Washington, D.C.: World Bank.

Burgess, S., Gardiner, K., Jenkins, S. and Propper, C. (2000) Measuring Income Risk, *ISER Working Paper*, 2000-15, Institute for Social and Economic Research, University of Essex.

Chandrasiri, S and de Silva, A. (1996) Globalisation, Employment and Equity: The Vietnam Experience, Regional Office for Asia and the Pacific: Bangkok, ILO/EASMAT project.

Central Institute for Economic Management (CIEM) (2000) *Vietnam's Economy in 1999*, Hanoi: Statistical Publishing House.

__________ (2001) An Overview of Vietnam's Trade Policy in the 1990s, manuscript. This is an updated version of An Overview of Vietnam's Trade Policies, by The Technical Group of TLCV in *Vietnam's Socio-Economic Development*, No.19, Autumn, 1999.

Centre of International Economics (CIE) (1998) *Vietnam's Trade Policies 1998,* Canberra and Sydney: CIE.

Deaton, A. (1989) Rice Prices and Income Distribution in Thailand: A Non-Parametric Analysis, *Economic Journal*, 99, 1-37.

__________ (1997) *The Analysis of Household Surveys: A Microeconomic Approach to Development Policy,* World Bank: The John Hopkins University Press.

Dercon, S. (2002) The Impact of Economic Reforms on Rural Households in Ethiopia: A Study from 1989 to 1995, *Poverty Dynamics in Africa Series*, Washington, D.C.: World Bank.

Falaris, E. M. (2003) The Effect of Survey Attrition in Longitudinal Surveys: Evidence from Peru, Côte d'Ivoire and Vietnam, *Journal of Development Economics*, 70, 133-157.

Gallup, J.L. (2004) The Wage Labour Market and Inequality in Vietnam in the 1990s, in *Economic Growth, Poverty, and Household Welfare in Vietnam* (Ed.), Glewwe, P., Agrawal, N. and Dollar, D., Washington, D.C.: World Bank.

General Statistics Office (GSO), various issues, *Statistical Yearbook*, Hanoi: Statistical Publishing House.

Glewwe, P., Gragnolati, M. and Zaman, H. (2002) Who gained from Vietnam's boom in the 1990s?, *Economic Development and Cultural Change*, 50(4), 773-792.

International Monetary Fund (IMF) (1998) Vietnam: Selected Issues and Statistical Appendix, *Staff Country Report*, No.98/30, Washington D.C.: IMF.

____________ (1999) Vietnam: Selected Issues, *Staff Country Report*, No. 99/55, Washington D.C.: IMF.

__________ (2000) Vietnam: Statistical Appendix, *Staff Country Report*, No. 00/116, Washington D.C.: IMF.

Justino, P. and Litchfield, J. (2002) Poverty Dynamics in Vietnam: Winners and Losers during Reform, *PRUS Working Paper*, No.10, Poverty Research Unit, University of Sussex.

__________ (2004) Welfare in Vietnam during the 1990s: Poverty, Inequality and Poverty Dynamics, *Journal of the Asia Pacific Economy*, 9(2), 145-169.

Kokko, A. (1997) Vietnam 1997: Managing the Transition to Free Trade: Vietnamese Trade Policy for the 21st Century, *Macroeconomic Reports*, 1997:4, Stockholm: SIDA.

Martin, W. (2000) Achieving High Growth: Experience of Transitional Economies in East Asia, *Paper for presentation to the International Conference on Achieving High Growth: Experience of Transitional Economies in East Asia*, Australian National University, September 6-7, 2000.

Minot, N., 1998, Competitiveness of the Food Processing Sector in Vietnam: a Study of the Rice, Coffee, Seafood and Fruits and Vegetables Subsectors, Appendix I of the Industrial Competitiveness Review, UNIDO.

Minot, N. and Goletti, F. (1998) Export Liberalisation and Household welfare: the Case of Rice in Vietnam, *American Journal of Agricultural Economics*, 80, 738-749.

Nielsen, C. P. (2002) Vietnam in the International Rice Market, *Fødevareøkonomisk Institute Rap*port, No.132, Copenhagen: Fødevareøkonomisk Institute.

Niimi, Y., Vasudeva-Dutta, P. and Winters, L. A. (2003) Trade Liberalisation and Poverty Dynamics in Vietnam, *PRUS Working Paper*, No.17, Poverty Research Unit, University of Sussex.

__________ (2004) Storm in a Rice Bowl: Rice Reform and Poverty in Vietnam in the

1990s, *Journal of the Asia Pacific Economy*, 9(2), 170-190.

____________ (forthcoming (2005)) Linking Trade Liberalisation and Poverty: An Illustration from Vietnam in the 1990s, in *Globalisation and Poverty: Channels and Policy Responses* (Ed.), Bussolo, M. and Round, J., Routledge.

O'Connor, D. (1996) Labour Market Aspects of State Enterprise Reform in Viet Nam, OECD Development Centre.

Ravallion, M. (1996) Issues in Measuring and Modelling Poverty, *Economic Journal*, 106, 1328-1343.

Ravallion, M. and van de Walle, D. (1991) The Impact on Poverty of Food Pricing Reforms: A Welfare Analysis for Indonesia, *Journal of Policy Modelling*, 13, 281-299.

Singh, I., Squire, L. and Strauss, J. (1986) A Survey of Agricultural Household Models: recent Findings and Policy Implications, *World Bank Economic Review*, 1, 149-79.

van Donge, J. K, White, H. and Nghia, L. W. (1999) Fostering High Growth in a Low Income Economy, Stockholm: SIDA.

White, H. and Masset, E. (2003) The Importance of Household Size and Composition in Constructing Poverty Profiles: An Illustration from Vietnam, *Development and Change*, **34**(1), 105-126.

Winters, L. A. (2000) Trade and Poverty, Is There a Connection?, in *Trade, Income Disparity and Poverty* (Ed.) Ben David, D., Nordstrom, H. and Winters, L. A., Geneva: WTO.

__________ (2002) Trade Liberalisation and Poverty: What Are the Links?. *The World Economy*, **25**, 1339-1367.

World Bank (1999) *Vietnam Development Report 2000: Attacking Poverty*, Donor-NGO Working Group, Consultative Group Meeting for Vietnam, December 14-15, 1999.

___________ (2000) Vietnam Living Standards Survey 1992-93: Basic Information, Washington, D.C. World Bank.

___________ (2001) Vietnam Living Standards Survey 1997-98: Basic Information, Washington, D.C.: World Bank.

*Trade Liberalization and Rural Poverty (Thomas Hertel, Purdue University and Terry Sicular, University of Western Ontario, organizers)*

# AGRICULTURAL TRADE LIBERALIZATION AND POVERTY DYNAMICS IN THREE DEVELOPING COUNTRIES

JULIE LITCHFIELD, NEIL MCCULLOCH, AND L. ALAN WINTERS

Many developing countries implemented sweeping agricultural reforms over the last decade. Reforms have included the removal of quotas and price controls, changes in international trade barriers, and the commercialization and privatization of state marketing boards for key crops. These reforms have often generated intense criticism from groups claiming that they hurt poor farmers and poor households. This concern has generated an extensive literature on the economics of agricultural trade reform in developing countries, much of which has focused on explaining the large variations in supply response across countries, regions and households (e.g., Key, Sadoulet, and De Janvry). In addition, a number of papers have attempted to simulate the impact on poverty using household survey data and actual or predicted price changes (e.g., Chen and Ravallion). However, in many cases the true impact of agricultural reform is difficult to determine. In part this is because the analysis is based upon household surveys at a single point in time, so that the final (post-adjustment) consequences upon individual households are unknown. Also, even where observations are available over time, it has so far proved difficult to disentangle the effects of trade and agricultural liberalization from other contemporary shocks.

This article reports the results of a research project on the empirics of Trade Liberalization and Poverty. It exploits detailed household survey data from more than one period in time to look at the impact of agricultural and other liberalization in three developing countries: Vietnam, China (Sichuan), and Zambia. The research is based on a conceptual framework that links trade liberalization to poverty (see, e.g., Winters; Winters, McCulloch, and McKay). This helps significantly with the identification of different effects. Given the framework and the fact that the surveys span periods of intense liberalization, this study offers an almost unique chance of identifying the poverty effects of liberalization *ex post*.

## The Conceptual Framework

Trade economists understand that liberalization can have distributional impacts and an extensive literature exists discussing the impact of liberalization on wage inequality, particularly in developed countries. However, traditional trade theory does not take us too far when trying to understand the impact of liberalization on poverty in a multifactor and multigood world. Winters therefore starts from a "farm household" model, in which poverty is related to the prices and quantities of the goods and services produced by the household (including factor services, most notably labor), other sources of income such as transfers and remittances, and, implicitly, household

Julie Litchfield is director of the Poverty Research Unit at Sussex and lecturer in Economics at the University of Sussex; Neil McCulloch is research fellow at the Institute of Development Studies, Brighton, and L. Alan Winters is professor of Economics at the University of Sussex.

The authors are grateful to Patricia Justino, Yoko Niimi, and Puja Vasudeva-Dutta for their excellent contributions and to several seminar participants including Bob Baulch, Rhys Jenkins, Lina Song, Andy McKay, Shujie Yao, Barry Reilly, and Linxiu Zhang, for their valuable comments.

This research was funded by the U.K. Department for International Development, "The Impact of Trade Reforms and Trade Shocks on Household Poverty Dynamics" (ESCOR-R7621) as part of the Globalisation and Poverty Research Programme.

This article was presented in a principal paper session at the AAEA annual meeting (Montreal, Quebec, July 2003). The articles in these sessions are not subjected to the journal's standard refereeing process.

structure. Two key transmission mechanisms from trade to household living standards are identified here. First and most direct is price changes. Even simple economies have several stages between the border, where trade policy/shocks bite, and the poor household, so one consideration is how much of the price change gets passed through to the poor. This depends on the nature of the distribution sector, especially its degree of competition. It is also important to consider how households accommodate shocks, for strong "second round" effects could affect prices and employment in local markets. Even more important is whether markets exist at all: trade reform can both create and destroy markets. Extreme adverse poverty shocks are mostly associated with losing market access, while strong poverty alleviation can arise when new markets provide opportunities for previously untraded or unavailable goods.

Trade reform is also likely to have major effects on labor markets: if it boosts the demand for labor-intensive products, it will boost wages and/or employment. However, the effects on poverty are a function of whether the poor depend heavily on the favored type of labor and where the new wages lie relative to the poverty line and, of course, on whether labor-intensive products are actually stimulated by reform. The latter will not always be true, especially for goods produced by the very least-skilled workers.

Winters also discusses the links to poverty via government tax and expenditures, and economic growth. These are likely to be important, especially the latter, but are very difficult to identify with the available short time series of household survey data. Hence we focus on the most direct transmission mechanisms: prices, wages, and employment.

## The Empirical Challenge

The research faces two important empirical challenges. First, identifying the effects of trade liberalization on household poverty dynamics is difficult because other factors may be important. Demographic events such as births, deaths or family splits and other events such as spells of ill-health change the ratio of household needs to income. Environmental shocks, such as unusually high or low rainfall levels or diseases, or other shocks, e.g., damage to roads, affect earnings ability. Even if movements in and out of poverty can be traced to shifts in employment, wages or prices, these need to be attributed to trade rather than other economic reforms. And of course, the trade reform itself may include several different events and affect several different sectors in offsetting ways.

Second, the research requires detailed and reliable household data before and after the trade reform. For Vietnam, we use a nationally representative panel data set of 4,302 households, the Vietnam Living Standards Survey (VLSS) (with data on household expenditures, employment, production, demographics, schooling and other household and community characteristics) for 1992/1993 and 1997/1998, a period with significant changes in trade policy, especially on rice. For China, we use a rich 5-year panel dataset with similar data on 3,311 households in rural Sichuan between 1991 and 1995, the most populous province, spanning a period of major changes in the central government's quota and pricing regime for the grain market—the most important market for the poor. Analytically Sichuan is equivalent to a small open economy facing exogenous shocks from the world economy. Finally, in Zambia a pseudo-panel has been constructed from three nationally representative Living Standards Measurement Surveys covering the 1990s—a period that included a major reform of maize pricing and marketing. From these data, we determine movements in and out of poverty and relate these to shifts in policy while controlling for demographic and other shocks and for unobserved heterogeneity across households.[1]

## Vietnam

The direct, static, impact of trade liberalization on poverty is first estimated for Vietnam.[2] The incidence of poverty fell strongly between the two VLSS surveys: from 58% to 37%.[3] However, the gains were not uniform: around 28% of individuals remained poor in both years, 5% fell into poverty, 27% escaped poverty and just under 40% were not poor in either year (Justino and Litchfield). Since the start

[1] We are grateful to the General Statistical Office in Hanoi, Vietnam, the Household Survey Division of the Rural Survey Organization in the National Bureau of Statistics, China, the Central Statistical Office in Lusaka, Zambia, and to the World Bank LSMS for access to the household data and documentation.

[2] See Justino and Litchfield and Niimi, Vasudeva-Dutta, and Winters (2003a) for details.

[3] The official poverty line is used here, and is based on a specific basket of goods that provide 2100 calories per person per day plus some nonfood expenses (World Bank).

of the *doi moi* reforms in the late 1980s, the Vietnamese economy has undergone a broad but sometimes halting and confused transition. A major challenge has been to separate the international trade reforms from other shocks and plot their transmission through to poor households.

The trade reforms included: (*a*) the removal of constraints on trade outside the Council of Mutual Economic Assistance (CMEA) bloc,[4] (*b*) the liberalization of foreign exchange controls, (*c*) the relaxation of quantitative controls and greater use of tariffs, (*d*) export promotion and the establishment of export processing zones, (*e*) integration with the world economy via regional and multilateral trading agreements, and (*f*) the adoption of the international Harmonised System (HS) for defining tariffs.

The multiplicity of instruments and reversibility of many reforms make it very difficult to assess the importance of particular tariff and other policy changes, so we relied on outcomes—observed prices and quantities—rather than policies to identify the impact of the trade liberalization. In outcomes we detect dramatic changes, and there must be at least a reasonable presumption that they have been heavily influenced by the policy changes noted. The share of international trade in GDP increased from about 52 to 71% between 1993 and 1998. Imports grew by 293% dominated by machinery and intermediate goods (amounting to approximately 70% of total imports), while exports grew by 213%—apparently in line with comparative advantage. Agriculture, forestry, and fisheriesexports expanded but by less than the share of coffee (a new product), handicrafts, and light industrial goods. One of the most dramatic changes was from being a net importer of rice in 1992, to the world's second largest exporter by volume in 1998. From around 1990, domestic rice prices were liberalized, export quotas removed and trading rights extended. Exports boomed and prices rose (by 29% in real terms relative to the CPI). Real fertilizer prices fell by 19% between 1993 and 1998, again as a result of policy change. Real prices of other tradables are also changed considerably, for example, seafoods by over +40% and woollens by –38%. These changes alone suggest that trade policy was effective.

Wage data are extremely confused in Vietnam, but trade affects wages by changing the output bundle, so we also identified the commodities for which exports and imports changed most over 1993–1998 and then traced these back to their producing industries and occupations. *Prima facie*, if trade "matters," these sectors and occupations would help most in explaining household poverty experiences. The export sectors are clothing, footwear, seafood, and food processing[5] and the import sectors are textiles, machinery, leather, chemicals and metal industries.[6]

We then determined the contribution of the observable liberalization-induced changes to the reduction of poverty at the household level. We estimated a multinomial logit model on household data, and asked whether the production activities and characteristics that would a priori dispose a household towards an escape from poverty actually did so. Starting from a "standard" demographic multinominal logit model of household poverty dynamics we add a number of additional variables to reflect the trade links: rice and coffee production, land and fertilizer use, and the proportion of household members working in export industries. With one exception, all the variables refer to households' characteristics or activities in the initial period. This is partly to avoid problems of simultaneity whereby poverty experience might determine the variables included on the right-hand side of the equation rather than vice versa. But it also reflects the desire to test the conceptual framework as a predictive tool. That is, to see how well the framework would predict the effects of trade reform if it were applied *ex ante* using only the information available in the initial period.

Collectively the trade variables are strongly statistically significant and loosely speaking, allowing for trade variables improves one's ability to explain poverty dynamics by around 10%. Table 1 reports the coefficients on the trade variables as relative risk ratios: *ceteris paribus*, a household whose production of coffee in 1992 was one standard deviation above the mean had more than double the mean chance of escaping from poverty in 1998. Similarly, a one standard deviation increase in rice output increases the chances of escape by 75% in general (although less in the Mekong Delta

[4] The CMEA consists of the former Soviet Union, socialist Eastern Europe and Cuba.

[5] We do not include agriculture because (*a*) it offers relatively little wage-employment and (*b*) most food is at least partly processed before it is exported.

[6] We also conducted a factor-content of trade analysis and found some evidence of increased demand for unskilled labor (Niimi, Vasudeva-Dutta, and Winters 2003b).

**Table 1. Relative Risk Ratios (RRR) for Escaping from Poverty in Vietnam**

| Agricultural Variables | RRR |
|---|---|
| Quantity of rice production | 1.75*** |
| In Mekong river delta | 0.60** |
| In Red river delta | 0.85** |
| Quantity of coffee production | 2.32*** |
| Quantity of fertilizer—for rice crops | 1.46*** |
| Quantity of fertilizer—for nonrice crops | 1.70* |
| Other trade variables | |
| Ratio of household members working in exports | 1.25*** |
| Change in the ratio of export workers | 1.17** |
| Pseudo $R^2$ | 0.27 |

Notes: Asterisks denote the statistical significance of each of the relative risk ratios: *** indicates that the relative risk ratio is significant at a 1% level; ** at a 5% level and * at a 10% level. All continuous variables are included in standardized form.
Source: Niimi, Vasudeva-Dutta, and Winters (2003a).

where farms are larger than average and hired labor is more common.[7] As fertilizer prices fell, heavy users could sustain increases in real consumption. We distinguished between rice and nonrice fertilizer effects, because the latter may reflect greater opportunities for exploiting the fall in price as farmers switch between crops rather than just increase use for a single crop.

There are at least three ways to link initial employment in an export sector to escape from poverty. Existing workers could get real wage increases or longer hours, or initial employment may indicate a location close to exporting firms and hence better chances of the household obtaining jobs as the firms expand. To explore the third more closely, we broke our rule of using only initial values as explanatory variables, and added the change in the proportion of adults with employment in export sectors. Initial employment in the export sectors does have advantages in escaping poverty but so too does a household's ability to supply new export workers. The lesson is that for predicting the poverty effects of trade liberalization, agricultural elements may be well captured by initial activity in the affected sector because mobility is relatively low in these sectors.[8] For manufacturing, however, although initial employment captures some of the likely effects, some will be less predictable because mobility into manufacturing jobs is high.

While the trade effects appear to be estimated precisely enough to reject the hypothesis that they have arisen by chance, we also should consider their contribution to explaining poverty dynamics. Adding the trade variables increases the pseudo-$R^2$ from 0.234 to 0.266 suggesting that trade adds a further 14% to the explained variation in poverty experience but much variation remains unexplained. The proportions of correct predictions from the model tell a similar story. The basic model classifies 59.90% of households correctly, over-predicting no-change outcomes and strongly under-predicting the changes. Adding the trade variables improves the overall success rate by about 1.5 percentage points or 2.5% and materially improves the predictions for escapees from poverty.

The results so far lend considerable weight to the conceptual framework proposed and to the view that "trade matters." They do not, however, tell us directly whether trade reform reduced poverty in Vietnam. For that, we need to simulate a counterfactual—"1998 without trade reform"—and it is here that uncertain attribution takes its toll. As noted above we use initial household characteristics as variables and then essentially infer the change in their value between 1993 and 1998 from the estimated coefficients. Hence, we can estimate the effects of trade reform on overall poverty by reducing the 'trade-related' coefficients in the multinomial logit and recalculating the predicted changes in poverty. To allow for the possibility that some of the benefits of being in rice or using fertilizer may reflect domestic reforms we halve the estimated values of the trade coefficients. In the absence of the trade component about 100 fewer households (out of 4,302)

---

[7] The effect of an increase in rice output in the Mekong by one standard deviation is an increase of 5%, that is, 100 × (1.75 × 0.60 − 1), in the chance of escaping poverty.

[8] Similarly negative shocks will hit hard in agriculture, as, for example, the decline in coffee prices since 1997 is reported to have done in Vietnam's Central Highlands.

would have escaped from poverty and nearly 300 more would have been in poverty in 1998—about 10% of the observed values in each case. Hence we conclude that for Vietnam, trade liberalization not only mattered but was directly responsible for a significant share of the dramatic poverty reduction observed during the period.

## China (Sichuan)

The effects of trade liberalization on poverty are next estimated for rural Sichuan.[9] Major reforms were undertaken in the Sichuan grain market during the early 1990s: parts of Sichuan eliminated mandatory procurement quota requirements in 1992; both the urban grain rationing and compulsory procurement system were successfully liberalized in the entire province by 1993 and some regions also relaxed restrictions on grain trade in free markets. However, these reforms were abruptly halted in 1994 after a severe grain price hike. Price controls were reimposed and reforms in the grain rationing system in urban areas were abandoned. To encourage farmers to meet their production quota, the government raised contract purchase prices by 44% in 1994 and again in 1995. By 1995, the old system of compulsory procurement through a two-tier system of quota and above-quota sales and subsidised grain for urban areas had been reintroduced in 29 of China's 35 major cities.

These reforms (and their reversal) are of particular interest because they are "trade like" reforms in the sense that they were centrally determined, uniform in their application and affected the price of the commodity of most importance to poor people. However, attribution is again a problem as there was a drought in many parts of the province in 1993, a rapid expansion in the number of Township and Village Enterprises (TVEs), and the government began a major anti-poverty initiative in designated "poor counties" some of which are included in our sample.

Our analysis of the effect of trade on poverty in Sichuan takes a slightly different approach because the household surveys include reliable information on income sources. Firstly, changes in per adult equivalent income giving rise to movements in and out of poverty were decomposed into the changes in the various sources of household income and changes in the number of adult equivalents in the household. This exercise showed that changes in household income were generally a much more important reason for movements in and out of poverty than changes in household composition: changes in household income were responsible for entries and exits in more than 90% of cases, and of these, changes in profit income (which includes farm profits) were by far the most common cause of a poverty transition, with changes in employment income accounting for less than 5% of all cases. When looking just at profit income, changes in farming income dominate, although changes in livestock income are also important. Interestingly changes in farming income are a much more important cause of exits from poverty between 1993 and 1994 than they are of entries into poverty—presumably reflecting the large rise in the government procurement price in 1994.

This decomposition analysis does not account for differences in household characteristics or external shocks faced by the household. To identify the impact of grain market reforms while controlling for these other factors, a discrete-time proportional odds model was estimated, with the results shown in table 2.[10] Several of the control factors play a strong and statistically significant role but here we focus on those variables that reflect trade reform (see McCulloch and Cao). Notwithstanding the many other factors, grain market variables play an important and statistically significant role. A higher grain quota price or market price significantly reduces the probability of entering poverty,[11] and being a net seller of grain greatly increases the chance of exit. Households who are both net sellers and who live in areas with high grain market prices substantially reduce their risk of entering poverty (although surprisingly it also reduces the risk of exiting poverty too). Interestingly, it is the market price that is doing all the work—the interaction of the quota price with net sales has no statistically significant effect.

Overall, these results do not prove that grain market reform had a predominant effect on poverty reduction—too much else is going on.

[9] See McCulloch and Calandrino and McCulloch and Cao for further details.

[10] This model assumes that the relative odds of entry into (or exit from) poverty is equal to the relative odds of a baseline hazard scaled by $\exp(\boldsymbol{\beta}'\mathbf{X})$.

[11] An "average" household in an area with a quota or market price one standard deviation above the mean would see a fall in their probability of entry into poverty of around 20%.

**Table 2. Discrete Time Proportional Odds Model of Poverty Entry/Exit in Sichuan**

| | Entry into Poverty | | Exit from Poverty | |
|---|---|---|---|---|
| | Odds Ratio | *z*-stat | Odds Ratio | *z*-stat |
| Grain market variables | | | | |
| Grain quota price | 0.67 | −3.50 | 1.03 | 0.74 |
| Grain market price | 0.68 | −3.04 | 1.02 | 0.24 |
| Net sales per adult equivalent | 4.09 | 0.70 | 13.04 | 2.34 |
| Net sales × grain market price | 0.14 | −1.72 | 0.23 | −1.69 |
| Net sales × grain quota price | 2.34 | 0.52 | 0.42 | −1.35 |
| Hazard | | | | |
| ln(time) | 15.20 | 11.64 | 102.10 | 15.15 |
| Pseudo $R^2$ | 0.204 | | 0.389 | |

Source: McCulloch and Cao.

However, they do show that the impact of grain reforms can be identified and that in rural Sichuan they do appear to have had a statistically significant effect in reducing entry into poverty particularly among households who were net producers of grain (and conversely for net consumers). This is exactly the result that our conceptual framework predicts.

## Zambia

Implementing the conceptual framework is especially difficult in the Zambian case study as there are no nationally representative panel survey data sets available. Instead the national LSMS-style households surveys are used to create a pseudo-panel of household types based on shared geographical and household characteristics (see Litchfield and McCulloch).

Some of the key reforms in Zambia during the 1990s were the removal of the ban on maize exports, abolition of the state maize marketing board (that previously provided inputs as well as purchased outputs) and the consequent end to pan-territorial and pan-seasonal maize pricing. In addition, the price of copper declined further during the latter part of this period.

Poverty in Zambia during the 1990s was persistently high: estimates from the cross-section suggest that poverty hovered between 70 and 80% between 1991 and 1998. For the pseudo-panel, which is based on aggregates, there was very little movement across the poverty threshold observed between 1991 and 1998 but much more movement across quintiles. Therefore, the limited dependent variable model approach adopted for Vietnam was replaced by a consumption growth model. Table 3 summarizes the trade-related results for the rural pseudo-panel. The first observation is that few coefficients are statistically significant, suggesting that grouping by age of household head and district creates some groups that are too small to yield precise estimates. The second observation is that only one of the trade-related variable coefficients is statistically significant: cohorts who initially sold a high proportion of their hybrid maize harvest

**Table 3. Cohort Regression of Consumption Growth in Rural Zambia (Selected Variables)**

| Employment | Coefficient | Agriculture | Coefficient | Sector | Coefficient |
|---|---|---|---|---|---|
| Self-employed | 0.23 | Hybrid maize | 0.16 | Agriculture | 1.98 |
| Govt. employee | 1.73 | Local maize | 0.78 | Mining | 0.45 |
| Parastatal | −0.65 | Hybrid maize sold | 0.54* | Light manu. | 18.26 |
| Private employee | −3.27 | Local maize sold | 0.06 | Heavy manu. | −0.37 |
| Employer | −25.12 | Non-agri hh | −2.01 | Utilities | 17.06 |
| Family worker | −3.19 | | | Services | −2.70 |
| Other | −5.92 | | | Public admin | −11.18 |
| *N* | 147 | | | | |
| Adjusted $R^2$ | 0.27 | | | | |

Notes: Results refer to changes in (ln) per adult equivalent expenditures between 1991 and 1998 for cohorts defined by age of household head and district. All variables are measured as proportions of households per cohort. An asterisk indicates coefficient is statistically significant at the 5% level or better.
Source: Litchfield and McCulloch.

experienced higher growth of consumption expenditures. However, even though almost all coefficients on the trade related variables are not statistically significant, most have the sign expected: cohorts with greater proportions of workers employed by parastatals, in the private sector and as employers performed relatively badly, as did those with high proportions employed in heavy manufacturing and services. Cohorts with more household heads engaged in agriculture and with fewer nonagricultural households did better than others, although the results are not statistically significant. Although the lack of statistical significance of the trade-related variables is somewhat disappointing the results do suggest that some trade effects can be identified using the conceptual framework described above.

## Common Themes and Conclusions

This paper is one of the first attempts to measure empirically, rather than simulate, the effects of trade reform on poverty using household survey microdata. In each of the three countries, trade liberalization of a major agricultural staple was analyzed: rice in Vietnam, grains in Sichuan, China and maize in Zambia. Each of these commodities was initially highly regulated but underwent considerable liberalization during the 1990s.

In Vietnam, a clear empirical link can be identified between movements in and out of poverty and households' status as producers of rice, including differences between regions (due to differences in the structure of the rice sector) and technology. In addition, the effects of liberalization on coffee producers and employees in other sectors are identified. In Sichuan, changes in grain prices affected movements in and out of poverty, but changes in the government grain quota had less impact. In Zambia, nonagricultural households were hurt by policy reforms, whereas the combined effect of output and input market reforms appears to have muted the impact upon rural farmers.

The policy significance of this work is not the generation of universal rules linking trade to poverty—that was never expected nor intended. Rather, we have shown the importance of trade in specific cases and shown how the conceptual framework can be used to predict the likely poverty impacts of policy reforms. Although trade reform is only one of several influences on poverty outcomes, it is one of the most easily and quickly manipulated. Thus this work contributes to the advice that liberal trade, supplemented where necessary with flanking measures, can help reduce poverty.

## References

Chen, S., and M. Ravallion. "Household Welfare Impacts of China's Accession to the World Trade Organization." World Bank Working Paper 3040, Washington DC, 2003.

Justino, P., and J. Litchfield. "Poverty Dynamics in Rural Vietnam: Winners and Losers During Reform." Poverty Research Unit at Sussex Working Paper 10, 2003.

Key, N., E. Sadoulet, and A. De Janvry. "Transaction Costs and Agricultural Household Supply Response." *American Journal of Agricultural Economics* 82(2000):245–59.

Litchfield, J., and N. McCulloch. "Poverty in Zambia: Assessing the Impacts of Trade Liberalisation in the 1990s." Poverty Research Unit at Sussex Working Paper 16, 2003.

McCulloch, N., and M. Calandrino. "Vulnerability and Chronic Poverty in Rural Sichuan." *World Development* 31(2003):611–28.

McCulloch, N., and Y. Cao. "What Caused Changes in Household Income and Poverty in Rural Sichuan in the Early 1990s?" Poverty Research Unit at Sussex Working Paper 21, 2003.

Niimi, Y., P. Vasudeva-Dutta, and L.A. Winters. "Trade Liberalisation and Poverty Dynamics in Vietnam." Poverty Research Unit at Sussex Working Paper 17, 2003a.

——. "Linking Trade Liberalisation and Poverty: An Illustration from Vietnam in the 1990s." Poverty Research Unit at Sussex Working Paper 22, 2003b.

Winters, L.A. "Trade, Trade Policy and Poverty: What Are the Links?" *The World Economy* 25(2002):1339–67.

Winters, L.A., N. McCulloch, and A. McKay. "Trade Liberalisation and Poverty: The Empirical Evidence." University of Sussex Discussion Paper in Economics 88, 2002.

World Bank. "Vietnam Development Report 2000: Attacking Poverty." Donor-NGO Working Group, Consultative Group Meeting for Vietnam Hanoi, December 1999.

*Review of Development Economics*, *13(4)*, *543–559*, *2009*
DOI:10.1111/j.1467-9361.2008.00483.x

# Why Isn't the Doha Development Agenda more Poverty Friendly?

*Thomas W. Hertel, Roman Keeney, Maros Ivanic, and L. Alan Winters**

## Abstract

Critics of the Doha Development Agenda rightly point to the lack of aggressive reform in wealthy countries for its role in dampening developing country gains. The authors find that the absence of tariff cuts on staple food products in developing countries also critically limits poverty reduction in those countries. Based on their analysis of the impacts of multilateral trade policy reforms in a sample of 15 developing countries, they find there is some evidence of poverty increases amongst the poor who work in agriculture when they lose protection for their earnings. However, these effects are minimized when agricultural tariffs are cut in *all* developing countries, and when the impact of lower food prices on low income consumers is taken into account in their 15 country sample.

## 1. Introduction and Motivation

The troubled progress of the World Trade Organization's Doha Development Agenda (DDA) has largely revolved around agricultural negotiations and the implications for developing country gains associated with these potential reforms. It is the connection between agricultural reforms and development that has arisen as the most contentious issue in the negotiations. For the current analysis, we adopt an operational definition of development—reduction in the extreme poverty headcount—and ask how different elements of trade liberalization contribute towards this goal. We find that a likely Doha package will be less poverty-friendly than it could have been when considering reforms already removed from the negotiating table. Previous analyses have identified the misplaced attention on industrial countries' agricultural subsidies as not particularly poverty-friendly (Hoekman et al., 2004; Anderson et al., 2006; Hertel et al., 2007). In the current analysis, we concur with this result and note additionally that the limited reform requirements placed on developing countries curtails the ability of the negotiations to reduce poverty in these same nations.

Based on the patterns of protection involved, our analysis suggests that developing country poverty reduction is enhanced both by liberalizing industrial countries' agricultural trade (and rising agricultural prices) and by liberalizing developing countries' trade (which reduces agricultural prices). We are able to resolve the paradoxical nature of these two results by decomposing poverty level income into changes in earnings, taxation, and cost of living effects in order to identify the sources of poverty reduction across a sample of 15 developed countries.

We follow previous simulation analyses of the DDA, such as Hertel and Winters (2006) and Hertel et al. (2007), by constructing plausible Doha round outcomes and

* Hertel and Keeney: Center for Global Trade Analysis, Purdue University, 403 West State Street, W. Lafayette, IN 47907, USA. Tel: 765-494-4199; Fax: 765-496-1224; E-mail: hertel@purdue.edu, rkeeney@purdue.edu. Ivanic: The World Bank 1818 H Street, NW, Washington, DC 20433, USA. Winters: University of Sussex Falmer, Brighton BN1 9SN, UK. Tel: 44 1273 877273; Fax: 44 1273 673563; E-mail: L.A.Winters@sussex.ac.uk.

translating them into reductions in agricultural support. Using these reforms, we employ a general equilibrium model (GTAP) to estimate the impacts on factor and commodity prices and government revenue in 34 countries and regions. In 15 of the developing countries we use detailed household data on factor earnings and consumption to calculate the effects on poverty across seven strata of households in those countries. These 15 developing countries span the continents of Africa, Asia, and Latin America, accounting for nearly 1 billion people and more than 150 million poor (evaluated at the $1/day poverty line). The basic scenarios and modeling approach in this paper are the same as in Hertel et al. (2007). Whereas that article looked at rich-country income distribution as well as poor, and only at the net effects on developing country poverty, here we focus on the decomposition of the effects of different policies and the contrast between developed and developing country liberalization. We believe it is the first systematic attempt to look at the poverty impacts of omitted developing country liberalization in the Doha round. We turn now to our analytical framework, which features a novel approach to decomposing the poverty impacts of trade reform.

## 2. Analytical Framework

*The Poverty Model*

There are many alternative approaches to estimating the change in poverty headcount due to trade reforms (Winters et al., 2004; Hertel and Reimer, 2005). The approach here builds on Hertel et al. (2004) using a sequential modeling strategy with results from a global trade model passed to a series of micro-simulation models. Beginning with a consumer demand system and the associated utility function, the *poverty level of utility* is defined. Evaluation of poverty changes is thus simplified to calculating the percentage of the population below this poverty level of utility.

In this study, we use Rimmer and Powell's (1996) AIDADS demand system to represent consumer preferences. AIDADS is particularly useful for poverty analysis as it devotes two-thirds of its parameters to consumption behavior in the neighborhood of the poverty line (Cranfield et al., 2003). Estimation of this demand system is undertaken using the 80 country, per capita consumption dataset offered by GTAP version 6.1, with the demand system estimates then calibrated to reproduce base year, per capita demands in each country.

A key finding in the work of Hertel et al. (2004) is the importance of stratifying households by primary source of income. Farm households in developing countries often rely on the farm enterprise for virtually all of their income. And national poverty tends to be concentrated in agriculture-specialized households in the poorest countries in our sample. In these cases, the poor are more likely to benefit from producer price increases. In other countries, the national poverty headcount is dominated by wage earners who will be more susceptible to food price rises. To delineate the patterns of earnings specialization we follow Hertel et al. (2004) in identifying five household groups that rely almost exclusively (95% or more) on one source of income: agricultural self-employment, non-agricultural self-employment, rural wage labor, urban wage labor, or transfer payments. The remaining households are grouped into rural and urban diversified strata.[1]

Given our emphasis on the poverty headcount, we focus on households in the neighborhood of the poverty line using a *highly disaggregated* poverty elasticity.[2] Our analysis begins with the cumulative density function of per capita income in region $r$ for the population stratum $s$: $F_{rs}(y)$. Thus $F_{rs}(\bar{y}_r^p)$ computes the poverty headcount ratio when $\bar{y}_r^p$ is the level of income required to attain the poverty level of utility in region $r$ at initial prices. Because preferences and consumer prices are assumed to be the same across all strata in the country, this poverty level of income is unique. We are interested in the elasticity of this poverty headcount with respect to a small change in the real income of households at the poverty line, in a given stratum $s$: $dy_{rs}^p$. Assuming unchanging commodity prices, and given the function $F_{rs}(\bar{y}_r^p)$, this may be computed as follows (where the elasticity is defined to be non-negative):

$$\varepsilon_{rs} = -\frac{dF_{rs}(\bar{y}_r^p)/dy_{rs}^p}{F_{rs}(\bar{y}_r^p)/y_{rs}^p}.$$

The top panel in Table 1 reports these (positive) stratum-specific poverty elasticities for the 15 countries in our sample. They range from a low of 0.0006 in the self-employed agriculture stratum in Zambia, where nearly all of the population is well below the poverty line, to a high of 3.63 in the urban diversified stratum of Brazil, where the population density at the poverty line is quite high.

The proportional change in real income of households at the poverty line in stratum $s$ of region $r$ can be written as the income share-weighted sum of the households' real after-tax factor earnings:

$$\hat{y}_{rs}^p = \sum_j \alpha_{rsj}^p(\hat{W}_{rj} - \hat{C}_r^p) \tag{1}$$

where $\alpha_{rsj}^p$ is the share of income obtained from factor $j$ by households at the poverty line in stratum $s$ of region $r$. These poverty earnings shares tend to be dominated by unskilled labor.[3]

The proportional change in after-tax earnings of factor $j$ in region $r$ is denoted $\hat{W}_{rj}$; $\hat{C}_r^p$ is the proportional change in the cost of living at the poverty line in region $r$, obtained by evaluating the consumer utility function for the level of expenditure required to *remain at the poverty level of utility*.[4] We can now express the proportional change in the poverty headcount in stratum $s$ of region $r$ as follows:

$$\hat{F}_{rs}(\bar{y}_r^p) = \hat{H}_{rs} = -\varepsilon_{rs}\cdot\hat{y}_{rs}^p = -\varepsilon_{rs}\cdot\sum_j\cdot\alpha_{rsj}^p(\hat{W}_{rj} - \hat{C}_r^p) \tag{2}$$

The national poverty headcount can now be expressed as a function of the stratum headcounts and stratum populations ($POP_{rs}$): $H_r = \left[\sum_s POP_{rs} * H_{rs}\right]\Big/POP_r$, where $POP_r = \sum_s POP_{rs}$. So the proportional change in $H_r$ is given by $\hat{H}_r = \sum_s \beta_{rs} * \hat{H}_{rs}$, where the share of stratum $s$ poverty in nationwide poverty in region $r$ is computed as $\beta_{rs} = [(POP_{rs} * H_{rs})/POP_r]/H_r = (POP_{rs} * H_{rs})\Big/\sum_k (POP_{rk} * H_{rk})$. These stratum poverty shares are reported in the bottom panel of Table 1 for our 15 focus countries. Agriculture specialized households and rural diversified households tend to dominate the poverty headcount, although exceptions are Colombia, Venezuela, and Peru, where self-employed, non-agriculture households contain a large share of the poor. Substituting (2) into this expression, we get the following equation with which to evaluate the change in the national poverty headcount in response to changing factor and commodity prices:

$$\hat{H}_r = -\sum_s \beta_{rs}\cdot\varepsilon_{rs}\cdot\sum_j \alpha_{rsj}^p(\hat{W}_{rj} - C_r^p) \tag{3}$$

*Table 1. Key Data for Focus-country Poverty Analysis*

| | Strata | | | | | | | |
|---|---|---|---|---|---|---|---|---|
| *Country* | *Agric.* | *Non-agric.* | *Urban labor* | *Rural labor* | *Transfer* | *Urban diverse* | *Rural diverse* | *Total* |
| *Elasticity of poverty headcount by stratum ($1/day) wrt total income** | | | | | | | | |
| Bangladesh | 1.64 | 2.02 | 1.58 | 0.63 | 0.56 | 1.74 | 1.09 | 1.24 |
| Brazil | 0.75 | 1.28 | 1.94 | 2.19 | 0.34 | 3.63 | 2.69 | 1.35 |
| Chile | 1.90 | 2.24 | 2.06 | 1.55 | 2.45 | 2.29 | 2.60 | 2.18 |
| Colombia | 0.79 | 0.60 | 1.73 | 1.72 | 0.93 | 1.14 | 1.00 | 0.82 |
| Indonesia | 2.35 | 2.14 | 2.38 | 2.89 | 1.17 | 2.58 | 2.87 | 2.47 |
| Malawi | 0.49 | 0.30 | 2.26 | 1.97 | 0.43 | 1.04 | 0.76 | 0.58 |
| Mexico | 1.73 | 1.90 | 3.33 | 2.08 | 2.28 | 1.63 | 1.80 | 2.02 |
| Mozambique | 0.28 | 0.94 | 0.97 | 0.76 | 0.48 | 1.58 | 0.99 | 0.64 |
| Peru | 1.50 | 1.32 | 2.37 | 1.73 | 0.44 | 1.09 | 1.05 | 1.07 |
| Philippines | 2.25 | 1.96 | 2.98 | 2.44 | 1.69 | 2.42 | 1.98 | 2.15 |
| Thailand | 2.30 | 2.42 | 2.98 | 2.45 | 2.78 | 2.42 | 2.59 | 2.57 |
| Uganda | 0.28 | 0.40 | 1.71 | 0.34 | 0.01 | 0.36 | 0.21 | 0.24 |
| Venezuela | 0.69 | 1.16 | 2.57 | 2.17 | 0.01 | 1.72 | 1.53 | 1.20 |
| Vietnam | 0.48 | 1.12 | 2.81 | 8.98 | 0.84 | 0.86 | 1.01 | 0.98 |
| Zambia | 0.00 | 0.64 | 2.28 | 0.91 | 0.45 | 1.29 | 0.37 | 0.61 |
| *Stratum contributions to the $1/day poverty population in each country*** | | | | | | | | |
| Bangladesh | 0.15 | 0.13 | 0.04 | 0.22 | 0.03 | 0.07 | 0.37 | 1.00 |
| Brazil | 0.14 | 0.09 | 0.24 | 0.15 | 0.32 | 0.04 | 0.03 | 1.00 |
| Chile | 0.26 | 0.01 | 0.09 | 0.09 | 0.28 | 0.15 | 0.12 | 1.00 |
| Colombia | 0.28 | 0.43 | 0.03 | 0.04 | 0.12 | 0.05 | 0.04 | 1.00 |
| Indonesia | 0.42 | 0.12 | 0.02 | 0.07 | 0.04 | 0.06 | 0.28 | 1.00 |
| Malawi | 0.54 | 0.11 | 0.00 | 0.03 | 0.07 | 0.01 | 0.25 | 1.00 |
| Mexico | 0.05 | 0.06 | 0.05 | 0.12 | 0.28 | 0.14 | 0.29 | 1.00 |
| Mozambique | 0.41 | 0.13 | 0.01 | 0.05 | 0.14 | 0.06 | 0.19 | 1.00 |
| Peru | 0.07 | 0.35 | 0.01 | 0.02 | 0.22 | 0.11 | 0.23 | 1.00 |
| Philippines | 0.12 | 0.06 | 0.03 | 0.05 | 0.03 | 0.23 | 0.49 | 1.00 |
| Thailand | 0.06 | 0.02 | 0.00 | 0.06 | 0.11 | 0.07 | 0.68 | 1.00 |
| Uganda | 0.10 | 0.04 | 0.00 | 0.03 | 0.02 | 0.07 | 0.75 | 1.00 |
| Venezuela | 0.08 | 0.24 | 0.17 | 0.10 | 0.28 | 0.08 | 0.05 | 1.00 |
| Vietnam | 0.04 | 0.11 | 0.00 | 0.00 | 0.05 | 0.10 | 0.70 | 1.00 |
| Zambia | 0.34 | 0.23 | 0.10 | 0.07 | 0.07 | 0.09 | 0.11 | 1.00 |

* Values in strata columns are elasticities of the poverty headcount with respect to changes in earnings. Total column gives the national elasticity which is the poverty share weighted aggregate elasticity for each country. Elasticities estimated by authors using country-specific household survey data.

** Values are shares of the impoverished population that are specialized in a particular stratum of earnings. Shares are derived from country-specific household surveys. Total column reflects that entire poverty population is allocated among the seven strata.

For purposes of subsequent analysis and discussion, it will be useful to further separate the tax component associated with the replacement of lost tariff revenue by another tax instrument. Hertel and Winters (2006) find that the choice of a revenue replacing tax instrument can have a significant impact on the poverty results following trade reform. Here, we follow those authors in adopting the rather neutral approach of an endogenous, uniform-factor income tax. Define the uniform *ad valorem* income tax on factor $j$ in region $r$ as follows: $TAX_{rj} = t_r W_{rj}^m \cdot L_{rj}$, where $t_r$ is the tax replacement instrument applied to market earnings, $W_{rj}^m$. Letting $T_r = (1 + t_r)$ be the *power* of the replacement income tax in region $r$, then, with fixed endowments, the proportional change in after tax income is given by $\hat{W}_{rj} = \hat{W}_{rj}^m - \hat{T}_r$. Substituting into (3) we have the following decomposition of changes in the poverty headcount in region $r$ into market earnings, replacement tax, and cost of living components:

$$\hat{H}_r = -\sum_s \beta_{rs} \cdot \varepsilon_{rs} \cdot \sum_j \alpha_{rsj}^p \left(\hat{W}_{rj}^m - \hat{T}_r - \hat{C}_r^p\right) \tag{4}$$

Finally, because only relative prices matter in the general equilibrium model, and because we wish to separate the "earnings" and "spending" effects of trade reform on households, it is useful to normalize both market wages and the cost of living by a common variable. The choice of normalization factor is arbitrary, because we will first subtract it from wages, before adding it back in with the cost of living. The normalization variable should be a national, nominal variable that does not vary by stratum or earnings type, and it should have some economic meaning when compared to a particular category of wages or to the cost of living. For the present analysis, we choose net national income in the region: $y_r$. Subtracting and adding $\hat{y}_r$ to the term in brackets in (4), recognizing that the tax replacement and cost of living effects are independent of stratum and earnings type, and making use of the fact that $\sum_j \alpha_{rsj} = 1$, we define the national poverty elasticity as the poverty share-weighted sum of the stratum elasticities: $\varepsilon_r \equiv \sum_s \beta_{rs}\varepsilon_{rs}$. This gives the final decomposition of the national poverty impacts of a trade reform in:

$$\hat{H}_r = -\sum_s \beta_{rs}\varepsilon_{rs} \sum_j \alpha_{rsj}^p \left(\hat{W}_{rj}^m - \hat{y}_r\right) + \varepsilon_r \hat{T}_r + \varepsilon_r\left(\hat{C}_r^p - \hat{y}_r\right) \tag{5}$$

The first term in (5) will be termed the "earnings effect" and it identifies the change in a particular wage, relative to net national income. The second term is the "tax effect" and the third term is the "spending effect," which identifies the change in cost of living at the poverty line, relative to net national income.

For expository purposes, let us now consider what (5) has to say about three different trade policy-induced changes: a rise in the unskilled wage rate, a rise in the power of the tax, and a rise in the price of staple foods. Because unskilled wages often represent an important part of poverty income (i.e. $\alpha_{rsj}^p > 0$), a rise in the wage rate relative to $y_r$ will boost real income, substantially moving some households across the poverty line. The proportional change in stratum headcount following the wage rise will depend on the density of the stratum population in the neighborhood of the poverty line as captured by $\varepsilon_{rs}$. If this density is high, and the stratum also contains a substantial share of the nation's poor, as captured by $\beta_{rs}$, then there will be a relatively large reduction in the poverty headcount *ceteris paribus*. Of course, other factors may change as well. If tariffs are cut, we expect that the income tax, $t_r$, will rise so that $\hat{T}_r > 0$, inducing a *rise* in poverty. Finally, if trade liberalization results in a rise in staple food prices for which the poor household's expenditure share is very large, then we expect a rise in the cost of living at the poverty line, relative to net national income, leading to a rise in poverty in region *r*.

In light of the fact that trade reforms considered here change all the relative prices as well as tax revenues, the decomposition offered by (5) is quite important for understanding the underlying drivers behind any change in the national poverty headcount. We now turn to the general equilibrium framework that will determine how these factor prices, commodity prices, and taxes change as a function of trade policies.

### *The Global General Equilibrium Model*

Our starting point for the global general equilibrium analysis of the impacts of trade policy is the GTAP version 6.1 database (Dimaranan, 2007). These data permit us to draw on the carefully constructed Doha reform scenarios developed and utilized in the recent books by Anderson and Martin (2006) and Hertel and Winters (2006). We conduct the necessary experiments to update key trade policies to 2005 to establish that year as the benchmark for trade liberalization, as well as modifying the standard GTAP CGE model to enhance our analysis of agricultural reforms and simulation of poverty impacts. While we retain the simplistic yet empirically robust assumptions of constant returns to scale and perfect competition typically featured in agricultural trade studies, we modify the model to shed new light on the distributional consequences of the Doha reforms—focusing particularly on unraveling the puzzle of why the DDA is not more poverty friendly. Specifically, we ensure consistency on the demand-side of the model by modifying the global model to incorporate the same AIDADS demand system used in the poverty module. Thus, aggregate preferences are consistent with the preferences used to evaluate the impact of price changes on households at the poverty line—although expenditure patterns differ due to differing income levels.

The other modifications relate to the factor markets for discerning earnings effects. We follow recent studies of global agricultural trade liberalization (e.g. Keeney and Hertel, 2005) in modeling farm/non-farm mobility by specifying a constant elasticity of transformation function which "transforms" farm employed versions of labor and capital into non-farm uses, and vice versa. This transformation function permits wages to diverge between the farm and non-farm sectors, a key driver for our distributional analysis. With segmented factor markets, the impact of reduced subsidies to agriculture in the rich economies will not be shared equally between the farm and non-farm labor forces or between farm and non-farm capital owners, and similarly for the benefits from higher farm prices in developing countries following rich country reforms. In order to parameterize these CET factor mobility functions we draw on the OECD's (2001) survey of agricultural factor markets.

We assume a constant aggregate level of land, labor, and capital employment, reflecting the belief that the aggregate supply of factors is unaffected by trade policy. In addition, we employ a macroeconomic closure which fixes the ratios of government spending, tax revenue, net national savings, and the trade balance, all relative to net national income. This (relatively standard) closure facilitates linking the aggregate and disaggregate welfare impacts of trade reform (see online Appendix (at https://www.gtap.agecon.purdue.edu/resources/download/3663.pdf) for a discussion of our closure assumptions and their implications).

Implementation of (5) requires us to map factor earnings in the general equilibrium model to household income sources. Agricultural labor and capital receive the corresponding farm factor returns from the general equilibrium model, as do non-agricultural labor and capital. Wage labor for diversified households reported in the surveys presents a problem because information is lacking for allocating it to either agricultural or non-agricultural activities. We simply assign to it the composite wage for labor determined by the CET endowment function. Finally, transfer payments are indexed by the growth rate in net national income.

## 3. Policy Scenarios

Our attention in this paper is on the developing-country poverty impacts of trade reforms undertaken in both rich and poor countries. We address these in two stages, focusing initially, and in isolation, on the poor-country poverty impacts caused by liberalizing rich-country agricultural policies. We then contrast this with agricultural trade reforms in the poor countries themselves. The latter have proven controversial—particularly with regard to their impact on poverty, with some policymakers emphasizing that lowering protection for agriculture in developing countries will hurt poor farmers. Others have argued that lower food prices will serve to reduce poverty. Our poverty decomposition from equation (5) allows us to identify both the earnings and spending sides of the problem, providing a natural framework for analyzing the combined impact on poverty in our sample of 15 countries. Finally, we bring in non-agricultural reforms (in rich and poor countries) to complete the global reform scenarios.

We consider full liberalization both as a benchmark and as a carefully constructed Doha scenario which derives from the so-called July 2004 Framework Agreement (WTO, 2004). The Doha scenario follows the core liberalization assumptions in Hertel and Winters (2006). Our treatment of Doha entails a combination of cuts to domestic support, export subsidies, and tariffs. We assume that industrial countries with domestic support in excess of 20% of production cut their bound commitments by 75%, while others cut by 60%. However, even with these ambitious reductions, the binding overhang means that effectively only five WTO members would be required to reduce actual support, based on 2001 notifications: Australia, EU, Iceland, Norway, and USA (Jensen and Zobbe, 2006). For developing countries domestic subsidy bindings are cut by 40%. In this case, Jensen and Zobbe (2006) estimate that only Thailand's subsidies would be affected. Export subsidies are assumed to be fully eliminated. Agricultural tariffs in the rich countries are reduced using a tiered formula, with a marginal reduction of 45% on the first 15 percentage points of the tariff, 70% reduction for between 15 and 90 percentage points, and 75% on the remainder of the tariff. The same approach is applied for developing countries with 20, 60, and 120% bound tariff levels in agriculture and marginal cuts of 35, 40, 50, and 60%, respectively.

Cross-sector trade-offs are at the heart of the WTO negotiations, so we also consider the impact of non-agricultural elements of a prospective DDA. We focus exclusively on market access in non-agricultural trade, because barriers to services and investment remain difficult to quantify and those WTO negotiations appear unlikely to yield significant changes in the near term. Non-agriculture tariffs are subjected to proportional reductions of 50% for developed countries and 33% for developing countries. Least developed countries are exempted from these reductions.

## 4. Results

### *Agricultural Liberalization by the Rich Economies*

In our empirical analysis, we make use of the poverty decomposition outlined in equation (5), working through this expression from the inside out, beginning with the fundamental "drivers" of poverty changes, namely factor prices, tax rate changes, and the cost of living change, by region. We then translate the earnings changes into poverty changes by strata, using the earnings shares and poverty elasticities in (5). Finally, we aggregate across strata to examine the national poverty impacts in each region which result from the effects of changes in earnings, taxes and cost of living. This approach provides significant new insights into the contrasting effects of trade reforms in rich and poor countries, as well as Doha vs full liberalization.

Table 2 reports the change in relative factor returns, cost of living, and income tax rates, by country resulting from agricultural trade liberalization by the rich economies.[5] We first note that relative returns to factors employed in agriculture (land, labor, and capital) increase throughout the sample, while returns to non-agricultural factors decline. Economy-wide returns to unskilled wage labor rise, while those associated with skilled wage labor fall. These results are to be expected, because rich country agricultural reforms tend to shift agricultural production from North to South, thereby boosting the demand for agricultural inputs and unskilled labor in general in developing countries. Observe that the impact on the "earnings" associated with transfer payments is zero, as these payments are indexed to net national income, which is also used to deflate all earnings types reported in Table 2.

The first row of the second block of Table 2 averages the changes across our focus countries, while the second row reports the average absolute value (AAV) of the price changes, which tells us how large the price changes are, regardless of sign. Thus, we see that the impact on factor price is largest for land, followed by agricultural unskilled labor, and then skilled labor and agricultural capital. The absolute size of the impacts on non-agricultural factor returns and economy-wide wages are much smaller. So we expect the earnings-driven poverty impacts from rich country agricultural liberalization to be greatest in strata where agricultural factors command large earnings shares.

The consistency of the results across sample countries is neatly summarized by the "sign consistency" statistic (Hertel and Ivanic, 2006) of a given variable (e.g. agricultural unskilled wages). This is the ratio of the average to the AAV of the price change, which is reported in the third row of the second block of Table 2. Because rich agricultural reforms boost unskilled wages in all countries, the sign consistency measure reaches its maximum value of 1.0 for these factors. On the other hand, when it lowers a relative price in all regions—as is the case with non-agriculture skilled wages—the sign consistency measure reaches its minimum value of –1.0. The most striking thing about the relative factor returns impacts under rich country agriculture liberalization is the great consistency of effects across this diverse group of countries (either 1.0 or –1.0 in all cases).

The final two columns in Table 2 report the percentage changes in the power of income tax and the cost of living at the poverty line. Because the rich agricultural reform scenarios involve no tariff reductions in developing countries, there is no need to raise income taxes to replace lost revenue. So the only tax changes are due to the interaction between trade, production, and consumption volumes and the associated taxes. In this case, we see that, in most cases, income tax rates increase slightly, thereby increasing the power of the tax. In the next column, we see that the cost of living at the poverty line rises in all focus countries, save Malawi. Both the tax and living cost factors have an adverse impact on poverty, *ceteris paribus*.

For purposes of comparison, we also report the summary statistics from the rich countries' partial reforms under Doha[6] at the bottom of Table 2. Note that the sign consistency measures share the same sign, but are somewhat muted—the results are mixed across the focus countries. Similarly, the AAV measures are considerably

*Table 2. Drivers of Poverty Change across Focus Regions: Rich Country Agricultural Reforms*

| Countries | Land | Ag. unskilled labor | Ag. skilled labor | Non-ag. unskilled labor | Non-ag. skilled labor | Wage labor unskilled | Wage labor skilled | Agricultural capital | Non-agricultural capital | Transfers | Taxes | Cost of living |
|---|---|---|---|---|---|---|---|---|---|---|---|---|
| ***Rich agriculture full liberalization*** | | | | | | | | | | | | |
| Bangladesh | 2.1 | 1.1 | 0.9 | –0.1 | –0.2 | 0.3 | –0.2 | 0.9 | –0.3 | 0.0 | 0.0 | 0.3 |
| Brazil | 41.5 | 17.7 | 16.3 | –0.6 | –1.0 | 1.6 | –0.8 | 16.2 | –1.3 | 0.0 | 0.3 | 0.8 |
| Chile | 13.5 | 7.0 | 6.3 | –0.2 | –0.5 | 0.9 | –0.5 | 6.3 | –0.6 | 0.0 | 0.0 | 0.7 |
| Colombia | 11.5 | 5.8 | 5.1 | –0.5 | –0.7 | 0.7 | –0.7 | 5.1 | –1.0 | 0.0 | 0.1 | 1.2 |
| Indonesia | 3.2 | 1.9 | 1.5 | –0.2 | –0.4 | 0.5 | –0.4 | 1.5 | –0.4 | 0.0 | 0.0 | 0.6 |
| Malawi | 1.0 | 0.4 | 0.1 | –0.4 | –0.7 | –0.1 | –0.7 | 0.2 | –0.7 | 0.0 | 0.1 | –1.3 |
| Mexico | 11.2 | 5.0 | 4.5 | 0.0 | –0.2 | 0.9 | –0.2 | 4.5 | –0.3 | 0.0 | 0.1 | 0.9 |
| Mozambique | 2.2 | 1.1 | 0.9 | –0.2 | –0.3 | 0.2 | –0.3 | 0.9 | –0.3 | 0.0 | 0.0 | 0.5 |
| Peru | 16.9 | 9.6 | 7.9 | –0.8 | –1.2 | 2.3 | –0.9 | 7.7 | –1.3 | 0.0 | 0.1 | 0.8 |
| Philippines | 3.1 | 1.9 | 1.5 | –0.1 | –0.2 | 0.8 | –0.1 | 1.4 | –0.4 | 0.0 | 0.2 | 0.6 |
| Thailand | 23.4 | 12.2 | 9.6 | –0.2 | –1.2 | 3.8 | –1.0 | 9.3 | –1.8 | 0.0 | 0.1 | 1.2 |
| Uganda | 0.1 | 0.0 | 0.0 | 0.1 | 0.0 | 0.0 | 0.0 | 0.0 | 0.0 | 0.0 | 0.0 | 0.2 |
| Venezuela | 2.4 | 1.3 | 1.2 | –0.1 | –0.1 | 0.1 | –0.1 | 1.2 | –0.1 | 0.0 | 0.0 | 0.3 |
| Vietnam | 4.9 | 2.7 | 2.3 | –0.3 | –0.5 | 0.4 | –0.5 | 2.3 | –0.4 | 0.0 | 0.1 | 0.3 |
| Zambia | 1.8 | 1.0 | 0.8 | –0.1 | –0.1 | 0.2 | –0.1 | 0.8 | –0.3 | 0.0 | 0.0 | 0.2 |
| Average | 9.2 | 4.6 | 3.9 | –0.2 | –0.5 | 0.8 | –0.4 | 3.9 | –0.6 | 0.0 | 0.1 | 0.5 |
| AAV | 9.2 | 4.6 | 3.9 | 0.3 | 0.5 | 0.8 | 0.4 | 3.9 | 0.6 | 0.0 | 0.1 | 0.7 |
| Sign cons. | 1.0 | 1.0 | 1.0 | –1.0 | –1.0 | 1.0 | –1.0 | 1.0 | –1.0 | 0.0 | 0.9 | 0.7 |
| ***Rich agriculture Doha liberalization*** | | | | | | | | | | | | |
| Average | 2.2 | 1.1 | 1.0 | 0.0 | –0.1 | 0.2 | –0.1 | 1.0 | –0.1 | 0.0 | 0.0 | 0.2 |
| AAV | 2.5 | 1.3 | 1.1 | 0.1 | 0.1 | 0.2 | 0.1 | 1.1 | 0.2 | 0.0 | 0.0 | 0.2 |
| Sign cons. | 0.9 | 0.9 | 0.9 | –0.3 | –0.6 | 0.8 | –0.5 | 0.9 | –0.5 | 0.0 | 0.8 | 0.9 |

*Notes*: AAV is the average absolute value of the data in the column; "sign cons" is the "sign consistency" of the data: the ratio of the average to the average absolute value of the variable.

*Table 3. Earnings-driven Percentage Change in the Poverty Headcount ($1/day) across Developing Country Stratums, when Rich Countries Reform Agriculture*

| *Countries* | *Earnings* | *Taxes* | *Cost of living* | *Total* |
|---|---|---|---|---|
| ***Rich agriculture full liberalization*** | | | | |
| Bangladesh | −0.46 | −0.04 | 0.39 | −0.11 |
| Brazil | −3.16 | 0.39 | 0.97 | −1.80 |
| Chile | −5.42 | 0.01 | 1.51 | −3.90 |
| Colombia | −1.28 | 0.05 | 0.95 | −0.28 |
| Indonesia | −2.68 | 0.05 | 1.40 | −1.23 |
| Malawi | −0.05 | 0.05 | −0.74 | −0.74 |
| Mexico | −1.74 | 0.12 | 1.93 | 0.31 |
| Mozambique | −0.23 | −0.01 | 0.31 | 0.07 |
| Peru | −1.32 | 0.07 | 0.85 | −0.40 |
| Philippines | −2.35 | 0.32 | 1.27 | −0.76 |
| Thailand | −9.63 | 0.16 | 2.84 | −6.63 |
| Uganda | −0.01 | 0.00 | 0.05 | 0.04 |
| Venezuela | −0.17 | 0.00 | 0.42 | 0.25 |
| Vietnam | −0.13 | 0.05 | 0.31 | 0.23 |
| Zambia | −0.01 | 0.02 | 0.13 | 0.14 |
| Average | −1.91 | 0.08 | 0.84 | −0.99 |
| AAV | 1.91 | 0.09 | 0.94 | 1.13 |
| Sign cons. | −1.00 | 0.93 | 0.89 | −0.88 |
| ***Rich agriculture Doha liberalization*** | | | | |
| Average | −0.46 | 0.10 | 0.16 | −0.19 |
| AAV | 0.52 | 0.11 | 0.31 | 0.42 |
| Sign cons. | −0.88 | 0.92 | 0.52 | −0.46 |

*Notes*: The total results in this table differ from the RichAgrFull poverty results in Hertel et al. (2007) because the results in this paper are computed as part of a full liberalization experiment using the methodology of Harrison et al. (2000). Thus the results in this table reflect interactions with agricultural policy reforms in the poor countries, as well as non-agriculture reforms. AAV is the average absolute value of the data in the column; "sign cons" is the "sign consistency" of the data: the ratio of the average to the average absolute value of the variable.

smaller. As a result, we expect the poverty impacts of the rich country agricultural liberalization to be similar in sign between full and Doha reforms, but smaller in size under the Doha scenario.

As previously discussed, our analysis of poverty changes and the elasticity of poverty is developed from the earnings and stratum level. In general, we find that poverty falls in the earnings specialized agricultural stratum and rises in the specialized non-agricultural stratum. In other strata earnings-driven poverty falls, driven by the rise in unskilled wages. Thus, apart from those households specialized in self-employment in non-agricultural activities, earnings impacts of rich country agricultural liberalization are favorable for poverty reduction. This general finding follows through in the Doha partial reform scenario as well—albeit with less sign consistency and a smaller AAV.

In order to determine the national poverty impacts, we must aggregate the earnings impacts across strata (weighting the stratum changes by the groups' shares in national poverty) and combine this with the poverty impacts of changing taxes and consumer prices. Table 3 depicts these results of the national poverty impacts separately for earnings, taxes, and cost of living changes, in addition to their sum, which is the total impact on the national poverty headcount. Earnings changes from rich country agricultural liberalization contribute to national poverty reduction in all cases. The rise in agriculture-related returns as well as unskilled wages is sufficient to reduce poverty, even in those countries where the non-agriculture stratum contains a relatively large share of the poor (e.g. Colombia and Peru). The tax effect is negligible, while the cost of living effect tends to raise poverty in all regions save one (Malawi).

With the earnings and spending effects working in opposite directions, it is now a question of relative size in determining the combined impact on national poverty. From Table 3, we see that the earnings effect dominates in nine of the 15 cases, and it is sufficiently large to boost the sign consistency measure to –0.88 (recall that uniform poverty reduction across countries would yield a sign consistency of –1.0). Thus we conclude that full agricultural liberalization in the rich countries is poverty reducing on average for this sample of countries. In contrast, the partial rich country reforms stemming from the Doha scenario yield summary measures (see bottom of Table 3) with a smaller sign consistency measure and an AAV about one-quarter the magnitude of full liberalization. Thus we conclude that rich country reforms under Doha are less poverty-friendly than they would be under full liberalization, and about one-quarter as large. This can be attributed to the heavy emphasis on elimination of export subsidies and the relatively modest cuts in tariffs and domestic subsidies (Hertel and Ivanic, 2006).

*Agricultural Liberalization by the Developing Economies*

Next we consider the impacts of poor country agricultural liberalization following the same scheme as we did in the previous section for rich countries. Table 4 reports the impacts by underlying "drivers" in each focus economy. Note that now it is non-agricultural labor and capital, as well as skilled labor, that realize the largest post-reform gains. This is as expected, because the tariff cuts are now implemented in the developing countries; they reduce the relative demand for unskilled labor and result in the loss of tariff revenue. The impact on deflated agricultural returns is mixed, with substantial declines in some cases and modest rises in those cases where agricultural exports to other developing countries rise as a result of increased South–South trade. With the exception of agricultural land and transfers (the latter's impact is zero due to indexing), the sign consistency summary measure is positive for other factors. The tax and cost of living impacts are quite consistent across countries, with income tax rates rising (to replace lost tariff revenue) and the cost of living falling as consumers get access to food at world market prices (sign consistency = –1.0).

As before, we aggregate the earnings effects across factors and translate them into poverty reductions, by stratum. We now find that the set of households specialized in non-agricultural self-employment realize the most consistent poverty reduction. The other strata show aggregate poverty reductions, but less consistently so. Not surprisingly, the largest AAV is for the agriculture specialized and rural diversified households, as these are the groups most directly affected (on the earnings side) by the agricultural tariff cuts. This pattern of poverty reduction presents a striking contrast with the stratum impacts of reforms in agriculture by wealthy countries. In the latter case, the non-agriculture stratum consistently experiences poverty increases. So combining agriculture reforms in the poor countries with those in the rich countries is quite appealing from an equity point of view because they benefit different segments of the poverty population.

*Table 4. Drivers of Poverty Change across Focus Regions under Poor Agricultural Reforms*

| *Countries* | *Land* | *Ag. unskilled labor* | *Ag. skilled labor* | *Non-ag. unskilled labor* | *Non-ag. skilled labor* | *Wage labor unskilled* | *Wage labor skilled* | *Agricultural capital* | *Non-agricultural capital* | *Transfers* | *Taxes* | *Cost of living* |
|---|---|---|---|---|---|---|---|---|---|---|---|---|
| **Poor agriculture full liberalization** | | | | | | | | | | | | |
| Bangladesh | −1.9 | −0.9 | −0.7 | 0.7 | 0.7 | 0.3 | 0.7 | −0.7 | 0.7 | 0.0 | 0.5 | −0.5 |
| Brazil | 1.9 | 1.3 | 1.2 | −0.1 | −0.1 | 0.1 | −0.1 | 1.1 | −0.2 | 0.0 | −0.1 | 0.0 |
| Chile | 3.0 | 1.6 | 1.5 | 0.1 | 0.0 | 0.4 | 0.0 | 1.5 | 0.0 | 0.0 | 0.2 | −0.1 |
| Colombia | −0.7 | −0.3 | −0.3 | 0.3 | 0.2 | 0.2 | 0.2 | −0.3 | 0.3 | 0.0 | 0.2 | −0.5 |
| Indonesia | 0.1 | 0.1 | 0.0 | 0.2 | 0.0 | 0.2 | 0.0 | 0.1 | 0.2 | 0.0 | 0.2 | −0.4 |
| Malawi | 3.7 | 2.3 | 1.8 | 0.2 | −0.1 | 1.1 | −0.1 | 1.8 | −0.4 | 0.0 | 0.6 | −0.8 |
| Mexico | −12.4 | −5.3 | −4.7 | 0.0 | 0.2 | −0.9 | 0.2 | −4.7 | 0.3 | 0.0 | −0.1 | −0.5 |
| Mozambique | 3.4 | 2.3 | 2.0 | 0.8 | 0.7 | 1.2 | 0.7 | 2.1 | 0.7 | 0.0 | 0.9 | −1.2 |
| Peru | −1.9 | −1.0 | −0.8 | 0.4 | 0.3 | 0.0 | 0.3 | −0.7 | 0.7 | 0.0 | 0.4 | −0.5 |
| Philippines | −2.3 | −1.4 | −1.0 | 0.4 | 0.4 | −0.3 | 0.4 | −0.9 | 0.8 | 0.0 | 0.2 | −1.1 |
| Thailand | 3.4 | 2.4 | 2.1 | 0.7 | 0.5 | 1.2 | 0.5 | 2.0 | 0.5 | 0.0 | 0.7 | −1.2 |
| Uganda | 0.3 | 0.2 | 0.2 | 0.1 | 0.1 | 0.2 | 0.1 | 0.2 | 0.2 | 0.0 | 0.2 | −0.3 |
| Venezuela | −1.6 | −0.7 | −0.7 | 0.3 | 0.2 | 0.1 | 0.2 | −0.7 | 0.3 | 0.0 | 0.2 | −0.2 |
| Vietnam | 5.7 | 3.9 | 3.6 | 1.8 | 1.6 | 2.3 | 1.6 | 3.5 | 1.4 | 0.0 | 1.5 | −1.4 |
| Zambia | −0.7 | −0.4 | −0.2 | 0.4 | 0.4 | 0.2 | 0.4 | −0.2 | 0.7 | 0.0 | 0.3 | −0.4 |
| Average | −0.0 | 0.3 | 0.3 | 0.4 | 0.3 | 0.4 | 0.3 | 0.3 | 0.4 | 0.0 | 0.4 | −0.6 |
| AAV | 2.9 | 1.6 | 1.4 | 0.4 | 0.4 | 0.6 | 0.4 | 1.4 | 0.5 | 0.0 | 0.4 | 0.6 |
| Sign cons. | −0.0 | 0.2 | 0.2 | 1.0 | 0.9 | 0.7 | 0.9 | 0.2 | 0.9 | 0.0 | 0.9 | −1.0 |
| **Poor agriculture Doha liberalization** | | | | | | | | | | | | |
| Average | −0.09 | −0.04 | −0.03 | 0.01 | 0.02 | −0.01 | 0.02 | −0.03 | 0.01 | 0.00 | −0.01 | −0.06 |
| AAV | 0.38 | 0.20 | 0.16 | 0.03 | 0.04 | 0.04 | 0.04 | 0.16 | 0.05 | 0.00 | 0.02 | 0.07 |
| Sign cons. | −0.24 | −0.22 | −0.18 | 0.50 | 0.53 | −0.16 | 0.53 | −0.20 | 0.26 | 0.00 | −0.42 | −0.90 |

*Notes*: AAV is the average absolute value of the data in the column; "sign cons" is the "sign consistency" of the data: the ratio of the average to the average absolute value of the variable.

*Table 5. Earnings-driven Percentage Change in the Poverty Headcount ($1/day) across Developing Country Stratums, when Poor Countries Reform Agriculture*

| *Countries* | *Earnings* | *Taxes* | *Cost of living* | *Total* |
|---|---|---|---|---|
| ***Poor agriculture full liberalization*** | | | | |
| Bangladesh | –0.10 | 0.56 | –0.63 | –0.17 |
| Brazil | –0.15 | –0.05 | 0.05 | –0.15 |
| Chile | –1.36 | 0.19 | –0.24 | –1.41 |
| Colombia | –0.03 | 0.14 | –0.39 | –0.28 |
| Indonesia | –0.30 | 0.39 | –0.92 | –0.83 |
| Malawi | –0.85 | 0.32 | –0.43 | –0.96 |
| Mexico | 1.84 | –0.15 | –1.08 | 0.61 |
| Mozambique | –0.78 | 0.48 | –0.78 | –1.08 |
| Peru | –0.07 | 0.34 | –0.50 | –0.23 |
| Philippines | 1.36 | 0.40 | –2.33 | –0.57 |
| Thailand | –2.61 | 1.02 | –2.96 | –4.55 |
| Uganda | –0.04 | 0.04 | –0.06 | –0.06 |
| Venezuela | –0.11 | 0.25 | –0.29 | –0.15 |
| Vietnam | –1.42 | 1.13 | –1.42 | –1.71 |
| Zambia | –0.19 | 0.17 | –0.27 | –0.29 |
| Average | –0.32 | 0.35 | –0.82 | –0.79 |
| AAV | 0.75 | 0.38 | 0.82 | 0.87 |
| Sign cons. | –0.43 | 0.93 | –0.99 | –0.91 |
| ***Poor agriculture Doha liberalization*** | | | | |
| Average | 0.01 | 0.01 | –0.10 | –0.07 |
| AAV | 0.07 | 0.03 | 0.11 | 0.09 |
| Sign cons. | 0.07 | 0.56 | –0.88 | –0.83 |

*Notes*: The total results in this table differ from the RichAgrFull poverty results in Hertel et al. (2007), since the results in this paper are computed as part of a full liberalization experiment using the methodology of Harrison et al. (2000). Thus the results in this table reflect interactions with agricultural policy reforms in the poor countries, as well as non-agriculture reforms. AAV is the average absolute value of the data in the column; "sign cons" is the "sign consistency" of the data: the ratio of the average to the average absolute value of the variable.

Table 5 summarizes the national poverty impacts of poor country agricultural trade liberalization. The first column represents the poverty share-weighted sum of the percentage changes in stratum poverty headcounts due to earnings. Here, we see that the impacts on poverty, while mixed, are on balance poverty reducing. This is somewhat surprising in light of concerns about agricultural tariff cuts on the poor. However, the reader needs to bear in mind that these are the impacts prior to tax replacement. Once the income tax adjustment is introduced (next column), the earnings picture is less rosy. Indeed, in all countries excepting Brazil and Mexico, income taxes rise and this has an adverse impact on poverty. Furthermore, the AAV of the tax rise is nearly half as large as the earnings effect, and it dominates the former for several of the focus countries.

Of course the primary benefit of agricultural tariff cuts with respect to poverty alleviation is to allow the poor access to food at world prices. This effect is evident in the cost of living column, where the deflated cost of living falls in all regions except Brazil, where increased export demand in other developing countries boosts food prices. The sign consistency measure is –0.99 for the cost of living contribution to national poverty changes and the AAV measure of 0.82 is even larger than the earnings AAV. The results

*Table 6. Percentage Change in the $1/day Headcount under Agricultural and Non-agricultural Reform*

| | *Full liberalization* | | | | *Doha* | |
|---|---|---|---|---|---|---|
| *Countries* | *Rich agric. reforms* | *Poor agric. reforms* | *Subtotal agric. reforms* | *Subtotal non-agric. reforms* | *Total full lib.* | *Total Doha lib.* |
| Bangladesh | −0.11 | −0.18 | −0.29 | 0.57 | 0.28 | −0.04 |
| Brazil | −1.79 | −0.15 | −1.94 | 0.53 | −1.41 | −0.80 |
| Chile | −3.89 | −1.41 | −5.30 | 0.31 | −4.99 | −1.29 |
| Colombia | −0.29 | −0.28 | −0.57 | 0.67 | 0.10 | −0.10 |
| Indonesia | −1.24 | −0.82 | −2.06 | 0.61 | −1.45 | −0.20 |
| Malawi | −0.74 | −0.96 | −1.70 | −0.14 | −1.84 | 0.36 |
| Mexico | 0.31 | 0.61 | 0.92 | 0.43 | 1.35 | 0.13 |
| Mozambique | 0.07 | −1.08 | −1.01 | 0.32 | −0.69 | 0.02 |
| Peru | −0.40 | −0.23 | −0.63 | −0.16 | −0.79 | 0.06 |
| Philippines | −0.76 | −0.56 | −1.32 | 0.57 | −0.75 | −0.25 |
| Thailand | −6.63 | −4.55 | −11.18 | 2.31 | −8.87 | −1.97 |
| Uganda | 0.04 | −0.06 | −0.02 | 0.08 | 0.06 | 0.04 |
| Venezuela | 0.26 | −0.15 | 0.11 | 0.75 | 0.86 | 0.21 |
| Vietnam | 0.22 | −1.70 | −1.48 | −4.37 | −5.85 | 0.89 |
| Zambia | 0.14 | −0.29 | −0.15 | 0.24 | 0.09 | 0.03 |
| Average | −0.99 | −0.79 | −1.77 | 0.18 | −1.59 | −0.19 |
| AAV | 1.13 | 0.87 | 1.91 | 0.80 | 1.96 | 0.43 |
| Sign cons. | −0.88 | −0.91 | −0.93 | 0.23 | −0.81 | −0.46 |
| ***Doha Reforms*** | | | | | | |
| Average | −0.16 | −0.08 | −0.24 | 0.04 | | −0.19 |
| AAV | 0.30 | 0.09 | 0.31 | 0.13 | | 0.43 |
| Sign cons. | −0.55 | −0.86 | −0.76 | 0.32 | | −0.46 |

*Notes*: AAV is the average absolute value of the data in the column; "sign cons" is the "sign consistency" of the data: the ratio of the average to the average absolute value of the variable.

presented in this table demonstrate clearly the beneficial impact of developing country agricultural liberalization on poverty, through the lowering of food prices.

The final column in Table 5 reports the total impact arising from agricultural trade reform in the poor countries, taking into account the combined earnings, tax, and cost of living impacts. It is striking to note that poverty falls in all but one country. And the sign consistency measure of −0.91 indicates that these reforms are even more consistently poverty friendly than the rich agricultural reforms in Table 3. On the other hand, the contribution of poor country agriculture tariff cuts under Doha (bottom panel of Table 5), while also poverty friendly, are negligible in magnitude, as indicated by AAV = 0.09.

Table 6 summarizes the poverty outcomes under rich, poor, and combined (Subtotal agric. reforms column) agricultural reforms. Here we see total poverty changes repeated from agricultural reforms as reported in Tables 4 and 5, along with their combined effect. Given the total impact of agricultural liberalization we see that our findings suggest that only Mexico and Uganda would see an increase in the poverty headcount attributable to agricultural reforms (due to rich country reforms for Uganda and reforms by both types of reforms for Mexico). Furthermore, the AAV summary measure of 1.91, indicating significant movement of persons across the poverty line due to agricultural reforms, suggests that the impact of combined rich and poor country reforms is significantly more important than either one taken alone. The sign consistency value of –0.93 is also higher than either of the two sets of reforms alone and indicates that global agricultural trade reforms are heavily weighted in the direction of poverty alleviation. This outcome is a direct consequence of the fact that both developed and developing country reforms reduce poverty—but each tends to do so for a different segment of the population; their poverty benefits are complementary in nature.

The bottom panel in Table 6 summarizes the results from the combined agricultural reforms taken under Doha. We find that only seven of the 15 countries realize a reduction in the poverty headcount due to partial agricultural reforms under the postulated Doha scenario. The limited poverty reduction impact is reflected in the small (one-third of full reforms) value for the AAV of 0.31 for agricultural reforms, and the lack of uniform cross-country reductions of these partial reforms is reflected in the more moderate –0.76 sign consistency value, considerably smaller than that under full agriculture reforms (–0.93).

*Beyond Agricultural Liberalization*

The fifth column of Table 6 reports the focus country poverty impacts of non-agricultural reforms and the sixth and seventh columns show the combined effect with agricultural reforms (full liberalization and Doha, respectively). The full reform of non-agricultural tariffs contributes to a poverty increase in the majority of our focus countries. However, the AAV of 0.80 is less than the values for full agricultural reforms in either the rich or poor countries, indicating a lesser absolute impact on poverty, and the sign consistency of 0.23 indicates a mixture of poverty increases and decreases (note the importance of the large reduction in Vietnam in this calculation). In the fifth column of the bottom panel these same impacts are reported for Doha reforms in non-agriculture and we see that the AAV is smaller, indicating less impact, but slightly more consistent (sign consistency = 0.32), indicating that the impact of the Doha reforms across this sample of countries is somewhat more consistently poverty raising than full reform.

The final two columns in Table 6 report the combined impact of all merchandise trade reforms on poverty in our focus countries. The full reforms reduce poverty in 9 of the 15 countries, with a sign consistency of –0.81 and an average absolute value of 1.96. On the other hand, Doha reforms (the last column) reduce poverty in only 7 of the 15 countries, with lower sign consistency and an AAV only about one-fifth as large. Thus, we conclude that the Doha reforms only generate about one-fifth of the poverty change as do the full reforms and are considerably less poverty friendly. This stems from the fact that both the agriculture and the non-agriculture Doha reforms are individually less poverty friendly than the full reforms.

## 5. Conclusion

We have examined the likely poverty impacts of trade reforms under the DDA and contrasted them with the poverty consequences of full reform. We expected partial reforms to generate smaller poverty responses than full reforms, and indeed we have found this to be the case, with lower AAVs (about one-fifth as large) for national poverty changes across our 15 focus countries. However, the two types of reforms are also *qualitatively* different. This is captured in our sign consistency measure, which reports how poverty friendly a given reform is, regardless of magnitude. By this measure, we judge that full reforms are nearly twice as poverty friendly as the Doha reforms.

There are two factors driving this result. The first is that rich country agricultural reforms under Doha emphasize those elements of policy reform—export subsidies and to a lesser degree domestic support—that are less important to developing countries as a whole (Hertel and Keeney, 2006) and are less favorable to poverty in particular (Ivanic, 2006). The latter is underscored by our comparison of the sign consistency of rich country agricultural reforms under Doha and full liberalization. Less well understood is the second reason why the Doha scenario is not more poverty friendly—it largely omits tariff cuts in the developing countries themselves. Our analysis shows that this is the most poverty friendly aspect of global trade reform and serves effectively to complement the poverty impacts of rich country reforms. While the latter tend to raise food prices, the developing country reforms lower food prices for the poor by reducing tariffs on these products. This generates rather widespread poverty reduction.

## References


Anderson, K. and W. Martin (eds), *Agricultural Trade Reform and the Doha Development Agenda*, Basingstoke: Palgrave Macmillan (2006).

Anderson, K., W.J. Martin, and E. Valenzuela, "The Relative Importance of Global Agricultural Subsidies and Market Access," policy research working paper 3900, World Bank (2006).

Cranfield, J.A.L., J.S. Eales, T.W. Hertel, and P.V. Preckel, "Model Selection when Estimating and Predicting Consumer Demand Using International, Cross-Section Data," *Empirical Economics* 28 (2003):353–64.

Dimaranan, B.D., *Global Trade, Assistance and Protection: The GTAP 6 Data Base*, Center for Global Trade Analysis, Purdue University (2007).

Harrison, W.J., J.M. Horridge, and K. Pearson, "Decomposing Simulation Results with Respect to Exogenous Shocks," *Computational Economics* 15 (2000):227–49.

Hertel, T.W. and M. Ivanic, "Understanding the Poverty Implications of the Doha Development Agenda," MS, Center for Global Trade Analysis, Purdue University (2006).

Hertel, T.W., M. Ivanic, P.V. Preckel, and J.A.L. Cranfield, "The Earnings Effects of Multilateral Trade Liberalization: Implications for Poverty," *World Bank Economic Review* 18 (2004):205–36.

Hertel, T.W. and R. Keeney, "What is at Stake: The Relative Importance of Import Barriers, Export Subsidies, and Domestic Support," in K. Anderson and W. Martin (eds), *Agricultural Trade Reform and the Doha Development Agenda*, Basingstoke: Palgrave Macmillan (2006).

Hertel, T.W., R. Keeney, M. Ivanic, and L.A. Winters, "Distributional Effects of WTO Agricultural Reforms in Rich and Poor Countries," *Economic Policy* 50 (2007):289–337.

Hertel, T.W. and J.J. Reimer, "Predicting the Poverty Impacts of Trade Reform," *Journal of International Trade and Economic Development* 14 (2005):377–405.

Hertel, T.W. and L.A. Winters, *Poverty and the WTO: Impacts of the Doha Development Agenda*, Basingstoke: Palgrave (2006).

Hoekman, B., F. Ng, and M. Olarreaga, "Agricultural Tariffs or Subsidies: Which Are More Important for Developing Countries?" *World Bank Economic Review* 18 (2) (2004):175–204.

Ivanic, M., "The Effects of a Prospective Multilateral Trade Reform on Poverty in Developing Countries," in T.W. Hertel and L.A. Winters (eds), *Poverty and the WTO: Impacts of the Doha Development Agenda*, Basingstoke: Palgrave (2006).

Jensen, H.G. and H. Zobbe, "Consequences of Reducing Limits on Aggregate Measurements of Support," in K. Anderson and W. Martin (eds), *Agricultural Trade Reform and the Doha Development Agenda*, Basingstoke: Palgrave Macmillan (2006).

Keeney. R. and T.W. Hertel, *GTAP-AGR: A Framework for Assessing the Implications of Multilateral Changes in Agricultural Policies*, GTAP technical paper 24, Center for Global Trade Analysis, Purdue University (2005).

Organisation for Economic Co-operation and Development (OECD), *Market Effects of Crop Support Measures*, Paris: OECD Publications (2001).

Rimmer, M. and A. Powell, "An Implicitly Additive Demand System," *Applied Economics* 28 (1996):1613–22.

Winters, L.A., N. McCulloch, and A. McKay, "Trade Liberalization and Poverty: The Evidence So Far," *Journal of Economic Literature* 27 (2004):481–506.

WTO (World Trade Organization), Decision Adopted by the General Council, August 1, 2004, WTO Secretariat, Geneva.

## Notes

1. A clear limitation of this approach stems from the rigidity of a given household's classification by earnings specialization. Obviously households may be induced to change their specialization or to diversify in response to changing relative factor returns. We believe that the relatively broad definition of strata circumvents this problem for the majority of households in the face of modest changes to earnings. However, this important qualification will be further considered in the results section.
2. We have chosen to focus on households in the neighborhood of the poverty line in order to permit generalization of impacts across countries. An alternative would be to explore the impacts on all households within a single country.
3. A complete set of shares for all strata is available in the online Appendix at https://www.gtap.agecon.purdue.edu/resources/res_display.asp?RecordID=2292.
4. In practice we expect that price changes for importables are likely to be attenuated and those for exportables magnified (see Winters et al., 2004). Because importables are differentiated from domestic goods in this model the pass-through of tariff changes will be below 100%, so that the prices of domestic varieties of importables move in the same direction, but by much less than border prices.
5. A complete analysis of the macroeconomic results of the trade scenarios is available in the online Appendix at https://www.gtap.agecon.purdue.edu/resources/res_display.asp?RecordID=2292.
6. The complete results from the Doha experiments are available in the online Appendix at https://www.gtap.agecon.purdue.edu/resources/res_display.asp?RecordID=2292.

Journal of International Economics 89 (2013) 379–392

Contents lists available at SciVerse ScienceDirect

Journal of International Economics

journal homepage: www.elsevier.com/locate/jie

# Trade as an engine of creative destruction: Mexican experience with Chinese competition☆

Leonardo Iacovone [a,*], Ferdinand Rauch [b], L. Alan Winters [c,1]

[a] World Bank, 1818 H Street, NW, Washington, DC, 20433, USA
[b] London School of Economics, CEP, Houghton Street, WC2A 2AE, London, United Kingdom
[c] Department of Economics, University of Sussex, Falmer, Brighton, BN1 9SL United Kingdom

ARTICLE INFO

*Article history:*
Received 21 June 2011
Received in revised form 5 September 2012
Accepted 6 September 2012
Available online 20 September 2012

*JEL classifications:*
D22
F14
F15
F61
L25

*Keywords:*
Competition
Trade
Firm-heterogeneity
Product-level
Mexico
China

ABSTRACT

This paper exploits the surge in Chinese exports from 1994 to 2004 to evaluate the effects of a competition shock from a low wage competitor for producers in an important middle-income country, Mexico. We find that this shock causes selection and reallocation at both firm and product levels and that its impact is highly heterogeneous at the intensive and extensive margins. Sales of smaller plants and more marginal products are compressed and are more likely to cease, whereas those of larger plants and core products seem relatively impervious to the shock. This implies a reallocation in terms of market shares within firms and between firms. We also show that the impact of expanded access to cheaper Chinese intermediate inputs has a similar effect, with larger plants benefiting more from the availability of cheaper imported inputs.


## 1. Introduction

Between 1990 and 2007 Chinese exports grew from 62 billion US dollars to 1.2 trillion USD, at the staggering average rate of about 20% per year. China became the world's largest exporter in 2009, and the second largest economy of the world in 2010. The emergence of China and its impact on producers worldwide has been a focus of attention for both policy-makers and researchers, and, at least among the former, has generally led to expressions of deep concern and calls for protection.[2]

While no set of countries is entirely insulated from competition from China, one might expect the effects to be most immediate on those middle-income countries whose established positions in manufactured markets have come under threat. This is the focus of this paper, in which we examine the impact of Chinese competition on Mexican manufacturing firms.[3] We do not claim that the results we derive pertain to all middle-income countries, but we believe that they have a

☆ The authors are grateful to Gerardo Leyva and Abigail Duran for granting us access to INEGI data at the offices of INEGI in Aguascalientes under the commitment of complying with the confidentiality requirements set by the Mexican Laws. Special thanks go to all INEGI employees who provided assistance and answered our questions, in particular to Gabriel Romero, Alejandro Cano, Araceli Martinez, Armando Arellanes, Ramon Sanchez, Otoniel Soto, Candido Aguilar, and Adriana Ramirez. We also thank Christian Hansen for his help with the implementation of the quantile IV regressions and Philippe Aghion, Tibor Besedes, Chad Bown, Ana Cusolito, Judith Dean, Aaditya Mattoo, Guy Michaels, Emanuel Ornelas, Stephen Redding, Daniel Sturm as well as the participants at the seminars of ETSG, USITC, Penn State, Boston University, University of Vienna, London School of Economics, St Andrews University, FREIT, the World Bank trade seminar, the Econometric Society World Congress and the University of Kent for helpful comments. The views contained in this paper are of the authors and not necessarily those of the World Bank. The financial support of the World Bank's Research Support Budget is gratefully acknowledged.
* Corresponding author.
*E-mail address:* liacovone@worldbank.org (L. Iacovone).
[1] Prof Winters is also associated with CEPR, IZA and GDN.

[2] Some examples from the media to highlight this point: "[We] must not repeat the mistakes of the nineties, when an 'invasion' of Chinese products destroyed entire sectors of our industry [...]" (Medium Enterprises Association of Argentina, April 6, 2004), or: "I made it very clear to Minister Bo Xilai that we will take the legal steps to give Brazilian industry the right to protect itself" (Brazilian minister for Industry, Development and Commerce after meeting with his Chinese counterpart, October 4, 2005). See also Arroba et al. (2009).

[3] Our data covers plants. As most plants are also firms, we use the terms firms and plants interchangeably.

0022-1996/$ – see front matter 
http://dx.doi.org/10.1016/j.jinteco.2012.09.002

relevance wider than just Mexico, if only as hypotheses that might be considered by policy-makers and researchers in other countries.

Methodologically, the paper aims to close two gaps in the literature. First, we provide a careful investigation of the causal impact of competition on the intensive and extensive margins of Mexican firms, using detailed plant-level and plant–product-level data over time. Moreover, we recognize that competition may be felt as strongly in export markets as at home, and hence evaluate these causal links not only for Mexican firms serving their home market but also for those serving its main export market – the USA. On both markets we find strongly heterogeneous effects of the competitive shock on the extensive (exit and survival) and intensive (sales) margins, which provide evidence of resource reallocation between firms and of product reallocation within plants as competition obliges them to focus on their core competencies.[4] Second, we show that, similar to the effect of competition, the effect of the increasing availability of cheaper Chinese intermediate inputs is highly asymmetric; however, taking this into account does not alter our main results on the effect of competition.

We reach these results by treating the emergence of China onto world markets as a quasi-natural experiment of a strong and sudden surge in the competition facing Mexican manufacturing producers. As depicted in Fig. 1, Chinese exports to Mexico and the United States increased substantially in terms of both value and share during the period considered. China's share of Mexican imports grew from around 0.5% in 1994 to 8% in 2004 – a factor of 16. This growth was primarily driven by the intensive margin, see Amiti and Freund (2010). In comparison, the import shares from Africa and Oceania to Mexico changed by a factor of 1.04, from other Asian countries by a factor of 1.35 and from South America by a factor from 1.41, while those of North America and Europe fell by factors of 0.96 and 0.84. In value terms, all these continental groups increased their exports to Mexico. This does not suggest that China has crowded out other developing country imports, but rather that China appears to be the larger part of a broad tendency raising the importance of developing countries in Mexican imports. This sizable growth was matched by a relatively moderate increase in trade flows in the opposite direction: the share of Chinese imports from Mexico increased from 1.9 to 2.8% from 1994 to 2004.[5] Hence we interpret the situation at hand as essentially a unilateral trade shock and not a mutual trade expansion.

The situation is similar in the USA – the third-country market where Mexico has confronted Chinese competition so strongly. China's share of total imports more than doubled from 6.5% in 1996 to 13.4% in 2004 (USITC Trade Online), while the corresponding expansion factors for Mexico were 1.15, for developing Asia 1.46, other Latin America 1.09, for Europe 1.05 and for developed Asia 0.64. In both cases we would argue that the broad thrust of Chinese export growth was largely unanticipated and exogenous to the countries we study. While those countries' import policies had to be permissive to imports (and in a few specific cases were less than perfectly so), the increases in Chinese output and exports were generated by China's internal policy changes which induced huge growth in productivity and investment, massive inflows of FDI and large increases in the labor force available to manufacturers.[6]

Turning to the effect on export markets, Mexico is one of the countries that is likely to be most strongly affected by Chinese competition, given that within NAFTA Mexico has had a comparative advantage in the production of labor intensive goods and that China's exports to the USA have increased so strongly. di Giovanni et al. (2011) estimate that Mexico is the seventh most technologically similar country to China. Given that over 85% of Mexican exports go to the United States, Chinese expansion in the US market will have been a major shock to Mexican exporters; and given, in turn, that Mexico's export to GDP ratio varied from 14% (1994) to 25% (2004), such competition is clearly likely to be a major issue for the Mexican economy as a whole.

The objective of this study is to provide an example of how trade can work as a force of creative destruction that leads to competition enhancing readjustments within and between firms. For this reason we focus on both reallocation between firms and within firms at the product level. We analyze how the rise of China affected production patterns in Mexico, and show that larger plants and core products are relatively shielded from the adverse effects that this competition generates. We interpret the size effect as a productivity effect, since size and productivity are strongly correlated, but we do not have the data required to make this link formally. Additionally, we show that it is important to take into account the role of intermediate inputs as an additional channel through which the expansion of Chinese exports could influence Mexican firms, and that this channel reinforced the asymmetric effect of the Chinese competition shock.

The rest of the article is organized as follows. Section 2 discusses the empirical and theoretical context of our study. Section 3 describes the data and our empirical strategy. Section 4 describes the principal results, while Section 5 provides some additional robustness checks and extensions. Finally, Section 6 concludes.

## 2. Related literature

Our work is related to several areas of research. First, there exist a large number of studies that rely on sectoral trade flow data to assess the competitive threat from Chinese exports to Latin American producers (Freund and Ozden, 2006; Hanson and Robertson, 2007; Lederman et al., 2008; Soloaga et al., 2007; Devlin et al., 2006; Lall et al., 2005). Other studies have evaluated the impact of Chinese exports on wages and employment for various parts of Latin America, see Levinsohn (1999) and Pavcnik (2002) for Chile, Pavcnik and Goldberg (2005) and Eslava et al. (2009) for Colombia, and Pavcnik et al. (2004) for Brazil. A sectoral study of the effects of Chinese exports to the US on Mexican exports to the US finds some evidence for crowding out on this third market (see Iranzo and Ma, 2006). In a large study Jenkins et al. (2008) emphasize that the emergence of China brings about winners and losers in Latin America, and that its effect tends to be asymmetrical. However, while sectoral analyses are interesting, adjustment is ultimately undertaken by firms which find their market positions eroded or enhanced, and it is at the level of firms that we see most of the response in terms of innovation, the introduction of new products, changes in the product mix, new investment, etc. A shock that could have different impacts on different plants, or bring about a reallocation within plants cannot be adequately described at sectoral level.[7] These are important elements in the discussion of the full impact of China's emergence on incomes and growth and require the use of firm-level data.

Firm-level studies have proliferated in recent years and we refer here only to a small selection of them to place our own work in context.[8] Several studies highlight that foreign competition not only hurts producers but also pushes them to improve their efficiency and organization. For example, Chen et al. (2009) find that openness to trade squeezes margins and pricing among European firms but typically raises productivity as well. Autor et al. (2012) postulate the same sort of forces, but trace the effects of competition from imports from China directly into local labor markets in the USA. The degree of import competition that a local market is exposed to is mainly related

[4] For related studies see Iacovone and Javorcik (2008), Eckel et al. (2010) and Liu (2010).

[5] Source: Comtrade. See also Dussel Peters (2007) or Eichengreen et al. (2007).

[6] Hsieh and Ossa (2011) suggest that productivity growth in Chinese manufacturing sectors over 1995–2007 ranged from 7.4% to 24.3% and averaged 13.8%.

[7] For an excellent review of the importance of using firm-level data in analyzing responses to trade shocks see Bernard et al. (2007).

[8] For a survey, see, inter alia, Bernard et al. (2011b).

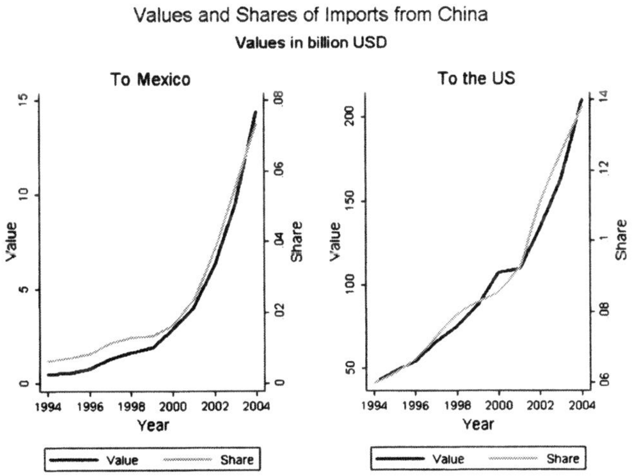


Note: The left scales of both figures show the import values in billion US dollars, the right scales the share of Chinese imports in total imports of the stated market. The data source for both graphs is Comtrade.

**Fig. 1.** Impact of Chinese exports on the US and Mexican market. Note: The left scales of both figures show the import values in billion US dollars, the right scales the share of Chinese imports in total imports of the stated market. The data source for both graphs is Comtrade.

to the share of imports in total US sales of the types of manufactured goods that it produces, and Autor et al. (2012) find that labor market stress is directly related to this measure. Mion and Zhu (forthcoming) find that Chinese competition induces skill upgrading in Belgium, while finding no effect on firm exit. Fernandes (2007) documents the link between tariff liberalization and plant productivity in Colombia, and Fernandes and Paunov (2011) in Chile. A common finding, in line with Aghion et al. (2005), is that responses to competition vary across firms, with stronger (variously, more productive, larger, exporting) firms more likely to survive and to respond positively to the competition shock. One example is Alvarez and Vergara (2010), who state that competition-enhancing reforms in Chile induce plant closures more strongly among smaller and less productive firms, although the way they model this heterogeneity relies on untested assumptions about functional forms and their result for tariff reforms is weak. Verhoogen (2008) studies the responses of Mexican plants to the peso devaluation in 1994. The devaluation led more-productive plants to increase exports, upgrade quality, and raise wages relative to less-productive plants within the same industry, but in doing so to increase the within-industry wage dispersion.

In a paper more closely related to ours, Bloom et al. (2011) find that in twelve European countries imports from China in a firms' sectors of production (expressed relative to total sectoral imports) increased the innovative activity of surviving firms in Europe, while decreasing the chances of survival and employment. In heavily exposed sectors, low-tech firms suffered declines in jobs and survival while high-tech ones were relatively protected. The positive association between competition and technology upgrading was made by Bustos (2011) for Argentina. Bernard et al. (2004) show that Chinese competition in the US boosts high wage and high skill companies, and causes the decline of low wage and low skill industries. Bernard et al. (2006) investigate how US firms react to exposure to international trade and show that plant survival and growth are negatively correlated with competition, while skill intensity and industry switching are positively correlated with it.[9]

In the developing world, Fernandes and Paunov (2009), find that imports from China and India boost Chilean firms' quality, but the only marked heterogeneity that they find is that this effect is stronger for firms in non-traded sectors. More recently Iacovone et al. (2011) provide evidence that competition from China raised the innovation activity of Mexican plants. They show that activities such as the use of ISO2000 certificates, Just in Time activities, or worker participation programs are more likely given higher competitive pressure from China.

The impact of trade on product-level and within-firm reallocations has featured less prominently in the literature to date. Bernard et al. (2010) find that the impact of product switching on US manufacturing growth is as large as that of firm exit and entry to the market. In an interesting study, Liu (2010) shows that increases in import competition make US firms more likely to drop their less important products (those with smaller shares of total sales) and less likely to drop their core product (with the largest share of sales). He finds that core products increase their shares of sales while less important ones face declines. Turning to trade liberalization, Bernard et al. (2011a) and Baldwin and Gu (2009), find evidence that competition reduces the diversification of Canadian producers, while Eckel et al. (2010) show that Mexican producers tended to react to NAFTA trade liberalization by focusing on their core competencies. Relatedly, Goldberg et al. (2010a) analyze multi-product firm dynamics in India without finding any evidence of a link between product rationalization and output tariff declines following trade liberalization.

[9] Additional views of the issues we discuss are available in, for example, Yusuf et al. (2007) and Arroba et al. (2009), who offer a non-model-based discussion of adjustment to import competition from China, and Teshima (2010) who relates general import competition to innovation among Mexican plants.

In terms of theory, numerous theoretical articles on emerging trade models and multi-product firms are closely related to our analysis, and provide us with various hypotheses that closely inform our empirical analysis. Bernard et al. (2011b) develop a model of multi-product firms that predicts the demise of the smaller firms and products resulting from trade liberalization. This conjecture is consistent with our results. Their model however does not predict the asymmetric sales shifts across and within plants that we describe, since it relies on a CES demand and thus constant markups. The model by Eckel and Neary (2010), which suggests that within-firm adjustments resulting from trade reforms might generate substantial gains due to higher efficiency, also plays a role in generating our predictions. Further related models include the neo-Schumpeterian growth models pioneered by Aghion et al. (2005).

Mayer et al. (2011) is closely related to our study as it extends Melitz and Ottaviano (2008) by introducing a multi-product dimension. This model predicts that a bilateral trade liberalization leads to an increase in competitive pressure, which in turn leads firms to drop their marginal products (the ones that also have a lower share in production), and reallocate their resources towards increasing the production of the remaining goods. The inter-firm reallocations generate an additional channel for aggregate productivity growth. For export markets they predict that more competition will lead to the dropping of less substantial products and firms. This model does not, however, lead to these predictions when a unilateral trade shock is analyzed (for example a unilateral productivity shock, or decrease of trade costs). Additional short-run assumptions are required to reach hypotheses that are consistent with our findings.

## 3. Data and empirical strategy

The main source of data is the Monthly Industrial Survey (EIM) data on Mexican plants provided by the Mexican Institute of Statistics (INEGI). This dataset covers about 85% of all Mexican industrial output.[10] This unique survey contains detailed information on sales and exports of each of the products manufactured by Mexican plants as well as information on employment broken down by skills.[11] The data tracks plants and products throughout the sample period including their introduction and exit from the market. The information on the entry of new plants, however, is not complete, as new plants are not systematically included. Further, we use trade data from Comtrade at the 6-digit level of the World Customs Organizations Harmonized System (HS-1996).[12] For bilateral trade transactions we rely on reported imports since it is generally believed that importer-reported data tend to be more accurate.

**Table 1**
Descriptive statistics. This table presents main variables used in the regressions. Among subscripts, *M* denotes the Mexican market and *U* the US market, *i* the plant, *k* the product, so that *ik* denotes plant-product level observations, and *t* time. $Ch-comp_{Mikt}$ and $Ch-comp_{Uikt}$ denote the shares of China in Mexican and US imports of product *k*; these vary only by product but we use the notation *ik* here to denote that they are averaged here over plant-product observations. $Share_{ikt}$ is the share of product *k* in *i*'s sales. For plants, denoted by subscript *i* alone, product-level data are weighted averages over the products produced by the plant, while $Skillshare_{it}$ is ratio of white collar workers and $Nr.Prod.s_{it}$ the number of products the plant produces. $Herfindahl_{it}$ is constructed as a weighted average of product level Herfindahl indices.

| | Mean | S.D. | Min. | Max. |
|---|---|---|---|---|
| Product data variables | | | | |
| $Ch-comp_{Mkt}$ | 0.02 | 0.06 | 0.00 | 0.96 |
| $Ch-comp_{Ukt}$ | 0.08 | 0.15 | 0.00 | 1.00 |
| $Share_{ikt}$ | 0.32 | 0.36 | 0.00 | 1.00 |
| $LnSales_{ikt}$ | 8.49 | 2.63 | 0.00 | 18.00 |
| $LnExportSales_{ikt}$ | 8.14 | 2.63 | 0.00 | 17.84 |
| Plant data variables | | | | |
| $Ch-comp_{Mit}$ | 0.02 | 0.06 | 0.00 | 0.86 |
| $Ch-comp_{Uit}$ | 0.02 | 0.09 | 0.00 | 0.95 |
| $Exportshare_{it}$ | 0.10 | 0.22 | 0.00 | 1.00 |
| $LnSales_{it}$ | 10.54 | 1.91 | 0.00 | 18.01 |
| $LnExportSales_{it}$ | 9.21 | 2.45 | 0.00 | 17.84 |
| $Skillshare_{it}$ | 0.31 | 0.20 | 0.00 | 1.00 |
| $Nr.Prod.s_{it}$ | 3.18 | 2.93 | 1.00 | 33.00 |
| $Herfindahl_{it}$ | 0.08 | 0.09 | 0.01 | 1.00 |

After merging the trade and plant-product level datasets we are left with information on 2744 products and a number of plants varying between 6219 and 4439 because of attrition during our sample period (from 1994 to 2004).[13] The main variables of this dataset are described in Table 1. The specific measure of exposure to foreign competition, calculated at individual product-level and applied to each plant producing that product, is the share of Chinese in total imports in the market concerned, while at the plant level we compute the weighted average of this measure for the products of each plant, where the weights are equal to the sales shares of products. At a product level, the average share of Chinese competition in Mexico in our data is only around 2%, since the full sample includes the years 1994–1998, during which Chinese competition was less intense, and gives more weight to these years because of attrition in the sample. Plants face similar level of competition. The average share of exports in sales is 10.5%, the share of white collar workers averages 31%. On average a plant produces three different products, the maximum number on this statistic we observe is 33. The Herfindahl index, which we compute as the sum of the squares of domestic firms' market shares on product level, gives a value of 0.08 on average.

Empirically, we aim to explain plant-product or plant-level outcomes over time by means of competition from China which varies over time at a product or, via weighted averages, plant level plus a number of control variables. Hence, using the combined dataset just described we estimate equations of the following form:

$$y_{i(k)t} = \beta_1 Z_{i(k)t-1} + \beta_2 Z_{i(k)t-1} x_{i(k)t-1} + \beta_3 X_{i(k)t-1} + D_t + F_{i(k)} + \varepsilon_{i(k)t}, \quad (1)$$

where $y_{i(k)t}$ is a product or plant specific outcome of interest for plant *i* or plant-product *ik* at time *t*, $Z_{i(k)t}$ a measure of the Chinese competition shock, $X_{i(k)t}$ a set of sector, firm and product characteristics, and $y_{i(k)t} x_{it}$ the interaction of the Chinese competition with $x_{i(k)t}$, a subset

[10] This survey does not include data on maquiladoras as these are separately collected by another unit within INEGI and maintained in a different location, hence making the access to both datasets at the same time difficult. In addition, there are confidentiality restrictions to the joint use of these datasets.

[11] These datasets have been used and described in previous studies, see for example Iacovone and Javorcik (2008).

[12] INEGI manufacturing survey relies on the Mexican Industrial Classification CMAP-1994 (Clasificacion Mexicana de Actividades y Productos) at product level (i.e. 8-digit), while the trade data is based on the HS-1996 classification provided by the World Custom Organization at 6-digit level. The Mexican eight digit data gives a detailed description of products. For example, in the category of alcoholic beverages it distinguishes between detailed products such as vodka, whiskey or gin. We match the individual product code manually using its description. We conduct this match of these databases relying on the English and Spanish HS 1996 classification obtained from the Export Helpdesk of the European Union (European Commission, 2009) and the Spanish language HS classification obtained from the SICA project from the Ecuadorian Ministry of Agriculture and Livestock (SICA, 2009). The only CMAP products that we do not consider are those for which a correspondence was not possible to make, mainly the broadly defined "other" categories. Whenever more than one HS code corresponds to one CMAP product we use the aggregate trade value across the different HS codes. The full created matching correspondence between CMAP and HS codes is available on request. See the online technical appendix for more details on the construction of the concordance.

[13] In our analysis we exclude some data outliers such as plants claiming to export more than they sell overall and plants characterized by extreme values in the rates of Chinese imports growth. Specifically, we exclude those instances in which Chinese imports increase by more than 300% or decrease by more than 90% within a year, since given that the trade values are weighted means of product competition such huge changes are more likely to reflect changes in the product mix than in actual competition. In total these outliers amount to about 10% of the data. Our results are robust to the inclusion of outliers, however.

of $X_{i(k)t}$. $D_t$ denotes a year fixed effect and $F_{i(k)}$ is a plant or plant-product fixed effect.[14] Our measure of Chinese competition $Z_{i(k)t-1}$ is the share of Chinese imports in total imports to either the US or Mexico, constructed from Comtrade data. Several other studies have used the import penetration rate from China or broader classes of low-wage countries, for example Broda and Romalis (2009), Bernard et al. (2006) or Bloom et al. (2011).

The control variables that we use for the firm-level regressions are plant size measured by log sales, the Herfindahl index of product market competition, which we compute as the sum of squared market shares of all CMAP – 8 digit products (at plant level this is again a weighted average), the export share and the ratio of white collar workers (skill share). In the product-level regressions we also control for the scope of the firm, proxied by the number of manufactured products, the export share of the product and the share of sales that the product has within the firm (which is a proxy of the extent to which the product can be considered a "core product"). Additionally in some equations we control for log total imports of the product to Mexico or the US respectively. The two outcomes of interest in this study, both at plant-product and plant level, are sales and exit. Exit is defined as:

$$y_{i(k)t} = \begin{cases} 1 & \text{in the last year that the plant or plant-product is observed in the sample} \\ 0 & \text{in all other years.} \end{cases}$$

For the firm-level regressions, a change of ownership would not count as exit in the dataset we use. In fact the data are collected and designed in such a way that the only reason for a product to disappear from the data is that it is no longer produced by the plant. Similarly, a plant that disappears from the dataset can only have closed down. Additionally, we drop the last year of the sample (2004) in the exit regressions, since for this year we can't distinguish plants (products) that exit from those that do not. We focus on these two outcomes, since hypotheses in recent theoretical papers have focused on sales and exit probability in their hypotheses, see the discussion in Section 2.

The model we estimate for the product level regressions is similar to the one we estimate for the plant-level analysis. The only difference is that we rewrite the equation in terms of plant-product $ik$, which involves product specific outcomes, control variables on product and plant level, and plant-product level fixed effects. In all our regressions we cluster standard errors on the level at which we observe the competition from China.[15]

Although we believe that the huge growth of Chinese exports is largely exogenous to our outcomes of interest, there is clearly a possibility that its details are influenced by Mexican plant and product behavior or by third variables that influence both Chinese exports and Mexican firms. Hence to try to avoid any resulting biases in our estimates of $\beta_1$ and $\beta_2$, we instrument the Chinese share of Mexican imports, and in the export equations, the Chinese share of US imports. Our instruments are the Chinese share of EU imports and, separately, the Chinese share of the imports into all countries in the world except the US, the EU and Mexico. These should reflect various product-specific developments in China that are shared by our main variables of interest. This strategy is similar to that adopted by Autor et al. (2012). In the regressions that use the interaction we create the interactions of these export instruments with $x_{i(k)t}$ which provides us with additional instruments for the regressions that involve interaction terms.

China's export strategy has mainly been to enter the market with products similar to existing ones but at lower prices (see for example Broda and Romalis, 2009). Thus, as is widely believed, at the heart of the rise of China as a global exporter lie the domestic policies of China that increase its output and reduce its costs – for example, high investment rates, infrastructure development, the mobility of labor from rural to manufacturing areas, the successful attraction of FDI and the establishment of joint ventures with Western firms (see Keefer, 2007 or Huang, 2003). All these are largely independent of strategic decisions of Mexican plants. Ideally an instrument would measure production or productivity within China directly, but absent detailed Chinese production data, we have to rely on Chinese exports to the instrumental destinations as a correlated measure.

A potential concern about the exogeneity of the instruments is that product-year specific global technological trends might affect both Chinese exports and Mexican firms and thus invalidate our instruments. While one can never be sure, two arguments suggest to us that this may not be an overwhelming difficulty. First, given that China is still catching up in manufacturing technology rather than driven by technological shocks at the frontier, its productivity is mainly determined by its incentives to imitate, which will tend to be somewhat idiosyncratic, rather than developments at the frontier, which could have common elements. Second, in robustness tests (see Table 11 below), we re-run our main specifications including two digit industry-year fixed effects which should pick up sector-specific global supply and demand shocks. As discussed below, apart from being less precisely estimated, the results are little changed by the inclusion of these additional fixed effects.

Another typical concern in related studies is the comparability of treatment and control groups, i.e. if plants and products affected by competition from China differ initially from those that are not. As depicted in Fig. 1, Chinese trade to Mexico increased considerably after 1998, while the Chinese shock before that period was less dramatic. To test the similarity of firms affected by future Chinese competition to those that were not, we create an indicator of Chinese competition that firms face during the years 1998–2004, and regress log sales at firm level for the years 1994–1998 on that variable. In this sample we do not find statistically significant differences in initial sales between firms facing later competition and firms that do not (with a p-value of 0.114 using industry fixed effects on the domestic market, and a p-value of 0.132 on the export market).[16]

A final concern is that when we estimate the equation with sales as outcome, we use a lag-dependent variable and an interacted lag-dependent variable alongside fixed effects. As shown by Nickell (1981), the fixed effect estimator of the coefficient on the lagged variable is likely to be downward biased, while the bias for the interaction of the lagged dependent variable with an exogenous one is, to our knowledge, unknown. The former bias is asymptotically decreasing in the number of time periods and to try to gauge its size in a sample of ten years (as we have), as well as to explore the latter bias, we have conducted an illustrative simulation in Appendix 1. In this the estimated coefficients on the lag-dependent variable, its interaction and the exogenous variable used in the interaction are all biased towards zero, with the strongest effect being felt on the first. If this were to be replicated in our actual estimates it would lead us to underestimate the true magnitude of the impacts of the included variables on sales and hence make us less likely to reject the null hypothesis of 'no effect'. Without much more research one cannot be sure that this result applies to our actual estimates, but the simulation offers at least a little comfort. One consequence of the under-estimation of the lag-dependent effect would be that we

[14] $D_t$ is a variable equal to zero in all years except $t$, and one in $t$; $F_{i(k)}$ is equal to zero for all plants or plant-products except for plant $i$ or plant-product $ik$.

[15] At the product level the competition varies at 8 digit CMAP codes, which is the cluster we apply. At the plant level competition varies at plant level only, since competition for each plant is a weighted mean of the competition faced by each one of its products and thus plant specific. Such clustering treatment is consistent with Moulton (1990).

[16] A similar exercise for exit cannot be undertaken in the same way, given that competition is plant-year specific, and we do not observe future competition for plants that exit.

would over-estimate the long-run effects of our independent variables, but since our interest is more in testing for the presence of such effects than their precise long-run value, this is not a fundamental problem.

## 4. Results

### 4.1. Product level

We start by considering a simple transition matrix. Table 2 focuses on plants in 1994 and tracks their development over time. Block 1 refers to firms facing below median competition from China and block 2 to those facing median and above competition, where competition is measured by the change in China's share of Mexican imports between 1994 and 2004. The blocks report the probabilities of firms starting with $n$ products in 1994 (along the rows) finishing with $m$ products in 2004 (the probabilities sum to unity along the rows). Although such unconditional transition probabilities inevitably reflect many forces, several features of the table suggest the sort of outcomes we have postulated. For example, comparing the high competition sample with the low competition one, there is higher exit overall (column 1), the probability of one-product firms evolving into two or more product firms is lower (row 1), the probability of five-plus product firms cutting back below five products or of exiting altogether is higher (row 5), and the probability of a change in product numbers is greater, with slightly larger chances of moving below the diagonal (cutting back) than moving above it (expanding).

Following Bernard et al. (2010) we can decompose a product's output according to the type of firms producing it. In the first panel of Table 3 we decompose output at the product level over the period 1999–2004, classifying products by their history: column (1) reports the share of output produced by "incumbents of five years' standing" (i.e. output of products by firms that have existed and produced the product for at least five years); column (2) is the share of "new products" (where the firm has existed for five or more years, but the product was introduced during the past five years) and column (3) the share of "new" firms (output by firms that entered during the past five years). In the second panel we again decompose output by year but this time looking forward, distinguishing the output of products that continued to be produced by the same firm for at least five years, of products that were dropped by their firms over the following five years (but where the firm continued to exist), and of products produced by firms that ceased to exist over the following five years. The table shows considerably higher shares for incumbent and continuing firm/product combinations than was found for the USA. This suggests that Mexico may be a less dynamic economy than the USA, but drawing such a conclusion requires great caution. The INEGI data is precise on the entry and exit of products, and on the exit of plants but is less precise on the entry of plants because INEGI does not always manage to readily identify entry of smaller plants. In addition, the INEGI sample includes only partial coverage of small firms and so may miss the more dynamic ones.[17] More relevant for our study, in Table 4 we recompute the entries and exits recorded in Table 3 for CMAP4 sectors, and regress these margins on competition from China. We find that in industries with higher competition products are more likely to enter and exit the market, and less likely to continue. This suggests a higher dynamic in markets where Chinese competition is stronger.

**Table 2**
Transition matrix. This table displays the share of firms by the number of their products in 1994 and 2004 separately for above and below median competition firms.

| | Low competition | | | | | | Share of all plants |
|---|---|---|---|---|---|---|---|
| | 0 | 1 | 2 | 3 | 4 | 5 | |
| 1 | 0.380 | 0.424 | 0.125 | 0.039 | 0.017 | 0.016 | 0.469 |
| 2 | 0.293 | 0.151 | 0.362 | 0.129 | 0.036 | 0.029 | 0.217 |
| 3 | 0.297 | 0.074 | 0.179 | 0.220 | 0.105 | 0.125 | 0.105 |
| 4 | 0.351 | 0.041 | 0.072 | 0.139 | 0.196 | 0.201 | 0.069 |
| 5 | 0.233 | 0.025 | 0.025 | 0.050 | 0.073 | 0.594 | 0.141 |
| Share of all plants | 0.330 | 0.246 | 0.164 | 0.086 | 0.050 | 0.124 | 1.000 |
| | **High competition** | | | | | | **Share of all plants** |
| | 0 | 1 | 2 | 3 | 4 | 5 | |
| 1 | 0.380 | 0.470 | 0.087 | 0.035 | 0.014 | 0.013 | 0.368 |
| 2 | 0.360 | 0.133 | 0.261 | 0.137 | 0.064 | 0.044 | 0.193 |
| 3 | 0.366 | 0.080 | 0.102 | 0.211 | 0.148 | 0.094 | 0.146 |
| 4 | 0.306 | 0.060 | 0.063 | 0.127 | 0.187 | 0.258 | 0.089 |
| 5 | 0.330 | 0.041 | 0.043 | 0.050 | 0.066 | 0.470 | 0.204 |
| Share of all plants | 0.357 | 0.224 | 0.112 | 0.091 | 0.069 | 0.146 | 1.000 |

**Table 3**
Decomposition of product output based on Bernard et al. (2010) The table shows the shares of output of products produced by firms that (a) produced them throughout the last/next five years, (b) introduced or dropped them over the last/next five years or (c) entered or left the market over the last/next five years.

| Year | Share of output in year $t$ due to | | |
|---|---|---|---|
| | Incumbents of 5 years | New products | New firms |
| 1999 | .87 | .08 | .05 |
| 2000 | .88 | .08 | .05 |
| 2001 | .89 | .07 | .04 |
| 2002 | .92 | .05 | .04 |
| 2003 | .93 | .04 | .03 |
| 2004 | .93 | .04 | .03 |
| **Year** | **Share of output in year $t$ that subsequently experienced** | | |
| | Continued Production for 5 years | Product exit | Firm exit |
| 1994 | .84 | .10 | .07 |
| 1995 | .87 | .08 | .05 |
| 1996 | .86 | .08 | .06 |
| 1997 | .86 | .08 | .06 |
| 1998 | .86 | .08 | .06 |
| 1999 | .85 | .09 | .06 |

In Table 5 we provide evidence on sales growth and exit of products from long-run regressions. In the first column of this table we consider only plant-products that were produced in both 1994 and 2004, the first and last year of our sample. For these products we compute the change in Chinese competition in Mexico, $\Delta Ch-comp_{MI}$ and find that products that faced greater competition from China grew by less. In the second column we additionally interact this competition with the initial shares of the product in its plants sales. The interaction coefficient is positive, which suggests that the competitive effect was less strong for larger products. In columns (3) and (4) we repeat the exercise looking at the exit of products from the market. In this sample we consider all plant-products that existed in 1994. We find that Chinese competition correlates with exit, and we find again some evidence that more important products (those with larger shares of total output) were less subject to this effect. In columns (5) to (8) we repeat this exercise for products that are sold on the export markets using competition in the USA, $\Delta Ch-comp_{Uk}$, as the driver variable. The results are substantially the same.

To exploit the information of the full panel, and to evaluate the shorter run dynamics of the Chinese shock, we now run similar regressions using annual data, exploring all combinations in plant, product, exit/sales and domestic/export market space. Table shows one example – the overall exit of products from the Mexican domestic market as a consequence of Chinese competition – and the online appendix provides the tables for the remaining combinations (Tables A2–A8). In this exercise we restrict the sample to multi

[17] Unfortunately, the degree of under-representation varies by year and since we do not have enough information to quantify it we cannot apply sample weights in our results.

**Table 4**
Plant-product dynamics. In this table we regress the shares computed in Table 3 at the level of CMAP-4 on Chinese competition in Mexico at that level. Robust standard errors are clustered on four digit product level, stars give significance at 1 (***), 5 (**) and 10% (*) level of significance.

| | (1) | (2) | (3) | (4) | (5) | (6) |
|---|---|---|---|---|---|---|
| | Product exit | Firm exit | Continued | Product entry | Firm entry | Continued |
| $Ch-comp_{Mik}$ | 1.189*** | 0.0511 | −1.240*** | 0.218** | 0.192 | −0.410* |
| | (0.403) | (0.150) | (0.405) | (0.103) | (0.165) | (0.235) |
| Margin | Exit | Exit | Exit | Entry | Entry | Entry |
| Observations | 300 | 300 | 300 | 300 | 300 | 300 |

**Table 5**
Long term impact 1994–2004. Robust standard errors are clustered on four digit product level, stars give significance at 1 (***), 5 (**) and 10% (*) level of significance. The competition growth variables ($\Delta Ch-comp_{jk}$) measure the growth of the Chinese share of Mexican imports between 1994 and 2004 ($\Delta Ch-comp_{Mk}$) for the domestic market and of the Chinese share of US imports between 1994 and 2004 ($\Delta Ch-comp_{Uk}$) for the export market; similarly sales growth and exit are measured over 1994–2004. Exit indicates plant-products that existed in 1994 and that no longer exist in 2004.

| | (1) | (2) | (3) | (4) | (5) | (6) | (7) | (8) |
|---|---|---|---|---|---|---|---|---|
| | $Sales\ growth_{ik}$ | $Sales\ growth_{ik}$ | $Exit_{ik}$ | $Exit_{ik}$ | $Sales\ growth_{ik}$ | $Sales\ growth_{ik}$ | $Exit_{ik}$ | $Exit_{ik}$ |
| OLS | | | | | | | | |
| $\Delta Ch-comp_{jk}$ | −1.474** | −1.649** | 0.687** | 0.883*** | −3.558* | −4.697* | 0.256 | 0.731*** |
| | (0.568) | (0.560) | (0.255) | (0.223) | (1.559) | (2.368) | (0.166) | (0.187) |
| $\Delta Ch-comp_{jk}\times Share_{ik1994}$ | | 0.0537* | | −0.125* | | 0.522 | | −0.410*** |
| | | (0.0245) | | (0.0596) | | (0.690) | | (0.0672) |
| $Share_{ik1994}$ | | 0.000691 | | −0.00301 | | −0.00307*** | | −0.00167** |
| | | (0.000837) | | (0.00171) | | (0.000450) | | (0.000604) |
| Market | Domestic | Domestic | Domestic | Domestic | Export | Export | Export | Export |
| Observations | 8087 | 8087 | 15,747 | 15,747 | 1103 | 1103 | 2375 | 2375 |

product plants, those plants that produce more than one product.[18] In all the product regressions we use plant-product fixed effects, such that product $p$ produced by plant $i$ differs from product $p$ produced by plant $j$, and also from product $q$ produced in plant $i$ and cluster robust standard errors by product categories at the level of CMAP 8-digit. In the first column of Table 6 we use our dummy for product exit on the left hand side, and our measure of Chinese competition in Mexico ($Ch-comp_{Mkt-1}$) – the Chinese share of Mexico's ($M$'s)imports of product $k$ in year $t-1$ – on the right hand side. We find a positive significant coefficient of the competition variable, which suggests that products that face more competition from China are more likely to be dropped.

In order to exploit the possibility that this impact is asymmetric between products, the second column introduces an interaction with the share of product $k$ within the plant $i$'s total sales ($Share_{ikt-1}$). We use sales shares instead of sales to get closer to predictions from the multi-product literature. We think of a product with a larger share as a more profitable product (Mayer et al., 2011) or "core products" (Eckel and Neary, 2010; Eckel et al., 2010). We find that the impact of Chinese competition is highly asymmetric between products. The interaction between the proxy measuring the extent to which a product can be considered a core product, the share of the plant's sales, and Chinese competition is negative. Products that represent a larger share of plant's sales, are less likely to be dropped. In columns (3) and (4) we repeat the exercise, but use IV as the estimation method instead of OLS. The estimates retain the same size and statistical significance as with OLS, and increase in absolute size.[19] Columns (Fs 3) and (Fs 4) show the first stages associated with columns (3) and (4). The variable $Ch-comp_{Rkt-1}$ is the Chinese export share to the rest of the world, while $Ch-comp_{Ekt-1}$ is the Chinese export share to the EU. The p-value of the Sargan test of the over-identifying restrictions and the F-statistic of the first stage are also displayed. The F-statistics suggests a strong explanatory power for the first stage, with strong positive correlations between the Chinese import shares in the EU and the rest of the world with those in Mexico. In the first stages for column (4), the interaction instruments have more explanatory power than the mean effects; the joint effect remains positive. Sometimes some of the instrumental variables are statistically insignificant, but they always show the expected sign.

In the online appendix we provide similar tables for product exit from the export markets, for product sales domestically and on the export markets, and we repeat the four exercises at the plant-level. We also reproduce all eight exercises including control variables such as the share of white collar workers, a Herfindahl index of product competition and the export share of plants. Our results consistently provide evidence of the asymmetric effect of Chinese competition on Mexican firms: smaller plants and products are more likely to exit, while larger plants and core products are largely shielded from the competitive shock. The outcome is summarized in Figs. 2 and 3. The x-axis shows sales centile or sales share centiles for plants and products respectively, while the y-axis gives the marginal effect of competition, derived from the corresponding IV regressions using the coefficient on Chinese competition and on the interaction term multiplied by the corresponding size. The shapes and significance of these curves reflect the results previously described: larger plants and products are less affected by Chinese competition in terms of sales and exit probability. Magnitudes can be readily obtained from these graphs; for example the exit graph in Fig. 3 suggests that an increase of one percent in imports of a specific product from China increases the probability of a Mexican producer of that product withdrawing it from the domestic market by 0.6 for a product at the 10th centile of plant sales, but has no effect on the exit probability for a product at the 90th centile of plant's sales. The interaction terms are large enough to reverse the sign of the competitive effect at the top end of the distributions; however, the positive effects significantly exceed zero only for the extensive margin of the top 10% of

[18] We focus on multi-product plants since we interpret our results as within plant reallocation. The results remain substantially unchanged when we include all plants.

[19] While the endogeneity which we feared above would suggest that the absolute size of the coefficients might decline, instrumenting potentially compensates for a variety correlations in the actual data as well as increasing the standard errors of the estimates, so we do not find these increases unduly surprising. Liu (2010), Lileeva and Trefler (2010) and Autor et al. (2012) all find the same outcome. The last suggest that it might, in part, be because actual imports contain an element related to positive demand shocks which raise sales and reduce the chances of exit at the same time as raising imports from China, whereas the instruments do not.

**Table 6**
Product exit. Robust standard errors are clustered on eight digit product level, stars give significance at 1 (***), 5 (**) and 10% (*) level of significance. The last three columns show one first stage equation for column (3) and two for column (4). Plant-product and year controls used.

| | OLS | | IV | | First stages | | |
|---|---|---|---|---|---|---|---|
| | (1) $Prod\ exit_{ikt}$ | (2) $Prod\ exit_{ikt}$ | (3) $Prod\ exit_{ikt}$ | (4) $Prod\ exit_{ikt}$ | (Fs 3) $Ch-comp_{Mkt-1}$ | (Fs 4) $Ch-comp_{Mkt-1}$ | (Fs 4) $Ch-comp_{Mkt-1} \times Share_{ikt-1}$ |
| $Ch-comp_{Mkt-1}$ | 0.115*** | 0.172*** | 0.328*** | 0.499*** | | | |
| | (0.0409) | (0.0595) | (0.122) | (0.161) | | | |
| $Share_{ikt-1}$ | | 0.0736*** | | 0.0775*** | | −6.307** | −0.00138 |
| | | (0.0181) | | (0.0143) | | (2.567) | (0.00169) |
| $Ch-comp_{Mkt-1} \times Share_{ikt-1}$ | | −0.243* | | −0.690*** | | | |
| | | (0.127) | | (0.261) | | | |
| $Ch-comp_{Rkt-1}$ | | | | | 0.0748 | 0.0274 | 0.0894 |
| | | | | | (0.0551) | (0.0188) | (0.0552) |
| $Ch-comp_{Ekt-1}$ | | | | | 0.516*** | −2.10e−05 | 0.484*** |
| | | | | | (0.0659) | (0.0104) | (0.0620) |
| $Ch-comp_{Ekt-1} \times Share_{ikt-1}$ | | | | | | −1.429* | 4.275*** |
| | | | | | | (0.864) | (0.807) |
| $Ch-comp_{Ekt-1} \times Share_{ikt-1}$ | | | | | | 0.642*** | 0.394** |
| | | | | | | (0.232) | (0.161) |
| Observations | 85,292 | 85,292 | 85,292 | 85,292 | 85,292 | 85,292 | 85,292 |
| F statistic | | | | | 19.80 | 14.59 | 22.96 |
| Sargan p-value | | | | | 0.129 | 0.262 | 0.262 |

products on the export market and the top 10% of products of the intensive margin on the domestic market.[20]

In Table 7 we provide a less parametric approach to evaluate the existence of heterogeneous responses. Using just the plants that produced at least five products in 1994, we rank these products by their sales share. Then for the products with each rank in turn (i.e. for all those ranked first in their plants sales, and then for all those ranked second, etc.) we regress the probability that a product is dropped from production by 2004 against competition from China, measured as the change in the Chinese share of Mexican imports of that product. We find that this probability is significantly positive for the smaller products with initial ranks of 3, 4 and 5, while it is significantly negative for the core product (rank 1).[21]

### 4.2. Quantile regressions

In the previous section we have shown that the impact of competition from Chinese exports operates as a force for creative destruction in the sense that it induces a reallocation of resources within plants and between plants within sectors, in a way similar to that predicted by models such as Melitz and Ottaviano (2008) and others. Our previous model is affected by two shortcomings. First, we imposed a linear restriction on the heterogeneous effect of size, and second, our results are subject to biases arising from the use of a lagged dependent variable in a fixed effect estimator. To explore the nature of these asymmetries further but without imposing a strong functional restriction or requiring a lagged dependent variable we perform quantile regressions and quantile IV regressions for domestic sales.[22] These results are presented in Table 8 and a similar table with OLS results is given in the online appendix, see Table A17. In this exercise we de-mean our variables at the plant level to mimic the inclusion of plant fixed effects.[23] The outcome variable in the quantile regressions is plant-level sales. The tables show quite clearly a concave relationship between competition and sales, with the regression coefficients on Chinese competition becoming progressively less negative or more positive as we consider larger plants.

So far we have used size as our indicator of firm strength and found that it explains a good deal of heterogeneity in the response to Chinese competition. In the context of the quantile regressions we can consider a further dimension of difference – plants' average skill levels. Table 9 adds the interaction between Chinese competition and the ratio of white collar workers to the previous one, and finds that responses to competition differ at the different decile points of size. Specifically, although among smaller firms, firms with higher skills show no difference from other firms, at the 30th percentile and above skilled firms weather the competitive pressure better than less skilled ones. At the top end of the range the effects are not quite significantly different from zero statistically but that probably arises because larger firms tend to have higher skills ratios so that at that point in the sample there is insufficient variance to identify the effects precisely. Fig. 4 plots firms' responses to Chinese competition against both size and the skills ratio; it shows that the greatest resilience to competition occurs when both are high.

The coefficients show a monotonically increasing relationship between plant size and the response of sales to Chinese competition and for the 90th percentile of firms, this response is significantly larger than zero. That is, in this case we find direct evidence not only of sales destruction, but also of sales creation – i.e. genuinely creative destruction.[24]

### 4.3. The role of intermediate inputs

Some of our results suggest a beneficial impact of Chinese competition for larger plants and core products. In addition to the responses to increased competition discussed above, Chinese exports might have an additional effect if they expand firms' access to cheaper and a larger variety of imported intermediate inputs (see Amiti and Konings, 2007; Goldberg et al., 2010b). To account for this possibility we generate a measure of the Chinese shares in firms' inputs using Mexican input–output tables and Chinese exports to Mexico.[25] For

[20] In the case of the product regressions the cutoffs are as follows: The graph crosses the x axis at 75% for domestic sales, 70% for export sales, 65% for exit from export markets and 90% for exit from the domestic market. These positive effects are not statistically significantly different from zero, however. The cutoffs where the crossing becomes significant are 85 for domestic sales and 80 for exit from the export market, and they do not become significant for export sales and exit from the domestic market.

[21] We verify that the results hold qualitatively also for other cutoffs on the number of products produced such as four or six.

[22] For the implementation of the quantile IV regressions we use the strategy and codes developed by Chernozhukov and Hansen (2006).

[23] Quantile regressions require balanced panels, hence we exclude plants that exited at any point in time during the period studied. This requirement also means that we cannot repeat the same exercise for plant exit.

[24] The relationship between size and sales response is slightly concave, but the linear interaction postulated above seems to be a good approximation.

[25] Mexican input–output tables are available from the INEGI webpage. Given their level of disaggregation the Chinese share of inputs can be computed only at a 32 sectors level.

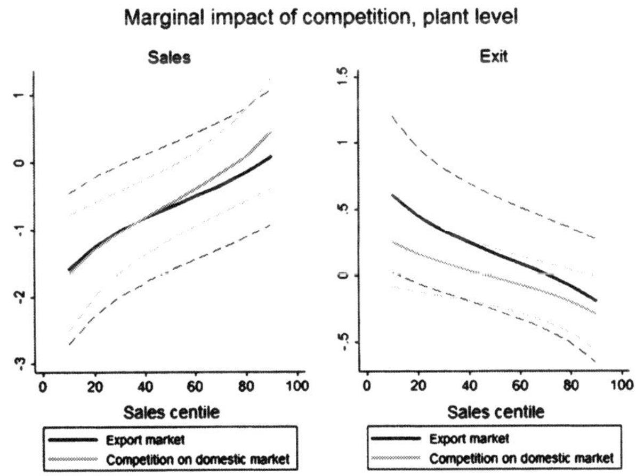


**Fig. 2.** Marginal effect of competition, plant level. The figure shows the marginal effects computed in the fourth column of the corresponding IV regressions similar to Table 6, as reported in the web appendix. From these columns we also compute 95% confidence intervals, which are shown in thin dashed lines.

the computation we weight the input–output coefficient of each sector listed as an input by its import share, and then by the Chinese share in imports for that sector. Summing these measures, we arrive at a measure that gives on average the weighted sum of inputs imported from China at a sectoral level, where the weights are given by the coefficients of the input–output table.

In Table 10 we introduce this measure of the Chinese weight in inputs and its interaction with the product share to the OLS specification above (only the coefficients of direct interest are reported). For product exit (column 1) we find that the inputs and interacted inputs have a similar effect to that found for competition, with positive coefficients on the non-interacted effects and negative coefficients in the product share interaction. This suggests that firms make better use of the availability of Chinese inputs for their core products, and that expanded access to cheaper Chinese inputs helps them to improve the competitiveness of their core products. The sales results are similar: output of core products expands more as a consequence of increased penetration of imported Chinese inputs, while marginal products less so or not at all. The coefficients on Chinese competition remain similar to our previous estimates in terms of signs, and in terms of statistical significance for sales; however, for product exit, they become statistically insignificant. This suggests that differences in ability to use imported Chinese intermediate inputs contribute crucially to the heterogeneity of the impact of Chinese competition. Columns (3) and (4) of Table 10 show similar results at plant level; again, the input coefficients follow the same pattern as the competition coefficients, which suggests that larger plants are better able to make use of Chinese inputs. We find similar effects in IV regressions, which we omit for reasons of space. Since the issue here is to disentangle the two possible effects of Chinese exports to Mexico

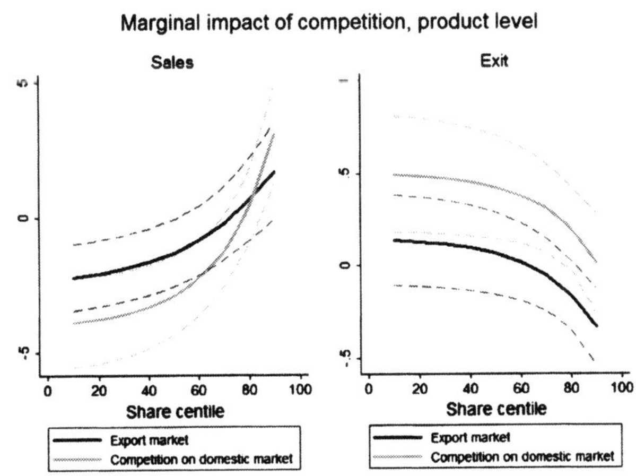


**Fig. 3.** Marginal effect of competition, product level. The figure shows the marginal effects computed in the fourth column of the corresponding IV regressions similar to Table 6, as reported in the web appendix. From these columns we also compute 95% confidence intervals, which are shown in thin dashed lines.

**Table 7**
Product exit by rank of product. This table regresses the probability of exit for products between 1994 and 2004 on the change in Chinese competition over that period for products with different initial ranks. Robust standard errors are clustered on eight digit product level, stars give significance at 1 (***), 5 (**) and 10% (*) level of significance. The panel used for this table is balanced, such that we consider products only from plants with at least five products.

| | (1)<br>Rank 1 | (2)<br>Rank 2 | (3)<br>Rank 3 | (4)<br>Rank 4 | (5)<br>Rank 5 |
|---|---|---|---|---|---|
| $\Delta Ch-comp_{Mk}$ | −0.0831*** | 0.0179 | 0.0236* | 0.0326*** | 0.0291** |
| | (0.0131) | (0.0131) | (0.0129) | (0.0124) | (0.0115) |
| Observations | 3363 | 3363 | 3363 | 3363 | 3363 |

**Table 8**
Quantile IV regression – plant sales.

| | Q1 | Q2 | Q3 | Q4 | Q5 | Q6 | Q7 | Q8 | Q9 |
|---|---|---|---|---|---|---|---|---|---|
| $Ch-comp_{Mit-1}$ | −0.4199*** | −0.2522*** | −0.1959*** | −0.1635*** | −0.1106*** | −0.0591 | −0.0336 | 0.0246 | 0.1112*** |
| | (0.0423) | (0.0433) | (0.0461) | (0.0411) | (0.0339) | (0.03) | (0.0362) | (0.032) | (0.0284) |
| $LnImports_{Mit-1}$ | 0.2127*** | 0.1655*** | 0.1323*** | 0.1164*** | 0.0812*** | 0.0485** | 0.0371 | −0.0027 | −0.0508*** |
| | (0.0311) | (0.0366) | (0.0363) | (0.0331) | (0.0261) | (0.0234) | (0.0301) | (0.0241) | (0.0208) |
| $LnSales_{it-1}$ | 0.7523*** | 0.7419*** | 0.7517*** | 0.7482*** | 0.7503*** | 0.7383*** | 0.719*** | 0.6841*** | 0.6036*** |
| | (0.0165) | (0.0136) | (0.0109) | (0.0104) | (0.0095) | (0.0086) | (0.0081) | (0.0095) | (0.0105) |
| $LnNr.employees_{it-1}$ | 0.03 | 0.0514** | 0.0448*** | 0.0429** | 0.0372*** | 0.0401*** | 0.0554*** | 0.0567*** | 0.0757*** |
| | (0.0251) | (0.0208) | (0.0168) | (0.0151) | (0.0129) | (0.011) | (0.0116) | (0.0135) | (0.0152) |
| $Herfindahl_{it-1}$ | −1.5433*** | −0.9707*** | −0.6478*** | −0.5031*** | −0.3769*** | −0.3545*** | −0.2624*** | −0.2546*** | −0.4116*** |
| | (0.2107) | (0.1664) | (0.1353) | (0.1167) | (0.0871) | (0.0917) | (0.1028) | (0.0941) | (0.1352) |
| $Exportshare_{it-1}$ | 0.1338* | 0.0739* | 0.0657 | 0.0613* | 0.0625* | 0.0688** | 0.0564* | 0.0477 | 0.0608 |
| | (0.0732) | (0.0498) | (0.0411) | (0.0393) | (0.0331) | (0.0289) | (0.029) | (0.03) | (0.0447) |
| $Skillshare_{it-1}$ | −0.3725*** | −0.1942*** | −0.0838* | −0.0557 | −0.0102 | 0.0076 | 0.0201 | 0.0468 | 0.0845* |
| | (0.0966) | (0.0589) | (0.0466) | (0.0431) | (0.0377) | (0.0335) | (0.0351) | (0.0416) | (0.0499) |
| Observations | 26,417 | 26,417 | 26,417 | 26,417 | 26,417 | 26,417 | 26,417 | 26,417 | 26,417 |
| Year fixed effects | Yes | Yes | Yes | Yes | Yes | Yes | Yes | Yes | Yes |
| Demeaned at plant level | Yes | Yes | Yes | Yes | Yes | Yes | Yes | Yes | Yes |

Note: Quantile IV regressions at the nine centiles of the distribution, Q1 gives the quantile regression at the 10th percentile. $Ch-comp_{Mit-1}$ was instrumented with $Ch-comp_{Rit-1}$ and $Ch-comp_{Eit-1}$. To mimic plant fixed effects all variables were demeaned at plant level. Stars denote significance at 1 (***), 5 (**) and 10% (*) level of significance. The table includes only plants that did not exit between 1994 and 2004.

(competition and inputs) we do not reproduce this exercise for Mexican export markets.

## 5. Robustness and additional findings

To demonstrate the robustness and plausibility of our results, we perform various robustness tests. A first concern is that some plants and products did not face any competition from China during the period analyzed, which could generate noise in the results. To address this concern we rerun the results at plant level separately for the 20% of plants most affected by competition and the 20% least affected, measured by mean competition. When we rerun estimations similar to the second columns of Table 6 in the sample of plants that are most affected by competition, we find coefficients on Chinese competition and the interaction of size and Chinese competition that are statistically significantly different from zero, and similar to the

**Table 9**
Quantile – skill interaction, plant sales.

| | Q1 | Q2 | Q3 | Q4 | Q5 | Q6 | Q7 | Q8 | Q9 |
|---|---|---|---|---|---|---|---|---|---|
| $Ch-comp_{Mit-1}$ | −0.024** | −0.012** | −0.011*** | −0.011*** | −0.009*** | −0.010*** | −0.008** | −0.003 | −0.002 |
| | (0.008) | (0.005) | (0.003) | (0.002) | (0.002) | (0.002) | (0.003) | (0.004) | (0.006) |
| $LnImports_{Mit-1}$ | −0.029** | −0.020** | −0.012** | −0.004 | −0.003 | −0.001 | 0.003 | 0.010 | 0.009 |
| | (0.012) | (0.006) | (0.004) | (0.004) | (0.003) | (0.003) | (0.004) | (0.006) | (0.009) |
| $LnSales_{it-1}$ | 0.749*** | 0.744*** | 0.748*** | 0.750*** | 0.742*** | 0.723*** | 0.703*** | 0.671*** | 0.612*** |
| | (0.020) | (0.009) | (0.005) | (0.004) | (0.004) | (0.004) | (0.005) | (0.008) | (0.015) |
| $LnNr.employees_{it-1}$ | −0.040 | −0.009 | −0.003 | 0.000 | 0.009* | 0.025*** | 0.038*** | 0.054*** | 0.091*** |
| | (0.022) | (0.011) | (0.006) | (0.005) | (0.005) | (0.005) | (0.006) | (0.008) | (0.014) |
| $Herfindahl_{it-1}$ | −0.959*** | −0.439*** | −0.369*** | −0.327*** | −0.301*** | −0.234*** | −0.276*** | −0.281** | −0.611*** |
| | (0.243) | (0.122) | (0.074) | (0.061) | (0.056) | (0.058) | (0.068) | (0.094) | (0.152) |
| $Exportshare_{it-1}$ | 0.031 | 0.024 | 0.029 | 0.053 | 0.046* | 0.055** | 0.055* | 0.070* | 0.117* |
| | (0.078) | (0.041) | (0.025) | (0.020) | (0.019) | (0.020) | (0.024) | (0.034) | (0.056) |
| $Skillshare_{it-1}$ | −0.271* | −0.162* | −0.136** | −0.098** | −0.075* | −0.068 | −0.086* | −0.039 | −0.038 |
| | (0.127) | (0.068) | (0.042) | (0.036) | (0.033) | (0.035) | (0.041) | (0.055) | (0.088) |
| $Ch-comp_{Mit-1} \times Skillshrare_{it-1}$ | −0.004 | 0.010 | 0.017* | 0.020*** | 0.017* | 0.019*** | 0.020** | 0.011 | 0.021 |
| | (0.019) | (0.011) | (0.007) | (0.006) | (0.005) | (0.006) | (0.007) | (0.009) | (0.013) |
| Year fixed effects | Yes | Yes | Yes | Yes | Yes | Yes | Yes | Yes | Yes |
| Demeaned at plant level | Yes | Yes | Yes | Yes | Yes | Yes | Yes | Yes | Yes |

Note: Quantile IV regressions at the nine centiles of the distribution, Q1 gives the quantile regression at the 10th percentile. $Ch-comp_{Mit-1}$ was instrumented with $Chcomp_{Rit-1}$ and $Ch-comp_{Eit-1}$. To mimic plant fixed effects all variables were demeaned at plant level. Stars denote significance at 1 (***), 5 (**) and 10% (*) level of significance. The table includes only plants that did not exit between 1994 and 2004.

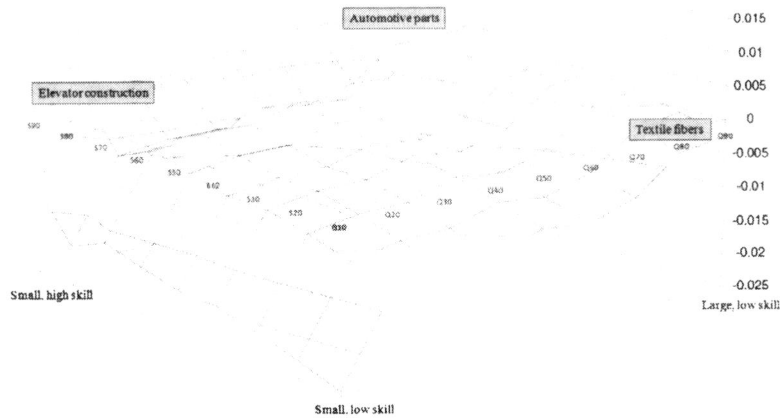


**Fig. 4.** Marginal effect of competition. This figure shows the marginal effect of competition as estimated in Table 9. The axis from left to right displays initial size percentiles, the axis running back and forth skill share percentiles, and the vertical axis the effect of competition on size. For example: The front corner shows a negative marginal effect of Chinese competition on size for the firm at the 5th percentile of size (Q5) and the 1% percentile of skill share (S1).

coefficients obtained in the full sample. In the sample of the bottom 20%, the competition coefficients are not significantly different from zero, which reflects the fact that in this sample there is little Chinese competition and so little information about competition effects.

A second robustness check is a response to concerns about potentially spurious results – specifically the possibility that sectors experiencing some other exogenous shock that affects plants asymmetrically, are also characterized by an increasing expansion of Chinese imports. To do so, we evaluate whether future competition from China has any impact on current plant sales – a sort of "placebo test". We cannot reject the null hypothesis that the coefficients on competition from China and its interaction are equal to zero. This provides some assurance that the emergence of Chinese competition was not anticipated and our results are not driven by some other spurious third cause.

Third, Mexican policy makers were active in filing anti-dumping cases against Chinese competition early on, which we can see in the anti-dumping data from Bown (2009). A sixth of the products in our sample were subject to anti-dumping complaints in Mexico. Anti-dumping might create a different link between competition and our outcome variables to the one postulated above. To address this we repeat analysis for only those products where no anti-dumping cases were attempted. Our results remain similar in terms of size and significance in the subsample where no anti-dumping cases were filed. Hence anti-dumping alone cannot explain the patterns we observe above.

A fourth concern relates to specific developments in the technology of certain goods, which may affect all Chinese exports and Mexican firm behavior directly and thus invalidate the IV strategy. To confront this concern we include industry-year fixed effects in the main

**Table 10**
Chinese exports as inputs to Mexican production. This table exactly reproduces the main effects from the main tables, but adds the Chinese share in inputs and its interaction with the share of products or the size of plants. Robust standard errors are clustered on eight digit product level, stars denote significance at 1 (***), 5 (**) and 10% (*) level of significance.

| Product level | | | Plant level | | |
|---|---|---|---|---|---|
| | (1) | (2) | | (3) | (4) |
| | $Prod\ exit_{ikt}$ | $Prod\ sales_{ikt}$ | | $Plant\ exit_{it}$ | $Plant\ sales_{it}$ |
| $Ch-comp_{Mkt-1}$ | 0.103* | −1.510*** | $Ch-comp_{Mkt-1}$ | 0.507 | 0.582 |
| | (0.0593) | (0.273) | | (0.325) | (0.691) |
| $Ch-comp_{Mkt-1} \times Share_{ikt-1}$ | −0.0918 | 2.385*** | $Ch-comp_{Mkt-1} \times LnSales_{it-1}$ | −0.0467* | −0.0390 |
| | (0.130) | (0.595) | | (0.0277) | (0.0603) |
| $Ch-shareininputs_{Mkt-1}$ | 0.239*** | −0.708** | $Ch-shareininputs_{Mkt-1}$ | 1.198*** | −5.165*** |
| | (0.0788) | (0.315) | | (0.263) | (0.501) |
| $Ch-shareininputs_{Mkt-1} \times Share_{ikt-1}$ | −0.632*** | 0.159*** | $Ch-shareininputs_{Mkt-1} \times LnSales_{it-1}$ | −0.0981*** | 0.416*** |
| | (0.115) | (0.376) | | (0.0216) | (0.0422) |
| Observations | 85,770 | 94,035 | Observations | 35,828 | 39,254 |
| R-squared | 0.485 | 0.922 | R-squared | 0.425 | 0.945 |
| | OLS | OLS | | OLS | OLS |

**Table 11**
Robustness, industry-year fixed effects, plant level.

| | IV | IV | IV | IV |
|---|---|---|---|---|
| | (1) | (2) | (3) | (4) |
| | $Exit_{it}$ | $Exit.export_{it}$ | $Sales_{it}$ | $Exportsales_{it}$ |
| $Ch-comp_{Mit-1}$ | 1.193** | | −6.736*** | |
| | (0.516) | | (1.393) | |
| $LnSales_{it-1}$ | −0.0549*** | | 0.644*** | |
| | (0.00241) | | (0.00663) | |
| $Ch-comp_{Mit-1} \times LnExportSales_{it-1}$ | −0.134*** | | 0.623*** | |
| | (0.0454) | | (0.130) | |
| $Ch-comp_{Uit-1}$ | | 1.562*** | | −3.916*** |
| | | (0.593) | | (0.963) |
| $LnExportSales_{it-1}$ | | 0.00139 | | 0.399*** |
| | | (0.00517) | | (0.0132) |
| $Ch-comp_{Uit-1} \times LnExportSales_{it-1}$ | | −0.136*** | | 0.313*** |
| | | (0.0516) | | (0.0808) |
| $Herfindahl_{it-1}$ | 0.0618* | 0.0311 | −0.524*** | −0.473* |
| | (0.0373) | (0.0938) | (0.0952) | (0.280) |
| $Exportshare_{it-1}$ | −0.0204* | 0.0240 | −0.970*** | 0.276*** |
| | (0.0120) | (0.0277) | (0.0322) | (0.0889) |
| $Skillshare_{it-1}$ | −0.00367 | −0.0239 | −0.0300 | −0.0976 |
| | (0.0148) | (0.0465) | (0.0391) | (0.142) |
| Plant fixed effects | Yes | Yes | Yes | Yes |
| Industry-year fixed effects | Yes | Yes | Yes | Yes |
| Observations | 35,376 | 12,089 | 38,774 | 11,771 |
| Sargan p-value | 0.0755 | 0.268 | 0.225 | 0.0918 |

Note: Robust standard errors are clustered on six digit product level, stars give significance at 1 (***), 5 (**) and 10% (*) level of significance. These regressions are identical to th fourth column of the main plant OLS regressions in the online appendix, except for the additional inclusion of 2 digit HS sectoral-year control variables. An example of such a contr variables is fertilizers in the year 2000.

specifications, to account for shocks such as to transportation costs, demand patterns or technology that might affect both Chinese exports and our outcome variables in one industry in one year.[25] The main results are reported in Table 11. They correspond to column (4) of Tables A13 to A16, respectively and are clearly similar to those in the original tables. That is, our main results are not due to the presence of common shocks at the 2-digit HS sector-year level.

A fifth concern relates to the use of the Chinese competition measure we employ. In Table 12 we repeat the annual exercise at the product level with different measures of competition. First, to address concerns about the functional form we replace the competition variable with a measure that just indicates whether competition is above or below the mean level of competition. Second, we provide the results using current competition, and not lagged competition, to address concerns about the timing. Third, we keep the imports from all countries (the denominator of the competition variable) constant at its value from 1994, and let only the numerator vary. Finally we compute a measure that indicates the penetration of Chinese imports, which we compute at the product level as imports from China divided by the sum of total imports into Mexico plus total Mexican production (which we can straight forwardly measure using our production data) minus exports (i.e. dividing by domestic absorption). All these different measures show the same signs of coefficients as our preferred specification above.

We further show in the online appendix (Table A18) that the results are robust to using the sales in the initial year as the interaction, and not sales that vary over time.

## 6. Conclusions

The substantial rise of Chinese exports in recent decades provides us with a quasi-natural experiment to evaluate the impact of a surge in competition on the extensive and intensive margins of firms at both the plant and the product levels. In this study we analyze the impact of such competitive pressures on Mexican manufacturin firms on both the domestic market and the export (US) market at sec toral, plant and product level.

We find that the surge of exports from China challenged Mexica firms, and led to plant exit, product exit and sales contraction. How ever, these effects were highly asymmetric and implied a reallocatio both between products within plants and between plants. First, an most crucially, while smaller, and thus perhaps less productive, plant are forced to shrink and sometimes exit from the market, this effect i attenuated for larger plants. Second, this process of creative destruc tion and market selection operates not only at plant but also at prod uct level. Such heterogeneous micro-level dynamics are hidden b average effects calculated at sectoral and even plant levels, pointin towards the importance of using plant- and product-level dat Third, we observe these effects not only on the domestic marke but also on the export market, which for Mexico effectively mean the USA. Fourth, Chinese competition brings with it access to cheape and possibly better and more diverse intermediate inputs. We sho that larger plants and core products benefit disproportionately fro such expanded access to imported Chinese intermediates. Th explains part of the heterogeneous impact of the Chinese trad surge, but the main asymmetric competitive result remains clearl identifiable.

These results confirm that the rise in Chinese exports has signifi cantly influenced production patterns in a major middle-incom country, a finding of potentially considerable relevance to polic makers and firms worldwide. By forcing plants to drop margin products, and forcing some smaller and less productive plants t close down, the heterogeneous effect of competition not only in creases average productivity at plant and sectoral levels but also ap pears to make room for some expansion at the top of the siz distribution. In the long run, higher productivity underpins highe real incomes, and thus contributes to higher economic welfare, bu our results cannot describe how the advent of China as a world trad ing power has affected overall economic welfare in Mexico. They pa no regard to consumers' benefits, nor to the extent to which compe tition in manufacturing has led to growth in other sectors, and n do they describe any distributional consequences. What the result

[25] These are based on HS-2 digit industry measures. A more disaggregated level such as HS-6 would be perfectly correlated with Chinese competition, and thus take out the variation of our explanatory variable of interest.

**Table 12**
Robustness to different measures of Chinese competition. The table exactly reproduces the main OLS results for product exit and sales, replacing the competition variable with different measures of competition. Only the main coefficients of interest are shown. Robust standard errors are clustered on eight digit product level, stars denote significance at 1 (***), 5 (**) and 10% (*) level of significance.

| | (1) | (2) | (3) | (4) | (5) | (6) | (7) | (8) |
|---|---|---|---|---|---|---|---|---|
| | *Prod* | *Prod* | *Prod* | *Prod* | *Prod* | *Prod* | *Prod* | *Prod* |
| | $exit_{ikt}$ | $exit_{ikt}$ | $exit_{ikt}$ | $exit_{ikt}$ | $sales_{ikt}$ | $sales_{ikt}$ | $sales_{ikt}$ | $sales_{ikt}$ |
| $Ch-comp_{Mkt-1}$ *above/belowmen* | 0.0014 | | | | −0.0329 | | | |
| | (0.0019) | | | | (0.0214) | | | |
| $Ch-Comp$*above/below mean* $\times Share_{ikt-1}$ | −0.0019*** | | | | 0.226*** | | | |
| | (0.00022) | | | | (0.079) | | | |
| $Ch-comp_{Mkt}$ | | 0.191*** | | | | −0.725*** | | |
| | | (0.0560) | | | | (0.214) | | |
| $Ch-comp_{Mkt}\times Share_{ikt-1}$ | | −0.226* | | | | 0.973** | | |
| | | (0.127) | | | | (0.484) | | |
| $Ch-comp_{Mkt-1}$, *fixeddenominator* | | | 0.0570*** | | | | −0.0979** | |
| | | | (0.0116) | | | | (0.0423) | |
| $Ch-Comp_{Mkt-1}\times Share_{ikt-1}$ | | | −0.0653*** | | | | 0.114** | |
| | | | (0.0131) | | | | (0.0490) | |
| $Absorption_{Mkt-1}$ | | | | 0.131** | | | | −0.407 |
| | | | | (0.0634) | | | | (0.376) |
| $Absorption\times Share_{ikt-1}$ | | | | −0.429*** | | | | 1.290*** |
| | | | | (0.0795) | | | | (0.422) |
| $Share_{ikt-1}$ | 0.076*** | −0.0873*** | 0.0745*** | 0.0739*** | 4.125 | 3.558*** | 51.19 | 55.51 |
| | (0.0172) | (0.0127) | (0.0194) | (0.0208) | (7.299) | (0.179) | (81.42) | (87.50) |
| Observations | 85,292 | 85,292 | 85,292 | 85,292 | 93,583 | 93,583 | 93,583 | 93,583 |

do show, however, is that despite understandable political resistance to competition from China, insulating the domestic market from competition is likely to be harmful to productivity as it would benefit less productive plants and marginal products. It would also be a partial solution to local economic stresses because competitive effects are also felt via export markets. While recognizing the possible distributional effects of competition, policy should aim to permit and facilitate change, rather than frustrate it by supporting failing firms. It should recognize the centrality of large and efficient firms to the national response, rather than focusing on less productive enterprises and marginal products and accommodate reallocation as a key to productivity growth.

## Appendix A. Supplementary data

Supplementary data to this article can be found online at http://dx.doi.org/10.1016/j.jinteco.2012.09.002.

## References

Aghion, Philippe, Bloom, Nicholas, Blundell, Richard, Griffith, Rachel, Howitt, Peter, 2005. Competition and innovation: an inverted-U relationship. Quarterly Journal of Economics 701–728.

Alvarez, Roberto, Vergara, Sebastian, 2010. Exit in Developing Countries: Economic Reforms and Plant Heterogeneity, vol. 58(3). University of Chicago Press, pp. 537–561 (04).

Amiti, Mary, Freund, Caroline, 2010. An anatomy of China's export growth. In: Feenstra, Robert, Wei, Shang-Jin (Eds.), Chinas Growing Role in World Trade. NBER and University of Chicago Press, Chicago, pp. 35–62.

Amiti, Mary, Konings, Jozef, 2007. Trade liberalization, intermediate inputs, and productivity: evidence from Indonesia. The American Economic Review 97 (5), 1611–1638.

Arroba, Angel A., Avendaño, Rolando, Estrada, Julio, 2009. Adapting to the rise of China: how can Latin American companies succeed? OECD and World Economic Forum.

Autor, David, Dorn, David, Hanson, Gordon, 2012. The China syndrome: local labor market effects of import competition in the United States. MIT Working Paper.

Baldwin, J., Gu, W., 2009. The impact of trade on plant scale, production-run length and diversification. In: Dunne, T., Jensen, J.B., Roberts, M.J. (Eds.), Producer Dynamics: New Evidence from Micro Data. University of Chicago Press, Chicago.

Bernard, Andrew B., Bradford Jensen, J., Schott, Peter K., 2004. Facing the dragon: prospects for US. Manufacturers in the coming decade. Working Paper. Yale University.

Bernard, Andrew B., Bradford Jensen, J., Schott, Peter K., 2006. Survival of the best fit: exposure to low wage countries and the (uneven) growth of US manufacturing plants. The Journal of Industrial Economics 68, 219–237.

Bernard, Andrew B., Bradford Jensen, J., Redding, Stephen J., Schott, Peter K., 2007. Firms in international trade. Journal of Economic Perspectives 21 (3), 105–130.

Bernard, Andrew B., Redding, Stephen J., Schott, Peter K., 2010. Multi-product firms and product switching. The American Economic Review 100 (1), 70–97 (28).

Bernard, A.B., Redding, S.J., Schott, P.K., 2011a. Multi-product firms and trade liberalization. Quarterly Journal of Economics 126, 1271–1318.

Bernard, Andrew B., Bradford Jensen, J., Redding, Stephen J., Schott, Peter K., 2011b. The empirics of firm heterogeneity and international trade. Nber Working Paper, 17627.

Bloom, Nicholas, Draca, Mirko, Van Reenen, John, 2011. Trade induced technical change? The impact of Chinese imports on innovation, IT and productivity. NBER Working paper, 16717.

Bown, Chad P., 2009. 'Global Antidumping Database', [Version 5.1, October]. (available at www.brandeis.edu/cbown/global-ad).

Broda, Christian, Romalis, John, 2009. The welfare implications of rising price dispersion. Working Paper.

Bustos, Paula, 2011. Trade liberalization, exports and technology upgrading: evidence on the impact of MERCOSUR on Argentinian firms. American Economic Review, American Economic Association 101 (1), 304–340 (February).

Chen, Natalie, Imbs, Jean, Scott, Andrew, 2009. The dynamics of trade and competition. Journal of International Economics 77 (1), 50–62 (February).

Chernozhukov, Victor, Hansen, Christian, 2006. Instrumental quantile regression inference for structural and treatment models. Journal of Econometrics 132, 491–525.

Devlin, R., Estevadeordal, A., Rodriguez-Clare, A. (Eds.), 2006. The Emergence of China. Opportunities and Challenges for Latin America and the Caribbean. Inter-American Development Bank, Washington, DC. ISBN: 1597820229.

di Giovanni, Julian, Andrei, Levchenko, Jing, Zhang, 2011. The Global Welfare Impact of China: Trade Integration and Technological Change. Mimeo, University of Michigan.

Dussel Peters, Enrique (Ed.), 2007. Oportunidades en la relacion economica y comercial entre China y Mexico. S.A. de C.V., United Nations, Mundi Prensa Mexico.

Eckel, Carsten, Neary, Peter, 2010. Multi-product firms and flexible manufacturing. The Review of Economic Studies 77 (1), 188–217.

Eckel, Carsten, Iacovone, Leonardo, Javorcik, Beata, Peter Neary, J., 2010. Multi-Product Firms at Home and Away: Cost- Versus Quality-Based Competence. Discussion Paper SeriesDepartment of Economics.

Eichengreen, B., Rhee, Y., Tong, H., 2007. China and the exports of other Asian countries. Review of World Economics 143 (2), 201–226.

Eslava, Marcela, Haltiwanger, John, Kugler, Adriana, Kugler, Maurice, 2009. Trade reforms and market selection: evidence from manufacturing plants in Colombia. IZA Discussion Paper, 4256.

European Commission, 2009. The export helpdesk for developing countries. HS 1996 Classifications downloaded from exporthelp.europa.eu in March.

Fernandes, Ana, 2007. Trade policy, trade volumes and plant-level productivity in Colombian manufacturing industries. Journal of International Economics 71, 52–71.

Fernandes, Ana, Paunov, Caroline, 2009. Does tougher import competition foster product quality upgrading? World Bank Policy Research Working Paper No. 4894.

Fernandes, Ana, Paunov, Caroline, 2011. Foreign direct investment in services and manufacturing productivity growth : evidence for Chile. Journal of Development Economics 97 (2), 305–321.

Freund, Caroline, Ozden, Caglar, 2006. The effect of China's exports on Latin American trade with the world. Working paper.

Goldberg, Pinelopi, Amit, K., Khandelwal, Nina Pavcnik, Topalova, Petia, 2010a. Multiproduct firms and product turnover in the developing world: evidence from India. The Review of Economics and Statistics 92 (4), 1042–1049.

Goldberg, Pinelopi, Amit, K., Khandelwal, Nina Pavcnik, Topalova, Petia, 2010b. Imported intermediate inputs and domestic product growth: evidence from India. Quarterly Journal of Economics 125 (4), 727–1767.

Hanson, Gordon H., Robertson, Raymond, 2007. China and the recent evolution of Latin America's manufacturing exports. Working paper.

Hsieh, Chang-Tai, Ossa, Ralph, 2011. A global view of productivity growth in China. NBER Working Paper No. 16778.

Huang, Yasheng, 2003. Selling China – Foreign Direct Investment during the Reform Years. Cambridge University Press.

Iacovone, Leonardo, Javorcik, Beata, 2008. Multi product exporters: diversification and micro-level dynamics. World Bank Policy Research Working Paper, WPS4723.2008.

Iacovone, Leonardo, Wolfgang, Keller, Rauch, Ferdinand, 2011. 'Innovation Responses to Import Competition', Mimeo.

Iranzo, Susana, Ma, Alyson C., 2006. The effect of China on Mexico–U.S. Trade: undoing NAFTA? Working Paper.

Jenkins, Rhys, Peters, Enrique Dussel, Moreira, Mauricio M., 2008. The impact of China on Latin America and the Caribbean. World Development 36 (2), 235–253.

Keefer, Philip, 2007. Governance and economic growth. In: Winters, L. Alan, Yusuf, Shahid (Eds.), Dancing with Giants. World Bank, Washington DC.

Lall, S., Weiss, J., Oikawa, H., 2005. China's competitive threat to Latin America: an analysis for 1990–2002. Oxford Development Studies 33 (2), 163–194.

Lederman, Daniel, Olarreaga, Marcelo, Rubiano, Eliana, 2008. Trade specialization in Latin America: the impact of China and India. Review of World Economics (Weltwirtschaftliches Archiv) 144 (2), 248–271 (Springer).

Levinsohn, James, 1999. Employment response to international liberalization in Chile. Journal of International Economics 47, 321–344.

Lileeva, Alla, Trefler, Daniel, 2010. Improved access to foreign markets raises plant-level productivity … for some plants. Quarterly Journal of Economics 125 (3), 1051–1099.

Liu, Runjuan, 2010. Import competition and firm refocusing. Canadian Journal of Ecc nomics 43 (2), 440–466.

Mayer, Thierry, Marc Melitz and Gianmarco Ottaviano, 2011, 'Market size, competitio and the product mix of exporters', draft.

Melitz, Marc, Ottaviano, Gianmarco, 2008. Market size, trade, and productivity. The Re view of Economic Studies 75, 295–316.

Mion, Giordano, Zhu, Linke, forthcoming. 'Import competition and offshoring to China a curse or blessing for firms?'. Journal of International Economics 101 (1 304–340.

Moulton, Brent R., 1990. An illustration of a pitfall in estimating the effects of aggregat variables on micro unit. The Review of Economics and Statistics 72 (2), 334–338

Nickell, Stephen, 1981. Biases in dynamic models with fixed effects. Econometrica 4 (6).

Pavcnik, Nina, 2002. Trade liberalization, exit, and productivity improvements: ev dence from Chilean plants. The Review of Economic Studies 69, 245–276.

Pavcnik, Nina, Goldberg, Penny, 2005. Short term consequences of trade reform for ir dustry employment and wages: survey of evidence from Colombia. World Econc my 923–939.

Pavcnik, Nina, Blom, Andreas, Goldberg, Pinelopi, Schady, Norbert, 2004. Trade polic and industry wage structure: evidence from Brazil. World Bank Economic Revie 18 (3), 319–344.

SICA, 2009. 'Tradado de Libre Comercio Chile–Panama – Anexo 3.3 Lista de Chile', H 1996 classifications downloaded from www.sica.gov.ec in March.

Soloaga, Isidro, Oarreaga, Marcelo, Lederman, Daniel, 2007. The growth of China an India in World Trade: opportunity or threat for Latin America and the Caribbear World Bank Policy Research Working Paper Series, WPS 4320.

Teshima, Kensuke, 2010. Import Competition and Innovation at the Plant Leve Evidence from Mexico. Mimeo.

Verhoogen, Eric, 2008. Trade, quality upgrading and wage inequality in the Mexica manufacturing sector. Quarterly Journal of Economics 123, 489–530.

Yusuf, Shahid, Nabeshima, Kaoru, Perkins, Dwight H., 2007. China and India reshap global industrial geography. In: Winters, L. Alan, Yusuf, Shahid (Eds.), Dancin with Giants. World Bank, Washington DC.

CPSIA information can be obtained at www.ICGtesting.com
Printed in the USA
BVOW05*0626070415

394974BV00001B/1/P

9 789814 571265